The

LOS ANGELES

REVISED EDITION

Editor
Colleen Dunn Bates

Contributing Editors
Charles Britton, Mark Ehrman, Liz Gardner, Kitty Morgan,
David Shaw, Merrill Shindler, Deborah Sroloff

Assistant Editors
Catherine Jordan, Jennifer Rylaarsdam,
Margery L. Schwartz,

Prentice Hall Travel Editor
Amit Shah

Operations
Alain Gayot

Directed by
André Gayot

PRENTICE HALL

New York ▪ London ▪ Toronto ▪ Sydney ▪ Tokyo ▪ Singapore

*Other Gault Millau Guides Available
from Prentice Hall Trade Division*

The Best of Chicago
The Best of France
The Best of Hong Kong
The Best of Italy
The Best of London
The Best of New England
The Best of New York
The Best of Paris
The Best of San Francisco
The Best of Washington, D.C.

Published by Prentice Hall Trade Division
A Division of Simon & Schuster, Inc.
15 Columbus Circle
New York, NY 10023

Please address all comments regarding *The Best of Los Angeles* to:
Gault Millau, Inc.
P.O. Box 361144
Los Angeles, CA 90036

Please address all advertising queries to:
Mr. Geoffrey Gropp, Vice President
Welsh Publishing Group, Inc.
300 Madison Avenue
New York, NY 10017
(212) 687-0680

Library of Congress Cataloging-in-Publication Data

The Best of Los Angeles / editor, Colleen Dunn Bates; contributing
editors, Mark Ehrman . . . [et. al.]; assistant editors, Jennifer
Rylaarsdam, Margery L. Schwartz.—Rev. ed.
    p.   c.m.
  ISBN 0-13-068248-9: $16.95
  1. Los Angeles (Calif.)—Description—1981- —Guide-books.
I. Bates, Colleen Dunn.
F889.L83B465   1990
917.94'940453—dc20   89-26491
                                                          CIP

Special thanks to the staff of Prentice Hall Travel for their invaluable
aid in producing these Gault Millau guides.

Manufactured in the United States of America

CONTENTS

INTRODUCTION

URBAN FRONTIER

It's much easier to picture Los Angeles in the '90s than it is such history-drenched cities as Boston and New Orleans. Which is not to say that L.A. doesn't have a rich history—it does. But from its inception, it has been a forward-looking city, always a metropolis of the future. Throughout the last century, while Easterners were crowding into smaller and smaller apartments, Angelenos of modest means were buying themselves rambling ranch houses with lawns and trees. L.A. was the urban frontier, like the pioneer frontier of 150 years ago (comparatively speaking, of course): you could stake a claim out here, get yourself a homestead and some open space and start a new life free of the social and economic restraints of an established, deeply structured community. People came out west to look forward, not backward. They came by the millions. And they're still coming.

Those frontier days are just about over, at least for Los Angeles proper. There are no more bean fields to be transformed into neighborhoods. Middle-class families looking to buy first homes have been priced out of the city, so they head for spanking-new developments in Riverside or Simi. But that freewheeling urban pioneer spirit lives on, and countless numbers still move here each year because of it—and for the sunshine and the ocean and the opportunities. They hail from the frozen northeastern United States and from the farthest corners of the world. Thus, the vast region known globally as Los Angeles has come to be one of the most powerful, dynamic, exciting (yes, and overdeveloped, overtrafficked, crime-plagued and smog-filled) cities in the world.

Angelenos no longer grow defensive when their city is compared to New York or San Francisco, both of which were once universally considered far superior culturally, intellectually and culinarily. True, L.A. still has, and probably will always have, its shallow, vacuous, showy side, but it helps Angelenos not take themselves so seriously (a lesson more than a few New Yorkers and San Franciscans could benefit from). In large part because of the plethora of successful TV shows set in L.A., the rest of the country—and the world—is now looking to Los Angeles. The clothing worn by L.A.'s young people becomes the rage in Japan and Germany a year later. The movies turned out by L.A.'s studios have a phenomenal global impact. The city's cultural life grows richer by the day; L.A. has a vibrant theater scene, a strong and growing art community, a tremendous wealth of music, from the classics to the cutting edge, and even some talented writers who churn out more than sitcom scripts (though they may do that, too). And L.A.'s restaurants are no longer the joke of the culinary world. Even San Franciscans, who have long reveled in belittling their overgrown southern neighbor, are storming the gates of Postrio, the newest restaurant of L.A. culinary wunderkind Wolfgang Puck.

It's clear that Los Angeles of the '90s is going to continue growing more and more sophisticated, yet without losing that wacky pioneer spirit that keeps it innovative. The denizens of the city will certainly see tremendous changes in the *way* they live here, much of it forced upon them by the ever-increasing sprawl and oppressive traffic. As the drive from point A to point B becomes slower, the neighborhood will become more important. We're already seeing an encouraging increase in excellent neighborhood restaurants (from Osteria Nonni in Atwater to Caffè Lido in Pacific Palisades) and theaters, and surely we'll be seeing more first-rate neighborhood shops, services and amusements (even if they are housed within the confines of a sterile mall). It is our firm belief that in order to attain optimum quality of life in L.A., residents must spend less time in their cars and more time in their local communities. This holds true for visitors as well. Of course, to see and do all there is to see and do in and around the sprawling megalopolis—actually an impossible undertaking—you'll need to master the at-first-daunting freeway system. But if you plan your trip well and choose a conveniently located hotel, you can make the most of this wonderful city without spending four hours a day in your rent-a-car.

In the pages that follow, we've attempted to distill the riches of this city into a single neat and readable package. As you can see, it's quite a large book—we distilled as best we could, but there's just too much worth writing about! How could we possibly leave out our favorite Chinese restaurant in El Monte, our favorite costume-rental place in Glendale, our favorite comedy club in Hermosa Beach, our favorite bookstore in Brentwood, our favorite bistro in Beverly Hills or our favorite inn in Santa Barbara? We've taken on much more than a city—we've taken on a conglomerate of communities and neighborhoods, each with its own personality and appeal. The most we can provide is a road map to the "bests" across the vast Southern California landscape. It's up to you to fill in the blanks—to have the experiences and meet the people and absorb the character of the city.

As always, we've made a Herculean effort to make this book as current as possible. Sadly, however, while it wends its way through the publishing process—printer, distributor and bookseller—businesses go out of business, new ones open and prices rise. So forgive us if you get a disconnected phone number or find that your restaurant bill is higher than our estimate. And if we've neglected one of your own "bests," please drop us a line and tell us all about it.

A DISCLAIMER

Readers are advised that prices and conditions change over the course of time. The restaurants, hotels, shops and other establishments reviewed in this book have been reviewed over a period of time, and the reviews reflect the personal experiences of the reviewers. The reviewers and publishers cannot be held responsible for the experiences of the reader related to the establishments reviewed. Readers are invited to write the publisher with ideas, comments and suggestions for future editions.

RESTAURANTS

INTRODUCTION

INTO THE NEW DECADE

Friends, colleagues and readers, to say nothing of casual acquaintances and complete strangers, always seem to be regaling us with stories about their newest restaurant discoveries. Almost invariably, they describe the restaurant as "great" (doesn't anyone ever discover a merely "good" restaurant?), and almost invariably, they rave first (or most) about the decor, service, location and/or prices, not the food. When we ask about the food, they usually say something like, "Oh, the food is great, of course, but . . . ," and they quickly resume talking about how close the place is to their house or how reasonable the prices are. "Of course" the food is great? No, not "of course."

There aren't that many restaurants serving truly great food—not in Los Angeles and not in any city in the world (except, perhaps, Paris). But there are a large and growing number of restaurants in Los Angeles that serve very good food indeed—and a few that really do serve great food.

Decor, service, location, convenience and prices are certainly important in choosing and enjoying a restaurant. Like you, we've had otherwise excellent dinners ruined by noisy, uncomfortable settings, rude, inattentive service and prices that seemed more appropriate for a Mercedes than a meal. (We've never resented a long trip for a truly fine dinner; we'll even venture 100 miles out of our way to go to a great restaurant.) But even we are thrilled that L.A. now actually has several excellent restaurants east of La Brea Avenue, where, until recently, no chef would have dared venture without swapping his toque for a pith helmet.

But as important as these other factors are, we go to a restaurant to eat good food. If the food is extraordinary enough, we'll forgive (well, almost) even the surliest waiter and the most extortionate prices. By "good" (or "great") food, we don't mean just exquisite French food served in a temple of haute cuisine (or exquisite Italian food served in a temple of alta cucina). We also love—and have favorite spots for—barbecue, steak, hot dogs, pizza, pastrami, hamburgers and virtually all the ethnic cuisines, especially Chinese, Moroccan, Thai, Indian, Vietnamese, Japanese, Mexican . . . well, you get the idea. But we want the food to be good, whatever it is. We'd much rather have a pastrami sandwich at the Stage Deli or a spicy Polish sausage at The Wiener Factory or barbecued ribs at Mom's or Mr. Jim's than eat at most fancy joints.

Good food of all kinds is increasingly easy to find in Los Angeles, we're pleased to say. In fact, Los Angeles is one of the best restaurant cities in the United States—a claim we would have dismissed as embarrassingly provincial as recently as three years ago. But the food at Citrus and Patina now rivals that at the best French restaurants in New York, and Valentino compares favorably with any Italian restaurant in New York, San Francisco or any other American city. Yes, both New York and San Francisco still have many more good neighborhood restaurants than L.A. does, in large measure because they have more true neighborhoods than L.A. But L.A. is improving even in this respect; there are now good neighborhood Italian, Chinese, Japanese, Lebanese, Thai and

Mexican restaurants (to name just a few) in neighborhoods all over town, from the Valley to Hollywood to West L.A.

Even more than most other large American cities today, L.A. has a polyglot population. The largest number of people of Mexican descent outside Mexico. The largest Filipino population outside the Philippines. More Salvadorans than in any city in the world except San Salvador. More Koreans than in any city in the world except Seoul. The largest concentration of Asian-Pacific people in the United States. The second-largest Jewish population in the world. When one of our contributors advertised for household help, he received responses from natives of almost 40 countries—not just from the various Latin American countries but from Indonesia, Sri Lanka, Ireland, Finland, Israel, France, Jamaica, Poland, Yugoslavia. . . .

When you have large numbers of people from a foreign country in a given city, you are likely to have wonderful authentic food from that country as well. And when you have large numbers of people from many foreign countries in a given city, you are likely to have a lot of wonderful authentic food of all kinds. L.A. is now such a city.

Yes, the L.A. restaurant scene still has problems—lots of them. Too many restaurants are too noisy. Too many diners would rather spend their money on what they put in their noses than in what they put in their mouths. Too many people here are still more interested in what's hot than in what's good; they'd rather go to the newest "in" spot, hoping to see Michael J. Fox, than go to a restaurant where the chef is more interested in sauces than celebrities. Moreover, the city's proximity to the ocean notwithstanding, we still don't have a fish restaurant that remotely compares to Le Bernardin in New York.

But L.A. is still a relatively young city—gastronomically and otherwise. A dozen years ago or so, the Italian food in New York and San Francisco was so far superior to L.A.'s that going out here for any Italian food other than pizza was an exercise in self-abuse. But today, you can barely get through West Hollywood without tripping over several excellent, authentic trattorias.

Au Petit Jean was, in many ways, the city's first serious French restaurant, but it was at La Chaumière that the seeds of the city's best restaurants were originally planted. The chef at La Chaumière was Jean Bertranou. Bertranou's next stop: L'Ermitage— where he began developing the first, faint touches of nouvelle cuisine in Los Angeles. Bertranou, born in the small Gascony village of Morlaas, periodically brought some of the best chefs in France to Los Angeles for a week apiece to cook special dinners at L'Ermitage, but it was Bertranou's own cooking that soon made L'Ermitage the best and most important restaurant in town.

Bertranou died in 1980 of an inoperable brain tumor, but the restaurant life of any city is far more than the lengthened shadow of one man, no matter how talented and how visionary he is. Bertranou's colleagues in the early days—Alexander Perino, Jean Leon, Ken Hansen, Raymond Andrieux and a few others—all made significant contributions. Today, there are different stars on the Los Angeles restaurant scene: names like Puck and Peel, styles ranging from Selvaggio to Sedlar to Splichal, superb French food from such Frenchmen as Michel Richard and Jean-Pierre Bosq and such Americans as Ken Frank and Patrick Healy. One man, Mauro Vincenti, has three top restaurants, one French and two (quite different) Italians.

And who will emerge as the next culinary geniuses? While L.A. rockets into the '90s, the field is wide open for the kind of talent, creativity and hard work that put the city's restaurateurs and chefs on the gastronomic map during the '80s. One thing's for sure: it will be fun to watch, napkin folded in lap, knife and fork poised at the ready.

SOME ADVICE & COMMENTS

- Specials of the day are generally interminable lists recited in a most irritating way; invariably the diner forgets the specials within seconds. Some restaurants, but not nearly enough, print these specials daily, a practice we wholeheartedly endorse. Are you listening out there, restaurateurs?

- Unlike in New York, most restaurants in this car-dominated culture have parking valets, who judge your social status by the car you are driving. Be prepared for a wait when retrieving your car, unless you drive a Silver Shadow. And be prepared to tip the valet $2 to $4—more if you want your Ferrari handled with TLC.

- L.A. doesn't usually dress up to go out, but it does dress in one or another version of its costume-party style. In the more conservative places, men still wear ties, and jackets are almost de rigueur. But in the trendy spots, anything goes—fur coats to leather miniskirts, T-shirts to baggy black suits, cloddy Dr. Marten's to chic Frizon pumps. One wouldn't want to overdress for Spago or Rebecca's or underdress for L'Orangerie or Rex.

- Oddly, it's hard to find superbly fresh Pacific seafood (although the salmon is good). In fact, it's hard to find superbly fresh seafood from any part of the world, except in the city's best sushi restaurants.

- There are very few outdoor cafés in this city, which would be so conducive to the pleasures of basking in the warm weather and watching the city roll by in its cars. L.A. would certainly benefit from more such cafés, but please, no more of the typical ones that feature a view of the parking lot.

- When you make reservations in a place with a famous chef, check to be sure he or she will be there that day, not traveling across the country demonstrating Californian cuisine.

- Chefs have good days and bad days, so don't be too put off if your experience is less stellar than was ours; with luck it will be better.

- A note on tipping: Only a small handful of restaurants handle tipping in the European fashion by adding 15 percent automatically to your bill. More common is the automatic 15 percent tip for large groups, which tend to undertip. Otherwise, keep in mind that 15 percent of your pretax bill (including drinks) is a customary tip. We like to reward exemplary service with an 18 to 20 percent tip, but we rarely tip less than 15 percent. Captains, waiters, servers and busboys depend on a share of that tip for their main source of income, and so often problems in service, such as a too-long wait for food, are more the fault of the kitchen than that of the serving staff.

- Our dear friends and associates, the local food critics, have up-to-the-minute information on restaurants; be sure to read Ruth Reichl, Colman Andrews and their colleagues in the *Los Angeles Times*; listen to radio reviewers Merrill Shindler and Elmer Dills on KABC (AM 790) and Paul Wallach on KIEV (AM 870), respectively; and read the restaurant coverage in such magazines as *Los Angeles*, *California*, *L.A. Style*, the *L.A. Weekly* and the *Reader*.

ABOUT THE REVIEWS

Restaurants are ranked in the same manner that French students are graded, on a scale of one to twenty. The rankings reflect *only* the quality of the cooking; decor, service, welcome and atmosphere are explicitly commented on within the reviews. Restaurants that are ranked thirteen and above are distinguished with toques (chef's hats), according to the following table:

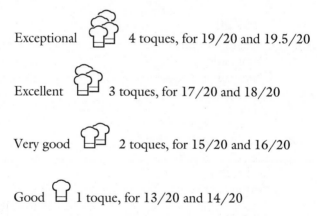

Exceptional   4 toques, for 19/20 and 19.5/20

Excellent   3 toques, for 17/20 and 18/20

Very good   2 toques, for 15/20 and 16/20

Good   1 toque, for 13/20 and 14/20

Keep in mind that we are comparing L.A.'s restaurants to the very best in the world. Also, these ranks are *relative*. One toque for 13/20 is not a very good ranking for a highly reputed (and very expensive) restaurant, but it is quite complimentary for a small place without much culinary pretension.

Unless otherwise noted, the prices given are for a complete dinner for two, including an appetizer, main course and dessert per person, along with tax, tip and a bottle of wine. It is, naturally, hard to estimate the cost of wine; for our purposes we assume a modest bottle at a modest restaurant and a good California wine (usually $30 to $40) at a more serious place. Lovers of the great Burgundies, Bordeaux or Champagnes will find their tabs higher than our estimations; conversely, those who like to eat lightly, sharing appetizers and desserts, will spend less. However, prices continue to creep up, so forgive us if a restaurant becomes more expensive by the time you visit it.

In many L.A. restaurants, chefs stay barely long enough to collect their first paychecks. This can—and frequently does—wreak havoc on a restaurant, which can go from good to bad overnight when the chef leaves. Menus are also subject to the winds of change, and the dishes we've described may no longer be available when you visit. We ask your forgiveness if a restaurant is somewhat different when you visit—we've done everything we can to keep up with the always-changing L.A. dining scene.

TOQUE TALLY

18/20
Citrus

17/20
Chinois on Main
Patina
Valentino

16/20
Antoine (Orange County)
Campanile
Champagne
Downey's (Santa Barbara)
Fennel
Norbert's (Santa Barbara)
Rex, Il Ristorante
Seventh Street Bistro
St. Estèphe
La Toque (Fenix)

15/20
The Dining Room
Fresco
Locanda Veneta
Marius (San Diego)
Matsuhisa
Michael's
L'Orangerie
Pascal (Orange County)
Pavilion (Orange County)
Pazzia

Primi
The Ritz-Carlton Dining Room
(Orange County)
Robata
Rockenwagner
Spago
Stonehouse (Santa Barbara)
Symphonie

14/20
Angeli Mare
Border Grill
C'est Fan Fan
Chaya Brasserie
Le Dôme
Empress Pavilion
Fino
Four Oaks
Hal's Bar & Grill
Harold & Belle's
Hotel Bel-Air
Ike-Ichi
Jitlada (San Fernando Valley)
Katsu
Kitayama (Orange County)
Koutoubia
The Mandarin
Pane e Vino (Santa Barbara)
Parkway Grill
The Ritz-Carlton Dining Room
(Palm Springs)

Ruth's Chris Steak House
Shiro
Tulipe
Tutto Bene
Warszawa
Wonder Seafood

13/20

Akbar (San Fernando Valley)
Akbar (Westside)
Angeli Caffè
Aunt Kizzy's Back Porch
Authentic Café
Le Bel Age
The Bistro
Bombay Cafe
Brigitte's (Santa Barbara)
Brother's Sushi
Café Blanc
Café Katsu
Café Pierre
Caffè Lido
Chapo
Le Chardonnay
Checkers
Chez Mélange
Chianti Cucina
Chianti Ristorante
China Sea
City Restaurant
Cuistot (Palm Springs)
Dobson's (San Diego)
Dragon Regency
El Emperador Maya
L'Ermitage
Five Feet (Orange County)
Five Feet Too (Orange County)
La Fonda Roberto's (San Diego)
Fragrant Vegetable
Gardens
Gaylord
Il Giardino
Gilliland's
La Gran Tapa (San Diego)

Harry's Bar & American Grill
Hugo's
Hu's Szechwan Restaurant
Hy's
Indigo
Ivy at the Shore
J'Adore
Jitlada (Los Angeles - Central)
Katsu 3rd
La Loggia
Louis XIV
Ma Bé
Madeo
Marouch
Morell's (Orange County)
Morton's
Off Vine
The Original Sonora Café
Orleans
Osteria Nonni
Otani (Palm Springs)
Oysters (Santa Barbara)
The Palace Cafe (Santa Barbara)
The Palm
Pane Caldo Bistrot
La Parrilla
Patout's
Peony
Prego (Orange County)
Prego (Westside)
Rainwater's (San Diego)
Rangoon Racquet Club
Rex of Newport (Orange County)
Ristorante Lido
Saddle Peak Lodge
72 Market Street
Shane
Shenandoah Café
Sofi Estiatorion
Sushi Nozawa
Tasca
The Towers (Orange County)
Trattoria Angeli
Trattoria Farfalla
Tribeca

Trumps
Versailles
Yang Chow

12/20

Ajeti's House of Lamb (Palm Springs)
Alouette
Bangkok 3 (Orange County)
Barnabey's
Benihana of Tokyo
Bistango (Orange County)
El Bizcocho (San Diego)
Broadway Bar & Grill
Brophy Bros. Clam Bar & Restaurant (Santa Barbara)
Café Jacoulet
Café Vallarta (Santa Barbara)
Camille's
Casa Carnitas
Casa de Oriente
Celestino
Cha Cha Cha
Chalet de France
Chan Dara
Chao Praya (San Fernando Valley)
Chartreuse
El Chavo
La Chêne
Chez Hélène
Chez Jay
Chez Loma (San Diego)
El Cholo
Il Cielo
Collage
Columbia Bar & Grill
La Costa (San Diego)
Cunard's (Palm Springs)
The Daily Grill
Dan Tana's
Da Pasquale
Engine Co. No. 28
The Epicurean
Five Crowns (Orange County)

Le Fontainebleau (San Diego)
Il Fornaio (San Diego)
Il Forno
Gardel's
George & Sigi's Knusperhauschen (Big Bear)
George's at the Cove (San Diego)
The Grill on the Alley
Habash Café
The Heritage
Hortobagy
Hymie's Fish Market
Iroha Sushi
JB's Little Bali
Jimmy's
Joss
JW's (Orange County)
Kaktus
Lawry's The Prime Rib
Ma Maison
Marix Tex Mex Norte
The Marquis West
Matuszek's Czechoslovak Cuisine
Michael's Waterside Inn (Santa Barbara)
Mille Fleurs (San Diego)
Mon Kee
Muse
Neptune's Net
Ocean Avenue Seafood
Pacifica Grill (San Diego)
Papadakis Taverna
Paradise Cafe (Santa Barbara)
Pastel
La Plancha
Plum Tree Inn
Remington's (San Diego)
Rincon Chileno
Ristorante Mamma Gina (Palm Springs)
Rondo
Scott's Seafood Grill and Bar (Orange County)
La Serre
Shame on the Moon (Palm Springs)

Shibucho
Shihoya
Siam Mania
Soho (Santa Barbara)
Studio Grill
Tommy Tang's
A Thousand Cranes
Tutto Mare (Orange County)
Val's
Walia
Wallaby Darned
West Beach Café
Yanks
Zumaya's

11/20

Aashiana
Al Amir
Los Arrieros
Babalu
Beaurivage
The Beaux Tie Grill
The Bistro Garden
The Black Whale
Café Prego (Catalina)
Carmelo's (Orange County)
Casablanca
Las Casuelas (Palm Springs)
Chao Praya (Los Angeles - Central)
Chopstix
The Chronicle
Cold Spring Tavern (Santa Barbara)
El Colmao
DC3
Duplex
Emilio's
L'Escoffier
La Especial (San Diego)
L'Express
Fama
La Famiglia
Gemmell's (Orange County)
Genghis Cohen
The Grand House

Grant Grill (San Diego)
Homer & Edy's Bistro
Horikawa
Inagiku
The Iron Squirrel (Big Bear)
The Ivy
Kachina (Orange County)
Kiyosaku (Palm Springs)
Knoll's Black Forest Inn
Lalo and Brothers
L.A. Nicola
Lawry's California Center
The Lobster
Kate Mantilini
Marix (Los Angeles - Central)
Marix (Westside)
Marrakesh (Orange County)
Maryland Crab House
Matteo's: A Little Taste of Hoboken
Maurice's Snack 'n' Chat
Mistral Brasserie
Moonlight Tango Cafe
Noodles
Old Town Mexican Café y Cantina
(San Diego)
Osteria Romana Orsini
Pacific Dining Car
Pancho's
Il Piccolino
The Ranch House (Santa Barbara)
Red Lion Tavern
Ristorante Villa Portofino (Catalina)
Rive Gauche Café
Romeo & Juliet
Rosalind's
Santo Pietro Bar & Grill
Siamese Princess
Simon & Seafort's
Sostanza
Stepps on the Court
Stoney Point
Talesai
Teru Sushi
Topanga Fresh Fish Market/
Reel Inn

Top o' the Cove (San Diego)
El Torito Grill (Westside)
El Torito Grill (Orange County)
Toscana
Le Vallauris (Palm Springs)
The Whale & Ale
The Wine Bistro
Yamato
Yankee Tavern (Orange County)

10/20

Abacus
Anthony's Star of the Sea Room
(San Diego)
Bernard's
Nicky Blair's
Borrelli's
Brentwood Bar & Grill
Caffè Giuseppe
Caioti
Dar Maghreb (Los Angeles -
Central)
Delmonico's Seafood Grille
La Dolce Vita
Dynasty Room
Fab's Italian Kitchen
The Great Greek
Hamlet Gardens
Hunan
McCormick & Schmick's
(Orange County)
McCormick & Schmick's
(San Diego)
El Mocambo
Musso & Frank Grill
The Nest (Palm Springs)
The Original Pantry
Panda Inn
Prezzo
Rebecca's
Spaghettini
Stratton's
La Strega
Tamayo

Tavern by the Sea (Orange County)
Teasers
Toledo
Tse Yang
Verdi
Zio & Co.

9/20

Adriano's
Baci
Bice Pomodoro
The Bottle Inn
Las Brisas (Orange County)
Las Casuelas Nuevas (Palm Springs)
Channel House (Catalina)
Chasen's
Crown and Coronet Rooms
(San Diego)
Dar Maghreb (Palm Springs)
John Dominis (Orange County)
555 East
La Frite Café
Louise's Trattoria
Matteo's
Orso
Paradise
Ritza
La Scala Boutique
La Scala Presto

8/20

Gustaf Anders (Orange County)
Antonio's
El Encanto Dining Room
(Santa Barbara)
Eveleen's (Palm Springs)
Frantrecôte
Gladstone's 4 Fish
Harbor Village
Malibu Adobe
Miriwa
Peppone
La Scala Malibu

Wally's Desert Turtle (Palm Springs)

7/20
Fung Lum
Lucy's Café El Adobe
Trader Vic's

6/20
Cabo Cabo Cabo
(Baja Beverly Hills)
Callender's

El Coyote
World Famous Malibu Sea Lion
U.S.A.

NO RANKING
Armstrong's Fish Market & Seafood
Restaurant (Catalina)
Café Montana
Maple Drive
Opera
St. Mark's

THE WORLD'S CUISINES

AFRICAN
Rosalind's
Walia

ALBANIAN
Ajeti's House of Lamb
(Palm Springs)

AMERICAN
Authentic Café
The Beaux Tie Grill
Broadway Bar & Grill
Callender's
Channel House (Catalina)
Chasen's
Checkers
Chez Jay
Chez Mélange
Cold Spring Tavern (Santa Barbara)
Columbia Bar & Grill
The Daily Grill
DC3
The Dining Room
Downey's (Santa Barbara)
Engine Co. No. 28
Five Crowns (Orange County)
555 East

George's at the Cove (San Diego)
Grant Grill (San Diego)
The Grill on the Alley
Hal's Bar & Grill
Hamlet Gardens
The Heritage
Hy's
The Ivy
Ivy at the Shore
L.A. Nicola
Lawry's California Center
Lawry's The Prime Rib
Kate Mantilini
Maple Drive
Michael's
Moonlight Tango Cafe
Morton's
Musso & Frank Grill
Off Vine
The Original Pantry
Pacifica Grill (San Diego)
Pacific Dining Car
The Palm
Paradise Cafe (Santa Barbara)
Parkway Grill
Rainwater's (San Diego)
Remington's (San Diego)
Ruth's Chris Steak House

Saddle Peak Lodge
72 Market Street
Shenandoah Café
St. Estèphe
Stratton's
Studio Grill
Tribeca
Trumps
World Famous Malibu Sea Lion
U.S.A.
Yankee Tavern (Orange County)
Yanks

ARGENTINIAN
Gardel's

AUSTRALIAN
Wallaby Darned

AUSTRIAN
Barnabey's

CAJUN/CREOLE
Homer & Edy's Bistro
Orleans
The Palace Cafe (Santa Barbara)
Patout's

CALIFORNIAN
Bernard's
Brentwood Bar & Grill
Brigitte's (Santa Barbara)
Las Brisas (Orange County)
Café Montana
Caioti
Chapo
Le Chardonnay
Collage
Cuistot (Palm Springs)
Duplex
Hamlet Gardens
Indigo
Lalo and Brothers

Michael's
Morell's (Orange County)
Muse
Noodles
Off Vine
Pacifica Grill (San Diego)
Paradise
Parkway Grill
Pavilion (Orange County)
The Ranch House (Santa Barbara)
Rockenwagner
Shane
Soho (Santa Barbara)
Spago
St. Mark's
Stepps on the Court
Tavern by the Sea (Orange County)
The Towers (Orange County)
West Beach Café

CARIBBEAN
Babalu
The Beaux Tie Grill
Cha Cha Cha
The Palace Cafe (Santa Barbara)

CHILEAN
Rincon Chileno

CHINESE
Abacus
Casa de Oriente
C'est Fan Fan
China Sea
Chinois on Main
Chopstix
Dragon Regency
Empress Pavilion
Five Feet (Orange County)
Five Feet Too (Orange County)
Fragrant Vegetable
Fung Lum
Genghis Cohen
Harbor Village

Hunan
Hu's Szechwan Restaurant
Joss
The Mandarin
Miriwa
Mon Kee
Panda Inn
Peony
Plum Tree Inn
Tse Yang
Wonder Seafood
Yang Chow

COLOMBIAN
Los Arrieros

CONTINENTAL
Gustaf Anders (Orange County)
Beaurivage
The Bistro Garden
Nicky Blair's
Chartreuse
Chez Mélange
The Chronicle
Crown and Coronet Rooms
(San Diego)
Cunard's (Palm Springs)
The Dining Room
Dynasty Room
The Epicurean
L'Escoffier
Eveleen's (Palm Springs)
Le Fontainebleau (San Diego)
George & Sigi's Knusperhauschen
(Big Bear)
The Grand House
The Heritage
Jimmy's
JW's (Orange County)
The Marquis West
The Nest (Palm Springs)
The Ranch House (Santa Barbara)
Shame on the Moon (Palm Springs)
Tavern by the Sea (Orange County)

Top o' the Cove (San Diego)
Val's

CUBAN
El Colmao
El Mocambo
Versailles

CZECHOSLOVAKIAN
Matuszek's Czechoslovak Cuisine

ENGLISH
Rangoon Racquet Club
The Whale & Ale

FRENCH
Alouette
Antoine (Orange County)
Le Bel Age
Bernard's
The Bistro
El Bizcocho (San Diego)
Café Jacoulet
Café Pierre
Camille's
C'est Fan Fan
Chalet de France
Champagne
Le Chardonnay
Chaya Brasserie
La Chêne
Chez Hélène
Chez Loma (San Diego)
Citrus
Cuistot (Palm Springs)
Cunard's (Palm Springs)
Dobson's (San Diego)
Le Dôme
El Encanto Dining Room
(Santa Barbara)
L'Ermitage
L'Escoffier
Eveleen's (Palm Springs)
L'Express

Fennel
Four Oaks
Frantrecote
La Frite Café
Gardens
Gemmell's (Orange County)
Grant Grill (San Diego)
Hotel Bel-Air
The Iron Squirrel (Big Bear)
J'Adore
JW's (Orange County)
Louis XIV
Ma Bé
Ma Maison
Marius (San Diego)
Michael's Waterside Inn
(Santa Barbara)
Mille Fleurs (San Diego)
Mistral Brasserie
Norbert's (Santa Barbara)
L'Orangerie
Pascal (Orange County)
Pastel
Patina
The Ritz-Carlton Dining Room
(Orange County)
The Ritz-Carlton Dining Room
(Palm Springs)
Rive Gauche Café
Rockenwagner
La Serre
Seventh Street Bistro
Shiro
Stonehouse (Santa Barbara)
Stoney Point
La Toque (Fenix)
Tulipe
Le Vallauris (Palm Springs)
Wally's Desert Turtle (Palm Springs)
The Wine Bistro

FRENCH-JAPANESE

Café Blanc
Café Katsu

Katsu 3rd
Symphonie

GERMAN

Knoll's Black Forest Inn
Red Lion Tavern

GREEK

The Great Greek
Papadakis Taverna
Sofi Estiatorion

HUNGARIAN

Hortobagy

INDIAN

Aashiana
Akbar
Bombay Cafe
Gaylord

INDONESIAN

JB's Little Bali

INTERNATIONAL

Babalu
City Restaurant
Gilliland's
Indigo
Lalo and Brothers
Moonlight Tango Cafe
Rangoon Racquet Club

ITALIAN

Adriano's
Angeli Caffè
Angeli Mare
Baci
Bice Pomodoro
Bistango (Orange County)
Borrelli's
The Bottle Inn
Café Prego (Catalina)

Caffè Giuseppe
Caffè Lido
Campanile
Carmelo's (Orange County)
Celestino
Chaya Brasserie
Chianti Cucina
Chianti Ristorante
Il Cielo
Da Pasquale
La Dolce Vita
Emilio's
Fab's Italian Kitchen
Fama
La Famiglia
Il Fornaio (San Diego)
Il Forno
Fresco
Gardel's
Il Giardino
Harry's Bar & American Grill
Hugo's
Locanda Veneta
La Loggia
Louise's Trattoria
Ma Bé
Madeo
The Marquis West
Matteo's
Matteo's: A Little Taste of Hoboken
The Nest (Palm Springs)
Orso
Osteria Nonni
Osteria Romana Orsini
Pane Caldo Bistrot
Pane e Vino (Santa Barbara)
Pazzia
Peppone
Il Piccolino
Prego
Prezzo
Primi
Rex, Il Ristorante
Ristorante Lido

Ristorante Mamma Gina
(Palm Springs)
Ristorante Villa Portofino (Catalina)
Romeo & Juliet
Rondo
Santo Pietro Bar & Grill
La Scala Boutique
La Scala Malibu
La Scala Presto
Shane
Sostanza
Spaghettini
Spago
La Strega
Dan Tana's
Toscana
Trattoria Angeli
Trattoria Farfalla
Tuttobene
Tutto Mare (Orange County)
Valentino
Verdi
Zio & Co.

JAPANESE
Benihana of Tokyo
Brother's Sushi
Café Jacoulet
Chaya Brasserie
Horikawa
Ike-Ichi
Inagiku
Iroha Sushi
Katsu
Kitayama (Orange County)
Kiyosaku (Palm Springs)
Matsuhisa
Otani (Palm Springs)
Robata
Shibucho
Shihoya
Shiro
Sushi Nozawa
Teru Sushi

A Thousand Cranes
Yamato

MEDITERRANEAN
Campanile
Fino
Opera

MEXICAN
Antonio's
Border Grill
Las Brisas (Orange County)
Cabo Cabo Cabo
(Baja Beverly Hills)
Café Vallarta (Santa Barbara)
Casablanca
Casa Carnitas
Las Casuelas (Palm Springs)
Las Casuelas Nuevas (Palm Springs)_
El Chavo
El Cholo
La Costa (San Diego)
El Coyote
El Emperador Maya
La Especial (San Diego)
La Fonda Roberto's (San Diego)
Kaktus
Lucy's Café El Adobe
Marix
Marix Tex Mex Norte
Old Town Mexican Café y Cantina
(San Diego)
The Original Sonora Café
Pancho's
La Parrilla
Rebecca's
Tamayo
El Torito Grill (Orange County)
El Torito Grill (Westside)
Zumaya's

MIDDLE EASTERN
Al Amir
Habash Café

Marouch

MOROCCAN
Dar Maghreb (Los Angeles -
Central)
Dar Maghreb (Palm Springs)
Koutoubia
Marrakesh (Orange County)

NICARAGUAN
La Plancha

POLISH
Warszawa

POLYNESIAN
Trader Vic's

RUSSIAN
Le Bel Age
Ritza

SCANDINAVIAN
Gustaf Anders (Orange County)

SEAFOOD
Anthony's Star of the Sea Room
(San Diego)
Armstrong's Fish Market & Seafood
Restaurant (Catalina)
The Black Whale
Las Brisas (Orange County)
Brophy Bros. Clam Bar &
Restaurant (Santa Barbara)
Channel House (Catalina)
China Sea
La Costa (San Diego)
Delmonico's Seafood Grille
John Dominis (Orange County)
Dragon Regency
George's at the Cove (San Diego)
Gladstone's 4 Fish
Hymie's Fish Market

The Lobster
Maryland Crab House
Matsuhisa
McCormick & Schmick's
(Orange County)
McCormick & Schmick's
(San Diego)
Mon Kee
Neptune's Net
Ocean Avenue Seafood
Oysters (Santa Barbara)
Rex of Newport (Orange County)
Scott's Seafood Grill & Bar (Orange
County)
Shiro
Simon & Seafort's
Topanga Fresh Fish Market/
Reel Inn
Wonder Seafood
World Famous Malibu Sea Lion
U.S.A.

SOUL FOOD
Aunt Kizzy's Back Porch
Harold & Belle's
Maurice's Snack 'n' Chat

SOUTHWESTERN
Authentic Café
Kachina (Orange County)
Kaktus
Malibu Adobe
The Original Sonora Café
St. Estèphe
El Torito Grill (Orange County)
El Torito Grill (Westside)

SPANISH
La Gran Tapa (San Diego)
Tasca
Toledo

STEAKHOUSE
The Black Whale

Frantrecôte
Hy's
Pacific Dining Car
The Palm
Ruth's Chris Steak House

SUSHI
Brother's Sushi
Ike-Ichi
Inagiku
Iroha Sushi
Katsu
Kiyosaku (Palm Springs)
Matsuhisa
Robata
Shibucho
Shihoya
Sushi Nozawa
Teru Sushi

SWISS
Chartreuse

THAI
Bangkok 3 (Orange County)
Chan Dara
Chao Praya
Jitlada
Siamese Princess
Siam Mania
Talesai
Tommy Tang's

VEGETARIAN
Fragrant Vegetable

Unless otherwise noted, restaurant prices quoted are for a complete meal for two, including an appetizer, main course, dessert and half bottle of wine each.

LOS ANGELES - CENTRAL

11/20 **Al Amir**

5750 Wilshire Blvd., Wilshire District
931-8740
MIDDLE EASTERN
Open daily 11:30 a.m.-midnight. All major cards.

Al Amir ("The Prince") sits in the midst of the Wilshire Courtyard, in a grandly opulent setting that makes you feel as if you're driving into the future as you head for the valet parker (permit parking rules this neighborhood, and the nearest parking lot is a few blocks away). Inside, the setting is simultaneously classic Middle Eastern and moderne. Service is respectful and most proper. Conversations are hushed.

Unfortunately, Al Amir doesn't offer the traditional meze combination, so you'll have to order appetizers individually. Though these appetizers aren't frightfully expensive, the portions are a bit small—the hummus is more of a taste than a bowlful. And $3.25 seems rather high for a bowl of pickled vegetables, though not as high as $11.50 for a small plate of grilled prawns. Nonetheless, we really can't complain: the menu lists many dishes we've never encountered before, such as the bazenjan makdous, a pair of Japanese eggplants filled with ground nuts, chilis and garlic (lots of garlic) moistened with olive oil. There are salads made with both lamb brains and lamb tongue, as well as no fewer than four raw-lamb dishes. There are even lamb testicles, served fried or grilled, as you wish (or if you wish).

Interestingly, many of the main courses are better bargains than the appetizers—most of the entrées are priced at just $10, not a bad price at all for lamb cutlets or grilled chicken in garlic sauce. Even the mixed grill, which offers a good deal of food for the money, is only $11.50. After the high enthusiasm level and conviviality of Marouch, we felt a bit odd having to dress for dinner at Al Amir and behave properly. The food is good (if sometimes a bit pricey)—the place just needs to be more fun. We're not suggesting belly dancers; perhaps all it needs is whatever's appropriate to help a prince to relax. Dinner for two, with wine, costs about $75.

12/20 **Alouette**

7929 Santa Monica Blvd., W. Hollywood
650-9119
FRENCH
Open Wed.-Thurs. 5:30 p.m.-9:30 p.m., Fri.-Sat. 5:30 p.m.-10 p.m., Sun. 5 p.m.-9:30 p.m. Cards: MC, V.

This is honest-to-goodness Mom's home cooking—if Mom's home is in Paris or Grenoble or Lyon. Homesick French expatriates and those who appreciate a good bargain frequent Alouette, a rustic little place with checkered red tablecloths and copper pots hanging on the walls. The inexpensive ($9 to $14) dinners include a bowl of simple, satisfying soup (usually some kind of cream of vegetable) and a fresh salad with a good vinaigrette. Entrée choices run the gamut of simple French standards, and all are tasty and well prepared. Roast chicken, either tarragon or provençale, is crisp-skinned and juicy inside, sweetbreads chasseur are tender and flavorful, and the crème caramel is smooth. This friendly, informal, honest restaurant provides a nostalgic alternative to all the hyper-trendy Franco-Italian cafés around town. About $40 for two, with the decent house wine.

⑬ **Angeli Caffè**

7274 Melrose Ave., W. Hollywood
936-9086
ITALIAN
Open Mon.-Sat. noon-11:30 p.m. (closing varies), Sun. 4 p.m.-11 p.m. (closing varies). Cards: AE, MC, V.

Before its expansion, Angeli was so small that, as the old joke goes, you had to step outside to change your mind. Or, perhaps, to make up your mind about which of the marvelous little dishes prepared by chef Evan Kleiman you'd order. Angeli is the antithesis of the old-style Italian-American restaurant, the kind with red-leatherette booths and cavelike lighting. At Angeli, the lighting is bright and the decor minimalist. The waiters are interchangeable with the customers. And the noise level is high, as it often is at restaurants that specialize in grazing. The central grazing dish here is pizza from the wood-burning oven, topped with true Italian ingredients:

pesto, onions, pine nuts, ricotta, mozzarella, Parmesan, prosciutto and sometimes simply olive oil and garlic. It's our favorite pizza in town, hands down. Aside from the pizza, try the arancini, simple rice croquettes filled with melted cheese, or the croquettes di patate, with potato replacing the cheese. There are perfect little antipasti plates, covered with bread scraped with garlic, various frittatas, smoked meats and lots of olives. For the most basic of snacks, try the panini, simple Italian sandwiches made with herbed ricotta, red peppers and black olives or with roast pork and pickled onions. Angeli's winning formula has led to two spinoffs, Trattoria Angeli and Angeli Mare, but this is the one we'll always love the most. Dinner for two, with a glass of wine, is about $40.

8/20   Antonio's

7472 Melrose Ave., W. Hollywood
655-0480
MEXICAN
Open Tues.-Fri. 11 a.m.-3 p.m. & 5 p.m.-11 p.m., Sat.-Sun. 6 p.m.-11 p.m. Cards: AE, MC, V.

Antonio's was once widely touted as L.A.'s best Mexican restaurant. Times were tough then. Choices were few. And anyone who added mole and birria to the typical taco/tamale/enchilada trilogy was considered avant-garde. But these days, experimentation with Mexican ingredients has reached a wide and wonderful level—and Antonio's is still living in the '60s. This is old-school Mexican: every plate arrives identically garnished, with rice at twelve o'clock, beans at six and a single carrot stick in the middle. And since most entrées are smothered in the same sort of brick-colored sauce, it's all too, too predictable. While Antonio's offers two pages' worth of tacos and tamales on its menu, the heart of the restaurant is clearly the daily specials. They *sound* good, even innovative, on paper: pollo en chipotle, ropa vieja, pollo en pipian (pumpkin seed sauce), chiles en nogada. But they come to the table overcooked, oversauced, overpriced and too much the same. And invariably, the specials for the other nights look far more appealing than those on the night you're visiting. The ambience is as behind the times as the menu: wrought iron, tiled arches, florid wall paintings. Dinner here will run about $50 for two, with wine.

11/20   Los Arrieros

2619 W. Sunset Blvd., Echo Park
483-0074
COLOMBIAN
Open Wed.-Mon. noon-10 p.m. Cards: MC, V.

Colombia is a land of temperate climate that grows such tropical fruits and vegetables as bananas, pineapples and plantains, along with such staples as corn, potatoes and beans. You can expect lots of seafood on Colombian menus, along with the usual chicken, pork and beef. (Colombian beef dishes tend to be tough, something chefs try to overcome by slow-cooking the meat for long periods. This technique rarely succeeds.) Los Arrieros (our waiter translated "arriero" as "a type of cowboy who rides on a donkey") is easily one of the most attractive South American restaurants in town, with dark-tile floors, polished wood tables and hanging wrought-iron lamps. The menu is a big one, with 26 entrées, many of which are convenient combination plates—bandeja especial, for instance, features a small, thin steak, a fried egg, pork skin, rice, plantains and a corn cake. On the fritanga plate you get pork ribs, small chunks of stewed beef, pork skin, fried liver and some very small pieces of veal tripe. Many of the grilled items are overcooked; more successful are the stews, particularly a seafood concoction served in a conch shell called concha Cartegenera, which overflows with shrimp, squid, fish and a too-heavy cheese sauce. Try the chorizo, a crumbly, dry sausage the chef makes himself. Dinner with wine will cost about $17 per person.

Authentic Café

7605 Beverly Blvd., Wilshire District
939-4626
AMERICAN/SOUTHWESTERN
Open Mon.-Thurs. 10 a.m.-3 p.m. & 6 p.m.-9 p.m., Fri.-Sat. 10 a.m.-3 p.m. & 6 p.m.-10 p.m. No cards.

It's easy to miss the Authentic Café, just a tiny storefront on Beverly Boulevard, a street where most people are accelerating and no one is walking. You could drive past the plain, blue-awninged facade a hundred times and never notice it. That would be a shame, for, as the large crowd *always* waiting in front knows, the Authentic is worth noticing. Hardly big enough to turn around in, it has just seven tall tables with high chairs and seven seats at the counter. In the kitchen—which is to say the other side of the counter—chef/owner Roger Hayot, formerly of Wave and the Cheesecake Factory, who cooks, answers the phone and mans the cash register. He has created a New Mexicanish café, complete with cacti on the tables, blankets on the walls and chilequiles on the plates. Though much of the menu runs toward nachos, tamales, sautéed chicken with tomatillos, and a cornbread-encrusted chicken casserole, the food takes odd twists and turns. There are curious pizzas (topped with chicken sausage and such), various pastas (including one made with chicken, corn and chipotle chile) and a smattering of good Chinese dishes, including great Szechuan dumplings. Is the Authentic Café authentic? We have no idea, but we'd be happy to eat there every day. As we write this, a spinoff restaurant was about to open in the same neighborhood. Bring your own beer or wine and expect to pay about $25 for dinner for two.

9/20 Baci

8265 Beverly Blvd., W. Hollywood
651-4776
ITALIAN
Open daily 11 a.m.-11 p.m. All major cards.

You can call the cuisine at Baci "Italian Lite," for there's no need to take the food seriously at this lightweight sibling of the insufferable Giuseppe! across the street. It's casual, it's easy, it's pleasant. It demands very little of you, which is probably why it's a popular neighborhood restaurant in neighborhoods not known for foodies (there's another branch on Pico in West L.A.). Baci may not change the way we eat, but it does feed us well enough—if we don't pay much attention to what's on our plates. It's the sort of place where women get together to gab about the problems they're having with men, and men get together to drink away the problems they're having with women. Baci makes passable renditions of fried calamari, linguine with bay shrimp and sun-dried tomatoes, and Italian sausages with sautéed onions and red peppers. There's also a "California sandwich" of alfalfa sprouts, avocado and Monterey Jack (no doubt for those feeling nostalgic for Woodstock, or so despondent about their own lives that they've lost the will to eat anything that has flavor), along with chicken and beef quesadillas, baby-back spareribs, chicken salad with a bland peanut-ginger dressing, and an assortment of hamburgers (including one topped with Gorgonzola and sweet onions). They make a decent pizza at Baci, probably the best thing to eat there. They also serve brunch, for those in need of heartburn on a Sunday morning. Dinner for two, with wine, costs about $40.

⒀ Le Bel Age

Le Bel Age Hotel, 1020 N. San Vicente Blvd., W. Hollywood
854-1111
FRENCH/RUSSIAN
Open Tues.-Sat. 6:30 p.m.-10:30 p.m. All major cards.

When you consider how much Russian cuisine owes to France (thanks to the nearly obsessive Francophilia of Peter the Great), it's not all that surprising that L.A.'s premier Russian restaurant is actually a French-Russian hybrid of sorts, with touches of nouvelle cuisine, California cuisine and hotel glitz. The style of the restaurant is probably best described as "drop-dead elegant"—which is to say swarms of maître d's, hordes of waiters and platoons of busboys, all catering to your every need and whim. The room, warm and soothing, is a virtual museum of pale shades. The banquettes are actually small couches with heavily upholstered arms. In one corner, a woman plays the piano while an intense-looking man concentrates on the balalaika; he's Emanuil Sheynkman, probably the greatest balalaika player outside the Soviet Union. This is a little like dining at Rex one night and finding the late Vladimir Horowitz quietly playing in the corner. The food is very expensive, very good and quite a bit more Russian than French. The cocktail of choice is any of the many flavored vodkas, infused with green peppercorns, lemon, orange, even Earl Grey tea. Of course, there's caviar (including beluga triple zero), borscht and chicken Kiev (filled with spinach and pine nuts and nestled in a Pinot Noir sauce). But there's also a rich chicken-and-lemon soup called chikirtma, plus a fabulous zakuska (appetizer) assortment of ratatouille, two types of salmon, two types of sturgeon, trout, sprats and sardines. Other dishes are an odd mix—coulibiac (a sort of salmon Wellington) comes with a very non-Russian sauce made with shallots and Loire wine; the exceedingly delicate quail Souvaroff is stuffed with foie gras and truffles; duck breast is sautéed in a Stroganoff sauce and served on a bed of fettuccine. It's a meeting of worlds that blend rather than clash. Peter the Great was really onto something when he formed an alliance between the foods of Russia and the cooking styles of France—a true culinary détente. Dinner for two, with wine, ranges from $100 to $140.

12/20 Benihana of Tokyo

38 N. La Cienega Blvd., W. Hollywood
655-7311
JAPANESE
Open Mon.-Thurs. 11:30 a.m.-2 p.m. & 5:30 p.m.-10 p.m., Fri. 11:30 a.m.-2 p.m. & 5:30 p.m.-11 p.m., Sat. 5:30 p.m.-11 p.m., Sun. 4:30 p.m.-10 p.m. All major cards.

The novelty of the Benihana specialty—watching the teppan chef dextrously wield his knife right under your nose—has paled a bit, but the grilled-at-the-table food is still good. Dishes include hibachi chicken, New York steak and filet mignon, sukiyaki and teriyaki steaks, plus three specials—the Benihana, with chicken and steak; the Imperial, a lobster tail and filet mignon; and hibachi lobster. All include soup or salad, a small shrimp appetizer, loads of fresh mushrooms and other vegetables. Decor is Japanese serene, with pale woods, shoji screens, and beams and stones from an eighteenth-century temple, and there is a pond providing a soft splash of water. Four other locations. Dinner is about $65 for two, with wine.

10/20 Bernard's

The Biltmore, 506 S. Olive St., Downtown
612-1580
CALIFORNIAN/FRENCH
Open Mon.-Fri. 11 a.m.-2:30 p.m. & 5 p.m.-10 p.m., Sat.-Sun. 5 p.m.-10 p.m. All major cards.

It's old history to rehash the fact that Bernard Jacoupy is no longer at Bernard's (he's at Le Méridien in Newport Beach). It's also old news that chef Gilbert Roland is no longer at Bernard's (he went to the little-known Califia, then on to the far more renowned Tulipe). But it is relevant to bring up these points simply because Bernard's has been such a revolving door in recent years that there's little consistency left to this rather grand hotel restaurant. When you boil it down to its bare

bones, all that's left of Bernard's is a pretty room, a menu that reads well, a harp player, good service and indifferent food. All style and no substance do not a great restaurant make. Consider, for instance, the signature bread basket, a curious combination of lahvosh (Armenian cracker bread) and banana bread. The well-written menu, clearly penned by someone who's never actually eaten here, waxes eloquent about sweet Maui onions and Roquefort in a salad that arrives with only enough onions and cheese to feed a hamster. And what is one to do with the terrine of turnips and carrots that holds a "chartreuse" of lobster, sweetbreads and chanterelles—at least that's how the menu described it, but we'd never guess what it was from the mush that arrived on our plate. Bernard's has long been a restaurant rich with promise and only occasionally with results. But it remains a restaurant in transition, where the chef seems to be in training. We wish him well, but we'd rather not have him learn his trade on our time—and our budget. Two will spend well over $100 for dinner with wine.

9/20 Bice Pomodoro

133 N. La Cienega Blvd., W. Hollywood
652-POMO
ITALIAN
Open daily 11:30 a.m.-midnight. All major cards.

During its heyday, Bistango was known for its distinctly cavalier attitude, both toward reservations and toward customers who didn't race in the fast lane. For a time its bar was the hottest spot in town, attracting the same fickle little-black-dress gang that eventually moved it's headquarters over to Rebecca's and DC3. Before long, as often happens with places of this trendoid ilk, a cannon fired off within the bar wouldn't have hurt a soul. Recently, the space was transformed into Bice Pomodoro (or Pomodoro by Bice, as they sometimes call it), the first L.A. branch of a Milanese Italian restaurant whose New York branch has been the talk of the Big Apple for a couple of years now. Bice Pomodoro is a puzzlement. Its postmodernist, futuristic decor (by famed New York restaurant designer Adam Tihany) is more interesting than comfortable. The food is decent but no more: carpaccio, pastas, risotti, gelati. And then there's the bar, which is usually busier than the restaurant itself. A good-looking but curious bar, it attracts Armani- and Versace-dressed sorts, like attracting like. On a small table near the reservations desk sit quite tasty bar snacks: chunks of good Parmesan, hunks of pizza bread, a pile of black olives. Unfortunately, there are no plates with which to carry them to your table. You have to borrow a paper napkin from the bar, then heap cheese and olives onto it and perilously carry the food from table to seat. Occasionally, an olive will fly in the direction of the tile floor, where it sits. We couldn't seem to find a waitress working the bar. And we thought about how one New York guidebook described the East Coast Bice: "as overbooked as an airline, with service to match." With that in mind, we suggest the next branch should be in San Francisco instead of Beverly Hills. Dinner for two, with wine, costs about $80.

10/20 Nicky Blair's

8730 Sunset Blvd., W. Hollywood
659-0929
CONTINENTAL
Open nightly 6 p.m.-2 a.m. All major cards.

We never ate at the original Nicky Blair's, which was a mainstay of the celebrity dining circuit from 1971 through 1975, when it burned to the ground. We also have no inclination to eat again at the revived Nicky Blair's, for this is the sort of Hollywood restaurant where you're either part of the scene or you're not. And if gold chains and shiny suits aren't your idea of good taste, then you're definitely not part of this particular universe. Just standing at the bar, nervousness begins to set in. The denizens of Blair's world are so utterly intense. Listening in on conversations, you hear chatter about points, the gross, the net, the package, the high concept, the low concept, the TVQ. People look well cared for, even pampered, in a glossy sort of way; the spirits of Giorgio, Bijan and Georgette Klinger hover over the room, and Ralph Lauren is nowhere in sight. Inside the dining room, things are slightly less wired. You're quickly evaluated for your status, and service depends on where you stand in the entertainment hierarchy. For us, service was slow—which was fine, because the food was heavy enough to give us pause. This is Italian/Continental cuisine in the style of, say, the old Perino's—not

bad, but definitely dated. This means standards like french-fried zucchini, calamari fritti, linguine with red or white clam sauce, veal piccata, whitefish with capers and lemon. Food isn't the point here; working the room is. Dinner for two, with wine, costs about $115.

⑭ Border Grill

7407 Melrose Ave., W. Hollywood
658-7495
MEXICAN
Open Tues.-Fri. noon-midnight, Sat. 11 a.m.-midnight, Sun. 11 a.m.-11 p.m. Cards: AE, MC, V.

The brainchild of chefs Susan Feniger and Mary Sue Milliken, (whose City Café occupied this spot before moving to La Brea and becoming City Restaurant), the Border Grill was the birthplace of nuevo Mexican cuisine in L.A.—Mexican minus the lard and the same old bean/rice/enchilada configuration, Mexican that doesn't depend on jumbo margaritas to make the meal exciting (though there is a good selection of beer and wine), Mexican that doesn't require a ten-hour recovery siesta. Milliken and Feniger have simply reinvented Mexican food, California style, with such instant classics as their grilled chicken—a tender boned breast, charred on the outside, juicy inside, smothered with sautéed roasted red peppers and onions, sitting on a bed of perfect yellow rice, accompanied by steamed chayote (a pale-green Mexican vegetable), chilequiles (a delicious mush of soft-fried tortilla pieces mixed with cream and cheese) and a cool, crisp salad of watercress and jicama. Even the three kinds of salsa that accompany the freshly fried tortilla chips are worth mentioning—one a chop of tomatoes, onions and cilantro, another a purée of tomatillos and the third a strange purée of smoked and dried jalapeños, which at first tastes like tennis shoes but quickly becomes an exotic addition. The guacamole, mini crab tacos, ceviche, sautéed squid, corn tamales, grilled scallops in tangy red sauce, veal tongue stew, fish Veracruzana (with a sauce of fresh tomato, capers, green olives and cilantro)—all are very good. Meat eaters will enjoy the sabaña, a pounded thin filet mignon grilled and folded over a paste of black beans, lime juice and scallions. For dessert, there's wonderful coconut and pumpkin flan and good, strong coffee, espresso or cappuccino. The crowd in this minimalist and miniature lime-green storefront café—and there is always a crowd—has remained a hip Melrosian mix. As we went to press, Milliken and Feniger announced plans to open another Border Grill in Santa Monica, early in March 1990. We'll be there, but in the meantime, we're happy to pay rather high prices for Mexican food that goes beyond Mexican food—as much as $60 for two if we're not careful.

Café Blanc

3706 Beverly Blvd., Hollywood
380-2829
FRENCH-JAPANESE
Open Mon.-Fri. 11:30 a.m.-3 p.m. & 6 p.m.-10 p.m., Sat. 6 p.m.-10 p.m. Cards: AE, MC, V.

Café Blanc, a tiny whitewashed storefront on a resolutely untrendy stretch of Beverly Boulevard (near Vermont), has only a small neon sign in its window to announce itself. On the site of the legendary Ishi's Grill, Café Blanc carries on its *Franco-Japonaise* tradition—and does it one better. Owned by a sweet young Japanese couple, it serves food that is simply exquisite, yet not at all precious. Lunches—complete meals including a light, oniony broth topped with a scattering of scallions, an entrée and dessert—are ridiculously cheap. Dinners are significantly more expensive but well worth the price. Café Blanc serves the best version of a Chinese chicken salad we've ever eaten, though this Japanese salad clearly has nothing to do with China. Served warm on exotic greens, the chicken is gently grilled, mixed with seasonal vegetables and lightly cloaked in a miso-scented dressing. The appetizers are dreamy, particularly the warm curried oysters with a cucumber sauce and salmon roe and the plate of beautiful steamed mussels with garlic sauce, which, like a truly breathtaking woman, needs no makeup for enhancement. Entrées are just as good, including a grilled chicken with mustard sauce whose nearly ephemeral hints of Japanese flavors seep subtly through. Other dishes—the roast duck with a distinctly uncloying orange sauce; the sautéed halibut (often the dullest fish in God's blue sea) in an elegant sea urchin sauce; the decidedly nongamey lamb with tenderly braised endive in a basil sauce—may

sound western, but the Asian tones are undeniable. For dessert, don't miss the remarkable jewel-like coffee gelatin served with thick, sweet cream—it's just the right note on which to end a Café Blanc meal. Dinner for two (bring your own alcoholic beverage) runs about $40.

10/20 Caioti

2100 Laurel Canyon Blvd., W. Hollywood
650-2988
CALIFORNIAN
Open Mon.-Fri. 11 a.m.-midnight, Sat. & Sun. 11 a.m.-1 a.m. Cards: MC, V.

We were sorry to see the second branch of Caioti close, for we found the Sunset Boulevard extension of this Laurel Canyon haunt preferable to its progenitor. Bad parking, a depressing room, terrible service and mediocre cooking did not make for a concept we were particularly charmed by. Despite our respect for Ed LaDou, the creator of Caioti and one of the driving forces behind the high-concept California pizza (LaDou's hand can be found in the pizzas served at both Spago and California Pizza Kitchen), or perhaps because of the admiration we feel for his creations, we were disappointed by his Laurel Canyon operation. Let us put aside, for the moment, any consideration of the lethargic waitresses and the Addams Family setting of Caioti in Laurel Canyon, and turn instead to the issue of pizza, L.A. style. It used to be that California pizza was defined mostly by the presence of goat cheese. But judging from the pizzas currently made at Caioti, the breed is defined by more than a touch of madness. Consider the pizza topped with chorizo, corn, cilantro, nopal cactus and salsa. Pizza topped with marinated pork, black beans, jalapeños, cilantro, onion and smoked Gouda. Pizza topped with chicken meatballs and a green-peppercorn curry sauce. Pizza topped with lamb sausage, grape leaves, red peppers and goat cheese. Pizza topped with prosciutto, cantaloupe, Gorgonzola, pine nuts and parsley. And there's more: pizzas made with shrimp and Thai flavorings, with barbecued chicken, with pancetta and leeks. LaDou also makes good appetizers of freshly baked focaccia topped with grilled leeks and goat cheese, and grilled shrimp wrapped in bacon and basil. The pastas are decent but no more—

try the fettuccine with sausage, tomatoes, fennel and goat cheese—and the salads can be failures. You'll even find a few entrées—vegetarian lasagne, catfish in a lemon-pecan sauce, half a grilled chicken. All of these could be very good, but we'll probably never know; we go to Caioti for the pizza. Everything else is simply a footnote. Even the lousy service. Dinner for two, with wine, costs about $40.

6/20   Callender's

5773 Wilshire Blvd., Wilshire District
937-7952
AMERICAN
Open Mon.-Fri. 11 a.m.-10 p.m., Sat. 11 a.m.-11 p.m., Sun. 10 a.m.-10 p.m. Cards: AE, MC, V.

Forget about those little branches of Marie Callender's found in suburban malls all around Los Angeles—this is the Callender's to be reckoned with: The Big One, the one unlike any of the others. In the midst of Wilshire's not-very-miraculous Miracle Mile, Callender's stands out like a refugee from Disneyland's Main Street. At night, with the exception of the new museum building, that particular strip of Wilshire defines terms like "dreary" and "dismal." Everything seems gray—except for Callender's. It beckons you in to sit at the long marble bar, to enjoy the piano bar and to eat some of the saddest food in town. There are pot pies on the menu, four of them, though the restaurant is often out of one or two. At one visit they didn't have the chicken or the Mexican pot pies. We chose the steak-and-mushroom-pepper pot pie over the turkey, and were sorry for it. The crust was good enough. But inside lurked a soup flavored, it seemed, with either Worcestershire sauce or A.1. steak sauce in it floated bits of gristle and some peppers that tasted like they'd been cooked since the earth was young. It was ghastly—but it was good compared to the lasagne we tried on our most recent visit, which was rubbery enough to play handball with. The hamburger that one of us had ordered arrived after the other entrées, and was not the version ordered; after a month or two passed, the proper one was delivered, a dry, tasteless thing with a side of frighteningly bad pasta salad. The dessert pies are numerous, and far too sticky sweet. Dinner for two, with a soda, costs about $35.

⑯ Campanile

624 S. La Brea Ave., Wilshire District
938-1447
ITALIAN/MEDITERRANEAN
Open Mon.-Fri. 7 a.m.-11:30 a.m., noon-2:30 p.m. & 6 p.m.-11 p.m., Sat. 6 p.m.-11 p.m. Cards: AE, MC, V.

"So, what kind of food would you say this is?" we asked our waiter on our third visit to Campanile, shortly after it opened in the summer of 1989. "Italian . . . I think," he replied, a quizzical look on his face. "What do you think it is?" We aren't exactly sure, but we can say that it's good—very good. Chef Mark Peel calls it "bourgeois, Provençal"; Nancy Silverton, Peel's wife, partner, baker and dessert chef, calls it "simple, rustic, nonfussy food." But with an Italian influence, right? "Southern California and Italy have a lot in common," Peel says, "climate, fresh ingredients, the chance for good, simple food. But we don't want to call our food Italian. If we do, someone will ask us to be authentic, and we don't know enough about Italian food to do that." Fair enough. But the wine list is filled with Italian (and Californian, but no French) names, the menu always lists a few pastas, and the appetizers include crostini, salami and figs; poached mozzarella with fresh pesto; and a ragoût of wild mushrooms on a bed of polenta. The menu also includes, however, wonderful soft-shell crab (with celery-root coleslaw), grilled Chiloé oysters, sautéed salmon, crisp, flattened chicken (sometimes rather dry) and (our favorite) grilled prime rib with white beans and sautéed bitter greens. The nightly grilled whole fish special is almost invariably excellent, and the fish soup—more a platter of fresh fish with some broth than a true soup—must be one of the healthiest dishes at any first-class restaurant in town. Interestingly, the pastas are generally less satisfying than many of the other dishes. Perhaps that's why we don't really consider Campanile an Italian restaurant. Then again, maybe it's best to forget ethnic labels at Campanile and just say the food is simple, hearty, rustic and, of course, good, whatever its origins. The breads and desserts are particularly notable; in fact, many other restaurants now order Silverton's bread from her La Brea Bakery, which adjoins the restaurant.

Peel and Silverton both worked at Michael's and Spago, two of the most celebrated pioneers in California cuisine, and they are now clearly about to become pioneers themselves. And they're doing it in one of the loveliest settings in Southern California. Architect Josh Schweitzer designed the restoration of the old building that houses the restaurant, and with its enclosed courtyard, Spanish-tiled fountain and hollow bell tower, it provides the ideal setting for a relaxed evening. The most desired tables seem to be the eight opposite the open kitchen, but it's quieter in the far corner of the restaurant proper or on one of the two mezzanines.

We must warn you: in its first few months, Campanile was having a difficult time serving customers promptly; many friends and acquaintances have had to wait an hour to get their food. From first-hand observation, this was clearly due to chef Peel's perfectionism and unwillingness to delegate. This perfectionism results in some wonderful cooking, but it's also sent too many guests home vowing never to return. We sincerely hope by the time you read this that the kitchen and service have become more efficient. (To be safe, we recommend coming early, before the rush; we've always been served promptly when we've arrived before 7:30 p.m.)

The wine list is neither unreasonable nor inspired. The Arneis from Ceretto ($26) is one of the better Italian whites, and the 1978 Rubesco Riserva from Lungarotti ($36) goes well with several dishes (even if it isn't nearly as good as the 1975). (As we go to press, the restaurant is open for dinner only, but it is expected to be open for breakfast and lunch by the time you read this.) Dinner for two, with wine, runs about $135.

12/20 Casa Carnitas

4067 Beverly Blvd., Hollywood
667-9953
MEXICAN
Open Sun.-Thurs. 11 a.m.-midnight, Fri.-Sat. 11 a.m.-1 a.m. Cards: MC, V.

This used to have good things going for it, besides very low prices: deep, rich, thick homemade soups, and Yucatecan side dishes of black beans, fried bananas and tomato-onion-cilantro salsas. Now it has more: some excellent entrées. Carne asada (steak) à la

Yucateca, formerly thin and dry, is still thin but is juicy and tantalizingly spicy. Arroz con camarones (rice with large, tender shrimp, green and red peppers, onions, peas) is saucy and delicious. Major surprises are a dozen sparkling-fresh oysters for $8.75 and a half lobster, perfectly grilled, with melted butter and guacamole dip, for about $8. A large seafood menu includes such delicacies as pulpo (octopus), and there are many Yucatecan beef and pork specials, as well as crab enchiladas. The crowd is mostly Latino, an unstated recommendation. The decor is primitive murals with some Day-Glo touches, and jukebox music jars the ear—but the food and prices are worth a little tackiness. With top-priced entrées, you'll spend about $30 for two, with beer, but it's not hard to keep the bill under $20.

⑭ C'est Fan Fan

3360 W. 1st St., Silverlake
487-7330
FRENCH/CHINESE
Open Mon.-Fri. 11:30 a.m.-3 p.m. & 6 p.m.-11 p.m., Sat. 6 p.m.-11 p.m. Cards: AE, MC, V.

On the site of the late, legendary Lyon (which reopened disastrously in Pasadena) and the late, legendary Chabuya (rumored to be reopening soon on the westside) is this sublime little gem. Located in a converted sushi bar, with counter seating for fourteen or so facing the tiny kitchen, C'est Fan Fan carries on its ethno-blendo tradition. But where the two earlier restaurants featured French-Japanese cuisine, C'est Fan Fan blends French and Chinese in almost equal measure. Though chef Hajime Kaki is Japanese, he's a veteran of both Wolfgang Puck's Chinois on Main and New York's acclaimed China Grill. Kaki is the whole show here—no prep or sous-chefs, just Kaki and a waitress. And he's quite a showman. Nothing is prepared in advance; when you order Kaki's revisionist chicken salad, he butchers a whole chicken, complete with head, right in front of you. It couldn't be fresher unless he slaughtered it, too. He spritzes oil, miso sauce and other mixtures from squeeze bottles into skillets with controlled abandon, arm poised aloft like Tinker Bell strewing fairy dust—and the results are truly magical. His movements are precise and lyrical, a Baryshnikov with a whisk.

You get the feeling that if a bomb went off behind him, he wouldn't flinch.

And his creations are exquisite. The aforementioned chicken salad is a subtle yet explosive mix of flavors—perfectly chosen greens, crisp rice noodles and surprising strips of deep-fried crêpes scattered on top, lightly and deliciously dressed, with a hint of peanut flavor. The chicken is spicy and warm, fresh from the skillet. The crabmeat crêpes are smooth and sly, with the unexpected addition of cheese as a sauce thickener, earthy slivers of mushroom and dabs of tart, made-on-the-spot papaya and raspberry purées as its crown. One of our favorite taste treats here is the simply named Chinese bread, an impossibly puffy pancake filled with chopped meat, mushrooms, veggies, a light touch of hoisin and lots of ginger. Entrées do not disappoint. Don't miss the Peking duck, one of the best versions of this old warhorse we've ever had the pleasure to introduce to our taste buds. Infused with garlic and plum sauce and served with scallion pancakes, the duck is nongamey, the sauce silky and buttery. The sautéed Louisiana shrimp with banana fritters (the shrimp are cleaned and deveined while you wait, the golden, ethereal banana puffs made to order) is both beautiful to look at and to taste. The shrimp, with heads and feelers intact, are fanned out on the plate around a pool of savory strawberry purée, with a gorgeous, glazy sauce over them. The squeamish should refrain from watching the preparation of the lobster—it's drawn and quartered while alive. Kaki sautés the lobster with soy butter and cilantro, twirling his chopsticks like Charlie Watts, pleased that he's executed a particularly difficult riff. The lobster is sauced with plum wine, Chardonnay and mushrooms and crowned with fried crêpes. Sweet, tender and rich with tomalley, its prized green liver, this dish is sheer perfection. The dessert menu is limited to ice cream, but the homemade confection is wonderful. The peach ice cream is creamy and chunky, enhanced with freshly cut cubes of peach and a squeeze of lime.

Fabulous vittles aren't the only reason to visit C'est Fan Fan; there are also the hundreds of dollars of (watch-while-you-wait) cooking lessons that are thrown in for free. Dinner for two, with wine, runs about $50.

12/20 Cha Cha Cha

656 N. Virgil Ave., Silverlake
664-7723
CARIBBEAN
Open Mon.-Fri. 11:30 a.m.-3 p.m. & 6 p.m.-11 p.m., Sat.-Sun. 11:30 a.m.-3 p.m. & 5 p.m.-11 p.m. All major cards.

When we wrote our last edition of *The Best of Los Angeles* a couple of years ago, Cha Cha Cha was one of the most annoyingly trendy spots in town, a colorful semidive in a seedy eastside neighborhood jam-packed with pretentious entertainment lawyers, good-looking, black-attired denizens of the art world and terminally cool scenemakers from all over the city. Now, of course, that fickle crowd has abandoned Cha Cha Cha for hipper pastures (at this writing, DC3, Maple Drive, Campanile and others, though the venues may well have changed by the time you read this). Our early experiences here, when Cha Cha Cha was *the* place in town, were less than good; the Caribbean-party atmosphere was undeniably infectious, but the food was atrocious. As much as we vowed never to return, we did, and we did again, and we had to admit that the food got better and better. And now that the trendoids have been replaced with low-key neighborhood locals of all kinds—meaning tables are easy to come by, even on a weekend—and now that wine and beer are served, Cha Cha Cha is an infinitely more enjoyable place to visit. Though the Caribbean-influenced cooking isn't earth-shattering, we quite like the flaky empanadas, the savory chicken-and-black-bean-filled sopes (like tiny tostada cups), the camarones al caribe (shrimp sautéed in butter, garlic and Caribbean spices) and the creamy house flan. The cooking is lively and robustly flavored, and it makes for an interesting change of pace from the usual Melrose Italian. Dinner for two, with beer, will run about $60 or so.

12/20 Chan Dara

1511 N. Cahuenga Blvd., Hollywood
464-8585
310 N. Larchmont Blvd., Larchmont Village
467-1052
THAI
Open Mon.-Thurs. 11 a.m.-11 p.m., Fri. 11 a.m.-midnight, Sat. 5 p.m.-midnight, Sun. 5 p.m.-11 p.m. Cards: AE, MC, V.

These days L.A. hot spots last about as long as it takes to say *"Franco-Japonaise,"* so it is quite remarkable that Chan Dara is still one of the best and most popular Thai restaurants in town. The two small, airy, casual dining rooms are jammed day and night with lively young regulars and more than the occasional celebrity. (Despite its handsome decor, the Larchmont branch is a little less popular and not quite as good as the original.) Typical dishes are done extremely well—a good, crunchy, not-too-sweet mee krob with fresh cilantro; chewy pad Thai noodles; a spicy beef pa nang; and commendable satays. The barbecued chicken, sadly, is available only on Thursdays, Fridays and Saturdays—talk about finger-lickin' good! The two-starred (for hotness) Thai barbecued sausage could stand some improvement in the taste and texture departments, but it is served salad style with lettuce and cucumber and is dressed in a wonderful ginger-lime concoction. There's a provocative crab and shrimp curry as well as spicy fried rice with fresh mint and chili. Beer, wine, Thai iced tea and coffee and even Thai lemonade are served. About $30 to $35 for dinner for two, with beer.

11/20 Chao Praya

6307 Yucca St., Hollywood
466-6704
THAI
Open Mon.-Thurs. 11:30 a.m.-11 p.m., Fri.-Sat. 11:30 a.m.-1:30 a.m., Sun. 11:30 a.m.-11:30 p.m. All major cards.
    At its worst, the food can be overly greasy and the service impossible. But Chao Praya, one of L.A.'s oldest and most established Thai restaurants, isn't usually at its worst. It does all the normal things quite well—satays, yum yai salad, Napa cabbage soup, Thai fried noodles, mint and chili with shrimp, chicken or pork—and doesn't try to be creative. Perhaps the best dish is the addictive barbecued chicken. It offers several different versions of fried whole fish (with mushroom, chili sauce, curry sauce, garlic sauce, ginger and so on) and also of squid, and a rather extensive selection of soups, most of them very good. The once-shabby Hollywood restaurant has been handsomely and dramatically remodeled. Another location (even better than the original)

in the Valley. About $25 for dinner for two, with beer.

13 Chapo

7661 Melrose Ave., W. Hollywood
655-2924
CALIFORNIAN
Open Mon.-Fri. noon-2:30 p.m. & 6 p.m.-11 p.m., Sat.-Sun. 6 p.m.-11 p.m. Cards: CB, DC, MC, V.
    As anyone who's visited Melrose in the last five years knows, the last thing that hopelessly trendy street needs is another restaurant. At least that's what we thought, until Chapo came along. At the time of this writing, this fine new practictioner of California cuisine was inexplicably struggling, having escaped notice of the throngs packing nearly every other Melrose eatery. How can this be? Is it because it dares to not be an Italian restaurant? Or because the atmosphere is simple and subdued, with candles on the tables? Whatever the reason, the lack of a mob scene makes dining here all the more enjoyable: you can hear yourselves talk, you can relax, you don't feel rushed. And the prices are moderate. Run by a young Belgian couple who met with great success at their Californian-cuisine restaurant in Antwerp (yes, we've even heard tell of a fabulously successful Cal-Mex restaurant in Switzerland, with $20 enchiladas, no less), Chapo actually seems more French than Californian, the grilled ahi with mango-papaya salsa aside. There's a strong Provençal leaning to the menu, with Italian thrown in for good Melrose measure.
    These are all dishes that suit Southern California to a T, from the fish and shellfish soup to the aforementioned grilled ahi (which, by the way, is delicious). We've tried about half of the small menu and were never once disappointed. Chapo plays with the Caesar salad recipe by using Belgian endive; the Parmesan and garlic croutons liven things up. Those seeking a lighter salad will be pleased with the mixed greens with a mild Xérès vinegar dressing. Pizzas are winners, their crusts boasting a pleasant touch of chewiness; our favorite is the one with prosciutto, goat cheese, mozzarella, Roma tomatoes and fresh basil. Entrées run to the likes of that old Cal-cuisine standby, grilled free-range chicken, here paired per-

fectly with a not-too-heavy goat-cheese sauce, sautéed leeks and tasty herb-and-chili-flecked fries. Meat eaters will love the excellent dry-aged New York steak with a peppercorn sauce, sautéed veggies and those great fries. And the desserts are homey and thoroughly satisfying, from the dense chocolate-raspberry terrine to the delicious warm apple tart with vanilla ice cream. Melrose may not need another jam-packed Italian caffè, but it's much improved with the opening of Chapo. Dinner for two, with wine, will cost about $65.

 Le Chardonnay
    8284 Melrose Ave., W. Hollywood
    655-8880
FRENCH/CALIFORNIAN
Open Mon.-Fri. noon-2 p.m. & 6 p.m.-10:30 p.m., Sat. 6 p.m.-10:30 p.m. All major cards.

The Parisian bistro that Le Chardonnay so closely resembles is the venerable Vagenende on Paris's boulevard Saint-Germain. As with Harry's Bar and American Grill in Century City, which is an almost exact replica of Harry's in Florence, Le Chardonnay is a loving re-creation, down to the most minute details. Gazing into Le Chardonnay as you drive down Melrose, it's almost impossible not to feel warmth radiating from within—the place smacks of a comfortable evening spent eating highly reliable comfort foods. It's a pleasure just to be there. All that fine brass and polished wood and all those glowing mirrors create an aura of activity and happy noise. In one corner, chickens slowly turn on a tall rotisserie, dripping juices into the pan below. In the rich, amber glow of the lighting, diners look particularly handsome and happy.

The menu itself is a bit of a compromise, falling somewhere between that of a French bistro and that of a regional California-cuisine restaurant. We've found this duality in some of the dishes, like the terrine of leeks with Louisiana crayfish in an olive-oil vinaigrette, the crispy sweetbread salad with sautéed oyster mushrooms and snow peas, and the grilled veal kidneys with wild mushrooms in a green-peppercorn mustard sauce—the basis of each dish is French bistro, but the ornamentations are Californian. And perhaps this is as it should be, for the bistro cooking of France has always been one of the purest reflections of the bounty of the land. The result is an awfully tasty hybrid that we'll call California bistro

cuisine. For the traditionalist, there's always the spitted wild Scottish pheasant, the sautéed calf's liver and the charbroiled New York steak. For the antitraditionalist, there are Louisiana crabcakes, grilled salmon trout in a tangerine sauce and grilled ahi in a ginger-lime sauce. Probably, if you ask nicely, they'll even serve you beer in a champagne glass . . . or Champagne in a beer glass. Dinner for two, with wine, will run in excess of $100.

12/20 El Chavo
4441 W. Sunset Blvd., Silverlake
664-0871
MEXICAN
Open Sun.-Thurs. 11:30 a.m.-10:30 p.m., Fri.-Sat. 11:30 a.m.-11:30 p.m. No cards.

You'll be serenaded by lovely Mexican guitar music as you grope your way through the gloom to your table at El Chavo, a commendable Mexican restaurant with a passionately devoted following. There's just enough light to read the menu, which offers many worthwhile dishes, from standard enchiladas to more imaginative creations. Our favorite is the terrific mole sauce, available with tongue or chicken. The poached Sonora chicken, perhaps El Chavo's most popular dish, can be a bit dry, but it is saved by a delicious, well-balanced sauce of tomato, bacon, onion, olives and chiles. There are a few dishes featuring tender, succulent pork; if you have an asbestos tongue, try the fiery pork chile verde. The classics—tostadas, enchiladas, chiles rellenos—are all terrific. Watch out for the tasty margaritas, which are automatically poured as doubles—two or three of them will have you doing the Mexican hat dance on your table. Dinner for two, with margaritas, will run $35.

 Chaya Brasserie
    8741 Alden Dr., W. Hollywood
    859-8833
ITALIAN/FRENCH/JAPANESE
Open Mon.-Thurs. 11:30 a.m.-2:30 p.m. & 6 p.m.-10:30 p.m., Fri. 11:30 a.m.-2:30 p.m. & 6 p.m.-11:30 p.m., Sat. 6 p.m.-11:30 p.m., Sun. 6 p.m.-10:30 p.m. Cards: AE, MC, V.

This place is very hip—Oriental waiters sporting chic black-and-white ensembles, a lively but discreet bistro atmosphere, fashionable rock (Talking Heads, Peter Gabriel) on the stereo, and walls hung with pine-framed mirrors that are tilted downward, so you can admire your new Comme des Garçons or Maxfield outfit. This is the kind of place where conversation centers on record deals, movie deals and how passé cocaine is. But don't let this L.A.-style yuppieness fool you into thinking that you won't eat well at Chaya Brasserie; quite the opposite is true. You can eat very well indeed at this offshoot of dearly departed La Petite Chaya, which was one of the first and most successful restaurants to combine French and Japanese cuisines. Despite a Japanese chef, however, Chaya Brasserie plays down its Japanese influence, opting instead for a marriage of Italian and French cooking with a slight Oriental overtone. And it's a marriage made in heaven. Everything we've tried here has been good: plump pan-fried oysters in puff pastry with a cream-sorrel sauce; fried zucchini stuffed with Camembert, and Japanese eggplant stuffed with mozzarella; a perfect grilled veal chop with Japanese mushrooms and earthy wild rice; slightly overcooked grilled salmon with a subtle pesto marinade and a very simple tomato sauce that tastes of the sun; and a lovely poached snapper stuffed with artichoke and served with a delicious herb-vermouth sauce. Chef Shigefumi Tachibe has a light touch and a talent for combinations that are interesting but not affected. Desserts can be less successful; the chocolate mousse cake is good, but the apple tart needs more apples and less density. All in all, though, the food at Chaya Brasserie is as consistently good as the ambience is fun. Despite the name, these are not brasserie prices— dinner for two, with wine, will run about $100.

 Checkers

Checkers Hotel, 535 S. Grand Ave., Downtown
624-0000

AMERICAN

Open Mon.-Thurs. 6:30 a.m.-11 a.m., 11:30 a.m.-2 p.m. & 5:30 p.m.-10 p.m., Fri.-Sat. 6:30 a.m.-11 a.m., 11:30 a.m.-2 p.m. & 5:30 p.m.-10:30 p.m. All major cards.

With rare exception, hotel restaurants in this country have long leaned more toward the predictable and mundane than the adventurous and first-rate; with even rarer exception, restaurants in downtown L.A. have been eminently forgettable. But there are signs that both trends are being reversed. The best res-

taurant in Washington (Jean-Louis) is in a hotel, the best restaurant in San Francisco (Masa's) is in a hotel, and several very good restaurants in New York are now in hotels. Downtown L.A.? With Rex, Seventh Street Bistro, Checkers and Engine Co. No. 28, both the quality and the variety of downtown restaurants are, suddenly, markedly improved. Checkers is owned by the same folks who own Campton Place, one of the best small hotels (and best restaurants) in San Francisco. Like Campton Place (the hotel), Checkers is small and luxurious. Like Campton Place (the restaurant), Checkers serves innovative American food. There's no one in the kitchen at Checkers with the skills and imagination of Bradley Ogden, who opened Campton Place (and who left to open his own restaurant), but you can eat well at Checkers anyway. And you can do so in pleasant surroundings: pastel walls, soft, recessed lighting, fresh flowers and plants, friendly (if a bit slow) service.

The grilled duck breast with peppered mangoes is especially good, as are the soft-shell crab with capered coleslaw and the double pork chop with mustard greens and baked beans. Among the appetizers, the chilled pea soup topped with sesame seeds and the smoked salmon tartare with ginger and shiso are most notable. The oven-roasted onion with a pine nut aïoli is also splendid. Desserts are excellent, especially the intensely chocolate devil's food cake, the Boston cream pie and the citrus and Mascarpone napoleon. Prices are a bit lower at lunch, but if you want to know the truth, the best meal of all at Checkers is breakfast. Fresh fruits and juices and a basket of scones, muffins and tiny Danish are followed by light, wonderful lemon poppyseed pancakes with citrus butter. Or ever-so-soft scrambled eggs with asparagus and Asiago cheese. Or waffles or duck hash or biscuits and poached eggs with chorizo gravy or. . . . Dinner for two, with wine, costs about $120.

 Chianti Cucina

7383 Melrose Ave., W. Hollywood
653-8333

ITALIAN

Open Mon.-Sat. 11:30 a.m.-midnight, Sun. 5 p.m.-midnight. Cards: AE, MC, V.

Cucina began as the baby brother of Chianti Ristorante, just an offspring opened in the kitchen of its far more opulent big brother. The irony is that this younger sibling has become much more popular than Chianti—in fact, it's one of the hottest (and noisiest) Italian restaurants in town. You are basically sitting in the kitchen; noise ricochets off the tile walls and floors and the marble counters. The din makes talking nearly impossible; even thinking about what to order is problematic. But the visuals are great—you can watch dishes for both restaurants being prepared and hustled off to their tables. It's like sitting in the middle of a very tasty three-ring circus. Most of the right side of Chianti Cucina is taken up by the kitchen area, where the chefs perform with a minimum of self-consciousness. At one end, there's usually a fellow making pasta with a hand-driven pasta machine. Farther along the counter, chefs stuff vegetables and put together platters of antipasti misti della casa, topping their carpaccio with thick curls of Parmesan cheese and laying the dried bresaola on top of heaps of arugula. Still others whip up aromatic pasta sauces and grill meat and fish over mesquite, a marriage of American and Italian ideas. The result: lovely small portions of marinated, grilled baby chicken, beef filets with green peppers, veal and lamb cutlets and satisfying pastas and risotti. The food is simple, as the best Italian food always is. A complete dinner for two, with wine, costs about $80; a simpler meal of salad, pasta and a glass of wine will run about $40 to $45.

⑬ Chianti Ristorante
7383 Melrose Ave., W. Hollywood
653-8333

ITALIAN

Open nightly 5:30 p.m.-midnight. Cards: AE, MC, V.

Unable to resist the temptation of joining the throngs of trendy Melrose minirestaurants, Spectrum Foods, Chianti's owner, opened Chianti Cucina next door. Chianti, fortunately, has retained its romantic, reserved, old-world atmosphere, making it a refreshing respite from the din found in every other Melrose hot spot. But the opening of Cucina seems to have put too much of a strain on Chianti's kitchen, which now services both places. The acclaimed homemade pastas are still delicately seasoned but can sometimes be overcooked and on the bland side. The service has also suffered; although reasonably attentive, the waiters can be amateurish, and the waiter-prepared Caesar salads aren't what they used to be. Still, Chianti has many wonderful dishes, including shrimp and clams in a robust, aromatic tomato-garlic broth, lobster tortelloni in a fine cream sauce and several interesting veal preparations. Although pricey, the wine list offers many excellent Italian bottles. Menu prices are reasonable, considering the atmosphere and style of cuisine: about $85 for two, with a bottle of Chianti.

12/20 El Cholo
1121 S. Western Ave., Mid-Wilshire
734-2773

MEXICAN

Open Sun.-Thurs. 11 a.m.-10 p.m., Fri.-Sat. 11 a.m.-11 p.m. Cards: AE, MC, V.

El Cholo has been around even longer than El Coyote—since 1927—and it's as fun as it's ever been. The menu is a little more ambitious than in the days when combination plates were the only real choice, and the food seems better and homier than ever. It's been a USC hangout since its opening; the students love it mostly for the incredible margaritas and the festive, typically Mexican atmosphere. But the food is good, especially the taco tray, a make-your-own meal of tortillas, chicken, beef, sauces and beans; the chicken breasts in flour tortillas with guacamole and zucchini; the salsa verde crab enchiladas; and the famous homemade green-corn tamales (from June to September). And we will always consider El Cholo's chicken enchiladas the best in town—the sort of dish that native Angelenos yearn for after being out of state for too long. You may have to wait up to an hour and put up with grumpy cocktail waitresses, but you won't mind if you nurse one or two of the perfect Cuervo Gold margaritas. About $25 for two, with margaritas.

11/20 Chopstix
7729 Melrose Ave., W. Hollywood
624-7789

CHINESE

Open Sun.-Thurs. 11 a.m.-1 a.m., Fri.-Sat. 11 a.m.-2 a.m. Cards: MC, V.

There is a certain faction of culinary purists out there who are certain not to think much of Chopstix. These purists will probably find fault in the menu that Chinese-cooking maven Hugh Carpenter has created for Chopstix. Those who feel that a Chinese meal is incomplete without an order of sea slug or a bowl of shark's-fin soup may not be happy here. Those who come from the "bouillabaisse can only be made in the style of Marseilles" school of dining will probably be put off by the radical menu. Those who think that Chinese food means one selection from column A and two from column B will find the place puzzling. But for those of us who enjoy the experience of being shocked by the new, Chopstix is just the right place at the right time. Rather than simply borrowing the idea of Chin Chin, Chopstix takes the concept of high-tech dim sum and turns it into "win sum dim sum"—complete with "new-wave noodles" and "radical rice." It's the perfect dim summery for the '90s, located exactly where it should be, on Melrose Avenue, and looking for all the world like one of those old White Castle hamburger stands, though significantly gussied up.

The menu, which is served until late (unfortunately rare in L.A.), begins with a section called Salads for the South Pacific, which includes a very good chicken salad, a Thai shrimp-papaya salad, a lemon-shrimp concoction and peanut-ginger sesame noodles, all of which are good warm-ups for the dim sum to follow. These are not the dim sum you eat with tea in Chinatown, though they're clearly relations—kind of like cousins who show up at your house sporting Mohawk hairdos and red high-tops. The Southern California potstickers seem familiar until you notice they're filled with chicken and spinach and glazed in orange sauce. Ditto for the shu mai that come stuffed with scallops, shrimp and scallions. The sea bass surprise is, not surprisingly, filled with sea bass and mushrooms. And then there's the marvelous Marco Polo pizza, a sort of Oriental bun topped with barbecued duck, mushrooms, scallions, ginger and melted cheese. The menu flows along in just that sort of fashion, running from mu shu and stir-fries through noodles and rice and into spareribs, satays and Oriental burritos. Where Chin Chin and Mandarette were the next generation of dim sum when they opened, Chopstix moves things yet further

along. It really is dim sum and then sum. And then sum more. Dinner for two, with beer, costs about $30.

 Citrus
6703 Melrose Ave., Hollywood
857-0034
FRENCH
Open Mon.-Fri. noon-2:30 p.m. & 6:30 p.m.-11 p.m., Sat. 6:30 p.m.-11 p.m. Cards: AE, MC, V.

No restaurant in Los Angeles has provided better, more creative food over the last two or three years than Citrus. An extravagant claim? Perhaps. But it's not a judgment made lightly. We have eaten here dozens of times since it opened, in groups both large and small, with chef Michel Richard in the kitchen and out of town. We've ordered off the menu and—much more often—we've asked Richard to serve us whatever he feels like making that day. Citrus has been packed to its whitewashed rafters since opening day, so Richard has had to make many of his most popular dishes over and over. Challenged, he's perfected them—and he enjoys making variations on them. But he also grows weary of them. What really pleases and challenges him is having customers who ignore the menu and just say, "Michel, make us dinner." "Are you hungry?" he'll ask. "Is there anything you don't like?" The best answers, of course, are "Yes" and "No," but if you want only one or two courses, or if you are allergic to shellfish or can't stand organ meats, just tell him and he'll create your dinner (or lunch) accordingly. At one lunch, for example, after a couple of small appetizers, he served us what he called a "fish ratatouille": diced salmon, scallops and tuna with vinegar, ginger, tomato, red pepper, zucchini and clam juice, topped with two perfectly cooked shrimp. Then we had the best striped bass we've ever tasted, the skin brushed with egg white, flour and couscous, then sautéed and served on a bed of couscous. The skin was crisp, the fish tender, the couscous chewy—the dish was magnificent. Next came short ribs, braised in a mushroom bouillon, then chopped and placed in a small dish atop a thin layer of mashed potatoes. Another layer of mashed potatoes was spread atop the meat, then covered with grated Parmesan and run briefly under the salamander for browning and crisping. Voilà: short ribs Parmentier.

Richard, born in a small town in Brittany, started out as a pastry chef, trained in Paris by Gaston Lenôtre, and it was as a pastry chef that he first attracted a following in L.A. His desserts can still buckle the resolve of the most determined weight-watcher, but he paints with a much larger culinary palette these days: a terrine made with alternating layers of smoked salmon and cucumber mousse. Venison in beet sauce with wild mushrooms. Foie gras in a crisp cornmeal crust with corn and chives. The regular menu at Citrus also features somewhat simpler fare, such as rack of lamb with an onion tart, tomato-eggplant terrine, Norwegian salmon in fennel sauce and sautéed scallops with deep-fried Maui onion rings. Richard is always experimenting, always changing, but he also knows his audience; there's usually a steak on the menu for the meat-and-potatoes crowd and several light dishes for the perpetually health-conscious and diet-crazy (although why anyone would go to a great restaurant and order a green salad and a piece of broiled fish, no sauce, is one of the great mysteries of our time). But Richard is more than a brilliant, innovative chef and a shrewd businessman; he's one of the warmest, friendliest, most generous men you will ever meet, a bearded, smiling teddy bear of a man who flirts (harmlessly) with women customers and smokes cigars (happily) with men customers. Forget all those stereotypes of the arrogant Frenchman, barely deigning to permit you to sample a morsel of his celestial cuisine. Richard is the kind of fellow who cries at your bad news, insists on drinking to your good news and says, "I want people to think of my restaurant as my home—as their home—as Mike's Place."

A few caveats amid all this acclaim: Citrus is busy and noisy, it can be difficult to get a table during prime dining hours, and when you get a table, you may not be able to hear what your companions are saying. Unless you're determined to sit on the patio, so you can be seen by others and look into the open kitchen beyond the large glass window, ask for a table inside, preferably one of the corner tables (numbers 1 and 8); they're much quieter and more private. Another caveat: the wine list is neither as complete nor as reasonable as it should be; more specifically, as with many relatively new restaurants, there just aren't enough mature red wines at affordable prices.

There are a few affordable choices among the whites, though, including the 1988 Ferrari-Carano Fumé Blanc ($20); if you want a white with more body, try the 1986 Sonoma Cutrer Chardonnay, Cutrer Vineyard ($32). Lunch at Citrus is a real bargain—appetizers $4 to $6, salads $8 to $13, main courses $10 to $15. Dinner for two, with wine, runs about $150, if you order from the menu. For just $45 per person, Richard will prepare a five-course feast—a *menu dégustation* of small, complementary courses that is not only the best meal in town but the best value available in any first-class restaurant in town. If you care at all about fine dining, you owe it to yourself to eat that way at least once here. In truth, the regular menu alone, as good as it is, would not earn Citrus this 18 ranking. But since Richard's special dinners are available to anyone who asks, at prices not much beyond those on the regular menu, it seems not only fair but essential to consider them in the ratings. And those dinners are worth 18—often even more.

 City Restaurant
180 S. La Brea Ave., Wilshire District
938-2155
INTERNATIONAL
Open Mon.-Sat. noon-midnight, Sun. 5 p.m.-midnight. Cards: AE, MC, V.

The desserts at City are so good that several of us went there just for dessert one night, to cheer ourselves up after a dreadful dinner at another restaurant. In fact, the desserts at City are so good that if you have a real sweet tooth, you might consider making a meal of dessert(s); skip appetizers and main courses, order three or four—or five or six—desserts and promise yourself you'll start dieting (and go to your dentist) tomorrow. Any desserts in particular? Virtually all of them. Just ask your waiter to accompany you to the large glassed-in dessert case between the dining room and the kitchen, and to describe each of the twenty or so desserts of the day, and then pick the one(s) that most appeal to your mood of the moment.

Unfortunately, although City enjoys the enthusiastic support of many of the city's more discriminating diners, we've never thought the rest of the menu was nearly as good as the desserts, even though we applaud the adventurous spirit of co-owners (and co-chefs) Susan Feniger and Mary Sue Milliken. Feniger and Milliken, who previously owned and cooked at what is now the Border Grill on Melrose Avenue, offer perhaps the most eclectic blend of cuisines in Los Angeles. They trained in France, Milliken travels regularly to Thailand, Feninger visits India, and both have spent time in Mexico. City's menu reflects all these influences and includes traditional American fare (and other cuisines) as well. On a recent visit, City was serving grilled short ribs, Thai melon salad, stuffed rigatoni, a tandoori special, a Portuguese stew of mussels and smoked black cod, and potato bhujia with mint chutney and yogurt (among other exotic dishes). The best dish we tried that day was the simplest: grilled baby salmon, perfectly undercooked, still pink inside, served with yellow tomatoes on a bed of spinach pesto. But the shrimp in beer batter was so overwhelmed by the batter that it had no shrimp flavor, and almost every other every dish we tasted was greasy, even the otherwise appealing parsnip chips—thin, crispy slices of cooked parsnip.

Saturday brunch may be the best meal here. Try the eggs Benedict on brioche with roast pork, or the brioche stuffed with pork and veal sausage and served with poached eggs. City Restaurant is a former carpet warehouse, with high ceilings, exposed beams and duct work and bare floors and walls. This strikingly minimalist decor contributes to the restaurant's resolutley hip image, and it remains one of the town's trendy spots. It's almost always crowded and noisy, and people-watching here can make for a most fascinating evening at a not unreasonable price: $130 for dinner for two, with wine.

11/20 El Colmao

2328 W. Pico Blvd., Downtown
386-6131
CUBAN
Open Wed.-Mon. 10 a.m.-9:30 p.m. No cards.

First, a word of warning: El Colmao is definitely for the more adventurous eater, simply because it's in the sort of neighborhood that necessitates an armed guard to patrol the restaurant's parking lot. Not much English is spoken, and service is a little loose. But the up side is that the food is simply wonderful, and it's so cheap you wonder how they can possibly make a profit. In what's basically a coffee-shop atmosphere (Cuban style), you can order a half chicken with a small mountain of sautéed chicken livers, which costs all of $6 and comes with a side of black beans, rice and fried yucca. The chicken is succulent and tender, the beans and rice musky and complex; a more satisfying dish would be hard to imagine. At the top end of the menu, where it gets expensive, are dishes costing as much as $11, like the shrimp with yellow rice (colored with achiote), a dish so good you'll eat far more than is prudent. To experience the sheer joy of Cuban cooking, there's also picadillo, a ground-beef stew into which a whole shelf of spices has fallen, and the classic shredded beef dish with the wonderful name of ropa vieja— "old clothes." Dinner for two, with beer, costs about $25.

12/20 Columbia Bar & Grill

1448 N. Gower St., Hollywood
461-8800
AMERICAN
Open Mon.-Fri. 11:30 a.m.-11 p.m., Sat. 5:30 p.m.-11 p.m. Cards: AE, MC, V.

Wayne Rogers has proven himself a smart restaurateur as well as a successful actor. He followed real estate's golden rule—location, location, location—when he established his handsome restaurant on Gower Street in Hollywood. No doubt he saw an area rich in upscale show-biz types, who work at nearby CBS and in local recording studios and production offices—and that they had nowhere to lunch. Sure, there are plenty of funky and/or ethnic restaurants around here, but no place for a proper lunch meeting. So Rogers created the perfect lunch-meeting restaurant, and it's been popular since opening day. It has all the right ingredients: a large, atrium-style central dining area with modern art on the walls, smaller, more private rooms in back, a comfortable bar, a brick patio protected from the street, handsome, friendly waiters, a good-looking New York–style decor, very nice wines by the glass and better than decent American bar and grill food. It's the kind of food that won't distract you from your discussion of residuals and options: properly grilled fish and steaks, fries, salads (Caesar and Chinese chicken), a couple of pastas, meatloaf, burgers, grilled chops and apple pie, all tasty and appealing. The crowds diminish considerably in the evening. About $35 or $40 for lunch for two, with a glass of wine, and about $95 for dinner with wine.

6/20   El Coyote

7313 Beverly Blvd., Wilshire District
939-2255
MEXICAN
Open daily 11 a.m.-10 p.m. Cards: MC, V.

There are two schools of opinion about this place, one of the first Mexican restaurants in L.A. To well over a thousand souls a day, El Coyote is the real thing; others (us, for example) label it the worst of Cal-Mex and are appalled at the glutinous orange cheese that seems to cover nearly every dish. But this hasn't deterred its fans from lining up outside for a chance to gorge themselves on dreadful, overflowing combination plates, tostadas that are mountains of sad canned vegetables topping fresh lettuce and tomatoes, and Mexican omelets puffed up to toque size. The decor combines the fake-peeling-plaster look with unappetizing Mexican art. But service can be excellent, and prices are as rock-bottom as the food, which (we hope) explains El Coyote's popularity. About $22 for an enormous meal for two, with potent but otherwise dismal margaritas.

10/20   Dar Maghreb

7651 W. Sunset Blvd., Hollywood
876-7651
MOROCCAN
Open nightly 6 p.m.-11 p.m. Cards: MC, V.

Flashbulbs pop, children stare and birthday-party groups giggle as the belly dancer (who's from Morocco by way of Redondo Beach) writhes about the restaurant, pausing here and there so the men in the audience can slip tips into her Middle Eastern bikini. This strikingly beautiful place, with its elaborate carved wood, mosaic tiles and hand-painted beamed ceilings, is an "occasion" restaurant—groups come here to celebrate all sorts of events, drawn more by its spirit of exotic adventure than its food. Fortunately, the food is a notch above tourist-trap standards. The prix fixe menu resembles that of other Moroccan places in town, and there are no surprises to be found if you've eaten in any of them. But most of the dishes are competently prepared, except for the dull couscous, which

oddly lacks the traditional spicy harissa sauce but has plenty of overcooked vegetables. The flaky, sweet-and-savory b'stilla is the highlight of the meal, and is in fact a meal in itself. The starter of cold marinated vegetables includes cucumber in yogurt and very good eggplant. Main courses vary, but usually include tasty lamb in honey-ginger sauce with prunes, a whole roasted lemon chicken and variations of squab and rabbit. This almost obscene feast is topped off with a basket of fresh fruit and nuts and a very sweet but refreshing mint tea. If you visit with a large group, follow the management's recommendations on wines for each course; otherwise, one of the bold German wines will complement your varied meal. A feast for two will run about $75 with wine.

Le Dôme

8720 Sunset Blvd., W. Hollywood
659-6919
FRENCH
Open Mon.-Fri. noon-1 a.m., Sat. 6 p.m.-1 a.m. All major cards.

Despite the fickleness of the movers and shakers in this town, Le Dôme—practically considered an éminence grise because it's managed to stay around for more than five years—has maintained its star-studded clientele and sterling reputation. The rooms have been redecorated to advantage, the lighting is more flattering than ever to women (and men), and the service is as professional yet warm to nobodies as it is to somebodies (well, almost). The crowd is pretty, polished and powerful, but aside from (or despite) all the foofaraw, the kitchen still turns out remarkably good bistro fare. There are plenty of salads to satisfy the lunching ladies, including a luxurious warm lobster on lightly dressed greens; grilled entrées of seafood and poultry that change daily; and the more substantial hearty cassoulet and nigh-unto-perfect osso buco. The desserts are still wickedly good, particularly the creamy, puckery lemon tart and the devour-every-crumb, warm caramelized apple tart. Of course, the added plus here is the people-watching—if you pay close enough attention, you may actually pick up some good gossip. Lunch for two, with a glass of wine, costs about $40.

11/20 Duplex

1930 Hillhurst Ave., Los Feliz
663-2430
CALIFORNIAN
*Open Tues.-Fri. 11:30 a.m.-2:30 p.m. & 6 p.m.-
11 p.m., Sat.-Sun. 6 p.m.-11 p.m. All major
cards.*

How exactly is one to define Duplex? The place calls itself an urban roadhouse. It sits in what used to be La Petite Chaya, just down the street from the eternally busy Katsu, on the single trendy street in the upwardly mobile Los Feliz/Silverlake area. Though not a lot has been done to the place, the decor has been de-Orientalized, the outside painted a sort of lime green and the inside funked up a little— but just a little. The sense of the place has changed from austere formality to casual ease; there's no need to dress up much for an evening at Duplex. It's far from polished in style, in execution, in its sense of what it is. But there's a feeling about the place of good intentions and sincere effort. The chef in the kitchen is one Mark Carter, formerly the pastry chef at Bernard's during its glory days, which implies that he knows a tart from a parfait. The food has its ups and downs, which might be a problem at higher prices; with the moderate prices at Duplex, goofs aren't such a big deal.

On our last visit, a good example of a goof was the salmon in an avocado sauce (which is decidedly not a roadhouse concoction). The salmon was good, carefully cooked so that it was a little crisp on the outside, a little raw on the inside. The avocado sauce would probably have been a good sauce under other circumstances. But the oiliness of the salmon and the oiliness of the avocado were not a marriage made in new-dish heaven. The ingredients were definitely not speaking civilly to each other. On the other hand, we liked the crafty appetizer of tea-smoked chicken with a spiced-noodle pancake, and the crab in the salad of crab, sautéed spuds and cucumbers was authentic crab (and plenty of it), not krab. Carter does good things with Snake River crappie (a fish that really deserves a better name), and he flavors a very tender veal steak with lots of thyme. The desserts are fine and dandy—would you expect otherwise? And those iced tea-aholics among us will love the

iced Earl Grey, iced camomile, and a combination of iced camomile and apple juice called Red Apple, a new taste under the sun. Dinner for two, with wine, costs about $55.

11/20 Emilio's

6602 Melrose Ave., Hollywood
935-4922
ITALIAN
*Open Mon.-Fri. 11:30 a.m.-3 p.m. & 5 p.m.-
midnight, Sat.-Sun. 5 p.m.-midnight. All major
cards.*

Rome has its Alfredo's, where tourists flock to taste bad versions of the gooey fettuccine dish allegedly invented at that shrine to overwrought Italian cooking. New York has Mama Leone's, where tourists either either precede or follow a play with a gut-busting trough full of ravioli à la Chef Boyardee and spaghetti with that's-a-some spicy meatball. And in L.A. those in the mood for a bit of high camp with their gnocchi go to Emilio's, where the food isn't actually bad, though it barely holds a candle to the ambience. If the people who built the Madonna Inn turned their attention to constructing Italian restaurants, the finished product would probably look very much like Emilio's. The place, which sits on the eastern edge of the hyper-trendy section of Melrose, is pure Fellini, with fountains gurgling colored waters, garish oils of rustic scenes lining the walls and overwrought wrought iron punctuating the whole affair. At the heart of it all is Emilio himself, an effusive *paesano* who used to run Jack Warner's private dining room at Warner Bros. and who has a taste for white suits worn with fire-engine-red shirts. He plays the concertina. He's worth the price of admission, which is not cheap. The menu is encyclopedic and, apparently, overwhelming to the kitchen, which rather than making a few dishes well, makes everything uninspired. Dinner for two, with wine, costs about $80.

🔲 Empress Pavilion

988 N. Hill St., Chinatown
617-9898
CHINESE
*Open daily 9 a.m.-2:30 p.m. & 5:30 p.m.-10
p.m. All major cards.*

Recently, Chinatown's culinary stature took a sudden and quite unexpected upward turn. At the Dodger Stadium end of Hill Street, a massive mall called the Bamboo Plaza opened. And within this plaza sits the exceedingly ornate and exceptionally fine Empress Pavilion, a restaurant that wouldn't be out of place on Hong Kong's Nathan Road. Like most Hong Kong–style restaurants, the place is awesomely large, with an assortment of sliding walls that can open with ease so it can accommodate 500 diners at a time. Normally about half the restaurant is open, which still makes for a good-sized room. Years ago, we were told that the one basic rule of Chinese restaurants is the smaller the place, the better the food, perhaps because in smaller restaurants, the food is usually hotter when it arrives at your table. But despite the Empress's size, the food there is as good as any in town. And thanks to a complex network of runners and servers, the dishes come zooming across the main room's expanse and land on your plate still sizzling and steaming.

In traditional Hong Kong style, there are 175 regular dishes to choose from, some of the best of which are listed as "Gourmet Selections" and "Mandarin Szechuan Specialties." No meal here should be without the fabulous sautéed prawns with honey-glazed walnuts, not just for the walnuts, which are a delightful little dessert tossed into the middle of the meal, but for the prawns, which are both plump and perfectly cooked—tender but solid, without a hint of rubberiness. The same can be said for the fried prawns in lemon sauce—perfect prawns with an understated lemon sauce (not to be confused with the lemon-pie filling so often served with this dish). Shrimp and chicken with black-bean sauce may not sound like much, but at the Empress, it's a piece of artwork—we've rarely tasted chicken this tender and this devoid of sinews and gristle. And the baked assorted seafood in garlic salt raised our old favorite, baked shrimp in spicy salt, to new heights; despite a sodium level that would have our doctors clucking with disapproval, the entire dish vanished in a twinkling.

We wholeheartedly suggest you order the Maine lobster or the Dungeness crab (both cooked however you wish), both of which come in heaping portions, more than you'd ever expect and expertly chopped so the meat comes out with ease. Empress Pavilion may just have the best beef in tangerine sauce in town as well. And for those who have long since given up on the idea of Chinese desserts, consider the honeydew melon in tapioca cream or the walnut purée. A superb dinner for two, with beer, costs about $50.

12/20 Engine Co. No. 28

644 S. Figueroa St., Downtown
624-6996
AMERICAN
Open Mon.-Fri. 11 a.m.-10 p.m., Sat. 5:30 p.m.-10:30 p.m. All major cards.

Saturday night, downtown L.A. It's as if someone put a deadly gas in the smog, emptying the sidewalks of all signs of life. We drive the Metrorail-mangled streets lit by the wan glow of empty office-building lobbies. We start to think that maybe there's no hope for the city's core, no chance that it will ever develop a soul and spirit. We start to think that maybe Beverly Hills isn't so bad after all. But then we hand our car over to a parking valet and walk into Engine Co. No. 28, a humble brick building tucked among downtown's latest crop of glass-and-granite towers. We could be in a timeless old San Francisco or New York joint, but we're not—these are L.A. people soaking in the charm of an honest-to-goodness old L.A. place. And a great-looking place it is, from its soaring ornate tin ceiling to its cubby-hole booths, from its burnished wood to its conservatively handsome upholstery. Even though swell old music—Billie Holiday, Frank Sinatra—is swirling overhead and every booth is filled with well-dressed downtown-business types, you don't have to strain to hear your dinner companions talk. It took years to restore this 1912-vintage historic landmark (the last firehouse built to handle horse-drawn trucks), and the care in the planning is evident—in the decor, in the superb (though not cheap) all-American wine list and in the service. Food and drinks appear promptly, the waiters know the menu, and even the busboys exude warmth and good cheer.

As you've probably gathered by now, we love this place. But wait—we forgot to mention the food. Okay, so it's not the best American cooking in town. But much of it is delicious, though, admittedly, we've had some losers. And unlike the 75,000 contemporary Italian trattorias around town, the Engine Co. is unique, a place downtown desperately needed. It's the kind of place you can return to again and again, gradually discovering which dishes to avoid and in the process finding a few personal favorites. Our favorites? The chewy grilled garlic bread. The thin, perfect french fries, either plain or kicked with red pepper. The fat, juicy cheeseburger, cooked as ordered and served on thinly sliced sourdough bread with a heap of fries and nice coleslaw. The first-rate pan-fried crabcakes, one of the four daily specials whose recipes are credited to firehouse cooks from across the country. The whisky-fennel sausages, juicy and mildly seasoned, accompanied with some of the best red cabbage we've ever tasted. And that eternal favorite, chocolate layer cake. We won't be reordering the bitter Firehouse chili, the humdrum smoked salmon, the massive, too-dry grilled pork chop or the gloppy rice pudding. But that's okay—there's plenty of good stuff to keep us coming back. And we'll be back. Dinner for two, with wine, ranges from $50 to $75.

⑬ L'Ermitage
730 N. La Cienega Blvd.,
W. Hollywood
652-5840

FRENCH

Open Mon.-Fri. 6:30 p.m.-10 p.m., Sat.-Sun. 6 p.m.-10:30 p.m. All major cards.

We're giving L'Ermitage thirteen points more as an act of homage than an act of equity. Somehow, out of respect for the late Jean Bertranou—the founder-chef of L'Ermitage and the man who gave Los Angeles its first world-class restaurant—we can't quite bring ourselves to strip the lovely but tired old house of its final, lonely toque. We really can't, however, recommend that anyone eat here. There is now better French food to be had at other restaurants in town, generally at lower prices and with better service and (in several instances) with as good or better an ambience.

At our last dinner at L'Ermitage, one of our party began with foie gras with haricots verts, the latter as cold as if they'd just been liberated from six months in an ice chest in deepest Antarctica, a jarring contrast to the velvety richness of foie gras. Worse, the seafood gazpacho was flat (except for what tasted like an excess of fennel). The special pasta was special only in that it was inedible. The scallops tasted

mealy. The duck with ginger and pineapple tasted like a bad sweet-and-sour concoction at, say, Trader Vic's or Don the Beachcomber's on a night when the chef was trying to break the world record for mai tai consumption.

We don't know whom to blame for the hard times that have befallen this kitchen. Michel Blanchet, who worked with Bertranou and did much of the cooking even when Bertranou was alive, is still the chef, but each time we go to L'Ermitage, his touch seems to have slipped further. We know he's very talented, but. . . Is he bored? Suffering a prolonged mid-life crisis? Whatever the reason, you know a restaurant is in trouble when you go there for dinner and wind up deciding that the best "dish" you tasted all night was a piece of Roquefort cheese (L'Ermitage being one of the few restaurants in town with a genuine cheese course). Even so, we couldn't help but notice that none of the cheeses were really ripe. Only the good-natured presence of our waiter, Scott, kept our mood from total desperation. At a recent dinner, when he mentioned the whitefish and lamb specials, he described them both carefully, in a normal tone of voice, then said, sotto voce but firmly, "Have the whitefish." The whitefish was just adequate, though, making us wonder—and shudder at—what the lamb might have tasted like. Moreover, L'Ermitage is so understaffed that even a good waiter looks bad; more than an hour passed between our arrival and the arrival of our first course, and we had long waits for everything else as well—including the check.

Needless to say, the check didn't improve our mood. Most appetizers are $16 to $20; soups are $7.50 to $10—except for "truffle soup in the style of Paul Bocuse," which is a trifling $38 (although, to be fair, that *is* $2 less than what we paid at Bocuse's own restaurant). Main courses are $27 to $32, and desserts $8 to $9.

The wine list is extensive and—compared to L'Orangerie, the other elegant French restaurant practically across the street—it's not unreasonable. There are seven California Chardonnays under $30 and a good number of Cabernets, Burgundies and Bordeaux for less than $40. The 1981 Haut Batailley ($30), the 1978 Bourgogne d'Auvenay from Leroy ($35) and the 1983 Clos des Lambrays ($45) are all well worth drinking, and they're fairly priced for a luxury restaurant. Even less expensive Beaujolais and wines from the Loire, Alsace and Rhône regions are also available. Dinner for two, with wine, will leave you some $210 poorer.

12/20 Gardel's

7963 Melrose Ave., W. Hollywood
655-0891
ARGENTINIAN/ITALIAN
Open Mon.-Sat. 6 p.m.-11 p.m. Cards: AE, MC, V.

Gardel's is named for Carlos Gardel, a legendary tango musician who died in 1935 but who lives on in the music of Argentina. The dishes served at Gardel's also go back in Argentinian history, to such classic preparations as matambre ("hunger killer"), a rolled, stuffed dish very much like the German dish Roulade. Normally, matambre is made with flank steak, but every now and then Gardel's makes it with chicken, filled with pickles, pimientos, hard-cooked eggs and sundry herbs. Most everything is made with a little twist at Gardel's. Consider, for instance, the ajo al horno, which is simply a head—an entire head—of garlic, baked then sliced across the top. Baking diminishes the strength of the garlic, giving it a rich, nutlike flavor. You eat it by taking the head in hand and giving it a good squeeze over a slice of bread; the thick garlic purée oozes out like so much toothpaste. Garlic also appears in the powerfully flavored vermicelli al pesto, so strong it almost burns. For a change, the parrillada gives you a less-garlicky assortment of skirt steak, grilled sweetbreads, dark, musky blood sausage, sweet and spicy Italian sausage and short ribs—but then the pollo de ajo brings us back to the world of garlic. It seems that when you marry Italian and Argentinian cuisines, their offspring is a head of garlic. Dinner for two, with wine, will cost you about $65.

⑬ Gardens

Four Seasons Hotel, 300 S. Doheny Dr., W. Hollywood
273-2222
FRENCH
Open Sun.-Thurs. 6:30 a.m.-2:30 p.m. & 6 p.m.-10 p.m., Fri.-Sat. 6:30 a.m.-2:30 p.m. & 6 p.m.-10:30 p.m. All major cards.

A few years back, one of the country's most talked-about chefs, Lydia Shire, opened the lovely Gardens in the equally lovely new Four Seasons Hotel; her food was eccentric, highly inventive and pretty good. As we suspected, however, the food was just too weird for a mainstream hotel dining room, and Shire and the Four Seasons soon parted ways. After a long in-between stage, the kitchen is now committed to a new cuisine under the direction of a new executive chef, Pascal Vignau (who's spent time in several fine French kitchens, including Jacques Maximin's), and chef Jean Pierre Lemanissier (who worked with Paul Bocuse and was chef at the old Ma Maison in the mid-'80s). Their food is much more suited to an upscale hotel dining room than Shire's was; though it's less exciting, it's also less threatening, which is important for a restaurant whose primary purpose is to serve often-harried, often-jet-lagged hotel guests.

Nothing has changed in the series of dining rooms, which are still as elegant, intimate and soothingly plush as ever (though the atmosphere can be a bit stiff at times). Service is formal yet friendly, though at our last dinner here, on a quiet Sunday night, the waiter was frazzled and inattentive (but we're fairly certain that this was an exception, not a rule). Also unchanged, happily, is the basket of assorted breads—breadsticks, toasted slices of buttery brioche, French bread, wonderfully crisp flatbread—plopped on your table when you arrive, a most refreshing change from the customary banal rolls. The new cuisine is a well-rounded collection of classic-contemporary French dishes—neither wildly inventive nor Continental-cuisine stodgy, with enough lightness and fashionable flavor combinations (grilled Pacific swordfish with first-pressed olive oil, tomato and basil) to call it modern, and enough conservatism (prime New York steak in a shallot-Cabernet sauce) to keep even the finickiest business traveler happy. Notable successes include the marvelous crab-and-wild-mushroom-filled ravioli, a perfect balance of flavors; the robustly Mediterranean oak-leaf salad topped with little rounds of excellent Italian goat cheese and dressed with a sort of mashing of sun-dried tomatoes and olive oil; and the thick, flavorful marinated rack of veal with a vegetable strudel and plenty of meaty morels. The desserts aren't knockouts, but they're well prepared and appropriately fancy; try the delicious warm hazelnut pudding soufflé with bourbon sauce and the classic apple crisp with vanilla ice cream.

Hotel dining rooms are too often sad, overpriced places serving boring, pretentious food to weary travelers. Not so Gardens. True, it is costly, but you get an intelligent, flavorful meal for your dollar, along with a beautiful setting, a romantic ambience, a minimum number of trendies and plenty of blessed quiet. Two will spend about $120 for dinner with wine.

 Gaylord
50 N. La Cienega Blvd.,
W. Hollywood
652-3838
INDIAN
Open daily 11:30 a.m.-2:30 p.m. & 5:30 p.m.-11 p.m. All major cards.

The Gaylord restaurant chain can trace its genealogy back to 1941, when the first Gaylord opened in New Delhi. Since then, branches have spread to Bombay, London, San Francisco, Hong Kong, Chicago, New York and, more recently, Los Angeles. Supposedly the chefs at each branch are trained at the original Gaylord in New Delhi. This is highly sophisticated Indian cooking, among the best in town, served in an elegant restaurant thick with mauves, pinks, grays and mirrored walls. Since it's hidden away in a La Cienega office building, L.A.'s Gaylord lacks the visual drama of some of its brothers (the San Francisco one, for instance, has a million-dollar view of the bay and the Golden Gate Bridge). But the bottom line is the food, which is always quite fine, though rarely extraordinary. The menu journeys through the usual territory: mulligatawny soup, fine tandoori dishes, reliable kebabs, jolly breads and so forth—good dishes that have, over the years, become old friends. We only wish the menu wasn't so predictable, even if it is predictably delicious. Dinner for two, with Indian beer, costs about $65 or $70.

11/20 Genghis Cohen
740 N. Fairfax Ave., Hollywood
653-0643
CHINESE
Open Tues.-Fri. 11:30 a.m.-2:30 p.m. & 5 p.m.-11 p.m., Sat. 5 p.m.-11 p.m., Sun. 5 p.m.-10 p.m. Cards: AE, MC, V.

At least the name of this place convinces us that America is still a melting pot, a country where a nice Jewish boy and a Mogul conqueror can join forces and open a humble Chinese restaurant. Genghis Cohen, located in the heart of L.A.'s Jewish community, attempts to offer both creative Chinese cooking and a sophisticated ambience. Although the results are not always successful, we like the place for trying. Hidden away in a nondescript strip center on Fairfax Avenue, Genghis Cohen is a sleek, contemporary place done in black, white and gray, with comfortable banquettes and recorded jazz music in the background. This cool setting is warmed by the management's hokey sense of humor: cocktails called the Lounge Lizard and the Ori-Yentl margarita, an appetizer assortment called Shanghai Schwartz's #1 Nosh and a selection of poultry dishes entitled Our Fowlest. The cuisine is a sampling of several Chinese provinces, with Szechuan, not surprisingly, being the favorite. Crispy fried chicken wings, accompanied by two excellent dipping sauces, are brought to your table when you sit down, followed by a small bowl of respectable hot-and-sour soup. Pan-fried dumplings are meaty and juicy, served with a delicious chili sauce. The kung pao chicken is fine, and the three-flavor mu shu, filled with shrimp, chicken and pork, is marvelous, each flavor distinct. But there are disappointments, especially the crackerjack shrimp, which are not as crispy as the name implies and are instead totally bland. Orange peel chicken is better, though not as good as it should be. Nonetheless, you'll enjoy Genghis Cohen, and you're sure to find a few favorites on the menu after some experimentation. About $40 for dinner for two, with drinks.

Harold & Belle's
2920 W. Jefferson Blvd.,
South-Central L.A.
735-9023
SOUL FOOD
Open Mon. & Wed.-Thurs. noon-10 p.m., Fri. noon-midnight, Sat. 1 p.m.-midnight, Sun. 1 p.m.-10 p.m. Cards: AE, MC, V.

One trip to RJ's or the Malibu Sea Lion is all you need to realize that massive portions do not make for good cooking. In fact, outsized portions are frequently a sign of trouble. But at Harold & Belle's, L.A.'s best (and most elegant) soul food restaurant, the quality of the food is as impressive as the gargantuan quantities. This means this place is always full, so you'll need to make reservations far in advance, especially for a weekend night and Sunday lunch (you'll also need to dress up a bit—this is no down-home dive). Harold & Belle's, which has been serving superb soul and Cajun/Creole food since 1969, is probably the single most popular restaurant in central Los Angeles. And for good reason—the food here is like a taste of spicy heaven, offered in portions too big for anyone to finish. Appetizers here are bigger than main courses in other restaurants, and main courses are suitable for groups of four. A heaping (and we do emphasize heaping) appetizer of wonderful Louisiana-style hot links neatly stuffed two of us with fine slices of thick, coarse sausage, rich with levels of spices, served with a dipping sauce that sparkles with fire. Clam chowder turns out to be a massive bowl of thick, moderately spicy soup-stew, heavy with clams and potatoes. The main courses are so large that people tend to laugh hysterically when they arrive on the table: piles of corn on the cob, fine potato salad and such entrées as redfish Suzette, which is three massive filets of pan-fried breaded redfish topped with a cream-laden crayfish sauce. There's much to choose from: fried catfish, soft-shell crabs, breaded Louisiana oysters, shrimp Creole, shrimp Ryan (with mushrooms and scallions in a brown sauce), even hyperbolic po' boy sandwiches. At the end of your meal, there are equally large desserts. Don't expect to eat much for the next day or two. Dinner for two, with drinks, ranges from $50 to $70.

11/20 Homer & Edy's Bistro

2839 S. Robertson Blvd., Rancho Park
559-5102
CAJUN/CREOLE
Open Tues.-Sat. 11:30 a.m.-2:30 p.m. & 6 p.m.-11 p.m., Sun. 5 p.m.-10 p.m. Cards: AE, MC, V.

For years, Homer & Edy's served the cooking of old New Orleans to a loyal following who came to this restaurant, which is decorated like a home in the Crescent City's Garden District to eat red beans and rice, sundry gumbos and decent jambalaya. Then, along came Paul Prudhomme and his newer style of Cajun/Creole cooking, and Homer & Edy's was suddenly left seeming very old-fashioned indeed. They probably never knew what hit them, and are no doubt still puzzled by the crowds that instantly descended on the now-defunct Ritz Café and the still-popular Orleans—crowds that never bothered to pass through the dining room at Homer & Edy's. To its credit, this restaurant has stuck by its guns, cooking the same dishes it's always cooked, without turning to blackened this and that. The food does have a pleasantly dusty quality to it, like cuisine from a museum. This is the cooking of Antoine's and Galatoire's, and it's prepared quite well. Seated in the living room or parlor, you can eat some eminently decent shrimp rémoulade, followed by four different gumbos, oysters Rockefeller and oysters Bienville, shrimp etouffée and poisson en papillote. The truth is that the food really is better at Orleans and Patout's. But with the exception of the occasional lapse—like the oyster stew and the flambéed spinach salad—the cooking is pretty reliable at Homer & Edy's. And it's the only New Orleans restaurant in town with a live jazz band playing every night. Dinner for two, with wine, costs around $80.

11/20 Horikawa

111 S. San Pedro St., Little Tokyo
680-9355
JAPANESE
Open Tues.-Thurs. 11:30 a.m.-2 p.m. & 6 p.m.-10 p.m., Fri. 11:30 a.m.-2 p.m. & 6 p.m.-10 p.m., Sat. 5:30 p.m.-11 p.m., Sun. 5 p.m.-10 p.m. All major cards.

When you enter Horikawa, you walk down a flight of stairs into a land of bamboo screens, gently burbling fountains and soft melodic refrains. On one side is a busy and quite jolly sushi bar; in the distance is a pleasant dining room; across the lobby is an attractive, very soothing bar, perfect for liaisons between people who are married, but not to each other. Perhaps best of all, though, is the teppan-yaki room, which serves dishes like those found at Benihana—only in this case, the dishes are really Japanese. The salad is a traditional sunomono, the tofu soup is pleasant, and the air is filled with refined anticipation. What you're waiting for is . . . the Chef. He arrives with happy hands, tossing handfuls of shrimp into the air, deveining, seasoning and butterflying them in midflight. They land on the grill and turn instantly from blue-gray to reddish-pink. Onions are chopped, mushrooms and zucchini sliced, bean sprouts herded about. After that come steaks (New York, filet mignon or ribeye), chicken, lobster tails and scallops. It's a group experience, all centering around the Chef. At the end of the meal, he inevitably receives an ovation, which is acknowledged with the most modest of bows. Dinner for two, with sake or beer, can run from $60 to $90, depending on what you order.

Hugo's
8401 Santa Monica Blvd.,
W. Hollywood
654-4088
ITALIAN
Open daily 6 a.m.-4:30 p.m. & 5 p.m.-11:30 p.m. Cards: AE, MC, V.

Hugo's was once one of L.A.'s best butcher shops; you could buy no better provini veal in town. The butchers still cut the best veal, but now you can sit down—along with all sorts of deal-making industry types—for breakfast, lunch and dinner, choosing from an exotic range of antipasti, salads, pastas and veal dishes (most of which can also be ordered to take home). We cannot fault the wild mushroom salad, the pasta with radicchio, the feather-light cannelloni stuffed with ground veal, or the light lasagne. The pastas are all lovely, especially the pesto and the carbonara; you also won't go wrong with the wild rice salad with fresh truffles or the true Italian torte, its perfect crust bursting with ground veal, prosciutto and spinach. But our favorite meal here is breakfast, especially the eggs carbonara and the pasta Mama, made with pancetta and eggs. The setting isn't as elegant as the food—it still looks like a gourmet butcher shop, albeit a very chic one—but it is cheerful, lively and reasonably comfortable. Despite the unrelenting trendiness of the crowd, a table is usually easy to come by. About $30 for a pasta lunch for two, with a glass of wine, and anywhere from $55 to $85 for dinner for two, with wine.

10/20 Hunan
980 N. Broadway, Chinatown
626-5050
CHINESE
Open Mon.-Thurs. 6 p.m.-10 p.m., Fri.-Sat. 6 p.m.-10:30 p.m., Sun. 5 p.m.-9 p.m. Cards: AE, MC, V.

In San Francisco, where the fog turns a midsummer afternoon into a wintry day (or, as Mark Twain once noted, "The coldest winter I ever spent was a summer in San Francisco"), Henry Fong's Hunan is all the rage—the searingly hot spices of Hunan are perfect for warming you up on a dank, chilly day. Down here in sunny Southern California, those peppers seem somewhat pointless (though, in actuality, spicy cuisines do a good job of cooling the body, by increasing perspiration; hence the hot cooking styles of India and Latin America). Hunan and Szechuan cooking has never become as much of an obsession here as it is in San Francisco and New York. And what little Hunanese cooking we have doesn't soar the way it does up north—this is good Chinese food, but rarely any better than that. In a coffee shop–like setting, Hunan's grumpy waiters serve adequate orders of spicy Chinese cabbage; well-garlicked, well-gingered Viceroy chicken; Szechuan dry-fried string beans; abalone with cinnamon sauce, and utterly addictive sweet crispy walnuts. The price is right, the service is brisk, the setting is down-home—for a Hunanese primer, it'll do just fine. Dinner for two, with beer, costs about $30.

12/20 Hymie's Fish Market
9228 W. Pico Blvd., Wilshire District
550-0377
SEAFOOD
Open nightly 5 p.m.-10 p.m. Cards: AE, MC, V.

Fish market by day, seafood restaurant by night, Hymie's still packs them in, despite hefty prices. One reason is the homey, unpretentious atmosphere: a cozy dining room with wood trim, marlin trophies and an aquarium filled with curious fish. Another is the warm service. But the most important reason is the fresh seafood, which is prepared very simply and very well. The dishes are either broiled or sautéed (absolutely no frying, salt or frills), served with garlic butter or Dijon mustard—

swordfish, John Dory, trout, red snapper, salmon or delicious sand dabs, all of which respond admirably to the bare-bones preparation. Try the oysters to start, and choose the decent salad over the too-floury chowder. Dinner for two, with wine, will run about $85.

11/20 Inagiku

Bonaventure Hotel, 404 S. Figueroa St., Downtown
614-0820

JAPANESE/SUSHI

Open Mon.-Fri. 7 a.m.-9:30 a.m., 11:30 a.m.-2 p.m. & 5:30 p.m.-10 p.m., Sat.-Sun. 5:30 p.m.-10 p.m. All major cards.

The biggest problem with Inagiku is getting there. It's hard enough to deal with the parking in downtown, where parking lots are the legalized equivalent of muggers. But it gets worse. Once inside the dreadful Bonaventure (which has been described as looking like the inside of a tooth), there's apparently no way to get to Inagiku. It's on the sixth floor, and no elevator goes directly there. So what you have to do is decipher the maze of elevators, go to another floor and walk up or down, while getting lost on the hotel's many balconies. When you finally get to Inagiku, you find that life has not become much simpler. You have to choose between sitting in a number of different worlds: a tempura bar, a sushi bar, a kaiseki (many small courses) room, a teppan-yaki room (grilled dishes), a Chinese room and an American room. You also have to decide whether you want to sit in a tatami room (on the floor) or at Western-style tables. It's enough to drive you to drink far too much sake. The food is good, though we're not sure it's worth all the trouble. The tempura, thanks to the tempura bar, is among the best in town, for tempura is best when it's at its hottest. The sushi is good, though not exceptional. Teppan is the cooking style that gave birth to Benihana, though it's done better here. Dinner for two, with sake, costs about $75.

Indigo

8222 W. 3rd St., W. Hollywood
653-0140

CALIFORNIAN/INTERNATIONAL

Open Mon.-Wed. 11:30 a.m.-2:30 p.m. & 5:30 p.m.-10 p.m., Thurs.-Fri. 11:30 a.m.-2:30 p.m. & 5:30 p.m.-11 p.m., Sat. 5:30 p.m.-11 p.m. All major cards.

Every once in a while, a new restaurant pops up that really gets the dining-experience gestalt right. It's sort of that indescribable wow—like a person of particular beauty or a movie that really touches you. The individual details or features may not be perfect, but the sum total of the parts works to impossible perfection. Relative newcomer Indigo does just that. Heading up the kitchen is Tony DiLembo, whose youth, affable charm and culinary know-how won him the position as Barbra Streisand's private chef several years back, after which he took over the reins of the now-defunct Beverly Restaurant & Market from super-chef Lydia Shire.

First off, DiLembo is a master of bread. The quartered boule of hot bread flecked with rosemary is simply delicious—we couldn't stop eating it. And the menu is a tough one in terms of making choices, simply because everything sounds so good. We tried the Chinese crisp-fried baby squid with spicy chili sauce and couldn't stop raving about it. The coating on the squid was goosed with five-spice powder—it really had a kick—and was completely greaseless. The chicken-and-spinach potsticker sautéed in sherry and served with a mint dipping sauce is another winner. This potsticker is more like a stuffed Chinese pancake, ribboned with cilantro and scallions, dotted with sesame seeds and embodying every flavor: sweet, sour, tart and salt. The pizzas sound like parodies of California pies, but the weird combinations work. The pizza with sautéed escarole, Provolone, Kalamata olives, capers, pine nuts and white raisins may seem whacked-out (it's actually a takeoff on a traditional Sicilian pizza), but it's delicious—the bitterness of the escarole, the smokiness of the cheese, the resiny chewiness of the pine nuts and the winey sweetness of the raisins play wonderfully together.

We couldn't get enough of the chicken saté with peanut sauce—the tender white meat was perfectly grilled, and the smooth, hot peanut sauce, with its hint of coconut, sneaks up on you. The hands-down winner in the entrée department is the chicken chili, which comes served in a huge ceramic bowl—a thick, musky chili clogged with cubes of chicken and topped with a pretty mess of blue-corn tortilla chips, Cheddar cheese and sweet red onions. It really is a dish and a half. The charred flank steak, infused with garlic and served with a red-onion-and-thyme relish and a side of excellent fried potatoes, was a little on the tough side but very, very tasty, and the Thai shrimp and papaya salad with grilled shiitake mushrooms, pine nuts and onion in a lime-ginger vinaigrette was graced with huge, juicy shrimp (but it is a bit pricey at $13.50, on a menu where the average price of an entrée is just $8.50). The one department that could use some muscle is the desserts. A couple, like the voluptuous banana cheesecake and the vanilla sundae with fudge, sprinkled with habit-forming candied pine nuts and served with sugar-dusted Mexican wedding cookies, are well worth the calories, but the cappuccino crème brûlée had too coarse a texture and a failed crackle of sugar crust on top. Indigo sure didn't leave us blue. Dinner for two, with wine, runs a very fair $50.

11/20 The Ivy

113 N. Robertson Blvd., W. Hollywood
274-8303

AMERICAN

Open Mon.-Thurs. 11:30 a.m.-3 p.m. & 6 p.m.-11 p.m., Fri.-Sat. 11:30 a.m.-3 p.m. & 6 p.m.-11:30 p.m. All major cards.

A major gathering place for stars on the rise and celebrities taking time out from gathering at the Bistro Garden and Morton's, The Ivy remains one of the town's hot spots—but, sadly, the food seems to get worse (and even more outrageously expensive) with each passing year. There's something rather avant-garde, even somewhat outré, about The Ivy. Perhaps it's the shabby little outdoor eating area, which allows you to breathe deeply of the fumes from Robertson Boulevard. Or perhaps it's the rustic, deliberately run-down look of the dining room. People like to pretend they're slumming when they go to The Ivy, and in a sense they are—one need not dress elegantly, though it's best that your casual clothes don't look as if they cost too little (Fred Segal's togs will do nicely). Service can be a bit scrambled—we once had a waiter explain to us that martinis were *supposed* to be murky and lukewarm. (We told him to try again, and he did.) The food is a cross-section of trendy cooking, starting with some decent California-style pizzas, topped with smoked Scottish salmon and sour cream (a waste of good salmon) or with sun-dried tomatoes. While the earthy anadama bread and the

crabcakes can be delicious, the Louisiana red-fish can be awful—we once had one that was half-cooked *and* half-spiced. The waiter didn't pretend that it was supposed to come that way. Unfortunately, it returned from the kitchen overcooked. Also steer clear of the dry, chewy shrimp with a dusty coating of Cajun spices. That notwithstanding, The Ivy can be fun, though it should be avoided on crowded weekend evenings, when service seems to crumble. Despite the scene at The Ivy's sibling, Ivy at the Shore, its cooking is tastier and more consistently prepared than what you'll get here. Dinner for two, with wine, is an outlandish $130.

13 Jitlada

5233 W. Sunset Blvd., Hollywood
667-9809

THAI

Open Tues.-Sun. 11:30 a.m.-10:30 p.m. Cards: MC, V.

Snuggled into a tacky mini shopping center in the heart of multiethnic Hollywood, Jitlada is easy to miss. That's a shame—for inside this warm, cozy family-run restaurant is some of the best Thai food in Los Angeles. Though it's been spruced up, it still isn't nearly as nice as its handsome sister restaurant in the Valley, but its food is almost as wonderful. Appetizers include perfect spring rolls, moist and peppery barbecued chicken, deep-fried fresh squid, and minced pork marinated in lemon juice, ginger and shallots. Soups are excellent, particularly the poh-taek, a hot-and-sour broth spiked with lemon grass and loaded with various fish and shellfish. Among the generally outstanding curry dishes are a very good beef pa nang, a beef tamarind with potatoes and onions, and fried catfish with green curry and bamboo shoots. Dish number 43, simply called "Shrimp Specialties," is momentarily shocking (and thereafter delicious) when it arrives on the table—three massive crustaceans served in the shell, each nearly the size of a baby lobster, slightly charred on a barbecue grill and eaten as you would eat the meat of a lobster claw, pulling it from the shell. Jitlada does well and often terrifically well with nearly everything—although, as is often the case in Oriental restaurants, the beef dishes are the least successful, not because of the preparation but because the beef itself is chewy and of poor quality. About $30 to $35 for two, with beer.

12/20 Joss
9255 Sunset Blvd., W. Hollywood
276-1886
CHINESE
Open Sun.-Fri. 11:30 a.m.-3:30 p.m. & 5:30 p.m.-11 p.m. All major cards.

When Joss opened a few years ago, it was hailed as the first truly authentic (forgive us for using the term) *gourmet* Chinese restaurant in Los Angeles. And indeed it may have been. Unfortunately, a combination of indifferent service (one critic left after waiting 90 minutes without tasting a dish), small portions and high prices kept the public at bay. Even today, though things are greatly improved, the restaurant was never full during any of our visits; its somewhat problematic reputation seems to have stuck. Revisiting Joss after some time, we found a restaurant that can be quite good and that seems to have a show-biz following, including a fair-sized sprinkling of rock musicians. But Joss still hasn't overcome a number of its problems. Service, on our last visit, was decidedly slow, marked by a vanishing-waiters act. But we can't deny that the food was quite good. Unfortunately, nothing has changed in terms of the small portions and the high prices—this is still more of a grazer's restaurant, sort of an expensive version of Mandarette.

The highly creative hand in the kitchen turns out good (though undersized) orders of light crab wontons in a nicely fiery Szechuan garlic-chili sauce; excellent cold steamed eggplant in the same good sauce; wonderful Napa cabbage in a peppery vinaigrette; exceptional pin-pei chicken, served à la Peking duck; and an exceptional casserole (they call it a mosaic) of catfish, Smithfield ham and black mushrooms. Yes, the food is quite tasty—when it finally arrives. But with so many good Chinese restaurants in Monterey Park, and the rise of the Panda and Plum Tree inns on the westside, we hesitate to spend as much as Joss can cost—crab wontons, for instance, are $8, the catfish is $28, the pin-pei chicken is $28, and Peking duck is a stiff $36. These are Beverly Hills prices, only marginally appropriate for a restaurant on the edge of Beverly Hills. Dinner for two, with wine, costs about $80.

14 Katsu
1972 N. Hillhurst Ave., Los Feliz
665-1891
JAPANESE/SUSHI
Open Mon.-Fri. noon-2 p.m. & 6 p.m.-10 p.m., Sat. 6 p.m.-11 p.m. Cards: AE, MC, V.

Katsu is so modernistic, so future shock, that visiting it is almost like stepping inside the lyrics of one of the minimalist songs from David Bowie's "Thin White Duke" period. The decor is black and white, the only color coming from the sushi on the plates and the skinny ties on the sushi chefs. You enter Katsu through a room decorated with oversized mottled-gray blocks, which leads you into a world of many strange shapes. The sushi arrives on plates shaped like frozen bolts of lightning or terraced gardens, and it is among the finest sushi in town—virtually perfect cuts of tuna (both lean maguro and the highly prized fatty toro), yellowtail (hamachi), sea bass (shiromi), salmon (shake), mackerel (saba) and crunchy jumbo clam (mirugai). There are hot dishes as well, along with an elegant kaiseki dinner of many small, odd dishes. But few diners order anything but the sushi. Like jogging and Perrier, it's good for you, and can cost too much—the perfect L.A. experience. Dinner for two, with sake, ranges from $45 to $60.

13 Katsu 3rd
8636 W. 3rd St., W. Hollywood
273-3605
FRENCH-JAPANESE
Open Mon.-Fri. 11:30 a.m.-2:30 p.m. & 5:30 p.m.-10 p.m., Sat. 5:30 p.m.-10 p.m. All major cards.

Master chef and ultra-minimalist designer Katsu began with the sushi bar that bears his name on Hillhurst in Los Feliz, a restaurant notable for having two rooms, one of which exists solely as a highly avant-garde art gallery. After that, he opened Café Katsu in a mini-mall on Sawtelle, where he serves California cuisine only vaguely touched by Japanese ingredients (except for the name, you probably wouldn't notice that the restaurant has Japanese roots at all). And now the often-present Katsu (you'll recognize him by his Marine-length crew cut, radiant grin and oddly baggy suits, worn with shirts buttoned to the top and no tie) can be found at Katsu 3rd, perhaps his most ambitious restaurant and a place that you can drive by several thousand times without noticing. That's because there's no real sign in front—just a green chalkboard on which Katsu 3rd is written when the restaurant is open. (Here's a hint: it's one door east of Locanda Veneta.) Inside, the design is every bit as underplayed—it's much like sitting inside a gigantic whitewashed bento box, almost shocking in its simplicity, yet filled with all sorts of odd little jokes. Consider the bright-green jalapeños that serve as rests for your chopsticks—it's not often that the dishware can be eaten at the end of the meal. (It reminded us of the observation that Jell-O wrestling is the only sport in which you can eat the playing field.)

The menu is so utterly eclectic that it can be pigeonholed in any of a dozen ways, all combining and recombining our basic concepts of the foods of Japan, China, Thailand, France, Italy, America, even Eastern Europe. This is surely the only Japanese-influenced restaurant known to man that serves beef brisket. And it's about as good as brisket gets, a small clump of ludicrously tender meat cooked in a Madeira wine sauce (which tastes surprisingly like miso), with carrots, potatoes and turnips. It doesn't look anything like the brisket at Nate 'n' Al's—it's almost delicate. The menu changes quite a bit from lunch to dinner (be sure to order the not-on-the-menu bento box if it's available for lunch; you can practially sample the whole menu in one sitting). But the theme of the dishes remains the same: exceedingly light yet richly flavored. Consider the salad of broiled salmon marinated in a citrus dressing, the grilled filet of beef stuffed with monkfish-liver mousse, or the poached tai fish in a pear-brandy sauce, served on a bed of shiitake, enoki and shimeji mushrooms. Think further of the beef sashimi with radishes marinated in chili sauce and a julienne of Hawaiian ginger root (a dish to clear out your psyche), the grilled duck served with apples in an orange sauce (as good and crisp as a duck can be), even the Wiener Shnitzel—yes, Wiener Schnitzel! It's actually a Japanese translation of the dish, made with Dijon mustard and a sprinkling of hard-cooked egg. It isn't like anything you've ever seen before. But neither is Katsu 3rd. Dinner for two, with wine, runs around $60.

11/20 L.A. Nicola

4326 W. Sunset Blvd., Silverlake
660-7217
AMERICAN
Open Mon.-Fri. 11:30 a.m.-2 p.m. & 6 p.m.-10:30 p.m., Sat. 6 p.m.-10:30 p.m. Cards: AE, MC, V.

Another in the continuing series of L.A.'s temporary shelters for traveling art shows, this friendly place has the requisite white walls, industrial gray carpet, pink linens and simple nondecor. What makes L.A. Nicola unique, we suppose, is the corrugated aluminum-hut architecture that reminds us of a tasteful POW camp. Owner Larry Nicola is a most charming and gracious host, a man who truly cares about his restaurant and his clientele, many of whom come from nearby KCET and KABC television stations. His cuisine is quite simple: good fried calamari served with a zesty tomato-onion salsa, good grilled steaks and fresh fish, pleasant salads and satisfying desserts. But over the years the cooking has remained consistently uneven (if that isn't too much of an oxymoron)—sometimes fresh and flavorful, sometimes overcooked and dull. All in all, L.A. Nicola is a well-intentioned, stylish neighborhood restaurant that serves good food—but never as good as you hope it will be. The prices aren't too bad, at $75 to $80 for dinner for two, with a good California wine.

11/20 Lawry's California Center

570 W. Ave. 26, E.L.A.
224-6850
AMERICAN
Open Mon.-Sat. 11 a.m.-3 p.m. & 4:30 p.m.-10 p.m., Sun. 4:30 p.m.-9 p.m. Cards: AE, MC, V.

Propelled by a starving and impatient crowd that overruns this immense eating factory, you will quickly be seated in an enticing garden. Because the place is mislaid in a sad industrial zone east of downtown L.A., you immediately expect the worst. But you are wrong. In spite of the more than 6,000 meals served daily in this charming California-Spanish patio, shaded by ancient trees, surrounded by flowering gardens and refreshed by an old-fashioned fountain, the dishes are always the same and are honestly prepared. After checking in at the door, you can buy your wine at the little wine boutique and then be seated right away. Just as quickly, a charming young waitress brings your salad with four different Lawry's dressings (which would be much better with olive oil), then leaves you to go select from the grill such specials as barbecued chicken, grilled salmon or tender, juicy New York steak. There is a certain gaiety in the air; mariachis hover around the tables (which you won't take up for too long, because of the waiting crowds), and you finally leave with admiration for Lawrence Frank, the man who some 25 years ago created this highly successful tourist attraction, which has mercifully avoided falling into mediocrity. Plan on about $65 for dinner for two, with margaritas.

12/20 Lawry's The Prime Rib

55 N. La Cienega Blvd., W. Hollywood
652-2827
AMERICAN
Open Mon.-Thurs. 5 p.m.-11 p.m., Fri.-Sat. 5 p.m.-midnight, Sun. 3 p.m.-11 p.m. Cards: AE, MC, V.

For many, Lawry's is the ultimate dining experience—huge slabs of savory prime rib cut tableside to order, with simple, crowd-pleasing accompaniments and reasonable prices. Never mind that you feel as if you're eating in an impersonal prime rib factory—you're getting your money's worth, so you probably won't mind. Carvers wheel carts around this huge, brightly lit dining room dominated by a fresco of Versailles and giant eighteenth-century portraits, stopping at tables filled with families celebrating high-school graduations and couples celebrating anniversaries. Fortunately, Lawrence Frank has built a small empire on the notion of doing simple things well, and the prime rib carved here is truly outstanding, marvelously tender and rich in taste and aroma. Everything else, however, is forgettable: huge baked potatoes, flat, tasteless Yorkshire pudding and boring salad (though the rich creamed spinach is pretty good). Service is chipper but sometimes slow. About $75 for two, with wine.

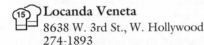

Locanda Veneta

8638 W. 3rd St., W. Hollywood
274-1893
ITALIAN
Open Mon.-Fri. 11:30 a.m.-2:30 p.m. & 5:30 p.m.-10:30 p.m., Sat. 5:30 p.m.-10:30 p.m. Cards: AE, MC, V.

We suppose some may find fault with this lively *locanda* (inn): they may feel claustrophobic at the elbow-to-elbow tables, or they may resent having to make reservations two weeks in advance for a prime dinner time. Well, you can't blame a place for being small or popular, and as for the crowding, we can't deny it, but we think it gives the place an aura of authentic Italian camaraderie. Besides, we'd eat this food in a mess hall.

Chef Antonio Tommasi (ex of Chianti Cucina) and owner Jean-Louis Di Mori (brother of Silvio, the man behind Tuttobene and the Tuttopastas) are onto something here: there may be dozens of hip Italian trattorias around town that on the surface seem just like Locanda Veneta, but this place has, as George Bush would say, that authentic thing. The minuscule dining room is authentically overcrowded, the decor is authentically simple (white linens, paver-tile floors), the windows are authentically open to 3rd Street outside, the wines are authentically Italian and simple, and the food is authentically fresh, generous and delicious. Tune out the West Hollywood chatter at the tables around you and you'd swear you were in Venice.

We've been here many times and have yet to be disappointed with a single dish. Some are standouts: frittura di bianchetti, an addictive heap of pan-fried baby whitebait served with an onion-vinegar confit; rich, creamy risotto with porcini mushrooms, a straight-ahead classic; perfect carpaccio with arugula, chunks of Parmesan and a drizzle of olive oil; delicate yet savory lobster ravioli dressed with a heavenly saffron sauce; and sweet, juicy, monstrous Hawaiian prawns, grilled masterfully. Cheeses are a pride of the house; Tommasi and a friend make mozzarella and other fresh white cheeses themselves. Mozzarella-lovers must order the trittico di mozzarelle, three thick slices of marvelous garden-grown tomato, each topped with a different mozzarella variety, fresh basil and a drizzle of olive oil. And if it's available, don't miss the casatela coa peperonata alla veneta, a ball of delicious, light-as-air homemade white cheese next to an incredible ratatouille made with some of the sweetest sweet peppers we've had. And the desserts . . . these send us swooning. The vanilla crème caramel is the newest honoree in our dessert hall of fame— the richest, creamiest crème caramel imaginable, half of which is topped with a deadly fudge sauce and half with an intense caramel sauce. And the tiramisu is as good as it gets. As with most Italian restaurants, your bill depends on how much you eat and whether you have a pasta or an entrée as your main course; the range here is $60 to $90 for dinner for two, with wine.

9/20 Louise's Trattoria

232 N. Larchmont Blvd., Larchmont Village
962-9510
ITALIAN
Open daily 11 a.m.-11 p.m. Cards: AE, MC, V.
See Restaurants, "Westside."

Louis XIV

606 N. La Brea Ave., Hollywood
934-5102
FRENCH
Open Mon.-Sat. 6 p.m.-midnight. Cards: MC, V.

Louis XIV looks much like someone's barn or attic, cleaned up and filled with paintings, chairs and tables. It's got an incredibly casual sense to it; so casual, in fact, that you'd probably feel overdressed in a sports jacket. This is, in classic terminology, the sort of place you dress down for—and happily so. In the great bistro tradition, the wine list is utterly minimal and inexpensive; the wine is almost generic, as if you were to simply ask your waiter to bring you a bottle of wine, period. The lighting is dim and a tad conspiratorial; at some of the larger tables, people look as if they're busily forming political parties and movements.

The classic bistro food is tasty and right to the point, without folderol or froufrou. For an appetizer, you can order a perfectly wonderful salad of mixed greens and tomatoes in an olive-oil vinaigrette; a simple tomato salad with fresh basil leaves; some nice marinated mixed peppers in a garlic-and-anchovy sauce; an artichoke with a vinaigrette sauce; a perfectly decent carpaccio topped with lots of Parmesan chunks; or a fine salad of grilled oyster mushrooms with breaded lamb in a mint sauce. The same no-nonsense style is seen in the main courses: steak with pommes frites (one of the triumphs of French cuisine), steak with green-peppercorn sauce, filet mignon with mushrooms, rack of lamb, chicken breast in a Dijon mustard sauce, trout amand-

ine, grilled salmon with fried baby onions. It's food so wonderfully simple, and so forgotten in our rush to trendiness, that you get the sense of eating the stuff for the first time. Dinner for two, with wine, costs about $50.

7/20 Lucy's Café El Adobe

5536 Melrose Ave., Hollywood
462-9421
MEXICAN
Open Mon.-Sat. 11:30 a.m.-11:30 p.m. Cards: AE, MC, V.

Once again, the famous have proved themselves to have frequently questionable taste. The walls at Lucy's are covered with autographed pictures of these celebrities, from the Eagles and Linda Ronstadt (who used to show up with her old beau, former governor Jerry Brown), to Ted Kennedy and the late Hubert Humphrey. Why John Denver, Brenda Vaccaro and Alan Cranston chose to bring fame to this simple Mexican restaurant is a mystery, for there are a thousand such places in L.A. serving far better food. We can only presume that the proximity to Paramount Studios (across the street) has helped its fame. The rooms are dark, with ersatz brick walls and plastic shrubbery beneath an imitation straw ceiling. The food is as dreadfully dull as ever; with each passing year the celebrities grow scarcer and the food seems more pathetic. Tamales appear to have been put through a deflavorizing machine, enchiladas are an oddly shapeless glop, and the chile relleno is buried beneath an absurdly thick omelet. The shredded beef in the ropa vieja is stringy and is served in an utterly boring sauce. The margaritas, however, are frothy and delicious—maybe *that's* the reason for Lucy's success! Dinner with margaritas will run about $30 for two.

Ma Bé

8722 W. 3rd St., W. Hollywood
276-6223
FRENCH/ITALIAN
Open Sun.-Thurs. 11:30 a.m.-midnight, Fri.-Sat. 11:30 a.m.-1 a.m. All major cards.

Call us shallow, call us superficial, but we love a great-looking restaurant. Sure, the cooking has to be good to make the place work, but most of us go out for more than just food—we go out to have fun, to relax, to buy into the illusion that, at least for an hour or two, all the world is attractive and well fed and full of *joie de vivre*. That's why we loved Ma Bé from the moment we walked in the door: this is one seriously handsome restaurant. It may have been designed to death, but it's a design that works, a seductively lit vision of burnished dark woods, chic blond woods, warm, restrained colors in the carpets and upholstery, and flowers galore. Downstairs are a bar, a comfortable lounge and cozy dining areas; upstairs are more large tables, an unspeakably beautiful lounge area around a fireplace, and a flower-lined terrace. Waiters bustle about efficiently, and the noise level is mercifully moderate. And the food? Well, it's not *quite* on a par with the setting, but it's plenty good enough. Chef Claude Segal offers a refreshing number of fairly hearty meat entrées, from the beautiful mesquite-grilled veal chop to the delicious garlic-roasted rack of lamb in a bread-crumb crust. The grilled calf's liver with crispy onions and garlic mashed potatoes is as perfect a liver dish as exists. Co-chef Sandro Marcato's Italian birth and training are revealed in the collection of pastas, served in both appetizer and entrée sizes (try the garlic linguine, which lives up to its name, or the black ravioli filled with crab and lobster), and the heavenly appetizer of grilled jumbo shrimp wrapped first in a basil leaf and then in a piece of lean pancetta. Another appetizer that absolutely must be ordered is the grilled seasonal mushrooms, a mountain of perfectly cooked funghi given just the right kick with garlic and olive oil. Less successful are the pastry-related dishes, such as the lamb loin in soggy puff pastry and the equally soggy tarte tatin. But the chocolate cake is everything that chocolate cake should be: rich, smooth and wonderfully bad for you. Our only other beef is with the wine list, which is overpriced and more limited than the extensive, fairly priced (given the big-bucks decor and the quality of food) menu. Dinner for two, with wine, costs about $100.

 Madeo

8897 Beverly Blvd., W. Hollywood
859-4903
ITALIAN
Open Mon.-Sat. 11:30 a.m.-2:30 p.m. & 6:30 p.m.-10 p.m., Sun. 6:30 p.m.-10 p.m. All major cards.

If the Guinness Book of World Records had a category for Restaurant with the Most Names in the Shortest Period of Time, Madeo would surely win hands down. First it was Boboli. Then within a week it was christened Gritti. A week later, it became Madeo, which is the name that's stuck. In its various incarnations, the restaurant has been connected with both Pane Caldo (across the street) and Il Giardino (a few blocks away). It also went through a period of being closed for redecoration and the installation of a pizza oven, about six months after it opened. Clearly, life has not been smooth for Madeo. Several steps below street level, Madeo is tucked into the building that houses International Creative Management (ICM). Not surprisingly, at both lunch and dinner, you'll find a fair-sized population of agents drinking martinis and Maalox and nibbling on carpaccio. It's a first-rate carpaccio, a large plate of raw filet mignon that's sliced (apparently) with a microtome and topped with bits of artichoke, thick slices of Reggiano Parmesan and a drizzle of greenish olive oil. Since the installation of the wood-burning pizza oven, there are also pizzas that feature excellent crusts and such toppings as Gorgonzola cheese and porcini mushrooms, along with a fine calzone and some nice matzohlike cracker breads. At lunch, a superb choice is the antipasti misti, which you prepare yourself from a heavily laden table near the front door. There are about a dozen dishes to choose from: fine, dry bresaola, steamed clams and mussels, creamy buffalo mozzarella, excellent risotto and so on. From the menu, there's an extraordinary thick Tuscan soup called ribolitta, made with bread and cabbage, and good ravioli filled with a fish called branzino (Italian sea bass). Service can be a bit odd, perhaps because many of the waiters appear to speak no English. Dinner for two, with wine, costs $100 or more.

 Ma Maison

Ma Maison Sofitel, 8555 Beverly Blvd., W. Hollywood
655-1991
FRENCH
Open Mon.-Sat. 11:30 a.m.-2:30 p.m. & 6:30 p.m.-10:30 p.m. All major cards.

Here we have the newest venture of one of L.A.'s most famous restaurateurs, Patrick Terrail, the man who created and ran that great power restaurant of the '70s, Ma Maison—a wildly popular, terribly expensive yet somehow shabby place that could have reached great heights only in L.A., where carefully studied casualness is an art form. Terrail had the smarts to hire more than a few immensely talented chefs, including Kazuto Matsusaka, the gifted chef at Chinois on Main, and Matsusaka's boss, the one and only Wolfgang Puck. For more than a few years, Ma Maison was *the* place to dine in L.A., and its many loyal customers were sad to see it go. Thankfully, Terrail is back at his all-new Ma Maison, part of the new Ma Maison Sofitel hotel. Terrail's new restaurant, detached from the hotel, is much more attractive, with a false-beamed, pseudo-French-country bar and a cheery, open, garden-style dining room, where every table is good and everyone can see everyone else. Except for the rare lapse, service is good, too, handled by pros. And the food? It's better than that of many a hotel restaurant and better than it probably needs to be. And the chef's ingenuity tells us that when things have settled down, there will be potential for some truly excellent dining here. A few dishes are solid winners, notably the Burgundy snails stuffed in an upended baked potato with chives and lots of garlic; the rich, slightly peppery corn chowder; the generous warm duck salad with Oriental spices and avocado (a lunch dish); and the exceptionally tasty charbroiled half chicken with a sharp Meaux mustard sauce. The rest of the menu is well prepared if not noteworthy, satisfying if not brilliantly creative. And Terrail is back where he should be, unchanged: kissing ladies' hands, spreading his ever-present charm among his patrons. Dinner for two, with wine, runs about $115.

11/20 Marix

1108 N. Flores Dr., W. Hollywood
656-8800
MEXICAN
Open Mon.-Thurs. 8 a.m.-11 p.m., Fri. 8 a.m.-1 a.m., Sat. 8:30 a.m.-1 a.m., Sun. 8:30 a.m.-noon. Cards: MC, V.

When Victoria Shemaria and Mary Sweeney turned a failing French restaurant called Marix into a rustic but thriving Tex-Mex eatery called Marix, they made a major contribution to the culinary lore of Los Angeles, by proving that Mexican food could succeed where French food could not—especially if the rice-and-beans basics were replaced with trendier dishes like fajitas, blue-corn-tortilla casseroles and good Mexican-style pizza. They also proved that Mexican restaurants, formerly the domain of chains, could be fun, hip, now and good for thin people. With their second branch in Santa Monica, they went on to prove that Tex-Mex could succeed where even sushi had failed, in the process winding up with what looks like a shogun's palace on the outside and a Mexican cantina on the inside (very Los Angeles). Not only did this particular brand of Tex-Mex succeed, it has become all the rage, so you can count on a party atmosphere (with a large, very chic gay crowd at this branch) and a long wait. The food is informal and tasty, if a bit sloppy: good fajitas, made with either beef, chicken or shrimp, perfect with grilled vegetables and charro beans; heavy chalupas and chimichangas from New Mexico; passable margaritas; salsas both mild and fiery. Mostly, Marix is great fun, no matter how imperfect the food sometimes is. And the price is right: $30 for two, with margaritas.

(13) Marouch

4905 Santa Monica Blvd., Hollywood
662-9325
MIDDLE EASTERN
Open daily 11 a.m.-11 p.m. Cards: MC, V.

Marouch—which sits in a seedy mini-mall in the Middle Eastern section of Santa Monica Boulevard just west of Vermont—offers one of the largest Middle Eastern menus in the city. Yet you really don't have to spend much time mulling it over, for the appetizer section alone is hugely satisfying. You can order a meze (appetizer) assortment for two ($20), four ($35) or six ($50); actually, the one for two does a pretty good job of feeding four, and so on exponentially upward. The meze for six comprises twenty dishes, most of them large enough to serve as main courses. The one for two includes eight dishes; it covers most of the table.

For us, Middle Eastern food is one of the great grazing cuisines of the world, an experience built around a multitude of flavors. From hummus to tabouli, from fattoush (salad made of pita bread, parsley, mint and tomato) to falafel, it all satisfies. But there's much more to the Marouch menu. Consider the marvelous baked kibbeh, a meatloaf cake of ground veal, beef, bulghur wheat and pine nuts—we can't get enough of it. Then there's the moughrabiye, a stew of couscous topped with the most tender chicken and beef imaginable, and the mehshi kousa, an assortment of squash, eggplant, grape leaves and bell peppers filled with rice and ground beef. Even the farroug, a barbecued chicken served with a garlic sauce, is a marvel; and the whole chicken costs all of $7 ($5 if you get it to go). Marouch is most likely the best Lebanese/Armenian/Middle Eastern restaurant in Los Angeles—at least for the moment. Dinner for two, with beer, costs about $40.

Matsuhisa
129 N. La Cienega Blvd.,
W. Hollywood
659-9639

JAPANESE/SUSHI/SEAFOOD
Open Mon.-Fri. 11:45 a.m.-2:30 p.m. & 5:45 p.m.-10:15 p.m., Sat.-Sun. 5:45 p.m.-10:15 p.m. Cards: AE, MC, V.

From the street, Matsuhisa doesn't look much different from any of a hundred other sushi bars scattered around the city. It doesn't look different from the inside, either. But there is a difference, and it quickly makes itself obvious. The basic sushi items on the menu are utterly beyond reproach—perfect orders of buttery salmon, musky sea urchin, sweet toro tuna. As you move down the menu, toward the sushi rolls, Matsuhisa's depth begins to show. We've never had a better California roll or asparagus roll, and the soft-shell crab roll is astonishing—a perfect piece of tiny deep-fried soft-shell crab in the middle of a roll filled with rice, asparagus, small fish eggs and more. We could have eaten a hundred. There's also a wondrous salmon-skin roll, wrapped in cucumber sliced translucently thin, and a fabulously spicy tuna hand roll, so piquant it demands extra sake. And then there are the "Special Dishes," which are defined in a sizable bound menu that is a virtual textbook on seafood. Of bonito, for instance, the menu says, "Bonito, also called the skip-jack tuna, has a deep red color with a firm texture and a rich flavor. . . . It is served as sushi or tataki, which is a beautiful arrangement of shredded daikon radish, large pieces of cucumber and thinly sliced garlic, garnished with green onions and momiji oroshi with plenty of tosaza sauce." This is nice reading. This is also the best baked black cod we've ever had, the most extraordinary tiger shrimp in a pepper sauce, the most breathtaking uni wrapped in a shiso leaf and then fried tempura style. Not only is Matsuhisa the best sushi bar in the city, it may also be the best seafood restaurant in the city. The bad news is that it's on Restaurant Row across from Ed Debevic's, which means the parking is lousy. A wonderful dinner for two, with beer, will run about $55 if you order off the menu; we prefer to ask chef Matsuhisa to make us dinner, which results in a dazzling succession of small seafood dishes. He stops sending out food when you tell your waitress you're full, so the bill depends on your appetite, and whether you request such pricey delicacies as abalone: anywhere from $50 to $100 for two.

12/20 Matuszek's Czechoslovak Cuisine
7513 W. Sunset Blvd., Hollywood
874-0106

CZECHOSLOVAKIAN
Open Mon.-Fri. 11:30 a.m.-2 p.m. & 6 p.m.-10 p.m., Sat. 6 p.m.-10 p.m. Cards: MC, V.

Though there's a tendency for us to lump most Eastern European cuisines under the general sobriquet of heavy and heavy with heavy, there is a certain delicacy to the cooking of Czechoslovakia that's not generally found in the dishes of Bulgaria, Rumania and Poland. This may stem from the simple fact that Czechoslovakia never had the time to develop a really heavy style of cooking—the country didn't come into being until the end of World War I, and like the nation itself, its cooking had to draw from immediate sources: partially from the more subtle cooking of Hungary and partially from the elegant cuisine of Austria. Call it Balkan Lite for lack of a better name. The Matuszeks, a lovely couple who had the foolish idea of opening a restaurant in the heart of tumultuous Hollywood, cook the food of their homeland as well as anyone in town. In a pretty, aubergine-colored setting, they create small wonders using chicken, veal and pork, mixed variously with sour cream, paprika and garlic. The spirit of the restaurant is fine, though it's not getting as much business as it deserves. Dinner for two, with wine, costs about $30.

11/20 Maurice's Snack 'n' Chat

5549 W. Pico Blvd., Wilshire District
930-1795
SOUL FOOD
Open Mon.-Thurs. noon-10 p.m., Fri. noon-11 p.m., Sat. 4 p.m.-11 p.m., Sun. 4 p.m.-9 p.m. No cards.

We aren't the biggest fans of Maurice's—service is eccentric at best and slow as molasses at worst, the decor is tacky and too bright, and some of the dishes can be made better at home. But that's not to say we don't like the place, because we do. It's fun and completely unpretentious, and there are plenty of good things to eat: heavy but tasty fried chicken, messy short ribs, wonderful yams, honest liver and onions and such comforting desserts as pound cake and cobbler. Most of the accompanying vegetables, however, are forgettable. As at any good soul food restaurant, it's impossible to leave hungry. Maurice's enjoys a loyal following, so make reservations if you plan to visit on a weekend—and don't forget to bring cash and your own beer or wine. About $30 for dinner for two.

8/20 Miriwa

750 N. Hill St., Chinatown
687-3088
CHINESE
Open daily 9 a.m.-2:30 p.m. & 5 p.m.-9:30 p.m. Cards: AE, MC, V.

Despite the coming and going of every manner of Chinese culinary trend—from the rise (and fall) of Szechuan and Hunanese cooking, through the advent of the age of Cantonese seafood, through the metamorphosis of Monterey Park from nondescript suburb to Hong Kong in a shopping mall—Miriwa has remained Miriwa: one of the most chaotic, least satisfying Chinese restaurants in town. Every weekend Miriwa is packed with Chinese families who show up to eat dumplings and drink tea in that grand ritual called dim sum. At Miriwa, trying to put together a good dim sum meal can lead to something of a minor breakdown, for the cart pushers seem to have learned from New York cabdrivers the fine art of not noticing those with their hands outstretched. At night, when the dim sum rests, you can study an oversized menu in the three or four seconds allowed you by a horde of exceedingly impatient waiters, who take your order, walk into the kitchen with it, and ten seconds later walk out with every dish you've ordered, delivered all at once. The same scenario is followed in both Hong Kong and Taipei, but here the food is mediocre at best. This is mass-produced cooking for the masses, who show up en masse. For those of you who argue that Chinese food is not subtle, here's your proof. The good news is that it's cheap—but not cheap enough. Dinner for two, with beer, costs about $30.

10/20 El Mocambo

8338 W. 3rd St., W. Hollywood
651-2113
CUBAN
Open Mon. & Sat. 6 p.m.-11 p.m., Tues.-Fri. & Sun. noon-3 p.m. & 6 p.m.-11 p.m. Cards: AE, MC, V.

The people behind El Mocambo surely noticed the nightly lines outside Culver City's Versailles, the chaotic Cuban dive with giveaway prices and the best roast chicken in town. They surely saw the potential in gussying up this appealing, fashionable cuisine and serving it in a cheerful, neo–Ricky Ricardo setting complete with bright colors, danceable Cuban music and high prices. It's a darn good idea, too, creating a "haute" Cuban restaurant that evokes the glamorous casino days of 1950s pre-Castro Cuba. Too bad it doesn't work. Oh, it's not a complete failure: the taped Cuban music is lots of fun (though you have to scream to be heard over it), the fanciful rum drinks are tasty, and the tropical decor is vibrant. But parsimoniously portioned appetizers for $8 to $10? Beef dishes for $15 to $18? At these prices, the service would have to be great, which it certainly is not, and the food would have to be the best Cuban imaginable. In fact, Versailles gives you much better food for less than half the price.

The best dishes by far are the appetizers: rich, sweet tamale soup, a sort of corn chowder with slivers of free-range chicken breast; Cuban-style Caesar salad, not discernibly different from a regular Caesar; and the "babaloo boat," a little boat-shaped dish filled with moist, savory-sweet dumplinglike balls of chicken, fruit and vegetables wrapped in sweet plantains, served with a pineapple-onion relish. If you stick with appetizers and a fun cocktail, you'll probably be quite content. But the entrées should be avoided. On our last visit, the Cuban roast chicken was dry and lifeless, lacking its signature intensely garlicky moistness; the ropa vieja (shredded beef) was bland, ordinary and swimming in salt. The hearty paella was better—for $25 it ought to be—but still problematic: its lobster and crab were succulent, but its chicken was banal and its pieces of fish overcooked. Desserts are as uneven as the rest of the meal, from the creamy, comforting flan to the tasteless custardy-fruity natillas, described on the menu as "Havana's version of crème brûlée," but in fact having nary a hint of "brûlée" (burnt sugar) on its top. El Mocambo may show you a good time, but it won't serve you a memorable meal. Dinner for two, with one rum drink each, will set you back about $75.

12/20 Mon Kee

679 N. Spring St., Chinatown
628-6717
CHINESE/SEAFOOD
Open daily 11:30 a.m.-3 p.m. & 3:30 p.m.-9:45 p.m. All major cards.

The years go by, but the crowds are still here—Mon Kee always seems to have a line out the door. And, happily, as the years have gone by, the food remains good. Mon Kee earned its place in local restaurant history by introducing countless L.A. residents (and visitors) to the joys of Chinese seafood, which can today be found in several excellent establishments around town, particularly in Monterey Park and Alhambra. The food here is uniformly tasty: juicy shrimp coated with rock salt, delicious stir-fried rock cod in a sweet-and-sour sauce, scallops with chicken and snow peas and, best of all, the generous, messy crab in either black-bean sauce or ginger sauce with scallions. Success has not inspired Mon Kee to redecorate—the crowded dining rooms are still done in typically tacky linoleum and vinyl. Expect a long wait for a table. About $35 to $40 for two, with beer.

Morton's

8800 Melrose Ave., W. Hollywood
276-5205
AMERICAN
Open Mon.-Sat. 6 p.m.-midnight. All major cards.

At Morton's, celebrities stop by for burgers. And at Morton's, no one pays them any mind. The Morton of Morton's is Peter Morton, creator of the Hard Rock Cafe, a fellow who

knows his roots well. He was one of the first restaurateurs to recognize that culinary Americana means good eats. And even though he could probably serve food that's not quite as good as it is—especially to the howling hordes who fill the Hard Rock—he's always made American food that's really about as good as it gets.

Though the menu here changes with some regularity, the dishes we tried on our last visit included a finely muscled black-eyed pea soup, thick with peas and ham, smoky and filled with a sense of cold New England winters and Appalachian rainstorms. A plateful of cold East Coast oysters was accompanied by a fairly delicate tomato salsa. Curly endive was tossed with goat cheese and bacon. A hodgepodge of wild mushrooms was lightly sautéed, served musky and dangerous and wholly irresistible. This all went well with a wine selection that's seriously committed to the pleasures of California, filled with names that read like a California wine hall of fame—Ggrich Hills, Acacia, Trefethen, Spring Mountain, Jordan and so forth. It's easy to meander from a good Chardonnay to an even better Cabernet as you move through Morton's main courses: exceptional Chesapeake Bay crabcakes kept company by a Dijon-mustard mayonnaise, pork chops with a chunky homemade apple sauce, grilled lime chicken (free range, of course). There's also a wonderful vegetable plate, one of the few really good vegetable plates in town. And the hamburger is a proud one—thick, juicy, elegant in its simplicity. On weeknights, particularly Monday, Morton's is a veritable commissary for Hollywood's heaviest of hitters; weekends see more ordinary mortals hoping for a glimpse of the immortals. Dinner for two, with wine, costs about $80.

12/20 Muse

7360 Beverly Blvd., Wilshire District
934-4400
CALIFORNIAN
Open Mon.-Thurs. 11:30 a.m.-2:30 p.m. & 6 p.m.-10:30 p.m., Fri.-Sat. 11:30 a.m.-2:30 p.m. & 6 p.m.-11:30 p.m., Sun. 6 p.m.-10:30 p.m. All major cards.

When Muse first opened in the early '80s, it was hard to say whether the place was an art gallery that served food or a restaurant that served art. At first, the place had no sign in front (even to this day, the sign is minimal)—

just a mass of gray concrete, with a look that never said anything akin to "Welcome" or "Come on in." Inside, the look was, and still is, Very High Art World. Extremely modern paintings and artworks line the walls and hang—like the cutout of a businessman that dominates the main dining room—from the ceiling. The back room has an intentionally unfinished bare-wood look. Even the fish tank behind the bar is peculiar, with a bubble pattern that drifts up across parallel planes of Plexiglas. In other words, for its ultra-high-tech look alone, this could be the quintessential L.A. restaurant. But the crowd is equal to the decor—not as show-biz ostentatious as the crowd at Citrus or The Ivy, not as artsy as the crowd at Rebecca's or City. Instead, there's a sense that these Italian-dressed folk may actually be working artists, out for a night on the town; at least they're people who look as if they could be artists, which, too often in the art world, is good enough.

As artists, what they're seeking at Muse—aside from whatever muse might dwell there—is artistic food. And that's exactly what the chefs create. Dishes along the lines of lettuce "tacos" filled with spicy minced chicken and a peanut vinaigrette (a Mexican dish meets a Chinese dish meets a Thai dish); plump grilled Louisiana shrimp in a little pool of sweet-and-sour nectarine sauce, served with deep-fried spaghetti; lobster and lobster mushrooms (who's ever heard of such a thing?) tossed with pasta shells; steamed steelhead salmon with a trio of Japanese caviars and lemon cream; charbroiled squab with mango and flying-fish caviar. . . . Wonderful food, creative food, food that could be pure, unmitigated nonsense, but that in this case isn't. Food touched, ahem, by the muse. Dinner for two, with wine, costs about $70.

10/20 Musso & Frank Grill

6667 Hollywood Blvd., Hollywood
467-7788
AMERICAN
Open Mon.-Sat. 11 a.m.-11 p.m. All major cards.

The stoic waiter looked surprised at our request; while shaking his head he mumbled, "Okay, but it might take a long time." This was not in response to a request for some elaborate dish—we were visiting for breakfast and had merely ordered plain scrambled eggs.

Normally we would be mystified by such a reaction, but not at Musso & Frank, a men's-clubbish Hollywood landmark that continues to be popular despite frequently insolent service (except at the counter, where the waiters are charming) and often mediocre food. But we are not completely immune to Musso's charms. The bar is great-looking and loaded with lore, the ambience will have you dreaming of Hollywood of the '40s, and some of the food (most notably the flannel cakes and the simpler grilled chops) is more than satisfying. By all means avoid the vegetables (they look and taste canned) and most of the overpriced salads. But do come here, at least for a drink—you haven't been to Hollywood if you haven't been to Musso's. Dinner with wine or drinks will be about $70 for two.

⑬ Off Vine

6263 Leland Way, Hollywood
962-1900
AMERICAN/CALIFORNIAN
Open Mon.-Sat. 11:30 a.m.-3 p.m. & 6 p.m.-11 p.m. Cards: AE, MC, V.

Having a meal at this charming newcomer is like dining at a friend's cottage in the Hamptons—a friend who happens to have extremely good taste and really knows how to cook. The atmosphere is comfortable and casually chic at this converted house in an unlikely location in Hollywood, complete with Herb Ritts photographs hanging over the fireplace and Adirondack chairs on the front lawn. There's a porch for outdoor dining, but the white-washed room indoors is so inviting and cozy that even if the weather permits, you may want to eschew the al fresco option altogether. The staff is efficient and friendly, the menu short and sweet. Every item mentioned is a good one (the chef, a young woman fresh out of the Culinary Institute of America, learned her lessons well). First courses include an admirable Caesar salad; slightly spicy, perfectly crisp and nongreasy fried calamari served with two dipping sauces; and cheese-stuffed chiles rellenos in a puddle of tomatillo sauce and topped with a chile-pepper purée. Our favorite appetizer, though, is the beautifully browned, waferlike potato pancakes, crowned with tiny dollops of sour cream, caviar and herbs. Entrées range from a grilled New York strip steak to a more ambitious tenderloin of veal in a fresh peach-and-green-peppercorn sauce, as well as a couple of different daily fish dishes and a few tasty pastas. Desserts are homemade and homey—we flipped over the fragrant blueberry crumble pie. Off Vine is a real treasure, a little patch of genteel civilization with a languid and friendly atmosphere, which accounts for a lot in this nutty age we live in. A complete dinner for two, with wine, will set you back a reasonable $65.

⑮ L'Orangerie
903 N. La Cienaga Blvd.,
W. Hollywood
652-9770

FRENCH

L'Orangerie remains one of the most beautiful and romantic restaurants in Los Angeles. But it is no longer, alas, one of the best restaurants in the city. For some reason, first-rate French restaurants in this country almost invariably seem to fade in the course of their second decade. Unlike the best restaurants in France, they lose their spark, their creativity, their consistency. They don't get bad; they just get, well, competent (as opposed to inspired). You can still eat well at L'Orangerie, but to do so, you must choose very carefully or get lucky—a burden one shouldn't have to endure at these prices.

The restaurant's trademark appetizers are still excellent: the eggs with caviar and the frisée aux lardons chauds, vieux vinegar et ouefs mollets (salad with poached eggs, hot chunks of crisp smoky bacon and a sharp vinegar dressing). So is the hot apple tart—caramelized, crisp, sweet and firm. The côte de boeuf for two—a thick slab of beef grilled to perfection—is also splendid. There are some good fish dishes as well, but too often they are overwhelmed by their sauces and accompaniments. The taste and texture of the skate fish is lost, for example, amid mushrooms, green beans, spinach, zucchini blossoms and, especially, too-sharp raspberry vinegar. On the other hand, there was little taste of mustard in the loup (sea bass) with chanterelles and mustard sauce. Because the setting is so pretty, L'Orangerie remains good for a special occasion, when frame of mind may count for more than food. Trees stand in each of the four corners of the main dining room. Green trellises covered with ivy are visible through the large window. Enormous vases of fresh flowers sit atop the divider between the two rows of banquettes. Arched doors and windows, soft lighting and high ceilings complete the mood. But even for a special event, your mood may be shattered by the right side of the menu. L'Orangerie almost succeeds in the impossible—making the prices at our favorite Paris restaurant look borderline reasonable. At our last dinner, five appetizers were $20 or more, and the average was $19—not including the caviar with wild-rice blini at $75. Main courses averaged $33. Desserts were $10 to $11.

The wine list is also overpriced, not to mention that L'Orangerie is the only fine restaurant we've been to in Los Angeles that has a corkage fee. And it doesn't have the excuse of being a new restaurant, obligated to buy older wines at exorbitant prices. Why should a 1975 Lynch Bages—not even one of the best vintages for this excellent vineyard—sell for $114.50 just a few months after it was auctioned to the general public at $39? Why should wines from the widely heralded (and still largely immature) 1982 vintage sell for such extravagant multiples of their actual cost that even Ivan Boesky would be embarrassed by the potential profit margins. If you'd like to sample the beauty and charm of this quintessentially French restaurant without depleting the entire contents of your wallet, consider going just for a drink. The bar is also pretty and romantic, and it's generally quiet, especially early in the evening. Dinner for two, with wine, will cost about $245 a couple.

10/20 The Original Pantry
877 S. Figueroa St., Downtown
972-9279

AMERICAN

Open daily 24 hours. No cards.

"We never close" has been the Pantry's motto for 63 years, and the menu, the waiters and the line at the door have been equally long-lived. It's the poor man's Palm: plain food cooked well (and plenty of it), served by veteran, no-nonsense waiters. Only here, the top of the line isn't a $75 lobster à la carte but a tenderloin steak at $8.75—and that includes the ever-present massive bowl of roughly scraped carrots, celery and untrimmed radishes, a stack of fresh sourdough bread, butter, homemade coleslaw and pan-fried potatoes. Among the most loyal patrons here are prominent L.A. attorney and businessman

Richard Riordan—who also happens to own the restaurant—and his circle of L.A.-business-elite friends. But all manner of other regulars can be found here too: they come for the delicious charbroiled steaks (sirloin, club, New York and more); they come for pork or lamb chops; they come for the daily specials (which might be macaroni and cheese, baked chicken complete with stuffing, mashed potatoes and peas, or sirloin tips over noodles); they come for the enormous (if somewhat greasy) breakfasts of eggs, very good bacon and pan-fried potatoes; they come for generous bowls of homemade soups that cost about a dollar. They certainly don't come for frills, ambience, chatty service or privacy. But where else can you feed a family of four for $30—and still need doggie bags? About $15 for dinner for two. No liquor.

⑬ The Original Sonora Café
445 S. Figueroa St., Downtown
624-1800
MEXICAN/SOUTHWESTERN
Open Mon.-Fri. 11 a.m.-2:30 p.m. & 5 p.m.-10 p.m., Sat.-Sun. 5 p.m.-10 p.m. All major cards.

Probably no trend, not even Cajun, came and went with greater rapidity than the Great Southwestern Panic of the late '80s. Like lemmings heading for the sea, otherwise sensible restaurateurs began serving blue-corn tortillas and dishes made with hard-to-pronounce chiles and charging lots of money for them. The bad news was that very few of these restaurateurs knew what they were doing. In time, Southwestern cuisine fell as flat as the tasteless gray tortillas most allegedly Southwestern restaurants were serving. The Original Sonora Café, a sibling of the El Cholo chain, is the notable exception to this rule. They know exactly what they're doing at this cool, downtown bank-building restaurant, with its high-concept stylized Santa Fe decor. The menu is filled with all the right dishes, only in this case they're prepared to taste like something you might actually want to eat. This is the best place in town to go for duck tamales, tequila-marinated fish, blue-cornbread madeleines (perhaps the only blue-corn concoction we've ever tasted that works), spectacular carnitas with earthy black beans—all delicious. The only bad news is that if you go during the day, parking in the bank

building will bankrupt you; go at night, when the parking is free. Dinner for two, with wine, costs about $60.

9/20 Orso
8706 W. 3rd St., W. Hollywood
274-7144
ITALIAN
Open daily 11:45 a.m.-11:45 p.m. All major cards.

Orso is an offspring of New York's Joe Allen, which in turn is a branch of the Orso on 46th Street in New York. There was a time when it was exciting for a New York restaurant to open in Los Angeles; that New York restaurants were interested in L.A. was a clear validation of the city's existence. But it's been a few years since L.A. has actually needed the approval of the New York culinary establishment. And in the case of Orso, though its presence is certainly appreciated, it's not doing anything to change the way we eat out here on the fault line. The room still looks like Joe Allen, only considerably brightened and opened up. You enter through a somewhat concealed side entrance, which always makes us wonder if we're going in the same way as the fruits and vegetables. Inside is a small bar and a somewhat larger dining room; like the late Dominick's, this is a small restaurant, considering the amount of chatter it inspires. The menu is smallish, too, especially when you consider that the right side is just a translation of the Italian left side.

Our favorite dish, without a doubt, was probably the simplest thing the restaurant makes: a crackly pizza bread, reminiscent of Armenian lahvosh, thickly coated with olive oil and garlic. It's just a big old cracker that goes great with a salad of buffalo mozzarella and tomatoes; as a light meal, it's hard to beat. Not so wonderful was the vitello tonnato, cold veal in a tuna sauce that had an unctuous, sweet-bitter taste (if you want vitello tonnato, try Harry's in Century City). The carpaccio also had its problems; when we asked for a drop of balsamic vinegar for the heap of arugula that came with the carpaccio, we were brought a bottle of Roland Brand balsamic, which is not one of the better vinegars; it was a little like bringing a can of Kraft Parmesan to the table. Nor were the pastas particularly inspired, especially the tagliatelle with grilled vegetables, which tasted like noodles flavored with nothing. And the roast potatoes with garlic were a downright shame—overcooked and somewhat shriveled, with a taste that made us wonder if they had been cooked a day or two early. . . . For $19, you can get a nice order of lamb chops from what appear to be the world's smallest lambs. Perhaps the single oddest dish we tasted, though, was the cheese course, a plate of two small slices of Parmesan, a huge hunk of butter and a pile of bread. Perhaps we're missing out on something, but we don't usually end our meals with bread and butter. Dinner for two, with wine, costs about $80.

⑬ Osteria Nonni
3219 Glendale Blvd., Atwater
666-7133
ITALIAN
Open Mon.-Thurs. 11:30 a.m.-3 p.m. & 5:30 p.m.-10 p.m., Fri. 11:30 a.m.-3 p.m. & 5:30 p.m.-10:30 p.m., Sat. 5:30 p.m.-10:30 p.m. Cards: MC, V.

Tucked between Los Feliz and Glendale, Atwater is the land that time forgot, a thoroughly unhip community of modest little prewar houses and sleepy businesses. It's a friendly, melting-pot community populated with working-class Latinos and Anglos and a new influx of Asians, a place where Chevy sedans, not Saabs, are the norm. But wait—isn't that little storefront next to a liquor store filled with men in ponytails and assorted cool types dressed in requisite black? Aren't they mingling quite happily with the Atwater moms and dads who also fill the place? Don't the decor and menu look exactly like those at Angeli Caffè? The answer is yes to all of the above. And while at first it might seem that an Angeli-style restaurant belongs in Atwater like Prince belongs at a Rotary Club meeting, the owners knew exactly what they were doing: word got out immediately in the area and in the restaurant-poor neighboring communities of Silverlake, Los Feliz and Glendale, and this warm, friendly trattoria is doing a bang-up business.

In terms of food, if you've been to Angeli's Melrose restaurant, you've been to Osteria Nonni. There's a reason for that: the founding chef was the pizza chef at Angeli, and he brought his incomparable pizza-dough recipe with him. That pizza dough is the core of the menu, going into the ten or so pizzas, the variety of lunchtime panini (sandwiches) and the basket of warm pizza bread on each table. And that pizza dough is a very good reason to come here. Osteria Nonni's pizzas are every bit as savory, crisp-chewy and totally delicious as Angeli's. The rest of the menu runs to a couple of simple starters, including an excellent antipasto assortment and a sharp, tangy green salad; a half dozen extremely simple pastas (spaghetti marinara, spaghetti with butter and Parmesan), which are sometimes a bit dull; a few grilled nightly specials; and, of course, tiramisu, no different than anywhere else but completely satisfying. The wine selection is as modest, inexpensive and appealing as the pizzas, and the caffè lattes are the real thing. And the prices can't be beat: salad, pizza and a glass of Chianti for two will cost just $30.

11/20 Pacific Dining Car
1310 W. 6th St., Downtown
483-6000
AMERICAN/STEAKHOUSE
Open daily 24 hours. Cards: MC, V.

As one of the oldest restaurants in Los Angeles, dating back to 1921, the Pacific Dining Car has built up a loyal and sizable following who swear by its steaks. Like The Original Pantry, it's a restaurant that—through sheer longevity—has moved some distance past criticism. And actually, we'd rather not be critical of it. But the truth of the matter is that no meal we've ever had at the Dining Car (save breakfast) has been noteworthy, and some dishes have been downright dreadful. It has some good things going for it, chief among them the fact that it's open 24 hours. And it's undeniably a fun place to visit; the front room looks like a fine old railway dining car from the glory days of the Union Pacific. The ambience is warm, comforting and rather clubby; the service is always good. And so, for that matter, are the breakfasts and many of the appetizers. The chili is exceptional, the smoky spareribs wonderful, the french-fried zucchini positively addictive. But the steaks, despite their primeness, tend to be disappointing. A sirloin, ordered medium rare, arrived black and blue, with a surprisingly flat flavor; a pepper steak was oddly dry. The Pacific Dining Car may have been the best steakhouse in town at one time, but that was a long time ago. And the prices! Dinner for two, with wine, will run $100 or more.

 The Palm
9001 Santa Monica Blvd.,
W. Hollywood
550-8811
AMERICAN/STEAKHOUSE
Open daily noon-10:30 p.m. All major cards.

The Palm is noisy; its waiters can be abrupt; its wine list is inadequate; its steaks aren't as good as those at Ruth's Chris or Hy's. So why is it almost always jammed? Why do so many people—ourselves included—really like it? Because it's fun. And because the steaks, while not the best, are still pretty damned good. Somehow, the din seems less offensive in a New York–style steakhouse, with sawdust on the floor and caricatures on the wall, than in an elegant French or Italian restaurant. Besides, The Palm serves the best accompaniment to a steak that you can find this side of a great bottle of red Burgundy—the finest cottage fries in town, thick and crisp and crunchy and addictive. A New York steak, cottage fries and a piece of The Palm's splendid, straight–from–New York cheesecake is one of the best simple dinners in Southern California. (Some people prefer the huge platter of chewy onion rings to the cottage fries, so you may want to compromise and order a half-and-half.) Like most steakhouses in our increasingly health-conscious age, The Palm serves far more than steak—not just other red meat but veal, chicken, fish and lobsters so large you'll think they're special effects created by one of the Hollywood crowd who frequent The Palm (and who invariably get the best tables: the four booths to either side as you enter the dining room). Come before 7 p.m. or after 9:30 p.m. and you might even be able to hear your companion speak. Regardless, bring money. Dinner for two will probably top $120, with wine, and $170 isn't tough to break if you have a couple of side dishes and a reasonably good bottle of wine.

 Pane Caldo Bistrot
8840 Beverly Blvd., W. Hollywood
274-0916
ITALIAN
Open Mon.-Thurs. 11:30 a.m.-3 p.m. & 5:30 p.m.-10:30 p.m., Fri.-Sat. 11:30 a.m.-3 p.m. &
5:30 p.m.-11 p.m., Sun. 5:30 p.m.-10:30 p.m. All major cards.

No wonder local agents love Pane Caldo—the uncomfortably crowded tables allow for excellent eavesdropping on one another's latest deals. This noisy, cheery place is packed during late lunch and weekend dinner, which also allows for plenty of elbow rubbing, an agenting pastime that ranks up there with eavesdropping. But we must commend these agents (and the designers and architects from the nearby Pacific Design Center) for their good taste, for Pane Caldo's menu is full of delights. We have sampled many delicious dishes here: spaghetti in a very flavorful clam sauce; fat spinach tortelloni in a sublime butter-and-sage sauce; a fine pesto pizza with a near-perfect crust; and a moist osso buco in a fresh tomato sauce. There are occasional disappointments, most notably the tasteless veal in the various scaloppines. But the rest of the ingredients are of a high quality. Best of all is the complimentary appetizer of chopped Italian tomatoes and croutons dressed with an excellent olive oil. This marvelous dish is served with a basket of good focaccia; you would leave happy after dining on just these simple delights. Try to avoid the peak times, when the otherwise charming waiters get overworked and the noise level gets annoying, and if the weather is good request a table on the patio, which offers a view of the Blue Whale and the Hollywood Hills. Lunch for two, with a glass of wine, is about $35; a hearty dinner with a bottle of Chianti Classico will run from $60 to $80.

 La Parrilla
2126 Brooklyn Ave., E.L.A.
262-3434
MEXICAN
Open Sun.-Thurs. 8 a.m.-midnight, Fri.-Sat. 8 a.m.-1 a.m. Cards: AE, MC, V.

Very little English is spoken at La Parrilla (which means "The Grill"). In fact, little English is spoken at any of the Mexican restaurants along Brooklyn Avenue in East Los Angeles, the heart of the Mexican barrio. La Parrilla is much prettier than most of its nearby neighbors, with earthenware bowls hanging from the walls and a large collection of decorative tiles. It's also better than its neighbors—in fact, it's one of the best Mexican restaurants in town. The menu is completely in Spanish, but the staff is eager to please, translating dishes in halting, giggly English. There are signs posted on the walls touting the wonders of the house menudo (a traditional hangover cure made from tripe), the pozole and the tamales, which are made fresh on weekends. The tortillas served with lunch are handmade. The salsa is fresh and strong, with the onions and cilantro still crisp. La Parrilla is at its best with Mexican seafood, especially the massive red snapper, which is deep fried and topped with a relatively light tomato-and-olive sauce. There is finally enough—in fact, more than enough—garlic on the camarones mojo de ajo. Dinner for two, with beer, will run about $30 to $35.

Patina

5955 Melrose Ave., Hollywood
467-1108

FRENCH

Open Mon.-Thurs. 11:30 a.m.-1:30 p.m. & 6 p.m.-9:30 p.m., Fri. 11:30 a.m.-1:30 p.m. & 6 p.m.-10 p.m., Sat. 6 p.m.-10 p.m., Sun. 6 p.m.-9:30 p.m. Cards: AE, MC, V.

If we were writing predictions for the future rather than evaluations in the present, we'd say that by the time this book is in your hands, Patina may well deserve an 18. After all, we have sampled the cuisine of chef Joachim Splichal many times before he opened Patina in the summer of 1989—first at the Regency Club and later at Seventh Street Bistro and Max au Triangle and even at Q.V. in New York, when he was a consultant—and we have long thought him to be one of the two or three most talented chefs in town. But as brilliant as Splichal is, Patina is just too new as we go to press for us to assure you that it deserves to be ranked at the same topmost level as Citrus, which we think is the best restaurant in town. Splichal—35, German-born, French-trained, a protégé of Jacques Maximin—has been working in restaurants since he was 19. When Splichal was at Max au Triangle, he dazzled critics and common folks alike with his inventive Mediterranean-style cuisine, but the restaurant was poorly located and underfinanced and it couldn't survive. This time out, with the help of his charming, lovely wife, Christine, who runs the front of the house—and with the financial support of 38 investors—Splichal has a much better shot at success. Patina is on the site of the old Le

St. Germain, a longtime L.A. favorite (hence the name: "We put a new patina on an old restaurant," Christine says). Patina is not as comfortable as it could be—seating on the banquettes seems a bit crowded—but it is pretty, and the service is attentive.

And Splichal's food is better than ever. His corn blini with marinated salmon is one of the best appetizers in town. His Santa Barbara shrimp with mashed potatoes and potato-truffle chips is equally good. Other appetizers we enjoy include the crabcakes with a red-pepper rémoulade and the braised suckling pig with cabbage. If you like fish, Splichal is your kind of chef; five of the twelve main courses listed on the regular menu are fish, including salmon with a clam vinaigrette; John Dory with calf's feet and oysters; and rock cod with fried garlic and baby artichokes. Splichal may have to broaden his menu a bit, though. Many of his creations are strikingly innovative, but not everyone (alas) likes innovation. Diners seeking the familiar, unwilling to be adventurous, may be uneasy here. In fact, we saw a party of six sit down one night, study the menu, get up and walk out, unable to find anything they wanted to eat. It's easy to say that's their mistake—and their loss—and both are true. Why would anyone go to Patina if all he wanted was something ordinary? The whole idea of a restaurant like Patina is to be extraordinary. On the other hand, the customer *is* always right—or at least, the customer is always the customer; if Splichal wants to pay his bills, he may have to serve at least one or two more traditional dishes.

Like Maximin, Splichal turns out unusual, and tasty, desserts, among them a corn crème brûlée, a peach galette with orange Champagne sorbet and a passion fruit macaroon with fresh-fruit ratatouille. The ice creams are a bit thin, though. Also like Maximin, Splichal has a special fondness for vegetables, evidenced by his nightly "garden menu," which is composed entirely of vegetables. One such menu ($42) includes a carpaccio of summer vegetables in virgin olive oil; a tomato tart with niçoise olives; baby turnips stuffed with shiitake and oyster mushrooms; and a raspberry gratin with citrus sauce. The main fixed-price dinner, also four courses and usually including an appetizer, fish course, meat or fowl and dessert, is $45. Both are bargains in this era of entrées running $30 and up. In fact,

CHAMPAGNE

Veuve Clicquot Ponsardin

MAISON FONDÉE EN 1772

REIMS
FRANCE

*"Une seule qualité:
la toute première"*

*"One quality...
the very finest"*

Madame Veuve Clicquot Ponsardin

REFLECTIONS OF GRANDEUR.

most of Splichal's menu is reasonable by today's standards, much more so than when he was at Max au Triangle: you can order an appetizer, main course and dessert for $32 per person (plus wine, tax and tip). Lunch is even more reasonable, particularly the two-course "American business lunch" for $18. Patina's house white wine is the excellent 1987 Sonoma Cutrer Chardonnay from Russian River Ranches at $5.50 a glass. You can also order it by the half bottle ($14) or full bottle ($22). Other good Chardonnays on the list include the 1988 Ferrari-Carano ($30) and several older vintages of Chalone. There are also a number of California Cabernets in the $22 to $39 price range and a French Burgundy—1983 Corton Clos du Roi from Dubreuil Fontaine ($47)—at affordable prices (by contemporary Burgundy standards, anyway). Splichal has been adding small quantities of French wines in the $30-to-$50-a-bottle range. The wine glasses at Patina are the best in town—especially the Burgundy glass; ask for it (particularly with the older vintages) even if you drink a Bordeaux or a Cabernet. Dinner for two, with wine, runs about $140.

Pazzia
755 N. La Cienega Blvd.,
W. Hollywood
657-9271
ITALIAN
Open Mon. & Sat. 6:30 p.m.-10:30 p.m., Tues.-Fri. noon-2 p.m. & 6:30 p.m.-10:30 p.m. All major cards.

Finding truly good Italian food in Los Angeles used to be about as easy as finding a parking space (or a cab) in midtown Manhattan at dinnertime. No more. There are now splendid Italian restaurants here in every possible variety: neighborhood trattoria, designer pizzeria, rustic country inn, temple of *alta cucina*. Nor are these restaurants limited to the chic westside. They can be found downtown and in Glendale as well as in Beverly Hills and Santa Monica. Mauro Vincenti owns two of these restaurants: the elegant, formal Rex and the casual, minimalist Pazzia (Italian for "madness" or "craziness"). Pazzia is a bright, noisy (some say cold) place, with high ceilings, an open kitchen and a glassed-in wine cellar. Waiters wear loud yellow shirts, smile frequently and do all they can to make you feel at ease. Vincenti himself is a warm, friendly fellow, given to open displays of affection—and to learned and impassioned disquisitions on the history of various dishes and the provenance of various ingredients.

The pappa al pomodoro—a seventeenth-century Tuscan dish made of bread, tomatoes and olive oil mushed together into a porridge—is the ideal appetizer for a chilly evening. The focaccia—round, thin bread heated and filled with melted Fontina cheese—is the ideal appetizer for any evening (or afternoon). Still better is the cold saddle of rabbit stuffed with black olives, basil and radicchio and served with lentils. Pastas here are universally excellent, whether light (tagliolini with tomato and fresh herbs) or robust (farfalle with a sauce of rabbit and porcini mushrooms); a special favorite is the maltagliati with clams, shrimp and squid ink. Among the fish, the salmon with black-olive paste, roasted sweet peppers and basil oil is the dish of choice. The veal with clams and a purée of garbanzo beans (another dish that Vincenti discovered in one of the old cookbooks he enjoys plowing through) is a most unusual taste combination. Most of the other main courses are less successful, and the pastries are even less so. But the gelati are excellent (as are the pizzas). In fact, Pazzia has an espresso bar and gelateria across the patio from the main dining room, and pizza, gelato and cappuccino or espresso make a wonderful (and affordable) light supper after a movie or concert. The wine list is reasonably good, but not reasonably priced. If you can afford a nice Barolo, be sure to save a few sips to have with a chunk of the best Parmigiana in town. Vincenti spends more time at Pazzia than at either Rex or his other restaurant, Fennel, but when he's not at Pazzia, the food sometimes suffers (a circumstance that does not apply to Rex or Fennel, the first being more established, the second being French and thus less dependent on him). Vincenti seems more interested in creation and inspiration than in execution and administration (translation: he loves starting new projects but seems to lose interest in them sooner than most), so we worry that Pazzia may ultimately decline if he finds a new challenge. Rex seemed to slip a bit a couple of years ago, in fact, but the new chef there has reinvigorated Vincenti. He's still very much excited by Pazzia, too, so go, eat, enjoy. Dinner for two, with wine, costs about $110; a pizza-gelato-espresso meal for two is about $45.

11/20 Il Piccolino

641 N. Highland Ave., Wilshire District
936-2996
ITALIAN
Open Tues.-Fri. 11:30 a.m.-3 p.m. & 5 p.m.-10:30 p.m., Sat. 5 p.m.-11:30 p.m., Sun. 5 p.m.-10:30 p.m. Cards: AE, MC, V.

Il Piccolino is a joiner in a very enjoyable trend, in which large, formal, perhaps even a bit stuffy restaurants open informal, easygoing offspring. There's La Scala's La Scala Presto, the Mandarin's Mandarette, Ristorante Lido's Caffè Lido, Chianti Ristorante's Chianti Cucina, Valentino's Primi and this place, Emilio's Il Piccolino. You'll notice that most of these offshoots are Italian—and what better food is there than Italian for utter casualness? If you don't mind the noise here, you can stay for hours at Il Piccolino, which is literally an offspring restaurant, since it is run by Emilio's son. "Piccolino" is the diminutive of "piccolo," which means tiny. So what we've got is a small tiny. Actually, it's larger than that—a room that combines casualness with understated elegance. The menu is familiar in an affable way. Pasta comes with tomato and basil, as does bufula mozzarella. Salads are made with clams, mussels, shrimp and calamari. But all is not standard-issue Italian. Pizza alla campagniolla is topped with spinach, asparagus, artichokes, peppers, broccoli, eggplant and more. There's a pizza topped with potatoes and rosemary. There's even a pizza made with polenta and topped with escarole, garlic and Gorgonzola. As is often the case with a true trattoria, the best dishes are the simplest. Our favorite is the patate fritte (french fries), a wonderful mound of great, crispy fries spiked with deep-fried parsley bits—a dish that demands eating to excess. Dinner for two, with wine, will run about $55.

12/20 La Plancha

2818 W. 9th St., Downtown
383-1449
NICARAGUAN
Open Tues.-Sun. 11:30 a.m.-9 p.m., Fri.-Sat. 11:30 a.m.-10 p.m. Cards: MC, V.

There are at least two reasons to eat at La Plancha. One is the fine Nicaraguan food, served at rock-bottom prices. The other is owner Milton Molina, an ebullient fellow who literally bubbles with enthusiasm. "Everything on the menu is fabulous," he tells us. "There is something in Nicaraguan food for everyone. You will taste things like you've never had before, and you will like them 150 percent." Order the empanada and the nacatamal (made by the Molina family at their nacatamal factory in Baldwin Park), and Milton exclaims: "You don't want the fried cheese? I get it specially from a man in San Francisco who sells it in 40-pound blocks. It is the best fried cheese you'll ever taste." Milton is right. Milton is always right. The cheese comes with a mild homemade salsa for dipping. The remarkable nacatamal is like a tamale that's decided to grow up—filled with anything and everything, from chicken, pork and whole chiles to carrots, tomatoes and prunes (watch out for the pits). There are many meat dishes; have the chopped or shredded ones over the often-tough steaks. All the entrées come with rice, a small salad of chopped cabbage and tomatoes, and a side order of both soft and crisp fried plantains. The decor would be dismal if it weren't for the bright light of Milton's personality. Dinner with beer runs about $28 for two.

12/20 Plum Tree Inn

937 N. Hill St., Chinatown
613-1819
CHINESE
Open Mon.-Thurs. 11 a.m.-3 p.m. & 5 p.m.-10 p.m., Fri. 11 a.m.-3 p.m. & 5 p.m.-11 p.m., Sat. 11:30 a.m.-11 p.m., Sun. 11:30 a.m.-10 p.m. Cards: AE, MC, V.

Though a bit garish, the Plum Tree is rather elegant by Chinatown standards. There's a bar for those waiting (and there is usually a wait), and service is friendlier than the norm. The setting may not be as handsome as those of its cousins, the various Panda Inns, but the food is superior. Favorites include classic Peking duck; deliciously spicy Hunan-style lamb, rich with black beans; admirable kung pao chicken; "pungent shrimp," a perfect balance of sweet and sour; and the mixed vegetable plate with a subtle sauce. We are less fond of the overly spicy hot-and-sour soup and the bland sizzling chicken. Still and all, the Plum Tree Inn serves consistently satisfying Chinese food. Dinner for two, with wine, will run $40 to $45.

11/20 Red Lion Tavern

2366 Glendale Blvd., Silverlake
662-5337
GERMAN
Open Mon.-Sat. 11 a.m.-2 a.m., Sun. 11 a.m.-midnight. Cards: MC, V.

German is the preferred language in this convivial neighborhood tavern, where German expatriates, students, hard-drinking local men and assorted in-the-know people come for good, hearty, inexpensive dinners. The small downstairs room has about a dozen tables and an eight-seat bar, with a simple, typically Bavarian decor; upstairs is a second dining room and another tiny bar, which is populated strictly with regulars. The charming, costumed waitresses (mostly German) keep busy visiting with the regulars, singing along with the guitarist, keeping the occasional overserved patron under control and delivering plates loaded with goulash, Wiener Schnitzel, sauerkraut, sausages, smoked pork, red cabbage and hearty sandwiches. There's a complete lack of pretension both in atmosphere and cuisine—this is very simple, generous and honest cooking that is well prepared and tasty. And dinners average just $7! There's excellent tap Ritter Brau and Munich Weissbeer, along with a small choice of German wines. Plan on $22 for two, with beer.

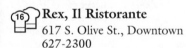

Rex, Il Ristorante

617 S. Olive St., Downtown
627-2300
ITALIAN
Open Mon. 7 p.m.-10 p.m., Tues.-Fri. noon-2 p.m. & 7 p.m.-10 p.m., Sat. 7 p.m.-10 p.m. All major cards.

When Mauro Vincenti brought Gennaro Villella to Los Angeles from his native Italy late in 1987 to become the chef at Rex, the two men agreed that Villella shouldn't rush to change the menu. They decided he should take a while to familiarize himself with American palates and products in general and with the taste and demands of Los Angeles and the clientele at Rex in particular. So, for a year, Villella did just that. He cooked the Rex menu, only gradually introducing a few of his own specials. Then, late last fall, he felt comfortable enough to create his own menu. We have not yet had the opportunity to eat our way through Villella's entire menu, but what we did taste was most impressive. Among these were a hearty soup made with potatoes and chunks of tuna, and an even heartier plate of borlotti beans topped with salmon and prosciutto. We also sampled a salad of walnuts, raisins and pieces of sea bream with arugula, as well as one of the best veal chops we've ever had, cut thick, undercooked and served atop alternating slices of tomato and zucchini. The pastas we liked best included tagliolini with squab, tomato and juniper in a rich Barolo sauce; tagliatelle with bits of rabbit, rabbit liver and rabbit kidney; and pappardelle (long, flat egg noodles) with quail and artichoke hearts.

The new menu includes many other dishes that we expect to have tried (and liked) by the time you read this. In fact, if we had tried them, we suspect we would have given Rex another toque, and a 17 ranking. But the new menu was too new for us to comfortably award that ranking when we went to press. Villella comes from the deep south of Italy, from a small town in Calabria, and he served most of his apprenticeship in Umbria, so perhaps it's not surprising that his cuisine is earthier and more robust than we've been accustomed to at Rex.

The portions at Rex are small, the presentations often precious and the influence of nuova cucina sometimes stifling to the simplicity that has historically been the true glory of Italian cuisine. No such problem with Villella's food. He manages to blend the sophisticated and the rustic and—for the most part—to eschew the excesses of nuova cucina. "You have to respect the ingredients," he says by way of explanation, and he generally does that. Two exceptions: lamb chops with mint and cantaloupe (an unhappy and ill-advised marriage, to say the least) and medallions of veal with a tomato and red-pepper sauce (a similarly unhappy mismatch).

Portions at Rex are now large enough that diners don't have to stop for a snack on the way home, so you can relax and enjoy both the food and the ambience. Rex is one of the most beautiful dining spots in the city. Black-granite tabletops. Lalique crystal table bases. Thick carpeting. Dark, polished wood. Glistening gold handrails. A sweeping stairway. Subdued lighting. Silver service plates, silver candle holders, silver sugar bowls, silver butter dishes, silver bread baskets. Vincenti patterned the interior and the appointments after the 1930s luxury liner, S.S. *Rex*, and the results are stunning. Rex actually used to be a famous men's store in the historic Oviatt Building, an art deco landmark built in 1928 (the tiny oak drawers that line the walls once held shirts; now they hold silverware).

The wine list has improved dramatically over the years; it now runs 48 pages and includes substantial offerings from California, France and Italy. More than 50 of the Californian selections are priced at $25 or less, but—with a few exceptions—we don't think California wines go well with Italian food. The French wines—which aren't always the best accompaniment to Italian cuisine, either—are considerably more expensive. Italian whites tend to be much less distinguished than Italian reds, but Rex has a broad selection of both, often terribly overpriced. Several Barolos are not unreasonable, given the price they generally fetch everywhere. The 1978s from Ceretto and Giacosa at $50 each are good buys—and super wines. The '78s won't be mature for several years, but if you ask your waiter to decant one and then wait ten or fifteen minutes to drink it, you'll have a good idea why Barolo is regarded as one of the world's great wines. A three-course dinner for two, with a modest wine, will run about $210.

12/20   Rincon Chileno

4352 Melrose Ave., Hollywood
666-6075
CHILEAN
Open Tues.-Thurs. & Sun. 11:30 a.m.-10 p.m., Fri.-Sat. 11:30 a.m.-11 p.m. All major cards.

Chile, which as we all know looks like a string bean on the map, is virtually all coastline, making seafood the dominant force in Chilean cooking. On any given night, the population at this tiny, nondescript restaurant will consist almost entirely of Chilean expatriates and emigrés savoring a small selection of dishes rarely found north of Valparaiso. Little English is spoken here, but with only eight tables, the place exudes warmth and conviviality. Ask them to sing "Happy Birthday" for you, and you'll hear "Feliz Cumpleaños." The dishes are cooked to Chilean tastes, not compromised for Americans. The abalone—served cold with papaas mayonesa or salsa verde—is chewy, the style preferred in Chile. The salsa verde, freshly made and thick with coriander, is magnificent, worth a visit all by

itself. Congrio, which they insist is fish and not eel, is flaky but a bit tasteless and filled with hundreds of tiny bones. The paila de mariscos Rincon Chileno is the Chilean version of bouillabaisse, and it's the best dish in the house—a spicy white broth filled with clams, crab, shrimp and whatever fish happens to be available. Eaten with an empanada, perhaps some anticuchos and a corn casserole called pastel de choclo, this is a fine and very filling meal. Argentinian Santa Fe beer comes in eighteen-ounce bottles, making sobriety difficult to maintain. About $30 for dinner for two, with beer.

9/20   Ritza

5468 Wilshire Blvd., Wilshire District
934-2215
RUSSIAN
Open Tues.-Sun. 11:30 a.m.-3 p.m. & 5 p.m.-10 p.m. Cards: MC, V.

Sitting in the old Ritza, on Hollywood Boulevard, it was easy to believe that you were actually in a restaurant in Tbilisi, somewhere between the Caucasus Mountains and the Black Sea. The place had a desperately shoddy air to it, including an inexplicable mural of Yosemite Valley on the wall and blinking Christmas lights strung up all year round. Then Ritza relocated to much fancier quarters on Wilshire Boulevard. It never really lost that shoddy sense, but it did lose a lot of its fun. The decor is mostly blue, with heavy chandeliers hanging overhead. There's a band of sorts that plays on weekends to large groups of emigrés who show up to eat, dance and drink too much vodka. Service can be perfectly dreadful; we once arrived when the restaurant was half empty, were told that the reservation we had made didn't exist, and that we wouldn't be served for an hour. True to their word, it took them more than an hour to serve us. Since this is Georgian Russian cooking, don't expect chicken Kiev. Instead, try appetizers of pkhali, a dip made of green beans, walnuts, garlic, olive oil and hot peppers; or bastourma, a smoked meat very much like pastrami, only far stronger. Lamb is the basic ingredient in most of the dishes—kharcho is a thick soup-stew made with lamb; cigar-shaped cabbage rolls called galoubchi are filled with spiced lamb; hashlama is a stew of lamb and vegetables; chihirtma is lamb with onions and paprika; chanakhi is lamb with okra. Dinner for two, with wine, costs about $45.

12/20 Rondo

7966 Melrose Ave., W. Hollywood
655-8158
ITALIAN
Open Mon.-Fri. 11:30 a.m.-2:30 p.m. & 6 p.m.-11 p.m., Sat. 6 p.m.-11 p.m. All major cards.

The bad news about Rondo, just a long narrow storefront, used to be that there was no place to wait for a table. And since it was always packed to the gills, waiting was something you often had to do out in the street. The good news is that Rondo expanded a while back into the storefront next door, more than doubling in size, giving those anxious to eat there lots of places to wait. The better news is that there are lots of good things worth waiting for. As at Primi, one feels inspired to graze here. Among the more substantial dishes are such good things as grilled lamb chops, an assortment of veal scaloppines and grilled salmon. But inveterate grazers inevitably go for the smaller dishes, which allow them to eat that many more items. Rondo serves one of the best calzones in town, thick with ham, cheese and fresh herbs. The exceedingly crisp pizza is topped with cheese and prosciutto—just a single pizza, nothing more. Crostini arrives with the same topping, and a lot more crunch—why do you think they call it crostini? Chubby gamberi (shrimp) come in a cream sauce, smaller scampi are paired with white beans. Risotto is made with artichokes, with seafood and with the ubiquitous porcini mushrooms. Many little dishes, we've found, easily add up to a few big ones. Many little dishes can also add up to quite a costly ticket—but the pleasure is too great to complain. Dinner for two, with wine, costs about $80.

11/20 Rosalind's

1044 S. Fairfax Ave., Wilshire District
936-2486
AFRICAN
Open daily 11:30 a.m.-11 p.m. Cards: MC, V.

Rosalind's used to be Rosalind's West African Cuisine, an atmospheric, somewhat campy one-of-a-kind restaurant on La Cienega Boulevard, famed for its ground-nut stew and Nigerian goat. Then Rosalind's moved to larger quarters on Fairfax, just south of the Jewish ghetto, into a space that used to be home to a Vietnamese and then an Ethiopian restaurant, down the block from a deli, a Chinese restaurant and an Italian restaurant and across the street from an Indian restaurant. Is it any wonder that we love L.A.? Rosalind's menu has expanded considerably, taking its exotic West African cooking—yam balls from Ghana, pilli pilli sauce from central Africa, pepper chicken from Liberia and so forth—and adding the even more exotic cooking of Ethiopia, a world of highly spiced stews with such names as yebeg alticha and yeawaze tibs, eaten with a type of millet pancake called injera that's cooked only on one side and looks like a washrag. Despite the exotic sound of the dishes, there are few ingredients you won't recognize here; they're just put together in different—and quite tasty—ways. Service is friendly, but slow; prices are ethnically low. Dinner for two, with beer, costs about $30.

Seventh Street Bistro

815 W. 7th St., Downtown
627-1242
FRENCH
Open Mon.-Fri. 11:30 a.m.-2:30 p.m. & 5:30 p.m.-10 p.m., Sat. 5:30 p.m.-10 p.m. All major cards.

When Joachim Splichal left the Seventh Street Bistro less than a year after it opened, many downtown diners were openly disgruntled. After all, apart from Rex, Bernard's and several Asian restaurants, downtown L.A. was then a gastronomic wasteland. Splichal had brought to the area an innovative approach to French food; he'd wowed everyone, then abandoned them. But Laurent Quenioux, Splichal's sous-chef, stayed behind, flourished and made the Seventh Street Bistro his restaurant—one of the most overlooked and underrated restaurants in town. Quenioux, now 30, was born in a small French town in the Loire Valley. He worked with Splichal under Jacques Maximin at Chantecler in Nice, then joined Splichal at the Regency Club before the two came to the Seventh Street Bistro. Like Maximin and Splichal, he prides himself on a "spontaneous cuisine," based on the availability of fresh ingredients and his own daily inspiration.

Our favorite appetizers here include a cold cream-of-tomato soup with basil and baby clams; lentil salad with smoked duck breast; and several salmon variations: a tartare of salmon with ginger, green peppercorns and sesame seeds; a "purse" of smoked salmon filled with crab and asparagus in a lemon grass crème fraîche; and thin cucumber slices topped with smoked salmon and served in a light tarragon cream. Quenioux also has a splendid salmon main course, which is served with a celery root purée, mustard sauce and mussels. Most of his fish dishes are excellent, but he also does well with birds, venison and lamb—the latter, for example, stuffed with ratatouille, wrapped in puff pastry and served with a red-pepper flan. Salads tend to be less successful, but desserts are superb (if a bit too preciously described on the menu: "Berry nice," "In the pink" and "Superb"). The lemon mousse terrine with a papaya-and-black-currant sauce is light; the tart of bitter-sweet chocolate and walnuts with Jack Daniels and Chantilly cream is not. Both are wonderful. At dinner, you can order half portions of virtually everything on the menu, provided you order at least one appetizer, one fish course and one meat course. So you can have three half portions, sample broadly and break neither the bank nor your diet. The wine list includes 22 California Chardonnays, sixteen Cabernets, fifteen white Burgundies and more than 50 French reds, though too few of the reds are mature, and those that are cost too much. Food prices are relatively reasonable, however. Main courses average just under $20. Three courses in half portions, plus dessert, would be just $130 per couple, including wine. Or you could ask Quenioux to prepare a special "spontaneous" dinner for what will amount to about the same price. Be sure to walk next door after you eat so you can peek inside the Fine Arts Building, one of the most attractive old lobbies in the city.

12/20 Shibucho

3114 Beverly Blvd., Silverlake
387-8498
Little Tokyo Square, 333 S. Alameda St.,
Little Tokyo
626-1184
JAPANESE/SUSHI
Open Mon.-Sat. 11:30 a.m.-2:30 p.m. & 5:30 p.m.-10:30 p.m. Cards: AE, MC, V.

In recent years, the entire sense of sushi in Los Angeles has changed radically, going from the yuppie/foodie dish of the moment to a culinary style that's both trickled down to the masses through all-you-can-eat sushi bars (an awful idea) and caused a growing panic among food fearists that raw fish is just squirming with nematodes, pox-infested bacteria and dire pollutants. Possibly it is, but then chicken has its problems, too. And so does breathing—in Los Angeles. Sushi bars are no longer quite as crowded as they used to be. But the two Shibuchos continue to function exactly as they always have, filled with Japanese hungry for real sushi (rather than the wacky rolls and casseroles that have come to pass for sushi in such rock 'n' roll sushi bars as Teru Sushi). This is not the sort of sushi bar where you can tell the chef to bring you fifteen pieces of sushi at once. Sushi is served casually, one piece at a time, at a rate the chef feels is appropriate. Try to act pushy and you'll find your meal slow down more and more, and when the bill comes, it will be very high—in a sushi bar with a nice price list, you can be charged whatever the management deems appropriate to your behavior. If they don't want you back, you'll know it from your bill. The sushi here is fresh, elegant and quite fine, particularly the belly cut of tuna called toro (in season). There's an elegance to eating at Shibucho that's quite, well, Japanese, particularly at the branch in the cubist Little Tokyo Square. Afterward, you can go bowling if you want—not a bad activity after too much yellowtail. Dinner for two, with beer, costs about $60.

11/20 Siamese Princess

8048 W. 3rd St., W. Hollywood
653-2643
THAI
Open Mon.-Fri. 11:30 a.m.-2:30 p.m. & 5:30 p.m.-11 p.m., Sat.-Sun. 5:30 p.m.-11 p.m. All major cards.

Siamese Princess has long been one of the most highly touted Thai restaurants in Los Angeles, lauded for its elegance, sophistication and fine food. However, on our last few visits, the princess's crown seems to have tarnished a bit. Where the whimsical decor (mismatched antiques, formal china place settings, dozens of portraits of multinational princesses decorating the walls, along with scads of rave reviews) once seemed dotty and sweet, it now looks a bit tatty and claustrophobic. The service tends to be poky and a bit absent-minded, but what's worse is the state of the food. On our last visit, the satays were tough and lacked flavor; the mee krob tasted like candied excelsior. We had better luck with the stuffed chicken wings, which were delicious, and the pla nam priew wan, a lightly fried fish in a ginger-scallion-vinegar sauce, which was terrific. Our noodle dishes were unmemorable, as was the bland curried chicken. Despite the fact that there are dozens of little neighborhood Thai restaurants throughout the city serving food that is far, far better than this, the Siamese Princess still continues to garner accolades and maintains a steadfast clientele. But with the drop in quality, and at these far-from-bargain prices, we wonder how much longer the hurrahs will last. Dinner for two, with wine, goes for about $70.

12/20 Siam Mania

7450 Beverly Blvd., Wilshire District
939-2466
THAI
Open Mon.-Fri. 11 a.m.-11 p.m., Sat.-Sun. 5 p.m.-11 p.m. All major cards.
Siam Mania remains one of our favorite Thai restaurants in town. The food is consistently good, and the room, while as sleek and high-tech as any around, remains soothing and quiet. You can actually talk, really talk, and still be dazzled by what comes from the kitchen. The sate is presented with one saucer of peanut sauce, another of chopped cucumbers and four toast points: a meal in itself. The stuffed chicken wings have been boned and filled with well-seasoned noodles and vegetables. The shrimp in red curry sauce, served in a pineapple shell, has a sweet coconut back taste that balances the hotness. Pad Thai is the only below-par dish we've had here in many visits: it can be an uninspired, glutinous pile. Most nights the specials are seafood dishes. If you live in the neighborhood, Siam Mania is great for take-out. Dinner for two, with beer, will run about $30 to $35.

Sofi Estiatorion

8030 W. 3rd St., W. Hollywood
651-0346
GREEK
Open Mon.-Sat. 11:30 a.m.-3 p.m. & 6 p.m.-11 p.m., Sun. 6 p.m.-11 p.m. Cards: MC, V.
Sofi is Sofi Lazaridis, a Greek-born former M.D. who decided to turn to cooking as a career when she moved to America with her architect husband Konstantine Konstan-

tinides (who is responsible for the restaurant's clean, modern look). The recipes Sofi uses in her kitchen are her own adaptations of the dishes made by her grandmother, who was supposedly the best Greek cook in Istanbul. The result is a style so non-Americanized that it's hard to believe you aren't eating in a small taverna on an Athens sidestreet. Too many of L.A.'s Greek restaurants are more cosmetic than good, but Sofi is just plain good. In fact, it's a lot better than good. Open your meal with an order of pikilia, a mixed appetizer that includes feta cheese doused with olive oil and scattered with crumbled oregano; keftedes, the definitive meatball; dolmadas, veal, lamb and rice in tiny grape leaves; and chtapodi, octopus in a vinaigrette. You can also begin your meal with a combination of Greek salads, mixing and matching tzatziki (yogurt and cucumbers), patzari (yogurt and beets), melitzana (eggplant and peppers), tarama (red caviar dip) and more. Needless to say, Sofi serves moussaka, a sublime creation that is very probably the best in town. There's tender souvlaki, plump, elegant shrimp wrapped in bacon, and a plethora of phyllo pies: kolokithopita (zucchini, feta, cottage cheese, eggs, dill), kreatopita (lamb, mushrooms, onions, pine nuts, lemon juice) and so forth. By meal's end, you'll feel so large you'll doubt you can get through the door. If you can bear it, drink the raw Greek retsina, which does wonders when it comes to cutting through the heaviness of Greek food. Dinner for two, with wine, costs about $50.

Spago

1114 Horn Ave., W. Hollywood
652-4025
CALIFORNIAN/ITALIAN
Open nightly 6 p.m.-midnight. All major cards.
Every time we go to Spago, we want to love it. We like and admire Wolfgang Puck—for his warm, puckish personality, his creativity, his energy and his imagination. Besides, several of our friends consider Spago one of the best restaurants in town. But every time we go, we're . . . not . . . really . . . dazzled. It's not that the food is bad, God knows. It's very good. But unlike Puck's other restaurant, Chinois—a true original—there's nothing at Spago that we can't get elsewhere, and usually better. In the beginning, yes, Spago was a pioneer; Puck helped create the "gourmet

pizza," and he helped define California cuisine. But now? Well, as good as the food at Spago is and as wide-ranging as Puck's talent is—who else has cooked first-rate French, Italian, Chinese and California cuisine?—there are places in town where one can eat comparable food. The pastas, in particular, seemed to us to have slipped in quality; who knows, maybe you have to be Italian—not Austrian, with French training—to make the perfect pasta, an achievement that seems to come so easily to so many Italian chefs far less skilled than Puck. The problem may be that Puck is spread too thin, what with Chinois and Spago, Postrio in San Francisco, a new restaurant coming in Malibu, his soon-to-open brewery and all those other ventures, from frozen foods to various consultancies. Or maybe Spago no longer challenges Puck. Or maybe his chef here isn't as good as Kazuto Matsusaka at Chinois. Whatever, the pizzas at Spago are still excellent, whether topped with duck sausage, with prosciutto, goat cheese and red onions or with peppered Louisiana shrimp, sun-dried tomatoes and leeks.

Some of the grilled entrées are also good. But the liver we had on a recent visit was curiously bland, the squab merely adequate and the desserts less dazzling than when Nancy Silverton was making them. The wine list is admirable, including more than 50 California Chardonnays, from $26 to $98 a bottle, and more than 40 Cabernets, from $24 to $168 a bottle. There is a smaller (and more expensive) selection of French wines and, surprisingly, only eleven Italian wines. But we've often felt that, for many, food and wine are only incidental to the experience of Spago. Spago is showtime, a movie-able feast, a restaurant frequented by stars and those who gaze at stars. The kitchen is open, the floral arrangements large and exotic, Puck's presence electric. Moreover, the help treats everyone like celebrities: despite the crowds and the noise, service is almost invariably friendly, attentive and efficient. Now almost nine years old, Spago is still one of the toughest tickets in this most fickle of towns. Call a week or two—or three or four—in advance for reservations and you're likely to be told, "We have tables at 6 and 10." Are all the tables already reserved at 7, 8 and 9? Don't be ridiculous. They're being saved for the "important customers"—celebrities and other regulars.

And some of these "regulars" are anything but celebrities. You don't have to be a celebrity, or an investment banker, to afford Spago. Many diners spend less on dinner here than they spend on the chiropractors who treat them for the stiff necks they get straining to see who's at the next table. The pizzas are $12.50 to $14, so you can order a pizza, a glass of wine and dessert and spend less than $60 per couple. If you have an appetizer, main course, wine and dessert, you're likely to spend about $140. Still not bad, considering the thrill of actually getting into the restaurant and the opportunity to see Puck and maybe a star or two.

11/20 Stepps on the Court
Wells Fargo Center, 350 S. Hope St., Downtown
626-0900
CALIFORNIAN
Open Mon.-Fri. 11 a.m.-2:30 p.m. & 5 p.m.-11 p.m., Sat. 5 p.m.-11 p.m., Sun. 4:30 p.m.-10 p.m. Cards: AE, MC, V.

Good restaurants, like good movies, are not created by MBAs and detailed market research. When the corporate approach to restauranting is taken, you usually end up with such dreadful places as Café Casino. Every rule has its exception, however, and Stepps is such an exception. The decor, the menu, the service: all of it was clearly designed by clever business-school types who took great pains to create a place that (dare we say it?) young urban professionals would flock to. They practiced first on Cutters, the Santa Monica singles spot that has an almost identical menu but a less consistent kitchen. They had the formula down perfectly by the time they opened this place; Stepps immediately attracted L.A.'s up-and-coming pinstripe crowd. Stepps's success is not surprising, but the quality of the food is. There are many dishes worth ordering from the sizable menu, which offers a sampling of nearly every kind of culinary fad. Pastas, of course, are a mainstay. The spinach tortellini in a light tomato-basil sauce is a winner, and the fettuccine topped with fiery Cajun chicken is tasty despite its temperature. Salads are interesting and usually quite good, and the daily fish specials (grilled on kiawe wood) are decent if boring. The complimentary focaccia is doughy and undercooked, but it has a nice flavor and there's plenty of it. Desserts include a fine lemon mousse and a smooth chocolate-espresso pot de crème. The attractive, open, split-level dining area is packed at lunch, making reservations a must; even at dinner, when most downtown places are dead, there's a crowd, especially in the bar. Parking in the building is free for either meal. About $30 for a simple lunch for two, with a glass of wine; $60 to $75 for a more complete dinner for two.

10/20 La Strega

400 S. Western Ave., Wilshire District
385-1546
ITALIAN
Open Mon.-Thurs. 11:30 a.m.-2:30 p.m. & 4:30 p.m.-11 p.m., Fri.-Sat. 11:30 a.m.-2:30 p.m. & 4:30 p.m.-midnight, Sun. 4:30 p.m.-11 p.m. All major cards.

"Strega" means sorceress, and the Merlin-esque masks, paintings and broomsticks that adorn the walls of this friendly, popular, more-than-a-pizza place keep the meaning firmly in mind. The lengthy menu supplements the artifacts with such dishes as a "Sorcerer's Crêpe, Specialty of the Realm" and the "Bodnicks and Broomstick" pizza, but the gimmickry is more sweet than annoying. In all ways La Strega aims to please, from the spirited (if amateurish) service to the carefully prepared and generously served (if dull) pastas to the truly astonishing wine list, one of the better in town. The diverse clientele—conservative Hancock Park couples, music-industry types from nearby Hollywood, dinner-date yuppies—mix well together under the subdued lights. And though some may order the acceptable but completely uninspired veal, homemade ravioli or Italianate seafood, the most dependable dish is the pizza. They are usually superb, often with such odd toppings as octopus or tuna; particularly luscious is the Sicilian (referring not to the crust but to its topping of Sicilian peppers and yellow chiles) and the marinated eggplant and Sicilian sausage. Next door is the rather sad and frequently deserted Lo Stregone, an overpriced, upscale version of La Strega that serves quite mediocre food. About $45 for a good pizza dinner for two, with wine.

12/20 Studio Grill

7321 Santa Monica Blvd., Hollywood
874-9202
AMERICAN
Open Mon.-Thurs. noon-2:30 p.m. & 6 p.m.-10:30 p.m., Fri. noon-2:30 p.m. & 6 p.m.-11:30 p.m., Sat. 6 p.m.-11:30 p.m. Cards: AE, MC, V.

A decade ago, the Studio Grill was one of the most innovative and exciting restaurants in town. Everything was topsy-turvy about the place, from its Pepsi-Cola sign in front (which was finally replaced a couple of years ago), to its location in a less-than-desirable section of Hollywood, to the trendy dishes on the menu. Today, the Studio Grill seems much less avant-garde; in fact, it seems almost staid and conservative. The food is still good, but it rarely excites and does little to fire the culinary imagination. The kitchen seems to have reached a point of contentment, staying there ever since. But the cooking can still be skillful, as with the shrimp poached in a superb lemon and ginger sauce, which demands sopping up with a slice of bread; the salad of smoked salmon tossed with romaine, watercress and arugula; and the cold pasta with crisp slices of duck. The more straightforward grilled dishes—swordfish, chicken, a veal chop—are usually just fine. The wine list has always been one of the best and most reasonably priced in town. It remains so, the absence of the Pepsi sign notwithstanding. Dinner for two, with wine, will run $75 to $80.

11/20 Talesai

9043 Sunset Blvd., W. Hollywood
275-9724
THAI
Open Mon.-Fri. 11:30 a.m.-2:30 p.m. & 5:30 p.m.-10:30 p.m., Sat. 5:30 p.m.-10:30 p.m. All major cards.

Once upon a time, Thai restaurants followed the style of most small ethnic restaurants, which is to say they looked like little holes in the wall. Then, as they gained acceptance, some of them began to look quite good. In fact, at Talesai, the ambience is downright elegant. There's nothing Thai at all about the design—with its cool, pale pastel colors, unusual postmodernist art and wide-open spaces, it could easily be a nouvelle California restaurant serving Pigeon Point oysters and golden caviar. Instead, the food here might be described as "inventive Thai."

There are items on the menu found nowhere else in town; there are also smaller portions and higher prices than just about any other Thai restaurant around. The mee krob, that ubiquitous sweet noodle dish, is good but a bit too sweet, with a dearth of shrimp and pork. The same dearth was noticeable in the yum yai, a traditional Thai salad of shrimp, pork, chicken, cucumber, onions and egg, tossed with lime juice and ground peanuts, but there's a reasonable amount of beef in the beef satay. And one dish is worth a trip to Talesai from just about any distance—called gai hor, it is an interesting mixture of chicken pieces marinated in a sea of herbs and spices, then wrapped in a corn husk and fried. The menu calls it "Everybody's Favorite." It is, and for very good reason. Dinner for two, with beer, costs about $55.

10/20 Tamayo
5300 E. Olympic Blvd., E.L.A.
260-4700
MEXICAN
Open daily 11:30 a.m.-2:30 p.m. & 5 p.m.-10 p.m. All major cards.

Tamayo, named for Mexican artist Rufino Tamayo, whose highly modern, dramatic paintings line the high walls of this 1928 Spanish mission-style structure, began as an attempt to introduce moderately expensive nuevo Mexicano cooking to the primarily Hispanic population of East Los Angeles. It didn't work, more because the cooking and service ranged from admirable on a good day to bad the rest of the time. After a considerable staff shake-up and the wholesale rolling of heads, Tamayo has settled down to being a good, standard-issue Mexican restaurant in an exceptional setting. The main dining room is grand and exciting, the sort of place that works beautifully for serious banquets, weddings and significant power meals, East L.A. style. Though the food has largely settled down to quesadillas, nachos and burritos, there are still many points of bright light: scallops sautéed in a jalapeño butter sauce, a chile relleno filled with seafood, a fine dish of grilled milk-fed goat (which the menu, curiously, doesn't translate from *cabrito*, as if it might scare Anglos away from ordering the dish). The prices are higher than at most East L.A. Mexican restaurants; you're paying for the ambience, but it's worth it. Dinner for two, with beer, costs about $40.

12/20 Dan Tana's
9071 Santa Monica Blvd., W. Hollywood
275-9444
ITALIAN
Open Mon.-Sat. 5 p.m.-1 a.m., Sun. 5 p.m.-midnight. All major cards.

Let's not mince words—Bruce Springsteen was sitting at the table next to ours at Dan Tana's the last time we were there. Even in a town notable for the presence of celebrities in restaurants, where you can see Michael Jackson shopping for vegetables at Gelson's in Encino, sighting the Boss at Dan Tana's is no small accomplishment. And it says a lot in terms of what this place is all about, for there were Bruce and Patty Scialfa sitting in a perfectly obvious corner booth, eating linguine and shrimp, with no one paying them any mind, no one approaching them for autographs. There wasn't even any evidence of bowing and scraping on the part of the waiter—he brought the food with the élan granted to one and all at Dan Tana's.

This dark, clubby, cozy celebrity hangout is one of the better New York–style Italian restaurants in town, serving all the old dishes, made as well as ever: spaghetti with meatballs, mostaccioli, ravioli with meat sauce, veal saltimbocca, veal piccata, shrimp Fra Diavolo, chicken cacciatore. The truth is, it's nice to rediscover just how good chicken Parmigiana really is. It's nice to watch the Monday night football game on the TV over the bar while chewing on garlic bread. And it's nice to discover that Bruce Springsteen eats with a knife and a fork—just like everyone else. Dinner for two, with wine, costs $100 or more.

12/20 Tommy Tang's
7473 Melrose Ave., W. Hollywood
651-1810
THAI
Open Mon.-Thurs. 11:30 a.m.-11 p.m., Fri. 11:30 a.m.-11:30 p.m., Sat. 5 p.m.-11:30 p.m., Sun. 5 p.m.-10:30 p.m. Cards: MC, V.

As one of the most famous restaurants in the middle of L.A.'s trendiest street, Tommy Tang's is always filled with orchidaceous creatures who are dressed oddly and look as if they're waiting for Godot. Aside from eating mee krob, the main activities here are posing, people-watching and posing some more. Surprisingly, the food is good, although the portions are smaller than the norm and the prices are a bit higher. The mee krob isn't too sweet, and it comes with a fair amount of shrimp and pork. The crispy eggrolls come with a mildly hot vinegar sauce. The Thai sausage arrives in a bathtub filled with lime juice, ginger, onion and garlic—a sauce that would make shoe leather taste decent. When it comes to hot dishes, Tommy Tang's is worth taking seriously—the squid with mint leaves and chili is perfect if sweating is your idea of a good time. The baby corn and mushrooms is a lot milder, sort of a point-counterpoint to the squid. The best drink here is the Thai lemonade, which is so acidic it puckers you—not a bad look for Melrose. We won't discuss the adjacent sushi bar, a sad-looking place that never seems to have more than one customer at a time. Dinner for two, with Thai beer, will run about $40.

⑬ Tasca

6266 Sunset Blvd., Hollywood
465-7747

SPANISH

Open Mon.-Thurs. 11:30 a.m.-10 p.m., Fri. 11:30 a.m.-11 p.m., Sat.-Sun. 5 p.m.-11 p.m. Cards: AE, MC, V.

In the past few years, when food writers have gone hunting for trends to make them look like culinary palm readers, they've often touted tapas as the next big thing. Perhaps that's true in other cities, but we sure haven't noticed tapas bars putting Thai restaurants out of business in these parts. Not that those marvelously savory little dishes don't deserve devotion—for whatever reason, they just haven't become the rage. But trend or no, we'll tell you one thing: the tapas at Tasca deserve to become the rage. In a handsome, beamed, rough-plaster setting, Tasca serves tapas and nothing but: 34 dishes, to be precise, plus a half dozen or so daily specials. Tapas, for the uninitiated, is a catch-all name for all sorts of Spanish dishes that are served in small- to medium-sized portions suitable for snacking; a few of them make for a dandy meal. At Tasca, the tapas have an emphasis on seafood and garlic (make that a passion for garlic). We don't have nearly the space to describe each of the many delicious dishes, so we'll just mention the real standouts: pimien-

tos en vinagre, perhaps the best sweet-red-pepper dish we've ever had, the peppers roasted to a perfect sweetness, dressed in a tangy-garlicky vinaigrette; ensalada rusa, a fresh-tasting combination of red potatoes, vegetables, albacore and sweet peppers; champinones al ajillo, a sauté of mushrooms in a heady garlic-sherry sauce; calamares a la romana, delicate Italian-style fried calamari; gambas al ajillo, beautiful butterflied shrimp with sweet peppers and a robustly flavored garlic-herb sauce; and el cordero, an incredibly savory dish of lamb stuffed with salty Serrano ham, spinach and manchego cheese, cooked in a coating of cilantro and basil and served with a potent red-wine sauce. Desserts include an excellent crema catalana, by any other name crème brûlée. Tasca is an ideal place for groups: the price is right, the food lends itself to sharing lots of little tastes, and the real sangría is served in festive pitchers. Two can feast well, with sangría, for $50.

12/20 A Thousand Cranes

New Otani Hotel, 120 S. Los Angeles St., Downtown
629-1200

JAPANESE

Open daily 6:30 a.m.-10 a.m., 11:30 a.m.-2 p.m. & 6 p.m.-10 p.m. All major cards.

In many ways, Japanese cooking embodies the fine art of trompe l'oeil—things that fool the eye and are therefore as satisfying to the visual sense as they are to the taste. In many ways, A Thousand Cranes is a self-contained masterpiece of trompe l'oeil. Sitting in its subdued lighting, surrounded by blond wood, waitresses in traditional dress, and a row of fine tatami rooms, you can look out leisurely on a neatly sculpted Japanese garden, with rocks and stones arranged in exactly the right places, water trickling gently into a waiting pool and small delicate shrubs blending one into another. Yet look just beyond the garden, and the mottled gray skyline of industrial Los Angeles looms before you. Thanks to the garden, the eye is fooled; it rarely gets as far as the skyline. Within A Thousand Cranes, there's a sushi bar, a tempura bar (quite rare in America) and a row of tables at which various stews are cooked over small tabletop heating elements. A Japanese brunch is served on Sundays, at which East and West collide. The best bet here is to go with either the sushi or the tempura, since the heavier casseroles tend to disappoint, and the multicourse kaiseki meal is annoyingly ordinary. When the tempura chef is on, he's the best in town, serving perfectly crisp morsels of a dish first introduced to Japan by the Portuguese—about the only good thing they gave Japan. Dinner for two, with sake, ranges from $70 to as much as $140, if you splurge on a kaiseki dinner.

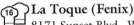 **La Toque (Fenix)**
8171 Sunset Blvd., W. Hollywood
656-7515
FRENCH
Open Mon.-Thurs. noon-2 p.m. & 6:30 p.m.-10 p.m., Fri. noon-2 p.m. & 6 p.m.-10:30 p.m., Sat. 6 p.m.-10:30 p.m. All major cards.

Ken Frank has been cooking superb French food in L.A. for more than a decade amid great critical acclaim and little financial reward. He is gastronomy's version of a fine television documentary; the reviewers love him but the public stays away in droves. Indeed, as you read this, La Toque may not even be La Toque anymore; it may be Fenix, the name Frank long ago selected for a completely remodeled and revitalized La Toque—and not, he insists, because the Phoenix rises from its own ashes. "I just like the name," he says. Okay. He's entitled. Frank has had a troubled career. —one can only sympathize with his endless misfortunes. A temperamental sort, he worked in seventeen restaurants before opening La Toque in 1979, leaving more than one place on terms that were less than amicable. In the early 1980s, he was a victim of Guillain-Barré Syndrome, a disease that ravages the central nervous system and left Frank paralyzed for a time "from the eyebrows down." After he recovered, La Toque went into Chapter 11 proceedings. Frank recovered from that, too. But for some reason, not even his dramatic recoveries have endeared him or his restaurant to the dining public. He gets a good review and people flock to La Toque for a few weeks and then business drops again. Why? Who knows. But Frank, tired of trying to figure it out, has decided to start all over with Fenix (if not now, soon), and we think it's a good idea. Although Frank continues to be one of the best chefs in town, his cuisine seems to have reached a plateau of sorts in the past couple of years. He hasn't continued to grow and develop as he might have. Perhaps the strain of fighting off both disease and creditors finally sapped his creative juices. Perhaps cooking for the small numbers of loyal customers who continue to patronize La Toque simply hasn't given him the challenge. On a given night, Frank can still be brilliant. But he isn't as consistently inventive and original and dazzling as he once was. Which is why (along with the disappointment of a recent meal at La Toque), as much as it pains us, we have lowered its ranking by one point. Perhaps Fenix, or even the mere anticipation of Fenix, will fire anew his innovative instincts.

Whether it's La Toque or Fenix or a restaurant by some other name, Frank's presence in the kitchen means superb sauces, a wonderfully light touch with fish and one of the best soft-shell crabs in town: sautéed with garlic and wild mushrooms. Frank's Rösti potatoes with caviar—the world's classiest potato pancake—is a perfect appetizer, and the swordfish grilled with calamata-olive sauce is as tasty as it is healthy. His grilled duck breast in red wine (or port and green peppercorns) and his venison in a foie gras sauce can be what a condemned man might beg for as his last dinner (assuming, of course, that the prisoner was a hit man for the local wine and food society). Frank has made so many other supernal dishes over the years that it's difficult to single out just a few. But if you see Santa Barbara shrimp on the menu, order it—whether in a soup with spinach or with Pernod or in a Pommery mustard sauce. La Toque remains a relatively reasonably priced restaurant, given the quality of the offerings. An à la carte dinner for two, with wine, runs about $160. Reduce that by $15 if you order the four-course "harvest menu"; increase it by $25 if you order the six-course "menu fantasie". Neither the wine list nor the bread is notable at La Toque, but that may change for Fenix. We hope so. Frank deserves success.

Trattoria Farfalla
1978 Hillhurst Ave., Los Feliz
661-7365
ITALIAN
Open Mon.-Fri. 11:30 a.m.-3 p.m. & 6 p.m.-10:30 p.m., Sat.-Sun. 6 p.m.-10:30 p.m. All major cards.

Hillhurst Avenue is home to a rather bizarre collection of restaurants, from the signless, ultra-minimalist Katsu, to the pale-green, homely-hip Duplex, to the newest comer, Trattoria Farfalla, which is about as big as a breadstick box. If you have to wait for a table—and you will, believe us—you'll have to stand on the sidewalk outside, for every inch of the minuscule interior is taken up with the open kitchen and the handful of crowded tables. Severe claustrophobics should stay far away from Farfalla. In fact, until the planned expansion into the neighboring podiatrist's office takes place, *everybody* should stay away, so those of us who live nearby can continue to revel in the fresh, tasty, inexpensive Italian food without having to wait three hours for a table. But our generosity of spirit forces us to tell you about the good food here, even if it does make the crowds even worse. The in-salata Farfalla, for instance, is a crisp Caesar-style salad served atop a round of equally crisp pizza bread (in lieu of croutons), a deliciously successful twist. Tagliolini is prepared with lots of sweet shrimp and garlic and just the right amount of olive oil. The roasted chicken is simple perfection. The pizzas (small and large) are terrific. And the creamy tiramisu goes down beautifully with an espresso. The setting is bare-bones, but the atmosphere couldn't be more convivial, and the price is right: about $33 for two. Bring your own wine.

Trumps
8764 Melrose Ave., W. Hollywood
855-1480

AMERICAN

Open Mon.-Thurs. 11:45 a.m.-2:45 p.m. & 6 p.m.-11:30 p.m., Fri. 11:45 a.m.-2:45 p.m. & 6 p.m.-midnight, Sat. 11:45 a.m.-2:45 p.m. & 6 p.m.-midnight, Sun. 6 p.m.-10 p.m. (tea Mon.-Sat. 3:30 p.m.-5 p.m.). All major cards.

Like City Restaurant, Trumps is much admired by L.A.'s gastronomic cognoscenti. We're not talking about the omnipresent (and oppressive) "foodies," those trendy folks who run pantingly after the newest hot chef so they can cut another notch in their Gold Cards and drop the chef's name (first name, of course) at their next dinner party. No, Trumps and chef Michael Roberts have many fans among truly discriminating diners who are too busy

eating to bother looking around to see who else is eating and who might notice them. But Roberts's food has just never engaged us. We like experimentation, even novelty, but he too often seems to step just over the boundary between the novel and the bizarre. Plantains and caviar? Cold beet and watermelon soup? Chinese roast duck with pickled pumpkin? A quesadilla of Brie and grapes with sweet-pea guacamole? Nothing seems to marry properly on our palates. Moreover, Trumps's more standard dishes—fried chicken, veal chop, rack of lamb—seem, ultimately, ordinary, clearly not worth the fuss made over the restaurant. Who has to sit in a place with a noise level that often approaches that of a busy airport runway and eat ordinary rack of lamb at $28 a pop? It's possible, of course, that we're wrong, that the food here is marvelous and that, for some quirky, indiscernible reason, it just doesn't work for us. We've all seen movies or read books, for example, that all our friends love and we hate. So maybe you should give Trumps a try, our criticisms notwithstanding. If you want to avoid a costly evening but still soak up the decadent atmosphere, you could go for a good late supper (after 10:30 p.m.) and order the $11 hamburger and fries or the $11 french toast and bacon (among other things). You could even try afternoon tea, a delightfully civilized repast. And, in fairness, the desserts here are sometimes delicious, at any time of the day or night. Whenever you come, you'll sit chic-by-jowl with westside trying-to-be trendies at massive concrete tables, surrounded by high white walls (changing art), topped by white beamed ceilings, awash in constant noise. You'll spend about $160 for dinner, with wine, for two.

Tulipe
8360 Melrose Ave., W. Hollywood
655-7400

FRENCH

Open Mon.-Fri. 11:30 a.m.-2:30 p.m. & 6 p.m.-10:30 p.m., Sat. 6 p.m.-10:30 p.m. All major cards.

In this era of $25 and $30 entrées and $200-a-couple dinner tabs in fancy French restaurants, it's a delight to find a place with talent in the kitchen and prices that don't force you to refinance your home. Roland Gibert, best-known to Southern Californians for his remarkable fish dishes at Bernard's downtown, and Maurice Peguet, formerly of L'Escoffier, teamed up recently to open a (sort of) minimalist French restaurant on Melrose, the site (sort of) of the original Ma Maison. The decor is spare, the waiters casual, the kitchen open and the prices reasonable by today's standards: $5.50 to $8 for most appetizers, $15 to $18 for most main courses. If you choose carefully, you can have a three-course dinner at Tulipe for $23.50 per person (plus wine, tip and tax). At these prices, you don't expect—and you don't get—the brilliance of the city's very best French restaurants, but you do get good, creative food. The daube de canard—duck braised in Corbière wine, baked in clay, chilled and served with baby carrots, onions and its own juices—is a lovely, hearty appetizer. The Fourme d'Ambert blue cheese and pears in a warm pastry shell is equally delicious as a starter, and the smoked salmon on a bed of Sauerkraut is an intriguing oceanic variation on the traditional choucroute. The ravioli of dry-cured duck and California snails is not as good (with the exception of Joël Robuchon and Alain Senderens in Paris, the French almost always seem to make their ravioli too thick and heavy). For main courses, the fish and seafood are almost uniformly good, particularly the salmon with wild mushrooms, the striped sea bass with a potato crust and the sea scallops with candied shallots. If you like osso buco–style veal shank, Tulipe's is excellent, served with spring vegetables and crunchy cabbage. Be forewarned that the meat is so tender it falls apart at first touch; if that texture doesn't appeal to you, try the lamb with garlic, spinach and tomatoes or the squab flavored with lime and rosemary. Skip the grilled duck breast with Acacia honey and Oriental spices; the flavors don't marry well, and the dish seems but a pale imitation of Senderens's famous canard Apicius. Desserts are $5 each and guaranteed to bring a smile to your dentist's face as well as your own. The chocolate puff pastry with bitter-chocolate cream and pistachio sauce is a chocoholic's fantasy come true; the hazelnut praline with espresso sauce and the apple tart with Calvados sauce are also worth saving room for. The wine list is intelligently

chosen and for the most part fairly priced, although many of the names may be unfamiliar. The few that are familiar are steep; $106 for a 1985 Léoville–Las Cases seems exorbitant. And the restaurant could do better than the overly sweet Weibel for its house Champagne.

⑭ **Tutto Bene**
945 N. Fairfax Ave., W. Hollywood
655-7051
ITALIAN
Open Mon.-Thurs. 11:30 a.m.-2:30 p.m. & 6 p.m.-11 p.m., Fri. 11:30 a.m.-2:30 p.m. & 6 p.m.-11:30 p.m., Sat. 6 p.m.-11:30 p.m. All major cards.

As we went to press for our last edition of this book, Silvio Di Mori had just abandoned Silvio's to open this place, which occupies the former site of that dreadful institution, Hollywood Diner. We loved Tuttobene from the start and are happy to report that, two years and many meals later, it has proved to be one of L.A.'s most consistently enjoyable Italian trattorias. Although always lively and convivial, it never got overwhelmed with the trendy set that suffocated Silvio's, and the service has remained very good. The setting won't knock you out, but it is comfortable and cheerful. And the menu is a winning collection of antipasti, pastas, risotto, salads and veal/seafood/chicken entrées, all full of fresh flavors. We can assure you that every single pasta and risotto is soulful and delicious; other don't-miss dishes include the rich, moist osso buco with creamy polenta and spinach, the juicy grilled veal chop, the simple but perfect green salad and the rich tiramisu. Healthy sorts will appreciate the kitchen's skill at grilling fish. Dinner for two, with a modest Italian wine, will range from $60 to $85.

12/20 Walia
5881 W. Pico Blvd., Wilshire District
933-1215
AFRICAN
Open nightly 5 p.m.-11 p.m. Cards: MC, V.

An African hut decor (with the tasteful accent of an early American chandelier) welcomes you, while Felliniesque voodoo music plays in the background. The lovely staff, native portraits, tentlike ceilings, batiked fabrics and rattan walls all make this Ethiopian restaurant winsome, although it's not exactly a front-runner for an interior design award. Be forewarned that the service can be extremely slow, which may press you into seeking out your own beer or Ethiopian wine to keep you company while studying the menu, which offers such exotic Ethiopian specialties as doro wat, yesega alecha, kifto, minchetabish and ye asa wat. Freely translated, you are in for a feast of fiery hot curries, stews and Ethiopian preparations of beef, chicken and fish. Everything is brought on a communal serving tray with collards, lentils, lettuce and a cooling dollop of sour cream. Native customs predominate: you are expected to eat these delicious morsels with your hands or with the help of the large swaths of tripe-like bread, which look like neatly folded napkins and taste like thick, spongy crêpes. Especially good are the sambusa (wonderful crispy meat turnovers with a chili sauce); red snapper in a tomato-based sauce; chicken pieces laden with red-pepper sauce, spices and hard-boiled eggs; the beef stew; Ethiopian fried chicken with green pepper; the light-as-air walnut baklava; and the delicious Ethiopian coffee. Walia provides both adventure and good food—and it's a bargain to boot: dinner will be $30 to $35 for two, with beer.

Yang Chow

379 N. Broadway, Chinatown
625-0811
CHINESE
Open Sun.-Thurs. 11:30 a.m.-9:30 p.m., Fri.-Sat. 11:30 a.m.-10:30 p.m. Cards: AE, MC, V.

Yang Chow's two dining rooms are always filled with happy diners who visit frequently. They obviously don't come for the decor, which is functional, tacky and brightly lit, like most Chinese restaurants. It's the cooking they come for: Szechuan wontons in a tasty, aromatic chicken-soy-garlic-chili broth; juicy pan-fried dumplings, among the best in town; shrimp in a fabulous tomato-based garlic sauce; a fine kung pao chicken; Yang Chow lamb, slices of lamb and broccoli stems in a rich brown sauce; Szechuan beef, which is a heavenly combination of chewy, crunchy, hot and sweet; slippery shrimp, the house special that is similar to Szechuan beef; and pan-fried noodles with mixed ingredients, a delicious tangle of hearty noodles, shrimp, chicken, beef and vegetables. Even that old warhorse, cashew chicken, is exemplary here. The many Szechuan dishes are spiced with a restrained hand, so the chilis don't overwhelm the other flavors. Every dish we've tried here, Szechuan or otherwise, has been at the least good and at the most wonderful. Dinner for two, with Chinese beers, will be about $25.

12/20 Zumaya's

5722 Melrose Ave., Hollywood
464-0624
MEXICAN
Open Mon.-Thurs. 11:30 a.m.-3:30 p.m. & 5:30 p.m.-10 p.m., Fri. 11:30 a.m.-3:30 p.m. & 5:30 p.m.-midnight, Sat. 5:30 p.m.-midnight. All major cards.

Despite the notation on its business card that it serves Latin cuisine, Zumaya's actually serves fairly classy Mexican chow at fairly reasonable prices. The menu is a simple one, yet there's much on it that begs to be ordered. Like the fabulous empanada, as crisp and brown as George Hamilton, with a rich filling of shredded beef, potato and a bit of mild red sauce. Or the super chicken wings, crusty and strikingly hot. Or the fine fish taco and strikingly tender abalone ceviche. The kitchen also turns out a terrific pair of enchiladas—not the gooey, cooked-till-they-drop type, but well-formed enchiladas filled with chicken or cheese and topped with either a red or a green sauce. Jumbo shrimp, butterflied and sautéed in garlic and butter, are about as good as any we've found at any of the Mexican seafood houses around town; in fact, for a change, these were not uncomfortably dry. The food here walks an interesting line—it's modern Mexican with trendy touches, but it's not trendy. In this case, it's the place itself, with its corps of spunky waitresses and customers from the Melrose neighborhood, that's trendy. This joint is full of spirit, buttressed by spirited cooking. Dinner for two, with beer, costs about $35.

SAN FERNANDO VALLEY

Akbar
17049 Ventura Blvd., Encino
(818) 905-5129

INDIAN

Open Mon.-Fri. & Sun. 11:30 a.m.-2:30 p.m. & 5:30 p.m.-11 p.m., Sat. 5:30 p.m.-11 p.m. All major cards.

This branch of Marina del Rey's Akbar is even more popular than the original; like its parent, it serves some of the best Indian food in Southern California. Everything is well prepared: the crisp samosas, the many breads, especially the onion kulcha, the cool raitha, the homemade chutneys and all the tandoori dishes, most notably the chicken tikka, which is first smoked, then broiled in the tandoor oven, and served on a sizzling platter with sliced onions. The cooking is imaginative and skilled, the ambience is pleasant, the service is good, and the wine list is better than you would expect of an Indian restaurant. The attractive decor is sometimes outshone by the diners, among whom the singing Jackson family can sometimes be found. About $55 for two, with wine.

11/20 The Beaux Tie Grill
7458 Lankershim Blvd., N. Hollywood
(818) 765-5965

CARIBBEAN/AMERICAN

Open Tues.-Sat. noon-10 p.m. Cards: MC, V.

One could try, if one were so inclined, to pigeonhole The Beaux Tie into any number of categories. It's Cajun and Creole, it's Carribean, it's Southern, it's nouvellish, it's down-home American, it's soul. It's lots of things—but it's primarily an expression of the culinary creativity of owner/chef Jardin Kazaar, an affable fellow who picked up kitchen experience cooking in (from the sublime to the ridiculous?) both France and Claremont, California. His Beaux Tie is a quirky little joint set in the midst of a dicey neighborhood, decorated on a budget that wouldn't pay for the flowers on Spago's bar. Aside from cooking, Kazaar is particularly talented at finding good waitpersons; Michelle and Dick are easily two of the friendliest we've ever encountered. Both add a slightly conspiratorial edge to the meal, with their on-the-

money suggestions about what to order. "I tasted the snapper in pili cream," said Michelle with a grin, "and whew! Is it hot!" And whew! Was it good!

The food meanders around the map some, from a dish as formal (and dated) as steak Diane to baked salmon with a jalapeño sauce, filet mignon in a green-peppercorn sauce, Cajun fried catfish, Jamaican chicken wings, Cornish hen charbroiled with a Champagne-mustard sauce, crab-stuffed shrimp and chile peppers stuffed with chicken and cheese. For dessert, the cobblers taste like a real person made them—they're imperfect, funky and finger-licking good. Do take note that The Beaux Tie has no liquor license, and the liquor store down the street leans more toward wines in screw-top bottles than Chardonnays from amusing little Napa boutiques—in other words, BYOB. Dinner for two costs about $30.

Brother's Sushi
21418 Ventura Blvd., Canoga Park
(818) 992-1284

JAPANESE/SUSHI

Open Mon.-Fri. 11:30 a.m.-2 p.m. & 5:30 p.m.-10 p.m., Sat. 5:30 p.m.-10:30 p.m. Cards: MC, V.

There may be a dearth of great French restaurants in the Valley, and its Italian and Chinese restaurants may leave much to be desired. But when it comes to sushi, the Valley can speak very well for itself. In the beginning, there was Teru Sushi, which began the trend toward raucous sushi bars back in the late '70s; later came the fine Iroha Sushi. Then along came Brother's Sushi, which gave Reseda a superb taste of Japan. Now Brother's has moved on to Canoga Park, but, thankfully, it's kept its attractive look and very good fish. There are tables, but few people sit anywhere but at the sushi bar, where most of the diners are usually Japanese. The bar is controlled by a pair of sushi chefs, one named Goro, who's been a master for nearly twenty years, and his assistant, Goto, who has a fine flair for sushi work. There's much that's superb here—the grilled bonito, for instance, which is ever-so-slightly grilled along one edge, then served as either sushi or sashimi. The miso soup, too often a boring, fetid pool, is prepared here with a pair of perfectly steamed cherrystone clams floating in the broth. It would be hard to imagine a dish more satisfying than the iced tray of salty, primal raw oysters, topped delicately with grated daikon radish and scallions. The deep-fried soft-shell crabs are easily among the best in town, with a crunch that's genuinely addictive. There's a fine, rather luxuriant lobster handroll that overflows with lobster chunks, and the very best, most exquisitely crackly salmon-skin roll we've found. Toro, the rarely encountered fatty underbelly cut of tuna, should be the dictionary's definition of the word "buttery." Dinner for two, with sake, will costs between $40 and $50.

10/20 Caffè Giuseppe

18515 Roscoe Blvd., Northridge
(818) 349-9090
ITALIAN
Open Mon.-Fri. 11:30 a.m.-3 p.m. & 5 p.m.-10:30 p.m., Sat.-Sun. 5 p.m.-10:30 p.m. Cards: MC, V.

For years, the best restaurant in the Valley was Via Fettuccini on Ventura Boulevard. When that went under, the Valley truly turned into Chef Boyardee land. Fortunately, the situation has improved a bit, partly because of the influence of Caffè Giuseppe, a little brother to Giuseppe! on Beverly Boulevard. The caffè, which anchors a small shopping mall, is ultra-spiffy—deep-green carpets, green walls, green banquettes, dusty-rose tablecloths and good graphics on the walls. It's a little too chic, perhaps, for the deep-Valley crowd—they don't seem to know what to make of this place. We once overheard a sizable fellow ask, "What kind of spaghetti you serve here?" When the waiter explained the various pastas and sauces, the fellow replied, "Yeah, but what kind of spaghetti you have?" At another table, we heard a waiter explain that fettuccine is the pasta and primavera is the sauce, not the other way around. This section of the Valley isn't used to so many choices: tortellini burina, tortellini bolognese, linguine with clams or mussels, lasagne al forno, fettuccine alla carbonara, rigatoni al pesto and more. However, a concession is made to the neighborhood—the rather heavy hot pastas are served in very large portions (though the cold pastas at the salad bar are a bit thin and bland).

The most popular item seems to be the good thin-crust pizza, especially the pesto pizza, which, however, isn't as good as the one made at Mario's in Westwood. About $45 to $50 for dinner for two, with wine.

12/20 Camille's

13573 Ventura Blvd., Sherman Oaks
(818) 995-1660
FRENCH
Open Tues.-Fri. 11:45 a.m.-2:15 p.m. & 6 p.m.-10:30 p.m., Sat. 6 p.m.-10:30 p.m. Cards: AE, MC, V.

A sadly neglected Valley French restaurant, Camille's seems to get lost in the shadow of nearby La Serre. It looks like the dining room of a hip grandmother—lots of rose and emerald colors, pictures in gilded frames and a fair selection of candelabra and well-aged vases. Stepping through the door off busy Ventura Boulevard, you'll be hit with some minor culture shock, for Camille's doesn't relate in the least to the street, or even the world, outside. The pace is leisurely and genuinely romantic without being saccharine; it's a good place to look deep into someone's eyes and say words you never thought you'd muster the courage to utter. You can do all that over some very good French dishes done with modern touches that bring them close to nouvelle in tone. A chilled tomato soup comes flavored with spinach and cucumbers. Filet of sole is given a counterpoint of smoked salmon. Veal contrasts cleverly with beef marrow and morel mushrooms. Scallops are done perfectly in an elegant saffron butter. The wine list has long been an especially good one, particularly regarding California wines. After a meal at Camille's, you'll feel like you've been let in on one of the Valley's great secrets. Dinner for two, with wine, will run about $100.

12/20 Chao Praya

13456 Ventura Blvd., Sherman Oaks
(818) 789-3575
THAI
Open Mon.-Thurs. 11:30 a.m.-11 p.m., Fri.-Sat. 11:30 a.m.-1:30 a.m., Sun. 11:30 a.m.-11:30 p.m. All major cards.
See Restaurants, "Los Angeles - Central."

12/20 La Chêne

12625 Sierra Hwy., Saugus
(805) 251-4315
FRENCH
Open Mon.-Sat. 5:30 p.m.-10:30 p.m., Sun. 10:30 a.m.-3 p.m. & 5:30 p.m.-10:30 p.m. All major cards.

Situated as it is on the Sierra Highway some ten miles from the nearest off-ramp of the Antelope Freeway, La Chêne genuinely appears to be in the middle of nowhere—or at least not far from the middle of nowhere. But there's great warmth to be found under its roof. As it says on the matchbooks: NO NEED TO TRAVEL TO FRANCE TO DINE IN A COUNTRY INN BY THE SIDE OF THE ROAD. The exterior design is river rock held together with stucco, a venerable look that seems strangely new, as if the place had just been sandblasted. The river rock is repeated on the inside, most notably in the fireplace in one corner of the dining room. But otherwise, the interior is disappointingly ordinary—with its picture of John Wayne on one wall, its paper placemats and its utilitarian banquet-hall chairs, it looks like a gussied-up Elks hall.

The menu is printed on a blackboard, and its listings run the gamut of country French dishes, with an occasional eccentric oddity. The choice of dishes is virtually encyclopedic: escargots, tongue vinaigrette, shrimp Escoffier, veal forestière, frogs' legs provençale, duck à l'orange, roast quail Veronique. And La Chêne does a first-rate job with the classics—the onion soup is rich with bread, cheese and that quintessential burnt-onion flavor that defines the beast. The filet mignon au poivre was one of the best steaks we've ever eaten—buttery soft, with a crunchy pepper crust. The beef tongue with capers melted in our mouths. La Chêne is a restaurant that fills you a wonderful sense of discovery. You can't wait to share it with your friends, to see their amazement at finding such a place on a quiet country road, so far from the madding crowd. Dinner for two, with wine, costs about $70.

11/20 Chopstix

14622 Ventura Blvd., Sherman Oaks
(818) 990-1111
CHINESE
Open Sun.-Thurs. 11 a.m.-11 p.m., Fri.-Sat. 11 a.m.-midnight. Cards: MC, V.
See Restaurants, "Los Angeles - Central."

11/20 L'Express

3575 Cahuenga Blvd. West, Studio City
876-3778
14910 Ventura Blvd., Sherman Oaks
(818) 990-8683
FRENCH
Open daily 7 a.m.-2 a.m. Cards: MC, V.

A typical California brasserie, more handsome than some but no better than others, L'Express is known for its tacky, twenty-page menu filled with paid advertisements. These two branches of the popular chain—one on the border of Hollywood and the Valley and one on the middle of Ventura Boulevard—attract a handsome crowd of local residents and entertainment-industry employees. Lots of tile and rock music on the stereo keep the noise level cheerfully high, and pretty good bistro fare keeps the chic patrons returning. Salads are your best bet—they're all good, especially the duck salad—along with the onion soup, omelets and croque-monsieur and -madame sandwiches. We're particularly fond of the near-perfect croissants. The pizza, however, is done much better elsewhere, as are the more elaborate entrées and specials. Wines are too expensive for a brasserie. A meal for two, with a glass of wine, will run anywhere from $30 to $70.

10/20 Fab's Italian Kitchen

4336 Van Nuys Blvd., Sherman Oaks
(818) 995-2933
ITALIAN
Open Mon.-Thurs. 11 a.m.-10 p.m., Fri.-Sat. 11 a.m.-11 p.m., Sun. noon-10 p.m. Cards: MC, V.

Hip Angelenos may claim to love all kinds of exotic international cuisines, from Vietnamese and Caribbean to Grenadan and Pago-Pagoan, but Fab's is proof positive that what everybody really loves is Italian food—that is, hearty, tomato-sauced Italian food. Fab's appeal is at first a mystery—why would all those people wait in line every night of the week to eat in such a bare-bones storefront café? But once you get a whiff of the kitchen aromas and look at the menu, you understand. This place serves old-fashioned Italian standards at very low prices, and they're generally pretty good, if unsophisticated and a bit heavy: generous, real-Italian-style pizzas; pastas with bolognese, marinara, clam and meat sauces; and such much-loved entrées as veal marsala, eggplant Parmigiana and whitefish pizzaiola. Try the very respectable calamari fritto, served with a side of fresh marinara sauce, and the deliciously cheesy veal saltimbocca. Entrées come with a side of good spaghetti with oil and lots of garlic. The wine list is limited, but there are a couple of decent Chiantis by the glass. Less than $40 for dinner for two, with a glass of wine and an espresso.

8/20　Frantrecote

15466 Ventura Blvd., Sherman Oaks
(818) 783-3007
FRENCH/STEAKHOUSE
Open Tues.-Fri. 11:30 a.m.-2 p.m. & 5:30 p.m.-10 p.m., Sat.-Sun. 5:30 p.m.-10 p.m. Cards: AE, MC, V.

Despite the almost universal obsession with cholesterol afflicting Southern California (where people speak of their cholesterol the way the French speak of their livers), in recent years not one but two Parisian-style entrecôte- and pommes-frites restaurants have opened. The superior of the two is L'Entrecote in Beverly Hills; the other is Frantrecote in the Valley. Frantrecote—a silly name—has a French-comic-book look to it, with framed posters on the walls and waiters with accents that are too thick to be entirely believable. With prices quite a bit higher than L'Entrecote's, where the basic meal costs under $15, Frantrecote serves a salad, a glass of mediocre wine, a presliced steak buried beneath a dreadful multi-ingredient sauce (it's one of those awful sauces that's supposed to impress us because it includes something like 1,700 ingredients), and pommes frites that could be quite a bit crisper. The sauce, a swamplike concoction, obscured the taste of the meat to such a degree that it just as easily could have been corrugated cardboard, and no one would have been the wiser. Possibly, it would taste better. Possibly, it would also be better for you. Dinner for two, with wine, costs about $60.

9/20　La Frite Café

15013 Ventura Blvd., Sherman Oaks
(818) 990-1791
FRENCH
Open Mon.-Thurs. 11 a.m.-11:30 p.m., Fri. 11 a.m.-12:30 a.m., Sat. 10 a.m.-12:30 a.m., Sun. 10 a.m.-11 p.m. Cards: AE, MC, V.

We're sad to say that standards seem to have slipped at this delightful little café owned by the people who brought us L'Express. Or have we simply become accustomed to a higher level of bistro cooking as L.A.'s restaurants have improved? In any event, our last meal was humdrum at best. The beloved salads, such as the one with spinach, chicken, avocado and bacon, are still huge, but the one we tried was ruined by a tidal wave of pungent vinaigrette. Everything else was ordinary and either too salty or flavorless. But we still like to hang out here, in this sweet, homey setting, complete with hanging plants, antique lights and ceiling fans. If you're looking for a pleasant spot for a simple snack or dessert and espresso, you could do worse than La Frite. About $25 for lunch for two, with a glass of wine; $60 for dinner with wine. There's another La Frite at 22616 Ventura Boulevard in Woodland Hills (818-347-6711).

7/20　Fung Lum

222 Universal Terrace Pkwy., Universal City
(818) 763-7888
CHINESE
Open Mon.-Thurs. 11:30 a.m.-2:30 p.m. & 5 p.m.-10 p.m., Fri.-Sat. 11:30 a.m.-2:30 p.m. & 5 p.m.-11 p.m., Sun. 11 a.m.-10 p.m. Cards: AE, MC, V.

This is probably the most gorgeous Chinese restaurant outside the Orient. Also probably the worst. Why painstakingly copy an antique building—down to the ornamental tiles, sculptured carpets and hand-carved woods—and then serve perfectly awful food? Blindfolded, you could mistake one dish for another, except for the texture. The years go by, the tourists come and go by the busload (Fung Lum is next to Universal Studios), and the food has seen little improvement. About $45 for two, with beer or the house wine.

10/20　The Great Greek

13362 Ventura Blvd., Sherman Oaks
(818) 905-5250
GREEK
Open Sun.-Thurs. 11:30 a.m.-11:30 p.m., Fri.-Sat. 11:30 a.m.-12:30 a.m. Cards: AE, MC, V.

Though you might feel this place is a desperate attempt to duplicate the *Zorba the Greek* experience, you won't mind after a while because you'll be having too much fun. Ouzo and retsina flow, the balalaika music's great, and pretty soon you'll have joined the line of dancers snaking through this Valley version of a Greek taverna. Photos of every Greek actor who ever walked across a TV screen or ate a dolmathe here grace the walls. The appetizers are the restaurant's main strength, particularly the Greek salad, spanakopita and very garlicky, delicious tzatziki. The entrées include all the usual suspects—moussaka, shish kebabs and so on—but they've been Valleyized, denatured. Such desserts as ice cream sundaes don't help much in the authenticity department. To get the most out of this Greek experience, we recommend concentrating on the retsina, the appetizers and the dancing—in which case the bill will come to about $30 for two. A larger meal will set you back about $50.

12/20 Hortobagy

11138 Ventura Blvd., Studio City
(818) 980-2273
HUNGARIAN
Open Tues.-Sat. 11:30 a.m.-10 p.m. No cards (checks accepted).

Eastern European restaurants are hardly known for the excellence of their decor, and so as Hungarian restaurants go, Hortobagy is actually rather handsome—simple but warm, with comfortable booths and windows that unfortunately face a Department of Water and Power building across the street. If you visit Hortobagy with a fellow carnivore, try the Hortobagy Wooden Platter—a groaning board for two piled high with spicy pork sausages, breaded slabs of veal and liver, vinegared potato salad, marinated red cabbage and a small hillock of rice. There's also a smaller version of the Wooden Platter, called the Farmer's Plate (disznotaros), which gives you more sausages but no veal or liver. The goulash is thick, hearty and honest, topped with a dollop of sour cream. For dessert, try one of the few Eastern European sweets that is actually edible—palacsinta, crêpes flavored with jam, cheese, walnuts or poppy seeds. Meals with beer run about $30 to $35 for two.

12/20 Iroha Sushi

12953 Ventura Blvd., Studio City
(818) 990-9559
JAPANESE/SUSHI
Open Mon.-Thurs. noon-2:30 p.m. & 6 p.m.-10:30 p.m., Fri. noon-2:30 p.m. & 5:30 p.m.-11 p.m., Sat. 5:30 p.m.-11 p.m. Cards: MC, V.

There's a hidden-away quality about Iroha Sushi that will make you feel as if you're in on a very special secret. Even though it's just a few feet away from La Serre and Marrakesh, the owners have done nothing to make Iroha seem particularly visible. In fact, they've hidden it quite well down a pathway behind the subdued Garendo Gallery. Once you've figured out where it is, you'll have found one of the Valley's best sushi shops, a peaceful place (not to be confused with such gong-bangers as the nearby Teru Sushi) where the chefs give the few discerning customers at the sushi bar all of their attention. Many say the single best sushi item here is the spiced tuna, and it is an impressive creation—a mass of very tender, delicately chopped tuna mixed with wasabe and some unidentifiable spices. The result is a sort of spiced tuna salad that is served either as a sashimi dish or in a roll. They've mastered the art of the roll at Iroha, serving a superlative salmon-skin roll (very crisp), and a first-rate California roll—a dish that may be looked down upon by traditionalists but that we've noticed is well loved by Japanese visiting from Tokyo. Dinner for two, with sake, costs about $45.

Jitlada

11622 Ventura Blvd., Studio City
(818) 506-9355
THAI
Open Mon.-Thurs. 11:30 a.m.-3 p.m. & 5 p.m.-10 p.m., Fri. 11:30 a.m.-3 p.m. & 5 p.m.-11 p.m., Sat. 5 p.m.-11 p.m., Sun. 4 p.m.-10 p.m. Cards: MC, V.

With its large windows and pleasant pastel decor, Jitlada may be the best-looking Thai restaurant in town. But, in the same way that no one ever leaves a musical whistling the set design, it isn't the decor that really matters at Jitlada. It's the food, which is nothing short of superb. As a rule, the food at most Thai restaurants is very good at worst; the number of bad Thai restaurants in town is minimal. But there are a few places that stand out above the rest, and Jitlada is one of them. Tasting mee krob here was like eating this ubiquitous dish for the first time; instead of a cloyingly gooey mound of noodles, we discovered a most subtle dish, strongly flavored with coriander and not particularly sweet, with lots of shrimp and chicken. The squid appetizer, in a batter that crunches like a Sousa march, is surely the best squid preparation in any local Thai restaurant. Nothing could be better than the barbecued chicken, so well spiced that the temptation to eat the bones is overwhelming. And those are only the appetizers! The salads are superlative, especially the pungent Thai sausage salad and the beautifully complex yum yai (cucumbers, carrots, onions, tomatoes, shrimp and chicken). We couldn't get enough of the crispy Bangkok duck, the intensely spiced, very garlicky pompano or the stir-fried asparagus with bacon and cashews. It's hard to believe that Thai food can get any better than this. Two can have dinner with Thai beer for $30 to $35; dishes will be prepared without MSG on request.

11/20 Lalo and Brothers

17237 Ventura Blvd., Encino
(818) 784-8281
CALIFORNIAN/INTERNATIONAL
Open Mon.-Thurs. 11:30 a.m.-3 p.m. & 6 p.m.-10:30 p.m., Fri. 11:30 a.m.-3 p.m. & 6 p.m.-11 p.m., Sat. 6 p.m.-11 p.m. All major cards.

Like Marlon Brando in *On the Waterfront*, for years Lalo and Brothers has been trying to become a contender. All the right elements seem to be in place: the space, basically a large cool restaurant stretching onto an effusive patio, is delightful, especially on a warm summer's night; the menu reads well, filled with creative touches; the service is smart. Unfortunately, all these great components don't add up to much. There's something flat and uninspired about the cooking at Lalo, as if the kitchen were trying too hard. This is the sort of restaurant that, at one time, actually served beer-battered shrimp in a strawberry sauce, which tasted every bit as bad as it sounds. What it does best is grill fish and chicken and put together pastas (like a memorable pasta dish tossed with sautéed scallops, scallop roe and shiitake mushrooms). What it does worst is try to be overly creative—like stuffing a baby chicken with a Vermont goat cheese so acrid the chicken smelled like a goat farm, or sautéeing Hawaiian ono with macadamia-nut butter scented with rose petals. Like many things in the Valley, the cooking at Lalo is a victim of excess—it's too much of a good thing. Dinner for two, with wine, costs about $100.

La Loggia

11814 Ventura Blvd., Studio City
(818) 985-9222
ITALIAN
Open Mon.-Fri. 11:30 a.m.-2:30 p.m. & 5:30 p.m.-10:30 p.m., Sat.-Sun. 5:30 p.m.-10:30 p.m. All major cards.

Okay, we'll admit it: we're Valley snobs, like so many who have long lived on the "right" side of the hill. We would never think of actually going to the Valley for dinner, so entrenched is our prejudice that its restaurants are no more than third-rate imitators of the real things over the hill. Yet we know that's not fair: there are plenty of good places in the Valley. And Valley residents don't want people like us coming out to their restaurants anyway. After all, we cityside dwellers have countless good places to eat, and food-wise Valleyites would just as soon keep their secrets safe.

One such secret, La Loggia, is certainly well-known to locals—it's packed night and day with an expensively underdressed crowd, most of whom are drawn from the hills to the south and the studios in Burbank, including a smattering of celebs (Molly Ringwald at one visit, Dweezil Zappa at another). They love La Loggia's intimacy, casual good cheer and straightforward Italian food—and they love the fact that they don't have to drive to West Hollywood for it. Except for the rather sad, commercial-tasting desserts (apple strudel in an Italian restaurant?!) and the fairly humdrum entrées, everything here is delicious—sometimes a touch underseasoned, but just a touch. The Caesar salad, for instance, is light on the anchovy, but it's a good, crisp, tasty salad nonetheless. One of the best dishes in the house is a $7.95 appetizer, tortino di gamberetti e funghi—it has twice the shrimp, and tasty ones at that, that you'll get with $25 entrées in most restaurants, along with an equally generous heap of wild mushrooms. Pastas are classic and reliably good; we're particularly fond of the bianchi e neri, a tangle of regular and squid's-ink pasta with plenty of bay scallops and shrimp in a wonderfully rich saffron-cream sauce. You'll also find the usual assortment of individual pizzas, which are very good. Perhaps tonight we'll get on that 101 and head out to the Valley for dinner . . . really, it's not such a bad place after all. Dinner for two, with wine, ranges from $50 to $75.

12/20 Marix Tex Mex Norte
16240 Ventura Blvd., Encino
(818) 789-5400
MEXICAN
Open daily 11:30 a.m.-2:30 p.m. & 5 p.m.-11 p.m. Cards: AE, MC, V.

The first branch of Marix (Marix Tex Mex Cafe) is in West Hollywood. The second branch (Tex Mex Playa) is in Santa Monica, just across the highway from the beach. Inevitably, the third, and grandest branch, has now opened in Encino. Marix Tex Mex Norte is one of the first Mexican restaurants in the Valley to rise above the starch-and-starch-with-starch boredom of El Torito and Acapulco y Los Arcos. It's a massive restaurant, with a semiopen kitchen and a glassed-in tortilla-making area, guaranteeing a constant supply of fresh hot tortillas. The large terracotta-tiled bar makes a good, strong margarita and attracts a sizable cross-section of Valleyites, especially the young exotics who go to bars to meet and greet; it may be one of the world's greatest conglomerations of acid-washed denim in one place. The thing to order here, as at all the Marix branches, is the fajitas, sizzling platters of chicken, beef, shrimp or vegetables that come steaming out of the kitchen like locomotives out of Grand Central Station. These come with grilled onions, tortillas, guacamole and salsa, and make for a substantial meal. Toss in some more guacamole, some queso fundido (melted cheese topped with chorizo), perhaps even a Mexican pizza, and you'll find the waistband on your distressed denims notably tight. This is food that's both fun and good; nobody said anything about it being good for you. Dinner for two, with beer, costs about $40.

11/20 Mistral Brasserie
13422 Ventura Blvd., Sherman Oaks
(818) 981-6650
FRENCH
Open Mon.-Fri. 11:30 a.m.-2:30 p.m. & 5:30 p.m.-10 p.m., Sat. 5:30 p.m.-11 p.m., Sun. 5:30 p.m.-10 p.m. All major cards.

They may call it a brasserie, but Mistral is really more of a bistro (brasseries are really glorified bars, while bistros are more for dining). And it's a very good bistro at that.

Mistral attracts a lively, upscale Valley crowd that ranges from the yuppies who congregate at the bar to the seniors who like to complain about the din while they dine. The decor is fairly authentic, with lots of dark wood, tiled floors and a mirrored bar, and while the food isn't great, it is satisfying. One of the best dishes is the pissaladière, a sort of pizza on a chou pastry crust heaped with caramelized onions, olives, herbs and anchovies, a dish that's musky and sweet at the same time. The steak tartare is terrific, as is the steak frites, served with skinny, perfectly crispy french fries. The chicken dishes, particularly the stewlike Provençal version, are fair, the pastas are nothing to get exercised over, and the desserts are so-so. Stick to the classic bistro dishes and you can't go wrong. You'll spend about $55 for dinner for two, with wine.

11/20 Moonlight Tango Cafe
13730 Ventura Blvd., Sherman Oaks
(818) 788-2000
AMERICAN/INTERNATIONAL
Open Mon.-Thurs. 11:30 a.m.-11:30 p.m., Fri.-Sat. 11:30 a.m.-12:30 a.m., Sun. 4 p.m.-11:30 p.m. All major cards.

The Moonlight Tango Cafe is the hottest thing to hit the Valley since high-top Reeboks and waterproof mascara. It's the most significant innovation on Ventura Boulevard since the invention of acrylic nails. And for good reason—it's absolutely the right restaurant in the right place at the right time. It's the latest creation of one Ernie Criezis, who also opened The Great Greek in Sherman Oaks, along with a dozen other restaurants in locations as varied as Paris and Houston. The overall concept is a born-again art deco nightclub in the style of the '20s and '30s—the sort of place that was always appearing in Marx Brothers and Bette Davis movies. Overhead hang wonderful frosted-glass and brass light fixtures that once shined in Houston's Majestic Theatre; photographs of Parisian café society taken by Brassai adorn the walls. In one corner, a band attired in white tuxedos, playing white instruments (including a beautiful stand-up bass), perform songs like "As Time Goes By." But don't expect bistro cooking of the Parisian nightclubs of a half century ago. What people eat at the Moonlight Tango are decent crabcakes (which could have been a bit crisper) with a biting red salsa; a whipped avocado-caviar purée that is virtually identical to the taramosalata served at The Great Greek (which we love); a salad of Cajun sausage and braised greens; angel-hair pasta with Sicilian sausage; grilled chicken breast stuffed with goat cheese and so forth. In other words, late-'80s and early-'90s food served in a revived 1920s ambience—hey, welcome to L.A. The bottom line, though, is the fun that people have here. Where else have you encountered (in recent memory) a conga line snaking its way through a restaurant? Where else have you come upon singing waiters who really can sing (and wait too!)? Where else can you find a place that plays "Hernando's Hideaway" as a birthday song? The Moonlight Tango is a hit; the Valley may never be the same again. Dinner for two, with wine, runs about $60.

10/20 Prezzo

13625 Ventura Blvd., Sherman Oaks
(818) 905-8400
ITALIAN
Open nightly 5:30 p.m.-1:30 a.m. Cards: AE, MC, V.

At first glance, Prezzo looks like any of a dozen Valley singles bars, filled with platoons of young women with long red fingernails and Madonna threads and men with too many gold chains. When we've visited in the past, the feel of the place wasn't helped by the tendency of the hostess to vanish for long periods of time, and then be rather rude when we suggested that her time would be better spent seating customers instead of gossiping with her friends. But, surprisingly, the food is actually decent at Prezzo. In the midst of all that mindless pick-up chatter and pounding rock, the kitchen somehow manages to do a better than serviceable job. The carpaccio alla campagnola, though a bit cold, is otherwise good—paper-thin slices of beef scattered with slivers of porcini and moistened with olive oil. A duck salad combines the muskiness of smoked duck with celery root. The pastas are good, if trendy: fusilli tricolori, capelli d'angeli with crab, ravioli stuffed with ricotta and goat cheese. The pizza is a son of Spago by way of the California Pizza Kitchen. There are many grilled dishes, which are usually well prepared. And if the cooking should fail, the mating rituals at the bar will always amuse. Plan on $55 for two, with wine.

11/20 Rive Gauche Café

14106 Ventura Blvd., Sherman Oaks
(818) 990-3573
FRENCH
Open Mon.-Fri. 11 a.m.-10 p.m., Sat. 11 a.m.-11 p.m., Sun. 10 a.m.-11 p.m. Cards: AE, MC, V.

One must spend a moment pondering the exact meaning of the name of this pleasant Valley café. If, indeed, this is the Left Bank, does that mean the large Ralphs market across the street sits on the Right Bank? Does this mean Ventura Boulevard is a metaphor for the Seine? It's all too confusing, and it makes one want to sit down and enjoy a glass of wine while trying to sort out the pieces. Like a number of the Valley's small French cafés (L'Express, La Frite, Le Café and others), Rive Gauche is popular among what Stephen Sondheim called "The Ladies Who Lunch." Though there may be many couples in here at night, during the day it is populated by well-pampered women from Sherman Oaks and Encino who drop by to eat lightly, admire each other's nails and discuss their husbands and/or boyfriends. The food is very simple café-French, including quiches and crêpes of good quality and with popular ingredients. At lunchtime, the coquilles St-Jacques make for a perfect appetizer, followed rather deftly by the eggs St-George—an eggs Benedict variation in which the Canadian bacon is replaced by crab. The food is simple and good, the windows admit lots of light, and the chatter at the tables would make a worldly priest blush. A light lunch for two, with a glass of wine, will run about $30; dinner is about $60.

⑬ Saddle Peak Lodge

419 Cold Canyon Rd., Calabasas
(818) 340-6029
AMERICAN
Open Wed.-Fri. 6 p.m.-midnight, Sat.-Sun. 11 a.m.-2 p.m. & 6 p.m.-midnight. Cards: MC, V.

Although Angelenos think nothing of driving an hour each way to work, they don't usually like to venture far for dinner. So the fact that the Saddle Peak Lodge is doing a bang-up business is indicative of its appeal, for it is a considerable drive from almost any part of L.A. Saddle Peak sits in the middle of the Santa Monica Mountains between Malibu and Calabasas; a visit here for a leisurely dinner or Sunday brunch will make you feel as if you've gone to the country for the weekend. The skillfully refurbished 50-year-old lodge (supposedly a former bordello) has several handsome, comfortably rustic dining rooms, some with fireplaces. Our favorite is the small room on the top floor, which has French doors and views of the surrounding mountaintops.

Once you get past the sometimes brusque welcome, you'll be advised and served by intelligent and opinionated waiters. Game—venison, pheasant, brook trout—is the specialty of the house, but there is much more: pâtés, vodka-cured salmon, hunter-style rack of lamb, sweetbreads, carpetbagger steak (a New York steak stuffed with oysters and served with a green-peppercorn sauce), Lake Superior whitefish and so on. The cooking is, for the most part, accomplished. True, there are lapses, but the exceptional quality of the ingredients and the marvelous atmosphere will prevent you from being too annoyed at the kitchen's faults. You won't go wrong if you start with the perfect salad of endive, watercress, goat cheese and walnuts. You may be tempted by the sautéed New York duck liver on a bed of mâche and red onion, but it doesn't work—the outstandingly tender liver is overwhelmed by the strong raspberry vinaigrette and the overabundance of pungent red onion. Much more discreet is the juniper-berry sauce served with the delicious roast venison. The skin of the lacquered Long Island duck (in a soy, sherry, ginger and wild-mountain-honey sauce) isn't always as crispy as promised, but the duck is tasty nonetheless. Accompaniments show thought, from the excellent vegetables to the wild-rice griddle cakes with black-currant jam. And the cheesecake, served in mountain-man portions, is perfect. A few hours in this charming mountain lodge won't come cheap—count on spending $110 for two, with one of the fairly priced California wines—but you'll leave well fed, rested and ready to cope with the city again. If the weather is good, take a Sunday drive out here for a lovely brunch.

11/20 Santo Pietro Bar & Grill

12001 Ventura Pl., Studio City
(818) 508-1177
ITALIAN
Open Mon.-Thurs. 11:30 a.m.-11 p.m., Fri.-Sun. 11:30 a.m.-midnight. Cards: MC, V.

You won't doubt for a minute that you're in the Valley. For one thing, this more ambitious branch of the ever-popular Bel Air pizza joint has the perfect Valley location—hidden in a new glass-box office building on (where else?) Ventura Boulevard. For another, it has a platoon of blond Valley-girl waitresses, most of whom are cheery and efficient. And it is filled with entire families from south of the Boulevard—prosperous, well-groomed people wearing colorful sweaters and white Reeboks. Their wardrobes provide the only color at Santo Pietro, which, with the exception of the open kitchen, looks like an office-building computer center stocked with tables instead of computers. The small California-style Italian menu is appealing; too bad the food doesn't always taste as good as it sounds. While you decide, you are presented with a plate of addictive rolls that have been brushed with olive oil, garlic and salt. The daily specials are frequently your best bet (though they can be much more expensive than menu dishes), such as the grilled jumbo prawns with various onions and a delicious rice-wine sauce, or the angel-hair pasta with a julienne of salmon and cucumbers. We can also recommend the variation on a Caesar salad, with rye croutons, toasted pine nuts and a tasty anchovy-mustard dressing. We've been disappointed with, ironically, one of the pizzas—the crust wasn't crisp and the "spicy" chicken sausage atop it was completely bland. There are a few desserts, the best of which is the classic cheesecake. Dinner for two, with wine, will run about $70; lunch or a simple pizza dinner will cost much less.

9/20 La Scala Presto

16234 Ventura Blvd., Encino
(818) 784-7499
3821 Riverside Dr., Toluca Lake
(818) 846-6800
ITALIAN
Open Mon.-Sat. 11:30 a.m.-10:30 p.m. All major cards.
See Restaurants, "Westside."

12/20 La Serre

12969 Ventura Blvd., Studio City
(818) 990-0500
FRENCH
Open Mon.-Fri. noon-2:30 p.m. & 6 p.m.-10:30 p.m., Sat. 6 p.m.-10:30 p.m. Cards: AE, MC, V.

Is $90 too much to pay for lunch—without wine? Not if you are served food that improves your life in some way, food that makes your taste buds sing with joy. But it's far too much for uninspired food that you can get at any number of places for much less money. We found ourselves in one of the cheery, white-trellised, flower-filled patio rooms, which are pretty but by no means elegant. Our waiter was very attentive, and he brought us food that was perfectly fine. But none of it made us pause from our conversation to pay attention to our plates. Starters were good: tender asparagus dressed with a well-balanced, mustardy vinaigrette, and delicate linguine in a tasty garlic-cream sauce with bits of dry sausage. Both dishes were correct and quite nice, if not exceptional. Entrées, however, were disappointing. Chicken in a honey-mustard sauce suffered from oversaucing and poor presentation: a half a chicken floated in an ungarnished bowl of thick, unattractive orange sauce. The strongly flavored sauce would have been tolerable in moderation, but it completely overwhelmed the chicken. Much lighter was the sauté of veal scallops and zucchini in a lemon-butter sauce. Unfortunately, the sauce was too light to improve the lifeless veal. Things picked up at the finale with a wonderfully simple raspberry tart and good coffee. If a producer from one of the nearby studios wants to bring you here, rest assured that you'll enjoy yourself—as long as he or she is paying. But if you're buying, take Laurel Canyon over the hill to Patina, Citrus or La Toque, where you will be served far, far better food for less money. Dinner for two at La Serre, with a good wine, will run about $140.

12/20 Shihoya

15489 Ventura Blvd., Sherman Oaks
(818) 986-4461
JAPANESE/SUSHI
Open Wed.-Mon. noon-2 p.m. & 5 p.m.-10 p.m. Cards: MC, V.

Shihoya is no place for diehard individualists, those who feel compelled to go their own way. It is a place of Japanese discipline, where you conform completely and do exactly as you are told. When you first arrive at the sushi bar, the schoolmistress/hostess asks if you have eaten there before. If you haven't, she begins her lesson in sushi-bar dogma. You're told not to dip the rice in the soy, you're shown in

mime what side to dip, and you're shown how to turn it over and place it in your mouth. You're told not to dip any sushi that already has a topping. You're told that the pickled ginger (gari) is served not as a salad but as a palate cleanser, and that no wasabe (green horseradish) is served, so the chef can control the spiciness of the food. And you're told that the sushi must be eaten in a particular sequence, from lighter fish to heavier, as listed on the sushi menu. Once you go to heavy, you cannot return to light. Deviance is not tolerated; if you do not wish to abide by the rules you will be seated in the dining room instead of at the sushi bar. There are other sushi bars this traditional in town, but none this authoritarian (usually they just write you off as an oaf).

Annoying as the lecture may be, it's not invalid—and the sushi served here is worth the bother. There are several elegantly arranged sashimi appetizers, including a marvelous landscape of deep-fried sculpin and some sharply spiced fuguzukui halibut, small rose petals of fish dotted with grated bits of horseradish. The lighter fish include jumbo clams, scallops, abalone, local yellowtail, halibut, bream, salmon, sea bass, shrimp and crab. The heavier dishes include oyster, barracuda, Spanish mackerel, Japanese mackerel, sea urchin (the beloved uni), sea eel, Japanese yellowtail, flying fish eggs, salmon roe and toro (the fatty belly cut of tuna). California rolls are not to be found, for they are not traditional. We were disappointed, however, that after following all the rules through a superlative sushi dinner, we weren't given gold stars for being such good boys and girls. About $60 for dinner for two, with sake.

10/20 Stratton's

16925 Ventura Blvd., Encino
(818) 986-2400
AMERICAN
Open daily 11:30 a.m.-2:30 p.m. & 5:30 p.m.-11 p.m. All major cards.

The Valley branch of Stratton's is like neither the haute Continental Stratton's across from UCLA or the noisy, rambunctious Stratton's Grill a few blocks away in Westwood Village. To get right down to it, it's a direct copy of The Grill, which is in turn a direct copy of Musso & Frank. The menus actually look so similar you have to check the matchbooks to figure out which one you're in. The difference is that the food is a tribute to Americana at The Grill and Musso & Frank; here it's just a carbon copy, and not a very good one at that. The restaurant sits over the bones of what used to be Hamburger Hamlet's Downtown Grill, a California pizza-and-pasta house that defied all odds by going under. But Stratton's Encino is succeeding in a big way, for no apparent logical reason except that when a place is hot, people flock to it just because it's hot—it's famous for being famous. The bottom line is that it's bustling and noisy, with confused service and passable salads, sandwiches and grilled items. The kitchen makes a good hamburger and a decent meatloaf with overly mashed potatoes and lumpy gravy. The fish in the fish-and-chips is coated in a dreadful crust. The Wild Turkey whisky sauce served with the New York steak tastes like spiced lighter fluid. This is good food for those who think quantity first, quality second. Dinner for two, with wine, costs about $70.

⑬ Sushi Nozawa

11288 Ventura Blvd., Studio City
(818) 508-7017
JAPANESE/SUSHI
Open Mon.-Fri. noon-2 p.m. & 5 p.m.-10 p.m.,
Sat. 5 p.m.-10 p.m. All major cards.

There's certainly no shortage of sushi bars in L.A. But in accordance with the law of averages, there are easily as many lousy ones as there are good ones. Enter Sushi Nozawa. Located in one of those accursed pod malls in Studio City (though we must confess that some of L.A's best new restaurants are tucked into these mini-mall extravaganzas—they're about the only places left with rents low enough for fledgling mom 'n' pop operations), Sushi Nozawa deserves to be ranked right up there with Matsuhisa and Katsu as one of L.A.'s best Japanese restaurants. It may lack Katsu's chic and Matsuhisa's buzz, but it's got the goods in the fish department.

Sitting at the bar, you're faced with a sign that reads SPECIAL TODAY—TRUST ME! And you'll do well to heed that notice. Just let chef Nozawa do his thing, and halt him when you can't eat another bite. Proud ("I only serve the best fish") yet self-effacing ("I've been a sushi chef 25 years, but my master—he's been for 40 years"), Nozawa makes bites that live

up to his bark. He really does use the best fish, refusing to buy or serve any that aren't up to his incredibly demanding standards. When we asked for toro, he shook his head and said the only good toro he could find was fearfully expensive, and that he'd rather not serve it at all.

Nozawa walks you through your meal: he'll tell you what to dip into soy sauce and what not to; what day the mussels are best; whether you should devour a piece of sushi in one or two bites. But rather than being offended by this dictatorialness, we found that his instruction rendered eating here a sensual experience—a culinary education we heathen Occidentals rarely encounter in restaurants. Nozawa also educates his guests regarding the provenance of his bounty: the fat, firm shrimp are from Santa Barbara, the briny, freshly harvested mussels are from New Zealand and so on. Nozawa dissuaded us from ordering uni, saying he could give it only an 80 percent guarantee and suggesting we return and try it on Thursday, when it's better and fresher. We ordered it anyway, and found it superior than any we've had anywhere else. We are in awe of Nozawa's sushi. His perfect, roseate salmon, layered with a glassy seaweed noodle and sprinkled with toasted sesame seeds, is heavenly; the mussels, bathed in a rice-vinegary broth and dabbed with a gentle yet tangy salsalike concoction, are divine. The hand rolls are deliciously complex and bound in the crispiest, toastiest seaweed sheets we've ever eaten. Each flavor comes out from behind another, like Chinese boxes. And just when you think you've tasted the best piece of sushi you've ever had, Nozawa will amaze you by serving you one that's even better. A sushi dinner for two, with beer, costs about $50.

11/20 Teru Sushi

11940 Ventura Blvd., Studio City
(818) 763-6201
JAPANESE/SUSHI
Open Mon.-Thurs. noon-2:30 p.m. & 5:30 p.m.-
11 p.m., Fri. noon-2:30 p.m. & 5:30 p.m.-11:30
p.m., Sat. 5:30 p.m.-11:30 p.m., Sun. 5:30 p.m.-
11 p.m. All major cards.

Many credit (though some also blame) Teru Sushi with starting the sushi craze in Los Angeles. There were sushi bars here before Teru, of course, but they catered mostly to Japanese businessmen. Teru was the first sushi bar that dedicated itself to the tastes of Americans. And it's been packed to the proverbial gills ever since. It's not only very good, it's also very theatrical, with a lineup of comical chefs in samurai-sushi outfits who yell at the top of their lungs every time a customer comes in or goes out. Without enough sake running through your veins, all that hubbub may give you quite a headache; with enough sake, you're sure to start yelling along. In recent years, as more and more sushi bars have appeared in L.A., Teru's quality has slipped a bit—perhaps there is too much competition for the best cuts of fish. But the level of fun hasn't changed, and the crowds haven't abated a whit—there's still a guaranteed long wait on weekends. This is the place to go for dishes like tiger's eye (salmon stuffed in squid, then baked and sliced), and for pretty little sea flowers (fish shaped into flower petals) made with sea bass. Some of the local yuppies have taken to asking the chefs to make ludicrous combinations, which they do as long as the recipient is willing to pay the price. And after too much sake and too much beer, that price can be high. Dinner for two, with sake, will run $60 or so.

12/20 Val's

10130 Riverside Dr., Toluca Lake
(818) 508-6644
CONTINENTAL
Open Mon.-Fri. 11:30 a.m.-2 p.m. & 6 p.m.-10 p.m., Sat. 6 p.m.-10 p.m. All major cards.

Like the people who laughed at the fellow who sat down at the piano (and stopped laughing when he started to play), we must admit that we chuckled when we found ourselves standing in front of Val's. Someone has clearly poured a lot of money into creating what looks like a branch of L'Orangerie. Yet they've given it a name as nonelegant as Val's (when we called directory service for the restaurant's number, they asked, "Do you mean Val's House of Pizza on Van Owen?"). They've opened it in Toluca Lake, where the residents are far more at home in the Smokehouse and Hampton's. And they've come up with a menu that is best described as haute Continental—which is not the trendiest of culinary styles at the moment. Cards on the tables call Val's "The World's Most Beautiful Restaurant," and despite that immodesty, it certainly is a fabulous space, with some of the best art we've ever seen in a restaurant (the huge renderings of ancient bowls in the dining room are amazing) and a great assortment of flowers cascading out of Volkswagen-size vases. Power seemed to ooze from the customers seated in the main dining room. Despite first impressions, Val's is clearly not someone's idea of an expensive joke.

Neither, for that matter, is the food, which ranges from the classic to the surprisingly innovative—from snails in mushroom caps and petite marmite (a clear consommé served from the earthenware marmite in which it is cooked) to saffroned mushroom soup and broiled shrimp wrapped in a scallop mousse and phyllo dough. These dishes have their moments, both good and bad. For instance, the chicken breast stuffed with shrimp and spinach in a red-pepper coulis is fine in concept and lovely to behold, but when we tried it the chicken was dry, the sauce underflavored and the accompanying vegetables problematic: overcooked wild rice, odd-tasting Chinese string beans and a tough cheese-topped tomato. Once again, there's lots of promise here, and lots of style. Add to this the new Bistro Garden in Sherman Oaks (scheduled to open after we went to press), and we seem to have the roots of the "elegantization" of the Valley. Dinner for two, with wine, costs $100 or more.

11/20 The Wine Bistro

11915 Ventura Blvd., Studio City
(818) 766-6233
FRENCH
Open Mon.-Thurs. 11 a.m.-10:30 p.m., Fri. 11 a.m.-11 p.m., Sat. 5:30 p.m.-11 p.m. Cards: AE, MC, V.

Back in the days when he was heading MTM Productions, before he went on to turn things around at NBC, Grant Tinker ate lunch at The Wine Bistro just about every day. His table was the first one inside the restaurant, a highly conspicuous spot worthy of an experienced power luncher. But the funny thing about The Wine Bistro, which is just around the corner from the CBS Center, is that it isn't the sort of place at which power lunchers would normally think of congregating. Unlike The Polo Lounge or The Bistro Garden, it's simply too friendly, too down-to-earth, too affable. But it's a power-lunching spot nonetheless, only because of its proximity to all those TV executives. The decor is pure-and-simple bistro, with lots of wood and glass and a tone of relaxation that allows you to slow down after a morning of frenzied meetings. The dishes are very simple: croque monsieur, filet of sole Veronique, calf's liver Bercy, scampi and so on. These dishes are rarely worse than good and are often very good, as in the case of the salmon with mustard sauce and the lovely cream of celery soup. At dinnertime, the local residents come in; coincidentally, they're often the same studio people who lunch here. Dinner for two, with wine, costs about $85.

10/20 Zio & Co.

5242 Van Nuys Blvd., Van Nuys
(818) 784-8051
ITALIAN
Open Tues.-Sat. 11:30 a.m.-10 p.m., Sun. 5:30 p.m.-9 p.m. Cards: MC, V.

There was a time when it was no small feat to find a decent plate of spaghetti and meat-balls in the Valley. These days, there's an abundance of both red-sauce and white-sauce restaurants (easily discernible by red-and-white tablecloths in the former and all-white tablecloths in the latter), ranging from the funky fun of Maria's Kitchen to the seriousness of La Loggia. Zio sits somewhere in between the two extremes, a combination trattoria and deli with a design scheme based on a gallery full of oversized papier-mâché characters standing against the walls and sitting at the tables, generally filling the room with waves of whimsy. The food is cheerful and simple, as befits a trattoria, including some of the best pizza in the Valley and a wide assortment of antipasti from the refrigerator case. You can find better Italian food in the Valley, but it would be hard to find a more casual space in which to eat your calamari and mozzarella. Zio is a good neighborhood Italian restaurant that serves better-than-neighborhood fare at Van Nuys prices. Dinner for two, with wine, costs about $30.

SAN GABRIEL VALLEY

12/20 Café Jacoulet

91 N. Raymond Ave., Pasadena
(818) 796-2233
FRENCH/JAPANESE
Open Tues.-Thurs. 11:30 a.m.-2:30 p.m. & 6 p.m.-9:30 p.m., Fri.-Sat. 11:30 a.m.-2:30 p.m. & 6 p.m.-11:30 p.m., Sun. 10:30 a.m.-2:30 p.m. & 5:30 p.m.-9:30 p.m. Cards: DC, MC, V.

Although Italian trattorias and California cafés are reproducing faster than rabbits, L.A. has surprisingly few true French-style bistros (good ones, at least)—places that serve simple albeit not unsophisticated French dishes to a fashionable clientele at reasonable prices. Café Jacoulet is just such a place, and its winning combination of good food, a handsome decor and low prices keeps it full day and night. Its popularity results in an occasional wait for a table, even with reservations, but you can put the time to good use by studying the shelves of French and California wines on display in the small retail and to-go area. (These wines are one of the best things about Jacoulet, because you pay a mere $2 corkage on top of the retail price.) Or wander over to the window looking into the kitchen and watch the crew prepare all sorts of tasty dishes, most of which are French with a Japanese touch: a perfectly fresh sashimi appetizer, good salads, comforting soups, juicy chicken chasseur, fine grilled yellowtail, an excellent hamburger with a peppercorn sauce, and satisfying desserts. None of these dishes will take your breath away, but all of them are honest and consistently well prepared. You'll dine in a crowded, attractive, rather noisy room decorated with huge upside-down umbrellas overhead and the graceful Japanese woodblock prints of French artist Paul Jacoulet, for whom the restaurant was named. About $25 for a simple lunch for two, with a glass of wine; with a good Acacia Chardonnay, dinner will cost two about $70.

12/20 Casa de Oriente

2000 W. Main St., Alhambra
(818) 282-8833
CHINESE
Open daily 10:30 a.m.-10 p.m. Cards: MC, V.

In a place named Casa de Oriente, we expected to find Peking duck in mole sauce or fajitas with fried rice. Instead, we found a huge, cheerful, thoroughly Chinese restaurant in a Latino neighborhood just east of downtown. Although the legions of happy Chinese diners were a good sign, the sheer size of the place made us wonder how the kitchen could turn out the quality for which it is reputed. But our fears were immediately allayed as plate after plate of delicious dishes appeared before us: war wonton soup thick with shrimp, squid and wontons; a whole chopped chicken in a robust, garlicky black-bean sauce; tender beef with fresh broccoli; and perfect kung pao shrimp, its sauce light yet fiery. Only the run-of-the-mill mu shu pork was disappointing. The high standards are maintained at lunch, when remarkable dim sum are served. The cooking alone at Casa de Oriente (so named in honor of the Latino neighborhood) is well worth the drive to Alhambra; the pleasant decor, attentive and informative service and reasonable check make a visit here all the more enjoyable. About $35 for two, with Chinese beer.

11/20 The Chronicle

897 Granite Dr., Pasadena
(818) 792-1179
CONTINENTAL
Open Mon.-Thurs. 11:30 a.m.-2:30 p.m. & 5 p.m.-10 p.m., Fri.-Sat. 11:30 a.m.-2:30 p.m. & 5 p.m.-11 p.m., Sun. 5 p.m.-10 p.m. All major cards.

What you may remember most about the Chronicle is the 74-page wine list. Even if you never eat, you'll be happy to spend an evening with any of the excellent, reasonably priced California wines. The place itself is simple and charming in the style of a men's lodge from the twenties. Tin ceilings, wood-paneled walls, a hunting trophy, a large central bar and nostalgic photos of old Pasadena dominate one small room; the other, more restful room has a cozy, living-room feeling. Like the average Pasadenan, the food is pleasant and reliable, if not dazzling. Starters are perfectly straightforward: fresh oysters and clams that mercifully don't taste like water, lovely cold poached salmon, an excellent crab crêpe, very creamy oysters Rockefeller and a perfect Caesar salad. The uncomplicated entrées will neither disappoint nor overly impress you:

broiled swordfish, very tender sand dabs, by-the-book snapper meunière and tasteless but tender veal piccata. The desserts are traditional and therefore rather dull. About $22 per person for lunch, with a glass of wine, and $45 per person for dinner, with a bottle of Chardonnay.

⑬ Dragon Regency

120 S. Atlantic Blvd., Monterey Park
(818) 282-1089
CHINESE/SEAFOOD
Open daily 9 a.m.-10 p.m. Cards: MC, V.

We never thought we would taste Chinese seafood better prepared than what is served at Mon Kee. And, indeed, Mon Kee's food remains near and dear to our taste buds. But where Mon Kee is merely great, Dragon Regency is ethereal. The chef, Chun Wong, used to cook at Imperial Dynasty in Chevy Chase, Maryland, a wealthy Washington suburb—and Washington's loss is definitely L.A.'s gain. Dragon Regency is on the edge of one of the many shopping centers that make up Monterey Park's burgeoning Chinatown. The large dining room is attractive, as Chinese restaurants go. The menu is divided into such categories as beef, pork, shrimp, lobster, fish snout, eel and frog. As is usually the case with these kinds of restaurants, there's too much to choose from. But good selections include braised whole abalone with oyster sauce, double-pleasure fresh Eastern sole (cooked twice, so the skin and bones are as edible as potato chips), pan-fried crab with garlic and black-bean sauce, pan-fried shrimp with special salt and the most marvelous frog in a powerful garlic sauce. By all means, do try the snake soup if it's in season. Everything is good: flavors are brilliantly intense but delicate enough to allow the taste of the seafood to come through. Dinner for two, with Chinese beer, runs around $40.

⑬ El Emperador Maya

1823 S. San Gabriel Blvd.,
San Gabriel
(818) 288-7265
MEXICAN
Open Tues.-Fri. 11 a.m.-9 p.m., Sat.-Sun. 10 a.m.-9 p.m. Cards: MC, V.

El Emperador Maya—the Mayan Emperor—is a small street-corner restaurant, attached to an even smaller combination kitchen and to-go window, specializing in the cooking of the Yucatán, a gigantic fist of land jutting into the Caribbean from the body of Mexico. The food of the Yucatán seems like a distant cousin of the more standardized cuisine found throughout most of Mexico. All the same ingredients are there, but they tend to be mixed together in entirely different ways. Consider, for instance, the panuchos—tiny tortillas stuffed with black beans and marinated turkey (turkey is often used in Yucatecan dishes), topped with pickled red onions; a better dish than this is difficult for us to imagine. Taste the cochinita pibil (probably the definitive Yucatecan dish), a stew of marinated pork flavored and colored with achiote (or annatto, a red dye from the fruit of a South American tree), among other things, steamed in a pot (originally in a pit, called a *pib* in Mayan, hence pibil), from which it emerges so tender and flavorful you wonder why you don't eat pork more often. Try its cousin dish, the poc chuc Don Belos, a pork chop coated with an assortment of herbs and spices so aromatic you'll find yourself wanting to lick the thing like an ice cream cone.

We will tell you, flat out, that we haven't tasted a single dish at El Emperador that wasn't utterly wonderful—from the enchilada in mole sauce to the nearly perfect guacamole, from the thick crunchy chips to the chicken with onions, peppers, tomatoes, olives, garlic and rice, and from the Mayan-style pork and beans (*buli cecen yete'l kutbi pac*—how's that for a mouthful?) to the best flans made in Los Angeles (one banana, the other cheese). We cannot imagine better Mexican food than this, served in a more unpretentious setting and at lower prices. With a cuisine like this, the Mayans should have conquered the world. Dinner for two, with beer, runs about $20.

12/20 The Epicurean

913 Foothill Blvd., La Cañada
(818) 790-5565
CONTINENTAL
Open Mon.-Fri. 11 a.m.-2 p.m. & 5:30 p.m.-9:30 p.m., Sat. 5:30 p.m.-9:30 p.m. All major cards.

'Fess up, all you restaurant-hoppers out there: aren't you just a wee bit sick of making every restaurant scene in town? After yet another night at a mobbed new hot spot, where you have to tackle a waiter to get his attention and risk going hoarse to hold a rudimentary conversation, don't you secretly long for a nice, quiet, romantic restaurant, a place that serves—gasp!—pleasant Continental food, a place that takes care of you, a place that even has a discreet pianist? If that describes your secret, and if you live on the eastside, head up La Cañada way to The Epicurean. You won't risk being embarrassed by running into any of your foodie friends (they won't be here, believe us), and you'll have a most relaxing evening eating good suburban French/Continental fare. It's not the most memorable food in town, but in general it does the job just fine: a delicious salad with duck and goat cheese, another with sun-dried tomatoes, oranges and walnuts, saucy osso buco with fettuccine, tasty sautéed breast of duck with Cognac, morels and shallots. One caveat: avoid any dish served with a sauce made of red wine or port; they tend to be unpleasantly intense, almost bitter, masking the taste of whatever they're accompanying. Otherwise, you can expect upscale comfort food that won't interfere with relaxed conversation and an entirely pleasant evening. Dinner for two, with wine, runs a fairly costly $90.

⑬ Fragrant Vegetable

108 N. Garfield Ave., Monterey Park
(818) 280-4215
CHINESE/VEGETARIAN
Open Mon.-Thurs. & Sun. 11 a.m.-9:30 p.m., Fri.-Sat. 11 a.m.-10 p.m. Cards: AE, MC, V.

In the beginning, Fragrant Vegetable was called the Vegi Food Kitchen, an unfortunate name that brings to mind brown rice, alfalfa sprouts and sitar music. Luckily the name was changed, because this surprisingly elegant restaurant, located in a Monterey Park shopping center, is far more a Fragrant Vegetable than a Vegi Food Kitchen. It's also a restaurant that would probably do better on the westside, where vegetarian cooking is more highly revered than it is in Monterey Park. In fact, its new West L.A. branch is doing beautifully.

When you enter Fragrant Vegetable you'll spy a small glass case on the left filled with different types of Chinese fungi, which the host will name for you: mushrooms, tree ears, black moss and so forth. He'll also explain that all the pork, beef, chicken and shark's-fin dishes on the menu are actually made with bean curd and served trompe l'oeil, which is surprisingly successful. The chicken, made with bean-curd skins, is eerily similar to white chop chicken. The bean-curd pork has the same red coloring as char siu pork. All told, there are 86 items on the menu at Fragrant Vegetable, with bean curd and mushrooms the dominant ingredients. The mushrooms tend to be quite musky and earthy, especially the stewed black mushrooms topped with black moss, a dish called Buddha's Cushions. This is vegetarian cooking that's too good for vegetarians; it has enough flavor to make a carnivore very happy. Dinner for two, with beer, costs around $35.

Fresco

514 S. Brand Blvd., Glendale
(818) 247-5541

ITALIAN

Open Mon.-Thurs. 11:30 a.m.-2:30 p.m. & 5:30 p.m.-10 p.m., Fri. 11:30 a.m.-2:30 p.m. & 5:30 p.m.-11 p.m., Sat. 5:30 p.m.-11 p.m. Cards: AE, MC, V.

When Mauro Vincenti opened Mauro's restaurant in late 1977, Glendale was better known as the headquarters of the American Nazi Party than as a mecca of gastronomy. Glendale still isn't known as a mecca of gastronomy, and Vincenti has long since departed, to open restaurants in three other Los Angeles-area locations. But Lino Autiero, a longtime captain at Valentino, and Antonio Orlando, longtime chef at Valentino and, later, at Primi, have taken over Mauro's and changed its name to Fresco. Fresco is now easily the best Italian restaurant in the entire San Gabriel/San Fernando Valley area and one of the best in all of Southern California. It still has the feel of Vincenti's native Rome, but the soft piano music, the white linen and the waiters in white jackets give the place a more formal feel than one customarily associates with that bustling, sunny metropolis. Autiero is also from the south of Italy (Naples), and when he recognizes a steady customer, he quickly dispenses with the formality and enjoys bantering and making recommendations for dishes not on the menu ("whatever you feel like today").

What we often "feel like" are the two calamari appetizers, either fried or sautéed Sicilian style (spicy!) with fresh tomato, capers, black olives and white-wine vinegar.

Other good appetizers include the mozzarella marinara and the fritto misto. But pastas are Fresco's specialty—everything from the traditional linguine with clams, tagliolini al pesto and spaghetti cacio e pepe (whole-wheat spaghetti with sharp cheese and black pepper) to such house specialties as rotelli with eggplant and ricotta, rigatoni with four cheeses and spinach cannelloni with a veal-and-ricotta ragù. Risotto is excellent as well; our favorites are risotto al frutti de mare (seafood) and risotto with asparagus and veal. As at most Italian restaurants, main courses aren't as good as the appetizers and pastas, but the steak Fiorentina and the giant scampi are better than most. Make sure to save room for dessert; the tiramisu is one of the best around. Lunch, when prices are generally lower, is a particularly good time to come to Fresco; it's quiet and relaxed, and if you eat late, you can watch the owners have lunch together and find out what they think is *really* good. Dinner for two, with wine, costs about $125.

8/20 Harbor Village

Landmark Center, 111 N. Atlantic Blvd., Monterey Park
(818) 300-8833

CHINESE

Open daily 11 a.m.-2:30 p.m. (for dim sum) & 5:30 p.m.-10 p.m. All major cards.

Harbor Village is the massive Los Angeles extension of a restaurant with two branches in giant Hong Kong malls and one in San Francisco's Embarcadero Center. The people behind the Harbor Village chain clearly have an affection for shopping malls—their latest venture is inside something called the Landmark Center, an imposing structure with lots of parking underground. Certain stratagems must be undertaken in terms of eating at Harbor Village (at least until the next big-deal Chinese place opens and *tout le monde* moves on): you should make a reservation for an early hour and then get there even earlier, for reservations are taken only semiseriously; you should eat something before going, since few dishes arrive within your first hour there; you should bring a parka or fur coat, for the air conditioning from the kitchen's freezer seems to have been diverted into the dining room; and you should lower your expectations, for despite Harbor Village's Hong Kong roots, the food has its ups and down. It's one of those places that's skilled at preparing complex, ornate dishes but falls to pieces when it comes to the tried-and-true favorites.

At one meal, for instance, we ordered shark's-fin soup made with a huge chunk of Smithfield ham that was as good as any shark's-fin soup we've eaten in Hong Kong or Taiwan—as subtle and delicate as a Lalique vase, yet filled with a bright rosebud of strongly flavored ham. The menu abounds with ornate-sounding dishes, some of which have won various and sundry awards: boneless pear and apple duck (winner of the 1987 Australian Pear and Apple Culinary Competition), sautéed fresh scallops with crab cream (selected for the 1986 International Chinese Culinary Arts Exposition), stewed winter melon with assorted meats (1986 Hong Kong Food Festival Golden Award) and so forth. But when it came down to ordering the dishes we always order to see what a Chinese kitchen is up to, all was not up to competition standards. The fried sesame fan-tail prawns (1979 *Travel/Holiday* Magazine Special Recommendation) arrived cold, oily and a bit mealy. Minced squab in lettuce cups featured badly aged lettuce that was brown, limp and unappetizing. Whoever made the kung pao chicken seemed to have forgotten the peppers—there were almost none, and the chicken was gristly. Pan-fried prawns with pepper-salt, one of our favorite dishes, was a major disappointment, lukewarm and rather soggy. And the crispy fried fresh oysters were anything but crispy, dripping enough oil to dress several other dishes.

Meanwhile, several dishes we ordered—such seemingly simple ones as a cold noodle salad—were unavailable. Additional glasses of club soda had to be begged for; our pot of tea vanished for a refill and never reappeared. In Hong Kong, where labor is plentiful, things probably work better. In Monterey Park, Harbor Village needs work. Dinner for two, with beer, costs about $40.

11/20 Noodles

215 N. Central Ave., Glendale
(818) 500-8783
CALIFORNIAN
Open Mon.-Thurs. 11 a.m.-10:30 p.m., Fri. 11 a.m.-midnight, Sat. noon-midnight, Sun. noon-10:30 p.m. Cards: MC, V.

Noodles looks for all the world like a chain restaurant, and in fact it has just opened its first offshoot up in Montrose. It's got all the trendy L.A.-restaurant gimmicks—baseball-capped cooks in an open kitchen, a mesquite-stoked pizza oven, exposed brick walls and ducts—but there's something about the place that smacks of Coco's-does-California-cuisine. Nonetheless, Noodles is exactly what Glendale needed—a lively café serving contemporary pizza-pasta-salad basics—which explains the full house every night. The food is exactly as good as it needs to be, no more and no less: herb-and-olive-oil-brushed rolls, tasty pizzas (except those that try in vain to imitate the California Pizza Kitchen's, like the too-sweet barbecued-chicken version), crisp Caesar salad and pastas topped with such trendy things as duck sausage and pesto. The best thing here can be had at lunch: a thick, excellent grilled-tuna sandwich served with addictive waffle fries. None of this will cause you to give up a prized 7:30 p.m. Spago reservation to come here, but if you live in this neck of the woods, it'll scratch that Cal-cuisine itch just fine. Dinner for two, with a glass of wine, is $35 to $45.

10/20 Panda Inn

111 E. Wilson Ave., Glendale
(818) 502-1234
3472 E. Foothill Blvd., Pasadena
(818) 793-7300
CHINESE
Open daily 11 a.m.-10:30 p.m. Cards: AE, MC, V.

The Panda Inn deserves a medal just for bringing Glendale and Pasadena out of the chop-suey era. Okay, so its Szechuan dishes compare to the real thing as André's does to Dom Pérignon, but that's not really the point. The Panda Inn has made it possible for San Gabriel Valleyites who don't want to venture to Monterey Park to get interesting, reasonably authentic, tasty Chinese dishes, all in a stylish atmosphere (complete with full bar) that puts Anglos totally at ease. Most everything is good, especially the soups (both the hot-and-sour and the war wonton), the assorted kung pao, the Hunan lamb, the mu shus, the Chinese chicken salad and many of the shrimp dishes. Prices are reasonable given the handsome decor and level of service.

There's another branch in the Westside Pavilion in West L.A. Dinner for two, with beer, runs $40.

⑭ **Parkway Grill**
510 S. Arroyo Pkwy., Pasadena
(818) 795-1001
AMERICAN/CALIFORNIAN
Open Mon.-Thurs. 11:30 a.m.-2:30 p.m. & 5 p.m.-10 p.m., Fri. 11:30 a.m.-2:30 p.m. & 5 p.m.-11 p.m., Sat. 5 p.m.-11 p.m., Sun. 5 p.m.-10 p.m. All major cards.

That the Parkway Grill is full night and day is no surprise—it's a textbook example of the popular restaurant, late '80s–style. The trees lining the valet parking lot are laced with tiny white lights. The mahogany bar sports a Cruvinet machine stocked with good California wines. From all points in the handsome restaurant you can watch the red-faced chefs in the open kitchen toss pizza dough and shake sauté pans. Smiling, well-dressed diners sit in the brick-walled, beam-ceilinged, split-level dining room, which is noisy enough to be lively without being annoying. And the menu offers a tempting selection of reasonably priced contemporary American and Californian dishes, all of which are good. In fact, every dish we've tried (and we've been here many, many times) has been consistently fresh, well prepared and delicious: crisp salads, al dente pastas with lots of good ingredients (fresh herbs, cheeses, sun-dried tomatoes, tender seafood), terrific California pizzas, perfectly grilled free-range chicken, unusually fresh and flavorful grilled salmon and classic cheesecake. But chef Hugo Molina is capable of more than just the California-cuisine basics. Try one of the daily specials; with these he feels freer to experiment with whatever interesting products he has found, from fresh venison to strange tropical fruits. The wine list is small but decent, the atmosphere is fun, and the service is good (though reservations are not always promptly honored). This is a great place to bring out-of-towners who want to see what California cuisine is all about. Meals for two range from $40 (for a simple pizza dinner with a glass of wine) to $85 or so (for a three-course dinner with a bottle of California wine).

⑬ **Peony**
7232 Rosemead Blvd., San Gabriel
(818) 286-3374
10990 Lower Azusa Rd., El Monte
(818) 575-3376
CHINESE
Open daily 11 a.m.-10 p.m. Cards: MC, V.

It's a long way from Beverly Hills to San Gabriel and El Monte. But it's a trip well worth the time and effort, for Peony is one of the best new Chinese restaurants to come along in quite some time. It is, in the parlance of the *Guide Michelin*, a restaurant worth going out of your way for. And that's quite a statement when you consider that the San Gabriel branch is inside a former IHOP across the street from Clearman's Northwoods Inn. It's a restaurant chain opened by a couple of fellows formerly connected with Joss in Beverly Hills, who have managed to take Joss's interesting cooking, straighten it out just a bit and remove all the pretension (and high prices). The result is a jolly restaurant that serves some exceptional food—and serves it with a smile. At the San Gabriel branch, the maître d' is a real charmer of a fellow, with a waspish wit and a great hands-on approach to restauranting (he seems to be everywhere at once).

But the real joy of Peony (such a pretty name) is the food, which seems to get better with each subsequent dish. There's a reasonably priced Peking duck ($22), which can feed a lot of people—great, crisp skin, served on puffy buns (rather than thin crêpes), accompanied by lots of meat and duck parts. Order the fried chicken salad and you'll find yourself in for quite a treat; rather than the usual concoction, this salad is made with mayonnaise, which may sound odd but tastes wonderful. When mixed with a few Szechuan-style Chinese pickles, it is transformed into the sine qua non of chicken salads. Though the stir-fried shrimp with spicy salt isn't quite up to the stuff made at Dragon Regency (Monterey Park) or Wonder Seafood (Alhambra), a house special of lobster with garlic and black-bean sauce was mind-boggling—we've rarely eaten a lobster so rich with wonderful chunks of meat. Of the 140 dishes on the menu, we've tried only a fraction, but we'll be back soon for more of this excellent Hong Kong–style Chinese seafood, served in a decidedly wacky setting. (The second Peony in El Monte is a bit more mundane looking.) It's just what the San Gabriel Valley needs; we wish there was a branch or two westward, too. Dinner for two, with beer, costs about $40.

⑭ Shiro

1505 Mission St., S. Pasadena
(818) 799-4774
FRENCH/JAPANESE/SEAFOOD
Open Tues.-Sat. 6 p.m.-10 p.m., Sun. 5:45 p.m.-9 p.m. Cards: MC, V.

Well-nigh the perfect neighborhood restaurant, Shiro makes us wish we lived in sleepy South Pasadena. Then we would surely return every week for a dinner of impeccably fresh seafood, an inexpensive bottle of Chardonnay and a flawless crème brûlée with berries. Owner-chef Hideo Yamashiro (who goes by the nickname Shiro) learned the tricks of the bistro trade at the immensely successful Café Jacoulet before striking out on his own (much to the detriment of Jacoulet's food, which has slipped a notch since his departure). It took neither advertising nor publicity to immediately fill up this modest yet comfortable storefront café—Shiro's piscatorial talent resulted in an instant cadre of loyal locals. Chef Shiro combines a Japanese eye for high-quality, ultra-fresh fish with the French art of saucing, and the resulting dishes are delicious. We can recommend everything on the small, daily-changing menu, though we do have some special favorites, most of which are usually available. One of the best dishes in the house is the seafood salad, a heap of shrimp, scallops, clams, mussels and calamari dressed in an unbelievably wonderful herb-oil sauce with a hint of saffron. Other memorable starters are large Chinese ravioli stuffed with a perfectly seasoned shrimp and salmon mousse and served with a vibrant tomato-basil sauce, excellent sashimi sharpened with a lime sauce, and a light yet robustly flavored Provençal-style clam soup. Entrées include whole sizzling catfish with ponzu (a soy-based sauce), moist Pacific king salmon with one of several herb sauces, grilled yellowtail with a sharp, savory, fabulous sauce of stone-ground mustard and sesame seeds and, for a change from fish, grilled free-range chicken with a rosemary-mustard-garlic sauce, the kind of supremely satisfying dish you find at good

bistros all over France. The rest of the details are carefully thought out: good desserts, handsome waiters who are there when you need them but disappear when you don't, and several tasty wines for well under $20. Though Shiro is stocked with the trappings of any successful bistro these days—an open kitchen, exposed ceilings, white walls—the noise level is quite within reason. And the tab is more than fair: about $70 for an excellent seafood dinner for two, with wine.

11/20 Stoney Point

1460 W. Colorado Blvd., Pasadena
(818) 792-6115
FRENCH
Open Mon.-Thurs. 11:30 a.m.-2:30 p.m. & 5:30 p.m.-10 p.m., Fri. 11:30 a.m.-2:30 p.m. & 5:30 p.m.-11 p.m., Sat. 5:30 p.m.-11 p.m. Cards: MC, V.

There's a postcard of Stoney Point, available at the door, that says much about how we used to dine—and sometimes still do. On it is a photograph of a room that is devoid of people and is done in tones of purple and pink, with black-leather banquettes, black chairs with casters and brown-and-red carpeting. Stoney Point actually looks much better than that in person, and it's a lot more lively when people are there. Hidden in the San Rafael–Annandale section of Pasadena, Stoney Point sits next to the freeway, which gives the air an odd hum. The menu describes the food as "French, Continental and nouvelle," and that's almost what it is. There are such satisfying old favorites as poulet dijonnaise, a pleasant, tender chicken breast carefully broiled and served in a forceful mustard-and-peppercorn sauce, and there's much pleasure to be derived from the sirloin steak cooked with shallots and a bordelaise sauce—a taste from way back in our memory. The dishes here are neither particularly simple nor especially complex. Stoney Point is quite fond of puff pastry, which is done well, especially the feuilleté of snails sautéed with leeks, or the millefeuille of mushrooms in a saffron sauce. Nightly specials run to such things as spinach pasta with salmon, or roast quail and venison. If there was one dish we'd go back for, it would be the ris de veau à la hunanaise, Franco-Hunanese sweetbreads served with sweet-and-sour ginger and a light garlic sauce.

The entrées come with carrots, green beans, red cabbage, zucchini, red potatoes and ratatouille—a quantity of food as old-fashioned as the decor. Dinner for two, with wine, costs about $85.

⑭ Wonder Seafood

2505 W. Valley Blvd., Alhambra
(818) 308-0259
CHINESE/SEAFOOD
Open daily 11:30 a.m.-10 p.m. Cards: MC, V.

While you wait to be shown to your table at Wonder Seafood, there are several entertaining activities in which you can involve yourself. You can watch the live shrimp in the tank do their little fandangos and pirouettes, blissfully unaware that they're about to be boiled—the only way to maintain the pure taste of live shrimp. You can also meditate on the small shrine, with its statues, red lights, oranges and rice, on the wall next to the kitchen. And, of course, you can watch the endless parade of superb dishes emerge from the kitchen, dishes that will fill you with both hunger and great anticipation. The menu is similar to those found at most of the better Chinese seafood restaurants around town. The kitchen does an exceptional job preparing baked crab with black-bean sauce, baked prawns with spicy salt, sizzling seafood, sliced abalone with black mushrooms, steamed clams with black-bean sauce and deep-fried whole fish with sweet-and-sour sauce. In fact, the crab and shrimp are among the best we've come across—immense crabs filled with tender lumps of sweet meat in a pinkish-brown sauce, and prawns so crisp they crackle when you bite into them. Though most of the nonseafood dishes (like the sad kung pao chicken) are best left unordered, the minced squab is a marvel. There are also great adventures available to those willing to go for the limit. The walls are lined with orange, green, red and yellow signs, all in Chinese, detailing daily specials. If you're friendly (or pushy) enough, you might convince your waiter to bring you one. We did—and what we got was the Chinese equivalent of corned beef hash, served with hoisin sauce and lettuce leaves. We were told it was pork "scrap," though perhaps they meant scrapple. It was also delicious. Dinner for two, with Chinese beer, will run about $35.

SOUTH BAY

12/20 Barnabey's

3501 N. Sepulveda Blvd., Manhattan Beach
545-5693
AUSTRIAN
Open daily 6:30 a.m.-2 p.m. & 5 p.m.-10 p.m. All major cards.

The management of Barnabey's Hotel had chef Andreas Kisler broiling steaks for a couple of years before they realized they had an expert in modern Austrian cuisine on their hands. They finally gave him a green light, and the result is . . . well, okay, it's still Middle European cooking, which means that it comes from the wrong side of the Rhine according to today's culinary trends. Nevertheless, Kisler turns out a fine schnitzel, a refined klare rindsuppe (clear beef soup) to start and plenty of excellent salads. Actually, Mitteleuropa is at one with most of the rest of the world in opting for a lighter cuisine, as Kisler explains in his book *Viennese Cuisine, the New Approach*. He demonstrates his touch in such dishes as poached salmon with leek sauce and the game platter of quail, venison and rabbit with black-currant sauce. For those who think that modernization has its limits, Kisler also turns out such *echt-wiener* specialties as paprika hendl mit Spätzle (a Viennese pasta dish) and, for dessert, Mohr im Hemd (Moor in a Shirt), warm chocolate cake with chocolate sauce. The Victorian setting could be mistaken for Biedermeier. The modest wine list includes a number of award-winning bottles, all priced at $16. Dinner for two, with a bottle of wine, runs about $80.

10/20 Borrelli's

672 Silver Spur Rd., Rolling Hills Estates
541-2632
ITALIAN
Open Mon.-Fri. 11:30 a.m.-10 p.m., Sat.-Sun. 5 p.m.-10 p.m. All major cards.

Clearly there's a taste for the sort of old-fashioned Italian food that flourished back in the days of the straw-clad Chianti bottle, especially down in the South Bay, where until quite recently high-tech Italian was virtually unknown. Proof of the undying love of this cuisine is found in the continuing success of Borrelli's. The food, like the ambience and the service, is certainly affable enough, and nothing's actually bad, though nothing will make you stand up and salute the chef, or even drop him a postcard. They do decent enough things with seafood and have a particularly tender way with calamari and scallops. One of the best dishes is called shrimp Capri, a whimsically named concoction of plump shrimp wrapped in prosciutto, with sautéed peas and mushrooms in a cream sauce—a dish with something for everyone. Pastas can be a bit exotic, as in fettuccine Michelangelo, which isn't flavored with the Sistine Chapel, but rather with sautéed chicken. Dinner for two, with wine, costs about $70.

9/20 The Bottle Inn

26 22nd St., Hermosa Beach
376-9595
ITALIAN
Open Sun.-Mon. 6 p.m.-9 p.m., Tues.-Thurs. 6 p.m.-9:30 p.m., Fri.-Sat. 6 p.m.-10:30 p.m. Cards: AE, MC, V.

Despite its situation in one of L.A.'s funkiest, wildest beach towns, on a small street just a few feet from the beach, The Bottle Inn is doing an amazing job of pretending it's somewhere else. No tip of the toque is made to either the beach life that swirls outside or the wacky nature of the residents of Hermosa. Instead, The Bottle Inn is steadfastly suburban, a restaurant that could be located in any of a hundred nearby shopping malls, serving food that is rarely bad but also never good enough to warrant a drive out of your way. The decor is worth looking at if you're a collector of those small liquor bottles served on airplanes; hundreds of them decorate the walls. The place looks like a cave, with nary a window to the outside world. Service is pleasant, though in the past it has been annoyingly lackadaisical. The fritto misto is competent, and the veal is nicely done:, especially the rolatini, which is stuffed with prosciutto, olives and cheese. The uninteresting desserts often look as if they've sat out on the display

tray a few hours too long. Dinner for two, with wine, costs around $75.

13 Café Pierre

317 Manhattan Beach Blvd.,
Manhattan Beach
545-5252
FRENCH
Open Mon.-Thurs. 11:30 a.m.-2:30 p.m. & 5:30 p.m.-10 p.m., Fri. 11:30 a.m.-2:30 p.m. & 5:30 p.m.-11 p.m., Sat. 5:30 p.m.-11 p.m., Sun. 5:30 p.m.-10 p.m. Cards: AE, MC, V.

There's no such person as Pierre. The place first opened as La Crêpière, which everybody called La Crêpe Pierre, so owner Guy Gabriele decided not to argue. In the years since, Café Pierre has grown into one of the South Bay's finest French restaurants, and most recently its menu has grown far more eclectic than anything Escoffier would recognize. Pastas now proliferate, and although you can find steak au poivre and frogs' legs, the bulk of the menu is given over to such entrées as saddle of venison with sweet-and-sour sauce, grilled lamb with mint pesto and terrific Tuscan-style beans, and a chicken cassoulet with duck sausage. Soft polenta with Gorgonzola makes a seductive opener. Gabriele, whose father is a charcutier in Nice, has begun to experiment with sausages, and so the kitchen now offers a mixed grill of rabbit boudin and lamb links with jalapeños. The wine list has expanded over time, and it now comprises well-chosen selections from most viticultural areas. But you'll probably best appreciate the section at the front of the list where bottles are offered at retail prices. Dinner for two, with a bottle of wine, runs about $75, but a pasta main course would cut that figure back a bit.

12/20 Chalet de France

23254 Roberts Rd., Torrance
540-4646
FRENCH
Open Sun.-Fri. 5:30 p.m.-10 p.m., Sat. 5:30 p.m.-11 p.m. All major cards.

Nestled on a hilltop, Chalet de France prepares classical French cuisine that offers no surprises but does present plenty of good, safe food at a fair price. The interior has a forgettable quasi-chalet decor with dated leather banquettes, but it is comfortable and quiet and has a pleasant outdoor terrace. The chef may not be overly inspired, but he is a technician who doesn't make mistakes—this is regional cuisine at its most traditional best. Starters, such as an excellent house pâté, seafood crêpes, the ever-popular scampi au diable, classic escargots bourguignon and a lovely smoked salmon, will not disappoint you. Entrées are equally predictable and good: sweetbreads à la financière, quail with raspberry sauce (a concession to nouvelle), salmon béarnaise, rack of lamb (presented with so many chops, it looks like a miniature campfire), veal normande (subtle and good), frog's legs provençale and those triple-play holdovers, veal Oscar, steak Diane and tournedos Rossini. There are a few too many flamethrower acts here (steaks, cherries jubilee, crêpes Suzette), but the clientele obviously enjoys them. There is an excellent napoleon and an even better cheesecake served with raspberry purée. Service is efficient, personable and professional. Dinner for two, with a French wine, will run $85.

 Chez Mélange
   1716 Pacific Coast Hwy., Redondo Beach
   540-1222
AMERICAN/CONTINENTAL
Open Mon.-Thurs. 7 a.m.-11:30 p.m., Sat. 7:30 a.m.-11:30 p.m., Sun. 8 a.m.-2:30 p.m. & 5 p.m.-10:30 p.m. Cards: AE, MC, V.
   The fact that Chez Mélange is inside a motel (the Plush Horse Motel, to be specific) would lead you to expect a restaurant like Denny's or Ship's. Instead, the big, complex, softly lit dining room is done in tones of peach, with cozy, oversized banquettes in which you can easily lose yourself. It's easy to linger here—and the first thing to linger over is the menu from the Champagne bar, which features four caviars, two American (golden and spoonbill) and two imported (beluga and osetra), along with smoked Scotch salmon, yellowtail sashimi, California rolls and oysters from both Long Island and Louisiana. Clearly, this is not your average motel restaurant. There are many fine dishes: lovely sausages, good grilled fish, wonderful desserts. The cooking is ambitious, though not always as successful as it might be. For instance, the angel-hair pasta tossed with duck, artichoke hearts, prosciutto, tomatoes, olives, mushrooms, garlic, oregano, parsley, fennel, olive oil and white wine sounded great on paper.

On the plate, it was thick and heavy, with watery artichoke hearts and not much of the other ingredients. Yet there's something good going on at Chez Mélange—a spirit, perhaps, that makes the place quite enjoyable despite the occasional failings of the kitchen. Dinner for two, with wine, runs about $60.

11/20 Chopstix
1430 Pacific Coast Hwy., Redondo Beach
543-1111
CHINESE
Open Sun.-Thurs. 11 a.m.-11 p.m., Fri.-Sat. 11 a.m.-midnight. Cards: MC, V.
See Restaurants, "Los Angeles - Central."

12/20 Collage
762 Pacific Ave., Long Beach
437-3324
CALIFORNIAN
Open Mon. 11 a.m.-2:30 p.m., Tues.-Fri. 11 a.m.-2:30 p.m. & 5:30 p.m.-11 p.m., Sat.-Sun. 5:30 p.m.-11 p.m. All major cards.
   Collage sits inside what used to be, of all things, a gas station. Ask the manager about it, and he'll show you where the pumps used to be and which room held the grease bays. Looking at this softly lit, pastel-colored room today, it's hard to believe Hupmobiles and Hispano-Suizas once parked where customers now eat grilled Japanese eggplant with a (to quote the menu) "Française-Szechuan sauce." Welcome to California cuisine, Long Beach–style. Actually, Collage calls it "Cuisine of Yesterday and Today." Today and tomorrow seem far better represented than yesterday, which appears on the menu mostly as a handful of such nostalgic entrées as frogs' legs (though there's nothing dated about the garlic butter and ginger-tomato sauce they come in), veal Calvados and spaghettini with garlic, basil, tomatoes and oil.
   Most everything else is new, and wildly eclectic to boot. The Cajun popcorn is made with crab (rather than crayfish) and is served in such an immense portion that it could do very well as a main course. (It could also do well to be served with the traditional spicy rémoulade rather than the mild sherry sauce.) A fine Sicilian caponata (vegetable salad) is served with light little lumps of buffalo mozzarella; other dishes include Santa Fe black-bean cakes and even a duck sausage and wild-mushroom ragoût with polenta and can-

nellini beans. One dish in particular defines the nature of the restaurant: the collage of salads—a plate of Moroccan beef salad (North African), tomato-cucumber salad (Greek), sesame chicken salad (Chinese), jicama-and-orange salad (Californian) and caponata (Sicilian)—which puts the whole world on a single plate. Entrées, please note, come with soup (a thick mushroom creation, at least on our last visit) or salad. The mixed-sausage platter is probably the most popular dish on the menu, and for good reason—you get one sausage made with turkey, basil and orange, one with duck, one with jalapeños and lamb. As you may notice, the name doesn't refer so much to the art on the walls as it does to the collages on the plates. Dinner for two, with wine, costs about $70.

Fino
Hillside Village, 24530 Hawthorne Blvd., Torrance
373-1952
MEDITERRANEAN
Open Mon.-Sat. 5 p.m.-10:30 p.m. Cards: AE, MC, V.

Chef Robert Bell and his partner, Michael Franks, spent a reported $150,000—a pittance by present-day standards—to open their second venture, Fino, in Torrance. With the money left over, they clearly cornered the market in garlic and olive oil. The fainthearted may find the two ingredients overrepresented in this variation of a Mediterranean bistro, but that leaves more for the rest of us. Bell is clearly smitten with the sunny food of Spain, France and Italy, and he serves up some of the tastiest dishes in Southern California. Don't miss his braised escarole stuffed with bread crumbs and prosciutto. The duck comes with savory white beans cooked with sausage—an almost-cassoulet. The sausage ragoût with grilled quail is an incitement to dig into the rich polenta. There are pastas, of course, but in a show of heresy, no pizzas. So we like to dabble the house bread in a sauce of fruity olive oil and eat it along with salty olives and a glass of fino (a pale, light sherry). We love this stuff. The wine list exemplifies the partners' policy of apt selection and fair prices. Desserts are similar to what you'll find at their Chez Mélange, but that's no reproach. Fino provides an informal ambience, and Bell and Franks have adopted a limited reservation pol-

icy so customers may find available tables if just dropping by. The lighter and cheaper dishes are substantial here, but for a three-course meal for two with a bottle of wine, allow about $75.

9/20 555 East
555 E. Ocean Blvd., Long Beach
437-0626
AMERICAN
Open Mon.-Fri. 11:30 a.m.-4 p.m. & 5 p.m.-11 p.m., Sat.-Sun. 5 p.m.-11 p.m. All major cards.

Situated inside an office building along Long Beach's main boulevard, 555 East is a bustling, noisy, somewhat daunting restaurant. On a Friday night, the party-hearty bar sounds not unlike the last moments of the Super Bowl, with hordes of secretaries and junior executives talking each other up with a desperate ferocity. If you don't have a Corona in your hand, it's only because you've put your drink down to grab some deep-fried calamari. On the restaurant side, life is only a bit more sedate. 555 East is often described as a New York–style steakhouse, no doubt by those who have never been to New York. The feel is definitely Southern Californian, from the smiley staff through the highly eclectic menu—New York steakhouses do not serve saffron tagliatelle with fresh scallops, or sautéed orange roughy in a caper-mustard sauce. The food is pretty good, though never better than that and sometimes much worse. On our last visit, steamed Santa Barbara mussels were cooked to the point of stringiness; charred raw beef arrived nearly frozen; angel-hair pasta with shellfish was gummy. A New York pepper steak was good, though the brandied mushrooms that came with the beef were not. The place rates right up there when it comes to people-watching, but not nearly as well when it comes to paying attention to what's on your plate. Dinner for two, with wine, will run about $85.

11/20 The Grand House
809 S. Grand Ave., San Pedro
548-1240
CONTINENTAL
Open Tues.-Fri. & Sun. 11:30 a.m.-2:30 p.m. & 6 p.m.-10 p.m., Sat. 6 p.m.-10 p.m. Cards: AE, MC, V.

Several years ago, the cuisine served in this pretty house in the midst of residential San

Pedro was an amalgam of French and Californian cooking; indeed, The Grand House was one of the first sub-haute restaurants in town to bring French-California cuisine to the masses. These days, though, The Grand House has either delved into a new, cutting-edge direction or simply retrenched and headed back to one of the least adventurous styles of cooking around—that amorphous thing called Continental. Though the setting remains lovely, particularly the pretty backyard with its massive, towering stone pine, the menu is more safe than interesting—baked Camembert, cheese triangles, calamari steak, Pacific red snapper, veal medallions, things flavored with pink peppercorns, that sort of cooking. The food is fine and dandy, nothing wrong with it, except that a day later we couldn't remember a thing about our meal. It's turned into just a house, without anything particularly grand about it. Dinner for two, with wine, costs about $70.

12/20   Habash Café

233 Pacific Coast Hwy., Hermosa Beach
376-6620
MIDDLE EASTERN
Open Mon.-Sat. 7 a.m.-9 p.m. Cards: AE, MC, V.

Some restaurants offer ambience, others innovation or elegance. Then there are the places with character. Welcome to the Habash Café, a Hermosa Beach landmark. For twenty years Mama Habash has been dishing up Middle Eastern specialities, including her definitive version of falafel. She believes in doing things the right way—that is, the way she has always done them. As a result, you get what amounts to Levantine home cooking. Longtime customers still speak in awe of Mama's reaction when someone asked her for ketchup for the falafel. It was something to the effect of, "Not in my house, you don't." Besides the falafel, the faithful keep coming back for the mjedara (lentil and rice salad), the hummus, the meltingly tender stewed squash and, most of all, the lentil soup, which may not cure whatever ails you but will at least give it a shot. The Habash Café is a pleasant, unpretentious place, rather like a coffee shop in appearance, except that the coffee is thick, sweet and redolent of cardamom. Prices here are family-style: you can be fairly certain of getting out the door for about $25 for two, maybe less.

 J'Adore

742 Yarmouth Ave., Palos Verdes Estates
541-3316
FRENCH
Open Tues.-Sat. 5:30 p.m.-10 p.m. All major cards.

J'Adore is one of the South Bay's hidden treasures—and given its location, it's likely to remain hidden. It's located off Palos Verdes Drive West, between wherever you are and Catalina Island. The journey is something of an expedition, unless you happen to find yourself on the Palos Verdes Peninsula. If you do, you should arrange your schedule to allow a dinner stop at this trim little restaurant in Lunada Bay, operated by José Dahan, from Toulouse via Redondo Beach, where he built up a following at Le Beaujolais. Now in his own kitchen, he has created a $29 fixed-price menu that ranks as one of the Southland's better cuisine values. Dahan's enthusiasm for cooking is infectious: "Right now I am offering abalone. It comes in fresh in the shell, I clean it, slice it very thin so it has to be pounded only slightly, then serve it sautéed on a bed of julienned carrots with saffron and Pernod. It's outrageous!" The fixed-price menu permits choices, such as tender venison with a suave version of pickled onions, or a more traditional rabbit in cream sauce with cèpes. As a midmeal break, an apple sorbet is as crisp as a new pippin. Desserts hold up their end of the menu, and the wine list, though small, provides some apt selections. Adding a bottle to a dinner for two will bring the bill to about $90.

12/20   JB's Little Bali

217 E. Nutwood St., Inglewood
674-9835
INDONESIAN
Open Thurs.-Sun. 5 p.m.-10 p.m. Cards: MC, V.

JB's fortunes must be improving. It went from being open four nights a week to being open three nights; now, happily, it's back to four nights. We say happily because this is by far the best Indonesian cooking in town. It's also practically the only Indonesian cooking in town. There's only one meal served at JB's—a rijstaffel, of course—referred to on the placemat menu as "The Works." In an atmosphere that smacks of latter-day Somerset

Maugham, Diane and Hans Oei start you off with a salad of gado gado: broccoli, bean sprouts, green beans, cabbage, cucumber, potatoes, hard-boiled eggs and pinkish and green shrimp chips, all moistened with a peanut sauce that shouldn't be confused with anything as mundane as peanut butter. The salad is followed with steamed white rice, the hub around which the rest of the meal is built. Dishes arrive at a frantic pace—a chili-flavored shish kebab (sate sapi), sweet ginger-sauced meatballs (pangsit goreng), coconut-milk–flavored beef (daging bumbu rujak), sweet shoestring potatoes (sambal goreng kentang) and more, much more. The dishes mix and match, passing through the unifying force of the rice. For dessert, there's a milky brown gelatin that tastes of brown sugar. Overhead, you can hear the jets descending into LAX. Dinner with beer costs about $18 per person.

11/20 Pancho's
3615 Highland Ave., Manhattan Beach
545-6670
MEXICAN
Open Mon.-Thurs. 11 a.m.-11 p.m., Fri.-Sat. 11 a.m.-midnight. Cards: MC, V.

This attractive two-tiered hacienda is filled with Spanish antiques, greenery, stained glass, questionable oil paintings and a cheerful clientele. For its size and brick-wall acoustics, it's amazingly quiet and intimate. This is primarily a hangout for locals who love the margaritas and the commercial Mexican food. Pancho's menu is so extensive that there is undoubtedly something to please every Mexican-addicted palate. Of course, there are a few concessions to the sunny Californian's sense of taste; nine potato-skin preparations are offered. But there are also six types of quesadillas (the combination is excellent), seven burritos, enchiladas, empanadas, tostadas and a plethora of combination plates. Most everything is served with heaping portions of sour cream and guacamole. You can also find more ambitious entrées, such as a passable pescado acapulqueño (sole stuffed with vegetables, wrapped in cabbage and covered with white sauce), a spicy sirloin steak, a stuffed zucchini and several shrimp dishes. There is also a variety of huevos for Sunday brunch. There is a very popular bar, with a stuffed marlin keeping an eye on the young crowd enjoying the

live music, generous drinks and one another. Dinner for two, with beer, will run about $40.

12/20 Papadakis Taverna
301 W. 6th St., San Pedro
548-1186
GREEK
Open Mon.-Thurs. & Sat.-Sun. 5 p.m.-10 p.m., Fri. 11:30 a.m.-2 p.m. & 5 p.m.-10 p.m. Cards: MC, V.

Forgive the lighting (bright) and forget the decor (Greek wall hangings and a tin ceiling) and instead concentrate on having a wonderful time. This is a warm, happy place with old-fashioned values and traditions that the owner and his family keep alive. The machismo waiters dance and sing, and Papadakis himself leads the ladies by hand to their tables with much ceremonial kissing. Everyone comes here to have fun—fun that entails eating enormous and very good Greek dinners, drinking plenty of wine and cheering the dancers as they snake through the dining room. You won't know what to choose between: there are anginares (artichoke hearts in phyllo), kalamaria Alexandra (stuffed squid), Greek cheeses and olives, stuffed grape leaves and many other phyllo starters. Pacing is essential if you want to have dessert—dinners come with salad and the traditional avgolemono (a delicious lemon-rice soup), and entrées are plentiful and generous. They include kavouri moustartha (crab in pastry with mustard sauce), moussaka (not as great as we had expected), mousgari vassiliko (veal in kasseri pastry topped with a memorable basil sauce), arni ala Papadakis (tender, flavorful lamb in pastry), psari ala Papadakis (sea bass in phyllo) or pastistio (pasta with meat and béchamel). By all means try the heavenly baklava and spice cake, but avoid the custard pie, which is too heavy after such a rich meal. Though on the costly side, the wine list includes several lesser-known boutique vineyards. Dinner with wine will cost about $85 for two, and you'll be happy to work off some of the calories by joining in and dancing to your heart's content.

9/20 Paradise
889 W. 190th St., Gardena
324-4800
CALIFORNIAN
Open daily 11 a.m.-3 p.m. & 5 p.m.-11 p.m. Cards: AE, MC, V.

The developers of this postmodernist outcropping at the junction of the Harbor and San Diego freeways obviously intend Paradise to be a dining adventure, but the greater venturesomeness is in its location, not exactly on a restaurant row. Some 500,000 motorists pass the location daily, but will they stop? Those who do discover that the designers have been given a free rein in this cubist idea of a Quonset hut, complete with a corrugated exterior and, on the inside, such objects as Frank Gehryesque aquaria, filled with artificial sea life and, among other jetsam, pink plastic flamingos. Admitting that you find this ridiculous will immediately stamp you a reactionary, so we'll say that the place is loads of fun and change the subject. The menu—something American, something Asian, something Mexican, quite a bit Italian—hits many of the same themes that you find in trendy restaurants everywhere. A pizza oven blazes away to good effect, and chickens turn on the rotisserie. Most of the dishes are decently prepared, and the salads have been more than decent, particularly leaves of romaine with plenty of Maytag blue cheese and pine nuts. Steer clear of the desserts. Dinner for two, with a glass of wine, costs about $60.

9/20 La Scala Presto

South Bay Galleria, 1815 Hawthorne Blvd., Redondo Beach
371-7222
ITALIAN
Open Mon.-Sat. 11:30 a.m.-10:30 p.m. All major cards.
See Restaurants, "Westside."

Shenandoah Café

4722 E. 2nd St., Long Beach
434-3469
AMERICAN
Open Sun.-Thurs. 4:30 p.m.-10 p.m., Fri.-Sat. 4:30 p.m.-11 p.m. Cards: AE, MC, V.
Since American cuisine is one of the styles of the moment, our palates are routinely subjected to all kinds of assaults, from a $19 piece of meatloaf at one of L.A.'s hottest spots to dried-out blackened "redfish" at every chain restaurant in town. But this is the real thing—unpretentious, authentic, reasonably priced and delicious. In the cheery dining areas done up like New Orleans drawing rooms, gingham-clad waitresses serve such dishes as beer-batter shrimp, beef brisket in barbecue sauce and a plate of wonderful country sausages. As you might expect of a good American place, the meat dishes are the best. Two in particular are worth a drive here: the riverwalk steak, a thinly sliced flank steak in a mustard-caper sauce, and the very juicy blackened swordfish, which will make you forget all the blackened disasters you have suffered through. Starters are unnecessary; dinners come with incredible warm apple fritters, a fine salad and homemade rolls. About $55 for two, with a simple California wine.

11/20 Simon & Seafort's

Catalina Landing, 340 Golden Shore, Long Beach
435-2333
SEAFOOD
Open Sun.-Thurs. 11:30 a.m.-2:30 p.m. & 5 p.m.-10 p.m., Fri.-Sat. 11:30 a.m.-2:30 p.m. & 5 p.m.-11 p.m. All major cards.
Simon & Seafort's is found at the end of a road and a ramp, in a business complex where humans never roam. You park in the multi-level lot, walk across a ramp to a door, and there you are. Chances are good they'll put you in the bar for a while, where you can gorge yourself on puffy herb pan bread, nondescript Buffalo chicken wings, undercooked calamari and such while you wait and wait. We waited an hour and a half on a Saturday night, which serves us right for going there on a weekend. Judging the restaurant by its bar appetizers, one would expect the food to be mediocre at best. Which is why, when you are finally led into the dining room, this functional, characterless restaurant is so surprising. The New England clam chowder is fine, not gooped up with starch but cleverly thickened with crushed New England common crackers and a plethora of clam chunks. The plain lettuce salad comes pleasantly moistened with a Maytag blue cheese dressing, made with what's probably the best cheese produced in the heartland. An order of Copper River king salmon was about as good as salmon gets, particularly the smaller "light cut," a filet rather than a steak. There's a perfectly decent red snapper in a ginger-cream sauce and some nicely turned Chilean swordfish in a vermouth-garlic butter. It's hard to believe that one kitchen produced the dreadful food served in the bar and the flavorful food served

in the restaurant. It's one more reason to resent being warehoused in the lounge, where you can only stare at the nearby *Queen Mary* and wonder what this monarch of the sea is doing in Long Beach. Dinner for two, with wine, costs about $70.

10/20 Spaghettini
3003 Old Ranch Pkwy., Seal Beach
596-2199
ITALIAN
Open daily 11:30 a.m.-2:30 p.m. & 5 p.m.-10 p.m. All major cards.

You can see the strangely named Spaghettini (does this foreshadow restaurants named Linguine, Ravioli and Veal Parmigiana?) from the San Diego Freeway as you rocket south in the general direction of Newport Beach. Seal Beach, which more or less sits at the border of L.A. and Orange counties, has never been a major culinary destination; it's a pleasant bedroom community with its fair share of restaurant chains. But the newly opened Spaghettini has sort of put the place on the map. It's not an earth shaker of a restaurant, but in a land where the Olive Garden is considered to serve pretty good stuff, Spaghettini is a real standout of a restaurant. It's a hypertrophic Tuscan palace (Orange County–style), with wings and rooms that never seem to end—and on weekend evenings, every one of them appears to be filled to the brim.

Not surprisingly, there are quite a few spaghettinis on the menu: topped with a tomato-basil sauce, grilled sausages, jumbo shrimp or a variety of seafood. Pastas come with a choice of soups, including a perfectly decent minicioppino—not a bad meal for $11 or $12. Indeed, though no dish knocked us for a loop, everything was certainly good. There's a fine selection of nice crunchy pizzas, more Italianate than Californian, topped with fontina, mozzarella and Provolone; salami, mushrooms, artichokes and mozzarella; or jumbo shrimp and Provolone. There's chicken marsala, grilled lamb chops and sautéed shrimp. But mostly there's pasta, and the pasta is just fine. This is an Italian restaurant that's fun and filling, bringing the gospel of good bread and olive oil to Seal Beach. Spaghettini isn't Spago—but the names are close, and so is the joyous spirit. Dinner for two, with wine, costs about $40.

St. Estèphe
2640 N. Sepulveda Blvd., Manhattan Beach
545-1334
SOUTHWESTERN/AMERICAN
Open Tues.-Fri. 11 a.m.-1:30 p.m. & 6 p.m.-9:30 p.m., Sat. 6 p.m.-9:30 p.m. All major cards.

John Sedlar is a warm, friendly young man—and a talented, playful chef who provides one of the most enjoyable dining adventures in Los Angeles. Born in New Mexico, trained at L'Ermitage, he blends the foods and techniques of France and the American Southwest in a unique and delightful fashion; best of all, he (and you) can have fun while he's doing it. On our last visit, we began with "tomato martinis," martini glasses filled with a spicy, fresh tomato broth spiked with vodka—sort of a cross between a Bloody Mary and gazpacho but better and more subtle than either. Then we had plates decorated with squiggles of smoked salmon, crème fraîche and capers. Next, a huge, round plate, black and white in pattern, covered—strikingly—with bands of chopped egg, onion, caviar and parsley (a variation on Sedlar's trademark "rattlesnake" appetizer, alternating bands of chopped raw salmon, spinach, eggs and parsley arranged in a serpentine pattern on the plate). Those were the "preappetizers." The real appetizer was duck-liver mousse with aspic "fireworks"—splattered as if it had exploded all over the gold plate on which it arrived. We then had jalapeño peppers carved in the shape of rats, with tiny olive-dot eyes, stuffed with anchovy, sardine and pepper. They were HOTTTTTT! Once palates recovered from that onslaught, we tried the shrimp enchiladas—large, fresh shrimp served under a square of blue corn tortilla—and a superb rare duck breast with posole chiles in a red-wine and garlic sauce.

You may never see more beautiful or unusual food presentation than Sedlar and his crew provide in this unique restaurant, redecorated with a Southwestern motif and tucked into a shopping center in one of the L.A. area's seemingly endless suburbs. His "chile relleno" is a dessert: a dark-chocolate "chile" shell filled with two kinds of chocolate mousse, served with a rich caramel sauce. His "salmon painted dessert" is a steamed salmon filet served atop three sauces, striations of green and orange that dazzle the eye and please the palate. Other Sedlar specialties include a salmon tamale, a pyramid of red and green chile pasta and a cassoulet of sweetbreads sautéed with chiles and cheese. For dessert, try the blue cornmeal crêpes with pumpkin ice cream or one of the "premodern Southwestern" creations. Some dishes look better than they taste, but if you enjoy experimenting, Sedlar is your man—and his partner, manager and maître d' Steve Garcia, will help you choose the right wines, not an easy task for this cuisine. A "normal" dinner—appetizer, main course, dessert and wine—will cost about $145 per couple. If you really want to enjoy yourself, though, don't bother looking at the menu; just ask Sedlar to make dinner for you. But be sure to first ask how much it will cost. We once ordered such a dinner and got stuck with a tab of $662.44 for four people—about double what we'd ever paid before for Sedlar's "special" dinners.

Symphonie
23863 Hawthorne Blvd., Torrance
373-8187
FRENCH-JAPANESE
Open Tues.-Fri. & Sun. 11:30 a.m.-2:30 p.m. & 6 p.m.-10 p.m., Sat. 6 p.m.-10 p.m. All major cards.

Symphonie is the creation of chef Susumu Fukui, formerly of La Petite Chaya. Exactly what motivated him to open in the South Bay is anyone's guess; it's a decision that probably guarantees him lower rent in exchange for giving up customers from the well-heeled Beverly Hills/Brentwood/Pacific Palisades culinary axis. It is, however, a restaurant worth going to, not just from the westside, but from all over L.A. This is one wonderful restaurant. There's something about the feel of the room, with its Japanese bistro mood, its flowing curves, its bluish light, that quickly relaxes you. And there's a perfection to the food that's absolutely undeniable. One combination offers mixed shellfish poached in a mustard sauce, grilled scallops with a pesto sauce and pan-fried tiger shrimp stuffed with tiger-shrimp mousse; another includes a julienne of roast duck in a miso sauce, marinated chicken breast grilled with anise and mustard seeds and a sautéed chicken leg simmered in a sauce of olives, garlic and tomatoes. What you may notice here is a great sensitivity toward con-

trasting preparations—in one case, poached, grilled and pan-fried; in another, roasted, julienned, grilled and sautéed. You really do get the sense that you're in the midst of a fine bit of culinary orchestration. There are movements, some adagio, some allegro. Crescendo and diminuendo are found from course to course. There are overtures, such as the terrific Peking duck with a julienne of vegetables, in essence a reinvention of a very old dish, or the terrine of tuna and vegetables wrapped in leeks. There are such high chorale works as the lobster pan-fried with jalapeños in olive oil, with shallots and peppers, a special note you must taste to believe. And every meal ends with a beautifully sweet coda, for the pastries are light but perfect—exactly the final note a meal at Symphonie demands. There's music on every plate at Symphonie. Dinner for two, with wine, costs about $100.

12/20 Wallaby Darned
617 S. Centre St., San Pedro
833-3629
AUSTRALIAN
Open Mon.-Fri. 11 a.m.-10 p.m., Sat.-Sun. 8 a.m.-11 p.m. Cards: MC, V.

Remember the jokes about the world's thinnest books? One was titled *Great Australian Dishes*. Still, good cooking has begun to take hold everywhere, and you can get an agreeable version of Aussie tucker in this simple San Pedro café. Curry is made in the creamy Western style, but it can have plenty of bite, and, of course, they throw a shrimp on the barby at the drop of one of those funny Aussie hats. Proprietor John Lindfield knows his way around a kitchen, and so his pavlova—the obligatory antipodean dessert—is rather like a classic vacherin, crisp of meringue and studded with fruit. Along with thin books, the Aussies are working on a rather thick tome, *Great Australian Wines*. The wine list here is replete with such deserving but not-yet-household names as Krondorf, Coonawarra and Taltarni, and you may find bottles that don't have regular distribution. There's plenty of beer, too. And for that final touch, the house offers all a Yank could want of the Aussie national food supplement (which isn't much), the dreaded Vegemite. Dinner for two, with a glass of house wine, runs about $40.

11/20 The Whale & Ale

327 W. 7th St., San Pedro
832-0363
ENGLISH
Open Mon.-Thurs. 11 a.m.-9 p.m., Fri.-Sat. 11 a.m.-10 p.m. Cards: AE, MC, V.

San Pedro is a community in transition, and among new developments is this simulacrum of a British pub, which might be described as standing somewhere between Paddington Station and L.A.'s RTD station. The Whale & Ale took three years to bring to fruition, three years mostly spent in the complexities of rehabilitating an old building. And a handsomely detailed place it is. Downstairs, you can have your fill of bangers and mash. Upstairs, two dining rooms take care of the more proper meals. The food here rates as pleasant rather than wonderful; part of the problem has been a kitchen that's really far too small. This will be remedied, however, and meanwhile there's enough space to keep up with the demand for duck in a sharp bigarade sauce, chicken with roast potatoes and steak-and-kidney pie. Service can be slow, and desserts remain a weak element. The beer flows freely, of course, and there's a modest wine list. As is only proper, tea is served in the afternoons. About $50 for dinner for two with beer or wine, less for pub fare.

WESTSIDE

11/20 Aashiana

11645 Wilshire Blvd., Brentwood
207-5522
INDIAN
Open Sun.-Fri. 11:30 a.m.-2:30 p.m. & 5:30 p.m.-10 p.m., Sat. 5:30 p.m.-10 p.m. All major cards.

Most of the walls at Aashiana are made of glass, so from your table you can look out at the traffic one story below, where cars swirl around the intersection of Wilshire and Barrington, off of which dozens of restaurants radiate. Interestingly, the chef at Aashiana, Sunil Ghay, was the man who cooked for the Indian ambassador and the Indian Olympic team. This means his cuisine is authentic—perhaps even too much so. There is, for instance, a drink on the menu called jal jerra, described as "a special thirst-quenching mixture of Indian spices and herbs, served chilled." One taste is enough for a lifetime—suffice it to say, jal jerra is a very acquired taste. So is the rice pudding, with its distinctly sour flavor. We're not saying either of these dishes is bad; they're just odd tastes to those of us who thought Indian food meant curry and naan. There are other oddities: the vegetable chat appetizer is just a plate of chopped onions, and the rogan josh has far too little lamb to be called a lamb dish, although it certainly tastes fine. On the other hand, the chicken pakoras, the Indian equivalent of chicken Mc-Nuggets, are excellent. And the breads are worth the trip: onion kulcha, fat and jolly and thick with onions; garlic naan; and very well-spiced paratha, one of the best parathas in town. Dinner for two, with Indian beer, shouldn't cost more than $50.

10/20 Abacus

11701 Wilshire Blvd., W.L.A.
207-4875
CHINESE
Open daily 11:30 a.m.-2:30 p.m. & 5:30 p.m.-10 p.m. All major cards.

One can grow pretty darned tired trying to keep up with the latest assessments of the quality level at this attractive, ambitious westside Cantonese seafood house, which sits on the second story of a pink mini-mall on Wilshire Boulevard just outside Westwood. The chefs here alternately run hot and cold, which has been a source of some embarrassment for us—we'll never forget showing up there with a group for a banquet, only to discover that the good chef who was there just weeks before had departed, leaving, as far as we could tell from the food, the dishwasher to prepare the Peking duck. When the food is good at Abacus, it can be very good. Few Chinese restaurants on the westside have a better way with shrimp, crab, lobster and whole fish, and the Peking duck can be among the best in town. But inconsistency, while admirable in a creative mind, is a pain in a restaurant. The pretty room is separated from the bar by an impressive aquarium. At Abacus, you pays your money and you takes your chances. Dinner for two, with beer, costs about $60.

9/20 Adriano's

2930 Beverly Glen Circle, Beverly Glen
475-9807
ITALIAN
Open Tues.-Thurs. 11:30 a.m.-2:30 p.m. & 6 p.m.-10:30 p.m., Fri.-Sat. 11:30 a.m.-2:30 p.m. & 5 p.m.-11 p.m., Sun. 5 p.m.-10:30 p.m. All major cards.

Adriano's—a high-rent northern Italian restaurant in a shopping center at the top of Beverly Glen—suffers from an unfortunate restaurant complex: the staff, convinced as they are that they work at one of the best eateries in town, tend to feel superior to their customers. The logic is simple: the diners do not work at Adriano's and therefore must be inferior to the staff, so as a rule they're treated as if they had just disembarked from steerage. On more than one occasion we've been tempted to send up a flare in the hope of attracting our waiter's attention. Usually the waiters seem terribly busy in the kitschy but posh room, but what they're busy doing doesn't seem to have much to do with customers' needs. Food lovers don't speak of Adriano's with enthusiasm, the way diners heading for meals at places like Tuttobene or Locanda Veneta do; instead, it's regarded as a solid, elegant restaurant that some like and some think is overrated. Count us in the latter camp. Dining at Adriano's, you are separated by a thin wall from the parking lot outside (dining next to a parking lot is a way of life in L.A.), in a room filled with diffused light and thriving greenery. Judging from the exceedingly steep prices, that greenery is being nurtured on mulched $20 bills. And it might actually be worth the price if only the food were better. On our last visit, the calamari fritti, though tender, were coated with soggy breading; the gnocchi, though reasonably light, sat in a pool of oil; the risotto was overcooked; the breaded veal was stringy; and the roast duck with olives was fatty. Despite our caviling, we should say that the food at Adriano's isn't terrible, it just isn't worthy of the price. Up at Adriano's they may think they're king of the hill, but we wish they'd take a look at what's happening in the lowlands to give themselves a sense of perspective. Dinner for two, with wine, costs well over $100.

⑬ Akbar

590 Washington St., Marina del Rey
822-4116
INDIAN
Open Mon.-Sat. 11:30 a.m.-2:30 p.m. & 6 p.m.-10:30 p.m., Sun. 11 a.m.-2 p.m. All major cards.

Outside, young roller-skaters without an ounce of cellulite, wearing skintight workout ensembles, glide by, their heads serenely bobbing to the melodies played on their Sony Walkmans. Inside, all is cool, dark and soothing, with sparkling crystal on the tables, white napery and wonderful, overpowering smells emerging from the kitchen. "Feel the grandeur of a Moghul," says the menu, perhaps a touch of an overstatement (who wants to go tiger hunting these days?), but one does feel cared for, even indulged. The menu is familiar to anyone who's dined on Indian food, and the dishes are prepared with care. For a good cross-section of appetizers, try the hors d'oeuvres combination that offers chicken tikka (smoked in a tandoor oven), samosa pancakes (filled with peas and potatoes), sheekh kebab (minced beef on a skewer, reminiscent of Middle Eastern kefta kebab) and that intriguing Indian spiced wafer called papadum. The tandoori dishes are the restaurant's raison d'être. The vindaloos are less hot than most, a concession to American taste. If you want them hotter, just ask. As a nod to the style of the ancient Moghuls, the gulab jaman, a dessert of sweetened yogurt, flour and butter, is decorated with a piece of silver leaf. Dinner for two, with Indian beer, costs about $40.

⑭ Angeli Mare

Marina Marketplace, 13455 Maxella Ave., Marina del Rey
822-1984
ITALIAN
Open daily 11:30 a.m.-10:30 p.m. Cards: AE, MC, V.

At the original Angeli Caffè on Melrose, the food is delicious, but the menu is limited, and the setting is crowded and often chaotic. At the second member of the family, West L.A.'s Trattoria Angeli, the rather dramatic modern setting is more open and relaxed, and the menu is more ambitious, but the food isn't always as good as we wish it would be. But now, partners Evan Kleiman and John Strobel have hit the mark square on with their brand-new venture, Angeli· Mare. The interior is considerably more inviting than those of the other Angelis: warm lighting gives a sparkle to the rich marble tables, soft music plays in the background, and curved polished wooden "beams" overhead give the feeling of being either inside an overturned boat or in the belly of a particularly classy whale. There's a full bar (unlike at the others), along with a small but appealing wine list. And the service is first-rate. As for the food, it's the best we've had at any of the Angelis. The main menu closely resembles its siblings, offering the same marvelous thin-crust pizzas (the three-cheese with prosciutto is our favorite pizza on the planet), the same salads (Caesar, caprese and a delicious panzanella, made with thick toasted bread, tomato chunks, capers and bell peppers), the same classic roast chicken. All those dishes are eminently worthy, but what really shines are the daily specials, which, as the name suggests, favor seafood. Since the specials change, we can't predict what you'll be offered, but we can tell you that every dish we've tried has been marvelous, from the robust, spicy Tuscan fish soup (with shrimp, clams, scallops, mussels and a thick slab of toasted bread) to the juicy salmon topped with smooth pesto. Finish with a perfect cappuccino and a heaping bowl of vanilla gelato topped with a crumble of homemade brownies, and you'll want for nothing. About $90 for a complete seafood dinner for two, with wine; considerably less for a light pizza meal.

(13) **Aunt Kizzy's Back Porch**
Villa Marina Shopping Center,
4371 Glencoe Ave., Marina del Rey
578-1005
SOUL FOOD
Open Sun.-Thurs. 11 a.m.-10 p.m., Fri.-Sat. 11 a.m.-midnight. No cards.
The problem with Aunt Kizzy's is the parking. The Villa Marina Shopping Center has a multiplex movie theater, major markets and assorted restaurants, so parking on a weekend night is virtually impossible. The other problem is the wait; reservations aren't taken, and on a weekend night or for Sunday brunch you may have to sit on one of the benches outside

for an hour or so, growing hungrier by the minute. So why do we love this place? For Chef Flossie's food, of course—the same recipes she made for almost 40 years down in Cleveland, Mississippi. This is Southern home cooking, as good as it gets anywhere in L.A.—food that just falls off the bone, with flavors as muscular as Arnold Schwarzenegger. These are dishes that come from America's collective culinary consciousness—superlative renditions of catfish and hush puppies, ultra-crunchy fried chicken, perfect beef short ribs, one of the best meatloafs in town, smothered pork chops—all served with inordinate quantities of red beans and rice, rice and gravy, blackeyed peas, okra, corn, collard greens and candied yams. Fresh-squeezed lemonade is served in a mason jar; for dessert, there are sloppy, sweet peach cobblers, pineapple-coconut cake and sweet-potato pie. Dinner for two, with lemonade, will cost around $30.

11/20 Babalu
1001 Montana Ave., Santa Monica
395-2500
CARIBBEAN/INTERNATIONAL
Open Tues.-Sun. 11:30 a.m.-2:30 p.m. & 5 p.m.-10 p.m. Cards: MC, V.
Babalu is as much fun as its name implies, and the cuisine just as jumbled—part Caribbean, part Mexican, part Italian, part Southwestern, part Asian and probably all Californian, the great culinary catch-all term of the '80s. The tone is set by its nutty decor—it looks like something a bunch of talented sixth graders might have done as a class project—and by its menu, which is rife with (intentional?) misspellings, strike-overs, ragged lines and upper case/lower case eccentricities, like PASTa PrIMervera (sic). The place is small, service is a little zany, and the food is pretty good. Not fabulous, but we'd go back without too much prompting. The crabcakes were all right, though they could have been much crisper. The coconut-lime-curry sauce that accompanied the chicken satay wasn't about to put the peanut-chile sauce makers of the world out of business. The chicken-and-chile sausage, served with an avocado relish, was rather bland. What are really fab here are the desserts, made in-house by one Ruth Milliken (the only name on the menu). You'll see her creations, beautiful pies and cakes, on the counter as you enter: Bavarian chocolate

pie, peach-raspberry pie, coconut flan, dynamite Key lime pie, all of which (for once) taste as good as they look. Consider the meal a pleasant prelude before dessert. Dinner for two, with wine, runs about $35.

9/20 Baci

9233 W. Pico Blvd., W.L.A.
205-8705
ITALIAN
Open daily 11 a.m.-11 p.m. All major cards.
See Restaurants, "Los Angeles - Central."

11/20 Beaurivage

26025 Pacific Coast Hwy., Malibu
456-5733
CONTINENTAL
Open Sun.-Fri. 11:30 a.m.-3 p.m. & 5:30 p.m.-10 p.m., Sat. 5:30 p.m.-10 p.m. All major cards.
The question arose the other day, as the question often does, about why there are so few good restaurants along the coast, and more specifically, why there are so few good restaurants along the coast in Malibu. The answers are many, few of which we find satisfying. Perhaps after making the monthly mortgage payments and ponying up the cash necessary to cover the cost of insurance on a beachfront eatery, there's simply nothing left to run a good kitchen. Perhaps all those affluent Malibu residents make ends meet by dining at home on peanut-butter-and-jelly sandwiches. Perhaps living next to the ocean is all one really needs in life, and food becomes irrelevant. But there are a few Malibu restaurants that at least *try*, chief among them Beaurivage, which serves Mediterranean cuisine just across Pacific Coast Highway from a radically different body of water.

Beaurivage looks much like the sort of small restaurant/villa found around such upscale beach towns as Forte dei Marmi—in other words, slightly worn, well aged and pleasantly elegant. Sitting on the outdoor patio, surrounded by bougainvillea, with live guitar music and the smell of the Pacific infusing everything, you could swear you're in France or Italy, though when the food arrives, it becomes clear that you're in Southern California. The food is what might best be described as Mediterranean More-or-Less. This being California, a chunk of the menu is filled with salads—a good cashew chicken in a mild curry dressing, a pleasant plate of grilled vegetables

with a pair of big scampi, a smoked-chicken Caesar (which could have done with a few more croutons), a Greek salad populated with eggplant, peppers, dolma, feta cheese and more. As a tip of the toque to the Mediterranean, there is an assortment of pastas: angel hair with tomato, garlic and feta; cannelloni filled with veal, ricotta and Gorgonzola; fettuccine with wild mushrooms and Madeira. For more serious eaters, there's swordfish, couscous, lamb chops in a puff pastry, venison sausages and stuffed veal. These are hefty dishes for those who live by the beach and dread every foolishly added ounce, but they're just fine for those of us who haven't been seen in a bathing suit since Roosevelt was in office. Dinner for two, with wine, runs about $80.

The Bistro

246 N. Cañon Dr., Beverly Hills
273-5633
FRENCH
Open Mon.-Fri. noon-3 p.m. & 6 p.m.-11 p.m., Sat. 6 p.m.-11 p.m. All major cards.
The actual bistroness of The Bistro often gets obscured by its celebrity status: the Hollywood faces who show up at this reasonably decent re-creation of a Parisian boîte distract most diners from the good solid food that makes its way out of the kitchen. But beyond the forbidding presence of owner Kurt Niklas (former head waiter at the legendary Romanoff's) at the door, and the stratified seating arrangement (in Hollywood, it is not, "I think, therefore I am" but rather, "I am seated prominently, therefore I am"), this is actually one of the few restaurants in town producing the sort of bistro cuisine that's so antithetical to a celebrity following. By all rights, based on the food served here, the dress of choice should be tweeds and berets. There are few onion soups better than The Bistro's, which is thick with the sweetness of long-cooked onions and the stretch of too much cheese. The oxtail soup is first-rate, and best on cold days; the salads are for summer and anorexics only. The steak tartare is nearly perfect, mixed to order at your table, along with a bestiary of dishes right out of the comfort-food hall of fame—veal cutlet Parmigiana, Hungarian goulash with Spätzle, roast duck à l'orange, tournedos Rossini, frogs' legs Provençal. Chances are good that you'll be seated in Siberia, where you can

concentrate on your food and not on who's sitting at the next table. Dinner for two, with wine, costs about $100.

11/20 The Bistro Garden

176 N. Cañon Dr., Beverly Hills
550-3900
CONTINENTAL
Open Mon. 11:30 a.m.-3:30 p.m., Tues.-Thurs. 11:30 a.m.-3:30 p.m. & 6 p.m.-10 p.m., Fri. 11:30 a.m.-3:30 p.m. & 6 p.m.-midnight, Sat. 6 p.m.-midnight. All major cards.

There is a class in Beverly Hills set apart from the general populace by its wealth, its glamour, its style—but most of all by its noontime habits. This class is known as the Ladies Who Lunch, and their semiofficial world headquarters is The Bistro Garden in Beverly Hills (the new branch in Sherman Oaks may soon be defined as the Ladies Who Lunch in the Valley headquarters). Though other trendy restaurants come (and go), occasionally attracting the Ladies Who Lunch for short periods of time, the place they always return to is The Bistro Garden, Kurt Niklas's pretty bower of flowers a quick ride by black-on-black Mercedes convertible from the shopping prerogatives of Rodeo Drive.

Such dishes as veal steak Romanoff, Schnitzel Holstein and ox-tongue marsala are served—really—though one wouldn't know it from watching the Ladies Who Lunch dine. Based on their eating habits, only the Soup Exchange uses more greens on a day-to-day basis than The Bistro Garden, for the Ladies Who Lunch live on salads: Bibb lettuce salad, spinach salad, mushroom salad, endive-and-watercress salad, the house salad. If you're not known, you'll be sent off into a darker corner of the restaurant to eat your matjes herring and, as the menu says, cold veal tonnato (is there such a thing as hot veal tonnato?), roast baby chicken and chicken curry. In the distance, in the garden, you'll see the Ladies Who Lunch, social X-rays every one of them, caring not a whit about the food, and doing nothing at all to keep the kitchen interested in itself. After all, just how many salads can one chef make before culinary senility sets in? Dinner for two, with wine, costs over $100; lunch with a glass of wine is about half that.

11/20 The Black Whale

3016 Washington Blvd., Marina del Rey
823-9898
SEAFOOD/STEAKHOUSE
Open daily 11 a.m.-1 a.m. Cards: AE, MC, V.

If you have a hearty appetite, you'll fit right in here. Actually, even more temperate diners will be starving after the one- to two-hour wait, depending on the day and the traffic. This is a real he-man place, filled with crusty characters who knock back drinks at the bar and hang around watching TV sports. The cluttered, nautical decor creates such a warm ambience (not to mention the golden light that makes everyone look younger), that even the more delicate will feel comfortable. Everyone maintains good spirits while waiting on the stairway for the chance to tackle the down-to-earth food at out-of-sight prices. To start, you can order three and a half pounds of steamers, a more moderate number of oysters on the half shell, king crab on ice (which will set you back a good $20) or large bowls of steaming clam chowder. Entrées are for the stouthearted; potatoes, salad and whale rolls are included with dinner. Red snapper, golden sea bass, salmon, trout and halibut are all baked—overly so, but they are still tasty. Shellfish—lobster, scallops, crab and shrimp—is the most popular thing to order here, and it is always very fresh and very good. Those hearty appetites are also sated with steak, prime rib and surf-'n'-turf combos that look like dinners for linebackers in training. The waitresses are as personable and as salty as the habitués, and they make every effort to make you feel at home (if home is a roadside tavern). It's definitely fun, frenetic and happy here. If you can't stand the wait, there is a small oyster bar upstairs. If you choose shellfish or a combination, dinner will run about $100 for two, with wine; a simpler meal will cost about $65 for two.

13 Bombay Cafe

12113 Santa Monica Blvd., W.L.A.
820-2070
INDIAN
Open Sun. & Tues.-Thurs. 11 a.m.-10 p.m., Fri.-Sat. 11 a.m.-11 p.m. Cards: MC, V.

Bombay Cafe is unlike any Indian restaurant we've ever been to. Like the East India Grill (see Quick Bites), it's probably not like any Indian restaurant in India either. What you have here is the continuing rise of California-Indian food, one of the least expected new cuisines of the '90s. The cheerful room, located on the second floor of a mini-mall at the busy corner of Santa Monica and Bundy, feels even larger than it is with its abundance of mirrors. Judging from the menu, it's run by people named Meeta, David, Neela and Bill (we're told the Indian-pizza equivalent called uttapam is Bill's favorite, that Neela makes the chutneys, and that Meeta and David once sold 800 masala dosa in a single night). Whoever these people are, they've come up with a brightly enthusiastic restaurant, featuring an open kitchen and a menu so full of wonderful-sounding items that you'll be tempted to say, "Just bring me one of each."

Consider, for instance, the sev puri, a quintessential bit of Indian street food consisting of crunchy little crisps, almost like Doritos, topped with chopped onions, potatoes, cilantro and a trio of chutneys (the food is chutney-intensive here). Or the curious fast food called frankies, which the menu says are a favorite at Bombay's Candy Beach; they bear a striking resemblance to burritos and are filled with chicken, lamb or cauliflower. We've never tasted anything quite like the crispy shrimp dish called haldi jhinga; the eggplant and yogurt purée called smoked bharta; the tandoori chicken sausages called reshmi kebabs; and the tandoori chicken salad, heavy with scallions and cilantro. It's a short menu, but a good one—there's hardly an item on it you won't want to order. And dishes change from day to day as well. In fact, the chutneys change with manic regularity, and there's a dhal of the day, a lentil stew prepared in as many fashions as risotto. Dinner for two, with beer, costs about $40.

10/20 Brentwood Bar & Grill

11647 San Vicente Blvd., Brentwood
820-2121
CALIFORNIAN
Open Mon.-Fri. 11:30 a.m.-11 p.m., Sat.-Sun. 11:30 a.m.-6 p.m. All major cards.
Judging from the name, and from the fact that the Brentwood Bar & Grill was opened by the people who run Bob Burns, we expected the food to be similar to that of the Broadway Bar & Grill and the nearby Daily Grill. And yes, there's a bar here (and a very fine one at that), a grill in the kitchen, and

many of the dishes are steak and fish. But beyond that, any resemblance between the Brentwood Bar & Grill and your basic bar and grill ends there. This is an exceedingly elegant restaurant, the type of place for which men dress in jacket and tie, the sort of place that charges significantly for the elegance it offers. It's a big, serious-looking restaurant, with flattering lighting, an open kitchen at one end and a plethora of serving folk who are always there when you need them.

The menu is awash with high-rent dishes and equally high prices—appetizers run from $6 to $11 (with the majority at the high end), and entrées go from $15 to $28 (once again, with more dishes above $20 than below). We rather enjoyed the yellow Finnish potato-and-onion tart with its black-truffle salad, though we wish we could have tasted some of the truffle (at $10 for a tart, one has certain unreasonable expectations). We saw the precious truffle bits, but they were from that breed of truffle that's seen but not savored. We also wish the wild-rice blini served with the caviars (osetra and salmon) were a bit lighter. For $28 we've come to expect a bit more than half an anemic lobster, so small it could have passed for a large prawn. And for $22, our wild Scotch salmon could have been apportioned more like an entrée than an appetizer; in addition, the saffron risotto on the side might have been a bit less gummy. The bottom line is that the food is not up to the prices, and the prices are shockingly high. The Brentwood Bar & Grill may do just fine in Brentwood, where cash flow is never a problem. But at these prices we'd much rather be eating at Citrus (actually, by comparison, Citrus is a bargain). Dinner for two, with wine, runs about $120.

12/20 Broadway Bar & Grill

1436 3rd St., Santa Monica
393-4211
AMERICAN
Open daily 11 a.m.-11 p.m., Sun. 10:30 a.m.-11 p.m. All major cards.
Bar & Grill has become a rather tired restaurant moniker, often no more than a sign that the restaurant seeks to cash in on the recent popularity of good ol' American cooking. But the Broadway Bar & Grill earns its name admirably. It's a comfortable, comforting San Francisco–style joint, complete with

private wooden booths (à la Tadich's in San Francisco), an appealing mishmash of a decor (combining a manly turn-of-the-century chop-house look with exposed brick, Ionic columns and art deco lighting and objets d'art), down-to-earth aproned waiters and a long, inviting wooden bar, blessedly devoid of Italian-suited trendoids. And the food is honest bar-and-grill chow—not always thrilling, but for the most part tasty and not the least bit threatening. The ideal meal here is a simple one: the Caesar salad and the hamburger. The only problem with the Caesar is that it's made of whole romaine leaves, a silly affectation that just makes it hard to eat. But once you've chopped the leaves yourself, it's an excellent Caesar, with plenty of Parmesan and a good kick to it. This hamburger reminded us why America fell in love with the burger in the first place. A fat, juicy, savory hunk of ground meat is sandwiched by a fine French roll; try it with Irish-style smoked bacon, which is quite lean and delicious. The burger comes with a heap of flawlessly crisp shoestring fries, for once properly thin. Almost as perfect as the burger are the very fresh, lightly battered fish-and-chips, and the grease-free deep-fried spicy calamari. As is generally the case with bar and grills, it is best to avoid anything particularly unusual or fancy. We gambled on the Mediterranean-style sausage flavored with pine nuts and sun-dried tomatoes, which turned out to be terribly overgrilled and consequently dried out and tasteless. Desserts are uniformly homey, hearty and wonderful, from the classic hot fudge sundae to the apple tart—more like apple pie, really—on a bed of lick-your-plate caramel sauce. And after-dinner indulgers will appreciate the surprisingly good choice of ports, Cognacs and the like. Dinner for two, with wine by the glass, will run about $50.

6/20   Cabo Cabo Cabo
(Baja Beverly Hills)
Century City Shopping Center,
10250 Santa Monica Blvd., Century City
552-2226
MEXICAN
Open daily 11:30 a.m.-11:30 p.m. Cards: AE, MC, V.

Bob Morris is the man responsible for such three-ring-circus eateries as RJ's—The Rib Joint, Gladstone's 4 Fish and World Famous

Malibu Sea Lion U.S.A. His restaurants are always full—always. Critics, as a rule, do not love them; the public, as a rule, does. In a way, they're the culinary equivalent of the *Police Academy* movies. If you actually pay any attention to them, they fall apart; but if you go in search of a good time, you'll probably find it. The point is to have fun, fun, fun. And the outlandishly oversized drinks certainly don't hurt in reaching that end.

What's wrong with Cabo is legion. The salsa-and-chip bar had no plates for the salsa and chips. When we asked for matches to relight the guttering candle on our table, no one could find matches. When we found the candle unrelightable and asked for a new one, no one could find one of those either. The taquitos were rubbery. The guacamole was dreadfully overripe. The mesquite-barbecued-chicken pizza was soggy, topped with chicken that was at the same time dry and sweeter than a Heath Bar. The quesadilla was mushy. If you want to see Cabo in all its frenetic glory, by all means go on a weekend night. You'll watch crowds ebb and flow between the cinema complex, the Stage Deli and Cabo, with the occasional stop at Brentano's bookstore in between. Go for the odd drinks, go for the jumbo beer list, go for the encyclopedic collection of tequilas . . . go even for the ambience, if you're in the mood for noisy, crowded bustling. But go for the food only if you dare. Dinner for two, with beer, costs about $25.

⑬   Café Katsu
2117 Sawtelle Blvd., W.L.A.
477-3359
FRENCH-JAPANESE
Open Mon.-Sat. 11:30 a.m.-2:30 p.m. & 6 p.m.-10 p.m. All major cards.

Café Katsu, the French-Japanese child of Katsu on Hillhurst (where sushi is the dominant motif), is, if such a thing is possible, even more minimalist in design than its parent restaurant. Were it not for some abstract art on the walls, the place could be a sensory deprivation tank. And when you add that Café Katsu is inside (yet another) westside minimall, you have a restaurant that borders on the surreal. The food, on the other hand, is quite down-to-earth and decently stable, albeit unquestionably exotic. The Japaneseness of the cooking is every bit as pronounced here as it is at Katsu, though with many a multiethnic twist. Just consider the linguistic-culinary implications of a dish called tempura de crevette with potatoes sauté and beurre fondue of chive and cayenne. What we have here is a Portuguese term (tempura) describing a treatment of a Japanese dish using French terminology (crevette, beurre fondue) and a number of ingredients native to the Americas (potatoes and cayenne)—an entire melting pot on a single tasty plate. There's also a strong Japanese influence in the grilled shiitake mushrooms with smoked mozzarella (Japanese-Italian cuisine?) and certainly in the delicacy of the entrées, most of which lean toward seafood: roast lotte with artichokes in a lobster sauce, striped bass poêle (sautéed, then grilled) with calamari and morels, grilled swordfish in a saffron sauce, sautéed scallops with lobster ravioli. Aside from St. Estèphe, this may be the best shopping-mall restaurant in the city. Malls may be the blight of L.A., but they're doing wonders for emerging cuisines. Dinner for two, with wine, runs about $60.

Café Montana

1534 Montana Ave., Santa Monica
829-3990

CALIFORNIAN

Open Tues.-Sat. 8 a.m.-3 p.m. & 6 p.m.-10:30 p.m., Sun. 5:30 p.m.-10:30 p.m. Cards: MC, V.

As we went to press, Café Montana opened the doors at its new location, just down the street from its old location. It's too early to give a proper review or ranking; all we can say is that the new place will certainly continue Café Montana's tradition of simple, handsome California cuisine that perfectly matches the moneyed, handsome, upper–Santa Monica clientele. Breakfast was always our favorite meal in this sunny place, and it'll probably continue to be so. But a complete lunch and dinner menu, strong on such light, healthy fare as pasta and grilled fish, is equally popular. Breakfast for two runs about $18; dinner with wine, about $80.

 Caffè Lido

147 W. Channel Rd., Santa Monica
459-8823

ITALIAN

Open Tues.-Thurs. noon-3 p.m. & 6 p.m.-10 p.m., Fri. noon-3 p.m. & 6 p.m.-10:30 p.m., Sat.
10 a.m.-3 p.m. & 6 p.m.-10:30 p.m., Sun. noon-3 p.m. & 6 p.m.-10 p.m. Cards: MC, V.

Caffè Lido is the kid brother of the somewhat (though not much) more formal Ristorante Lido found up the hill in Pacific Palisades. The café that grew out of Lido sits on the site of the old Yellow House restaurant, on a block that tends to eat restaurants alive— both West Channel Road's Casa Mia and Les Anges are no more. Like Lido, Caffè Lido reminds us a great deal of being in Italy. It has a spare, casual feel to it, an ease that is both seductive and wholly open to whatever you want to make of it. You can come here dressed down or in a natty Italian suit; in either case, you'll feel right at home. The food, in the style of some of the new little Italian restaurants that have recently opened (such as Trattoria Farfalla and Osteria Nonni), is simple and thoroughly basic, as the best Italian food always is.

We were delighted by the focaccia sandwiches (if the kitchen has the bread; it tends to run out) bearing the pretty name of focaccinne ripiene, which you can have filled with prosciutto and cheese, cooked peppers, green peas (a green-pea sandwich? you ask), cooked onions and clams. There are all the politically correct salads: caprese (mozzarella and tomatoes), seafood capricciosa (tuna and egg). And, of course, there are the pastas: tagliatelle bolognese (with meat sauce), linguine with clams, angel hair with tomatoes and basil, linguine with garlic and olive oil. The handful of meat and fish dishes—grilled game hen with rosemary, breaded veal, shrimp with tomatoes and garlic—were not disappointing. We asked the waiter if the cooks prepare risotto, and he told us they don't because the kitchen isn't equipped to handle such a complicated dish. Most restaurants would just go ahead and make it anyway, but at Caffè Lido it won't be done unless it can be done right. And they do it quite right. Maybe even right enough to put to rest the curse of West Channel Road. Dinner for two, with wine, runs about $40.

11/20 Casablanca

220 Lincoln Blvd., Venice
392-5751

MEXICAN

Open Sun.-Mon. 11 a.m.-10 p.m., Tues.-Sat. 11 a.m.-11 p.m. Cards: MC, V.

What does it mean when the waiters who bring the tortillas wear fezes? Or when Mexican seafood dishes are named after Ingrid Bergman and Paul Henreid? We don't care what it means, as long as the calamari steak—the dish to order here—stays so tender and terrific. This strange mix of Middle Eastern, movie nostalgia and Mexican can't be analyzed too closely. Just accept it for what it is: a silly, romantic mélange of palms, ceiling fans, mariachis, margaritas and good food. Meals begin with handmade flour tortillas served with chunks of cheese in a salsa verde—the kind of starter that has you saying "I could quit now" just before the entrée arrives. Giant calamari steaks are served seven ways, including with lemon butter, salsa fresca, veracruzana, borracho and mojo de ajo. This last one has so much ajo—garlic—that it looks smothered in mozzarella in the dim light. The rest of the menu (heavy on seafood) is just average—it's the calamari that makes a trip here worthwhile. Dinner will run $45 to $50 for two, with margaritas.

12/20 Celestino

236 S. Beverly Dr., Beverly Hills
859-8601
ITALIAN
Open Mon.-Fri. 11:30 a.m.-3 p.m. & 5:30 p.m.-11 p.m., Sat. 5:30 p.m.-11 p.m., Sun. 5:30 p.m.-10 p.m. Cards: AE, MC, V.

Back in the '70s, when good pasta was as scarce as a cruising taxi in Los Angeles, we would have been grateful for Celestino. Taxis are still scarce in Los Angeles, but pasta—good pasta—is now pervasive here, and a restaurant should offer something more than just good pasta if it wishes to distinguish itself. The pasta at Celestino is good, but it's not as good as the pasta at, say, Primi or Locanda Veneta (not to mention such higher-priced establishments as Valentino and Rex), and the main courses are generally disappointing, so it's difficult to get excited about coming here. Nevertheless, should you find yourself in the neighborhood, with a craving for pasta, you could do much worse than a plate of Celestino's angel-hair pasta with fresh tomatoes and basil, farfalle with fresh asparagus or spaghetti cooked with seafood in a parchment bag. For appetizers, try the veal carpaccio, served with balsamic vinegar, the venison carpaccio in a Gorgonzola dressing or the bufala mozzarella with tomatoes and basil. You'll spend about $105 a couple, with wine—more if you have both pasta and a main course.

 Champagne
10506 Santa Monica Blvd.,
Century City
470-8446
FRENCH
Open nightly 7 p.m.-10:30 p.m. All major cards.

Chef Patrick Healy looks quintessentially American: big and boyish, with tousled, sandy-blond hair and a warm, open, utterly unpretentious manner. But his restaurant, with its white walls, timbered ceiling and brightly colored pictures, feels more like a French provincial inn. One reason: Healy's charming wife, Sophie, is French, born and raised in Cannes, and in true French fashion, she runs the front of the house. At evening's end, she and Patrick sit down to dinner together in a corner of the restaurant, near the entryway, where they can bid *à la prochaine* to departing guests. The Healys also decorated and painted the restaurant themselves, with a French provincial theme clearly in mind. And best of all: Healy spent five years working and studying in France—with Michel Guérard, les frères Troisgros and Roger Vergé (Moulin de Mougins). We first encountered him when he was the chef at Le St. Germain, the longtime bistro favorite on the site of what is now Patina. We next encountered Healy at Colette and found his cuisine stunning. It's even better at Champagne (albeit, with all the cream sauces, a tad heavy at times).

Healy has essentially four different menus: "contemporary California," "spa," "rustic French" and "gastronomic." The last is a six-course dinner that changes nightly; the others are augmented by specials that also change nightly. At our last dinner, the "gastronomic menu" began with a salad of haricots verts, summer truffles and crispy sweetbreads, followed by lobster and asparagus in a Champagne-grape cream sauce. Grilled sea scallops came next, perfectly complemented by a Provençal compote of artichokes, tomatoes and olives. Instead of a sorbet, Healy offered as a palate cleanser a demitasse of herb-infused consommé—delicious but too much so to cleanse anyone's palate. The main course was grilled squab with a raisin sauce. Our dessert was as simple as it was sinful: pecan mousse in a dark-chocolate cup. The rustic French is the best of the regular menus, featuring such specialties as cassoulet, braised veal shank (or braised rabbit leg), pan-fried rib-eye steak and poulet au pot, half a free-range chicken poached with vegetables and served in bouillon or a cream sauce. The best "rustic" appetizer is the terrine of wild pheasant and wood squab. Healy's California menu includes several salads, among them asparagus in a ginger-and-citrus sauce with freshly minted scallions. Even better are the "sandwich" of shiitake mushrooms, lobster and risotto in a tomato, fennel and saffron coulis, and the "cake" of crayfish, eggplant, onions, black olives and bell peppers, all layered. Normally, at a fine restaurant, we avoid anything labeled "spa," but that would be a mistake here. Healy's roasted eggplant soup with a red-pepper purée—a mere 150 calories—brings smiles to weight-watchers and gastronomes alike. Desserts are delicious, and service is attentive without being obsequious.

The wine list—understandably disappointing when the restaurant opened on a shoestring in 1987—has improved considerably, although it's still not as good as it should be. One reason: Champagne has discriminating diners who almost invariably drink up the most attractive buys on the list. On our last visit, the restaurant was out of our first choice in both white and red. Healy is slowly building an excellent collection of Rhône wines, still vastly underappreciated and often underpriced. Because of the different menus, it's difficult to estimate what you'll spend for dinner here. Appetizers range from $5.75 for the eggplant soup to $19.50 for the terrine of domestic foie gras; main courses range from $14.75 for a plate of fresh vegetables to $26.50 for such nightly specials as saddle of venison marinated in red wine and served with a celery-roasted chestnut mousse and juniper-berry sauce. It isn't cheap, and the gastronomic dinner, at $68 a person, is severely overpriced. Dinner here for two, with wine, costs about $135.

12/20 Chan Dara

11940 W. Pico Blvd., W.L.A.
479-4461
THAI
Open Mon.-Thurs. noon-11 p.m., Fri. noon-midnight, Sat.-Sun. 5 p.m.-11 p.m. All major cards.
See Restaurants, "Los Angeles - Central."

12/20 Chartreuse

1909 Wilshire Blvd., Santa Monica
453-3333
SWISS/CONTINENTAL
Open Mon.-Fri. 11:30 a.m.-2:30 p.m. & 6 p.m.-10 p.m., Sat. 6 p.m.-10 p.m. Cards: AE, MC, V.
It is'nt really clear to us whether Chartreuse was named after the luminescent liqueur that is often confused with cough medicine, or after the term for a small French country house, or after the mountain in the Alps (the three bear the same name). It sat for its first decade in a lovely brick structure on Pico Boulevard near the 20th Century-Fox studios, until the city, in its infinite wisdom, decided that the venerable building the restaurant was housed in was not earthquake-proof, which inconveniently put chef Bruno Moeckli out of business. The result is a new, somewhat less charming Chartreuse in the space that used to be home to a confused restaurant called Tosh, in the midst of a sort of mini–restaurant row along Wilshire Boulevard in Santa Monica. The space may not be wreathed in charm, but the restaurant continues to be one of the best (and only) Swiss eateries in town, proof that there's more to Swiss cooking than fondue and Raclette. The menu here is more occasionally Swiss than Swiss, showing its Alpine roots in such dishes as the delicious Roquefort soufflé, the crispy potato Rösti topped (parsimoniously) with sour cream and two caviars, and the salad served with a lump of fried Camembert. Beyond that, the menu dashes from lamb curry to roast duck with gooseberries, from risotto with mushrooms and shrimp to a classic entrecôte with a Café de Paris sauce. The portions are large, the food filling and good. Depending on the mood of the owner, you may be presented with a complimentary glass of Chartreuse, an excellent drink come the winter flu season. Dinner for two, with wine, costs about $70.

9/20 Chasen's

9039 Beverly Blvd., Beverly Hills
271-2168
AMERICAN
Open Tues.-Sun. 6 p.m.-1 a.m. No cards.

We are visited occasionally by a dreadful nightmare: that one day, Los Angeles will be leveled by the Big One. That when it comes, all of Wolfgang Puck's enterprises will crumble to dust. That every one of our favorite eateries in the city will be instantly reduced to a collective heap of rubble. Yet Chasen's, untouched by natural disaster, time, or the outraged cries of its many poorly fed customers, will still stand. Chasen's has outlived both Perino's and Scandia, at one time the other two points of the troika of restaurants that defined dining in Los Angeles, for better or (more likely) for worse. Chasen's is still there, with a brace of papparazzi in front, and service so lackadaisacally rude, it's almost entertaining. Even the bartender at Chasen's behaves in a swinish manner; we inquired politely why a model of the space shuttle hangs over the bar, and he grunted something like, "Because it's there,"before resuming his previous position of ignoring us. In all fairness, those who have been regulars at Chasen's for the last half century or so do insist that they're treated well. George Burns is revered here. So are the Reagans. And the chili, unlisted on the menu as always. Those of us not to the manor born, unfortunately, are seated back in East Jesus, where it seems few waiters work. Cheese bread will eventually arrive—cold. The hobo steak (also not on the menu) is a tough piece of meat, no doubt reflecting the hard life of the cow from whence it came. Salads are not the forte of the house either; apparently, the rule in the kitchen is never to use oil when vinegar can be used instead. Deviled beef bones were a culinary farce: a greasy heap of strings and sinews, basted with ballpark mustard. We have found bones in the chicken pot pie, and on our last visit, we had what tasted suspiciously like Hershey's chocolate syrup on our sad vanilla sundae. For all this, you'll pay $120 or more for two, with wine.

12/20 Chez Hélène

267 S. Beverly Dr., Beverly Hills
276-1558
FRENCH
Open Tues.-Sat. 11:30 a.m.-3 p.m. & 6 p.m.-10:30 p.m., Sun. 6 p.m.-10:30 p.m. All major cards.

Chez Hélène used to be located on West Washington in Venice, where it survived for years in a neighborhood that had more than its share of crime. But when business waned, owner Micheline Hebert moved her funny little French auberge to greener pastures in Beverly Hills, where Chez Hélène is doing quite well, thank you. What's intriguing is how utterly old-fashioned the place is. It's reminiscent of the small French bistros we used to eat at in the late '50s and early '60s—the friendly little places where the service was casual, the food good and the ambience conducive to lingering for hours over a good cup of steaming cappuccino. Outside, there's a lot of brick and greenery. Inside, there's polished wood—and a nicely subdued air. Nobody's in a rush here. The dishes are made for casual dining—simple food that can be picked at without interfering with confidences exchanged between old friends. The small menu offers a good cream of tomato soup, a garden-variety French onion soup, escargots de Bourgogne and a trio of quiches: Lorraine, spinach and seafood. The lamb stew is hardy, pungent, musky and solid, the sort of dish found at *routiers* across France. Equally filling is the saucisses à la bière, a rich stew of sausage, beer, tomatoes and herbs. The herbed, grilled chicken couldn't be simpler. The bread pudding is truly a marvel. And, of course, there are poires belle Hélène. In a restaurant named Chez Hélène you expected tapioca pudding? Dinner for two, with wine, ranges from $60 to $90, depending on what you order.

12/20 Chez Jay

1657 Ocean Ave., Santa Monica
395-1741
AMERICAN
Open Sun.-Thurs. 11 a.m.-10:30 p.m., Fri.-Sat. 11 a.m.-11:30 p.m. All major cards.

It's a bit difficult to say whether this legendary refuge for beach bums, writers and artists is a restaurant with a bar attached or a bar with a restaurant attached; the general consensus would probably lean toward the latter, for this is the sort of high-class dive where such mottos as "Work is the curse of the drinking class" take on a special depth of meaning. There's sawdust on the floor, mirth and mayhem in the air, and good food on the well-worn tables, all orchestrated by an affable adventurer (hot-air balloons, sunken treasure, that sort of thing) named Jay Fiondella, who keeps the mood going full tilt, the drinks pouring freely and the potatoes baked with bananas flowing out of the kitchen. Despite the rough-and-ready ambience, this is a fine place to go for a thick steak (steak au poivre is the pride of the house, and rightly so), shrimp curry, even lobster thermidor. And for those in the know, there's a secret back room, accessed through a door in the rear of a closet in the restaurant's office, where groups can do as they wish, and often do just that till the small hours of the morning. (Rumor has it that Chez Jay will be moving to a larger location, though the restaurant would not confirm this as we went to press.) Dinner for two, with beer, costs about $60.

 China Sea
2130 S. Sawtelle Blvd., Ste. 200, W.L.A.
473-8948

CHINESE

Open Sun.-Thurs. 11:30 a.m.-9:30 p.m., Fri.-Sat. 11:30 a.m.-10:30 p.m. All major cards.

It was one of those dumb Sunday nights. We had just gotten out of a movie, and what we really wanted was a meal that was modest in size but intense in flavor. It was only a little after nine, but everywhere we drove things were closing down. Cruising down Sawtelle Boulevard in search of at least a good sushi bar, we noticed a Chinese seafood place called China Sea. From the street (it's on the second floor), it appeared to be a clean, well-lit sort of place. And since we can always do with an order of braised shrimp, we parked in the virtually empty lot, climbed the stairs and found ourselves in an equally empty restaurant. We apologized to the people working there, who appeared to be in the process of cleaning up, and said if the kitchen was closed, we'd just leave. Without a moment's hesita-

tion, they said there was no problem. Even though the hour was late, and people were getting ready to go home, they whipped up a wonder of a meal—the sort of meal that much fancier places couldn't put together even with lots of advanced notice.

In a matter of minutes, we were eating wonderful sticky chicken wings, neither too sweet nor too sour. We plowed into an exceptional shrimp confetti salad, a fine late-night toss of bean sprouts, julienned carrots, snow peas, bay shrimp and black sesame seeds. (The menu also lists a dandy-sounding Chinese chicken salad, a minced duck salad and a fine bean-thread noodle salad.) From the barbecue section, we ordered homemade forcheong sausage (wholly different from, and far better than, the more commonly encountered lapcheong sausage) and some divine barbecued chicken and spareribs. We exclaimed over the sybaritic joys of the fabulous shrimp with honey-glazed walnuts (is there a better combination under Heaven?), and made immediate plans to return for the double-sauced yin yang shrimp, the Szechuan shrimp and the salty crispy shrimp. We could only dream about the lemon scallops, the spicy fried calamari, the crispy pepper-skin chicken. We would be back. How fine it was to find a place where customers are more important than the hours posted on the door—and where the food is excellent to boot! Dinner for two, with beer, costs about $30.

 Chinois on Main
2709 Main St., Santa Monica
392-9025

CHINESE

Open Wed.-Fri. 11:30 a.m.-2 p.m. & 6 p.m.-10:30 p.m., Sat.-Tues. 6 p.m.-10:30 p.m. All major cards.

It would be difficult to think of an L.A. restaurant that consistently serves food as interesting and unusual as that served at Chinois. Words like *interesting* are, of course, often euphemisms or circumlocutions for "I don't really like it but don't want to sound like a rube." *Unusual* frequently serves a similar purpose—as a substitute for "bizarre" or "ridiculous." But there's no need for circumlocutions or euphemisms in describing Chinois, and if many of the dishes are unusual, they are neither bizarre nor ridiculous. No mousse of porpoise with tuna testicles en brochette here. The food is Chinese. Sort of. After all, how Chinese is a cuisine likely to be when it's cooked by a Japanese under the guidance of an Austrian who was trained in France and is best known for helping to popularize a new blend of Californian/Italian food? The Austrian is Wolfgang Puck of Spago fame, who is also executive chef and (with wife Barbara Lazaroff) coproprietor of Chinois. The Japanese is Kazuto Matsusaka, the chef and the man responsible for most of the dishes on the menu these days.

Appetizers at Chinois include barbecued eel with sweet turnips and cucumbers; warm, sweet curried oysters with salmon pearls; and barbecued Szechuan sausages with sweet-and-sour cabbage. Main courses include wok-charred salmon with zucchini blossoms; Shanghai lobster risotto; grilled filet of striped bass in a plum-wine sauce on a bed of Chinese pesto (made with cilantro instead of basil) and the pièce de résistance: whole sizzling catfish with ginger-and-ponzu sauce. There's something for almost every palate at Chinois: chicken, lamb, veal, beef, fish, duck, pork—and it's one of the few restaurants we know about which we can say, "Order almost anything on the menu; you won't be disappointed." Notice that we said "almost anything." If you're a Peking duck aficionado, skip the Szechuan pancakes with stir-fried duck; it's just similar enough to remind you of Peking duck but not nearly as good. We have also been disappointed in the sauce served with the grilled Mandarin beef—a blend of plum, chili, mint and ginger that just doesn't work with beef.

What kind of wine does one drink with this cuisine? Good question. Whites generally are best, and Chinois has 22 California Chardonnays, ranging in price from $22 to $46. If you find Chardonnay a bit heavy, you might prefer one of the Sauvignon Blancs. Dining at Chinois is not just about food and wine, though. It remains one of the hottest restaurants in the city, difficult to get into during prime hours, crowded and *very* noisy at any hour. (Two tips: go early and ask for a table along the wall or the front window; they're a little quieter.) Chinois makes as great an impact on the eye as on the palate. Designed by Lazaroff, it features two large mul-ticolored cloisonné cranes in the middle of the dining room; large Oriental vases; a sixteenth-century hand-carved wooden Buddha; huge Oriental fans; and a window looking out on an orchid garden. (Hundreds of flowers in every hue are pressed tightly against the window, a stunning sight.) The colors turquoise and rose predominate, but the tables are green, the chairs black (and not very comfortable), the lighting high-tech and the kitchen open. An evening amid such splendor costs about $165 for two, with wine. It may not be cheap, but it's a one-of-a-kind experience; think of it as dinner theater—dinner *as* theater—especially if you're lucky enough to spot one or two of the many celebrities who frequent the place.

12/20 Il Cielo

9018 Burton Way, Beverly Hills
276-9990
ITALIAN
Open Mon.-Fri. 11:30 a.m.-3 p.m. & 6 p.m.-10:30 p.m., Sat. 6 p.m.-11 p.m. All major cards.

Il Cielo means "the sky," which is exactly what you see (smog and fog willing) when you look heavenward from the lovely outdoor patio that surrounds this place. Il Cielo used to be En Brochette, before following the changing tide in local taste and transmuting from an out-of-date French restaurant into a modern Italian one. It's an oddity of a restaurant, basically a sweet little house in the middle of a neighborhood that is affluent but charmless—all those condos along Burton Way have made the street rather sterile. Il Cielo is happily out of its element, a place where water trickles from the mouth of a stone lion, plants run riot through the rear garden, and lovers draw close together to ward off the evening's chill—or perhaps just to draw close together. The food is good; in fact, the food is very good, in the style of such local favorites as Pane Caldo, Tutto Bene and Chianti Cucina. While sitting under the Beverly Hills stars (and possibly next to a few), you can eat carpaccio with bits of white truffle and shavings of Parmesan, smoked scamorza cheese with baked eggplant, baby frogs' legs grilled with shallots and garlic, plump shrimp cavorting in risotto blackened with squid's ink, lobster grilled with garlic and lemon, and filet mignon with some of the best-tasting spinach we've ever found. In other words, good, honest Italian cooking, served in a setting that's perfect for people who either are in love or would like to be in love before the evening is over. Two will spend about $80 for dinner with wine.

12/20 The Daily Grill

11677 San Vicente Blvd., Brentwood
442-0044
AMERICAN
Open daily 11 a.m.-11 p.m. All major cards.

The Daily Grill is the first offspring of The Grill in Beverly Hills, which itself is a gussied-up version of Musso & Frank. The Grill serves some of the city's finest steaks, chops, fish and potato dishes, at prices that are moderate for the talent impresarios of CAA and ICM but a little beyond the dinner budget for the rest of us. At The Daily Grill, the prices are dramatically lower but the food quality (and quantity) is more or less the same. The trade-off is the style of the place, which is much more casual, a lot noisier and based on a good deal of turnover. One goes to The Grill for the evening; one goes to The Daily Grill for the hour. The menu is a virtual Smithsonian of Great American Dishes, a delightful compendium of everyone's favorite grub. The names of the dishes alone inspire Proustian remembrances of meals past: linguine and clams, mushroom barley soup, shrimp Louie, Joe's Special, chicken pot pie, calf's liver with bacon and onions, steamed spinach, potatoes Lyonnaise, potatoes O'Brien, tapioca pie. This is comfort food incarnate, the perfect stuff to eat after a tough day hacking through the jungles of show-business litigiousness. We're always happy to sink our teeth into an order of The Daily Grill's fine Caesar salad (served in both appetizer and main-course sizes, as are all the salads), followed by the superb broiled garlic chicken (which has rid Brentwood of vampires), accompanied by mixed fried potatoes and onions, followed by the too-wonderful-for-words tapioca pie or the house rice pudding, or both. We've found that in the rush to serve so many, some dishes are cooked less than they should be—specify that you want your potatoes fried very crisp. We're also not crazy about the steamed broccoli that comes with just about everything, probably because we prefer steamed carrots or spinach. Expect joyous chaos and you won't be disappointed. Dinner for two, with wine, costs about $50.

12/20 Da Pasquale

9749 Santa Monica Blvd., Beverly Hills
859-3884
ITALIAN
Open Mon.-Sat. 11 a.m.-11 p.m. No cards.

If you're looking for atmosphere and a posh setting, skip this place. But if it's *molto authentico* rustic Italian food you have in mind, make a beeline for it. Da Pasquale is named for the former Angeli pizza chef who owns this tiny café, located on that no-man's-land stretch of little Santa Monica Boulevard that marks the transition of Beverly Hills into Century City. At the time of this writing, the only seating area consisted of a counter (tables are promised for the future), and the menu was somewhat limited. However, just about everything on the menu is terrific. Pasquale doesn't serve pizzas, per se; instead, you'll find pizzalike versions of focaccia, as well as overstuffed calzones, topped and filled with fresh mozzarella, ricotta, goat cheese, sausage, capers and so on. The pastas are very, very good, the best being a linguine with fresh tomatoes, sun-dried tomatoes, radicchio, basil, garlic and a delicious fetalike dried ricotta. There are also several varieties of panini (sandwiches) and daily specials, including a delectable osso buco and a half chicken stewed in tomato sauce. The ambience is casual, the service a little ditzy but friendly, the prices absurdly cheap, and the food an absolute delight. Dinner for two, with beverages, costs about $30.

11/20 DC3

Santa Monica Airport, 31st St. entrance,
Santa Monica
399-2323
AMERICAN
Open Sun.-Fri. 11:30 a.m.-2:30 p.m. & 6 p.m.-11 p.m., Sat. 6 p.m.-11 p.m. All major cards.

We wandered into DC3 in its first week and were confronted with the crowd that packs every hot new westside restaurant: show-biz scenemakers, well-to-do artists and Billionaire Boys' Club–type youngsters in Maxfield duds who drive convertible BMWs. Normally, this herd would stampede to a new pasture the second the next restaurant-of-the-moment opened. But several months later, they still thronged the huge rectangular bar and filled the many tables and booths. Of course, that's exactly what one would expect, since DC3 is the latest venture of Bruce Marder, the man who gave us the West Beach Café and Rebecca's, two of the hottest scene restaurants in town. Although the West Beach was in the vanguard of the Californian-cuisine movement of the late '70s and early '80s, Marder's restaurants are known more for their fashions than for their food, thanks in part to their popular bars. DC3 is no different from its older siblings. The people-watching can't be beat. The soaring interior is quite dramatic, with its huge windows overlooking the runways of the puny Santa Monica Airport. The multitextured decor, designed by Venice artist Charles Arnoldi, is loads of fun. And the food? Well, let's just say that it perpetuates Rebecca's tradition of overpriced mediocrity.

The regularly changing menu is a collection of the sort of simple American/international dishes currently in vogue: oysters, smoked salmon, salads, pasta appetizers, grilled meats . . . you know the type. Marder seems to have a fire fetish: about half of the dishes are "charred," and some that aren't charred may be accompanied with "burnt" butter. We were doubtful about all this charring, since burnt is way up there on our list of least-favorite flavors. But some of these dishes turned out to be among the kitchen's finest efforts, notably the juicy charred dry-aged New York steak in a restrained black-pepper sauce and the fine charred rack of lamb with a veal glaze, herbes de Provence and fried goat cheese. Dishes to avoid include the tiny cucumber-and-feta salad, which has been known to arrive sans feta; the sad, overcooked, lukewarm french fries; the pathetic appetizer of shrimp-stuffed ravioli—each ravioli had a few micrograms of filling that had not the slightest shrimp taste, and the whole heap sat in an uninteresting pool of oil—and the charred jumbo shrimp and sea scallops with a lime-tarragon dip, so stingily served that it'd leave an anorexic hungry. As for dessert, the burnt rice pudding (there's that incendiary mania again) was an unmitigated disaster, tasting much like a small pot of glue. Despite excellent berries, the raspberry brown-butter tart was dry and humdrum; the apple napoleon was no better. We can think of loads of other restaurants in town where we'd rather spend the $120 it'll cost two of you to dine, with wine. We will say that the scene can be fun to check out—but that can be done from the bar for the price of a drink.

10/20 Delmonico's Seafood Grille

9320 W. Pico Blvd., W.L.A.
550-7737
SEAFOOD
Open Mon.-Fri. 11:30 a.m.-11 p.m., Sat. 5:30 p.m.-11 p.m., Sun. 5 p.m.-10 p.m. All major cards.

To paraphrase Lloyd Bentsen's classic remark to Dan Quayle about John Kennedy, Delmonico's is no Grand Central Oyster Bar. It's also no Legal Seafood and no Tadich Grill. Not that there's anything wrong with the place; we just wish it hadn't put itself up against the best of the best. Delmonico's (named, as a further bit of hyperbole, for the legendary robber-baron watering hole in turn-of-the-century New York) is a good, functional seafood restaurant. It used to be the Ritz Café, L.A.'s first hot-spot Cajun restaurant, which then went through a menu shift to new American/Southern cooking when Cajun began to wane. Because it's been born again as a seafood restaurant, fish must be the food of the moment. If mutton becomes the food of choice next week, we suppose the name can easily be changed to Delmonico's Sheep Grille. The New Orleans–mess hall look of the place has been warmed up a bit with the addition of dividers and banquettes in the middle of the room, and a fish mural adds a finny air to the place, but basically, it still looks like the Ritz Café, and there's nothing wrong with that. But the menu has been completely purged of Cajun/Creole influences.

Actually, the new menu is more Italianate grill than seafood house—one section deals with pastas, another concentrates on steaks and chops, and a third lists such specialties as osso buco, paillard de veau (grilled veal scallop) and grilled quail. And you won't find such venerable seafood classics as Maryland she-crab soup, oyster pan roast or Florida stone-crab claws. Instead, the choice of dishes is a bit prosaic: an overly thickened Boston clam chowder, a good (though salty) Maine-lobster bisque, various grilled fish (halibut, ahi, mahi mahi, salmon) and various pan-sautéed seafood (rubbery calamari, scallops, catfish, trout and so forth). We've enjoyed a fine two-pound Maine lobster, nicely broiled (for a reasonable $24; by contrast, half a desiccated dwarf lobster at the Brentwood Bar & Grill goes for $28). On the other hand, we've also ordered a dull crispy calamari salad that was only vaguely crispy and even more vaguely flavorful. We also tried a bowl of something called potato and garlic pie that was just an overbuttered mush. All things considered, we long for the old Ritz, with its blackened steak and its wonderful cornbread in the shape of little cobs. Dinner for two, with wine, costs from $50 to $65.

 The Dining Room
Regent Beverly Wilshire,
9500 Wilshire Blvd., Beverly Hills
275-5200
CONTINENTAL/AMERICAN
Open daily 7 a.m.-10:30 a.m., 11:30 a.m.-3 p.m. & 5 p.m.-11 p.m. All major cards.

We've been to more than our share of hotel dining rooms, and we can say unreservedly that they're usually dreadfully boring. Some have very good food, such as Gardens at the Four Seasons. But they're still dull (at Gardens, for instance, we felt like we had to whisper). There's something innately stuffy about these places, perhaps in part because of the service, which is usually stiff and formal. One would certainly expect The Dining Room to fall prey to such an ailment. After all, this is the Beverly Wilshire we're talking about, and the new owner, The Regent group, is known for its ultra-luxurious hotels (it spent zillions to restore its newest possession). But The Regent is also known for the best service in the hotel business, and it's clearly a reputation that is well deserved. What really sets this service apart is not its efficiency or professionalism—both of which are generally ample at top hotels—but its total lack of pretentiousness. The maître d'/manager seems more like a friendly salesman than a maître d', and the waiters are warm and refreshingly casual (but not flip). Happily, both the food and the setting live up to the service. The multilevel dining room is open yet intimate, rich with glowing wood, excellent lighting, white linens and fine crystal, warmed with piano music drifting over from the nearby bar. The open-kitchen trend is acknowledged, albeit discreetly—small windows afford views of a phalanx of stiff-toqued cooks manning the gleaming kitchen of white marble and tile.

Like any good hotel menu, this one (printed anew each night) is diverse but not overwhelmingly large, well balanced with representatives from the classic and the creative, with something for everyone. And the prices are not as high as you would expect of such a fancy joint: appetizers for $4 to $14, with most in the $6 to $9 range, and entrées in the $14 to $24 range, with plenty for less than $20. It's not cheap, but there are plenty of places around town that charge more and offer much less. All the dishes we tried were skillfully prepared and delicious, from salads to pasta, fish to meat. Only the desserts were even slightly disappointing (and just slightly, as with the crème brûlée, a bit too sweet). We'd have to call the food contemporary Continental: French, Italian, Californian and good old American (i.e., steak and cheesecake). Don't pass up the world-class sautéed Napa Valley foie gras with wild mushrooms and garden greens: unspeakably good foie gras, cooked to just a bit of crustiness on the outside, with huge, tasty mushrooms and the welcome sharpness of the salad. Grilled Norwegian salmon with a Chinese-mustard marinade was beautifully prepared, the marinade providing a well-balanced blend of sweet and hot. And the veal chop with mashed potatoes and garlic was exactly as wonderful as we hoped it would be. Desserts vary regularly; a favorite is the chocolate-mousse cake, which is exceptionally light but still rich with chocolate flavor. If you're in Beverly Hills and want a first-class restaurant for romance or business, you can't beat the Beverly Wilshire. Dinner for two, with wine, will run about $110.

10/20 La Dolce Vita
9785 Santa Monica Blvd., Beverly Hills
278-1845
ITALIAN
Open Mon.-Sat. 5 p.m.-11 p.m. All major cards.

There's a whimsical saying about the California Lottery: it doesn't matter whether or not you buy a ticket, because the chances of winning are about the same in either case. Much the same can be said of writing about the food at such old-fashioned restaurants as La Dolce Vita, because no one really goes to restaurants of this ilk for the cuisine. Blue-haired Beverly Hills matrons and aging celebrities show up here to be coddled, cared for, fussed over. Service is delightfully unctuous (if you can bear such treatment without feeling smothered), and the room is thick with such clichés as curved leather banquettes and bad art. Everyone feels very comfortable here, and no one, as far as we can tell, ever complains that the food tastes like the sort of Italian food you might prepare at home. Perhaps that's the point—this is home cooking for people who don't have to cook at home, at prices that can be staggering. There are no surprises on the menu, which is how this crowd likes it—stuffed mushrooms, baked clams, minestrone, veal piccata, veal marsala, spaghetti carbonara, linguine with clams. Steak Sinatra, made with green peppers, pretty much defines the style of the house—it's a fine steak, but not one we'd go out of our way for. Dinner for two, with wine, costs about $95.

10/20 Dynasty Room

Westwood Marquis, 930 Hilgard Ave., Westwood
208-8765
CONTINENTAL
Open nightly 6 p.m.-10:30 p.m. All major cards.

What is one to do with the Dynasty Room? It sits within the plush Westwood Marquis, the UCLA-adjacent branch of the rock star–intensive Sunset Marquis. The hotel serves, from a gazebo in its Garden Room, what many consider to be the finest (and most expensive) buffet brunch in the city. The Westwood Marquis's big-deal dining room wants respect. It wants to be considered a player. It sponsors a big reception every year for the chefs who participate in Wolfgang Puck's sparkling American Wine & Food Festival to benefit Meals on Wheels. Of course, the hotel's chef, Philippe Reynaud, has a booth at the event. And interestingly, it's at that event that the weaknesses of the Dynasty Room's cooking become most apparent. There, surrounded by the likes of Dean Fearing, Larry Forgione, Bradley Ogden and Jeremiah Tower, the cooking of the Dynasty Room seems . . . well, out of shape. It's out of date and fussy. It's not the sort of food anyone takes seriously anymore. And that's exactly the kind of experience we've had eating there. It reminds us of a slightly less shabby Perino's, serving dishes that try to be modern—like Dungeness crab ravioli, or loin of lamb with couscous—but that, in this mummified setting, only seem weary. The menu reads well, but the plate is heavy with cream and butter.

The food is dulling, the service excessive, the setting moribund. They try their best—but their best just isn't good enough. Dinner for two, with wine, costs $120 or so.

11/20 L'Escoffier

The Beverly Hilton, 9876 Wilshire Blvd., Beverly Hills
274-7777
FRENCH/CONTINENTAL
Open Mon.-Fri. 6:30 p.m.-midnight, Sat. 6:30 p.m.-12:30 a.m. All major cards.

It's a pity that the Marx Brothers are long dead and gone, for this would be the perfect setting for one of their egalitarian farces, in which they mock the pseudo-pomposity of Margaret Dumont, Walter Woolf King and Sigmund Ruman. We can just see Groucho, Harpo and Chico lighting the paper cigarette holders that sit on every table, without first putting cigarettes inside them. We can see Groucho, with his greasepaint mustache and ubiquitous cigar, tangoing an overheated Dumont across the dance floor while the petrified orchestra plays a slow box step. We can see Harpo pulling out a fire extinguisher to quench the flames of a flambéed something or other being prepared with flourishes by the tuxedoed captains. L'Escoffier, appropriately named for a long-dead chef, is the last of a dying breed of restaurant—the old school French/Continental that comes complete with a dramatic view (of Century City) and a dance floor with a band playing slow music for those with creaky bones. The food is expensive, rich with names like Rockefeller, Diane, Rothschild and Henry IV, creamed and buttered to a turn, and rather dull—this is a restaurant where the presentation is far more important than the flavors. It's a fine place to take your rich old uncle on his birthday. He'll love the scene. He'll write you into his will. Then you'll be able to afford to eat a lot better, at fine restaurants where there's never a band playing, ever. Dinner for two, with wine, costs upward of $120.

11/20 Fama

1416 4th St., Santa Monica
451-8633
ITALIAN
Open Mon.-Fri. 11:30 a.m.-2:30 p.m. & 6 p.m.-11 p.m., Sat.-Sun. 6 p.m.-11 p.m. All major cards.

Fama is the eccentric Italian offspring of the equally eccentric nouvelle-French Rockenwagner, both run by Hans Rockenwagner and his wife, Mary Fama Rockenwagner. Though their first restaurant is a minuscule storefront in the midst of a small restaurant row in Venice, the new place is every bit as high-tech, noisy and modern as City, Citrus and DC3. Sadly, it's not nearly as good a restaurant as Rockenwagner. Perhaps the Rockenwagners work best under crowded conditions, perhaps Italian cooking is simply not their forte, or perhaps this is further proof of the workings of the Peter Principle—like the fat in a chicken soup, they've risen to the top, where they've solidified. Goodness knows, as big fans of Rockenwagner, we wanted to like Fama a lot. We like the ultra-trendy look of the place very much, especially all the odd angles and the peculiar lighting system (which looks something like Martians walking a tightrope). We like the fact that it is conveniently located a few steps from one of Santa Monica's free downtown parking structures. We even like the menu, which features all the right buzz terms: Maui-onion pizza, seared tuna, potato Rösti, saffron rice and so forth. The food is good, we'll go that far, particularly the crispy (and quite small) pizzas with odd toppings: ratatouille, cilantro and salsa, that sort of thing. But the appetizers aren't quite as thrilling as they sound—an eggplant mousse was flavorless, and clams stuffed with bread crumbs were as awful as clams stuffed with bread crumbs usually are. And both the pastas and entrées bordered on insipid: dull gnocchi, ordinary ricotta-filled ravioli, pointless stuffed swordfish, wholly unappealing breaded chicken cutlets. Rockenwagner still rocks, but Fama has a ways to go before it becomes worthy of fame. Two will spend about $70 for dinner with wine.

11/20 La Famiglia

453 N. Cañon Dr., Beverly Hills
276-6208
ITALIAN
Open Mon.-Fri. 11:30 a.m.-2:30 p.m. & 5 p.m.-10:30 p.m., Sat. 5 p.m.-10:30 p.m. All major cards.

La Famiglia is anything but trendy, which is why many celebrities of a certain age like to frequent it—there are no papparazzi hovering by the door, as at some chic eateries. They are comfortable here in the red-leatherette decor, which has a Beverly Hills touch: paisley linens, delicate crystal, mirrored paneling, and Tiffany lamps hanging from the cozily low ceilings. Owner Joe Patti is forever in attendance, greeting customers who have known him since he tended bar at La Scala seventeen years ago, preparing his homemade spinach and beet pastas tableside and proudly sending out free samples of his homemade gelati. The expected northern Italian veal and chicken dishes are prepared competently, if not brilliantly; it's all quite edible but quite unmemorable. What makes La Famiglia notable, however, is its interpretation of nuova cucina, spa-cuisine style. Patti has devised low-calorie, Italianish dishes to please his figure-conscious clientele, and they love the delicate whitefish and lemon sole, poached quickly in white wine instead of butter, and topped with capers, lemon chunks or tiny bay shrimp. Calamari are cooked in a spicy tomato broth and served in a tiny kettle rather than deep-fried. The not-so-low-calorie Caesar salad is wonderful, as are the feather-light french-fried zucchini sticks. The wine list has a good number of reasonably priced Italian vintages for such a small restaurant. Choose La Famiglia more for basic renditions of old favorites than for new adventures in eating; you can be relatively sure of a pleasant meal in pleasant surroundings. About $100 for two, with wine.

Fennel

1375 Ocean Ave., Santa Monica
394-2079
FRENCH
Open Mon. & Sat. 6:30 p.m.-10:30 p.m., Tues.-Fri. noon-2 p.m. & 6:30 p.m.-10:30 p.m. All major cards.

A recipe for disaster. That's what several knowledgeable, dedicated restaurant-goers predicted when Mauro Vincenti first spoke of his concept for Fennel. "How the hell can an Italian run a French restaurant in Los Angeles with four chefs as partners, all of them based in France?" several friends asked. Good question. But it's worked. Why? Well, the fax machine, long-distance telephone calls and discount airline fares have helped, but we think Jean-Pierre Bosq deserves much of the credit. Bosq—as talented as he is handsome—is the permanent, in-residence chef at Fennel, and while the four visiting chefs who fly in regularly from France generate most of the excitement and attract most of the giddy publicity, it's Bosq who keeps the kitchen humming on a day-to-day basis.

One Bosq lunch began with a robust, flavorful duck confit, shredded, dressed with mustard and balsamic vinegar and served on a bed of crisp greens. The duck breast with olive sauce and turnips was equally good, and the cold passion-fruit soufflé with raspberry sauce was a perfect summer dessert. Even though Fennel's original pastry chef has departed, his trademark hot chocolate tart with pistachio sauce remains, as seductively sublime as ever. But there are many other splendid dishes: tarts made with fresh salmon and with ratatouille and zucchini; soups made with tomato, red pepper and cucumber and with frogs' legs and chanterelles; sea-urchin soufflé; veal Parmentier; duck carpaccio with tagliatelle; thin slices of raw scallop, marinated in olive oil and lime juice, served atop a timbale of sweetbreads, oyster mushrooms and haricots verts. In fact, Fennel's food is often better than at our other 16-point restaurants; if we had a 16.5 rating, it'd be deserved here.

Bosq and his four transatlantic colleagues work together creating dishes and send ideas back and forth via fax, and they have a lot of help outside the kitchen as well. Dominique, the attentive maître d', will see to your every need. There is extra excitement when any of the chefs from France flies in; one usually comes each month, for about a week at a time, on a rotating basis. Michel Rostang, from the superb Paris restaurant that bears his name, is probably the best of the four, but the others—André Genin from Chez Pauline and Yannick Jacquot from Le Toit de Passy, both in Paris, and Michel Chabran of the restaurant that bears his name in Pont de l'Isère—have also delighted us with their originality and creativity.

Not that every dish is a success. We sampled duck with cabbage, for instance, that was curiously bland, and other dishes have misfired on occasion. Moreover, some diners have complained that service is slow, that reservations aren't honored and that if the staff doesn't know you, you may get stuck waiting interminably at the small bar. Those problems seem to have diminished considerably in recent months. But the wine list is still absurdly overpriced, and the restaurant isn't terribly comfortable. If we took all these factors into consideration in our ratings, Fennel would merit only a 15 ranking. But as noted in the introduction, "rankings reflect *only* the quality of the cooking," and the cooking here is quite fine indeed. Try lunch at Fennel; it's one of the best-kept secrets in town. The restaurant is sparsely populated and very quiet, and if you ask for a table by the window, across the street from the Pacific Ocean, you can pretend that you're in a charming seaside town in the south of France—except for the occasional sad encampments of homeless people in the park across the street. Dinner for two, with wine, runs about $165.

12/20 Il Forno

2901 Ocean Park Blvd., Santa Monica
450-1241
ITALIAN
Open Mon.-Fri. 11:30 a.m.-11:30 p.m., Sat. 5:30 p.m.-midnight. Cards: AE, MC, V.

Il Forno is yet another mini-mall find. This unpretentious trattoria is a neighborhood favorite—a lively, friendly place that also happens to serve authentic, delicious regional Italian fare at reasonable prices. It may be located across the way from DC3, but it's worlds away in cuisine and attitude; you actually feel welcome at Il Forno, and you actually walk away feeling well fed rather than ripped off. Yet, in its own way, Il Forno is just as much of a scene as DC3 is. The antipasto bar is a terrific experience: you make your selections and they're dished out to you. These range from a simple, fresh insalata caprese with firm white mozzarella and ripe tomatoes to more elaborate concoctions employing seafood, sun-dried tomatoes and pasta. The arancini di riso, little rice croquettes with porcini mushrooms and a melt of cheese in the center, are irresistible, as are a northern Italian rendition of carpaccio bathed in a fragrant olive oil with capers, served on a bed of shredded radicchio and dusted with parsley, and a sizzling crostini with a smoky mozzarella and prosciutto, troubled only by a tad of sog in the bread. The pizzas, particularly the rustica with sun-dried tomatoes, smoked cheese, basil and olive oil, are a dream, with thin, crisp crusts. The pastas are perfectly al dente; the main dishes, such as the fine osso buco, are also very good. Il Forno also features a spa menu, and the healthy items on it don't sacrifice a bit of taste in their quest for lower cholesterol and calorie levels. In fact, if you order from the spa menu, you may feel virtuous enough to eat dessert, although recovering alcoholics and pregnant women should eschew the tiramisu—it's loaded with Strega liqueur. You'll leave Il Forno thoroughly contented, and the friendly staff and general buzz of the place are bound to help along that good mood. Two will spend $40 to $45 for dinner with wine.

 Four Oaks
2181 N. Beverly Glen Blvd., Beverly Glen
470-2265
FRENCH
Open Sun.-Thurs. 11 a.m.-2:30 p.m & 6 p.m.-10 p.m., Fri.-Sat. 11 a.m.-2:30 p.m. & 6 p.m.-10:30 p.m. All major cards.

For the longest time, Four Oaks held its reputation as a lovely little restaurant that you really didn't look forward to eating at. Nestled in the midst of Beverly Glen, Four Oaks spent years being the prettiest place with the most mediocre food. But in recent years, it's gone through two changes of ownership. The first was an utter failure—if anything, the place became worse. But the most recent ownership seems to have finally come up with a kitchen that's a match for the lovely French-provincial decor and idyllic country-in-the-city setting. The new chef, Peter Roelant, is a young graduate of Girardet and L'Orangerie. And though he's clearly learned his classical lessons well, there's an antic drummer somewhere in his head to which he feels compelled to march. Roelant is the sort of fellow who absorbs all the rules, then happily discards them and starts all over the again at the beginning.

Four Oaks's food has evolved into a tidy sort of French/Californian mélange, with small touches from Italy and Japan—in other words, an eminently modern menu. It's home to one of the most elegant (and soothing) tomato soups in town, flavored lightly with tarragon and sweet roasted garlic. Where else can you find a salad of those ubiquitous baby mixed greens, hugely improved with candied lemon skin? How about a nigh-on perfect salad of baby Maine lobster with fresh peaches in a Champagne sauce? Or a rather nifty tuna-and-salmon tartare flavored with shallots and lime? Main courses are fantastically eclectic yet entirely accessible: a fabulous chicken-and-

vegetable pot-au-feu served with a completely contradictory five-pepper sabayon (peasant food meets haute cuisine in a perfect marriage); a terrific lamb filet served with a sweet garlic pancake and creamed turnips; ravioli filled with pesto-flavored cottage cheese in a saffron-and-tomato sauce; lovely veal medallions with rosemary, served with a lemon-flavored pasta. And there's plenty of it—the portions here are anything but nouvelle. This is wonderful food: new but not too new; modern but still filling. It's the right food for a night in the canyon, in a restaurant with a strong foundation that nevertheless seems almost unreal in its prettiness. Dinner for two, with wine, will run $120 or so.

 Fragrant Vegetable
11859 Wilshire Blvd., W.L.A.
312-1442
CHINESE/VEGETARIAN
Open Mon.-Thurs. 11 a.m.-9:30 p.m., Fri.-Sun. 11 a.m.-10 p.m. Cards: MC, V.
See Restaurants, "San Gabriel Valley."

 Il Giardino
9235 W. 3rd St., Beverly Hills
275-5444
ITALIAN
Open Mon.-Fri. noon-3 p.m. & 6 p.m.-10:30 p.m., Sat. 6 p.m.-10:30 p.m. All major cards.

When Il Giardino opened several years ago, it was a new and welcome kind of Italian restaurant in Los Angeles—a rustic, simple sort of place in an out-of-the-way section of baja Beverly Hills, with the authentic feel of Italy. The authentic feel remains, but the quality and originality of the food have slipped badly. Pastas and risotti often seem overcooked, ingredients don't marry well, and few dishes provide the satisfaction they once did. Part of the problem may be that our standards are higher now; new and better Italian restaurants have been steadily opening all over the city. But that isn't the only explanation, because such other old favorites as Valentino and Rex have improved while Il Giardino has declined. Celebrities continue to frequent the place, but that only confirms our theory that the quality of a restaurant's food is inversely proportional to the quantity of its celebrity clients.

A recent dinner began with a tired seafood salad (none of the appetizers seem inspired or inspiring) followed by risotto with chicken livers. At least, that's what the menu said. Our serving had more carrots, peas, zucchini and tomato than liver, and before we were halfway through, we had an unattractive, oily pool in our bowl. On our last visit, virtually everything about Il Giardino suggested that management was bored. The carpets were worn. The carrots in the complimentary bowl of fresh vegetables were limp. The wine list has more than 100 selections but none with vintages listed, and virtually every time we ordered one from it, we were told, "We don't have that one anymore." A few pastas are still good, though, and the tiramisu remains among the better desserts to be found on the westside. The waiters are friendly and helpful, even if a few have trouble with English. That used to add to the genuine charm of the place; now, at least sometimes, it's just another annoyance. Dinner for two, with wine, runs about $130.

⑬ Gilliland's
2424 Main St., Santa Monica
392-3901
INTERNATIONAL
Open Mon.-Fri. 11:30 a.m.-2:30 p.m. & 6 p.m.-11 p.m., Sat. 6 p.m.-11 p.m. Cards: AE, MC, V.
Like City Restaurant across town, Gilliland's has cuisine that is at once Mediterranean, East Indian, Irish and melting-pot American. Unlike City, Gilliland's is absolutely devoid of pretension and high prices—in fact, at one point a couple of years ago, owner Gerri Gilliland actually lowered her prices to make the place more populist. At the bar, you can get all kinds of little nibbles, such as light cubes of cornmeal polenta, Indian samosas and a marvelous blarney-cheese-and-onion tart. No matter when you go to Gilliland's, order those tarts—they are the very essence of comfort food, Irish style. You should also try (if it's on the ever-changing menu) the chicken thigh stuffed with goat cheese and flavored with a gentle rosemary butter. Luxuriate, if you will, in the sheer joy of the thick leg of lamb, flavored with mint, garlic and rosemary and grilled with red onions and eggplant. Dive headfirst into the audacious duck confit with jalapeño peppers and garlic fettuccine. And do order the shame-

lessly traditional Irish beef stew, thick and motherly, served with a chopped potato-and-onion concoction called champ. Dinner for two, with wine, costs about $60.

8/20 Gladstone's 4 Fish
17300 W. Pacific Coast Hwy.,
Pacific Palisades
GL-4-FISH
SEAFOOD
Open Sun.-Thurs. 7 a.m.-11 p.m., Fri.-Sat. 7 a.m.-midnight. Cards: MC, V.
By the time most diners are seated at this madhouse, they're so bombed from the huge tropical drinks that they wouldn't know if they were eating Mrs. Paul's or the real thing. It is the real thing—which means the fish is usually fresh and sometimes mesquite-grilled—but it may as well be Mrs. Paul's for all the flavor it has. The rich chowder is respectable, but little else is worth trying. Be sure to avoid the foot-high slabs of foam rubber that are disguised as pieces of chocolate cake. What makes people willing to wait up to two hours for a table here is the great beachfront location, the very pleasant ocean-view deck and the reasonable tab: $55 for two, with mai tais.

12/20 The Grill on the Alley
9560 Dayton Way, Beverly Hills
276-0615
AMERICAN
Open Mon.-Sat. 11:30 a.m.-midnight. All major cards.
We were instantly set at ease when we walked into the Grill, a quintessentially American place unspoiled by the vicissitudes of culinary fads. Settling into our spacious, comfortable booth, surrounded by the likes of Elliot Gould, Marsha Mason and prosperous-looking local stockbrokers, we were pleased to discover that the large menu is devoid of such fashionable dishes as blackened redfish, blue-corn tacos and shiitake pizzas. They can certainly be wonderful, but sometimes one gets a hankering for the kind of basic American food one grew up with, if one was blessed with a good cook for a mother. That's what you'll find at The Grill—cooking that is honest and simple, emphasizing high-quality ingredients: perfectly fresh clams and oysters on the half shell, excellent steaks and lamb chops, an aromatic and flavorful grilled garlic chicken, steamed vegetables that are, amazingly, fresh

and not overcooked, a near-perfect hamburger and a delicious pecan pie. Salads, on the other hand, can be disappointing, especially the niçoise, a poorly presented heap of iceberg lettuce and tuna. But you'll be quick to forgive such faults, for they are more than made up for by the handsome men's-club decor, the friendly but unobtrusive service and the sophisticated clientele. Prices reflect the neighborhood and the quality; the limited wine list is overpriced. Two can dine for about $95, with a simple wine.

Hal's Bar & Grill
1349 W. Washington Blvd., Venice
396-3105
AMERICAN
Open Mon.-Fri. 11:30 a.m.-1:30 a.m., Sat.-Sun. 9 a.m.-1:30 a.m. Cards: AE, V.

Not far from the insufferable scenes at Rebecca's, the West Beach Café and DC3 is another hip, arty, airy new restaurant serving simple American/international dishes: Hal's Bar & Grill. Except Hal's is less ambitious and pretentious than its neighboring counterparts, has a much more capable kitchen and is less expensive. Add relaxed, friendly service, comfortable booths, a long, roomy bar, good soul and jazz on the stereo and an interesting, Venice-style clientele, and you've got an all-around terrific place, just the right addition to Washington Boulevard's burgeoning restaurant row. The weekly changing dinner menu is refreshingly short and simple: a couple of salads, three appetizers and about ten entrées. The lunch menu has about the same number of dishes, with more of an emphasis on sandwiches and salads. And the wine list is equally brief—too much so, though there are several fine choices for well under $20. Dinner entrées come with soup of the day or salad (either the house mixed green or the delicious Caesar), so appetizers aren't necessary. But we like to get one or two for the table anyway—they're worth the calories and expense. We liked the marvelous steamed salmon "purse" filled with a mousse of scallops and yellow peppers and dressed with a perfect Dijon mustard sauce, cream and thyme, and the robust, stewy, delicious risotto with tomatoes, basil and black olives. In fact, every dish we've tried has been excellent, from the duck breast on a bed of risotto with wild mushrooms, thyme and aspagarus, to the simple, perfect grilled

New York steak with a shallot and rosemary mayonnaise and good fries, to the delicate Norwegian salmon on a bed of capellini pasta with ribbons of carrots and leeks and a lemon cream sauce. This is not fancy food, but chef Greg Gevurtz and staff cook it with the degree of care and precision found in the most elegant French fare. That standard is continued with the desserts, which are neither too heavy nor too petite: delicious crème caramel of an exceptional smoothness and richness, an individual apple brown-butter tart with a satisfyingly earthy brown-sugar taste, and the best of the bunch, Hal's sundae—a scoop of seriously chocolate, almost chewy chocolate, ice cream, a scoop of vanilla-bean ice cream, a dollop of thick fudge, a dollop of intense caramel sauce and a light dusting of ground nuts. It'll make you swear off frozen yogurt forever. You'll spend about $80 for a complete dinner for two, with a simple wine; the marvelous weekend brunch is only about $12 a person, with juice.

10/20 Hamlet Gardens
1139 Westwood Blvd., Westwood
824-1818
AMERICAN/CALIFORNIAN
Open Sun.-Thurs. 11:30 a.m.-10:30 p.m., Fri.-Sat. 11:30 a.m.-11:30 p.m. Cards: AE, MC, V.

Imagine a Hamburger Hamlet gone all grown up and nouvelle and you have Hamlet Gardens, Hamburger Hamlet Inc.'s bid for L.A.'s upscale market and a prototype for more outlets like it. Instead of the Hamlet's ersatz olde English decor, here is every cliché of the California outdoors-indoors '80s look—ficuses that reach to the skylights, terracotta floors, weathered brick walls. It's actually quite pleasant and airy, but its version of California cuisine, like the hamburgers at Hamburger Hamlet, is only a facsimile—a sort of generic nouvelle cuisine that gives the sense not of someone creating in the kitchen, but of a functionary putting fish, chicken and veal through its fresh-ingredients-simply-prepared paces. "Very Fresh Salmon Tartar" is very tasteless; Wiener Schnitzel is dull; grilled lavender-fennel-pepper steak is done in. The place tries so hard to be upscale that we feel embarrassed for it. While a pianist serenades dinner guests, an eager young waiter wheels a cart up to the table and proceeds to make guacamole—mashing avocados, folding in chopped onions and spices. What tableside gimmick will they think of next? Tableside tuna fish salad? But everything in perspective. This is Westwood, after all, and with few decent places to eat nearby, Hamlet Gardens (we keep wanting to call it Hamburger Gardens) provides edible, if overpriced, dinners, generous cocktails, pleasant service, a delicious pizza with pesto, prawns and sliced red onions, and some wonderfully gooey desserts, such as a hot fudge sundae topped with glazed sugar-fried walnuts, and warm bread pudding with caramelized apples on crème anglaise. The tab can run as high as $100 for two, with wine.

⑬ Harry's Bar & American Grill
ABC Entertainment Center,
2020 Ave. of the Stars, Century City
277-2333

ITALIAN

Open Mon.-Fri. 11:30 a.m.-3 p.m., Sat.-Sun. 5 p.m.-10:30 p.m. All major cards.

Unless you work in Century City, it's easy to let Harry's slip from your consciousness, what with new Italian trattorias opening practically every day. What one really forgets, however, is just how good it is. Clubby and warm, it lets you forget that you're in sterile Century City, not to mention L.A. The bar, while something of a singles scene, is nonetheless quite civilized; in fact, Harry's manages to be urbane without an attitude. (On the other hand, we doubt Ernest Hemingway, who immortalized the Harry's mystique, would connect with the crowd of high-powered suits, nor would he care to jot down their conversations about leveraged buy-outs and pay-or-play deals; Century City attracts a different kind of adventurer.)

What separates Harry's from most power-lunch boîtes is the quality of the food. The bread and breadsticks are fresh and taste as if they were baked by real people. The appetizers and salads are delicious, from the simple insalata caprese to the lovely, roseate carpaccio with scatterings of capers and an anointing of good olive oil. The vitello tonnato, that much-abused dish of cold veal blanketed in a tuna sauce, is as good as it gets, and the air-dried, wafer-thin bresaola (dried salt beef filet) is tender and flavorful. Harry's also does a good job with grilled meats, especially the steaks and veal chops, and while the pastas may not reach the pinnacle of noodledom, they are certainly up there in the lofty sphere. Desserts, too, are fine, but the cappuccino soufflé is exceptional, a must. Although Harry's is perfect for postmovie or -theater dining, it shouldn't be relegated exclusively to those occasions; it's a true and fine place to eat, as Papa might say. Dinner for two, with wine, costs about $90.

12/20 The Heritage
2640 Main St., Santa Monica
392-4956

CONTINENTAL/AMERICAN

Open Mon.-Fri. 11:30 a.m.-5 p.m. & 6 p.m.-10 p.m., Sat. 6 p.m.-10 p.m., Sun. 5 p.m.-10 p.m. All major cards.

At The Heritage (not Heritage, mind you, but *The* Heritage), one feels obliged to dress properly. Nearly a century ago, when this grand old Victorian was designed by one Summer P. Hunt, it was known as the Kyte House. In 1979 it became the western branch of The Chronicle restaurant (the remaining Chronicle is in Pasadena). Then just recently, the people responsible for the Saddle Peak Lodge, another dramatic structure, turned it into The Heritage. Its food is something of a gentrified reinterpretation of the rustic cooking at Saddle Peak. While you eat wild boar at Saddle Peak, at the Heritage things get no wilder than the broiled chopped buffalo steak and the wild honey with which the California quail is glazed. This cooking is both very American and very genteel. It's also very good, though it can be a bit, oh, saucy. We wouldn't have minded a tad more crispness in the crabmeat pancakes, or the potato blini with smoked salmon. And when broiled tuna is described on the menu as "rare," that's how we want it; perhaps we should have specified sushi-style rare. Still, overall, the food is quite flavorful and well prepated: fine braised veal shank, terrific steak tartare, excellent culotte steak broiled over bay leaves. It's worth noting that entrée prices, which are mostly in the mid-teens, include big plates with lots of side items. Vegetables can be ordered à la carte as well, though we found them wholly redundant. The Heritage has its roots in another era, when people ate big. And it hasn't given up those roots. Dinner for two, with wine, costs about $100.

Hotel Bel-Air
701 Stone Canyon Rd., Bel Air
472-1211
FRENCH
*Open Mon.-Sat. 7 a.m.-10:30 a.m., noon-2:30
p.m. & 6 p.m.-10:30 p.m., Sun. 11 a.m.-2:30
p.m. & 6 p.m.-10 p.m. All major cards.*

Some go to the grand and glorious Hotel Bel-Air for lunch. Some go for dinner. But most go for the weekend brunch, an event of unsurpassed elegance and charm. You must approach the experience with a certain amount of mental and physical preparation. You must dress properly, find a day on which you have plenty of time (for a leisurely meal and strolling the grounds to admire the myriad blooms like a lord) and choose your weather carefully. You should also be prepared to spend a proverbial arm and leg, for this is one of the most expensive brunches in town. You get to the Bel-Air by threading your way past some of the grand estates of L.A.; be prepared to give your car to a Ralph Lauren-esque parking attendant. Then you meander across a complex of small stone bridges, over ponds crowded with swans, to the main dining room, which, like everything at the Bel-Air, is easy to miss; this is not a land of neon signs or small stone jockeys pointing in the direction of the spa. At the Bel-Air, one is expected to simply know where things should be; if you don't know, you probably don't belong. The dining room is as elegant as we've ever seen, with bowers of flowers flowing out of monstrous vases and a fireplace crackling in one corner (despite the fact that the temperature outside may be in the 90s).

Brunch at the Bel-Air is inclusive, served in a manner best described as stately. You begin with a choice of juices or Champagne (try the tart tangerine juice). The appetizers run to some fair exotica: superb tortilla soup, mango fritters with lime crème fraîche, some of the best smoked salmon we've ever tasted with microbagels, a strudel of smoked chicken and ricotta. On the table is a basket of freshly baked croissants and pastries. By itself, this is brunch enough. But then there are the entrées to deal with: from the relative simplicity of cinnamon apple pancakes with walnut butter to what may be L.A.'s best chicken pot pie served with Cheddar-cheese twists, a lobster relleno fried in a wholly unique ancho chile–

cinnamon batter, crab and Swiss chard raviolis, even a fine turkey hash with poached eggs. After all this, dessert is wholly superfluous (there is a small add-on charge). The cost is serious, but so is the meal, so is the setting and so is the contentment felt as you drive back down to the hill to the real world. Brunch at the Hotel Bel-Air is not something we would have every weekend. But it's nice to feel rich now and again, for the same price as you might pay for a parking ticket in Beverly Hills. Brunch for two costs about $75.

 Hu's Szechwan Restaurant
10450 National Blvd., Palms
837-0252
CHINESE
*Open Sun.-Thurs. noon-2:30 p.m. & 5 p.m.-
9:30 p.m., Fri.-Sat. noon-2:30 p.m. & 5 p.m.-
10:30 p.m. Cards: MC, V.*

You don't have to venture to Monterey Park or Chinatown for wonderful Chinese food—you can find it on the westside in (of all places) Palms. Hu's bare-bones dining room is always full and almost always has a wait. Its popularity has never faded, because its Szechuan food has stayed terrific: fiery Szechuan dumplings, tender kung pao chicken, aromatic curried chicken, rich and pungent shrimp with a Szechuan tomato sauce, savory dried-fried string beans with ground pork, and a Mandarin chicken salad that is a bit sweet but is a perfect foil to the spicy dishes. There are some disappointments, mainly the too-sweet lemon chicken and the gooey "ants climbing a tree." The degree of hotness depends on the chef's daily whim; don't be too shy to request it extra hot. Bring your own beer and plan on spending a very reasonable $25 for two.

Hy's
10131 Constellation Ave.,
Century City
553-6000
AMERICAN/STEAKHOUSE
*Open Mon.-Fri. 11:30 a.m.-2:30 p.m. & 6 p.m.-
11 p.m., Sat. 6 p.m.-11 p.m. All major cards.*

For many years, Hy's was a large, relatively fancy, not very good Mexican restaurant, Señor Pico's. Then, briefly, it was a large, relatively fancy, mediocre French restaurant, the Princess. Now it's a large, relatively fancy, very good steakhouse. The first time we had a steak at Hy's, we thought it was the best steak we'd ever had in L.A.—maybe the best steak we'd ever had anywhere. But no Hy's steak since then has been its equal. Not that the steaks at Hy's have been poor. They're almost always good—very good. But none has been as celestial, as perfect, as that first one; the consistency here isn't quite what it is at Ruth's Chris Steak House. But Hy's has some advantages over other westside steakhouses. It's quieter and more pleasant. It has a better wine list. Some of its appetizers and nonsteak dishes are better than those generally found in a steakhouse—especially the Caesar salad, the rack of lamb roasted in a garlic cream sauce and some of the fresh fish. Vegetables can be done nicely, too, particularly the asparagus (but ask them to hold the hollandaise; it tasted like yellow library paste the last time we tried it). Steaks at Hy's have shriveled since our last edition and are now smaller than at the other major steakhouses in town. The restaurant used to serve a fifteen-ounce New York strip sirloin for $20.95; now the steak is thirteen ounces and it costs $21.95. Deflation and inflation simultaneously, no doubt. All the steaks are cooked over Hawaiian kiawe wood on an open grill, which is visible from most of the dining room. A full steak dinner for two, including wine, will cost about $135.

(14) Ike-Ichi
11951 Santa Monica Blvd., W.L.A.
477-1390
JAPANESE/SUSHI
Open Tues.-Thurs. 11:30 a.m.-2:30 p.m. & 5 p.m.-10 p.m., Fri. 11:30 a.m.-2:30 p.m. & 5 p.m.-11 p.m., Sat. 5 p.m.-11 p.m., Sun. 5 p.m.-10 p.m. Cards: MC, V.

To say that a Japanese restaurant should be good just because it's the offshoot of a restaurant in Japan is a specious argument at best. But still, there's always the hope that the connection will create some sort of special magic. And in the case of Ike-Ichi, which dates back nine generations to a sushi bar in Osaka, something quite special is afoot. Ike-Ichi isn't the best-looking sushi bar in town; it certainly doesn't compare with the high-tech elegance of Katsu. But it's comfortable enough, and its food is a pleasure to behold. The chefs, Tatsu and Taka, know their knives and their fish, and

they enjoy a good bottle of beer. They strike the perfect balance of reserve and affability—especially after a couple of beers. But there's more to Ike-Ichi than fun and games. For starters, there are excellent appetizers: the aoyagi-sumisoaye, for instance, a lovely dish of orange clam in a fiercely pungent vinegar and miso sauce; the eggplant dengaku, which is simply broiled Japanese eggplant tossed with miso; and the elegantly crispy soft-shell crab. You'll find sushi here that is rarely encountered anywhere else in town. If you want tuna, you'll find not only the standard-issue, lean maguro, but also the fattier, highly prized o-toro and chu-toro. There are clams upon clams—jumbo clams, orange clams, cockles and blood clams; and row upon row of roe—uni, salmon eggs, herring eggs, smelt eggs, flying-fish eggs and cod roe. And there are all kinds of unusual fish—kohada, shako, white salmon (extraordinary!) and ankimo (anglerfish liver; not for the amateur sushi eater). At the end of your meal, you draw a folded paper from a bowl, which allows you to win a T-shirt, a beer or even a free meal. It's redundant, because the simple act of eating at Ike-Ichi makes you a winner. Dinner for two, with sake, costs about $50.

(13) Ivy at the Shore
1541 Ocean Ave., Santa Monica
393-3113
AMERICAN
Open daily 11:30 a.m.-2:30 p.m. & 6 p.m.-11 p.m. All major cards.

Ivy at the Shore is sort of a postmodern Trader Vic's, except the food's good. It attracts a celebrity crowd and it's a major hangout and watering hole, packed to the rafters every night. The decor is what you might get if you crossed Miss Sadie Thompson with avant-wacky architect Brian Murphy—a sort of sophisticated bamboo shack, with vintage Hawaiian shirts hanging on the walls next to some Very Important Art. The lounge area is quite comfortable, with bamboo-and-tropical-print sofas and chairs; it's a good place to enjoy a late-night dessert or drink and get an eyeful of people-watching. As for the restaurant itself, it's really much better than it has to be. The optimum place to sit is the semi-enclosed outdoor patio, directly across the street from the Santa Monica Pier and the Pacific (though you have a much better view of the former than the latter—along with a view of the considerable homeless population outside, a tragic juxtaposition of opulence and poverty), but the main dining room is where the buzz of the biz is most palpable. Owners Lynn von Kersting and Richard Irving (who began their miniempire with L.A. Desserts, which begat The Ivy on Robertson, which begat Ivy at the Shore, which begat Indigo Seas, a home-furnishings emporium that's a design extension of the restaurants) haven't strayed too far from the original Ivy's menu; why mess with a good thing?

The salads are generous and delicious, particularly the Caesar, and the crabcakes are the best in town (served with very good black beans), despite their minuscule size. The Cajun pizza is a real hit, as are the fresh-fish dishes, whether they're simply grilled or done Louisiana-style. For carnivores, the prime rib and meatloaf are excellent, and the side orders of crackling Maui-onion rings and crispy french fries are a must. Desserts are delicious (especially the tarte tatin), and the tropical drinks are guaranteed to give you a world-class headache the next day (they can be ordered virgin). What we really love about Ivy at the Shore, though, is its Sunday brunch: light, puffy pancakes, fluffy omelets and a good selection of salads, which can be enjoyed while sitting out in the cool Santa Monica breeze, watching the passing parade. Dinner for two, with drinks, costs about $100.

12/20 Jimmy's

201 S. Moreno Dr., Beverly Hills
879-2394
CONTINENTAL
Open Mon.-Fri. 11:30 a.m.-3 p.m. & 5:30 p.m.- midnight, Sat. 5:30 p.m.-midnight. All major cards.

Lunch at Jimmy's is like the theater on opening night. Amid the incessant murmur of an aviary, people look at one another, recognize one another and speak to one another with the nods that the chic have perfected, while the women judge out of the corners of their eyes the clothes and jewels of their rivals, and the powerful affect that inimitable air when getting their Rolls at the door, with the security of knowing they feel at home wherever they go. If you want to understand the eternal Beverly Hills comedy in one glance, you must come here. The chinoise decor is

charming, but at the same time it has that nearly invisible touch of bad taste that gives chic restaurants their warmth and gaiety. If you have the chance to get a table under one of the large white parasols in the garden courtyard, you will be so happy you won't notice that over 30 minutes have passed and your first dish still hasn't arrived. It's just as well, because the lobster has no more taste than the crab; mercifully there is a good sauce to wake them up. The duck salad is delicious, the thick, fresh salmon in a light peppercorn sauce is delightful, and the simple rack of lamb is flawless in both quality of meat and preparation, if a bit dull. Perhaps you have understood that Jimmy's isn't a restaurant, but rather a club for beautiful people who only eat because it's time to. Fortunately, the food is much better than it needs to be. The immensely successful owner, Jimmy Murphy, who was maître d' at The Bistro, can consult his bank account with no worry. He should, however, advise his captains that a little more warmth and a lot more attentiveness would encourage his less famous customers to return sooner (the servers, however, can be charming). About $75 for two for lunch and $140 for dinner, with wine.

12/20 Kaktus

400 N. Cañon Dr., Beverly Hills
271-1856
MEXICAN/SOUTHWESTERN
Open Mon.-Thurs. 11:30 a.m.-4 p.m. & 5:30 p.m.-10 p.m., Fri.-Sat. 11:30 a.m.-4 p.m. & 5:30 p.m.-11 p.m., Sun. 5:30 p.m.-10 p.m. Cards: AE, MC, V.

Those seeking authentic Mexican food usually have to head east, to such places as East L.A.'s La Parrilla or San Gabriel's El Emperador Maya. But those of you who break out in hives when you venture east of La Cienega need not fear—you can find reasonably authentic Mexican food (along with a good dose of inauthentic Southwestern) at Kaktus in Beverly Hills. Of course, you'll have to put up with the all-too-Beverly-Hills crowd: women in décolletage ensembles and men in $400 sweaters, most of whom are table-hopping, kissing one another and radiating the aura of big deals about to close. And you'll have to put aside the concerns you'll certainly have about the silliness of the name. Kaktus is crowded, bright and lively, with an open kitchen and a decor resembling an upscale coffee shop. But despite the crowd, the location and the name, Kaktus serves surprisingly good food.

The first thing you'll try, apart from the drinks (the margaritas are run-of-the-mill), is reason enough to come here: a basket of warm, thick, just-made flour tortillas, served with a big crock of terrific salsa. These tortillas are served in lieu of chips, and they're a welcome change—roll one up, dunk it in the salsa and enter Mexican-food heaven. Also worth a drive here from any part of town are the flans, particularly the sublime sweet-potato flan. In fact, we could visit Kaktus for a beer, a couple of baskets of tortillas and an order of flan and go home supremely content. But that's not to say that the middle parts of the meal aren't worthwhile. They may not be as memorable, but they're just fine. Starters include tangy, tasty ceviche made with swordfish; tamalitos, three tiny, deliciously sweet corn tamales; and caldo loco, a stewy soup with chicken, rice, avocado, cheese, onions and peppers. Entrées cover the basics—fresh, tasty chiles rellenos, soft tacos filled with carnitas, chicken or beef—and venture on to such fancy dishes as filete chipotle, a thick, tender filet of beef grilled with a layer of Ranchero cheese on top (like a haute-Mex cheeseburger), placed atop a couple of tortillas and covered in a deliciously spicy and pungent chile sauce. And, of course, seafood lovers are attended to, with such dishes as brochetta de camarones marinados, a generous row of fat shrimp soaked in a tasty lime-cilantro marinade, charbroiled and served with a pot of clarified garlic butter. Two will spend about $55 for dinner, with beer.

11/20 Knoll's Black Forest Inn
2454 Wilshire Blvd., Santa Monica
395-2212
GERMAN
Open Tues.-Fri. 11:30 a.m.-2:30 p.m. & 5:30 p.m.-10:30 p.m., Sat.-Sun. 5:30 p.m.-10:30 p.m. All major cards.

This doesn't look or feel much like a Black Forest inn; the thin veneer of German decor (beer mugs, Tyrolian clocks, deer trophies) doesn't quite disguise the former resident's taste. Hilde, the charming hostess, greets you in native dress, as do the waiters, who seem to be primarily Iranian. But the ambience is warm and cheerful, and everyone has a very good time. Try the herring with apples and onions, coated in thick sour cream, or the equally good sausage salad to start; although entrées come with soup and salad, we cannot truthfully recommend them. Main courses tend toward meat, potatoes and red cabbage. One of our favorites is the roast veal for two, served sliced from the bone at table, with plenty of second helpings. Roast pork is also good, as is the Bratwurst and Knackwurst. If you can manage, the heavy artillery is waiting in the wings—German pastries and cakes, each one richer than the last. There is a comprehensive list of German wines; some of the Rieslings have a subdued fruitiness that is perfectly suited to this cuisine. About $75 for two, with wine.

 Koutoubia
2116 Westwood Blvd., Westwood
475-0729
MOROCCAN
Open Tues.-Sun. 6 p.m.-9:30 p.m. Cards: AE, MC, V.

There are dinners, and then there are dining adventures. And by adventure, we don't mean getting up from the table and wondering if you'll wake up at 3 a.m. with heartburn . . . or food poisoning. Michel Ohayon makes every meal at Koutoubia an adventure. And a pleasure. He greets his guests with a big smile and a native Moroccan costume, a floor-length *djellaba*, and you eat in native Moroccan style—seated or reclining on soft cushions, sofas and hassocks around a large, circular brass plate that serves as a table. The waiter comes by before your first course to pour warm water over your hands and give you a large towel to dry with. You keep the towel and use it as a napkin, which you'll need because you're encouraged to eat with your hands—picking up the food with the thumb and first two fingers of your right hand, to be precise, or using the anise-flavored bread to help scoop it up. The colorful cushions, carpets and walls (draped with fabric and designed to look like the inside of a Moroccan tent) lend an air of charm and mystery to the evening. On weekends, a belly dancer undulates her way between the tables, and if you really want a treat, Ohayon will bring the entire show (plus a live camel) to your home and set things up in your backyard.

Our favorite dish at Koutoubia is the b'stilla, a light, flaky pie (sort of) filled with pieces of chicken (or squab) and almonds and topped with cinnamon and powdered sugar. A warning: it's extremely hot, so resist the temptation to immediately stick your fingers through the crust and into the pie. Our second-favorite dish is the spicy merguez sausage, served with couscous. We can also recommend the lamb, the lemon chicken, the brains and the assorted Moroccan salads— beets, marinated carrots, a mixture of eggplant, olive oil, tomatoes and peppers and another of chopped onion, cucumber and tomatoes. For some reason, the fish here is not generally as good as the other dishes. But your best bet, here as in so many other good restaurants, is to ask for recommendations. Ohayon likes to please. Ask him to recommend a wine, too. He has a few older Burgundies that go particularly well with the lamb. You'll probably spend about $80 for dinner for two, with wine—more if you order a multi-course feast and a bottle or two of those Burgundies.

11/20 The Lobster
1602 Ocean Ave., Santa Monica
394-9751
SEAFOOD
Open Tues.-Sun. 11:30 a.m.-10:30 p.m. Cards: CB, DC, MC, V.

This odd little shack, with its NO BARE FEET sign outside the door, has sat seemingly forever at the foot of the Santa Monica Pier. On summer nights the line for a table can be endless, but the theater of the sea is pleasantly distracting. Once seated, you're confronted with an enormous list of seafood to choose from, some fresh, some not: rainbow trout and catfish; mahi mahi and black cod; shark and swordfish; fried oysters and cracked crab; shrimp Louie and shrimp Creole; and, of course, several varieties of lobster—Creole, thermidor, broiled, sautéed and cold. The meals are huge; dinners come with coleslaw, superb sourdough bread, a seafood cocktail, red clam chowder, french fries or a baked potato, vegetables, dessert (ice cream, pie or sherbet) *and* coffee, tea or milk. Thus, for $14.95 you can get a Florida lobster dinner, and for $15.25 you can get a broiled salmon dinner. Only one detail mars this dining Utopia: the fish just isn't that good. Broiled lob-

ster is tough, dry and lacking flavor. The cold seafood plate bears copious amounts of lobster, crab and shrimp, but the flavor is nothing remarkable. But the onion rings are perfect— and it's a great deal of a meal when you're feeling beachy, casual and loose. About $55 for dinner for two, with wine.

9/20 Louise's Trattoria
1008 Montana Ave., Santa Monica
394-8888
342 N. Beverly Dr., Beverly Hills
274-4271
10645 Pico Blvd., W.L.A.
475-6084
264 26th St., Santa Monica
451-5001
ITALIAN
Open daily 11 a.m.-11 p.m. Cards: AE, MC, V.

Louise's just keeps growing and growing, each branch more popular than the next. Well, we're absolutely befuddled by this mediocre chain's success—especially since the folks responsible for Louise's jettisoned two very good eateries that they also owned, Ruby B's (where the Pico branch is now located) and the Beverly Restaurant & Market (now the Beverly Hills Louise's, and where chef Tony DiLembo, presently at Indigo, plied his trade). We suppose we shouldn't be so naive; the trattorias are absolute gold mines. The original two branches, on 26th Street and Montana Avenue, were legendary for the waits to get a table. Yes, the food is cheap and plentiful, and the atmosphere lively and cheery, and families with young children can dine there without fear of rebuke, but the food ranges from just decent to downright inedible. On one visit, we had a plate of pasta with olive oil, garlic, mushrooms and Parmesan—a simple dish, to be sure—that not only looked like one of those plastic Japanese food-display models, but the entire gummy mass came up from the plate when lifted with a fork. The pesto sauce is heavy and gooey, the entrées not worth bothering with, and the desserts undistinguished, too often tasting overly refrigerated. The best items here are the pizzas (sometimes a tad heavy but nonetheless very tasty), the salads and the fresh bread. Obviously, Louise's has hit upon a formula that works—the inexpensive neighborhood restaurant with a menu that reads well, a restaurant that gives the impression of being much better than it really is. It serves the same purpose as California Pizza Kitchen, yet CPK does a far superior job. Dinner for two, with wine, runs about $40.

8/20 Malibu Adobe

23410 Cross Creek Rd., Malibu
456-2021

SOUTHWESTERN

Open Sun.-Thurs. 11:30 a.m.-2:30 p.m. & 5:30 p.m.-10 p.m., Fri.-Sat. 11:30 a.m.-2:30 p.m. & 5:30 p.m.-11 p.m. All major cards.

Here we are in Santa-Fe-by-the-Sea, at Malibu Adobe. It's an *Architectural Digest* dream of adobeisms: saltillo tile floors, white plaster walls, lodgepole-beamed ceilings, cowhide bar chairs and—what's this?—pictures of dudes hanging ten! Why, we're not in Santa Fe at all! At the bar is a platoon of giggling gals in acid-washed denim miniskirts being pursued by a couple of huge, blow-dried professional athletes. A few tables over is Stallone's ex, Sasha. Around us are tan, trim men in $200 sweaters, accompanied by women with leather outfits and weaved hair. Why are they here? Not because the food's any good, because it isn't. They're here because it's a great-looking place designed by a great-looking actress (Ali McGraw), whose involvement in the place attracted great-looking people who don't want to bother with the riffraff down the coast at Gladstone's. They're delighted that Malibu now has a handsome spot where they can listen to live new-age-ish jazz, meet their friends, drink watery, slushy margaritas, look good and, oh yes, eat.

Granted, we're biased about the food, because with a few notable exceptions, we think Southwestern cuisine has its limitations. Especially the kind of Southwestern offered at Malibu Adobe: a different salsa comes with every dish, each one tasting of little more than just "hot." The only dish we liked here is one of the few that has neither salsa nor chiles: the pleasantly earthy quesadilla with wild mushrooms, Sonoma goat cheese, roasted pine nuts, scallions and herbs. The rest of the food is totally uninteresting. Grilled chicken flautas were served with an unpleasantly bitter ancho-tomatillo sauce. Marinated pork loin was as dry as adobe, served with a banal roasted red pepper-almond-chipotle salsa. Also dry was the grilled ahi tuna topped with a poblano pesto, a misguided experiment that allowed

the chile's hotness to completely obscure the delicate basil flavor. And the apple tart, apparently made with dried apples, was as dusty as the Texas plains. But as we said, food isn't the point here. It would just distract the crowd from looking at one another, looking at the decor and looking good. Dinner for two, with drinks, is about $75.

The Mandarin

430 N. Camden Dr., Beverly Hills
272-0267

CHINESE

Open Mon.-Sat. 11:30 a.m.-11 p.m., Sun. 5 p.m.-11 p.m. All major cards.

Among aficionados of things culinary, Chinese food isn't mere sustenance, it's downright totemic, often as close to a religion as many agnostics get. The search for the quintessential Chinese restaurant can be tantamount to a nomadic search for the Holy Grail; when an eatery that American Mandarins deem to be the latest best is discovered, it attracts more loyal minions to its apse than even Jerry Falwell could once attract, and it becomes as devout a place of worship as any synagogue, its rafters ringing with as much joy and praise as any Baptist church. This constituted part of the reason why we looked forward to revisiting the revamped Mandarin in Beverly Hills. The Mandarin had been a venerable force in Chinese cuisine since 1975, when Madame Cecilia Chiang opened a branch of her upscale San Francisco restaurant down south. It was met with great and deserved acclaim, and it was one of the first Chinese restaurants to elevate L.A.'s Chung King–dulled taste buds into another realm. But by the time The Mandarin was ravaged by fire a couple of years back, it had lost some of its éclat. The once-elegant rooms looked a little tired, and while the food remained excellent, the menu was in need of some revamping. Madame Chiang handed the restaurant's reins over to her most charming and creative son, Phillip (proprietor of the chic-funky, minimalist Mandarette, which serves sassy, spiffed-up versions of Chinese street food), who wisely kept The Mandarin's good bones intact and gave both the decor and the food a flattering face-lift. Physically, the place has been opened up and stripped down; it's still as lovely as ever but now looks less fussy and more inviting.

As for the menu, many of the items are available in "small tastes" portions, which allows you to sample a number of taste treats (beware if you're on a budget, though: these little tidbits tot up quickly). From this list, don't miss the minced chicken in a lettuce cup, a perfect summer dish that's cool and crispy. The fried shrimp in a puffy batter are wonderfully fresh and nongreasy—a textbook example of how batter-fried foods should be prepared. The spicy boiled wonton sprinkled with chopped scallions and vegetable preserves are light and piquant, but for us the paramount Mandarin appetizer is a marvelous dish of glazed walnuts served cold on a bed of fried spinach leaves. This dish is an amazement. The fried spinach is as dry and transparent as parchment, almost cellophanelike, crumpling as easily as an autumn leaf. The walnuts nestled on this rustling bed are honeyed and chewily crisp—we could eat this dish forever. . . . The Chinese chicken salad is what Chinese chicken salad should be, instead of the soggy, bastardized version that's trickled down to every Coco's and its ilk in town. The dumplings and breads, such as the steamed threaded biscuit sprinkled with sweet-smoky Virginia ham, are delicious. The Mandarin also does one of the best Peking ducks in town; just remember to order it at least two hours in advance. Though at $35 it isn't cheap, it's as good as it gets. The meat is larded with just enough fat to give it a full-bodied flavor without being greasy, and the skin is crisper than potato chips. We have just one small complaint about the place: why does it charge a steep $5.75 for a small dish of pickled vegetables—the type that arrive at the table gratis in just about every Chinese restaurant in Monterey Park? Dinner for two, with wine, runs about $80.

11/20 Kate Mantilini

9101 Wilshire Blvd., Beverly Hills
278-3699
AMERICAN
Open Mon.-Thurs. 7:30 a.m.-2 a.m., Fri. 7:30 a.m.-3 a.m., Sat. noon-3 a.m., Sun. 10 a.m.-midnight. Cards: AE, MC, V.

Named for a hardboiled female fight promoter in the '40s, Kate Mantilini is Hamburger Hamlet queen Marilyn Lewis's jump on the all-American bandwagon. Lewis has more or less successfully pulled off an incongruous marriage: a large, straightforward, Musso & Frank–style menu of American food circa 1947 (with white-aproned waiters to match) and a dramatically modern, almost stark interior created by L.A.'s hippest architectural team, Morphosis. Though the food is no more than decent, Kate Mantilini has some good things going for it. For one, it's open until at least 2 a.m., making it one of L.A.'s very few late-night spots with edible food. For another, it's well located on the corner of Wilshire and Doheny. And, best of all, it serves wonderfully huge bowls of steaming cappuccino. Otherwise, expect generous breakfasts, simple roast chicken (which can be overly greasy), grilled steaks, chops and liver and onions, back-to-basics hamburgers, retro salads, homey sides (mashed potatoes, french fries) and deep-dish apple pie. The friendly waiters and busboys are more than attentive—you run the risk of having your plate whisked away if you set your fork down. Your tab will vary considerably depending on what you order: anywhere from $12 a person for a snack and a cappuccino to $45 a head for a complete steak dinner with wine.

Maple Drive

345 N. Maple Dr., Beverly Hills
274-9800
AMERICAN
Open Mon.-Fri. 11:30 a.m.-2:30 p.m. & 5:30 p.m.-11 p.m., Sat.-Sun. 5:30 p.m.-11 p.m. All major cards.

Show-biz-restaurateur Tony Bill chose quite an odd location for his second restaurant venture, Maple Drive—but then, everyone thought his *succès d'estime*, 72 Market Street, was out in the hinterlands when it opened in Venice. Bill has proven once again that he's crazy like a fox; Maple Drive became an instant gathering spot for the chic I-only-shop-at-Maxfield crowd. Maple Drive is housed in a sleek, granite-faced office building in the light-industrial area of Beverly Hills just around the corner from Il Giardino. The multileveled room is a triumph of Bauhaus/Corbusier/Schindler design warmed by the prodigious use of exotic woods, including a gorgeous bird's-eye maple bar and tabletops with intricate marquetry and inlays. In fact, the overall decor could perhaps be characterized as neo-Flintstonian, with bold forms of steel and concrete erupting through all that wood. At this writing, with the place brand-spanking new, it has hit the same level on the trend barometer as Bruce Marder's boîtes, though the Maple Drive crowd is a little older than DC3's and Rebecca's and less haute-artsy than the West Beach Café's (or 72 Market's, for that matter). It's basically the same demographic: mon-eyed, status-conscious and anxious to be part of the happening-at-the-moment scene.

At the time of this writing, Maple Drive was only a couple of weeks old, and the kitchen had not yet hit its stride. The menu reads beautifully, with such American/Asian/Med-iterranean/Franco-Italian dishes as duck foie gras sautéed with apples, turnips and turnip greens; grilled quail with string beans and mixed lettuces; and leg of lamb with Sicilian and Kalamata olives. But the execution isn't quite up to the descriptions—at least not yet. The fried calamari were on the soggy side, the risotti were raw tasting and lacked flavor, and the promising oyster ragoût with oyster plant and oyster mushrooms was a misbegotten mess. But while on the subject of oysters, we must add that there's a wonderful oyster bar (at which anything on the menu can be or-dered), with a good selection of raws. Since executive chef Leonard Schwartz does such a good job at 72 Market Street, things should change for the better; we have high hopes for this one. For now, we'll hold back on a rating. Dinner for two, with wine, will run about $125.

11/20 Marix

118 Entrada Dr., Pacific Palisades
459-8596
MEXICAN
Open Sun.-Thurs. 11 a.m.-11 p.m., Fri.-Sat. 11 a.m.-1 a.m. Cards: MC, V.

Like its West Hollywood counterpart, this '80s-style cantina is always packed to the gills. The reasons for this are plentiful: a great location (just off Pacific Coast Highway north of Sunset), low prices (entrées for about $7), tasty, trendy Mexican food (fajitas, Mexican pizzas, blue-corn tortilla casseroles) and free-flowing drinks (good margaritas, Mexican beer). It all adds up to a cheerful party atmo-sphere: pitchers of margaritas are passed around, fresh tortilla chips are devoured, con-versation is lively, and the noise level is loud.

The food is satisfying and sloppy, which suits this hang-loose ambience. You won't go wrong with the fajitas, a sizzling platter of grilled vegetables, beans and chicken, beef or shrimp. No reservations are taken, so expect a long wait—it may turn out to be the best part of the evening. Dinner for two, with margari-tas, will run about $35.

12/20 The Marquis West

3110 Santa Monica Blvd., Santa Monica
828-4567
ITALIAN/CONTINENTAL
Open Mon.-Fri. 11:30 a.m.-2:30 p.m. & 5:30 p.m.-10:30 p.m., Sat.-Sun. 5:30 p.m.-10:30 p.m. All major cards.

If you're under 40, this looks, feels and tastes like the kind of place your parents liked: heavy, substantial, safe and big, with crests on the walls, dark booths, a wine-cellar room for private parties, and people who look like Ron-ald and Nancy Reagan's friends (if a bit less chic) drinking Manhattans. Copious portions of food are expensive and well prepared, though hardly brilliant enough to be exciting. Much attention is paid to seafood—mussels, calamari, oysters, clams, shrimp and crab for appetizers; lobster, frog's legs, salmon, more calamari and various fresh fish specials for entrées. There's also the Friday special, bouil-labaisse, which happens to be quite good, its aromatic broth tasting faintly of anise (though it lacks the classic garlicky rouille). Pastas are competently done, particularly the green fet-tuccine with Italian sausage and the linguine puttanesca, done here with capers, olives, mushrooms, garlic and chili pepper. Caesar salad is prepared tableside, and all the right ingredients are there, although the croutons seem to come from a box. The wine list is as large and varied as the menu, with some good Italian bottles. About $100 for two, with wine.

11/20 Maryland Crab House

2424 W. Pico Blvd., Santa Monica
450-5555
SEAFOOD
Open Tues.-Thurs. noon-2:30 p.m. & 5 p.m.-9 p.m., Fri. noon-2 p.m. & 5 p.m.-10 p.m., Sat. noon-10 p.m., Sun. noon-9 p.m. Cards: CB, DC, MC, V.

A thoroughly agreeable, friendly, family-run seafood house that is, to the best of our knowledge, the only place in L.A. to get hot spiced hard-shell crabs from Eastern waters. If you order them—by the dozen—the waiter will spread your table with brown paper, hand you a bib and a mallet and let you go to it. Or you can choose to be lazy—with the backfin crabcakes, deviled crab, broiled fresh fish of the day, one of the broiled, garlicky Norfolk preparations of shrimp, crab or scallops, or one of the amazingly light and greaseless fried offerings—and your table will sport paper mats and cloth napkins. Main dishes come with homemade rum buns and rolls; dill pickles; a choice of baked potato, french fries or a potato mashed with sour cream and chives and topped with melted Cheddar; and a choice of crunchy homemade coleslaw, fresh vegetables of the day or the salad bar. For the foolish and for families, there are hamburgers, steaks and chicken. From $60 to $75 for two, with wine.

9/20 Matteo's

2321 Westwood Blvd., W.L.A.
475-4521
ITALIC
Open Tues.-Sun. 5 p.m.-midnight. Cards: AE, MC, V.

The night to show up at this affable, old-fashioned Italian restaurant is Sunday, when the stars descend on Matteo's in droves. Looking around the restaurant—which feels like a private club on Sunday night—you'll see enough famous faces to last you for weeks, many of them belonging to fading stars who gather here to curse the new generation of upstarts who are on display at Spago or DC3. Working the room is really the only reason to go to Matteo's; the food is merely an after-thought. Dishes are representative of the Italian food of the '50s, named for the many regulars: pork chops pizzaiola Steve Allen; cauliflower mostacciole Walter Matthau; manicotti Dolly Parton; and spaghetti bolognese Ernest Borgnine. But no one pays attention to the food here; they're too busy blowing kisses across the room—which happens so often that the place can resemble a kissy shooting gallery. Dinner for two, with wine, costs around $95.

11/20 Matteo's: A Little Taste of Hoboken

2323 Westwood Blvd., Westwood
474-1109
ITALIAN
Open Mon. 11 a.m.-10 p.m., Tues.-Sat. 11 a.m.-8 p.m. Cards: MC, V.

Few who have eaten in the Italian restaurants of Hoboken would deny that there's a special something that can be referred to as the Hoboken Style. It's there—and it's also here, at this small, casual diner next to Matteo's. For Matteo's to open such a snappy, inexpensive, easy-to-drop-by place is a little like L'Ermitage opening a next-door hot dog stand. Where there are tablecloths at Matteo's, you eat off Formica at Hoboken. Where the lights are dimmed at Matteo's, you could perform brain surgery on the tables at Hoboken. Where service is fairly proper at Matteo's, it's affable to the point of comical at Hoboken. Where you might have to plan a few days in advance to go to Matteo's, Hoboken is the sort of place at which you drop by on a whim. This is Italian soul food, served in an atmosphere where it seems just fine to pick your teeth after the meal.

The Hoboken culinary style is well defined at A Little Taste, though it doesn't necessarily obviate a journey to the source (something food-wise New Yorkers often do, traveling into the belly of the beast on the PATH trains that zip beneath the Hudson River). The style is mostly southern Italian and Sicilian—one does not find carpaccio, risotto with porcini and vitello tonnato in Hoboken. Red sauce abounds, as do massive, extraordinarily excessive portions. No one leaves a Hoboken-style restaurant hungry; usually you're not hungry the next day either. If you want to feel pleasantly gorged, begin with the superb broccoli salad (which is nothing but steamed broccoli in a garlic dressing), the heavily breaded stuffed artichoke, the scungilli (a sort of giant snail) salad or the fried calamari (one of the best in town). Progress to the sausage, pepper and potato hero, which is a totem of heartburn. If you dare, continue through the thick, unutterably rich lasagne, manicotti, baked rigatoni or baked eggplant. Conclude with spumone or cannoli. Trust us, you'll dream afterward of Hoboken, though Alka-Seltzer may help. Dinner for two, with wine, costs about $30.

Michael's
1150 3rd St., Santa Monica
451-0843
AMERICAN/CALIFORNIAN

Open Mon.-Fri. noon-2 p.m. & 6:30 p.m.-10 p.m., Sat.-Sun. 10:30 a.m.-2 p.m. & 6 p.m.-10 p.m. All major cards.

The food at Michael's may be more difficult to evaluate fairly than the food at any other first-rate restaurant in Los Angeles. Why? Because there are so many other factors that inevitably intrude on one's judgment here. To begin with, there's the setting; the garden at Michael's may be the prettiest spot to eat in the entire city—especially on a warm summer evening or at lunchtime. (In fact, brunch at Michael's on Saturday or Sunday is a delightful meal; be sure to order the pork sandwich with molasses.) If we included ambience in our ratings, Michael's would merit a 16, maybe more. On the other hand, prices were much too high for what you got; if we considered value in our ratings, Michael's would probably have rated only a 12. But as noted in the introduction, rankings reflect *only* the quality of the cooking, and the cooking here has become both predictable and uneven. To give credit where it is due, Michael's was a pioneer in what has come to be known as "California cuisine." But in the decade since the restaurant opened, Michael McCarty—who once spoke of himself proudly as "the chef," even though he didn't actually do the cooking—now calls himself "a businessman/restaurateur." Indeed. He has restaurants in New York, Washington and Denver, and he's building a luxury hotel on the beach in Santa Monica and . . . well, one senses that he just doesn't pay as much attention to the kitchen as he did when Michael's was his only enterprise. The problem may well be that McCarty believes what he has often said—that it doesn't matter who's cooking; *he's* really the chef. Well, back when he had Ken Frank, Jonathan Waxman, Mark Peel and other top-flight talent in the kitchen, he could get away with that. No more.

Not that the food is bad at Michael's. It isn't. Most of it is good, and some of it is excellent. The Norwegian salmon with chervil and the swordfish with yellow tomatoes and basil vinaigrette could make a fish-lover of almost anyone. The pork tenderloin with dou-ble-blanched garlic is even better, and most of the birds are superb, particularly the duck with port and figs, and the squab with foie gras, ginger and scallions in a rich Pinot Noir sauce. But virtually every dish comes with the same assortment of vegetables (don't some dishes go better with one vegetable than another?), and the pastas tend to be overcooked; those served in cream sauces often end up tasting almost like porridge. Given the rash of innovative cuisine that can be found in Los Angeles these days, one is left with a sense that Michael's is just coasting much of the time, trying to get by on its reputation and a little razzle-dazzle on the menu. Dishes often have so many ingredients you'd think the chef is trying to see how many he can crowd into one recipe without laughing. (How about "spaghettini with Chicago sweetbreads, shiitake and tree-mushroom cream sauce, red and yellow peppers, baby asparagus, fresh herbs and pine nuts"?) Also, there's something a bit too precious about listing the origin of so many ingredients; we know that Norwegian salmon is among the best in the world (along with Scottish salmon), but what's so special about "Chicago sweetbreads," "Lancaster saddle of rabbit" and (honest!) "Hackensack bresaola"? Is this McCarty the businessman/promoter or McCarty the chef/restaurateur at work? Michael is a promoter; make no mistake about that. Many people are put off by his manner. They find him arrogant. We often find his cockiness and candor refreshing; we like him. But Michael was never candid about what seemed to bother people most about his restaurant: the high prices. He simply denied that his prices were all that high, which was a bit like Wilt Chamberlain denying that he is all that tall. So Michael finally swallowed his pride and lowered his prices . . . twice. First, he cut the automatic service charge from 18 percent to 15 percent and eliminated the set prices of $16 for appetizers and $32 for main courses. In their place, he instituted a menu with slightly lower prices in each category, then cut those prices again, by almost one third. Now, appetizers average slightly less less than $12, and main courses average about $22—considerably less than some of the other fancy spots in town. Desserts, which used to average $11, now average $8.50. So Michael's is no longer among the most expensive restaurants in Los

Angeles. It will be interesting to see how long that remains true.

The wine list at Michael's is excellent in both its Californian and French selections, although it's not as reasonable as it once was. There are, however, several half bottles on the list, which is more than one can say for most restaurants in this country. If you have an appetizer, main course, dessert, coffee and modest bottle of wine, you'll spend upward of $170 a couple—more if you take advantage of the wine list and order a good bottle.

12/20 Neptune's Net

42505 Pacific Coast Hwy., Malibu
457-3095
SEAFOOD
Open daily 11 a.m.-8 p.m. (though hours vary). No cards.

The quintessential California beachfront restaurant is found at the northernmost outpost of Los Angeles County, just a short distance below the Ventura County Line. In fact, to many, this overgrown shack, which is properly named Neptune's Net, is known as County Line. Across the highway from County Line is Leo Carrillo State Beach and its ample supply of surfers, many of whom can be found at Neptune's Net, drinking beer, eating french fries and digging happily into mounds of shrimp, crab, clams, oysters and lobster, along with corn on the cob and some of the best clam chowder this side of the Saint Lawrence Seaway. This is a rough-and-ready sort of oceanfront seafood restaurant, where you have to do everything yourself and don't mind it one bit. The routine here is a simple one: you head for the tank room, where you order shrimp (like olives, they come large, jumbo and colossal), lobster (both Eastern and Western), crab (rock and king), clams and oysters, all by the pound. Corn costs 75 cents an ear; chowder is sold by the pint. You pay for your food, then head for the general store next door, where you can order drinks, along with baskets of deep-fried shrimp, oysters, clams, scallops, fish and french fries. You wait for your order at one of the long, gnarly wooden tables on the deck. And when your number is finally called out, you find yourself confronted with an array of unwieldy paper plates. The plastic utensils require some skill, particularly when it comes to picking the meat

out of a lobster. Amenities are few. And easily washable clothing is highly recommended, for this is the sort of food that gets all over you; these most memorable of meals are sloppy, over-the-edge and hedonistic. And as such, County Line attracts a broad cross-section of eaters, from the Porsche set to pickup-truck drivers who have gun racks an old dog hunkering in the truck bed. The Beach Boys might have wished they all could be California girls; we only wish all California seafood restaurants could be like this one. Dinner for two, with beer, costs about $40.

12/20 Ocean Avenue Seafood

1401 Ocean Ave., Santa Monica
394-5669
SEAFOOD
Open daily 11:30 a.m.-2:30 p.m. & 5:30 p.m.- 11 p.m. All major cards.

When this bustling, optimistically upscale seafood restaurant/oyster bar opened a few years ago, it got off to about as bad a start as any restaurant in recent memory. Our first meal there was so dreadful that we went back a few nights later, just to make sure we hadn't dreamed the whole thing. Unfortunately, we hadn't. Aside from dishes that were either cooked to mush or served still cold, one of our most memorable plates was an artichoke, a simple artichoke, that arrived as hard as a rock. If a restaurant can't cook an artichoke, it certainly can't cook a piece of fish. But Ocean Avenue has managed to do what few restaurants have: turn itself around. It is now one of the better seafood restaurants in a town where there are no really great ones, just a handful of good ones. Service has improved tremendously (at our earlier visits, we had to keep reminding our waiter what we had ordered), the atmosphere seems a lot more cheery, and the kitchen turns out an impressive selection of crab tacos, New England clam chowder, smoked Hawaiian ahi with a biting horseradish cream sauce, crisp crabcakes and a fine blackened catfish filet. This is still neither New York's Grand Central Oyster Bar nor San Francisco's Tadich Grill. But what it is, is just fine—until something better comes along. Dinner for two, with wine, costs about $70.

Opera
1551 Ocean Ave., Santa Monica
393-9224
MEDITERRANEAN
*Open Tues.-Sat. 6 p.m.-10:30 p.m., Sun. 11
a.m.-3 p.m. & 6 p.m.-10:30 p.m. Cards: AE,
MC, V.*

When Opera opened not too long ago, it attracted lots of attention, for a variety of reasons: its prime Santa Monica location, its fashionable Mediterranean cooking (one of the cuisines of the moment) and, most of all, its affiliation with Trumps, one of L.A.'s most popular and acclaimed Californian-cuisine restaurants. Many raved about Opera, and we admit to admiring the setting, service, enclosed patio and fair prices—but though it showed great promise, the food left us cold. Now, just as we go to press, we've learned that the Trumps people have sold Opera to an unknown husband-and-wife team of restaurateurs, who say they aren't exactly sure what direction the kitchen will take. So for now, no ranking; let's hope the new owners can realize the potential of this pleasant place. About $85 for dinner for two, with wine.

⑬ Orleans
11705 National Blvd., W.L.A.
479-4187
CAJUN/CREOLE
*Open Mon.-Thurs. 11:30 a.m.-2:30 p.m. & 5:30
p.m.-9:30 p.m., Fri. 11:30 a.m.-2:30 p.m. &
5:30 p.m.-10:30 p.m., Sat. 5:30 p.m.-10:30 p.m.,
Sun. 6 p.m.-9:30 p.m. Cards: AE, MC, V.*

Orleans serves among the best Cajun/Creole food in town. Unfortunately, that may not be saying much. Perhaps Cajun/Creole food is an acquired taste, but we find it often oversauced and overcooked, more fad than fine food, especially outside its native habitat. Yes, there are some remarkable culinary creations in the Cajun/Creole repertoire. A good gumbo—and the seafood gumbo at Orleans is very good indeed—is a splendid symphony of tastes and textures. Tasso (ham) with oysters, sautéed with butter and green onions and tossed with pasta in a spicy cream sauce, is as zesty as it is original. A good bread pudding with a properly balanced bourbon sauce is one of God's great, hearty desserts. But the purported charm of many other standard Cajun/Creole dishes—jambalaya, shrimp rémoulade, crayfish etouffée, Cajun pop-

corn—continues to elude us. To each his own redfish, though, and if you like this kind of food—or if you've spent the past few years on Mars and have never tried it but would like to—The Master, Paul Prudhomme himself, chef/proprietor of K-Paul's, pioneer and popularizer of the modern Cajun/Creole cuisine, was a consultant in the transformation of Orleans from the old Williamsburg Inn, and his mark is still upon the kitchen. Orleans does a fine job with eggplant and with blackened prime rib (or pork chops) and with several preparations that use the spicy andouille sausage (a chicken gumbo, a chicken Creole and—if you want to go all the way—red beans and rice with andouille sausage and ham hocks). Orleans is noisy, but the atmosphere is as lively as the food. Dinner for two, with wine, will run about $80.

11/20 Osteria Romana Orsini
9575 W. Pico Blvd., W.L.A.
277-6050
ITALIAN
*Open Mon.-Sat. noon-2:30 p.m. & 6 p.m.-10:15
p.m. All major cards.*

Some time ago, the venerable Orlando-Orsini mutated into Osteria Romana Orsini, a transformation that's difficult to detect for all but the most observant. The room looks the same, there's still a private dance club upstairs, and the menu is still built around the cooking of Rome, which means some of the dishes are from the north and some from the south—or as Romans might say, all the dishes are from Rome. The cooking is, at heart, a bridge between the old-style Italian cuisine of Peppone and the new style of Angeli, with more weight in the old than the new. The kitchen continues to make an excellent lunchtime antipasto buffet, one of the better deals in town, a fine groaning board of little tastes of this and that—you can make a lovely lunch out of the mozzarella salad alone. Dinner is more serious, more tie-and-jacket in tone, despite the casualness implied by the word *osteria* (which means "inn"), with heavy veal chops, classic pastas and lots of meat and fish. We've eaten well here, particularly when we've stuck to the pastas. But we've also eaten better elsewhere, had more fun doing it and spent less money. Stuck between Beverly Hills and Century City, Osteria Romana Orsini is a product of its location—a businessperson's restaurant that could never really be turned into a true osteria. Dinner for two, with wine, costs about $80.

12/20 Pastel

Rodeo Collection, 421 N. Rodeo Dr., Beverly Hills
274-9775
FRENCH

Open Mon.-Sat. 11:30 a.m.-11 p.m. All major cards.

Despite the fact that it is housed within the mausoleum-like Rodeo Collection, which has been the graveyard of many restaurants in the past, Pastel is a fine survivor—at least during the day. On a warm spring afternoon, you'll find an assortment of Hollywood wives happily negating those hours spent at Jane Fonda's gym, nibbling on cold poached salmon, superlative chicken with nigh-on perfect french fries, pasta with roast lamb, a terrific spinach salad—the right dishes for the right crowd. And Pastel should get things right; it is, after all, owned by L'Orangerie. But at night, a strange change comes over Pastel, the Rodeo Collection and Beverly Hills as well. The streets are empty, noiseless, devoid of humanity, like a set for a film about some failed world of the future. A few tourists window-shop past the closed stores, but otherwise, you could probably shoot off a cannon right down Rodeo Drive and hit nothing but a couple of forlorn pigeons. The Rodeo Collection at night turns into an imposing marble edifice that seems about as appropriate to its location as the Colloseum in Rome—it looks like the overblown dinosaur that it is. Down in Pastel, things tend to be quiet. And this is a pity, for the kitchen does some of its very best work at night. On Wednesday, Thursday, Friday and Saturday nights, there's an exceptional French country menu, a fixed-price affair that involves what must be a Guinness record for the largest crudité basket served by any restaurant anywhere—the crudités alone would feed a family of four for a week. And the spit-roasted chicken that follows is nearly as good as the legendary chicken served at the late, lamented Café Colorado in the Colorado Place complex. Dinner, with wine, costs about $70 for two.

⑬ Patout's

2260 Westwood Blvd., W.L.A.
475-7100
CAJUN/CREOLE

Open Sun.-Tues. 6 p.m.-10 p.m., Wed.-Thurs. 11:30 a.m.-2:30 p.m. & 6 p.m.-10 p.m., Fri. 11:30 a.m.-2:30 p.m. & 6 p.m.-11 p.m., Sat. 6 p.m.-11 p.m. Cards: AE, MC, V.

The truth of the matter is that we didn't go to Patout's the first time because the Patout family runs the best Cajun restaurant in New Iberia, Louisiana. Nor did we go there because we were dying for an order of lady fish (grilled redfish with a thick topping of crabmeat, shrimp, cream and butter) or veal Alex (grilled veal loin topped with oysters, cream and butter). We went there because Patout's was one of the only decent restaurants in the Westwood area that was open late (sadly, it's since shortened its hours). The second time, though, we went back for the food. Ditto the third time. For what they do at Patout's is better than good—it's joyous, enthusiastic fun. The cooking is somewhat creamier and more rich with butter than the food at Orleans. But it isn't overdone (though they actually make their own sweet butter and herbed butter, which are so good, you'll eat much more than you wisely should). Patout's looks like a deep-South bistro, with moss hanging from the roof, leaves on the walls and a stained-glass skylight in the middle of the room. The food tastes too gentrified to be authentic, yet it's absolutely real. The menu changes daily, but many dishes repeat—like the exquisite shrimp rémoulade and the marvelous tournedos Patout, a dish of smoked beef served on a bed of eggplant and topped with a crawfish cream sauce. The singular disappointment is the gumbo, which is rather thin. The greatest joy (aside from the food) is the service, which defines the term "Southern hospitality." These folks are so friendly, you'll be tempted to take them home for some bourbon and branch water. Dinner for two, with wine, is about $85.

8/20 Peppone

11628 Barrington Ct., Brentwood
476-7379
ITALIAN

Open Tues.-Fri. 11:30 a.m.-2:30 p.m. & 5:30 p.m.-11:30 p.m., Sat. 5:30 p.m.-11:30 p.m., Sun. 4:30 p.m.-10:30 p.m. All major cards.

Outside of Beverly Hills, we've been to few restaurants where it's been made so evident that some diners are friends of the house and others are just cattle, to be fed, billed and dispensed with as soon as possible—or at least, dispensed with at the restaurant's leisure. During our last meal at Peppone, an Italianate dinosaur from the pre-Angeli/Prego/Chianti Cucina/Celestino school of formal spaghetti and veal houses, we felt as if we were dressed in country-bumpkin coveralls, with hayseeds sticking out of our ears. Despite a reservation, we waited in the bar while small platoons of regulars were seated. At our table, in a restaurant so dark and gloomy that bats must live in its corners, we had to ask for *everything*: water, a wine list, a menu, coffee, our check. Had the food been phenomenal, the wait would have been worthwhile. Instead, most of what we were served tasted weary, tired of life, exhausted by a kitchen utterly disinterested in what gets put on the plate: leaden gnocchi, gummy cannelloni, shoe-leather calf's liver Veneziana, stringy roast lamb, bitter chicken livers. At an easy $100 (or more) for two, with wine, one expects much better. Perhaps the regulars eat well; for us at least, unknowns certainly don't.

 Prego

362 N. Camden Dr., Beverly Hills
277-7346

ITALIAN

Open Mon.-Sat. 11:30 a.m.-midnight, Sun. 5 p.m.-midnight. All major cards.

We have several knee-jerk reactions that make us not want to like Prego. First of all, it's part of a chain, which more often than not bodes poorly for the food. Secondly, the chain of Pregos is owned by a large company that controls all kinds of restaurants, from American grills (MacArthur Park) to an upscale Mexican place (Guaymas). And, finally, Prego is in the north-of-Wilshire part of Beverly Hills that seems to attract dull, sedate, set-in-their-ways restaurants. So how can we explain the fact that Prego is one of our favorite Italian restaurants? Perhaps it's because it is a genuine (or least genuine Beverly Hills) trattoria, with reasonable prices, very good food and an ambience that is loads of fun. When you enter Prego, the first thing you see is the wood-burning pizza oven, puffing fire and smoke and disgorging some excellent, not especially trendy pizzas—cracklingly crisp crusts topped with tomatoes, mozzarella, sun-dried tomatoes, prosciutto, eggplant and so forth. There isn't a goat-cheese pizza in sight. The atmosphere, as befits a trattoria, is intensely relaxed, with happily chummy service and the sorts of dishes you don't have to be introduced to: lovely carpaccio, reasonably light gnocchi, pappardelle (flat noodles) in a tomato-and-rabbit ragoût, and wonderful grilled chicken, lamb and veal. When you leave, you expect to find Milano outside instead of valet parking. Dinner for two, with wine, will run $55 to $65.

 Primi

10543 W. Pico Blvd., W.L.A.
475-9235

ITALIAN

Open Mon.-Sat. 11:30 a.m.-3 p.m. & 5 p.m.-11 p.m., Sun. 5 p.m.-11 p.m. All major cards.

Primi is an interesting case study (object lesson?) on the Los Angeles restaurant scene. When it opened, in mid-1985, it was a trendsetter, serving only appetizers, pastas, risotti and desserts—no main courses. Primi was an early experiment in what came to be called "grazing" restaurants; it was also a response of sorts to the major criticism of owner Piero Selvaggio's older, more formal restaurant, Valentino: that its main courses weren't as good as the rest of its menu. Primi quickly became one of the hottest restaurants in town, then, almost as quickly, it cooled off. Welcome to L.A., where the typical restaurant patron, it sometimes seems, has an attention span approximately half that of a hummingbird's. Primi has survived, but business is uneven—in part because of competition, in part because of the fickle public, but also in part because the food and service can be uneven. Not even Selvaggio, the most diligent and attentive of restaurateurs, can be in two places simultaneously. His restaurants require his presence and—with a beautiful and enchanting wife, two delightful toddlers and a demanding "mistress" (he always speaks of Valentino as his mistress)—he just doesn't have the time to lavish on yet another amour. Selvaggio spends some time at Primi, but he can't possibly spend enough. Donato, the maître d', is a warm, friendly fellow. But friends haven't always been made to feel so welcome. Both food and service can be ragged in a way that just wouldn't happen if Selvaggio were always present. Still, you can eat very well here, so it clings to the 15 ranking it received in our last edition. Start, for example, with the simple, rustic affettati, cured meats served with warm toast and a pool of the purest virgin olive oil, the oil that drips from the olives, crushed only by their weight on one another in the gondola, before the first pressing. The duck crêpe and calamari fritters are also splendid appetizers, and most of the pastas and risotti are hearty and authentic. We especially like the risotto with lamb and Barolo (an Italian red wine). Primi has added a few main courses in recent years—veal, sausages, swordfish, chicken and (our favorite) a ragoût of calamari. But you're probably best off sticking with the appetizers, pastas and risotti. Dinner for two will cost about $115.

 Rangoon Racquet Club
9474 Santa Monica Blvd.,
Beverly Hills
274-8926

ENGLISH/INTERNATIONAL
Open Mon.-Fri. 11 a.m.-2:30 p.m. & 6 p.m.-11 p.m., Sat. 6 p.m.-11 p.m. All major cards.

The white wicker latticework, sepia photos of Queen Victoria, and waiters in epauletted uniforms give you a momentary impression of an 1890s British officers' club in some exotic empire outpost—but the lively bar scene, celebrities and high prices bring you back to the reality of Beverly Hills. Service is cordial and efficient, and the complimentary Scotch egg, served as you are seated for dinner, represents the hospitality here. The menu is a hodge-podge of outstanding hamburgers, vaguely Indian dishes, basic grill fare and such odd but good dishes as Woody's world-championship chili and fried potato skins filled with peanut butter. Curries are served with an elaborate tray of condiments, including various chili sauces and a very good homemade chutney thick with fresh plums, peaches and cherries. In true English style, the coffee is dreadful; wines are as overpriced as the food. Desserts include a wonderful chocolate mousse cake and a banal English trifle topped with ice cream. If you order well, you'll enjoy the simple, hearty, well-prepared cuisine—until you are shocked with the check. About $45 for a hamburger lunch for two, with a glass of wine, and more than double that for dinner.

10/20 Rebecca's
2025 Pacific Ave., Venice
306-6266
MEXICAN
Open Sun.-Thurs. 6 p.m.-midnight, Fri.-Sat. 6 p.m.-2 a.m. All major cards.

As we went to press for our last edition, there wasn't a hotter, trendier, more "in" place to be seen than Rebecca's. Usually such culinary shooting stars burn out fast, but Rebecca's is still one of the city's leading see-and-be-seen restaurant/bars. The irony of this is that Rebecca's is a Mexican restaurant (albeit new-wave, upscale Mexican)—a cuisine as common in Los Angeles as hamburgers and hot dogs. Like many of the new Mexican places in New York, Rebecca's really sizzles—and not just because of the orders of steaming carnitas and antojitos that go flying through the air. The design, which is very hip and postmodern, is by Frank Gehry, who has floated alligators and an octopus in the air, creating a room in which it's hard to tell which direction is up. The concept is by Bruce and Rebecca Marder (of the West Beach Café across the street and DC3 over in Santa Monica). The crowd is defined, as is the case in L.A., by their cars—an endless stream of Mercedeses, Porsches and BMWs.

As you might expect, the design and the scene overshadow the food, which is served at prices formerly reserved for nouvelle French and California cuisine. A lot of what's served here needs work (regulars say things keep getting better, but that hasn't been our experience). The margaritas are small and not particularly good. The guacamole is perfectly decent, though no better than the guacamole found at any of a hundred nontrendy Mexican restaurants. Enchiladas—filled with spinach and Jack cheese, with lobster or shrimp, or with carnitas—are buried under a not particularly pungent ancho-chile sauce and are usually soggy. Of the appetizers on the plato de antojitos, the chicken taco is strikingly dull, and the pork picadillo tamale is a meager creation. The worst of the entrées must be the charred lobster with a pink-grapefruit salsa—charred is one thing, but dry as a bone is another. And for $24 (or more), one might expect the tail and claws along with the rest of the beast. Far better are the sundry grilled fish: Chilean sea bass Veracruz-style (in a tomato sauce with chiles and onions), fried baby red snapper in a garlic sauce and charred swordfish with refried beans of amazing ordinariness. Dinner for two, with beer or margaritas, ranges from $75 to $100.

⑬ Ristorante Lido
15200 Sunset Blvd., Ste. 106,
Pacific Palisades
459-9214

ITALIAN
Open nightly 6 p.m.-10:30 p.m. Cards: MC, V.

Italian restaurants have been opening in Los Angeles faster than mushrooms growing after a spring rain. And many of them, for better or worse, are pretty much the same restaurant—a variation on the Pane Caldo theme of good pizzas, pastas and salads. In other words, heavy on the light dishes and light on the heavy dishes. One of the most exceptional practitioners of this new wave of nuova cucina can be found in a nondescript room in an office building in restaurant-poor, money-rich Pacific Palisades—a restaurant that, more than almost any other we've been to in Los Angeles, makes us feel as if we're eating in Italy. This feeling comes not just from the food, which is better than very good, especially the extraordinary gnocchi al pesto, the perfect carpaccio topped with Parmesan and baby artichokes, the exceptional risotto with an excess of porcini, and the amazing portions of seafood, from exotic Italian orata to Hawaiian prawns the size of small lobsters. This feeling also comes from the heartfelt service—the bottles of San Pellegrino water that arrive continuously, the flourishes of the waiters as they bone fish tableside, the love so evident in their descriptions of the food. Close your eyes and you could be sitting at the edge of Lago Maggiore, with the Balearic Islands in the distance, instead of just down the street from Gladstone's. Dinner for two, with wine, will run about $100.

⑮ Robata
250 N. Robertson Blvd., Beverly Hills
274-5533

JAPANESE/SUSHI
Open Mon.-Fri. 11:30 a.m.-2:30 p.m. & 6 p.m.-10 p.m., Sat. 6 p.m.-10 p.m. All major cards.

Centuries ago in Kyoto, culinary Zen masters developed a style of cuisine that was more ritual than sustenance, a meal called *kaiseki*, which translates loosely as "warm stone in the belly." It's nothing less than a feast in which each course is a precious jewel, a tiny gem that demands consideration and contemplation. The presentation is every bit as important as the taste, perhaps even more so—you feel almost guilty actually eating the food in a kaiseki meal. In Kyoto, where the style was born, it's not unusual to spend as much as $1,000 a person for a kaiseki feast, served on lacquerware 300 or 400 years old and enjoyed at great leisure sitting cross-legged on the floor (wishing, perhaps, that you'd taken that yoga class). In L.A., a number of restaurants serve an American version of a kaiseki meal, but none approximate the real thing—except for Robata. This ultra-modern, high-tech restaurant just south of The Ivy is the sort of restaurant that separates the casual sushi eater from the rabid culinary Sinophile. This is food served at such a high level of perfection that each dish draws gasps, and each dish forces you to pay strict attention to what's in front of you.

There are three kaisekis available—one with ten courses, one with eleven and one with twelve—each progressing through a slow arc from soup and sashimi to grilled, fried and stewed dishes. The flow of the meal, fueled by a selection of expensive sakes (preferably served cold), is inexorable, undeniable, awesome. That a meal here, with sake, could easily cost well over $200 for two (making this potentially the most expensive restaurant in town) is definitely sobering; the best rationalization is that it would cost a lot more in Kyoto.

⑮ Rockenwagner
1023 W. Washington Blvd., Venice
399-6504

FRENCH/CALIFORNIAN
Open Tues.-Fri. 6 p.m.-9:45 p.m., Sat.-Sun. 5:30 p.m.-9:45 p.m. Cards: MC, V.

Despite its less-than-trendy location on the wrong side of the tracks in Venice, a name that's more memorable than pronounceable and a design that can make us feel as if we're eating in a long hallway, Rockenwagner is one of the most desired reservations in town, and for good reason—the food is terrific, the Rockenwagners (Hans and Mary, both from Chicago) are sweet and caring, and the overall sense is of being let in on one of L.A.'s best-kept culinary secrets. Inside Rockenwagner, diners-to-be sit at a sort of modern lunch counter, sipping California Chardonnay by the glass and waiting for customers to shake themselves free of their tables. This does not happen quickly, for Rockenwagner is a comfortable shoebox of a restaurant. You want to linger here, to talk about things that matter, to dwell on issues of the day. And to luxuriate over the food.

This food is quite personal, very much the vision of a single chef, though this vision was, of course, helped along by the time German-born and Swiss-trained Hans spent working with Jovan Trboyevic at Le Perroquet in Chicago—an apprenticeship with a legendary chef in a legendary restaurant. California has certainly suited Rockenwagner well, for his food is right at home in the land of the lotus and poodle—in other words, edibly eccentric in the most positive meaning of the term. As at most really good restaurants, the cooking is extremely simple. "Sashimi-grade" tuna is cooked very rare on a bed of mâche, with wild mushrooms and a sesame-oil vinaigrette: the perfect salad. Grilled sea scallops and baby asparagus are served in a feather-light puff pastry with a sweet-and-sour port sauce. Eating a dish like the roast medallion of pork tenderloin, rolled in cracked black pepper and topped with melting chèvre, you cherish each bite, not wanting the dish to end. Actually, for pure variety, there's nothing better there than the chef's fish platter, which consists of three fish in three sauces—a trio that rarely seems to be the same. It's as if Hans Rockenwagner had taken on the challenge of being able to match dozens of fish with dozens of possible sauces as a mathematical problem, which he solves on your plate. Oh, and the desserts are just fine as well—try the apple pizza, the nougat parfait or the orange gratin with sabayon sauce (but skip the glazed pecans in puff pastry with chocolate sauce). Dinner for two, with wine, costs $100 or so.

11/20 Romeo & Juliet

435 N. Beverly Dr., Beverly Hills
273-2292
ITALIAN
Open Mon.-Fri. 11:30 a.m.-2:30 p.m. & 6 p.m.-10:30 p.m., Sat. 6 p.m.-10:30 p.m. Cards: AE, MC, V.

In much the same way that Osteria Romana Orsini is dark and masculine, Romeo & Juliet is light, pretty and quite feminine. Which isn't to say that it's filled exclusively with the Ladies Who Lunch; it's also a favorite of Beverly Hills's male power brokers, who can be seen on phones at their tables, wheeling, dealing and making multimillion-dollar decisions over plates of food that are better than you might expect. Unlike nearby La Dolce Vita, where the food can be so dull, Romeo and Juliet's food has a little sparkle. The pesce fritto misto of fried squid, scallops, sole and shrimp can be very good, quite light and easy to handle. There are excellent fried artichokes and some superlative pastas, among them a delicate angel hair with fresh basil and a spicy tomato sauce, and a feather-light agnolotti filled with spinach. A scaloppine of veal with porcini and truffles is an exaltation of mushrooms, cooked in a strong brandy-and-wine sauce, but roast duckling in a cherry sauce is far too sweet, on a duck that is too dry. In the evening, the maître d' has been known to burst into song in the lounge. Apparently he cannot be tipped *not* to sing. Dinner for two, with wine, costs around $100.

⑭ Ruth's Chris Steak House

224 S. Beverly Dr., Beverly Hills
859-8744
AMERICAN/STEAKHOUSE
Open daily 11:30 a.m.-9:30 p.m. All major cards.

The best steak we've ever eaten in Los Angeles was served at Hy's in Century City. But the ten best after that were all served at Ruth's Chris Steak House. Ruth's Chris consistently serves excellent steaks, cooked exactly to order—and our order isn't easy: "Black and blue, warm center." Not many steakhouses can char a steak on the outside and have it blood-rare inside without leaving the center cold. Ruth's Chris does it right. Every time. Ruth Fertel, a divorced mother of two college-bound sons, opened the original Ruth's Chris in New Orleans in 1965 with an $18,000 loan. Now she runs a $30-million, 30-city restaurant empire. In all her restaurants, the steaks are USDA Prime, dry-aged, cooked in specially designed high-temperature broilers and served still sizzling, drenched in butter: cholesterol bliss. But if you're going to have a steak, you might as well have a great one. The sixteen-ounce New York strip is just that, at $21.75. The porterhouse for two is $42. Or you can have a filet (large or small) or a rib-eye. Ruth's Chris also serves veal chops, lamb chops, chicken, fish and a variety of appetizers, salads, vegetables and potatoes—the best of the latter being the extra-thin, crisp shoestrings. The two best desserts are the pecan pie and the bread pudding with whisky sauce. A tip: if you like quieter surroundings than you normally find in a steakhouse, ask to sit in the private dining room in the rear if it's available or, best of all, take one of the booths in the bar. About $125 for a steak dinner for two, with wine.

9/20　La Scala Boutique

410 N. Cañon Dr., Beverly Hills
550-8288
ITALIAN
Open Mon.-Sat. 11:30 a.m.-11:30 p.m. No cards.

We were hardly fans of the old La Scala on little Santa Monica, so it was with trepidation that we set out for the "new" La Scala, the result of a merging between the stuffy old place and the slightly more casual La Scala Boutique. What we found is the same old La Scala Boutique with a slightly different menu, including some of the old La Scala faves. And we found that the "new" La Scala is much more popular than the old one, which had become kind of sad. Every table was filled with people who could live only in Beverly Hills—aging men wearing dark-brown hairpieces and Gucci loafers, aging social X-ray women whose skin cracks when they smile, and loud-mouthed yuppie agents. Owner Jean Leon knows how to keep this crowd happy, but he certainly doesn't know how to make good Italian food, or even how to hire a decent Italian chef. While chatting and people-watching, and without even glancing at their plates, his faithful put away forkfuls of food that is at best ordinary and at worst leaden. L.A.'s Italian revolution, which has brought us no end of marvelous, authentic restaurants, completely bypassed La Scala; here you can still get heavy mozzarella marinara drenched in too much sauce, linguine with clams, spaghetti bolognese and tasteless breaded veal cutlets. And, of course, you can get the famous chopped Leon salad, an edible enough Ladies Who Lunch mainstay for years now. Steer quite clear of the seafood risotto, which, the day we were there, featured an abudance of bay scallops that tasted as if they'd been transported across country by pony express. Even the gelato wasn't up to par, being studded with bits of ice. And the service was distracted and inexcusably slow. Now that virtually every L.A. neighbhorhood has a good trattoria, we can't think of a single reason to come here—unless you're a potential Italian restaurateur who wants to know what *not* to do. Dinner for two, with wine, runs $80 to $90.

8/20　La Scala Malibu

3835 Cross Creek Rd., Malibu
456-1979
ITALIAN
Open Tues.-Thurs. 11:30 a.m.-2:30 p.m. & 5:30 p.m.-10:30 p.m., Fri. 11:30 a.m.-2:30 p.m. & 5:30 p.m.-11 p.m., Sat. 5:30 p.m.-11 p.m., Sun. 5:30 p.m.-10:30 p.m. All major cards.

Now that La Scala and La Scala Boutique have moved from little Santa Monica Boulevard to Cañon Drive, in the process becoming a sort of upscale version of the restaurant's downscale La Scala Presto chain (if this seems confusing, it is), the only vestige of the old snobbism that defined the original La Scala can be found at La Scala Malibu, a snippy watering hole for the Malibu Colonists. The success of the place is based on the old concept of the captive audience. In Malibu, the rich eat bad food because the nearest alternative is too far away; they figure it's a small price to pay for living by the beach. Admittedly, La Scala Malibu is prettier than La Scala BH ever was. Its sweet patio helps you forget the fact that you're sitting in the middle of a shopping mall, not far from the popular Deli Malibu. Perhaps it's best to describe La Scala Malibu as a museum collection of aging Italian dishes served by waiters with annoyingly good tans. If you long for inexpertly prepared renditions of mozzarella marinara, ratatouille niçoise, lasagne al forno and spaghetti carbonara, this is the place to find them. Sauces are heavy, pastas either under or overcooked (they never seem to hit right in the middle), and fish dishes apparently cooked to mush as a matter of policy. In exchange for this mediocrity, you'll pay a king's ransom. But at least you'll be near the beach, which for many seems to be fair compensation. Dinner for two, with wine, costs well over $100.

9/20   La Scala Presto

11740 San Vicente Blvd., Brentwood
826-6100
ITALIAN
Open Mon.-Sat. 11:30 a.m.-10:30 p.m. All major cards.

Like the inexplicable Louise's chain, La Scala Prestos keep popping up like wild mushrooms; unfortunately, they haven't a clue about what to do with the noble fungus. The food here isn't terrible, it's just bland and mediocre, and we can't help but wonder what Jean Leon really thinks of the culinary merits of his little La Scala-ettes. For one thing, you could be driven mad by the constant, staccato sound made by the cooks preparing the ubiquitous chopped salad; it's like being trapped in a Woody Woodpecker cartoon. Most everything here—salads, pastas and pizzas—tastes watered down, as if food with too much flavor might offend the masses. To be fair, the portions are quite ample and the prices are fairly low, so of course all the branches do a land-office business, although with places like Toscana and California Pizza Kitchen in close proximity to the various La Scalas, one wonders how and why.

Service varies wildly from branch to branch (see also San Fernando Valley and South Bay); Brentwood seems to be the best and most consistent, while the Encino branch appears to be staffed mainly by Valley girls who are more interested in reapplying their frosted lipstick and tossing their frosted hair than waiting on their customers; you could write a screenplay while waiting for a busboy to decide to refill your coffee cup. Yet more mass-produced Prestos keep opening, customers keep filling them, and that's the name of the game. Dinner for two, with wine, runs about $60.

13   72 Market Street

72 Market St., Venice
392-8720
AMERICAN
Open Sun.-Fri. 11:30 a.m.-2:30 p.m. & 6 p.m.-11:30 p.m., Sat. 6 p.m.-11:30 p.m. All major cards.

Let us, for a moment, put aside the ineffable trendiness of 72 Market Street, which is owned by actor/director/producer Tony Bill and chums Dudley Moore and Liza Minnelli, and forget about the serious problem this place sometimes has honoring reservations. Instead, let's consider the wonderful retroness of the food served at this beach-adjacent eatery. Back in the days of the Plymouth Colony in Massachusetts, the Pilgrims didn't eat their first meal of the day until many hours of hard, back-breaking work had passed. They'd arise at dawn, tend to their milking and farming, and only then, when the sun was high in the sky, would they settle down to a breakfast befitting those who worked harder in a day than most of us work in a month. Lunch was an equally awesome repast; dinner was even larger. A typically substantial meal of the period might include codfish cakes, baked beans, steamed brown bread and a pitcher or two of ale—and that's just breakfast. As a rule, people don't eat like that these days. But at 72 Market Street, you'll find a fair amount of hearty eating going on, despite the unbearable thinness of most of the clients.

The menu is highly eclectic, beginning with a wide assortment of appetizers from the oyster bar that sits in the restaurant's bustling first room. There are oysters and clams, briny and reasonably sublime, served raw on the half shell. Oysters are broiled and topped with pesto and salsa, mussels are cold and flavored with saffron and tomato. Scallops and snapper are ceviched; crayfish are garlic-mayonnaised. From the kitchen hails a Caesar salad that's as good as it gets, fine smoked Scottish salmon with walnut-wheat toast and a world-class bowl of red, appropriately named "kick ass" chili. The cooking may be American rustic, but the crowd (and decor) is distinctly smart—the last time we ate here, at noon on a Sunday, Steve Martin was trying to disguise himself with a funny-looking hat in one corner (sorry, we couldn't tell what Steve was eating; his hat was in the way). On this particular day, we were eating french toast (made with the Southern-Pacific rail recipe, which makes it sort of a pan-regional dish), pecan waffles with berries, an eggs Benedict variation using artichoke bottoms, grilled free-range chicken in a nice garlic, oregano and tomatillo sauce, even an amazing bit of steak tartare made of prime filet served with a salad of haricots verts, Maui onions, artichokes and tomatoes. It may have made a mere snack for the Pilgrims, but for us it was a full-scale feast. Dinner for two, with wine, costs about $100.

⑬ Shane

2932 Beverly Glen Circle,
Beverly Glen
470-6223

ITALIAN/CALIFORNIAN

Open nightly 6 p.m.-11 p.m. All major cards.

The trick at Shane, we've found, is to sit upstairs. Downstairs, the noise level is daunting. Tables are ridiculously close together. Smartly dressed folks waiting for tables tend to cluster. The activity level is almost too intense for words. Upstairs, on the other hand, the tables are well spaced. The din diminishes significantly as it drifts upward. The serving people make a point of bounding up the stairs—they must have leg muscles like the Joyner kids. And if you're lucky enough to get one of the two tables on the balcony's edge, giving you a great view of the activities down below, you can spend the whole evening playing Beverly Glen voyeur, watching the Mercedes and BMW set eat, chat and communicate via body language—and their choice of dress. At meal's end, you might feel tempted to give the diners down below a rousing ovation. Shane is just your basic, run-of-the-mill Barbara Lazaroff–designed, hidden-in-the-back-of-the-Beverly-Glen-Circle-shopping-center Italian/Southwestern restaurant. Nothing special about it at all—except that it's probably the only one of its kind on the planet. The decor is pure love-it-or-hate-it stuff, with tile snakes crawling around the room, a setting that would light up director Ken Russell like a proverbial pinball machine. This is definitely not neutral and beige. Even the dishware is distinctive: a black-and-white cowhide design from Metlox.

Oddly, the food that sits atop these plates is fairly recognizable, despite its eccentric Italian/Southwestern roots. The pizzas are all fine and dandy, the culinary siblings of the ones made at Spago: lamb sausage, sage and red chile; chicken and tomatillo salsa; pancetta and shiitake mushrooms—standard late-twentieth-century California chow. The calamari fritti could be more fritti (it's a persistent problem), but the saffron garlic sauce accompanying the dish is very nice. Equally nice are the wonderfully tender lamb scaloppines, which come with a stew of Tuscan white beans. The duck tostada and the beef quesadilla are a lot better than they are at most other places in town, with more duck and better duck (ditto the beef). The pastas, available as both appetizers and entrées, are worthy; try the saffron farfalle (butterfly-shape pasta) with Louisiana shrimp. If all else fails, order the grilled chicken with rosemary and lime, and skinny, crispy fries. Enjoy the view. Enjoy the easy parking. Enjoy the fact that no matter where you live, it's a downhill ride from way up here. Dinner for two, with wine, runs about $60.

11/20 Sostanza

12100 Wilshire Blvd., W.L.A.
207-4273

ITALIAN

Open Mon.-Thurs. 11:30 a.m.-3 p.m. & 6 p.m.-10 p.m., Fri. 11:30 a.m.-3 p.m. & 6 p.m.-11 p.m., Sun. 6 p.m.-10 p.m. All major cards.

There's something about restaurants inside office buildings that leaves us cold. Perhaps it's the thought of all those worker ants toiling away upstairs that depresses us, all that pointless labor conducted to move large amounts of paper from one side of a desk to another. Or perhaps it's simply because office-building restaurants tend to be such cold places, a problem that Sostanza has never managed to get around, despite its two grand murals and floor-to-ceiling windows; you feel as if you need a sweater, no matter what the weather. The modern Italian menu is filled with dishes that read better than they taste: an undergarlicked bagna càuda, made with vegetables that could have been a bit fresher; calamari fritti that could have been crisper; a variety of pizzas that could have been crunchier, topped with more than the smattering of duck sausage and goat cheese; seafood risotto that could certainly have been cooked into something other than rice mush. Our gripes notwithstanding, the food is decently average, the prices a bit above average, the service rather sleepy. Dinner for two, with wine, costs about $70.

St. Mark's

23 Windward Ave., Venice
452-2222

CALIFORNIAN

Open Mon.-Fri. 6 p.m.-10 p.m., Sat.-Sun. 10 a.m.-3 p.m. & 6 p.m.-10 p.m.; late supper nightly 10 p.m.-1 a.m. All major cards.

This too-trendy-for-words jazz supper club had just opened as we went to press, so we don't think it's fair to give it a ranking. Besides, based on our first experience here, St. Mark's would be the hardest place to rank in the whole book. We rank on food only, and the food we tried was good, particularly the entrées (tender, thin-sliced leg of lamb with a marvelous, slightly hot harissa sauce, perfect roast chicken with crisp fries). But the experience was nightmarish. Here we have a jazz club that charges about $15 a person (on top of the pricey dinner) for the show—and then seats diners in an upstairs loft with absolutely no view of the stage. When we complained to the haughty maître d', saying that we shouldn't pay the same price as those downstairs who could see the stage, she coolly replied, "You can hear the music just fine here." We said okay, we'd just eat dinner and leave, not paying for the show. She said, "If you're here when the music starts, you have to pay the $15." When we asked if others had complained about this bizarre arrangement, she said no—and after we spent some time eyeing the crowd, we believed her. These plastic scenemakers didn't care one whit about the performance. itself. After the maître d' tossed back her blond mane and stalked off, we were then treated to perhaps the worst, most confused service we've ever experienced; it would take many paragraphs to describe the entire comedy of errors.. So how could we give that first meal the solid 13/20 it deserved when the service, attitude and physical design of the place were worth a 5/20? In time, perhaps, the waiters will learn the fundamentals and the front desk will gain a touch of humility, which could make St. Mark's a pretty good restaurant. But it can never be a good jazz club, not with this confused, disjointed interior that shows no respect for the performer. About $110 for dinner for two, with wine; if you stay for the 9:30 p.m. show on weekends, you'll also pay about $15 per person admission.

10/20 Toledo

11613 Santa Monica Blvd., W.L.A.
477-2400
SPANISH
Open Tues.-Thurs. 5:30 p.m.-10:30 p.m., Fri. 11:30 a.m.-2:30 p.m. & 5:30 p.m.-11 p.m., Sat. 5:30 p.m.-11 p.m., Sun. 4:30 p.m.-10 p.m. Cards: AE, MC, V.

This small two-room Spanish restaurant works hard to be charming. Crammed full of quaint Castilian touches, it rushes to encase diners in a feeling of old-world coziness: dried flowers, wine bottles, copies of Goyas on the wall, lace curtains, a fireplace. Unfortunately, the charm often ends with owner Pedro Calle. He is brusque with some diners, soothing with others, but never quite seems like the affable host the part calls for. The food is more dependable than inspired. The word "tapas" has been added to the menu next to the "appetizers"—a sign of the times rather than a change in menu. These tapas include shrimp in garlic sauce, baby eels with garlic, mushrooms with garlic sauce—notice a common theme here? Garlic lovers will find plenty to praise, but those who stick to the moderate one-garlic-dish-per-meal dictum will have to choose carefully, since the entrées include garlic chicken, shrimp with garlic and other dishes that may not list garlic on the menu but that turn up smothered in the restaurant's signature creamy garlic sauce. The star of the menu is, naturally, paella, and it is artfully presented to the table in a huge flat dish and then dished up tableside by the waiter. Overall, Toledo's food is hearty and homey, if unexceptional. Dinner will run about $65 or $70 for two, with wine.

11/20 Topanga Fresh Fish Market

Topanga Canyon Blvd., Malibu
455-1728

Reel Inn

Pacific Coast Hwy., 100 yds. N. of Topanga Canyon Blvd., Malibu
456-8221
SEAFOOD
Open Mon.-Sat. 5 p.m.-9:30 p.m., Sun. 11 a.m.-9:30 p.m. No cards.

On any given evening, all things considered, we'd much rather be sitting at either the Topanga Fresh Fish Market or its nearby larger branch, the Reel Inn, than wearing a jacket and tie and eating some fancy dish in a cream sauce that's going to mess up our cholesterol count for months to come. The Fresh Fish Market and the Reel Inn have the same menu and the same blatant disregard for numerical addresses (neither has one). And both serve some of the best simple seafood in

Southern California—in funky settings that always make us think we're sitting inside a building made of salvaged wood. Yes, this is Shack Cuisine at its very best. In both cases, you order your meal at one window, pay for it, then pick it up at another window. At the somewhat funkier Topanga branch, you eat off paper plates; at the Malibu branch, the plates are plastic. A blackboard lists the exceptional fish dishes, served with the best of all possible spuds sautéed with onions, and the finest coleslaw in Los Angeles, bar none (assuming that you believe, as we do, that coleslaw should be jaw-achingly crunchy). By all means order the fish chowder, which defines the genre quite nicely. As an appetizer, we suggest you split the seafood quesadilla, which will just about ruin your appetite for anything that follows—though that's never kept us from eating on. Then you'll have a choice of mahi mahi, shark, snapper, salmon, halibut, swordfish, scallops in a buttery broth, scrumptious shrimp and some delicious lobster (the most expensive item on the menu, though still under $15). These restaurants are sufficiently anarchic that you can't help but wonder who's in charge. Clearly, somebody is—somebody who knows how to cook fish with the élan of a true zen master. Dinner for two, with wine, costs about $30.

11/20 El Torito Grill

9595 Wilshire Blvd., Beverly Hills
550-1599
MEXICAN/SOUTHWESTERN
Open daily 11 a.m.-11 p.m. Cards: AE, MC, V.

In Beverly Hills, paying full price is a badge of honor. But even big spenders like the occasional bargain, which explains in part the immediate and tremendous success of the sprawling El Torito Grill. The rest of its success can be explained by its excellent location (Wilshire and Camden), its vivid Southwestern decor, its Sauza Gold margaritas and the fact that every Southern Californian worth his or her salsa adores Mexican food. After meeting with similar success in Newport Beach, El Torito's yupscale rider on the Southwestern bandwagon brought its mass-market contempo-Mex fare to L.A. The food isn't spectacular, but if you order carefully you can get a lot of bang for your buck (along with enough noise to make a wrecking crew feel at home—if you want to talk, ask for a booth

along one of the walls). We could have done without the smoked grilled meats (chicken, sausages and more), which were dry and too strongly smoked. And the barbecued-chicken tostada was a misguided mess. But the baby-back ribs aren't bad, the complimentary warm, slightly underdone homemade tortillas are delicious, and the huge appetizers are usually quite tasty. Try the quesadilla with oven-smoked chicken, sweet red peppers and corn; the blue-corn nachos with black beans and cheese; the Texas sundae, layers of bean dip, chile, cheese, red chile, avocado sauce and sour cream, a perfectly awful mess that tastes swell; and the crisp red-corn taquitos stuffed with chicken or beef. In fact, skip the entrées entirely and order a collection of appetizers—it's a fun way to eat well for less in this, the nouveau-riche capital of the western world. From $30 to $45 for two, with margaritas.

11/20 Toscana

11633 San Vicente Blvd., Brentwood
820-2448
ITALIAN
Open daily 11:30 a.m.-10:30 p.m. All major cards.

How popular is Toscana? We called a week in advance and were told nothing was available but 6:30 p.m. and 9 p.m. We showed up at 8:45 p.m. for our 9 p.m. reservation and found eighteen people (by actual count) waiting for tables, which is problematic when you consider that Toscana has no bar and no waiting area; all you can do is crowd around the maître d' and glower at him, which on that particular night a number of people were doing. By 10 o'clock, tables began to free up, and the clot at the door finally loosened. And by that time, the restaurant gave up on the group of twelve who had reserved the one large table near the kitchen and never showed up (an act of near-homicidal rudeness in a restaurant this small), and sat us there, along with another party, which was fine—we rather enjoy the serendipity of sharing a table with strangers. We were, as you can imagine, not too happy by this time. And yet there was something about the feel of the place, and especially about the look of the food, that cheered us up. Under other circumstances, we'd have walked out, but something told us it was a good idea to stick around.

We're glad we did, for the food at Toscana is worth a wait. It's prepared by Agostino Sciandri, who used to do such good work at Il Giardino over in Beverly Hills. His feet may be planted in Brentwood, but his heart is planted in Tuscany. You'll taste Tuscany in every bite of his ribollita, a classic soup of the Italian hill country, an incredibly thick stew of vegetables, white beans, various cheeses and bread, which is traditionally eaten for lunch in such medieval towns as San Gimignano (where they serve a classic ribollita at La Cisterne, the hotel on the town's central plaza). Newly rediscovered classics abound— pasta e fagioli, the simplest imaginable dish of pasta and beans; salsicce all'uccelletto, which is nothing more than a wonderfully reassuring stew of sausage, white beans, tomatoes, olive oil and garlic; a mass of good risotti, cooked with seafood, or vegetables, or Mascarpone and Parmesan or, of course, porcini. Florence is a city of steak eaters, so of course there's steak on the menu, pounded and cooked with rosemary and garlic or grilled in olive oil. Toscana also makes a heck of a lamb chop and a heck of a veal chop. By the end of the meal, we had forgotten the nightmarish wait—almost. And we do admit that it was at least partially our fault—never go to a trendy restaurant on a Saturday night. Dinner for two, with wine, runs about $75.

Trattoria Angeli

11651 Santa Monica Blvd., W.L.A.
478-1191

ITALIAN

Open Mon.-Sat. noon-2:30 p.m. & 6 p.m.-10:30 p.m., Sun. 11 a.m.-2:30 p.m. & 6 p.m.-10:30 p.m. Cards: AE, MC, V.

For the past few years, Angeli Caffè on Melrose has been one of the city's preeminent joints for the foodwise intelligentsia. From day one, artists, chefs, writers, actors and assorted cool people have crowded around the tiny black tables in this architecturally outrageous storefront. Strangely, in this strange-food town, what draws them is not Brie quesadillas or passion-fruit chutneys. Instead, they are addicted to Angeli's remarkably untrendy Italian food: modest salads, little fried croquettes and no-frills pizzas with nary a hint of lamb sausage or Iowa Maytag blue cheese. But at Angeli, no frills doesn't mean no taste: pizza doesn't get any better than this.

Angeli, however, is not without its short-comings. If you're not in the mood for pizza, you may find the menu too limited, and the two small rooms are usually cramped and noisy. Owners Evan Kleiman and John Strobel worked to solve these problems when they created the westside's Trattoria Angeli. They skillfully kept the best of the original— the same terrific pizzas and salads and a similar architectural-statement decor that is as fun as it is weird—while improving on the formula by judiciously expanding the menu, offering a well-rounded wine list, hiring a sharp serving and management staff and creating a setting that is not overly noisy or crowded. And despite the metal catwalk and floating loft overhead, despite the long-haired waiters, despite the very L.A. crowd, this is a true Italian trattoria, a lively place where happy groups share bottles of Chianti and plates of authentic, unfussy Italian food. As in most such trattorias, the food is meant to satisfy, not dazzle, so don't come expecting the kind of carefully crafted dishes found at, say, Valentino. Perfection isn't always attained here; the risotto milanese, that classic dish of rice, saffron, chicken broth, butter and Parmesan, was rather soupy (though flavorful), and the simple angel-hair pasta with goat cheese and pancetta was bland. But there are plenty of good things to eat, from little tastes to big plates, and you'll have a good time eating them. The pizza alla checca, with fresh tomatoes, mozzarella, basil and garlic, and the pizza Angeli, with smoked mozzarella, garlic and a tomato-basil sauce, may make you swear off California pizza forever. The aforementioned disappointing angel hair was compensated for by terrific spaghetti alla carbonara (egg, cheeses, pancetta, onion and fresh basil). Other winners include the tasty potato-onion pie with mushrooms; the verdure alla griglia, an antipasto assortment of grilled vegetables; the scamorza alla griglia, a large, thin slice of barely melted smoked mozzarella topped with olive oil and fresh tomato, a dish so good you'll want to order two or three more; and the perfect pollo arrosto, a crisp-skinned, garlicky roast half chicken. Fortunately, given the dismal desserts found in most Italian restaurants, Trattoria Angeli breaks with authenticity to offer some lovely non-Italian cakes and fruit tarts. But, as befits Angeli's culinary simplicity, the two best are also the simplest: a heaping bowl of Häagen-Dazs vanilla ice cream topped with a fresh-brewed cup of espresso, a well-nigh perfect dessert; and a heavenly lemon tart with a chewy crust and a sublime sweet-tart filling. Two will spend anywhere from $60 to $90 for dinner with wine.

 Tribeca

242 N. Beverly Dr., Beverly Hills
271-1595
AMERICAN
Open Mon.-Thurs. 11:30 a.m.-midnight, Fri. 11:30 a.m.-1 a.m., Sat. 6 p.m.-1 a.m., Sun. 6 p.m.-midnight. Cards: AE, MC, V.

We suppose we really shouldn't like Tribeca (a few of our trusted friends don't), simply because of the crowd that packs the ground-floor bar and keeps every seat in the upstairs restaurant full: smug thirtysomething men in Armani power suits, smug businesswomen whose outfits cost more than many people make in a year, smug, tiny-ponytailed, art-dealerish men and leggy blond gals with perfect makeup and clingy little black dresses. We also probably shouldn't like it for its trendy Americana menu, full of blackened this-and-that and other such culinary clichés. It's true, we don't like the loud bar, except when it quiets down after ten or so on weeknights. But though we've tried hard on several visits to find fault with Tribeca as a restaurant, we always come away pleased—with the welcome, the friendly, prompt service, the comfortable booths, the airy, open-raftered lower–New York decor and, most of all, the kitchen's skill and efficiency. Blackened meatloaf with mashed potatoes may be a current cliché, but at Tribeca it's a cliché that tastes swell, a surprisingly mild meatloaf that can't help but make you feel warm and well fed. The clam chowder is herby and rich, not a work of genius but another excellent feel-good dish. In fact, just about every dish here is just the thing to cheer you up after a hard day screaming on the phone with agents and casting directors—from the moist, marvelous crabcakes on a bed of Creole rémoulade to the faultless Caesar salad to the down-home desserts (apple-blackberry pie, pumpkin cheesecake, chocolate–macadamia nut torte). After you tuck all this good food away, the people sitting around you may not appear to be so annoyingly smug after all. Two will spend about $95 for dinner with wine.

10/20 Tse Yang

151 S. Doheny Blvd., Beverly Hills
278-8886
CHINESE
Open daily noon-3 p.m. & 6 p.m.-11 p.m. All major cards.

Where most Chinese restaurants in Los Angeles have roots in Hong Kong, Tse Yang has an entirely different and surprising set of forebears—in New York, Paris, Frankfurt, Geneva and Düsseldorf. It was actually born in Paris, where the first branch opened in 1980, which explains why the menu is written in both English and French. This also explains the French accent found in many of the dishes—there aren't many Chinese restaurants that offer grenouilles au rôti or poulet au citron vert. Actually, both Tse Yang and Chinois serve food that is essentially French-Chinese, though the menus bear no resemblance to each other at all.

Tse Yang clearly cost a Mandarin's ransom to build. Everywhere you look are highly polished brass, elegant woods, exotic silks. Even the ceilings—or more properly, especially the ceilings—are filled with carvings, ornate filigree and polished highlights. We've spent a lot of time looking around the rooms, shaking our heads in wonderment. Unfortunately, this was a better way to spend our time than eating the food, which runs from decent to quite disappointing. The menu is of a distinctly different culinary milieu than that of L.A.'s current crop of Chinese restaurants, with their roots in Hong Kong, New York and San Francisco. This is Chinese food filtered through the more conservative cooking styles of old Europe. And though it might suit the needs of the populace there, it doesn't do much for us. Your best bets are the appetizers, particularly "les délices de Pekin à la vapeur" (or, in a simpler world, steamed dumplings). You get a precious few for your $6.25, but what you get are good. As are "les hors d'oeuvres arc en ciel" (rainbow appetizers), a trio of cold dishes: smoked beef, chicken and trompe l'oeil tofu. The Tse Yang smoked salmon is absolutely wonderful, and possibly the first salmon we've encountered in a Chinese restaurant. Less successful, alas, are the entrées, in particular the Peking duck ("la véritable canard laque comme à Pekin"), oily rectangles of duck skin wrapped in pancakes so skinny that globs of hoisin sauce tend to drip through. For $35, it would be nice to get a little duck meat as well. The green-lemon sauce that's served with a number of dishes was a frightening thing, with the texture of Vaseline and a taste reminiscent of cough medicine—a truly horrific sauce that ruined everything it came in contact with. The jade phoenix giant shrimp are both large and rather greasy. We rather liked the fruit-cup-with-ice-cream dessert, though we wish the fruit hadn't been soaked in Triple Sec; but then, we've never been fond of alcoholic desserts. Service is very good, though the kitchen is a bit slow; dishes are served in the French style, which means the waiter makes up your plate. In a Chinese restaurant, this is a nicety that obviates the fun of Chinese restaurants. Dinner for two, with wine, will set you back more than $100.

Valentino

3115 Pico Blvd., Santa Monica
829-4313

ITALIAN

Open Mon.-Thurs. 5:30 p.m.-11:30 p.m., Fri. 11:30 a.m.-2:30 p.m. & 5:30 p.m.-11:30 p.m., Sat. 5:30 p.m.-11:30 p.m. All major cards.

Italian food has become the rage in chic dining circles. Maybe people are weary of French food, maybe they're more health-conscious or maybe they just don't want to have to mortgage their homes so they can pay for one nice dinner out. Whatever the reason, more good Italian restaurants have opened in Los Angeles (and elsewhere) in recent years than you can shake a breadstick at. But Valentino remains unchallenged, the best of them all—and not just in Los Angeles. We continue to consider Valentino one of the top few Italian restaurants in the United States—and since its remodeling in 1987, it is an extremely attractive and romantic restaurant as well. In fact, if you consider everything, from food to wine, service to ambience, Valentino may well be the best dining experience in L.A.

Not that Valentino is the ideal destination for the budget-minded. Appetizers are $8 to $12.50, pastas $10 to $15 and main courses $18.50 to $24. But that's still a lot less than what's charged in tonier French establishments and in several other Italian restaurants as well. You won't find any $21 ravioli on Valentino's menu, for example, as you do at San Domenico in New York. On the other hand, if you're going to do Valentino right, you really shouldn't bother looking at a menu. Just put yourself in the hands of owner Piero Selvaggio, the best restaurateur in the city, if not the country. Either let him orchestrate your entire dinner or ask him to tell you the evening's specials and compose your dinner from those. We don't generally like lengthy recitations of daily specials; why can't restaurants simply have them printed on a small card and give it to you to peruse? Who can remember more than three specials, especially when the waiter is standing over you, pencil poised over order pad as if passing judgment on your palate? But Selvaggio infuses his recitation with so much warmth and genuine excitement that it only enhances the evening's pleasure. A cautionary note: the list of specials is long-long-long; on one typical night, it numbered four cold appetizers, five hot appetizers, five pastas, four risotti, four fresh fish and five meat dishes. How to deal with all that? We always take notes as Selvaggio reads, then ask him to return in a few minutes while we discuss among ourselves before consulting him for our final choices. The choices aren't easy. Although the regular menu has many traditional dishes, the specials are innovative and challenging. Almost everything sounds irresistible. One evening, the cold appetizers included a carpaccio of four fresh fish and a rabbit salad; hot appetizers included a tortino of wild mushrooms, a veal carpaccio with black truffles and Parmigiana and a warm eggplant crespella (a pancake, generally stuffed like a crêpe) with mortadella. Pastas? How about rigatoni with fava beans and smoked ricotta? Or orecchiette with rapini and chives? Risotto? It was made with saffron and veal tongue. And with Barolo, sweetbreads and radicchio. And with frogs' legs. And with peppers and corn. The fish and meat courses were similarly imaginative, but we have to say that we usually find them less successful than the rest of the dishes—and since our ratings are based on food alone, that's why Valentino just misses getting 18 points. So we often order two appetizers and a pasta, or an appetizer, a pasta and a risotto. But a few of the fresh fish are good, and the pigeon, grilled rare in a sauce of red wine and its own liver, is wonderful. Having a multi-course dinner like this can cost $175 to $225 per couple, including wine, but how often do you get the opportunity to have the best of anything?

In all honesty, we must tell you that a few friends don't share our enthusiasm for Valentino. If they go with people who know Selvaggio, they find his personal, tableside ministrations a bit excessive; if they go anonymously—as typical diners, without his ministrations—they say the food can be uneven. But we find Selvaggio, and dinner at Valentino, almost invariably a delight, and most knowledgeable diners we know share that judgment. Moreover, food isn't all Valentino has to offer. The restaurant also has one of the best wine lists in the country, at prices far more reasonable than at virtually any other first-rate restaurant we know, anywhere. Selvaggio has 100,000 bottles of wine, most of them cataloged on his 64-page list—and not just Italian wines but French and Californians as well. The California list alone runs twenty pages and includes thirteen vintages of B.V. Private Reserve (five of them in half bottles). Although the list includes all the Napa and Sonoma Valley heavyweights, it also has more than 100 California choices at $25 or less. Selvaggio's French list runs 24 pages and includes seventeen vintages of Château Margaux (dating back to the 1865, for a mere $2,700) and 23 vintages of Château Lafite Rothschild (dating back to the 1893, for only $6,000). The Burgundy section has three and a half pages on just the wines from the Domaine de la Romanée Conti. But with the French selections, too, there are bargains to be had—albeit not nearly as many of them. Valentino is an Italian restaurant, though, so we always order Italian wines. Again, let Selvaggio be your guide. We love Barolo, and he has three and a half pages of them, by all the best producers (Giacosa, Conterno, Ceretto, Mascarello, Ratti), ranging in price from $29 to $185. Be sure to save a few sips to have with a chunk of fresh Parmigiana, one of the best ways we can imagine to end a meal (although desserts, long a weak point, have improved considerably in recent months, and we now, alas, must save room for them as well). A three-course dinner off the menu, with wine, will run about $125 for two; a larger Selvaggio-composed feast can add $50 to $100 to that tab.

10/20 Verdi

1519 Wilshire Blvd., Santa Monica
393-0706
ITALIAN
Open Tues.-Sun. 6 p.m.-2 a.m. All major cards.

What has happened here? Verdi used to offer fine northern Italian cuisine, served with nightly entertainment ranging from opera (hence the name) to Broadway show tunes, with a bit of Kurt Weill thrown in for good measure. Verdi was also an architectural landmark—it was the first restaurant by the Morphosis design team, which went on to build Angeli, 72 Market Street and Kate Mantilini, among others—with a comfortable, modern interior. The good news is that the entertainment is still as enjoyable as ever (and continues, most nights, until 1 a.m.), and customers are treated with deference and respect (it's one of the few restaurants in town that doesn't flinch at patrons who show up at nine on Saturday evening wanting only dessert and cappuccino). But has the kitchen fallen upon hard times, or have our Italian taste buds grown more sophisticated? Whatever the reason, the diva is missing notes—the food is disappointing. Part of the problem seems to be subpar ingredients; our insalata caprese suffered from overly salty, overly fishy anchovies and flavorless mozzarella, which wasn't improved any by a sprinkling of olive oil that only made matters heavy and commercial-tasting. The fish in the various seafood dishes was tough and stringy on more than one occasion, and the pastas were overcooked and bland. And if a restaurant insists on using frozen or refrigerated bread, it should have the alacrity to warm it before serving; the center of ours was cold and as hard as a stone. Verdi should remember its beginnings, when it served wonderful regional Italian food—and was a pioneer for doing so. If we're going to listen to people sing for their supper, we at least want the food to be good. Dinner for two, with wine, runs about $100.

Versailles

10319 Venice Blvd., Culver City
558-3168
CUBAN
Open daily 11 a.m.-10 p.m. Cards: MC, V.

A palace the Versailles is not. In fact, it might be mistaken for the bunker of the used-car dealership with which it shares a parking lot. What Versailles is, however, is a lively, noisy, crowded little Cuban restaurant highlighted by illuminated beer advertisements and filled with insistent Latin music blaring from a radio. The clientele is a mix of types from nearby MGM, hipsters, artists, shoe salesmen, actual Cubans—a cross-section, we've observed, of L.A. rich and poor—because who doesn't love a bargain? The prices are low and the food is fresh and good. There are fresh-squeezed orange and carrot juices and delicious mango shakes. Some complain that the food is greasy, but that's because they've been foolish enough to order roast pork or deep-fried whole Florida pompano instead of Versailles's roast chicken, which is, simply, some of the best roast chicken available anywhere in town. Crisp-skinned, this giant half chicken tastes of a wonderful lime-vinegar marinade laced with plenty of garlic, and is served with slices of sweet raw onion, fried plantains, a plate of white rice and a cup of black beans. The beans aren't the absolute best in town, but at $25, including tip, for two chicken dinners, a couple of beers, deliciously strong espresso or caffè latte and a shared dish of candied mangos and cream cheese for dessert—who cares?

 Warszawa

1414 Lincoln Blvd., Santa Monica
393-8831

POLISH

Open nightly 5:30 p.m.-10:30 p.m. All major cards.

What was once a private home is now Warszawa, in the heart of Santa Monica's business district. The restaurant's interior is a series of small, softly lit, lace-curtained rooms, and the gracious, homey mood is enhanced by classical music. The diners, who range widely in age, appearance and company, come for this warmth, but most of all they come for the robust, flavorful, completely enjoyable food. The soups, for example: a truly superb hot borscht or a dense pea with bits of smoked ham, which satisfy the soul as well as the body. A full meal could happily be made of the soup, the crusty pumpernickel bread and the herring filets in a suave sour-cream sauce, with perhaps the crunchy sweet-and-sour Warszawa salad, composed of sauerkraut, apples, carrots and caraway. But then you'd miss the glorious bigos (hunter's stew), a fragrant and spicy

traditional dish of sausage, sauerkraut, beef and bacon, served with dumplings. Better to come with a group and order all of the above, as well as the crispy and well-seasoned duck, stuffed with caraway, lemon and apple and served with an amazing dark, herby applesauce; the stuffed cabbage, encasing ground meat, rice and onion; and one of the changing daily specials, which might be veal paprikash, horseradish-sauced beef tongue or roasted game hen stuffed with herbs. Because the portions are huge and the food is peasant-hearty, you'll certainly be sated—but dessert is a must. The homemade cheesecake is lovely, in a spicy brown-sugar crust, and we love the rum-walnut torte. There is a decently varied wine list (which would benefit from a few more German and Eastern European selections, considering the cuisine) and a few imported beers. About $70 for dinner for two, with wine.

12/20 West Beach Café

60 N. Venice Blvd., Venice
823-5396

CALIFORNIAN

Open Mon. 11:30 a.m.-2:45 p.m. & 6 p.m.-10 p.m., Tues.-Fri. 8 a.m.-2:45 p.m. & 6 p.m.-10:30 p.m., Sat. 10:30 a.m.-2:45 p.m. & 6 p.m.-11:30 p.m., Sun. 10:30 a.m.-2:45 p.m. & 6 p.m.-10:30 p.m. All major cards.

The West Beach was Bruce Marder's first restaurant, and it remains his best, simply because (unlike the problematic Rebecca's and the even more problematic DC3) it's almost completely gimmick-free. What we have here is nothing more than a shoebox-shape restaurant, with lots of modern art on the walls, a crowded bar on one side and tables so close together you can hear the people sitting next to you inhaling and exhaling. The service by aspiring actors (who had better be better thespians than they are waiters) is lacking—these young people seem to have a distinct problem with such high concepts as water and coffee (at times the concept of bringing food from the kitchen to your table tends to elude them as well).

On the positive side, the West Beach has a wondrous jolt of energy, a good deal of excitement and some generally fine, often creative food. There are chicken, duck and shrimp salads, but there were far more ingredients listed on the menu for each of these than we found on the plate (Mexican shrimp with arugula, sliced garlic, hothouse cucumbers, Roma tomatoes, Manchego cheese, Ardoino-brand extra virgin oil and such). The pastas are exotic (fedelini and Pacific tuna in a garlic cream sauce), the burgers reputable, the oyster-and-potato casserole a bit too oily. Entrées lean in the direction of pumpkin tortellini in lamb sauce, grilled skinless trout filets (with a mignonette of eggplant and porcini mushrooms, served with a slice of baked banana squash with nutmeg—do we really have to know all this?), and roast rack of lamb with sage (served with a gratin of eggplant, zucchini and tomatoes glazed with Locatelli Romano cheese). Dishes may not always work, but you'll never be bored. We certainly haven't been bored here, being too busy constantly wondering how many times you have to ask for: a) more mineral water; b) bread; c) dessert; d) sweetener for the coffee; and e) the check. And the check itself can be quite an adventure, for entrée prices average from the mid-$20s into the low $30s. The place only *looks* like a small beachside café; the prices are pure haute, and pure pain. Dinner for two, with wine, costs $120 or more.

6/20 World Famous Malibu Sea Lion U.S.A.

21150 Pacific Coast Hwy., Malibu
456-2810
AMERICAN/SEAFOOD
Open daily 10 a.m.-10 p.m. Cards: AE, MC, V.
The fork was sitting on the floor in the middle of the aisle near our booth as our excessively smiley waitress seated us. Over the next two hours, dozens of busboys, waiters and waitresses walked past it. And not one, not a single one, bent to pick it up. Malibu Sea Lion is another Bob Morris creation, based on the belief that if you throw enough food at the public, at low prices, they'll beat a path to your door. Morris is also responsible for RJ's—The Rib Joint, Gladstone's 4 Fish and Cabo Cabo Cabo, all of which are notable for serving large portions, sort of a twist on the old Woody Allen joke, "The food was terrible, and the portions were so small." In this case, you get huge portions. At the massive salad bar, a Bob Morris signature item, you can crowd you plate with several pounds of food. At the end of the line stood a young

smile machine who asked if we'd like some sort of glutinous dressing on our greens. We said yes, a small amount. She then took our carefully composed salad, dropped it into a bowl and drowned it in what tasted like hydrocarbon products and salt, returning to us a gummy mush that was far from what we had in mind. As in Hollywood, everything is bigger than life: the ribs are from the Pleistocene, the potatoes are the size of pumpkins (and just as tasty), and the chocolate cake looks like a small houseboat. People take lots of food home from this place. Dinner for two, with beer costs about $30.

11/20 Yamato

Century Plaza Hotel, 2025 Ave. of the Stars, Century City
277-1840
JAPANESE
Open Mon.-Fri. 11 a.m.-2:30 p.m. & 5 p.m.-11 p.m., Sat. 5 p.m.-11 p.m., Sun. 4:30 p.m.-10:30 p.m. All major cards.
An ethnic restaurant connected to a major hotel always hints of a tourist trap. But Yamato offers fine, well-prepared food at fair prices (especially the "twilight dinners," served until 6:30 p.m., which are only $8.50 to $12.75). The menu is standard Japanese, with many combination plates, but there are such things as crab cocktail, avocado salad and pork cutlet to appease the less adventurous. Tempura is very light and crisp. Teriyaki steak is not, as so often happens, oversauced; it is tender and as rare as requested. King crab legs are moist and buttery. Taki awasi is a delight—a mound of custardy tofu that is quickly deep fried for a crisp crust, then smothered with lightly cooked mushrooms, other vegetables and bits of meat. Side dishes are well prepared, especially the delicately sauced greens. Initial service can drag, but once the food begins to arrive, courses are served at proper intervals. The dining room is hardly exciting, but there's a fresh flower at every table and soft lantern light; there are also a small sushi bar, teppan grill room and shoji-screened private rooms. Tired travelers, depressed with the prospect of eating in the hotel, will be happily surprised here. About $60 for two, with sake.

12/20 Yanks

262 S. Beverly Dr., Beverly Hills
859-2657

AMERICAN

Open Mon.-Thurs. 11:30 a.m.-2:30 p.m. & 5:30 p.m.-10 p.m., Fri.-Sat. 11:30 a.m.-2:30 p.m. & 5:30 p.m.-11 p.m., Sun. 5:30 p.m.-10 p.m. All major cards.

Yanks is such an affable restaurant that you feel tempted to nudge the place a bit, in the hope that things might turn just a bit more persnickety. This is a Beverly Hills version of down-home eats. The waiters may not walk about wearing overalls and clodhoppers, but they're just so gosh-darn friendly, you have to wonder if they're for real. Far as we can tell, they are. They're friendly, the food they serve is friendly, the ambience is friendly. This is Iowa come to Beverly Hills. Not that Yanks looks like a restaurant in the Corn Belt. The design is clean and spare, in a warm sort of way. You're comfortable sitting at the bar, you're even more comfortable at the tables, which are set far enough apart that you don't have the sense that the people seated next to you are taking notes on the more intimate elements of your conversation. The food is reminiscent of what's served at other good local American modern restaurants, from the Columbia Bar & Grill to 72 Market Street. The Cajun meatloaf is reasonably spicy, with a mild burn as it descends the gullet. Like most of the down-home dishes served at Yanks, the meatloaf is good without approaching—or attempting to approach—great. There are, for instance, very nice Louisiana (*Louisiana,* of course, is the code for *hot*) crabcakes, served with a chunky, freshly made tartar sauce. Chili is served Cincinnati-style (that is, with red pinto beans). A Yankee salad of chicken, bacon, blue cheese, tomato and yellow and red peppers sounded good but lacked character—the ingredients just sat there on the plate, staring at one another, not sure of what to say or do. There's a good chicken pot pie (though we prefer the one served at DuPar's), roast chicken with herbs and garlic, grilled swordfish with a tomato chutney, grilled salmon with lime butter. In the bar, you can eat homemade potato chips, which are interesting because they're homemade, though they're not really better than most commercial brands. Dinner for two, with wine, costs about $70.

QUICK BITES

THE SIMPLE PLEASURES

L os Angeles has no shortage of wonderful restaurants, from extravagant, elegant temples of fine cuisine to lively, crowded bistros. But you'll be missing out on some of L.A.'s finest if you limit your eating to formal restaurants, because L.A. has some of the country's best fun food—incomparable taco stands, respectable barbecue, great burgers, heavenly breakfasts, authentic deli and inspired pizzas (both "real" pizza and its fashionable California-style derivative). No matter that the places on the following pages represent good bargains. At many of them you'll find some of the town's wealthiest people—people who appreciate good food whether it's served in a chic restaurant or from a Formica counter.

There are literally thousands of quick-bites places in the L.A. area; we've sought out the best, but we couldn't possibly find them all. Forgive us if we've left out your favorite hot dog stand or diner—for now, at least, your secret is safe!

BARBECUE

Benny's Barbecue
4077 Lincoln Blvd., Marina del Rey
821-6939
Open Mon.-Sat. 11 a.m.-10 p.m., Sun. 4 p.m.-10 p.m. No cards.

The way to identify good barbecue is to follow your nose. And you can smell the food cooking at Benny's from at least two blocks away. Though there are a few tables, this is really take-out food—from the superb ribs bathed in a fiery sauce to what may be the best hot links in town, more like meatloaf in a skin, with lots of peppercorns and plenty of bite. About $18 for two.

Carl's Bar-B-Q
5953 W. Pico Blvd., Wilshire District
934-0637
Open Mon.-Sat. 11:30 a.m.-midnight, Sun. 2 p.m.-11:45 p.m. No cards.

Carl's is one of L.A.'s best barbecue joints—out of its huge brick barbecue emerge messy, wonderful hickory-smoked ribs and chicken, superb hot links and tender roast beef and pork, all awash in a barbecue sauce that is sweet, vinegary and spicy at the same time; it comes medium or hot; the medium is bold and the hot will take your breath away. Don't miss the robust dirty rice, Carl's mother's recipe. The atmosphere is appropriately funky.

About $18 for an eat-there or a take-home barbecue feast for two.

Dr. Hogly Wogly's Tyler, Texas, Barbecue
8136 N. Sepulveda Blvd., Van Nuys
(818) 780-6701
Open daily noon-10 p.m. No cards.

We're happy to report that the recent change of ownership of this landmark 'cue joint hasn't changed the place one whit; the kitchen and floor staffs are intact, as are the recipes Hogly Wogly built its reputation on. The fame of this unpretentious restaurant has spread so much that there's usually a crowd lining the walls, waiting for a table and a huge plate of barbecue. Named for original owner Johnny Greene, who got his nickname in 1932 when he was a chubby delivery boy for a Piggly Wiggly market in Texas, this simple place, done in Early American vinyl and Formica, serves good Texas hot links, fantastic spareribs, tender chicken and delicious beef brisket. It's all good, except for the sometimes dry barbecued pork. All the meat is smoked on the premises, and two wonderful sauces, mild and hot, accompany the meals, so you can season to taste (the hot sauce is actually on the mild side). Portions are huge, and there are all the standard accompaniments, from coleslaw to baked beans. You'll be so full it'll be hard to succumb to the tempting pecan and sweet-potato pies. Dinner for two, with beer, will run about $30.

Mom's Bar-B-Q House
14062 Vanowen St., Van Nuys
(818) 786-1373
Open Mon.-Thurs. 11 a.m.-9:30 p.m., Fri.-Sat. 11 a.m.-11 p.m. No cards.

Deep in the heart of Van Nuys lies an unprepossessing mini-mall that houses two of L.A.'s best little finds, one of which is Mom's (the other is the foolishly monikered Gee, I Can't Believe It's Fish). Mom's has been a hit since it opened, and recently expanded—no surprise, since it dishes up some of the city's best barbecue. The decor is strictly rec-room, but the beef and pork ribs, chicken, hot links, fried chicken, fried chicken livers and rib tips will render you blind to your surroundings. While the meats aren't quite as tender as those at Dr. Hogly Wogly's, they're absolutely delicious and authentically smoky. The sides are terrific, too, especially the macaroni and cheese and the long-cooked baked beans. Even after the mammoth portions here, don't eschew the pineapple-coconut cake: the perfect antidote to the heat of Mom's sauce. Dinner for two runs about $20.

Mr. Jim's Pit Bar-B-Que
3809 S. Vermont Ave., South-Central L.A.
737-9727
5403 S. Vermont Ave., South-Central L.A.
778-6070
10303 Avalon Blvd., Watts
757-0221
Open daily 11 a.m.-4 a.m. No cards.

That inimitable hickory barbecue smell hits you about a block before you reach Mr. Jim's, a little take-out restaurant near USC and the Coliseum that draws barbecue fans from across the city. The incredible pork spareribs are the best thing here; beef ribs are tasty but a little tough. Order your ribs medium, and you'll get a smoky, rather sweet sauce; a hot order is true to its word. Rib dinners are served with the typical bland white bread, excellent, thick baked beans and good potato salad. If you can possibly save room for one of the delicious little sweet-potato tarts, it will be worth it. Mr. Jim's is not for the meek of heart who never leave Encino—the neighborhoods around all the branches can be intimidating. The eponymous Mr. Jim passed on not too long ago, but so far, the quality hasn't wavered at the various branches. About $18 for a barbecue orgy for two.

Warren's BBQ
4916 W. Slauson Ave., Ladera Heights
294-2272
Open Mon.-Thurs. 11 a.m.-9 p.m., Fri.-Sat. 11 a.m.-9:30 p.m., Sun. 2 p.m.-7 p.m. No cards.

Located in an upscale black neighborhood, Warren's is a spic-and-span barbecue haven, in an area that has no lack of good barbecue. You can eat in or take out, and owner Warren Gray is a knowledgable guide through the world of wood-smoked meats. The hot links are spicy and wonderfully grainy; the ribs and chicken are falling-off-the-bone tender. Warren also serves Cleveland-style pork sandwiches and heavenly barbecued boudin blanc sausage. The beans are smoky, the slaw is tart, and the sweet-potato pie is so good that you won't mind if its sweetness makes your fillings ache. A robust dinner for two will run about $18.

CAFES

LOS ANGELES - CENTRAL

Bullock's Wilshire Tea Room
3050 Wilshire Blvd., Mid-Wilshire
382-6161
Open Mon.-Sat. 11:30 a.m.-5 p.m., Sun. noon-5 p.m. Cards: AE, MC, V.

If you want to step back into a genteel and proper world, the Bullock's Wilshire Tea Room offers a welcome retro respite from a world gone bonkers. The building itself is a gorgeous art deco landmark (this was the first department store in Los Angeles to feature the main entrance in the back, off the carport)—all ziggurat moderne angles, mosaics commemorating the history of transportation, and escalators with beautifully detailed doors and real live operators. The Tea Room is on the fifth floor, and chances are that if your hair isn't a certain shade of blue and you're not clad in Chanel, you'll be considered slightly suspect. But that's okay—the maître d' is a charming pro, the waitresses are friendly, and the food is comforting and much better than you may expect. Salads and sandwiches are fresh and tasty, the breads and muffins in a basket on the table are homemade, and the afternoon tea is a quiet riot of finger sandwiches, scones and pots of jams and Devonshire cream. Lunch for two is about $25.

Note: As we went to press, it was announced that Bullock's Wilshire will become an I. Magnin store in 1990. The merchandise mix, and perhaps the customer mix, will change somewhat, but the Tea Room should carry on as ever.

Café des Artistes

1534 N. McCadden Pl., Hollywood
461-6889
Open Mon.-Fri. & Sun. noon-2:30 & 7 p.m.-11 p.m. All major cards.

This is not a street you're likely to find yourself on, unless you're attending the neighboring Stages Theater, which is owned by the same couple who run this terrific spot. Don't let the grimness of the block deter you from venturing past the row of hedges that protects this beautiful little converted bungalow from the street. On the bright patio or in the serene dining room, a pre- and post-theater crowd—as well as locals in on the secret—lunch, dine or brunch on a small but fine selection of salads, pastas and simple entrées. We have been least pleased with lunch, but we could not have been more pleased with the lovely Sunday brunch, when a classical trio plays, and an impeccable array of fruit, juices, sparkling and still wines, breads, salads, meats and desserts are laid out and fluffy omelets are made to order. It's one of our favorite brunches in town, and at $15 per person, it's a good deal (though not quite the bargain it once was). At brunch or dinner, be sure to try the delicious salad of chicken and almonds dressed with a balsamic vinaigrette, and the unspeakably marvelous crème caramel. Brunch for two runs $35, with wine.

Café Figaro

9010 Melrose Ave., W. Hollywood
274-7664
Open daily 11:30 a.m.-midnight. Cards: MC, V.

For years Café Figaro has been immensely popular with L.A.'s under-30 set. Much of this popularity was due to L.A.'s former lack of simple French and Italian cafés, though now places much better than Café Fig, as it's called, are abundant. But these big, rather shabby rooms still fill up fast on the weekends; we attribute this to the low prices, good location, relatively late hours and comfortable, casual atmosphere. Certainly the food isn't the draw—the hamburgers, sandwiches, omelets, simple entrées and generous desserts are all mediocre. Wine and beer are served. Two will spend about $28 for a simple supper with a glass of wine.

Cafe Habana

7465 Melrose Ave., W. Hollywood
655-2822
Open Sun.-Wed. 11 a.m.-10:30 p.m., Thurs.-Sat. 11 a.m.-11:30 p.m. Cards: AE, MC, V.

The best of the new Cubans that have been popping up around town lately, Cafe Habana is right in the center of the melee that is Melrose, and its picture windows provide excellent people-watching opportunities. Slickly designed, this tiny storefront serves the usual Cuban specialties—garlicky shrimp, roast pork—and, while the roast chicken here isn't quite the epiphany that Versailles's is, Cafe Habana's version manages to acquit itself nicely. But the Cuban sandwich here is the real deal—a veritable Dagwood piled with roast pork, ham, pickles and Swiss cheese on a loaf of sweet Cuban bread that's been slathered with mayonnaise, butter and mustard. And just in case you need some more carbs after all that, the flan is silky and delicious. About $30 for dinner for two, with beer; lunch runs about $18 for two.

Café Mambo

707 Heliotrope St., Hollywood
663-5800
Open Sun.-Thurs. 11 a.m.-3 p.m. & 6 p.m.-10 p.m., Fri.-Sat. 11 a.m.-3 p.m. & 6 p.m.-11 p.m. Cards: AE, MC, V.

Situated in a rather grimy no-man's-land between Hollywood, Los Feliz and Silverlake, just off the only stretch of Melrose that is (at this writing) truly hip, Café Mambo is an eminently likable café. The Caribbean influences are tasteful and not overdone, the clientele is hip but not annoyingly trendy, the room is rarely overcrowded, and the food is simply very good. Late breakfast (served until 3 p.m.) is our favorite Mambo meal: big glasses of fresh juice, marvelous chilequiles with blue-corn tortillas, thick french toast with fresh fruit, good coffee. Lunch and dinner run to pastas (tasty carbonara), creative sandwiches and Caribbeanish grills. Service is cheery and laid-back. About $15 to $20 for breakfast or lunch for two.

Caffè Latte
6254 Wilshire Blvd., Wilshire District
936-5213
Open Sun.-Mon. 7 a.m.-3:15 p.m., Tues.-Sat. 7 a.m.-3:15 p.m. & 6 p.m.-11 p.m. Cards: MC, V.

Caffè Latte is run by young, affable Tom Kaplan, whose family owns Hugo's in West Hollywood, and he's learned his lesson well: Caffè Latte is as big a hit as papa's place. About to expand as this is being written, Caffè Latte is yet another gem in a mini-mall, popular not only with neighborhood residents and doctors, dentists and ad-agency and publishing types from the surrounding office buildings, but with designers, writers and other creative sorts who've been somewhat disenfranchised by the heavy industry buzz that permeates Hugo's. The decor is sweet, if rather haute, coffee shop, and the food is solid and enticing. For breakfast, there are lots of egg dishes, pancakes and freshly baked pastries (as well as a version of Hugo's gut-busting Pasta Mama); lunch and dinner feature lots of sandwiches (including a first-rate BLT), pastas and grilled things. Caffè Latte also proudly serves Jody Maroni's supernal, exotic sausages (such as chicken with fig and duck with orange and cumin) and coffee roasted right on the premises, sold in bulk as well as by the cup.

Caffè Notte
7463 Melrose Ave., W. Hollywood
655-2222
Open Sun.-Thurs. 11 a.m.-midnight, Fri.-Sat. 11 a.m.-2 a.m. Cards: MC, V.

Caffè Notte is set apart on café-clogged Melrose by its generally uncrowded room, its late hours and its coffeehouse style—the food is as simple as can be, and if you just want to hang out for an hour over a cappuccino and a tiramisu, that's fine with the folks here. The menu is divided into four areas: salads (big enough for two; try the tangy, tasty bow-tie pasta with chicken), pizzas (thick-crusted, cheesy, rich and good), desserts (all the Italian standards, including delicious tiramisu) and beverages (primarily espresso/cappuccino creations; no liquor). Prices are as low as the pretension level: $22 for a pizza supper for two, with cappuccino.

Cocola
410 Boyd St., Downtown
680-0756
Open daily 11:30 a.m.-2 a.m. Cards: AE, MC, V.

Cocola is composed of equal parts modern, minimalist design, sniffy pretension and relentlessly ordinary food. The upside of this popular café is that it's close to the Temporary Contempory and MOCA (and the rest of the downtown art scene), it's open until 2 a.m., and the people-watching is sublime. There's something amusingly surreal about the place, akin to Griffin Dunne's tumble down the rabbit hole in the film *After Hours*, but don't make any detours to get here.

El Conchinito
3508 W. Sunset Blvd., Silverlake
668-0737
Open Mon. 10 a.m.-3 p.m., Tues.-Sat. 10 a.m.-8 p.m. No cards.

The owner of this plain little diner is from Montuleño in the Yucatán, and this is the place to find the very appealing cuisine of his homeland. It's Mexican-style food with a West Indies influence; the tacos, tortas and so on are less spicy and more delicate than their typical Mexican counterparts (though the dark-red chile sauce on the table is rich and hot). Try the salbute, a puffy corn tortilla topped with lettuce, onion and turkey, beef or pork; the panucho, a delicious tortilla with a thin layer of black beans inside, with toppings like the salbute; or the pollo Montuleño, a small, marinated half chicken atop a thin layer of black beans and a tortilla, then topped with another tortilla, bright-red tomato salsa and grated cheese. And by all means try one of the liquados, a marvelous kind of Mexican shake with fruit, milk and ice. About $12 for two.

Gasoline Alley
7219 Melrose Ave., W. Hollywood
937-5177
Open Tues.-Thurs. 10 a.m.-1 a.m., Fri.-Sat. noon-3 a.m., Sun. noon-2 a.m. No cards.

An early addition to L.A.'s recent coffee-house renaissance, Gasoline Alley is perhaps a bit too slick-looking for true authenticity (though at least you don't feel as though you need an inoculation after a visit, as you do at the Pikme-Up), but the feeling is warm and friendly, and the espresso, cappuccino, teas, light meals and desserts are just fine. And fear not—the de rigueur board games, newspapers and magazines are all on hand. About $12 for a light snack and beverage.

Gorky's Café
536 E. 8th St., Downtown
627-4060
1716 N. Cahuenga Blvd., Hollywood
463-4060
Open daily 24 hours. No cards.

Both branches of Gorky's are located in the seedier parts of town—one on the fringes of the garment district, where the homeless congregate en masse, and the other in the Hollywood jungle that Guns N' Roses sings about, where tattoo-drenched locals stagger about in a narcotic haze. But these worlds are left behind once you step into these high-ceilinged rooms filled with an amusing mishmash of executives, artists, eccentrics, women taking a break from the rigors of garment-district bargain hunting and, in the case of the Hollywood location (the site of the late lamented Tick Tock), those who are simply slumming. The menu aptly describes Gorky's as a "Russian avant-garde café with working people's prices." The decor is cheery but strictly utilitarian: long Formica tables, rustic booths, high-tech hanging lights and plastic cafeteria trays, on which you pile such simple, generous peasant fare as piroshki, Polish sausage with sauerkraut, and blintzes. There are also some fine salads and sandwiches, good omelets from the omelet bar and a couple of hearty daily specials. Also note that the downtown location recently added a brew pub that's

become all the rage in the evening. All the food is plain, good and wonderfully cheap— $16 will fill two starving Cossacks. Gorky's also features plenty of imported beers, rich desserts and an uneven roster of musicians.

Grand Avenue Bar
Biltmore Hotel, 515 S. Grand Ave., Downtown
624-1011
Open Mon.-Fri. 11:30 a.m.-2:30 p.m. (bar to 1:30 a.m.). All major cards.

A little Siberia, but a very chic Siberia, with high ceilings, marble tables, Mies van der Rohe chairs and a big screen TV, in front of which sit solid executive sorts who line up at the elegant, daily-changing buffet. It's the best lunch value downtown—for $15.95, you can dine to your heart's content on such good things as seafood or vegetable terrines, duck pâté, a ballotine of turkey, cold pastas, delicate salads, thin-sliced prime rib and beautiful desserts. After 5 p.m. the local offices empty out and the bar fills up with a crowd of businesspeople of both sexes, who don't necessarily come to discuss the stock market.

The Gumbo Pot
Farmer's Market, 6333 W. 3rd St., Wilshire District
933-0358
Open Mon.-Sat. 9 a.m.-6:30 p.m., Sun. 10 a.m.-5 p.m. No cards.

No need to spend $20 to $40 a head at Orleans or Patout's—not when you can come to the Gumbo Pot in touristy Farmer's Market, spend about $8 and get great Cajun/Creole food. The best things here are the incredible muffelata sandwiches, the very flavorful gumbo yaya with chicken, shrimp and andouille sausage, and the moist, delicious cornbread studded with whole corn, sweet roasted chiles and cheese. Also good are the sinful beignets, the not-too-hot Cajun meatloaf and the sweet-potato salad with apples, pecans and raisins. The gumbo, jambalaya, cornbread and salad are also available to go. Get a soda from a neighboring stand and plan to spend about $6 to $8 per person for lunch.

Hard Rock Cafe
Beverly Center, 8600 Beverly Blvd.,
W. Hollywood
276-7605
Open daily 11:30 a.m.-midnight. Cards: AE, MC, V.

Parents who worry about the effect rock concerts have on their kids' ears would be well advised to ban them from the Hard Rock—the noise level here on a Saturday night rivals front-row seats at a Metallica concert. L.A.'s after-dark teen scene is right here; carefully coiffed kids line up outside, anxious for a chance to get inside, where they can show off their outfits, see their friends, meet new ones and contribute to the din. Though the '50s and '60s rock still plays and the room is still full, lunch seems a little less loud and trendy, perhaps because you see more over-25 business sorts and large groups of pointing-and-gawking tourists during the lunch hour. The sea-foam–green Cadillac plunging through the roof, the classic music, the '50s movie-and-music memorabilia, the hopping bar, the white-uniformed waitresses—it's all great fun. Surprisingly, the food is pretty good, too, especially the burgers, chili, lime chicken and apple pie à la mode. A must-visit for out-of-towners, especially younger ones. About $15 to $18 per person, without drinks.

Hot Wings Café
7011 Melrose Ave., Hollywood
930-1233
Open Mon.-Thurs. 11 a.m.-midnight, Fri.-Sat. 11 a.m.-2 a.m., Sun. 5 p.m.-midnight. No cards.

A great place to know about, if only because it's one of the cheapest places to eat on ever-upscale Melrose (and it's open late). Hot Wings is a simple, storefront café with a collegiate atmosphere and good, simple food: juicy Reuben sandwiches, good burgers and French dips, classic New York cheesecake, and honest cappuccinos. The specialties of the house are all imports from the East Coast, from tasty buffalo chicken wings with fiery dipping sauces to Philly steak sandwiches and generous grinders. About $9 for a sandwich and an imported beer.

Java
7286 Beverly Blvd., Wilshire District
931-4943
Open Mon.-Thurs. 8 a.m.-2 a.m., Fri. 8 a.m.-3 a.m., Sat.-Sun. 10 a.m.-3 a.m. No cards.

The newest addition to L.A.'s coffeehouse population, Java is easily the most accessible. Opened by a trio of art students, this small storefront is surprisingly beautifully designed and eclectically decorated, with comfy antique chairs, tables and sofas. Delicious pastries by Il Fornaio are served, as are a small yet good selection of salads, to accompany the cappuccino, espresso, teas and juices. We're pleased to say that there isn't a shred of attitude here, and the crowd is nicely mixed—i.e., you won't feel out of place if you aren't clad all in black, shod in Doc Martens and coiffed à la Mixmaster. Also, on Sunday evenings, there are readings by such prominent local poets and writers as Wanda Coleman, Eve Babitz and Carolyn See. Espresso and dessert for two runs about $10.

Kokomo
Farmer's Market, 6333 W. 3rd St.,
Wilshire District
933-0773
Open Mon.-Sat. 8 a.m.-7 p.m., Sun. 8 a.m.-6 p.m. No cards.

The times certainly are a-changin'—who'd ever expect to find a neohip café like Kokomo ensconced in that Valhalla for tourists, Farmer's Market? It's just an orange pit's throw away from the Gumbo Pot, the owners of which are also responsible for Kokomo, tucked away in a corner of the market that isn't too beset by folks bedecked in plaid polyester Sansabelt Bermudas. The fare is of the hyper–coffee shop variety, including a BLT made with organically grown tomatoes, thick-sliced bacon and pesticide-free lettuce; it's one of the best BLTs in town. Kokomo also does mean burgers and chicken sandwiches and wonderful sweet-potato fries, as well as hearty morning fare. In fact, Kokomo has become a major power breakfast and lunch scene for music and show-biz folk; among the patrons are David Byrne and Axl Rose. The aspiring actors behind the counter are mostly very sweet and competent, but they're occasionally inclined to fits of major attitude. But with prices this low and food this good, that's a small price to pay. About $12 for lunch for two.

Mario's
7475 Beverly Blvd., Wilshire District
931-6342
Open Mon.-Sat. 8 a.m.-9:30 p.m. Cards: AE, DC.

For months we drove by this former gas station, watching its remodeling progress, hopeful that the developing Italian deli would prove to be as good as it looked—this neighborhood could really use a decent Italian deli/café/caterer. Happily, the food turned out to be every bit as appealing as the clean-lined design of the deli and the sponge-painted, frescoed, marble-countered dining room. Glass deli cases hold gorgeous salads (smoked chicken and roasted red pepper; roasted fennel; pasta creations), trays of savory rotisserie-roasted chicken, every kind of prepared meat and an array of cheeses; baskets hold beautiful Italian breads. The kitchen also prepares thick sandwiches made with the dense, flavorful house bread (many are less than $4 and are accompanied by a green salad), a pasta or two of the day and one or two simple entrées, all for less than $10. You can eat your delicious, self-service food in the dining room or at one of the outdoor tables, or take it home. At breakfast, the counter is laden with Italian breads and breakfast pastries, and the cappuccino machine is kept humming. As we write this, Mario's was about to start full lunch and dinner service, but deadlines won't allow us to give a full report. Lunch for two, with a cappuccino, runs from $12 to $20.

The Melting Pot
8490 Melrose Ave., W. Hollywood
652-8030
Open Mon.-Thurs. & Sun. 8 a.m.-11 p.m., Fri.-Sat. 8 a.m.-midnight. All major cards.

This holdover from the '70s is a pleasant and centrally located spot for lunch, whether you're on the cheery patio or in one of the comfortable dining rooms. Inside you get the feeling of being in an old country cottage, with low, beamed ceilings, antique mahogany-framed mirrors and bare-wood tables. The food isn't thrilling, but it's well intentioned and quite edible. Chinese chicken salad is especially good, as is the mushroom burger,

but the broiled baroque sandwich (tuna, tomato, avocado and mozzarella) is somewhat bland and heavy. All the Melting Pot's ingredients are scrupulously fresh, and service is friendly and prompt. Lunch with a glass of wine will run about $24 for two.

Mongolian Bar-B-Q
5401 Hollywood Blvd., Hollywood
464-6888
Open Tues.-Thurs. 11:30 a.m.-2:30 p.m. & 4:30 p.m.-9:30 p.m., Fri. 11:30 a.m.-2:30 p.m. & 4:30 p.m.-10 p.m., Sat. 4:30 p.m.-10 p.m., Sun. 4:30 p.m.-9:30 p.m. No cards.

A good find for those on a budget. At dinner, $6.95 gets you a small bowl of soup (usually pretty bad), a bowl of rice, all you can eat of the addictive sesame rolls and two high-as-you-can-pile-'em bowls of tasty Mongolian barbecue. You work your way around the buffet, heaping your bowl with your own combination of beef, lamb, pork, turkey and/or all kinds of vegetables: bean sprouts, carrots, celery, cabbage and so on. You then give this bowl to one of the proprietors, who douses it with sauce, as hot (or mild) as you want. The whole mess is then quick-cooked on the large, open Mongolian barbecue grill, and best eaten stuffed inside the aforementioned hollow sesame rolls. There's no atmosphere and no frills, just a lot of good food for the money.

Moustache Café
8155 Melrose Ave., W. Hollywood
651-2111
1071 Glendon Ave., Westwood
208-6633
Open Mon.-Fri. 11:30 a.m.-1 a.m., Sat. 11 a.m.-1 a.m., Sun. 11 a.m.-midnight. Cards: AE, MC, V.

The Moustache is hardly suffering from a lack of business, though we certainly won't be rushing back. True, the trellis- and plant-lined "enclosed patio" (read: former parking lot) is a charming spot to lunch, though the tables are crammed uncomfortably close together. Some of the dishes are pretty good, like the seafood salad and the Swiss cheese and tomato crêpe. But some of the dishes don't quite make it: the more elaborate entrées are best left unordered, and the much-acclaimed chocolate soufflé is uneven. Service is notoriously slow, no doubt because the kitchen is too small for such a crowd. But this hasn't stopped the throngs of Hollywood starlets and minor moguls from making the Moustache a resounding success. Lunch with a glass of wine will cost two about $28.

Netty's

1700 Silverlake Blvd., Silverlake
662-8655
Open Tues.-Sat. noon-9 p.m. Cards: MC, V.

Netty's is a real find: a hole-in-the-wall (actually, it's a converted gas station) neighborhood joint that serves terrific, right-on-target food—and there's even an herb garden in the back. The eponymous Netty's background includes stints at the late, lamented Mangia and at Angeli; her husband was a chef at the defunct Ritz Cafe. Together, they've put together an eclectic menu that spans the map from Italy to Salvador. The pasta dishes are delicious, the cold case is always filled with fresh, flavorful salads, the entrées and pastas are served with yummy pesto bread and the tamales are a real treat. The menu is a repertory of about 100 dishes, and while most of the business is tak-eout and catering, you can dine on the outdoor patio—the place has a certain charm. Two can dine sumptuously for about $20, without wine.

170 Café

170 S. La Brea Ave., Wilshire District
939-0170
Open Tues.-Sat. 11:30 a.m.-3 p.m. All major cards.

If you've had enough of the galleries at the 170 Art Center, wander upstairs to take a lunch break in this little museumesque café. Surrounded by contemporary art that you can take home if your aesthetic moves you, you can lunch on such simple fare as omelets, quiche, pasta primavera, salads and soups. The food is less inspired than the art, though most of it is tasty enough. There is a good house wine, and desserts can be lovely. About $30 for lunch for two, with a glass of wine.

Onyx Sequel

1802 N. Vermont Ave., Los Feliz
660-5820
Open Sun.-Thurs. 9 a.m.-1 a.m., Fri.-Sat. 9 a.m.-3 a.m. No cards.

Local coffeehouse aficionados were broken-hearted when the original Onyx on Sunset Drive next to the Vista Theater closed, but—this is Hollywood, after all—the Onyx didn't die, it just went into turnaround and sequelized itself. The new digs are down the street from the Los Feliz Theater and Chatterton's Books, on one of L.A.'s few streets that actually show signs of human life after dark. The atmosphere is the same as before—wonderfully bohemian, with denizens who actually have meaningful, philosophizing conversations with one another, or who, if alone, read a book. The fare is simply espresso, cappuccino, various teas and desserts, the price is certainly right, and the ambience is decidedly cerebral and civilized. Onyx Sequel also features live music and readings on Sundays; call for schedules. Two can commune over cappuccino and dessert for about $10.

Il Panini

Museum of Contemporary Art,
250 S. Grand Ave., Downtown
617-1844
Open Tues.-Sun. 8 a.m.-6 p.m. No cards.

MOCA visitors and denizens of the local business behemoths have a terrific lunch spot in Il Panini, a simple Italian café on museum grounds. The sandwich is elevated to a lofty state, each as creative as it is delicious; try the inspired smoked salmon and Mascarpone. Pasta salads are just fine, and there are wines by the glass to accompany lunch and espressos to end it. If the weather is hot, try to get one of the few inside tables—the outdoor tables are shaded by umbrellas, but the sun heats the marble underfoot and bakes diners like so many cookies. Lunch for two, with a glass of wine, will run about $22.

Le Petit Four

8654 W. Sunset Blvd., W. Hollywood
652-3863
Open Mon.-Sat. 9 a.m.-11 p.m., Sun. 9 a.m.-5 p.m. All major cards.

This charming little café doubles as a patisserie and gourmet food shop, featuring Fauchon products. The dining area is in the back, where colorful Delacroix posters line the walls. The delicious aroma of just-baked cakes and tarts is worth a visit in itself; so are the terrines, croquettes, Caesar salads and quiches, which are a cut above those at most other cafés in town. The diminutive portions will leave you hungry for dessert, which is fortunate—the pastries, all made on the premises, are outstanding (try the chocolate praline cake). Many of the better restaurants in town pass off Le Petit Four's pastries as their own. Service is friendly and provides such nice touches as a little crock of pâté with your bread. Mineral waters and good espresso and cappuccino are served, but no wine. About $30 for a most satisfying lunch for two.

Il Piatto
7306 Melrose Ave., W. Hollywood
937-8234
Open Mon.-Thurs. 11:30 a.m.-10 p.m., Fri.-Sat. 11:30 a.m.-11 p.m. Cards: AE.

If you don't want to deal with the crowds and prices at Chianti Cucina and Angeli, walk east a block or two to this quiet, unpretentious café, which serves tasty Italian-Argentinean food at very fair prices. The food may not be as terrific as what's served at its more upscale neighbors, but you'll be more than pleased with the empanadas, the little croquettes and any of the pastas. A simple dinner for two, with a glass of wine, will cost less than $30.

Pikme-Up
5437 W. 6th St., Wilshire District
939-9706
Open Sun.-Thurs. noon-2 a.m., Fri.-Sat. noon-4 a.m. No cards.

The Pikme-Up is one of those places we really wanted to like, since we're big fans of coffeehouses, but we came away feeling old, out of place and unwanted. With good reason: (1) none of the staff and clientele was over the age of 23; (2) everyone was clad in funereal black and looked as if he or she hadn't slept in a fortnight, and (3) we were treated so shabbily and snobbily, probably due in part to reasons 1 and 2, that we felt quite uncomfortable here. On top of that, this is one of the most depressing public spaces outside of the Hotel Fontenoy we've seen in many a moon: old, sagging furniture with sprung springs that attack you; dingy, cigarette-stained walls—even the coffee drinks aren't very good. We suppose that to the floating club-going crowd, the Pikme-Up is the closest thing on this continent to the Pigalle of the twenties. Maybe we're just getting crotchety

in our dotage, but give us Java or the Espresso Bar any day. About $10 for dessert and espresso for two.

La Poubelle
5909 Franklin Ave., Hollywood
462-9264
Open Mon.-Sat. 5:30 p.m.-midnight. Cards: MC, V.

La Poubelle is reminiscent of a multitude of neighborhood cafés in France, which no doubt explains the numbers of French among the clientele. The food, like the somewhat shabby decor, is basic, comforting and unexceptional—the omelets, crêpes, onion soup, salads and simple entrées are tasty and reasonably priced, though not worth a trip from another part of town. The friendly French owner, Mme. Koster, often provides the relaxed service personally. Supper with a glass of French wine will be about $30 for two.

The Source
8301 W. Sunset Blvd., W. Hollywood
656-6388
Open Mon.-Fri. 8 a.m.-midnight, Sat.-Sun. 9 a.m.-midnight. All major cards.

The white-robed spiritualists are long gone, and a more traditional dining experience marks the sign of the times at this L.A. health-food institution, which Woody Allen poked fun at years ago in *Annie Hall*. But it hasn't changed *too* much—you can still get loads of sprouts, healthy salads, brown-rice vegetarian burgers, juices, sandwiches and vegetable concoctions—but no alcohol. The food is quite good, the prices reasonable, breakfast a delight, and the clientele an interesting mix of locals and vegetarian devotees. Request a table on the outdoor patio, which has a good view of Sunset Boulevard's passing parade. About $28 for lunch for two.

Sweet Lady Jane
8360 Melrose Ave., W. Hollywood
653-7145
Open Mon.-Thurs. 9 a.m.-8:30 p.m., Fri.-Sat. 9 a.m.-11:30 p.m. No cards.

L.A. has all too few sit-down dessert cafés; luckily, one of the newest is also one of the best. Located on the west end of Melrose in the middle of interior-design showrooms and overwrought art galleries, Sweet Lady Jane looks like a cozy London tea room, and serves divine, homemade desserts. The cheesecakes are perfection (they come in a bouquet of varieties), the lemon tart is heaven, and the cookies are big and soft—the kind you want to bury your face in. The coffee is served French-filter–style, and there's also an assortment of teas and other coffee drinks. Service is quite friendly, and two can indulge in desserts and beverage for about $15. On weekend evenings after nine or so, there may be a wait to get in, but it's well worth it.

SAN FERNANDO VALLEY

Gee, I Can't Believe It's Fish!
14066 Vanowen St., Van Nuys
(818) 988-3474
Open Mon.-Sat. 11 a.m.-10 p.m., Sun. 1 p.m.-9 p.m. No cards.

We almost avoided this place (hereafter to be called Gee) because of its dreadful moniker; it reminded us of that awful shampoo, "Gee, Your Hair Smells Terrific!" But, to paraphrase the old adage, you can't judge a restaurant by its name, and this is certainly true of this place. Located in the same mini-mall that houses the excellent Mom's Bar-B-Q House (are these mini-malls the Main Streets of the '90s?), Gee is little more than a kitchen, a counter and a few tables, but it's a powerhouse of a place, serving up authentic Cajun seafood. The Cajun craze may be moribund, but don't tell these folks that; the owners are straight from bayou country, and they crank out excellent fried clams, hush puppies, gumbo, jambalaya and catfish to beat the band. In fact, Gee actually gives the superlative Gumbo Pot a run for its money. Two can eat copious amounts of food (without liquor) for about $20.

Maria's Kitchen
13353 Ventura Blvd., Sherman Oaks
(818) 906-0783
Open Mon.-Sat. 11 a.m.-11 p.m., Sun. 3 p.m.-9 p.m. Cards: MC, V.

There's always a wait to get into this simple little Italian deli and café, one of the most popular places in the Valley. Its popularity can be attributed to two things: the low prices and the down-home, retro Italian food. This is the kind of simple Italian food that everyone loves, from Italian-style pizza to linguine with pesto to meaty lasagne. If you can't stand the crowds, you can get food to go. A very reasonable $15 per person for a plate of pasta and a glass of wine.

Millie's Country Kitchen
10318 Sepulveda Blvd., Mission Hills
(818) 365-7597
Open Sun.-Thurs. 6 a.m.-11 p.m., Fri.-Sat. 6 a.m.-midnight. Cards: AE, MC, V.

This upscale coffee shop is as perky and bright as a calico apron, and it serves immense portions of good-ol'-boy food that's more than a cut above all the Marie Callender's–Coco's clones. When you've got a hankering for chicken-fried steak, fried chicken with mashed potatoes, biscuits and gravy, pot roast and deep-dish pies, you could do a lot worse than Millie's. It's a great place for kids (and seniors as well)—kind of a campy bit of exurban America, at preinflation prices. Two can let a couple of notches out of their belts for about $20, with beverages. Various other locations throughout Southern California.

Mogo's
4454 Van Nuys Blvd., Sherman Oaks
(818) 783-6646
Open Tues.-Thurs. 11:30 a.m.-2:30 p.m. & 5 p.m.-9:30 p.m., Fri.-Sat. 11:30 a.m.-2:30 p.m. & 5 p.m.-10 p.m., Sun. 5 p.m.-9:30 p.m. All major cards.

Hidden away in a corner mall, Mogo's is an upscale version of Hollywood's Mongolian Bar-B-Q. There's the same buffet stocked with meats and vegetables, the same open barbecue, the same pile-it-as-high-as-you-can attitude. But Mogo's has spacious, comfortable tables, a soothing decor, more relaxed service and meats that seem fresher. The only thing it lacks is Mongolian Bar-B-Q's delicious sesame rolls. But this place offers a great meal in a bowl, a create-your-own mix of beef, pork, turkey, lamb, vegetables and savory or spicy sauces. As you might expect, you pay a little more for the atmosphere: about $30 for dinner for two, with beer.

Stanley's

13817 Ventura Blvd., Sherman Oaks
(818) 986-4623
20969 Ventura Blvd., Woodland Hills
(818) 346-4050
Open daily 11:30 a.m.-midnight (bar open to 2 a.m.). Cards: AE, MC, V.

If you're looking for love *and* a good hamburger, salad or piece of grilled fish, head for Stanley's, a Valley hot spot. The bar scene hustles and bustles, to say the least; playing second fiddle to the nightly action is the café, which serves better California-style bar-and-grill fare than you might expect. Ingredients are fresh, the cooking is consistent, if uninspired, and the prices aren't bad. About $35 for a light dinner for two, with a glass of wine.

SAN GABRIEL VALLEY

Birdie's

17 S. Raymond Ave., Pasadena
(818) 449-5884
Open Mon. 7:30 a.m.-2 p.m., Tues.-Thurs. & Sun. 7:30 a.m.-9 p.m., Fri.-Sat. 7:30 a.m.-10 p.m. Cards: MC, V.

Muffins are the specialty of the house at Birdie's, a friendly, '70s-style café with a small outdoor patio. The muffins are huge, fresh and uniformly delicious, from the healthy bran to the decadent chocolate chip. Breakfast is the best meal here—very fresh juice, good omelets and egg dishes and, of course, muffins—but we also like Birdie's for lunch and dessert. The muffins and baked goods are also available to go from the bakery counter by the door. About $15 for breakfast for two.

Burger Continental

535 S. Lake St., Pasadena
(818) 792-6634
Open daily 6:30 a.m.-10:30 p.m. Cards: MC, V.

Despite its name, there's a lot more to Burger Continental than burgers. Much of the food is Greek and Armenian (huge plates of lamb kebabs and rice pilaf, moussaka, hummus with pita bread, baklava), some of it is American (charbroiled fish and prime rib) and some of it is Italianish (very garlicky scampi). While you stand in line at the counter, one of the gregarious brothers who own this place will come by to take your order; chat with him for a minute and he'll probably throw in a free appetizer. Not that you'll need it—dinners come with a simple salad bar and heaps of rice and vegetables, and portions are more than hearty. You'll eat this heavy but very tasty and inexpensive meal in the brick outdoor patio, which is kept warm with heaters at night. It's popular with local college students, who put away pitchers of beer and platefuls of food. We love Burger Continental much more for its chaotic nuttiness than for the food—but you won't be disappointed with either. About $28 for a huge meal for two, with beer.

Crocodile Café

140 S. Lake Ave., Pasadena
(818) 449-9900
Open Mon.-Thurs. 11 a.m.-11 p.m., Fri.-Sat. 11 a.m.-midnight, Sun. 11 a.m.-10 p.m. All major cards.

Gregg and Bob Smith, owners of the Parkway Grill, are two very smart businessmen. They saw the emergence of California cuisine and brought it (quite skillfully) to Pasadena; their handsome restaurant has been packed ever since. Then they brought Melrose Avenue's café craze to Pasadena with the Crocodile Café, which has also been packed since the doors opened. Is the food worth the hour or so you'll have to wait during peak dinner hours? Probably not. But if you come at an off-time—a late lunch, an early dinner—you'll enjoy the fashionable California café fare. There are some failures from time to time, but the salads, pastas, pizzas and chic sandwiches are all tasty and inexpensive. Weather permitting, skip the bright, bustling interior (replete with open kitchen, naturally) and sit on the quieter patio tucked a couple of steps below Lake Avenue. About $17 per person for a simple salad, a grilled chicken pizza and a glass of wine.

The Espresso Bar

34 S. Raymond Ave., Pasadena
(818) 356-9095
Open Mon. 6:30 p.m.-1 a.m., Tues.-Fri. noon-1 a.m., Sat. noon-2 a.m., Sun. noon-midnight. No cards.

L.A. could use many more places like The Espresso Bar, an honest-to-goodness coffeehouse tucked in an alley in ever-gentrifying Old Town Pasadena. Assorted intellectuals, artists, hip teenagers and neighborhood shoppers sip espresso, cappuccino, caffè latte or all-American coffee around small tables in this high-ceilinged, wood-floored old room, complete with fireplace, old upright piano and amateurish art. The ancient jukebox, stocked with uniformly great vintage rock and country, keeps the mood up, as does the occasional live music. You can also get teas, juices, croissants, delicious desserts (try the cheesecake) and, at lunch, a few simple salads. Expect a full house on weekend nights.

In Arty's

36 E. Holly St., Pasadena
(818) 793-3723
Open Tues. 6 p.m.-12:30 a.m., Wed.-Thurs. 2 p.m.-12:30 a.m., Fri. 2 p.m.-1:30 a.m., Sat. 6 p.m.-1:30 a.m., Sun. 2 p.m.-7 p.m. No cards.

The coffeehouse reaches new heights at In Arty's, a stylish new Old Town Pasadena spot that combines the hang-loose informality of a coffeehouse with the comfort and atmosphere of an upscale lounge. For the price of a cup o' java, you can settle in at a comfortable table or booth, chit-chat to your heart's content and listen to amiable live jazz. Unlike at L.A.'s other coffeehouses, wine, Champagne and beer are also served; the food offerings run to desserts and simple appetizers and snacks. In Arty's is at its best during its lazy afternoon high tea and on weekend nights, when the mood is at its most convivial.

Julienne

2649 Mission St., San Marino
(818) 441-2299
Open Mon.-Tues. 8 a.m.-6 p.m., Wed.-Fri. 8 a.m.-9 p.m., Sat. 8 a.m.-5 p.m. Cards: MC, V.

Not that we don't love San Marino, but when we visit Julienne we are happily transported to France (except for the rather unsettling fact that this lovely café is located directly across the street from a branch of the John Birch Society). You can tell the food will be great just from the decor—a loving re-creation of a tiny small-town French bistro. Umbrella-shaded marble bistro tables greet you on the sidewalk; inside is a romantic vision of tile, faux and real marble, blackboard menus and a few authentically French accents. Sue Campoy opened this take-out shop and café as an adjunct to her deservedly successful catering business, and now her fame has spread beyond Pasadena's protected borders

and across the city. Fresh rosemary, the house herb, shows up in several wonderful dishes, chief among them the amazing rosemary-raisin bread and the lovely chicken Normandy. There are always several delicious salads, a different quiche each day, a seasonal soup or two, a handful of tempting entrées (roasted lemon-herb chicken, for one) and fabulous, unfussy desserts, from brownies to lemon bars. When the weather turns cool, we stop at Julienne for a lunch or take-out dinner of soul-satisfying lasagne or sausage-potato stew. Lunch for two, with a glass of wine and dessert, will run $25 to $30.

Old Town Bakery

166 W. Colorado Blvd., Pasadena
(818) 792-7943
Open Sun.-Thurs. 9 a.m.-11 p.m., Fri.-Sat. 9 a.m.-midnight. No cards (checks accepted).

Southern California is suddenly going through a bakery renaissance, and along with Nancy Silverton's superlative La Brea Bakery, Old Town Bakery is leading the pack. Owned and operated by elfin pastry chef Amy Pressman, Old Town (located next to the dread Ritz Grill) offers about a dozen varieties of bread (including potato-onion, Italian olive, rosemary and even tomato-oat bran), homemade breadsticks, brioche buns stuffed with things like ham and cheese or fresh fruit (or rolled in cinnamon sugar) and delicious currant cream biscuits that are perfect with a cup of tea. Pressman's cakes and pies are truly amazing. They look like cartoon-size confections (one half expects a flock of birds to emerge from the pies), but they taste seriously divine. We love the gooey Milky Way cake, the sophisticated chocolate terrine, complete with edible gold leaf, the fresh-fruit shortcakes and the pies made from fruits in season. Old Town also serves a variety of salads to munch on, but that would be like going to Lourdes for the scenery. There's an outdoor patio to dine on as well as the tables inside. Two can snack guiltily for about $12 with beverages.

Robin's

395 N. Rosemead Blvd., Pasadena
(818) 351-8885
Open Sun.-Thurs. 7 a.m.-11 p.m., Fri.-Sat. 7 a.m.-1 a.m. Cards: AE, MC, V.

If you fear places that are bright, cheerful and cater to children, skip this one, but if you're looking for a family restaurant that not only tolerates the little monsters but actually encourages their visits, you're in the right place. Robin's is basically an upscale coffee shop that serves the usual coffee-shop fare (though it gets a little more ambitious with such things as eggs carbonara and omelets filled with goat cheese and French garlic sausages), but it's done very well and with some imagination. The kids have their own menu, though you may find yourself sampling more than a taste of Baby Fred's french toast, which is encrusted with corn flakes and raisin-nut cereal. There's also a decidedly more adult version made with King's Hawaiian bread (more cake than bread), dipped in a cream batter spiked with Cointreau and cinnamon. Breakfast for two runs about $14 with beverages.

WESTSIDE

Babalu
1001 Montana Ave., Santa Monica
395-2500
Open Tues.-Sun. 11:30 a.m.-2:30 p.m. & 5 p.m.-10 p.m. Cards: MC, V.
   Babalu is a terrific addition to the generally mediocre Montana Avenue restaurant scene. The decor is in a colorfully wacky Caribbean mode, and while the food isn't exactly gourmet fare, it's imaginative and tasty, served by friendly waitresses and waiters. While Caribbean is the prevalent culinary influence here, the menu jumps all over the map: pastas, burgers, chicken satay with coconut-lime sauce, homemade sausages. The desserts are a treat, from the Key lime pie to the coconut flan and various cakes and tarts. Babalu is a great place to take a load off after a heavy day of shopping Montana, and lunch will only set two back about $20, with beverages.

Café Beverly Wilshire
Regent Beverly Wilshire, 100 S. Rodeo Dr., Beverly Hills
275-4282
Open daily 6 a.m.-midnight. Cards: AE, MC, V.
   When the Regent hotel folks redid the tired, old Beverly Wilshire, a gorgeous phoenix, far

more beautiful than the original, rose from the ashes. Yet the powers that be wisely left one little corner intact. The hotel's revamped café replaces the former Pink Turtle (the silly name alone was a dead giveaway to the frivolous era in which it thrived), and the place is now quite soigné, but some of the great old dishes remain. In fact, the good old American breakfast menu is virtually unchanged (except that the quality of the ingredients and cooking is far better). For dinner and lunch, habitués can still order the famed McCarthy salad (iceberg lettuce, beets, Swiss and cheddar cheeses, egg yolk, egg white, diced tomato, bacon and turkey—a mouthful), a most delicious chili and an adorably fun platter that consists of a miniature hot dog, hamburger and Reuben sandwich—it's perfect for finicky kids, and it captivated us older diners, too. The french fries are to die for, and save room for goodies from the fountain, especially the decadent sundae of chocolate-marshmallow and honey ice creams washed in a rich coffee sauce and garnished with biscuit leaves. Dinner for two, with beverages, runs about $22.

Café SFA
Saks Fifth Avenue, 9600 Wilshire Blvd., Beverly Hills
275-4211
Open Mon.-Wed. & Fri.-Sat. 10 a.m.-5 p.m., Thurs. 10 a.m.-8:30, Sun. noon-5 p.m. All major cards.
   If you aren't bored to death with quiche and spinach salad, you'll enjoy the simple light-lunch fare served in this little café lurking behind Saks's gourmet kitchen department. It's a very pretty, feminine-looking place, in shades of rose and terra cotta, with satisfying food that will help you recover from a tiring shopping spree. About $30 for a light lunch for two, with a glass of wine or an invigorating cappuccino.

Caffè Roma
350 N. Cañon Dr., Beverly Hills
274-7834
Open Mon.-Sat. noon-2 a.m., Sun. 4 p.m.-2 a.m. All major cards.
   Caffè Roma is yet another sleazy/chic meeting spot for the Beverly Hills lunch crowd—a crowd tending toward men wearing

gold chains and silk shirts and women wearing lots of makeup and really high heels. We fail to understand the popularity of this café. The noise level is deafening, the service abominable, the clientele uninteresting, the prices high, and the food completely banal. The little pizzas are good, and the lunch buffet is acceptable, but the antipasti, pastas and Italian standards are much better elsewhere. About $45 for lunch for two and $80 for dinner, with wine.

Central Park Café
11604 W. San Vicente Blvd., Brentwood
826-6686
Open Mon.-Fri. 11:30 a.m.-3 p.m. & 5:30 p.m.-11 p.m., Sat.-Sun. 5:30 p.m.-2 a.m. Cards: DC, MC, V.

This café has several things going for it. First is its handsome, New York decor—wood floors, brick walls, prints of Central Park, posters of Broadway shows and an old park bench stocked with *New Yorker* magazines. Second is its friendly atmosphere and service. Third is its late hours. And fourth is its food, which, if you stick to the basics, can be very good. Avoid the steaks and the more complicated dishes and try the great clam chowder, the fine salads, the fresh oysters and clams and the straightforward grilled fish. Be careful at dinner, when the tab can creep up far too high for a café. About $22 for lunch for two, with a glass of wine, and about $70 for dinner with wine.

Cutters
Colorado Place, 2425 Colorado Ave., Santa Monica
453-3588
Open Mon.-Thurs. 11:30 a.m.-3 p.m. & 5 p.m.-10 p.m., Fri.-Sat. 11:30 a.m.-3 p.m. & 5 p.m.-11 p.m., Sun. 4 p.m.-9:30 p.m. Cards: AE, MC, V.

Junior executives zip over here in their junior BMWs, perhaps after a quick stop at the health club, to have a few drinks and nibble on generic California cuisine (meaning hip dishes from everywhere but California)— Cajun pastas, Italian pastas, salads with Chinese, Japanese and Thai influences and grilled fish from Hawaii and the Pacific Northwest. Making the scene and making new friends is more the point than the food, though it is all completely edible, and sometimes even tasty. It's all, however, done better elsewhere, which is where we recommend you go if you aren't interested in a loud, yuppie-bar ambience. Cutters is most pleasant for an early lunch, when it's relatively peaceful. Two of you will spend $25 to $30 for lunch and $40 to $65 for dinner with wine.

Il Fornaio
301 N. Beverly Dr., Beverly Hills
550-8330
Open Mon.-Thurs. 7:30 a.m.-9 p.m., Sun. 8:30 a.m.-9 p.m. Cards: MC, V.

This successful import from Italy is both a good café and a wonderful bakery, where you can find all kinds of delicious and very authentic Italian breads, tortes and cookies. Businesspeople, sightseers and professional Rodeo Drive shoppers fill the café at lunchtime, nibbling on one of six daily pastas, Italian sandwiches, pizzas (genuine Italian, not California), calzone and pastries. The noisy, crowded room is plain but handsome, with blond wood and lots of windows to keep diners in touch with the street scene. The pastas and pizzas are honest and delicious, and the prices aren't bad: about $25 for a pasta, pastry and cappuccino lunch for two. If you're in a hurry, you can get a piece of pizza to go.

Gianfranco
11363 Santa Monica Blvd., W.L.A.
477-7777
Open Mon.-Thurs. 9:30 a.m.-11 p.m., Fri.-Sat. 9:30 a.m.-11:30 p.m. Cards: MC, V.

One of the city's earlier casual pasta cafés, Gianfranco is a lively, charming eat-in/take-out Italian deli. The bright, modern room is dominated by huge deli cases stocked with beautiful antipasti, salads, pastries, hot and cold pastas, cheeses and meats. Most of the homemade pastas are quite nice (try the green fettuccine al pesto), and the salads and antipasti are always tasty. The pastries and the veal and chicken dishes, however, are disappointing. But there are plenty of good, inexpensive Italian wines, delicious gelati and rich cappuccinos. Two can lunch well for $30 or less.

Humphrey Yogart

Brentwood Gardens, 11677 San Vicente
Blvd., Brentwood
207-2206
*Open Mon.-Thurs. 9 a.m.-10:30 p.m., Fri.-Sat.
9 a.m.-11:30 p.m., Sun. 11 a.m.-10:30 p.m. No
cards.*

One of the hottest dining scenes on the westside isn't Italian, isn't French-Japanese, isn't even really a restaurant—it's a frozen-yogurt shop. More than that, it's a yogurt shop in a mall! Let it be said, however, that this mall houses a Daily Grill, a California Pizza Kitchen and some very tony boutiques, and it's got the crowd to prove it. Miles of shiny hair, expanses of perfect teeth, lengths of bare midriffs—the beautiful people indeed. What's the attraction? Why, the best frozen yogurt in Los Angeles, that's what. Humphrey's serves about a zillion different varieties, via mix-ins (the yogurt isn't soft-serve; it's scooped from hard-pack containers into grinders that soften and blend it with the added ingredients), including cinnamon-espresso, peanut butter and fresh fruit. It also serves sandwiches and salads, but why bother? Come for the yogurt, the cappuccino and the show. Yogurt and cappuccino for two comes to about $10.

Michel Richard

310 S. Robertson Blvd., Beverly Hills
275-5707
Open Mon.-Sat. 8 a.m.-10 p.m. Cards: MC, V.

Although the twinkly Richard sold his pâtisserie to a friend (who was tragically murdered here in 1989), this small, modest shop on Robertson is rarely empty, and after tasting the croissants, strawberry tarts, "mado" with hazelnuts, "fleur d'automne" and "auteuil" of chocolate and the "opéra" (a Lenôtre creation that is famous worldwide), you can understand why. There are also about 30 little tables, indoors and along the sidewalk, which are almost always full. For $10 to $14, you can have spinach quiche or a feuilleté of mushrooms and chicken. Other choices include good salads, omelets and such daily specials as the sauté of lamb with rosemary. Avoid the Valley branch; Richard no longer owns it, either, and the quality has plummeted.

The Rose Café

220 Rose Ave., Venice
399-0711
*Open Mon.-Fri. 8 a.m.-11:30 p.m., Sat. 9 a.m.-
11:30 p.m., Sun. 9 a.m.-5 p.m. Cards: MC, V.*

High-tech meets Venice coffeehouse at the Rose Café, one of Venice's premier hangouts. The building itself is enormous—high-ceilinged and airy enough to accommodate the inevitable weekend swarms. It's self-service, so you can linger over your croissant and wine or dessert and cappuccino for as long as you wish—and most of the patrons, who seem to have no end of time on their hands, take full advantage of this. The salads, quiches and pastries are sadly no longer what they used to be, and we'd advise that you avoid the more complicated dishes, which range from the boring to the pathetic. But though the beachy-bohemian atmosphere far surpasses the food, in this case, that's more than all right. About $25 for lunch for two, with a glass of wine or an espresso.

The Sidewalk Cafe

1401 Ocean Front Walk, Venice
399-5547
*Open Mon.-Thurs. 9 a.m.-10 p.m., Fri. 9 a.m.-
midnight, Sat. 8 a.m.-midnight, Sun. 8 a.m.-11
p.m. All major cards.*

Probably the only café in town where roller skates are the preferred footwear. This crowded outdoor patio abuts the Venice Beach boardwalk, making a visit here immensely entertaining, especially on a summer weekend. Unfortunately, to enjoy the passing parade you'll have to put up with drab food, a shabby patio, and a truly dingy and depressing interior. Keep your choice as simple as possible—a no-frills omelet or burger. About $20 for two, with a glass of wine.

Tavern on Main

2907 Main St., Santa Monica
392-2772
Open daily 11 a.m.-11 p.m. Cards: MC, V.

Santa Monica's busy Main Street suffers from no lack of nosheries and cafés, but one of the best to pop up of late is Tavern on Main, a fine-looking boîte serving up revisionist Americana food in pleasant surroundings. The decor is of the '30s-era grill variety, complete with a long bar, tiled floors and lots of dark wood. There's also a charming outdoor patio, which is especially nice for brunch and lunch. The food is unexpectedly fresh and well prepared: burgers, delicious homemade macaroni and cheese, chicken pot pie, spaghetti and meatballs, chili. The waffle-cut french fries are excellent, and there's a good selection of salads and lighter fare. Prices are amazingly low, and you leave very well fed. Dinner for two, with beer or good wine by the glass, is about $30.

Yokohama Ramen
11660 Gateway Blvd., W.L.A.
471-2321
Open Wed.-Mon. 11:30 a.m.-9 p.m. No cards.

For comfort food, it's hard to beat noodles as a palliative, especially Japanese noodles. The Japanese revere noodles, and the art of noodle-making is taken seriously. At Yokohama Ramen, a small, efficient-looking café in (of course) a mini-mall, the noodles are excellent. There's usually a line of people waiting to get in, and for good reason. You can choose between noodles with soup; noodles stir-fried with a variety of ingredients, such as barbecued pork and vegetables; pan-fried soft noodles and delicious cold noodles. Yokohama also serves delicious pan-fried dumplings, as well as a terrific version of Chinese chicken salad. Two can dine like gluttons for about $20, with beer.

Zabie's
3003 Ocean Park Blvd., Santa Monica
399-1150
Open Mon.-Fri. 7:30 a.m.-9 p.m., Sat. 8 a.m.-5 p.m., Sun. 9 a.m.-8 p.m. No cards (checks accepted).

Ocean Park Boulevard, formerly an aircraft-biz industrial wasteland, has come into its own in the last couple of years, and is becoming a real hotbed of restaurants—DC3 (like it or not, it's a force to be reckoned with), Il Forno, Ocean Park Cafe and now Zabie's, a little storefront café. The place is minuscule, with just a few tables and a counter (most of the business is in take-out and catering), but it's charmingly decorated and the food is wonderful. The menu changes regularly, but some of the standbys are a spicy vegetarian black-bean chili, tangy sesame noodles, hot Szechuan green beans and a first-class Caesar salad. There are also sandwiches, hot and cold pastas and various prepared salads. Zabie's also boasts a marvelous pastry chef, who turns out beautiful Shaker lemon pies, fruit turnovers wrapped in cream-cheese crusts, buttery shortbread cookies studded with pine nuts, and rich, fudgy brownies. Zabie's packs quite a punch in its tiny space. Lunch for two, with beverages, is about $20.

CHICKEN

Kokekokko
360 E. 2nd St., Little Tokyo
687-0690
Open Mon.-Sat. 5:30 p.m.-midnight. Cards: MC, V.

Just in case you weren't aware that roosters crow in different languages, the Japanese word *kokekokko* translates as *cock-a-doodle-do*. That settled, Kokekokko is a terrific Little Tokyo newcomer, and its menu is limited to chicken yakitori—which has far more scope than one might predict. Since the menu isn't in English, we asked our waiter to simply bring us dishes until we cried "uncle," which he happily did. We were brought skewers full of chicken livers, grilled chicken, gizzards, chicken skin, wings and chicken meatballs, and chicken kebabs with okra and squash, all traditionally followed by chicken soup and chopped chicken and rice. And the dishes were so different, we didn't feel as if we were getting "chickened" to death.. Kokekokko is really a kick—the crowd is young and exclusively Japanese, and the staff is enthusiastic and helpful. For something different, Kokekokko is something to crow about. Dinner for two, with sake, runs about $40.

Koo Koo Roo

3450 W. 6th St., Mid-Wilshire
383-6414
8393 Beverly Blvd., W. Hollywood
655-9045
Open daily 11 a.m.-10 p.m. No cards.

We're not quite sure from which language it is that *koo koo roo* translates as *cock-a-doodle-do*, but it must be from a language of a people who are very health-conscious. Both branches are bright, better-than-average fast-food joints, but the food here can definitely be classified as the un-McDonald's. The chicken is skinless, and it's grilled simply over an open flame after being marinated in a blend of vegetable juices. It's served with a crispy lavoshlike bread, with side orders of a cucumber-and-onion salad, tomato and onion salad, bulgar wheat, mixed-bean salad or warm eggplant salad. This food is very tasty, very fresh and very healthy. Dinner for two, with beverages, costs about $18.

Pollo Dorado

4830 Hollywood Blvd., Hollywood
663-3628
Open daily 11 a.m.-9:30 p.m. No cards.

We couldn't possibly cover all the Mexican grilled-chicken places—the El Pollo Locos, Pollo Ricos, Pollo Pollos and so on—because there are far too many of them. They're all similar, they're all cheap, and most all of them are as good as this place. Here $6.99 will get you a whole chicken, marinated and barbecued on a huge open grill, along with ten corn tortillas and your choice of salsas from the salsa bar. The chicken is salty, tender and quite tasty, and it's much healthier than fried chicken. You can eat at the fast-food-style tables or, better yet, take it home.

Zankou Chicken

5065 Sunset Blvd., Hollywood
665-7842
Open daily 10 a.m.-midnight. No cards.

This little joint is fast food at its best. Zankou serves Armenian/Middle Eastern food that is unbelievably good and astoundingly cheap. The real draw here are, obviously, the chickens: big, fat birds roasted on a rotisserie until they're crisp and crackling. Infused with garlic, these chickens are served with even more garlic in the form of a thick, scrumptious dipping sauce, and with side dishes of tabouli and hummus dip, all of which can be tucked into the pita bread that accompanies all the above. Zankou also serves excellent stuffed grape leaves, shwarma, shish kebab and falafel, and while there are tables at which to enjoy it all, we suggest you take it home. Maybe "Zankou" means "thank you," which, given the goodness of the food, makes perfect sense. Dinner for two costs less than $15.

COFFEE SHOPS & DINERS

Barron's Café

4130 W. Burbank Blvd., Burbank
(818) 846-0043
Open Mon.-Fri. 7 a.m.-7:30 p.m., Sat. 8 a.m.-1 p.m. No cards.

Let Ed Debevic's play all-American make-believe—this place is the real thing, as American as they come. The neighborhood is bare-bones Burbank, the interior is cozy, cluttered, kitschy Americana, the waitresses are friendly pros, and the food is good, hearty and cheap. Breakfast is the meal to go for: rich french toast, good pancakes, crisp bacon and simple eggs are served on mismatched flowery china, along with plenty of good coffee. You'll dine among the blessedly unpretentious—men wearing Cat caps and work boots, women tending to small children—and be taken care of by the friendly family that runs this Burbank institution. About $12 for a very good breakfast for two.

Beverly Hills Breakfast Club

9671 Wilshire Blvd., Beverly Hills
271-8903
Open Mon.-Sat. 7 a.m.-5 p.m., Sun. 8 a.m.-3 p.m. Cards: AE, MC, V.

Okay, so this place is a little too self-conscious and the food is a little uneven. But it's hard to fault a fun, attractive restaurant that's located in the heart of ultra-rich Beverly Hills and costs only $7 a head for breakfast or lunch.

You won't go wrong with the eggs, the delicious french toast, the respectable tuna-salad sandwich or some of the simpler salads. It's well located for a break from a Neiman's-Saks-Magnin's shopping spree. About $14 for breakfast or lunch for two.

Café '50s

838 Lincoln Blvd., Venice
399-1955
Open Sun.-Thurs. 7 a.m.-11 p.m., Fri.-Sat. 7 a.m.-1 a.m. No cards.
4609 Van Nuys Blvd., Sherman Oaks
(818) 906-1955
Open Sun.-Thurs. 8 a.m.-midnight, Fri.-Sat. 8 a.m.-1 a.m. No cards.

One of the early contenders in the neodiner movement, Café '50s is great fun. Fifties posters line the walls of these cheery but authentically dingy diners, which are full night and day. Perky waitresses and busboys sing in full voice with the great (but loud) jukebox oldies; patrons also sing along sometimes, when they aren't busy eating the simple fare named for Patsy Cline, Fats Domino, Richie Valens and *Leave It to Beaver.* Luckily, the food is all good (especially the burgers) and the prices are low—$16 for two, with a beer.

Ed Debevic's

134 N. La Cienega Blvd., Beverly Hills
659-1952
Open Sun.-Thurs. 11:30 a.m.-11 p.m., Fri.-Sat. 11:30 a.m.-1 a.m. Cards: MC, V.
23705 S. Hawthorne Blvd., Torrance
378-5454
Open Sun.-Thurs. 11:30 a.m.-10 p.m., Fri.-Sat. 11:30 a.m.-midnight. Cards: MC, V.

The owner of Ed Debevic's (named for no one in particular) knows a good trend when he sees one—and when he saw his Chicago retro-diner make it big, he came right out to California, where he was instantly successful. These huge, slick diners are campy and theatrical, but what they lack in authenticity (and great food) they make up for in zany fun. Outlandish, gum-cracking waitresses serve up decent but lifeless diner standards (meatloaf, burgers, chili, french fries) while busboys clown and sing along with blaring rock oldies, and people can't get enough of it—Debevic's is packed night and day. The '50s theme is more important than the actual quality of the food; they're proud of the fact that their

vegetables are frozen. The chaos and mediocre food gives us a headache, but we can't be too critical: you can make the scene, get fed and get out for less than $20 for dinner for two, with beer—at what other red-hot Beverly Hills restaurant can you do that?

Dinah's

6521 S. Sepulveda Blvd., Inglewood
645-0456
Open Mon.-Thurs. 6 a.m.-10 p.m., Fri.-Sun. 6 a.m.-11 p.m. No cards.

Dinah's is that sprawling, tacky-looking coffee shop with signs announcing its all-you-can-eat fried chicken and all-you-can-eat spaghetti meals (every night of the week offers a different pigathon) that you always pass on the way to LAX. Next time, don't just pass it by—stop in and enjoy some pretty darned good plain ol' food. Dinah's draws quite a crowd; the food's cheap, plentiful and tasty. Aside from the much-publicized poultry and pasta, it serves the usual stuff—burgers, meatloaf, sandwiches, blue-plate specials—but breakfast is the unsung treat here. The pancakes (served in several varieties) are the size of Frisbees, and the puffy, skillet-baked German pancake served with sautéed apples and powdered sugar is enough for a family of five. Omelets and other egg dishes are also of grand proportions—if you eat breakfast here, it's the only meal you'll need all day, possibly the next day as well. Breakfast for two is about $15.

Duke's

8909 Sunset Blvd., W. Hollywood
652-9411
Open Mon.-Fri. 7:30 a.m.-9 p.m., Sat.-Sun. 7:30 a.m.-4 p.m. No cards.

Duke's has survived its move to Sunset Boulevard and a more contemporary, fashionable decor, though we miss the charm of the old place in the worn Tropicana Motel on Santa Monica Boulevard. Duke's is legendary in L.A., sort of a Polo Lounge for the hip and happening who line up on the sidewalk every weekend morning. Breakfast is the meal to have here, and for good reason—it's simple, generous and very good. Nothing fancy, just the eggs-bacon-omelet-pancake basics. About $14 for breakfast for two.

DuPar's Coffee Shop

12036 Ventura Blvd., Studio City
(818) 766-4437
Open Sun.-Thurs. 6 a.m.-1 a.m., Fri.-Sat. 6 a.m.-3 a.m. Cards: MC, V.

There are branches of DuPar's all around Los Angeles, but this one is by far the best. The food is no different than what you'll find at the other locations, but the clientele makes this one of the hippest Valley early-morning/late-night hangouts. Studio executives, trendy teenagers, actors and Sherman Oaks suburbanites all frequent DuPar's, drinking the good coffee and eating excellent french toast, pancakes, egg dishes and pies (the rest of the food is decent but mediocre). The other locations attract a gray-haired, golf-sweater crowd. About $14 for breakfast for two.

Jan's

8424 Beverly Blvd., Wilshire District
651-2866
Open daily 8 a.m.-1 a.m. No cards.

Jan's is the quintessential '50s coffee shop, complete with Googie-style architecture, acres of Formica and Naugahyde, waitresses who wear little aprons, with matching doilies on their heads—and homey, down-to-earth food that's as good as coffee-shop fare gets. Jan's has been in this spot near the Beverly Center since that behemoth was still a neighborhood amusement park, and it's managed to maintain its family-run integrity all these years. (The family also owns Astro in Silverlake and Theodore's in West Hollywood.) The crowd is eclectic—you'll find seniors, punkers and nerds dining on generous portions of meatloaf and mashed potatoes cheek-by-jowl. There are no surprises on the menu (burgers, salads, blue-plate specials, homemade pies and puddings), but everything is fresh and properly cooked. Breakfasts are huge and satisfying, and if you're a root-beer-float fan, Jan's whips up one of the best in town. Dinner for two is about $16..

Millie's Inc.

3524 W. Sunset Blvd., Silverlake
661-5292
Open Mon.-Fri. 8 a.m.-3 p.m. & 6 p.m.-midnight, Sat. 8 a.m.-3 p.m. & 6 p.m.-4 a.m., Sun. 8 a.m.-3 p.m. & 6 p.m.-10 p.m. No cards.

Until its expansion, there was always a wait at Millie's, and on weekend mornings, there's still a line—partly because of its popularity and partly because with only a handful of counter seats, it's not hard to keep a place full. Millie's is a real insider's place, where regulars (musicians, artists, assorted Silverlake folks) hang out and trade jokes and insults with owner Magenta and her wacky crew. The food is hearty, homemade, cheap and good. Heavy biscuits and gravy are the thing to get here, along with eggs and seriously spicy home-fried potatoes. The decor is bare-bones retro diner, and the countertop jukebox music is always great. About $12 for breakfast or lunch for two.

John O'Groats

10516 W. Pico Blvd., W.L.A.
204-0692
Open Mon.-Fri. 7 a.m.-3 p.m., Sat.-Sun. 7 a.m.-2 p.m. Cards: MC, V.

We hate to publicize this wonderful place—part of its charm lies in its tiny size and relative obscurity, and we would love to continue to be seated quickly here. It's nondescript on the outside and cheery on the inside, with a single U-shape counter, flowered wallpaper, Scottish fishing memorabilia and owners Robert and Angelica Jacoby behind the counter. On the back of the tattered menu is a map of the Scottish Highlands that shows John O'Groats, a tiny town that so impressed the Jacobys, they named their restaurant for it. They serve up a very inexpensive breakfast and lunch: omelets stuffed with spinach or homemade salsa, marvelous biscuits, home-fried potatoes, light fish and chips, tasty soups and wonderful shortbread, all made here. Since the kitchen is tiny and the staff is small, expect a lag time between ordering and eating—but it's worth the wait. About $12 for breakfast or lunch for two.

Original Pantry Bake Shoppe

875 S. Figueroa St., Downtown
627-6879
Open daily 6 a.m.-9 p.m. No cards.

This little gem is right next door to the Original Pantry Cafe and, up until a couple of years ago, served only as the bakery for that institution. But the Pantry folks, who know a gold mine when they see one, expanded the bakery into a full-fledged diner, and the result is a winner. The place is tiny—just a handful of tables and a counter—and the menu is small, basically that of the Apple Pan: burgers, sandwiches (tuna, ham and Swiss), chili and fries. Breakfasts are gut-busting feasts of omelets, various other egg permutations, home fries, thick bacon, slabs of ham and the best sourdough bread for miles around. The waiters are delightful old pros, and the bakery counter sells such guilty pleasures as sticky buns, cinnamon rolls, old-fashioned pan dowdies and sinful brownies. This is a real don't-miss; it's convenient to MOCA and the Music Center, and is worth a detour even if you're not in the neighborhood. Lunch for two runs about $15, with beverages.

Rae's
2901 Pico Blvd., Santa Monica
828-7937
Open daily 5:30 a.m.-10:30 p.m. No cards.
   This small, turquoise-blue joint is a classic '50s diner—the real thing, not a re-creation. As at most of L.A.'s good breakfast spots, patrons line up outside on weekends, waiting patiently for a chance to be served good pancakes, french toast, omelets and biscuits with gravy by frenetic uniformed waitresses. Hardly elegant, but good, home-style breakfasts at thoroughly reasonable prices: $12 for a feast for two.

Reuben's/Edie's Diner
4211 Admiralty Way, Marina del Rey
823-5339
Open Sun.-Thurs. 6:30 a.m.-2:30 a.m., Fri.-Sat. 24 hours. All major cards.
   Noteworthy mainly for being open 24 hours on weekends, Edie's has some neodiner trappings, such as old jukebox rock, singing waitresses, coffee-shop fare. But it lacks that spark you find at Café '50s and Ed Debevic's. The food is so-so (but then true diner food is usually uninspired), and the service is slow. But if you're starving at 2 a.m., Edie's chili, sundaes, meatloaf and burgers will taste just fine. From $15 to $20 for a midnight snack for two, with a beer.

Rose City Diner
45 S. Fair Oaks Ave., Pasadena
(818) 793-8282
Open daily 6:30 a.m.-2 a.m. No cards.
   Rose City is evidence enough that this pseudodiner business has gone far enough. In a glistening, neo-'50s setting that reeks of phoniness, dolled-up waitresses serve dismal diner fare to a happy crowd that seems to thrive on the retro look and cheap food. Personally, we'd rather have a simple tuna sandwich at home, or eat at an honest, all-American coffee shop like Baron's, or even DuPar's—places where we feel perfectly comfortable stuffing ourselves. About $16 for burgers and shakes for two.

Vickman's
1228 E. 8th St., Downtown
622-3852
Open Mon.-Fri. 3 a.m.-3 p.m., Sat. 3 a.m.-1 p.m., Sun. 7 a.m.-1 p.m. No cards.
   Vickman's, like the Pantry, is an L.A. institution. Its two vast, bare-bones rooms are reminiscent of an Eastern European mess hall, with rows of long wooden tables and benches. It opens so early—3 a.m.—that it could almost be considered a late-night spot, but most of its wee-hours diners are workers just starting their day at the nearby produce and flower markets. Breakfasts here are basic fare—eggs and pancakes—but the baked goods are far more than basic. Vickman's is a bakery more than anything else, and its sweet rolls, coffee cakes, pies and cakes are absolutely delicious, if a bit on the heavy side. The line at the order counter stretches out to the sidewalk on Saturdays, when people come from all over town for an inexpensive, generous and satisfying breakfast. You'll spend a mere $10 for two, with coffees.

Village Coffee Shop
2695 Beachwood Dr., Hollywood
467-5398
Open Mon.-Fri. 8 a.m.-6:30 p.m., Sat. 8 a.m.-5 p.m. No cards.
   Known as the Beachwood Café to its many regulars, this simple coffee shop in the Hollywood Hills is a favorite of the many actors who live in the neighborhood. The menu lists classic coffee-shop fare, from pancakes and various omelets to juicy french dips and hamburgers. The food is plain and good, especially the breakfasts, and the atmosphere is friendly and unhurried (except on Saturdays, when a crowd gathers to while away the morning hours, reading the papers filling up on honest food). About $14 for breakfast or lunch for two.

DELIS

Art's Deli
12224 Ventura Blvd., Studio City
(818) 769-9808
Open daily 7:30 a.m.-8:30 p.m. Cards: MC, V.

Art's is certainly one of the best delis in town, though it's probably also the most expensive, aside from the Carnegie. Addicts come from all over to be crowded into this big room, done in gold tones of vinyl and Formica, and served by the usual abrupt, unsmiling waitresses. But you aren't here for atmosphere or service—you're here for outstanding lean corned beef, wonderfully fresh lox, a first-rate smoked-fish platter, fresh-baked bagels and rye bread and monstrous combination sandwiches. Giant color photos of these creations line the walls, along with signs proclaiming, EVERY SANDWICH IS A WORK OF ART. We can forgive the smiling, rotund patron, Art Ginsberg, though—anyone who prepares deli so consistently well can make all the bad puns he wants. About $25 to $30 for two.

Canter's
419 N. Fairfax Ave., Wilshire District
651-2030
Open daily 24 hours. No cards.

Located in the heart of L.A.'s Jewish community, Canter's is certainly the best-known deli in town. Unfortunately, its reputation is undeserved, unless you're a native and have a sentimental, Proustian attachment to the place (as we do). The serving staff has almost no patience and even less charm, and the bland chicken soup would be hard pressed to cure even the sniffles. The rest of the deli fare is decent but not much more, and in good deli

Have a favorite Quick Bite that we've overlooked? Drop us a line and let us know: Editor, Gault Millau, Inc., P.O. Box 361144, Los Angeles, CA 90036. Your secret is by no means safe with us!

tradition, the desserts are awful. But Canter's deserves praise for staying open 24 hours a day—it's one of the few places in town where you can get edible food at 4 a.m. And take note: it's the only deli in L.A. that feels truly authentic. About $22 for two.

Carnegie Deli
300 N. Beverly Dr., Beverly Hills
275-DELI
Open Mon.-Thurs. 7 a.m.-12:30 a.m., Fri.-Sat. 7 a.m.-2 a.m., Sun. 7 a.m.-11 p.m. Cards: AE, MC, V.

The king of the New York delis has finally made it to L.A., thanks to the largesse of large billionaire Marvin Davis. (He got tired of having his goodies airlifted from New York to Beverly Hills, so he decided to open a branch here: noblesse oblige.) It hasn't lost anything in the translation, except that the rye bread in Manhattan is better, and the sumptuous rugelach cheesecake hasn't yet crossed the Rockies. In any case, the place itself is beautiful (an anomaly among delis, to be sure), designed by San Francisco restaurant-design czar Pat Kuleto—it looks like a 1930s hash house, complete with dark wooden booths and panoramic views of bustling Beverly Drive. The food is quintessential deli fare: great corned beef and pastrami, tender brisket (get it with the authentically lumpy mashed potatoes), the best smoked fish outside of Barney Greengrass in New York, state-of-the-art potato pancakes and blintzes, a soul-satisfying mushroom-and-barley soup and the best cheesecake in the known world. The portions are beyond gargantuan, so keep that in mind when you initially blanch at the prices—just about anything you order should probably be shared. Dinner for two, with drinks, is about $40.

Deli Malibu
3894 Cross Creek Rd., Malibu
456-2444
Open Mon.-Thurs. 8 a.m.-9 p.m., Fri.-Sat. 8 a.m.-11 p.m., Sun. 8 a.m.-8 p.m. Cards: AE, MC, V.

A good deli in Malibu? Who would believe it? Well, it's true—and it's not just good for

Malibu; it could easily hold its own in Los Angeles proper. Aside from the silly syntax of the name (it was supposed to be called simply "Malibu Deli," but someone thought this sounded classier), this newcomer is wildly popular among Malibuites starved for good food. The room itself is bright and tastefully decorated, and the two gents who operate the place have a wealth of deli experience behind them, having served lots of time at Nate 'n' Al's and Art's. The Nova Scotia lox is absolutely fresh and delicious (as are all the smoked fish), the pastrami is lean and peppery, the corned beef tasty and rich, and the chopped liver as good as grandma's. There's also a good selection of salads and sugar-free desserts (this is Malibu, after all), which are surprisingly good; don't miss the brownies sweetened with fruit juice and the fresh-fruit cobblers. You're guaranteed to see a few stars, making the inevitable wait for a table much easier to endure. Lunch for two, with beverages, will run about $25.

Greenblatt's Delicatessen

8017 W. Sunset Blvd., W. Hollywood
656-0606
Open daily 9 a.m.-2 a.m. Cards: AE, MC, V.

Deli-lovers accustomed to standard deli decor—rather, the total lack of any—will be pleasantly surprised at Greenblatt's. Its small upstairs dining room is handsome and comfortable, a place where you can sit and schmooze for hours over a hot pastrami and coffee without being rushed. While not great deli, the food is perfectly fine, if a little expensive. Don't miss the great cheesecake, but pass on the pecan pie. We miss the days when 'Blatt's was just a hole-in-the-wall that was renowned for its barbecued chickens; it's a bit soulless now. It does, however, double as a good wine shop that generally has some fine bargain wines. About $32 for a deli dinner for two, with a glass of wine.

Junior's

2379 Westwood Blvd., Westwood
475-5771
Open Mon.-Thurs. 6 a.m.-11 p.m., Fri. 6 a.m.-12:30 a.m., Sat. 7 a.m.-midnight. Cards: AE, MC, V.

"The Cadillac of delis," Junior's calls itself, and the only reason we can find to justify this boast is that it's big and gassy. The decor is nouveau deli tacky, though plush by deli stan-dards, with hardwood floors and booths designed to look like the interior of a Bentley (owner Marvin Saul is a car buff). The kitchen is frustratingly inconsistent (no doubt because of the incredible volume of business here), but the bagel brunch is a pretty safe bet, featuring smoked fish flown in from New York. There's a small bar near the entrance stocked with coffee, beer and wine to sustain those waiting. But with two New York transplants nearby, the Carnegie and the Stage, we see no reason to eat here. Dinner for two, with a glass of wine, will run about $40; less for a simple lunch.

Langer's

704 S. Alvarado St., Downtown
483-8050
Open daily 6:30 a.m.-1 a.m. Cards: MC, V.

A sign in the window reworks an old adage: "When in doubt, eat hot pastrami." Wise advice, especially if you eat Langer's pastrami, which is lean, delicious and copiously served. We counted at least 27 pastrami dishes on the extensive menu, the rest of which lists all the deli classics: blintzes, lox, chopped liver, gefilte fish and so on. The corned beef is terrific, the various soups are tasty, and the rye bread is the best in town. Despite the bad neighborhood, and the suicidally dismal atmosphere, Langer's is one of our favorite delis in L.A. Go figure. About $18 for lunch for two.

Nate 'n' Al's Delicatessen

414 N. Beverly Dr., Beverly Hills
274-0101
Open daily 7:30 a.m.-8:45 p.m. Cards: DC.

Nate 'n' Al's is one of the most established "industry" hangouts in Beverly Hills (the industry being Hollywood, of course)—which, knowing Hollywood's taste, makes it suspect from the start. Actually, the food isn't bad, though it isn't nearly as good as at Art's or the Carnegie. Nate 'n' Al's is smaller than you might think, given its fame, and the decor is coffee-shop basic. The real decor, however, is the clientele: a strange assortment of slick studio executives, well-to-do Beverly Hills matrons, TV actors and cigar-chomping men whose shirts could use a few more buttons. The huge menu presents the full range of moderately priced deli fare, which has a tendency to be dull—just-average lox, tasteless corned beef sandwiches and soups that are sometimes bland. But the cheese blintzes are terrific, the pickles great, and most of the sandwiches respectable. Deli aficionados run the risk of being disappointed, but stargazers and eavesdroppers will love it—unless by the time you read this they've all decamped down the street to the Carnegie, which is entirely possible. About $20 for lunch for two.

Pico Kosher Deli

8826 W. Pico Blvd., Rancho Park
273-9381
Open Sun.-Thurs. 9 a.m.-7:30 p.m., Fri. 9 a.m.-2:30 p.m. No cards.

One of the few genuine kosher (not "kosher-style," a euphemism for "nonkosher") delis in town, Pico Kosher is a nondescript-looking room filled with people chewing on superb corned beef and pastrami sandwiches. It may not have the panache of Nate 'n' Al's, but the food is as good, if not better. About $20 for lunch for two.

Stage Deli

Century City Shopping Center,
10250 Santa Monica Blvd., Century City
553-3354
Open Mon.-Thurs. 7 a.m.-11 p.m., Fri.-Sat. 7 a.m.-midnight, Sun. 7 a.m.-10 p.m. Cards: AE, MC, V.

We're sad to report that New York's legendary Stage Deli has fallen down a bit from its strong opening. And with the opening of the Carnegie Deli in Beverly Hills, the Stage would be well advised to clean up its act a bit. (These two delis are locked in mortal competitive combat in Manhattan.) On the up side, it's a good-looking place, cavernous and decorated with old movie posters, and the food is generally quite good, as long as you stick to the sandwiches, salads and such standards as potato pancakes, blintzes and stuffed cabbage. Unfortunately, the soups taste bland and packaged—a deli that serves a poor chicken soup should be ashamed of itself—and the desserts often seem tired. Our biggest complaint, though, is the lack of attention to detail. Ketchup and mustard bottles are too often running on empty and could use a good wiping. Service varies wildly from professional and attentive to sloppy and indifferent. We were great supporters of the Stage at first (for one thing, it's a great spot for pre- or post-movie and theater dining in Century City), and we hope it takes stock of itself before things get too out of hand. Dinner for two, with beverages, is about $30.

Starkey's Deli

Beverly Center, 8500 Beverly Blvd.,
W. Hollywood
659-1010
Open daily 8 a.m.-10 p.m. All major cards.

Although Starkey's is no more authentic a deli than Charles Pierce is a woman, it's still a good place to know about, if only because it's a good alternative to the Beverly Center's usually dismal fast food. It's a comfortable, handsome, pseudo–New York place with all the deli basics—none of which are wonderful, though the sandwiches are more than edible. Don't go out of your way for Starkey's, especially if you have an aversion to dinging-pinging pinball machines, but it's good for a quick meal. About $20 for lunch for two.

DIM SUM

Although L.A.'s Chinese community has been going out for tea lunches—otherwise known as dim sum—as long as Chinatown has been around, the rest of the city has only recently discovered the many joys of this fine tradition. "Dim sum" loosely translates as "delights of the heart," which are exactly what they are—delicious, savory (and sometimes sweet) small dishes, from buns and dumplings to tiny spring rolls and spareribs.

You'll find dim sum served in two ways. The first and most authentic is found at Chinese restaurants in Chinatown or the Monterey Park/Alhambra area. Chinese women navigate stainless-steel carts through the large dining rooms, showing off the carts' contents for anyone interested. If their English is no better than your Chinese, you can just point to the dishes that intrigue you. They usually run from $1.25 to $2 each; your tab is figured when you're full by counting the number of empty plates on the table or the number of rubber-stamp marks on your check.

The newest way to eat dim sum is in one of the slick, trendy, anglicized dim sum cafés springing up around town. In these places you order your dim sum—along with noodle and salad dishes—off a menu. Though not always authentic, the dim sum at these places can be quite good. You'll pay more than in Chinatown, but you still won't pay much—dim sum is as inexpensive as it is satisfying and fun.

ABC Seafood

708 New High St., Chinatown
680-2887
Open for dim sum daily 8 a.m.-2:30 p.m. Cards: MC, V.

ABC is a well-respected, better-than-average Chinese seafood restaurant that serves very good dim sum every day. Young women who can sometimes be less than friendly work the large, open room, hawking their wares: open-faced meat dumplings called shu mai, shrimp hidden in thick rice noodles, barbecued pork, baked and steamed bao buns and all manner of other exotic dishes. The selection is usually broader than at most Chinatown dim sums, and the quality is much better than average. About $12 to $15 for a tea lunch for two.

Bao Wow

17209 Ventura Blvd., Encino
(818) 789-9010
Open Mon.-Thurs. 11:30 a.m.-10 p.m., Fri.-Sat. noon-11 p.m., Sun. noon-9 p.m. Cards: MC, V.

One of the new breed of dim sum restaurants, Bao Wow has combined a hip, high-tech decor and a square Encino mini-mall location with surprisingly decent dim sum. While tables of teenage Valley girls giggle around you, you can sample delicious "dancing shrimp," crisp pan-fried shrimp dumplings; "dumplings on fire," which have quite wonderful flavors but little fire; good shu mai and pan-fried wontons, both of which are generous with meat; and fine lo mein noodles. The house specialty, bao buns, can be very good if they are fresh and not so good if they've been sitting in the steamer for a few hours. About $25 for a dim sum dinner for two, with beer.

Casa de Oriente

2000 W. Main St., Alhambra
(818) 282-8833
Open for dim sum Mon.-Fri. 10:30 a.m.-3 p.m., Sat.-Sun. 9 a.m.-3 p.m. Cards: MC, V.

A good dinner restaurant as well, Casa de Oriente serves one of the best dim sums in town. It's a large, opulent, handsome place, with much better than average service and uniformly good food. All the dim sum are great—bao buns, potstickers, rice noodles and much, much more—but the real winners are the sweets, from sesame balls with red bean paste to incredibly delicious coconut snowballs filled with a sweet peanut purée. Try to restrain yourself when the carts are wheeled by—if you take too much at first, you'll be too full for the great dishes that are sure to come by next. Less than $16 for a feast for two.

Chin Chin

8618 Sunset Blvd., W. Hollywood
652-1818
11740 San Vicente Blvd., Brentwood
826-2525
Open Sun.-Thurs. 11 a.m.-11 p.m., Fri.-Sat. 11 a.m.-midnight. Cards: AE, MC, V.

Yuppie dim sum mania started right here on Sunset Boulevard in this tiny, noisy, always-jammed sidewalk café. If you're claustrophobic, visit the Brentwood branch instead, which is more spacious and less crowded, with a pleasant outdoor patio. Though somewhat Americanized, the food here is delicious—very fresh Max's noodle soup, with lots of fresh vegetables, good shredded chicken salad, flavorful curried-beef turnovers, comforting bao buns, crisp spring rolls and succulent soy-ginger duck. Two can have a quite agreeable light meal with a glass of wine for $20 to $25.

Chopstix

See "Los Angeles - Central" in the Restaurants chapter.

Empress Pavilion

988 N. Hill St., Chinatown
617-9898
Open for dim sum daily 9 a.m.-2:30 p.m. All major cards.

Chinatown's most promising new restaurant in eons is also one of the city's finest dim sum houses. The setting is grand in the Hong Kong style, with a series of sliding walls that can make the restaurant either huge or intimate. For dim sum, it's authentically huge, though not quite as chaotic as it can get elsewhere. Waitresses who are a tad friendlier than most (though they're still not about to chat you up) wheel by the usual carts laden with the usual range of dim sum delights, but the freshness and flavor of each is much better than usual. Our only complaint is that the selection seems fairly ordinary. But the prices is right: less than $12 for two.

Grandview Gardens

944 N. Hill St., Chinatown
624-6048
Open for dim sum daily 10 a.m.-3 p.m. Cards: AE, MC, V.

This small and simple establishment serves an eloquent dim sum in a style no different from that of the other Chinatown places, though the dishes are better than most and the service is more attentive. The sweet rice with chicken and sausage is a good bet, as is fun goon, a steamed noodle roll with vegetables and meat. Also try the pork or beef shu mai (open-faced dumplings). If basic dumplings bore you, try the yeong aup jeong, otherwise known as stuffed duck's feet. About $13 for two.

Mandarette

8386 Beverly Blvd., W. Hollywood
655-6115
Open Mon.-Thurs. 11 a.m.-3 p.m. & 5 p.m.-11 p.m., Fri. 11 a.m.-3 p.m. & 5 p.m.-midnight, Sat. 5 p.m.-midnight, Sun. 5 p.m.-11 p.m. Cards: MC, V.

Not just a dim sum place, Mandarette was among the first L.A. restaurants exclusively dedicated to grazing—an unfortunate term that connotes herds of yuppies stampeding trendy eateries to nibble on bite-sized dishes. Philip Chiang, son of the Mandarin's Cecilia Chiang, wisely spotted this developing trend toward eating a variety of small tastes instead of one large entrée. And, fortunately, most of the tastes served in this contemporary, comfortable room are agreeable: juicy steamed pork dumplings, good onion pancakes, earthy cold eggplant in a garlic-soy sauce, classic bao buns filled with tasty barbecued pork, and so on. That's not to say these dishes are exceptional, just good. If you stick to the smaller dim sum dishes, two can eat for about $25, with a beer.

Mandarin Deli

Chinese Food Center, 727 N. Broadway, Chinatown
623-6054
Open daily 11 a.m.-9 p.m. No cards.
356 E. 2nd St., Little Tokyo
617-0231
Open daily 11 a.m.-11 p.m. Cards: MC, V.

The sign over the original Mandarin Deli says NOODLES AND DUMPLINGS, and if you look in the window you'll see the chefs making those very dishes. The flawless pan-fried dumplings come to your table still steaming and are best eaten flavored with a bit of hot chili oil and a splash of white vinegar. There are also boiled-fish and pork dumplings. The savory, heart-warming noodle soups work especially well if coupled with the Mandarin-style cold noodles, which are bathed in a richly spiced sesame sauce. Like garlic butter, sesame sauce both improves and overwhelms whatever it's mixed with. Atmosphere is nonexistent at the Chinatown branch, but the newer Little Tokyo branch boasts comfortable booths and an attempt at a decor. About $15 for a huge meal for two.

Miriwa

747 N. Broadway, Chinatown
687-3088
Open for dim sum daily 9 a.m.-3 p.m. All major cards.

Elegant and huge, Miriwa resembles a traditional Hong Kong tea house and boasts a vast selection of reasonably priced dim sum. Consequently, the crowds can be oppressive and the wait interminable. But you'll be rewarded with exceptionally light and fluffy bao buns filled with pork or beef; tender har gow, a steamed dumpling with shrimp; and such unusual items as abalone and yellowfish shu mai. Our favorites are the guotie—pan-fried pork dumplings also known as potstickers. Dim sum is the meal to eat here; dinner is a disappointment. About $15 for two.

Tai Hong
845 N. Broadway, Chinatown
485-1052
Open for dim sum daily 8 a.m.-2:30 p.m. All major cards.

Tai Hong is a Chinatown mainstay, crowded and cheerful, with lots of large families. Sometimes the carts are slow to come, but once they do you'll find plenty of good dim sum. Try the sweet rice dumpling and the beef satay, both of which are unusual dim sum offerings. The sweet egg custard tarts are excellent, but the potstickers are disappointing. Service can be cool. About $12 for two.

Yum Cha
3435 Ocean Park Blvd., Santa Monica
450-7000
Open daily 11 a.m.-2 p.m. & 5 p.m.-9 p.m. Cards: DC, MC, V.

We have something here that is halfway between a concept and a restaurant. The idea is to create a vast chain of Chinese dim sum/grazing shops from coast to coast; the first of this planned nationwide chain occupies the ground-floor corner of a Santa Monica office building. And while it may someday grow up, at the moment it feels like the staff is still learning how to cook. We found mediocre Chinese chicken salads (there are three of them, almost identical), oily scallion pancakes, not-very-spicy Szechuan noodles and decent dim sum. It's acceptable when you consider the dim sum options in this area—but it would be laughed right out of Monterey Park. Dinner for two, with tea, will run about $20.

HAMBURGERS & SANDWICHES

The Apple Pan
10801 W. Pico Blvd., W.L.A.
475-3585
Open Tues.-Thurs. & Sun. 11 a.m.-midnight, Fri.-Sat. 11 a.m.-1 a.m. No cards.

The acclaimed Apple Pan is a godsend for the absolutely starving—your order will be hurled at you in about 45 seconds. The cooks/waiters race around inside the horse-shoe-shape counter (no tables—service would take too long), spewing forth hamburgers (try the hickory burger), Virginia ham sandwiches and apple pie à la mode, all of which are delicious and quite satisfying. Those waiting for seats will stare ravenously at you, making sure you devour your food as quickly as it was thrown at you. About $9 for a burger, Coke and pie.

Barney's Beanery
8447 Santa Monica Blvd., W. Hollywood
654-2287
Open daily 10 a.m.-2 a.m. Cards: AE, MC, V.

Not for the indecisive—Barney's offers some 150 hamburgers, 20 hot dogs, 50 sandwiches, 90 omelets, 25 scrambled egg dishes and 65 variations of chili. Needless to say, with a menu this monstrous you can't expect the finest cuisine. It's all perfectly edible, but you don't come to Barney's for the food—you come for the appealingly scruffy atmosphere and the fantastic beer selection: more than 200 labels from around the world. The place is a maze of pool tables, coffee shop–like booths, video games and a long, dark bar. The recently formed city of West Hollywood may have forced Barney's to take down the NO FAGGOTS ALLOWED sign that was over the bar, but the clientele is still much straighter than the neighborhood. About $12 for a chiliburger and an excellent beer.

Cassell's Hamburgers
3266 W. 6th St., Mid-Wilshire
480-8668
Open Mon.-Sat. 10:30 a.m.-4 p.m. No cards.

Hard-core fans of the classic burger swear by Cassell's, considered by most to serve the best hamburger in town. You won't be able to get sprouts, avocado, caviar or other such trendy nonsense on your burger here. Instead, you'll get a simple, large (one-third or two-thirds of a pound) hamburger made with Cassell's freshly ground beef, huge, specially made buns, homemade mayonnaise and fresh lettuce, tomatoes and pickles. The spicy homemade potato salad is as good as its reputation warrants. At lunchtime you'll have to stand in line with the local pinstripe-suit set at the order counter; no attempt at decor, comfort or ambience has been made. About $8 for a burger and fresh lemonade.

Hampton's
1342 N. Highland Ave., Hollywood
469-1090
4301 Riverside Dr., Toluca Lake
(818) 845-3009
Open Mon.-Thurs. 11 a.m.-10 p.m., Fri.-Sat. 11 a.m.-11 p.m., Sun. 10 a.m.-11 p.m. Cards: AE, MC, V.

Hampton's may rival Cassell's as the best hamburger place in town, but the two places couldn't make a more different burger. Where Cassell's is good ol' plain and old-fashioned, Hampton's is fussed up and heavy—burgers topped with everything imaginable, from bacon, avocado and chili to caviar and grape jelly. Stick to the simpler combinations, which can be very good. For the health-conscious, there's a delicious turkey burger; for the splurger, there's a wonderful cheesecake. The Toluca Lake branch is one of the best secret star-spotting spots in town, given its proximity to the Valley studios. Both restaurants are handsome in a '70s sort of way, with lots of wood and greenery—which means these burgers will cost more than those at Cassell's. About $14 per person for a hamburger lunch with a beer.

Johnny Rocket's
7507 Melrose Ave., W. Hollywood
651-3361
474 N. Beverly Dr., Beverly Hills
271-2222
14561 Ventura Blvd., Sherman Oaks
(818)501-1000
Open Sun.-Thurs. 11 a.m.-midnight, Fri.-Sat. 11 a.m.-2 a.m. No cards.

Mix the counter-only setup of the Apple Pan with the slick neodiner look so omnipresent these days, throw in a mob of self-conscious Melrosians and the most hyperactively cheerful staff imaginable, and you get Johnny Rocket's, L.A.'s fastest-growning chain burger joint. The fare is limited to burgers, fries, fountain drinks and pies, and it's all pretty good, especially the juicy, smallish burger (the meat of which has been seasoned) and the generous shakes. There's always a crowd, and there's no order to the wait—arguments over who gets seated next sometimes flare up among the hungry people lining the wall. They've now added some tables outside, though, which means you can forego the pseudo-authentic diner experience inside and watch the fascinating mix of passersby while you eat. The other branches are popular with parents and kids. About $8 for a burger, fries and Coke.

Philippe's Original Sandwich Shop
1001 N. Alameda St., Downtown
628-3781
Open daily 6 a.m.-10 p.m. No cards.

Philippe's is an L.A. classic. Since 1908, businesspeople, tourists, truck drivers and the unemployed have been lining up at the huge counter to order wonderful beef, pork or lamb french-dip sandwiches. The decor of this cavernous landmark is early fast food: sawdust on the floors and high stools along shared tables. Philippe's claims to have invented the french dip, a claim that is, of course, contested by many. But few serve so many french dips a day at so low a price ($3.10). Round out your sandwich with a decent potato salad and one of the many imported beers, or try Philippe's coffee, still Depression-priced at ten cents a cup. It isn't the greatest coffee in town, but it's a dime well spent. And support Philippe's while you can: it may soon fall prey to the city's development mania.

Pie 'n' Burger
913 E. California Blvd., Pasadena
(818) 795-1123
Open Mon.-Fri. 6 a.m.-10 p.m., Sat. 7 a.m.-10 p.m., Sun. 7 a.m.-9 p.m. No cards.

A no-frills place with a no-frills name that says it all. The pecan pie is to die for, all the other pies are very good, and the simple, all-American hamburger is fresh and tasty. Otherwise, except for good fries and soft drinks, forget it. The decor and prices are coffee-shop classic; the service ditzy and perfunctory. About $9 for a burger, fries and pie.

Russell's
5656 E. 2nd St., Long Beach
434-0226
Open Sun.-Thurs. 7 a.m.-10 p.m., Sat. 7 a.m.-11 p.m. No cards.

Without a doubt one of the very best burger places in Southern California. Burgers are juicy, messy and completely delicious, especially when topped with the great homemade chili. The other winners in this cheery café in the charming Naples area of Long Beach are the wonderfully crisp hash browns and the astonishingly tall and light meringue cream pies. You will not be disappointed by the sour cream, chocolate, banana, coconut, pumpkin or peanut-butter pies, or the panoply of fruit pies, shakes, sundaes and malts. Service is friendly, and the atmosphere is lively with local gossip and beach talk. About $8 per person for lunch.

Tommy's
2575 W. Beverly Blvd., Rampart
389-9060
Open daily 24 hours. No cards.

Anyone who's lived in L.A. for more than a few months will already know about Tommy's—an amazing reputation for a tiny, greasy neighborhood burger joint. We don't dare criticize Tommy's, or an army of its incredibly devoted fans will surely burn every book in print. So we'll say this: the burgers themselves aren't much, but the topping is—a glob of messy, spicy, intensely aromatic, impressively tasty chili that seems to have some magical addictive powers. No matter what hour, you'll find a crowd eating chiliburgers along the makeshift counter lining the parking lot, while armed guards wander aimlessly around (the neighborhood has seen better days). The old axiom is true: Tommy's tastes best at 2 a.m., though your stomach will hate you for it in the morning. There are many Tommy's around town now, but to purists, this is the one and only. About $6 per person.

Wolfe Burgers
46 N. Lake St., Pasadena
(818) 792-7292
Open daily 6:30 a.m.-midnight. No cards.

Hamburger heaven: these delicious char-broiled burgers range from one-sixth of a pound (for kids) to two-thirds of a pound (for football players), and come with or without cheese. Dress your burger the way you like it at the condiment bar, and by all means accompany it with an order of the fantastic onion rings, among the best in town. Everything's fresh and delicious, from the hot chili to the creamy, light flan for dessert. Our only complaint is that the burgers are sometimes overcooked. Wolfe's recently added breakfast to its repertoire. There are two plant-filled rooms in which you can enjoy this most American of foods, with a bottle of Corona or a root beer float. About $15 for two.

HOT DOGS

Law Dogs
14114 Sherman Way, Van Nuys
(818) 989-2220
Open daily 10 a.m.-10 p.m. No cards.

Started by a bored lawyer, Law Dogs is a no-frills stand with two main choices: the smaller Jury Dog or the larger (quarter-pound) Law Dog, both of which feature the usual mustard-relish trimmings (cheese is extra). You'll eat your good (but not exceptional) hot dog at the stand-up counter in this heart-of-the-Valley neighborhood.

Jody Maroni's Sausage Kingdom
2011 Ocean Front Walk, Venice
821-1950
Open Tues.-Fri. 10 a.m.-5 p.m., Sat.-Sun. 9:30 a.m.-6 p.m. No cards.

Even if Jody Maroni's little stand wasn't located right on zany Venice beach it would be worth driving to—from any part of town. Jody makes his own sausages, selling them as hot dogs to the beach people and in quantity to L.A. restaurants and home kitchens. He usually has about a dozen varieties available to eat at the stand, from old favorites (Knackwurst, Italian sausage) to his own fanciful inventions (Mexican jalapeño sausage, Indian sausage). They are all wonderful beyond belief—once you try one, you'll want to try them all.

Pink's Chili Dogs
711 N. La Brea Ave., Hollywood
931-4223
Open daily 7 a.m.-2 a.m. No cards.

Much ado has been made about Pink's chili dogs, which are indeed very tasty. But you'll have to put up with dirty tables, an unsavory Hollywood neighborhood and often-lukewarm sodas. Still, the delicious all-beef hot dogs (served with lots of messy all-beef chili on request) make Pink's worth a visit.

Rubin's Red Hots
15322 Ventura Blvd., Sherman Oaks
(818) 905-6515
Open Mon.-Fri. 11 a.m.-9 p.m., Sat.-Sun. 11 a.m.-10 p.m. No cards.

Rubin's main distinction is that it unequivocally has the nuttiest architecture of any hot dog stand we've ever seen. It looks like a combination car wash/jungle gym, and there's even a little Parisian-style kiosk selling magazines and flowers—go figure. Unfortunately, Rubin's hot dogs aren't as great as we had hoped they would be. We're serious hot dog fiends, and these Chicago-style dogs just don't crackle and spit the way they should. Don't get us wrong—they're quite tasty, but we prefer the Wiener Factory's. The relish seems to be a bizarre product of modern chemistry—it's a livid, poisonous-looking shade of green that most likely glows in the dark. Rubin's also serves veal bratwurst, steakburgers, chicken-breast and swordfish sandwiches (in a nod to the health-conscious; what the hell are they doing at a hot dog stand, anyway?) and salads. The chili is first-rate, as are the french fries. Lunch for two, with soft drinks, runs about $12.

Tail of the Pup
329 N. San Vicente Blvd., W. Hollywood
652-4517
Open Mon.-Sat. 5 a.m.-9 p.m., Sun. 5 a.m.-8 p.m. No cards.

One of the few remaining examples of L.A.'s roadside-pop architecture of the twenties (and consequently a favorite subject of photographers who have tried to capture the essence of the city), the landmark Tail of the Pup was moved from La Cienega (where the Ma Maison hotel is presently located) to a less visible spot on nearby San Vicente. The stand is little more than a huge stucco hot dog, and it's worth a visit just for a look at this rare gem of programmatic design. While you're studying the architecture, try one of the good hot dogs or hamburgers.

The Wiener Factory
14917 Ventura Blvd., Sherman Oaks
(818) 789-2676
Open daily 11 a.m.-9 p.m. No cards.

Quite simply, the best hot dog in town can be had at The Wiener Factory. It's an amusing little dive with an outdoor take-out counter and a rustic indoor area with tables. The basic dog is great, but our unsurpassed favorite is the thick, juicy, spicy Polish dog, which is quite addictive. This is worth going out of your way for.

MEXICAN FAST FOOD

Burrito King
2109 W. Sunset Blvd., Echo Park
413-9444
Open daily 7 a.m.-midnight. No cards.

Once the king of the burrito stand, Echo Park's Burrito King is now up against some pretty tough competition, from Yuca in Los Feliz to such chains as La Salsa on the westside. Its quality also seems to have slipped a bit—the carnitas burritos, soft tacos and large tostadas can still be very good, but not consistently so. Its late hours make it a worthwhile place to keep listed in your little black book. About $10 for two.

Mrs. Garcia's
11106 W. Olympic Blvd., W.L.A.
473-6322
8510 W. 3rd St., Wilshire District
657-1002
Open daily 8:30 a.m.-11 p.m. No cards.

These little mini-mall taco shops were an immediate success, and for good reason. The tacos al carbón are authentic and good—two small, soft corn tortillas, topped with grilled steak or chicken, marinated pork or beans, cheese and guacamole; you then take your tacos to the salsa bar and choose one or more salsas, from very mild to very hot. The steak (carne asada) is done better elsewhere, but it's still good; the chicken and pork are delicious. You can also get hearty burritos, fresh tostadas and enchiladas. About $12 for two.

El Nopal
10426 National Blvd., W.L.A.
559-4732
Open Mon.-Thurs. 11:30 a.m.-10 p.m., Fri.-Sat. 11:30 a.m.-11 p.m., Sun. 5:30 p.m.-10 p.m. Cards: AE, MC, V.

Billed as "The Home of the Pregnant Burrito," El Nopal is a fine neighborhood place that serves good, fresh Mexican food for very low prices. The famed pregnant burrito, a giant mass of chicken, avocado, green peppers, onions, beans and cheese, is definitely enough for two. The nachos, quesadillas, enchiladas, tacos and taquitos are also good bets, and service is quick and friendly. Dinner for two, with beer, runs about $20.

Poquito Mas
3701 Cahuenga Blvd. W., Studio City
(818) 505-0068
Open Sun.-Thurs. 10 a.m.-midnight, Fri.-Sat. 10 a.m.-1 a.m. No cards.

Poquito Mas vies with Yuca's as our favorite taco/burrito place in town. In a sort of no-man's-land on Cahuenga Boulevard paralleling the Hollywood Freeway (across from Universal Studios), Poquito Mas makes incomparable carnitas, which go into generous, delicious burritos and soft tacos. Tasty fish tacos are usually on offer, and the tostadas are perfection. You can eat inside in a tiny room, or outside on a makeshift patio. There's always a crowd, but the friendly crew keeps the food coming. Count on spending about $19 for two, with beers.

La Salsa
11075 W. Pico Blvd., W.L.A.
479-0919
Open daily 10 a.m.-midnight. No cards.
10959 Kinross Ave., Westwood
208-7666
Open Sun.-Tues. & Thurs. 10 a.m.-10 p.m., Wed. 10 a.m.-11 p.m., Fri.-Sat. 10 a.m.-midnight. No cards.

Probably the most popular taco al carbón chain in town, and for very good reason. Great soft tacos and burritos are filled with succulent meats (including grilled chicken, for you red-meat phobics); you then douse your taco or burrito with a variety of salsas from a well-stocked salsa bar. One plus here for those who burn for the real thing: the salsas marked "hot" really are. The Westwood Village branch can get mobbed on weekends, so beware if you get claustrophobic amid throngs of boisterous college students. You'll get away spending about $17 for two

El Tepayac Café
812 N. Evergreen Ave., E.L.A.
268-1960
Open Sun.-Mon. & Wed.-Thurs. 7 a.m.-9:45 p.m., Fri.-Sat. 7 a.m.-11 p.m. No cards.

Burrito lovers from all over the city make regular pilgrimages to El Tepayac, sort of the Pantry or Tommy's of East L.A. You'll probably have to wait in line before you get a seat in the garish little dining room, but you're sure to make friends with some of the many El Tepayac fanatics in line with you. The menu lists lots of Mexican standards, most of which are good, but burritos are the thing to get. They're huge beyond belief, chock-full of all kinds of delicious things: machaca, chile verde, beans, rice, guacamole and more. Watch out for the seriously hot salsa served with the good chips. About $16 for two, with a beer.

Yuca's Hut
2056 N. Hillhurst Ave., Los Feliz
662-1214
Open Mon.-Sat. 11 a.m.-6 p.m. No cards.

We know New Yorkers who land at LAX and head straight for Yuca's. As well they should—this is the quintessential L.A. taco stand, the kind of place you can find nowhere else in the country. The little stand sits in the parking lot between a Los Feliz liquor store and real estate office, and there's always a line at lunch, when Dora and her family dispense some of the best carnitas and carne asada tacos and burritos we've ever had the honor to taste. Get a Corona or Dos Equis from the liquor store, grab one of the rickety tables in the sunshine, order a couple of tacos, and enjoy one of L.A.'s great small pleasures. Dinner for two, with a couple of beers, will cost about $20.

PIZZA

California Pizza Kitchen
207 S. Beverly Dr., Beverly Hills
272-7878
Beverly Center, 121 N. La Cienega Blvd.,
W. Hollywood
854-6555
Brentwood Gardens, 11677 San Vicente
Blvd., Brentwood
826-3573
330 S. Hope St., Downtown
626-2616
*Open Mon.-Sat. 11:30 a.m.-midnight, Sun. 4
p.m.-11 p.m. Cards: MC, V.*

This burgeoning empire just keeps on growing. There are now branches throughout Southern California, as well as in Atlanta, Chicago and Hawaii and rumors of more to come in Europe. The smart people behind these booming cafés have brought Spago-style cuisine to the masses, and the masses can't get enough of it. The individual-size designer pizzas may not be as good as those at Spago, but they're good enough. We prefer the less complicated pizzas (fresh tomato, garlic and basil; duck sausage, fresh spinach, sun-dried tomatoes and roasted garlic) to the overly complicated and cutesy numbers (the BLT, with bacon, tomato, lettuce and mayonnaise, or the Thai chicken, with peanut-ginger-sesame chicken, green onions, bean sprouts, carrots, cilantro and peanuts). You can also select from ten salads, a couple of calzones and a dozen or so generous and good pastas. Expect to part with about $18 per person for a pizza, a glass of wine and a shared salad.

Casa Bianca
1650 Colorado Blvd., Eagle Rock
256-9617
*Open Tues.-Thurs. 4 p.m.-midnight, Fri.-Sat. 4
p.m.-1 a.m. No cards.*

Casa Bianca is a no-nonsense, old-fashioned (it's been around since 1955) pizza place, where everyone seems to know one another, and the room is decorated with Chianti bottles and posters of Naples. The pizza is excellent, with a crisp, thin crust, hearty tomato sauce and the perfect amount of cheese. The spaghetti and meat balls and the linguine with clam sauce are the kind you dream about, and the lasagne is about as comforting and homey as food can get. Definitely worth a detour. Dinner for two, with wine, runs about $25.

Jacopo's
490 N. Beverly Dr., Beverly Hills
858-6446
15415 Sunset Blvd., Pacific Palisades
454-8494
11676 Olympic Blvd., W.L.A.
477-2111
8150 Sunset Blvd., W. Hollywood
650-8128
*Open Sun.-Thurs. 11:30 a.m.-midnight, Fri.-
Sat. 11:30 a.m.-2 a.m. Cards: AE, MC, V.*

Decent pizza but often an unpleasant atmosphere—it's best to take out. The brick-floored and -walled dining area is cramped and uncomfortable at the Beverly Hills branch, and the others are rather cold and prefab looking. The service can be dreadful, and the food varies from branch to branch, with Beverly Hills coming out as the lesser of the branch evils. Despite that, Jacopo's is extremely popular with the designer-sweatsuit crowd, who seem to love the cheesy pizza. We've had better. A pizza meal for two, with beverages, costs about $20 to $25.

L.A. Wine Bar
8570 W. 3rd St., W. Hollywood
271-0498
Open daily 11:30 a.m.-10 p.m. Cards: MC, V.

Don't let the name fool you—this place, close to the Beverly Center and Cedars-Sinai, really feels like a café in New York's Little Italy. L.A. Wine Bar makes the best breadsticks we've had in a long time: puffy, garlicky and hot from the oven. The pizzas and calzones are first-rate (and there are a number of vegetarian versions), as are the salads and the pastas, which include a terrific three-cheese lasagne. Service is friendly and cheerful, and that, along with the food, makes this an excellent neighborhood pizza joint. Dinner for two, with wine, runs about $35.

Lamonica's N.Y. Pizza

1066 Gayley Ave., Westwood
208-8671
Open Sun.-Thurs. 10 a.m.-11 p.m., Fri.-Sat. 10 a.m.-1:30 a.m. No cards.

Lamonica's sells good New York–style pizza, whole or by the slice, to the hordes of Westwood pedestrians. The crust is thin and light, the sauce and cheese delicious, and the toppings simple. You can eat inside, but it can get crowded and stuffy. We like to do it New York style: outdoors, people-watching along Village sidewalks. And if you don't want to face the bustle of the Village, Lamonic'a's delivers to westside locations.

Little Toni's

4745 Lankershim Blvd., N. Hollywood
(818) 763-0131
Open nightly 5 p.m.-2 a.m. All major cards.

Little Toni's is the kind of nondescript neighborhood Italian restaurant one would visit only upon a recommendation. So here it is: Little Toni's makes an excellent pizza. Get the thin crust—it's delicious and evenly crisp—with several of the generous and fresh toppings (we like bacon, onion, green pepper and sausage). This is a cheese-lover's pizza, favoring mozzarella over sauce. Wash it down with a pitcher of imported beer and you'll have experienced one of life's more inexpensive and satisfying pleasures.

Mario's

1001 Broxton Ave., Westwood
208-7077
Open Mon.-Fri. 11:30 a.m.-11:15 p.m., Sat. 11:30 a.m.-12:30 a.m., Sun. 11:30 a.m.-11:30 p.m. All major cards.

One of the few restaurants worth going to in the Westwood morass, Mario's is a cartoon version of an Italian restaurant, with checkered tablecloths and Chianti bottles hanging from the ceiling. The pizza is better than good, and the pizza topped with pesto and bacon, however bad for you, is a marvel. Other Italian standards can be underwhelming. About $30 for two, with a glass of wine.

Palermo

1858 N. Vermont Ave., Los Feliz
663-1430
Open daily 11 a.m.-10:30 p.m. No cards.

The years have gone by and the location has changed, but Palermo remains as popular as ever. Locals and fans from across the city don't mind the long wait, as long as the house keeps the free industrial-strength wine flowing. The big draw here is the pizza: thick crust (Sicilian style), marvelously spicy and flavorful, and loaded with toppings. True, it's too heavy for more refined palates (nothing here, save Mama's cannoli, can be described as delicate), but what a taste! The heavy pastas are also good in a rustic way, but by all means avoid anything even slightly fancy, particularly the scampi and the veal. About $25 for two for pizza with a glass of wine.

Santo Pietro

2954 Beverly Glen Circle, Bel Air
474-4349
Open daily 11:30 a.m.-midnight. No cards.

This chic pizza joint sits atop Beverly Glen in the high-rent shopping center that also houses Adriano's and Shane's (you're better off at the latter). The clientele is unfailingly handsome and has perfected that L.A. look of being very carefully and expensively underdressed. But, the food is mediocre—except for those addictive little garlic dough balls that are served in generous platefuls with drinks and with dinners. The folks here swap gossip and talk deals while they drink simple wines, eat so-so pizza and linger over cappuccinos. There's also an equally disappointing Santo Pietro Bar & Grill in Studio City, and branches on both Westwood and Brentwood.. About $38 for a pizza-and-salad dinner for two, with wine.

Silvio's Pizza

10251 Santa Monica Blvd., Century City
277-9911, 286-1797
Open Mon.-Fri. 11 a.m.-3 p.m. & 5 p.m.-9 p.m., Sat.-Sun. 4 p.m.-9 p.m. No cards.

This sweet little place occupies a space vacated by a branch of Piece o' Pizza, and the delicious product here is worlds away from its dreadful predecessor. Silvio's is located directly across the street from the Century City

Shopping Center, which makes it a great pre-movie stop, and it's well worth the detour to the other side of the road. The pizzas and pastas are old-fashioned and delicious, and the owners are as sweet as can be, constantly refilling sodas gratis and making sure that everything is okay. Silvio's is a mom-and-pop restaurant that deserves a lot of support, and we hope it makes its way among the corporate pizza Goliaths. If we have anything to do with it, though, they'll keep selling pizzas for a long time to come. Dinner for two, with beverages, is about $20.

Vittorio!

16646 Marquez Ave., Pacific Palisades
459-3755
Open Tues.-Sat. 11 a.m.-10 p.m., Sun. 11 a.m.-9 p.m. No cards.

The best-kept secret in the Palisades, Vittorio!'s pocket-size pizza-and-pasta shop hidden off Sunset Boulevard serves terrific food in an ambience of utter Italian chaos. Not only will your waiter be an aspiring actor, he'll probably sing to you as he sprinkles Parmesan on your spaghetti. The pizza is classic and very good.

HOTELS

INTRODUCTION

BIG-DEAL BUNGALOWS

Los Angeles certainly isn't famous for its luxury hotels—in this car-obsessed town, perhaps the perfect hotel would be a classy R.V. park. In fact, in L.A. there's almost a reverse snob appeal regarding luxury; secluded and often rustic bungalows with private gardens are sought after by both the ultra-chic and the nouveau riche. True to its stereotype, L.A. expends a great deal of effort pretending it's somewhere else. Hotels hire British beefeater look-alikes; suites are decorated like futuristic-space-colony spas; and there are Japanese tea gardens, grounds that look like *Snow White* scenery and enough circular architecture to create a field of perfectly upright towers of Pisa. The better hotels cater to the entertainment industry, whose members often hole up in these bungalows to make deals, write and rewrite scripts, take over studios, and hire and fire one another. Be warned that tourists who venture into these temples can be ignored by the star-struck Midwestern staffs.

All such carping aside, L.A. is currently enjoying an unprecedented abundance of good accommodations, and with the Asian and Australian currency flooding Southern California, new hotels are opening right and left. The Ashkenazy brothers alone have provided hundreds of exceptionally comfortable and well-located suites, and such hotels as the Shangri-la, the Hotel Bel-Air and the Regent Beverly Wilshire provide a respite from the typical L.A. cookie-cutter hotel room.

The future looks good, too. The Four Seasons, which opened in 1987, is an established hit, and it set a new standard in small-scale opulence. The super-ultra-mega-rich Sultan of Brunei bought the landmark Beverly Hills Hotel from merely super-ultra-rich Denver oil mogul Marvin Davis, who had bought it from the, er, financially troubled Ivan Boeskys (Seema Boesky is the daughter of the original owners), with even greater promises than the ones Davis made to renovate the pink lady. And the unsinkable Patrick Terrail finally saw the completion of the hulking Ma Maison Sofitel, across the street from the even more hulking Beverly Center. Unfortunately, the hotel is almost as devoid of physical charm as the old Ma Maison restaurant was; it's just not as luxe as was hoped and promised.

A couple of old war-horses have undergone major transformations. The Beverly Hilton, now owned by former talk-show host/game-show impresario Merv Griffin, has been completely redecorated by designer-to-the-stars Waldo Fernandez. The Beverly Wilshire was bought by the superlative Hong Kong–based Regent chain, rechristened the Regent Beverly Wilshire and transformed into an absolutely drop-dead gorgeous place—with great service, to boot. The long-awaited Brit-deco St. James's Club finally opened on Sunset Boulevard; Santa Monica at last gained a semigrand seaside resort when Loews recently landed on the beach; a little gem named Checkers in the heart of downtown was brought to us by the folks who gave us Campton Place in San Francisco; and another Asian hostelry giant, the Peninsula group, plans on unveiling the ultra-swank Belvedere very soon.

There are countless hotels and motels in the L.A. area, but we have room to list only several dozen. We've included our favorites, from bare-bones motels with bargain prices to high-style luxury hotels, and you're sure to find a comfortable home-away-from-home in the pages that follow.

A word regarding price: we've quoted each hotel's full, regular rate. Keep in mind that many offer corporate discounts and/or special package deals.

SYMBOLS & ABBREVIATIONS

Our opinion of the comfort level and appeal of each hotel is expressed in the following ranking system:

Very luxurious

Luxurious

Very comfortable

Comfortable

Symbols in red denote charm.

Credit Cards
  AE: American Express
  DC: Diners Club
  MC: MasterCard
  V: VISA

LOS ANGELES - CENTRAL

 Le Bel Age

1020 N. San Vicente Blvd.,
W. Hollywood, 90069
854-1111, Fax 612-4800

Obviously the Ashkenazy brothers believe that if there's one thing West Hollywood needs, it's more hotel rooms. Their other fine establishments (Le Parc, L'Ermitage and Le Dufy) must have been regularly packed, because in the last couple of years they have invested in four more hotels, all in the same area: Le Bel Age, Le Mondrian, Le Rêve and Valadon. Le Bel Age is a lovely place. Like many Ashkenazy hotels, it's cleverly disguised as an ugly stucco apartment building on a quiet street just off the Sunset Strip, which makes guests feel as though they are hiding out—in a most discreet place, of course. Behind the banal facade is a handsome lobby done in blond-wood paneling and marble, with a fashionable taupe-rose-cream color scheme and beautiful wood chandeliers. Pieces from the Ashkenazys' fine-art collection adorn the walls, and classical music plays in the background. Like its brother hotels, Le Bel Age is composed entirely of suites, which feature rosewood and pecan furniture, wet bars, large TVs, private balconies and myriad amenities, from bathrobes to multiline phones. Guests may use the hotel's limousine, or hire one from the Dav-El office in the lobby. The hotel also offers secretarial services and poolside paging. By all means dine at the Bel Age restaurant, an elegant room serving delicious Franco-Russian cuisine.

Suites: $225-$270.

 The Biltmore

515 S. Olive St., Downtown, 90013
624-1011, Fax 655-5311

A few years ago, this grande dame was given yet another face-lift, and the interior is once again aglow. The former lobby has been transformed into a lovely bar, complete with mellow live jazz, a tiled fountain, lush plants and beautiful beamed and painted ceilings high overhead. A handsome new lobby has been created out of one of the old meeting rooms. The other meeting rooms have been cleaned and brightened, and the Crystal Ballroom is as grand as ever. The renovation has a downside, though: an ugly office tower and motor court entrance have been added on to the graceful old building.

Most of the rooms are colorful, modern and entirely too small, but there are some lovely old-fashioned suites with large living rooms and fireplace mantels; Jim Dine paintings are still found throughout. Sadly, Bernard's restaurant is no longer the wonder it once was. But the Grand Avenue Bar is still a chic place for drinks or an elegant buffet lunch, and the lobby lounge makes for a fine rendezvous spot. The Club floor caters to business travelers, who are greeted personally by a valet who oversees operations to ensure their comfort and pleasure. Complimentary breakfast, cocktails and hors d'oeuvres are provided for Club floor guests. Despite the poorly conceived new entrance and office addition, The Biltmore is one of L.A.'s most gracious and lovely hotels; it is particularly recommended for businesspeople who want to stay downtown but dislike the modern sterility of the big chain hotels.

Singles: $150-$200; doubles: $180-$230; suites: $370-$1,800.

 The Bonaventure

5th & Figueroa sts., Downtown,
90071 - 624-1000, Fax 612-4800

This self-contained minicity looks to some residents like a mirrored espresso machine. It reflects American designers' fascination with mirrored towers, hyper-speed glass elevators and restaurants that rotate diners through dinner. The interior is dreadful, a meandering,

---

Hotel prices quoted are for the "regular" rates. Don't forget that discounts are frequently offered, particularly weekend packages. And some hotels will even bargain!

hopelessly confusing tangle of concrete reminiscent of freeway on-ramps. The Bonaventure was designed for conventions; it has no less than 1,474 rooms, 28 meeting rooms and a honeycomb of boutiques, discos, bars and restaurants. You'll need a tour guide just to find your way around, especially if you're trying to reach one of the upper-floor restaurants. The hotel's finest suite is the five-bedroom Huntington Suite, which is stocked with rosewood furniture, Chinese antiques and dazzling crystal chandeliers. Otherwise, the rooms are cramped and run-of-the-mill, though the ones on the upper floors can have terrific views.

Singles: $130-$175; doubles: $200-$255; suites: $325-$2,000.

Château Marmont
8221 W. Sunset Blvd.,
W. Hollywood, 90069
656-1010, Fax 655-5311

Since it prides itself on its hotel's discretion and privacy, policies that attract celebrities, Château Marmont's management had to be extremely upset with the notoriety it received when actor John Belushi died here of a drug overdose. Fortunately, the Marmont didn't suffer from the attention, and the stars still stay in these ersatz Louis XV and Formica rooms. The staff makes the celebrated feel at home, so much so that even the most idiosyncratic are comfortable. The poolside Cape Cod bungalows provide sanctuary from the glitter and tinsel of Hollywood, and these highly coveted accommodations come with fully equipped kitchenettes for those who aren't keen on having their photos snapped at Spago. Château Marmont also has an impressive wine cellar and a romantic view of L.A. at night, when the real stars come out and the movie stars go in.

Singles: $95; cottage rooms: $130; suites: $180; bungalows: $300.

Checkers
555 S. Grand Ave., Downtown,
90071 - 624-0000, Fax 626-9906

The Ayala Hotel Group, which gave San Francisco a four-star jewel in Campton Place, now has a lovely establishment in downtown L.A. called Checkers. Located between The

Biltmore and Library Square, this small (190-room) hotel has all the earmarks of success—beautiful, muted furnishings (no expense has been spared here; there's quite a cache of antiques scattered about), a business communications center, on-site laundry and dry cleaning services, 24-hour room service, a rooftop spa with tanning, Jacuzzi and massage facilities (it hopes to add a lap pool soon), as well as saunas, a steam room and an exercise studio. While the rooms aren't exactly spacious, they are luxurious, and each has phones with call-waiting and phone-mail systems. There's also a cozy library and four meeting rooms. And the handsome restaurant, as at Campton, is of the first order, serving contemporary California/American cuisine. Checkers is exactly the kind of first-class hotel downtown needs to encourage further urban revitalization.

Singles & doubles: $190-$285; suites: $450-$975.

Le Dufy
1000 Westmount Dr.,
W. Hollywood, 90069
657-7400, Fax 854-6744

One of the Ashkenazy brothers' best hotels, Le Dufy combines contemporary art with comfort and reasonable prices. Like L'Ermitage and Le Parc, this all-suite hotel looks and feels more like an apartment building; the atmosphere is quiet, sophisticated and most discreet. The 120 compact suites are attractively decorated in trendy colors with contemporary furnishings; most have sunken living rooms, gas-powered fireplaces and small balconies. It's a pretty, well-located place, and weary travelers can relax by the pool or in the rooftop Jacuzzi that shows off a dazzling panoramic view on a clear day.

Suites: $175-$230.

Holiday Inn Hollywood
1755 N. Highland Ave., Hollywood,
90028 - 462-7181, Fax 466-9072

If you don't mind sharing the sidewalk with motorcycle-gang members, punk rockers, bewildered tourists, record producers, a stray lady of the evening or any of the other characters who make up the Hollywood scene, then you might enjoy this Holiday Inn. The

468 rooms are cozy, comfortable and of the predictable Holiday Inn design school. The location is great for visiting the Hollywood Bowl and local tourist sights, and the revolving restaurant on the 23rd floor provides a wonderful view. A good bet for the price.

Singles: $79-$135; doubles: $91-$175; suites: $185.

Hollywood Roosevelt

7000 Hollywood Blvd., Hollywood, 90028 - 466-7000, Fax 462-8056

In recent years this once-grand hotel, built in the twenties, had become seedy and scary, with head-banging punkers hanging around outside; travelers started staying away in droves. But a few years back millions of dollars were pumped into it, and the Hollywood Roosevelt is once again a lovely, peaceful hotel. The spacious lobby is a wonderful place to linger, with its dusty-rose-and-taupe color scheme, beautiful tilework, painted ceilings, baby grand piano, photos of Gable and Lombard and vintage jazz. Overhead you'll see the balconied mezzanine, which is a minimuseum of Hollywood history and lore. Film, TV and record executives have rediscovered the Roosevelt (so named for Teddy); they like to hold meetings in the wonderful old meeting rooms.

The hotel is home to a terrific '40s-style supper club, the Cinegrill, which features excellent jazz cabaret singers. Although some of the rooms can be small, they are all decorated in the lobby's tasteful color scheme. If you sign that big three-picture deal, celebrate in the fantastic two-story Celebrity Suite, worth every penny of its $1,500-a-night tag. The Roosevelt is located across from Mann's Chinese Theatre, just at the edge of Hollywood Boulevard's gaudy stretch to the east; to the west are an abundance of entertainment companies.

Singles: $110; doubles: $130; suites: $160-$1,500 (lower rates during fall & winter).

Hyatt on Sunset

8401 W. Sunset Blvd., W. Hollywood, 90069 656-4101, Fax 650-7024

In rock 'n' roll's wild 'n' woolly era, the late '60s through the late '70s, this hotel was better known as the Riot House. In this "safe" era, however, things have calmed down a bit, and nostalgia buffs will enjoy the art deco lobby of this aging Hyatt on the Sunset Strip. Popular with movie and record types, the Hyatt has a typical and forgettable decor and equally ordinary service and amenities. It does, however, offer a good location, perfect for travelers who want to walk to Spago or Tower Records or to stroll along the very fashionable Sunset Plaza section of the Strip. A small, comfortable, modest place.

Singles: $115; doubles: $135; suites: $150-$450.

Hyatt Regency

711 S. Hope St., Downtown, 90017 683-1234, Fax 629-3230

At press time, the Hyatt Regency was undergoing a complete and total renovation. We'll report back in our next edition.

Singles: $145-$160; doubles: $155-$170; suites: $250-$600.

Los Angeles Hilton and Towers

930 Wilshire Blvd., Downtown, 90017 - 629-4321, Fax 488-9869

After several years of ongoing renovation, this well-located Hilton has finally been completed. The lobby is now quite attractive, though as impersonal as ever, and its several new restaurants include the elegant Cardini, which serves sophisticated Italian cuisine in a series of intimate dining rooms that are handsome but sterile. The rooms are just what you would expect of a big-city, business-oriented Hilton: comfortable and devoid of personality; the rooms located in the Towers do have fabulous views. For those interested in more than mergers and real estate deals, the hotel is within walking distance of the Seventh Street Marketplace (a fine shopping center, featuring Bullock's, Ann Taylor and Godiva Chocolatier, among the shops) and the Seventh Street Bistro.

Singles: $139-$184; doubles: $159-$204; suites: $325-$550.

Ma Maison Sofitel

8555 Beverly Blvd., W. Hollywood, 90048 278-5444, Fax 657-2816

The long-awaited Ma Maison Sofitel has raised an interesting architectural controversy.

Some love its postmodern château exterior; others find the reference to the French Middle Ages a bit ill-placed at this bustling commercial intersection across from the Beverly Center. The rooms are nicely appointed and decorated in a sort of California-ized French-country scheme; also on the up side are its terrific location—on the edge of West Hollywood and smack in between Santa Monica and downtown—and its restaurants. While Patrick Terrail's updated version of Ma Maison: The Sequel doesn't quite have the luster of the original, it's still an unequivocally good place to eat for locals and visitors alike. And the hotel's more casual café, La Cajole, serves terrific French bistro–like cuisine, and it features a bar that's quite the scene. Amenities include a heated outdoor pool, sauna, fitness center and massage facilities. The hotel also has an arrangement with nearby golf courses and tennis courts, and seven meeting rooms (one of which holds 240 people) with audio-visual capabilities. At the time we went to press, it was too early to assign the hotel a rating., so we'll leave that task to its visitors.

Singles & doubles: $160-$190; suites: $300-$600 (special executive & weekend rates available).

Le Mondrian

8440 Sunset Blvd., W. Hollywood, 90069 - 650-8999, Fax 650-5215

This time the Ashkenazy brothers have carried their love for combining fine art with fine hotels a bit too far. Painted (and signed) by Yaacov Agam, the twelve-story Le Mondrian is described in the hotel brochure as a work of "contemporary art." We'll buy the contemporary part, but this supposed tribute to Piet Mondrian's paintings must have him doing cartwheels in his grave. The marble lobby—small, cold and uninviting—isn't much better. On the other hand, Le Mondrian is a fine all-suite hotel featuring cozy suites that are well designed and comfortable, with contemporary furnishings and carpets in black, gray, navy and the occasional primary color. And we love the view—Le Mondrian sits on the highest part of the Sunset Strip, and on a clear day the views stretch to the ocean. Other amenities include a complete health spa, a large pool and whirlpool, and pleasant outdoor patios for sunning or lunching.

Suites: $185-$320.

The New Otani

120 S. Los Angeles St., Downtown, 90012 - 629-1200, Fax 622-0980

If you're homesick for Tokyo and its geisha pamperings, don't fret. You can come spend $325 a night at The New Otani for a tatami suite with futon beds, Ofuro baths and first-class service. East meets West in this modern hotel, where the Garden in the Sky presents a serene half-acre Shinto garden to ease the pains of a harrying business day. Although the rooms have all the charm of a samurai's Spartan quarters, there is a certain soothing appeal to the less-is-more design. The Otani is more than a hotel—it offers cultural introductions to Zen archery, flower arranging and a host of Japanese arts for fine (but simple) living. The multilingual staff is as gracious, courteous and polite as you would expect the Japanese tradition to yield.

Singles: $110-$142; doubles: $125-$157; suites: $275-$700. Special packages available.

Le Parc

733 Westknoll Dr., W. Hollywood, 90069 - 855-8888, Fax 659-7812

The Ashkenazy brothers have done it again with this intimate, genteel hotel in a quiet residential area. The upwardly mobile clientele appreciates Le Parc's proximity to West Hollywood's countless galleries, restaurants and designers. Some of the signature art collection of these entrepreneurial businessmen is scattered throughout the 152 compact suites, each of which features a sunken living room, fireplace, wet bar, kitchenette, bedroom and bathroom. The roof is a veritable miniresort, sporting a gym, tennis court, pool, spa and sun deck, designed to keep the music and advertising industry guests in good shape. The restaurant, Café Le Parc, is open only to guests. A very good West Hollywood hotel.

Suites: $165-$245.

Ramada West Hollywood

8585 Santa Monica Blvd., W. Hollywood, 90069 652-6400, Fax 652-2135

A Ramada is a Ramada is Ramada—but this is a *Ramada!* From the outside, with its Max

Fleischer–on–acid lampposts, sculptures and mobiles, it looks like the unholy offspring of deconstructionist architect Frank Gehry and postmodern artisan Peter Shire. And the lobby, which you enter through *the parking lot*, looks like the waiting room of an airport on Mars, with its brightly colored, overstuffed cartoon furniture and throw-pillowed banquettes. Take note that the Ramada is located on the site of the beloved, sleazy old Tropicana Motel, once home to the likes of Tom Waits and Rickie Lee Jones, as well as the home of the original Duke's coffee shop. Unfortunately, the ditziness of the Duke's staff seems to have been telepathically transferred to the Ramada's staff; we wouldn't want to count on them to do anything more taxing than moussing their hair. But the rooms and suites are nicely decorated in a moderne mode, and amenities include a swimming pool, telephones with call-waiting, and the use of health-club facilities (including aerobics classes) at the Sports Connection across the street. As yet, there's no restaurant in the hotel, but the location is so central that you can take a five-minute trip over to "restaurant land," on Melrose Avenue or La Cienega Boulevard.

Singles & doubles: $69-$159; suites: $109-$239.

 ## Le Rêve
8822 Cynthia St., W. Hollywood,
90069 - 854-1114, Fax 657-2623

Those darn Ashkenazy brothers just can't restrain themselves from turning nondescript apartment buildings in quiet, residential areas into small hotels. Le Rêve, one of their newest creations, is very well located—adjacent to Beverly Hills, close to the galleries and shops, yet isolated enough for the privacy-minded (and since so few locals have even heard of it, you'll have privacy in spades). There are 80 suites in all, each tastefully decorated in a French-country prints-and-pine mode. Most of the suites have fireplaces, some have kitchenettes and balconies, and all offer multiline telephones so you don't have to worry about missing that big call from your agent. There's a rooftop garden with a heated pool (is there any other kind in Los Angeles?), and while Le

Rêve has no restaurant or liquor license yet, room service is available from the on-premises kitchen from 7 a.m. to 11 p.m. And, thankfully, the underground parking is complimentary.

Singles: $115-$175; doubles: $130-$190.

 ## St. James's Club
8358 Sunset Blvd., W. Hollywood,
90069 - 654-7100, Fax 654-9287

The St. James's Club tries to be all things to all people: a tony, private club; a chic, members-only hostelry and restaurant; and a hotel. We'll deal with it as a hotel here. No, you don't have to be a club member to stay here; a temporary membership fee of $8 per night will be tacked onto your bill. To us, the real attraction of the club is the building itself, a dazzling deco beacon that began life as the swanky Sunset Towers in 1931, home to luminaries like Errol Flynn, Jean Harlow, Clark Gable and Marilyn Monroe. It was placed on the National Registry of Historic Places in 1979, at which time it had fallen into a state of disrepair. When the St. James's folks took over in 1985, they pumped $40 million into its restoration, and the results are, well, mixed. While the exterior is absolutely gorgeous, the interiors are a bit *de trop*—a bit more deco than anything in that period ever was. But for those who like to feel important and like—dare we say—members of the club, this could be just the ticket.

The smallish rooms have two-line telephones, and for recreation there's a truly beautiful swimming pool, an outdoor lounging area that really does feel like something out of a much grander era, and a fully equipped health spa, with massage facilities available. You can also take advantage of the business center, meeting rooms, extensive film and book library and secretarial services. The restaurant (for members and hotel guests only) is truly wonderful—the food is excellent, and the atmosphere is right out of an Astaire-Rogers movie. The Club Lounge and Bar is a lovely place to unwind, and, last but certainly not least, the panoramic views of the city are spectacular.

Singles: $165; doubles: $180; suites: $280-$1,000.

SAN FERNANDO VALLEY

 La Maida House

11159 La Maida St., N. Hollywood,
91601 - (818) 769-3857, No fax

Scattered throughout the Valley's countless tract houses are the occasional mansions, reminders of an era gone by, the days when the Valley was populated by wealthy ranchers. La Maida House is one such mansion, and, happily, it has been converted to a luxurious bed-and-breakfast for hotel-weary travelers. The 7,000-square-foot Mediterranean villa, built in the 1920s, is nestled among grounds lush with magnolia trees, orchids and hundreds of roses. Owner Megan Timothy has decorated the seven spacious rooms and suites in good taste, with polished floors, wicker furniture, ceiling fans, pretty fabrics and tiled bathrooms. The atmosphere is refined and relaxed, the rooms are comfortable, and the breakfast (featuring eggs freshly hatched by La Maida's chickens) is lovely. Timothy prides herself on her cooking; with advance notice she prepares gourmet dinners for guests. A good bet for travelers who want to be near the Valley's movie studios but who can't stand huge, sterile hotels.

Rooms & suites: $80-$210.

 Registry Hotel

555 Universal Terrace Pkwy.,
Studio City, 91608
(818) 506-2500, Fax (818)509-2058

While the next-door Sheraton Universal attracts tourists headed for Universal Studios, the relatively new Registry (formerly the Sheraton Premiere) goes after well-heeled business and creative types in town to visit the production offices of the nearby movie studios. The gleaming 24-story tower encases an attractive plant-filled lobby, some good restaurants and handsome, spacious rooms. Ask for a room on an upper floor; you'll have a fabulous nighttime view of the valley. Service is as good as you would expect of an upscale Registry hotel.

Singles: $150-$165; doubles: $165-$175; suites: $260-$1,100.

 Sheraton Universal

333 Universal Terrace Pkwy.,
Studio City, 91608
(818) 980-1212, Fax (818) 985-4980

The lobby may look like a set from *Frankenstein*, and the rooms may be routine, but the location is great for visiting Universal Studios, the Universal Amphitheatre, The Burbank Studios and the Hollywood Bowl. Some of the upper rooms have great views, and all the rooms are comfortable. This large hotel constantly teems with tour groups and families.

Singles: $125-$180; doubles: $145-$205; suites: $375-$700. Summer discounts available.

 Warner Center Marriott

21850 Oxnard St., Woodland Hills,
91367 - (818) 887-4800,
Fax (818) 340-5843

The area of Woodland Hills known as Warner Center has mushroomed at the hands of bullish developers: office buildings, department stores, chain restaurants and tract housing, and it's still growing like mad. Even Angelenos are astounded at this enormous growth in the hinterlands. The newish Warner Center Marriott was created to serve this bustling community. It's a huge place with an emphasis on meeting and convention facilities; there are meeting rooms of every conceivable size, and a full kosher kitchen that can serve 60 to 600. Predictably, this Marriott immediately became a popular west Valley wedding spot. Rooms are comfortable and pleasant in that cookie-cutter, chain-hotel way. This is an ideal location if you have business or pleasure in Encino, Warner Center or the rest of the west Valley area. If you visit the dark glitter-and-glitz bar here, you'll find yourself grabbing for your sunglasses when you hit the bright sunshine outside.

Singles: $128; doubles: $148; suites: $350-$1,500; weekend package: $99.

SOUTH BAY & AIRPORT

 Barnabey's
3501 N. Sepulveda Blvd.,
Manhattan Beach, 90266
545-8466, Fax 545-8466

There is something rather bizarre about having a piece of Victorian England sequestered in a community more renowned for its surfer mentality than its cultural heritage. Nonetheless, Barnabey's has an ersatz, old-world charm that some find wonderful, and others (ourselves included) find ticky-tacky and silly—a more sedate version of the Madonna Inn, with a major attack of the cutes. The rooms are filled with antiques, deep, full carpets and lots of bronze, oak and carved marble. The Victorian dining room serves Continental cuisine (the chef is Viennese) that's actually very good—even though the room's a bit claustrophobic—along with high tea presented by servers in Victorian dress. Despite the old-fashioned atmosphere, however, all the modern conveniences are provided, making a stay here comfortable—provided you like this sort of thing. It's also very close to LAX. However, if you have an aversion to ruffles, frills and bric-a-brac, save yourself a nervous breakdown and stay at the nearby Radisson Plaza. And keep in mind that you may have to fight for time on the hotel's grounds, as Barnabey's is extremely popular for local wedding parties and assorted soirees.

Singles: $108; doubles: $118-$128; suites: $175.

 Hotel Queen Mary
Pier J (end of Long Beach Fwy.),
Long Beach, 90802
432-6964, Fax 437-4531

If you're looking not only to get away from it all but to get away in the style of the Carnegies, Gettys and Vanderbilts, stay at the Hotel Queen Mary, resplendent in its authentic deco decor. Wood paneling, marvelous overstuffed vintage furniture and ship-style bathrooms reflect the golden age. And it's a far cry from the oil rigs in Long Beach Harbor. Some of the rooms have been remodeled, and the luxury-ship feeling has been well pre-served. There are more than 380 rooms on three decks, in shapes accommodating the ship's hull; request an outside room, as the inside chambers, although less expensive, have no cheery portholes. Treat yourself to a more decadent visit to the past in one of the ultra-first-class suites, complete with two parlors, two bedrooms, two baths and *two* maid's rooms. There are a few concessions to the present; each room has a telephone and the ubiquitous TV set. Nostalgia fans can be married by the ship's captain and honeymoon in splendor.

Singles & doubles: $95-$140; suites: $185-$650.

 Marriott Los Angeles
5855 W. Century Blvd., Westchester, 90045 - 641-5700, Fax 337-5358

This ten-story high-rise, once the flagship of the chain, has been renovated and redecorated in a typical upscale-chain-hotel style. The expansive sunken lobby bar employs a harpist at cocktail hour to soothe the tired business travelers and tourists who stumble back to the hotel after a taxing day in L.A. You'll notice an attention to detail for which the Marriott chain is famous, and the rooms are spacious and comfortable, if not fancy. The three restaurants range from coffee-shop basic to hotel-Continental elegant; other amusements include a disco and a pool area with a lush tropical garden and outdoor bar. This hotel is ideal for corporate travelers who want to conduct business in a resortlike setting just minutes from the airport.

Singles: $66-$150; doubles: $134-$165; suites: $250-$1,000.

 Portofino Inn
260 Portofino Way, Redondo Beach, 90277 - 379-8481, Fax 372-7329

Despite its commanding view of King Harbor, this waterfront hotel is almost undone by its graceless architecture. An ideal getaway for people who intend only to sleep in their rooms, the Portofino Inn is surrounded by yachts, dinghys and power boats, and the views from the 133 rooms and suites are spectacular. There is a coffee shop and a restaurant, but we can't honestly recommend them.

Singles & doubles: $79-$160; suites: $130-$210.

Radisson Plaza Hotel
1400 Parkview Ave.,
Manhattan Beach, 90266
546-7511, Fax 546-7520

This newish, largish (400 rooms) West Coast flagship of the Radisson chain is pretty spectacular business for a mass-market chain hotel—and you do get quite a bit for your money. The grounds are lovely, with lots of fountains and waterfalls; indoors, in the atrium lobby, are acres of glitzy marble, terrazzo, etched glass and woods. One of the main draws here is the golf course (complete with pro shop); additional recreational facilities include a fully equipped health spa, a swimming pool and bicycle rentals. As with the more upscale Hyatts, there's a Plaza Club Level that provides 24-hour room service, laundry and pressing service, twice-daily maid service and a lounge. The rooms are good-sized and attractive in that fancy-corporate-hotel mode, and there are a business center and voluminous meeting facilities. The restaurant, Califia, serves surprisingly tasty California cuisine, or if you wish to dine more casually, the indoor/outdoor Terrace Bistro is a good spot.

Singles: $115-$145; doubles: $130-$165. Packages available.

Sheraton La Reina
6101 W. Century Blvd., Westchester,
90045 - 642-1111, Fax 410-1267

If you need to stay near the airport, the La Reina is as good a choice as any. We can't say much for the cold, sterile lobby, which is about as personal as an airport waiting room. The staff, however, offers some warmth to the conventioneering clientele that keeps this place active. The compact rooms feature a minimalist decor with little style, but the suites are spacious and comfortable. If you're satisfied with efficiency and a predictable, impersonal atmosphere, this Sheraton's will do.

Singles: $110-$145; doubles: $130-$165; suites: $165-$300.

WESTSIDE

Bay View Plaza
530 Pico Blvd., Santa Monica, 90405
399-9344, Fax 399-2504

The Bay View Plaza is actually a Holiday Inn, or rather, HI's version of a luxury hotel. It may be glossier and plusher than the average Holiday Inn, but the corporate-hotel mood prevails. Service is perfunctory, but the place looks fine enough, it's only five blocks from the beach, and the prices won't bankrupt you. Extras include two swimming pools, a health club and Jacuzzis in some of the suites. Don't bother with the cafés, though—just walk a few blocks to Main Street instead.

Singles & doubles: $95-$105; suites: $250.

Bel Air Summit
11461 W. Sunset Blvd., Brentwood,
90049 - 476-6571, Fax 471-6310

Formerly the Bel Air Sands, this unobtrusive hideaway recently went through a major overhaul. Though the redone exterior somewhat resembles a cross between Der Führer's bunker and a missile silo, the Summit is a quite pleasant hotel well located near the San Diego Freeway, making it a convenient central point for those who have business on the westside. It's easily accessible for the East Coast and movie-colony clientele, as well as for local executives who use it as a convenient meeting place and watering hole. The interior now has an ultra-moderne decor, very cool and sleek, yet comfortable; the 181 rooms are spacious and attractive, and each comes complete with a VCR (there's a video library as well); the meeting and banquet rooms can handle up to 300 people; and active sorts can use the swimming pool and tennis courts. Echo, the airy restaurant, has an interesting French/American/Caribbean menu and a most pleasant bar—all of which appeal to the many local couples who come here for quiet weekend retreats.

Singles: $125-$140; doubles: $140-$155; suites: $160-$350.

Beverly Crest Hotel

125 S. Spalding Dr., Beverly Hills,
90212 - 274-6801, Fax 273-6614

This nondescript 54-room hotel is so dull you might not notice it, though its loyal clientele swears by its service and convenient location. Its most compelling feature is its proximity to the shops along Wilshire Boulevard. The compact rooms lack character and style, but they are clean and neat. The pool area is a haven for tired shoppers who have just returned from sorties on Rodeo Drive. One has the impression that this is the kind of hotel where wealthy doctors sequester their mothers-in-law. A good value if you can tolerate the grim decor and small rooms.
Singles: $85-$95; doubles: $95-$110.

Beverly Hillcrest Hotel

1224 S. Beverwil Dr., Beverly Hills,
90212 - 277-2800, Fax 203-9537

High atop a knoll, with a commanding view of Beverly Hills, this tacky monument to the '60s can make you long for Frank Sinatra records and big cars with fins. Much of the Beverly Hillcrest's success and its loyal following are attributable to the experienced staff, some of whom have been with the hotel since it opened in 1965. All the rooms are sizable and have a private balcony or lanai patio, but the decor is strictly Miami Beach moderne. The rooftop restaurant is worth a visit if only for the wonderful nighttime view of the sparkling city. Given its prestigious location and excellent service, this hotel is a good value.
Singles: $115-$125; doubles: $125-$140; suites: $280.

The Beverly Hills Hotel

9641 Sunset Blvd., Beverly Hills,
90210 - 276-2251, Fax 271-0319

The Beverly Hills Hotel is a great shooting-star show. This is where we rediscover America's famous and near-misses, all vying for the attention and favors of the staff. (After a first trip to this mythological institution, one could have less-than-stellar memories, particularly after being closeted in a room the size of servants' quarters, which reaffirms the you-have-to-know-someone theory.) The pool is a legend unto itself; every socially important person takes a dip in it sooner or later, or at least takes a poolside phone call. The Polo Lounge is equally legendary, though it seems a bit drab and passé to us. The pink-stucco facade is hidden away on acres of lawn decorated with royal palms and banana and jacaranda trees. If you hit the proverbial jackpot, try out the $3,100-a-day four-bedroom suite, complete with wood-paneled bar, patios, oversized TV screen and other hedonistic appointments. Most of the 325 suites and bungalows are pleasantly decorated, albeit a bit tatty around the edges (just when is its current owner, the Sultan of Brunei, going to part with some bucks and spruce the place up, anyway?). Unless your name appears regularly in *Daily Variety*, prepare yourself for perfunctory service.
Singles: $160-$280; doubles: $215-$305; suites: $375-$3,100.

The Beverly Hilton

9876 Wilshire Blvd., Beverly Hills,
90212 - 274-7777, Fax 285-1313

Once upon a time, this was one of L.A.'s most chic hotels, famous around the world. But its gestalt remained mired in the '60s long after that era had passed, and the Hilton became just another tacky monument to kitsch. But then, just like out of one of the MGM musicals he once starred in, the chameleon-like Merv "singer-cum-actor-cum-talk-show-host-cum-game-show-mogul" Griffin, in a Trump-like move, bought the old dinosaur, gussied her up and is making her a star once again. While the architecture still looks dated, at least it's not that dread mustard-and-dinge color anymore. Griffin brought in designer-to-the-stars Waldo Fernandez (perhaps best known for his work on Trumps), who completely redid the lobby and the landscaping and is currently tackling the rooms. The result is a vast improvement over the original, and while there are still vestiges of time warp here (like the restaurants, Trader Vic's and L'Escoffier), they're nice, comforting anachronisms that deserve to live on.
Singles: $155-$195; doubles: $175-$215; suites: $195-$1,000.

The Beverly Pavilion

9360 Wilshire Blvd., Beverly Hills, 90212 - 273-1400, Fax 859-8551

This hotel has several things going for it: a fine location, within walking distance of Beverly Hills's shopping district; a rooftop pool and a sundeck with 320-degree views of the city; excellent, friendly service; and a good restaurant, Colette. The lobby is a little cramped, though it's nicely appointed, and the 110 small rooms and suites are quiet and attractive. Try to get a west-facing room on one of the top floors—you'll be rewarded with a lovely sunset view.

Singles: $120; doubles: $140; suites: $170-$390.

 Beverly Rodeo Hotel

260 N. Rodeo Dr., Beverly Hills, 90210 - 273-0300, Fax 859-8730

If you want to be the first one on the block to get inside Bottega Veneta and avoid the touristy throngs, or if you have an early-morning appointment at Bijan to pick up your $5,000 suit, then the Beverly Rodeo is the perfect place to stay. Other than its location, though, there is little to recommend it. The rooms are small and ordinary, featuring a standard-American-motel design. But most people don't spend too much time indoors when they have all that conspicuous consumption at their credit-card-ready fingertips. The quasi-sidewalk-café makes for good people-watching (but don't dare breast-feed your baby here; a nursing mom who committed this heinous infraction recently lost a precedent-setting lawsuit against the café, making us dislike it all the more), but we suggest you drop in for drinks rather than for the mediocre cuisine.

Singles: $120-$140; doubles: $140-$160; suites: $250-$390.

 Beverly Terrace Motor Hotel

469 N. Doheny Dr., Beverly Hills, 90210 - 274-8141, No fax

We find it fascinating that this unassuming little place has such a loyal following; you must book well in advance to stay in one of the 37 homey rooms. Despite its plain-Jane motor-hotel decor, it's a favorite with designers and other interior-decorator types associated with the nearby Pacific Design Center—no doubt because of its outstanding location-to-price ratio. The adjacent restaurant, Checco (formerly the legendary Scully's), is an offshoot of Madeo, but we found it overpriced, too clubby and most unattractive—like dining in your aunt's rec room. Parking is free, which makes it a doubly good value.

Singles: $55; doubles: $65.

 Century City Inn

10330 W. Olympic Blvd., Century City, 90064 553-1000, Fax 277-1633

This new addition to the Century City hotel scene is a small, workmanlike faux-château that's inexpensive and decently appointed; rooms have VCRs, refrigerators and microwaves, and the business center has computers, fax machines and copiers. It's a perfectly decent place to stay for those on business or those who don't want to waste all their vacation dollars on accommodations—and you can't beat its westside location. Service is perky.

Singles & doubles: $99-$129; suites: $129-$159.

 Century Plaza

2025 Ave. of the Stars, Century City, 90067 - 551-3300, Fax 551-3355

In the heart of Century City, on what was once the 20th Century-Fox back lot, this gigantic curvilinear monument to Cinemascope is a perfect symbol of today's Hollywood: a big screen with little inside. Despite its prestigious reputation, this hotel, one of the Westin chain, lacks charm and verve—and it's so big that you'll feel lost in the teeming throng of conventioneers, business travelers and black-tied folks attending the almost-nightly parties and dinners in the huge banquet rooms. The sunken lobby is a cold, mirrored cavern, and the 1,072 large rooms lack distinction. But in Los Angeles, location is all-important, and what most commends this hotel is its proximity to some of the best shopping, cinemas and live theater in Los Angeles. For other amusements, the Century Plaza has a pool, tennis courts, several restaurants, a coffee shop and a piano bar. The rooms in the newer 30-story tower are more attractive, and some have wonderful views. On the down side, the hotel charges $12 a night to park your car. No doubt because of the Century Plaza's size and facilities, it has been a favorite of presidents visiting L.A.—there's plenty of room for all those Secret Service agents.

Singles: $155-$185; doubles: $185-$215; suites: $375-$4,000.

 ### Century Wilshire
10776 Wilshire Blvd., Westwood, 90024 - 474-4506, Fax 474-2535

With 66 no-nonsense suites (and some singles and doubles) that are best suited for long-term visitors, the Century Wilshire is functionally banal. Popular with executives who prefer its convenient westside address, this hotel does try to make guests feel comfortable: each suite comes with a fully equipped kitchen and a daily newspaper. But while the rooms are large, the decor is basic motel material. This is a no-frills hotel at a chic address—and at the right price.

Singles: $65-$75; doubles: $75-$85; suites: $85-$250.

 ### Channel Road Inn
219 W. Channel Rd., Santa Monica, 90402 - 459-1920, No fax

Los Angeles suffers from a dearth of bed-and-breakfasts, especially on the westside and, more particularly, near the beach. Of the few that exist, the most charming is the recently opened Channel Road Inn. (Unfortunately, the lovely Casa Alma in the same neighborhood has closed.) A rare specimen of shingle-clad Colonial-revival architecture, this inn is a former residence, built in 1910 by a self-proclaimed outlaw and Indian fighter named Thomas McCall, and it originally stood on Second Street in Santa Monica. It was moved to its present location in the early '60s, and was bought and lovingly restored by the current owners in 1988. The fourteen rooms and suites all have private baths; most have ocean views. Home-baked breads and muffins are served as part of the Continental breakfast each morning, refreshments are offered in the afternoons, secretarial services are available, there's a hillside spa overlooking the Santa Monica Bay, and bicycles are available, as well as picnic lunches. There are also nearby horse-

back-riding and tennis facilities—and, best of all, you're within walking distance of the beach (just a block away). Not to mention the fact that the tariff's awfully gentle; the location alone could command far more.

Rooms & suites: $85-$145.

 ### Chesterfield Hotel Deluxe
10320 W. Olympic Blvd., Century City, 90015 201-5084, Fax 203-0563

A little glitzier than its neighbor, the Century City Inn, the Chesterfield offers low rates, decent rooms and lots of little touches—free morning paper, free breakfast and free meals in the café for kids age 12 and under. For grown-ups, there's a cocktail lounge and a Jacuzzi; the kids can watch movies on cable or closed-circuit TV after they've exhausted themselves at Disneyland and Universal Studios. A number of entertainment packages and student rates are available.

Singles & doubles: $86-$140.

 ### The Comstock
10300 Wilshire Blvd., Westwood, 90024 - 275-5575, Fax 278-3325

If you're looking for a westside home-away-from-home, this may be the place. It's a converted apartment building, and it still looks like one, the tiny white lights decorating the entryway notwithstanding. Each of the 73 suites has a living room, and all are tastefully decorated, featuring Chippendale furniture and a comfortable ambience. The inner courtyard (with a pool) makes for relaxed California living at its best. There is also a charming little bistro, Le Petit Café.

Suites: $135-$280.

 ### Del Capri Hotel
10587 Wilshire Blvd., Westwood, 90024 - 474-3511, Fax 824-0594

Half hidden by high-rise luxury condos, the Del Capri boasts simple charms that remain undiminished by time or real estate developers. Once a favorite haven for such international movie stars as the late Ingrid Bergman, this hotel provides privacy for its guests, as well as all the comforts of home at a very reasonable price. Most of the 80 suites have full kitchenettes, cable TVs and adjustable beds. While not luxurious, it is neat, clean and hospitable, and the veteran staff is efficient and friendly. Half of the suites overlook the free-form swimming pool and flower garden, which give this intimate hotel a cheery and relaxed ambience. A serene establishment at a trendy address.

Singles: $79; doubles: $89; suites: $104-$114.

L'Ermitage
9291 Burton Way, Beverly Hills,
90210 - 278-3344, Fax 278-8247

Arthur Rubinstein stayed here. If Mozart had visited Los Angeles, he would have stayed here, too. It's that select and elegant. The proprietors are the Ashkenazy brothers, who arrived penniless from central Europe after a long stay in Paris and who obviously know how to make (and, more lately, lose) a fortune in real estate, landscaping and art dealing. L'Ermitage is in a class of its own; not the least of its distinctions is its unique small size in a city of huge hotels. It looks more like a genteel European apartment house than a hotel, even though the masterpieces on the walls are all fakes. There are only suites here, and they're all beautifully appointed, with the exception of the overabundance of plastic used on the bars. Guests receive a score of amenities and faultless service; there's more than one employee per customer. A rooftop pool and a private restaurant protect guests from the public. And only in Los Angeles: L'Ermitage recently unveiled a next-door annex, Le Petit Ermitage, with sixteen suites that cater to—what else?—guests recovering from plastic surgery! Amenities at this new offshoot include nursing care, meals, transporation to and from the doctor's office and a physician on 24-hour call, natch.

Single-bedroom suites: $255-$295; two-bedroom suites: $325-$550; penthouse suite: $1,500; Le Petit Ermitage suites: $275-$475.

The Four Seasons Hotel
300 S. Doheny Dr., Beverly Hills,
90211 - 273-2222, Fax 859-3874

The Four Seasons is one of L.A.'s newest hotels, and it's also one of its loveliest. Canada's Four Seasons chain creates human-size hotels in the best of taste, catering to a prosperous clientele that likes the convenience of a modern hotel without too much ostenta-tiousness. With 285 rooms, The Four Seasons is small by modern hotel standards, ensuring a good level of service and a reasonably serene lobby. Each large, handsome room is equipped with a private balcony, two two-line phones, a fully stocked minibar, a remote-control TV in the bedroom and a black-and-white TV in the bathroom, a built-in hair dryer and terry robes. All the expected amen-ities are supplied—from the fourth-floor pool, spa and sundeck to the 24-hour concierge service—and the flower-filled common areas are gorgeous. In The Four Seasons' early days, its restaurant and café drew much attention with acclaimed chef Lydia Shire at the helm, but her cutting-edge cuisine proved to be a bit too radical for Beverly Hills. While the current regime in the kitchen isn't as revolu-tionary, it isn't as erratic, either; in fact, the food is excellent. One of L.A.'s very best hotels.

Singles: $245-$265; doubles: $270-$290; suites: $330-$750.

Holiday Inn Westwood Plaza
10740 Wilshire Blvd., Westwood,
90024 - 475-8711, Fax 475-5220

This Holiday Inn is more posh than you might expect; the rooms in its nineteen stories were decorated to match the upwardly mobile neighborhood. You may be surprised to be greeted by a doorman, welcomed in the at-tractive lobby and housed in a tastefully dec-orated room; after all, this chain has a reputation for banality and impersonal, for-gettable service. This branch is a find, not only for its great location (near UCLA, Westwood Village and Beverly Hills) but for its under-stated elegance, quality of service, free parking and reasonable prices.

Singles: $115; doubles: $125; suites: $200.

Hotel Bel-Air
701 Stone Canyon Rd., Bel Air,
90077 - 472-1211, Fax 476-5890

If Sleeping Beauty were to wake up in Southern California, no doubt she'd find her-self in the enchanted gardens of the Hotel Bel-Air. The grounds here are so beautiful that they almost seem to be a fairy-tale parody. You will be charmed by the swans, the ancient trees, the eleven acres of private park, the welcoming reception with its crackling fire and the quasi-country-château architecture. If staying or dining here is beyond your means, be sure to come for a drink on the patio just before twilight—it's one of the most magical, peaceful spot in all of Los Angeles.

The Bel-Air was recently sold to a Japanese investment group for more than $110 million—that's nearly $1.2 mil per room—by Caroline Hunt Schoellkopf, who had placed her refined stamp on the hotel's decor, service and attention to detail. Her skillful renovation added 26 rooms and a decor that is as stunning as that of her Mansion on Turtle Creek in Dallas and the Remington in Houston. Even though she's gone, we doubt that much here will change. Whether you're looking for a safe haven on a business trip, pampering yourself while taking a tourist tour of L.A. or spending your wedding night, the Bel-Air will meet your every need and provide first-class service and the treatment you deserve. One of the most beautiful and well-maintained luxury hotels in Southern California.

Singles: $195-$315; doubles: $230-$360; suites: $385-$1,300.

 Loews Santa Monica Beach Hotel

1700 Ocean Ave., Santa Monica, 90401 - 458-6700, Fax 458-6761

The Byzantine vicissitudes of Santa Monica's zoning laws, the Coastal Commission and various and sundry political machinations of which we have little understanding have kept Santa Monica's beachfront-hotel population to close to zero, in yet another instance of L.A.'s stubborn denial of its geography. However, inroads are being made, and several oceanfront hotels in Santa Monica, Venice and Malibu are currently in the planning stages (including one being developed by *restaurateur terrible* Michael McCarty). The first entry to open this sandy sweepstakes is the new, large (350 rooms and 35 suites) Loews resort, which looks like a postmodern amusement park (isn't it time to retire this worn-out architectural idiom?). The interiors, however, including the lobby, take their design cues from British colonialism—if Singapore's Raffles were to be rebuilt now, this is probably what it would look like. Of course, the real magnet here is location: right on the beach, close to the undeniably scuzzy

Santa Monica Pier (but across the street from the la-di-da Ivy at the Shore) and just a skip away from Main Street and the nutty Venice Boardwalk. Sadly, all too many of the neighborhood's denizens live out of shopping carts in nearby Palisades Park, giving the hotel a whiff of a "let them eat cake" air, but if you're able to put blinders on, you'll have a grand old time here. Amenities include an indoor/outdoor swimming pool (for those who wisely choose not to swim in the polluted—though that's up for debate—Pacific) that overlooks the beach, a health spa and fitness center complete with personal trainer, an executive business center, 17,000 square feet of meeting space and a couple of nice eateries: Riva, an Italian seafood restaurant, and the Coast Café, where you can dine outdoors or in; an afternoon tea is served in the lobby bar facing the beach.

Singles: $155-$230; doubles: $175-$250; suites: $300-$1,500.

 Marina Beach Hotel

4100 Admiralty Way, Marina del Rey, 90292 - 822-1010, Fax 301-6890

The most luxurious of the three-hotel Marina Hotel group, the Marina Beach positively reeks of that generic yet thoroughly tasteful muted-California-pastel look so prevalent these days. During the week, business travelers keep its couple of hundred rooms filled; on the weekends, when rates drop considerably, you'll find a lot more fun-seekers, here for a weekend of poolside lounging, tan-improving, sailing and joining the yuppies strolling boutique-and-restaurant-lined Main Street in nearby Venice. The rooms are soothing in design and perfectly comfortable. On the ground floor is Stones, serving overly precious yet skillfully prepared California cuisine; on the top floor is a terrific window-lined lounge that makes for an ideal rest stop around sunset time.

Singles: $180-$250; doubles: $200-$270; suites: $230-$650. Weekend discounts available.

J.W. Marriott Hotel

2151 Ave. of the Stars, Century City, 90067 - 277-2777, Fax 785-9240

Nineteen eighty-nine witnessed a veritable hotel boom in Century City, which theretofore had only the Century Plaza and The Beverly Hilton. The most upscale and largest (375 rooms) of the new bunch is the J.W. Marriott, just down the road from the convention-crazed Century Plaza. Our response to this Marriott is, well, mixed. From the street, and particularly at night, it looks spectacular, but up close a lot of little flaws show up. The fountain in the entrance driveway was strewn with litter on our last visit, and our treatment in the lobby bar was downright surly. Hopefully, the Marriott will work these bugs out, because otherwise it's a nice hotel (if a little too glittery for our more austere tastes). Amenities abound, from complimentary limousine service to a complete fitness center, indoor and outdoor swimming pools, a complete business center and an afternoon tea where you may unwind after all that activity.

Singles & doubles: $209-$249; suites: $275-$2,000.

Ramada Hotel Beverly Hills
1150 S. Beverly Dr., Beverly Hills, 90212 - 553-6561, Fax 277-4469

If you're bargain hunting in Beverly Hills, this may be your best find. The price is right for the overpriced location, and the place is pleasant, efficient and modest. For media junkies, the videocassette players in each room offer some diversion from the tedious decor. Suites are comfortable and have spectacular views of Century City and Beverly Hills. It's friendly around the Ramada, and you'll appreciate the professional staff.

Singles: $106-$116; doubles: $116-$126; suites: $185.

The Regent Beverly Wilshire
9500 Wilshire Blvd., Beverly Hills, 90212 - 275-4282, Fax 274-2851

It was no secret that this old dowager was in dire need of a physical and spiritual lift, and when the Hong Kong–based Regent Hotel group bought her a couple of years back, it promised to more than restore her to her former glory—it vowed to transform her. And that they did. This beauty is absolutely unrecognizable to those who knew her in her original incarnation. The lobby is a trove of gorgeous antiques, woods, marbles and glass; it looks like a Regency/Directoire–era dream.

The white-gloved service is crackerjack, and the rooms are positively luxurious, with gigantic marble bathrooms, silky bed linens, period furniture and double-glazed windows to obviate any street noise. The ghost of the old El Padrino Room is nowhere to be found in the sumptuous dining room, which also happens to serve some of the best food in the city. There's also a café that replaced the beloved yet hopelessly dated Pink Turtle (though some of its most popular dishes have been carried over), and nibbling and sipping afternoon tea in the new Lobby Lounge is just too sophisticated for words; you can rest your tootsies here in between shopping bouts at Armani and Chanel. (Note: As we went to press, the newer Beverly Wing was still under renovation.)

Singles & doubles: $275; suites: $325-$2,500.

Royal Palace
1052 Tiverton Ave., Westwood, 90024 - 208-6677

This small, economical 36-room hotel is neither royal nor palatial. It does have an excellent Westwood location, close to the entertaining street life, shops and UCLA student scene, and the price can't be beat. The rooms are Spartan but come with well-equipped kitchens, which are appreciated by the many visiting professors who make this their temporary shelter. The friendly service doesn't quite compensate for the sterile decor. Parking is free, which is cause enough for celebration.

Singles: $55-$60; doubles: $61-$100.

Shangri-la Hotel
1301 Ocean Ave., Santa Monica, 90401 - 394-2791, Fax 451-3351

This marvelously located art deco hotel should have been the setting for a Raymond Chandler detective story; as things stand, it's an offbeat lodging choice for such luminaries as Diane Keaton and Robert De Niro. The Shangri-la's suites have been restored to their original '30s decor—in most cases, quite successfully. Shell lamps illuminate the pink-and-mauve color scheme, frosted mirrors adorn the walls, and deco-style furniture graces the rooms. Some of the smaller rooms are cramped and slightly tacky, but because of the

Shangri-la's open, galleried design, all 50 rooms are cross-ventilated and have beautiful ocean views. Among its droll charms are suites with Murphy beds in the kitchens. The area is wonderful for people-watching, especially on Wednesday, when the streets are cordoned off and transformed into a festive outdoor farmer's market. The Shangri-la isn't for everybody—if such amenities as room service are important to you, go elsewhere, but if you're a fan of the charming and eccentric, this place is for you.

Studios: $99; singles & doubles: $130-$142; suites: $190-$210; penthouse: $365.

 ### Sheraton Miramar
101 Wilshire Blvd., Santa Monica, 90401 - 394-3731, Fax 458-7912

This Sheraton is so steeped in history that there's a house historian who keeps track of all the gossip. Its sixteen bungalows have been havens for Greta Garbo, Humphrey Bogart and Howard Hughes. Betty Grable used to sing here. And the Pacific is still just a few yards away. The large 292-room complex has a '60s decor housed in the ten-story tower; there's a superb view of Malibu and a lovely garden. Unfortunately, though the staff is attentive, the place desperately needs a rehab (hey, Four Seasons—here's a prime property for you!). Still, the hotel is a popular weekend destination for couples (some even locals) who just want to get away from it all. The approach to this historic monument is perhaps the most impressive: wrought-iron gates open to a stately old Moreton Bay fig tree. Perhaps it is because of the grounds that the Miramar has often been referred to as the Little Beverly Hills Hotel. Thank heavens we don't have two Polo Lounges to contend with.

Singles: $125-$165; doubles: $145-$185; suites & bungalows: $200-$400.

 ### Westwood Marquis
930 Hilgard Ave., Westwood, 90024 208-8765, Fax 824-0355

Elegance, warmth and an attentive reception come as a surprise from behind the severe, stark lines of the raw concrete exterior, and these surprises explain the hotel's good reputation. The excellent Westwood Village (near UCLA) location is another plus. We've been disappointed, however, by the service and the condo-tacky construction. The decor in the suites varies from clean, contemporary lines to updated antique charm. Penthouse suites include a butler, complimentary breakfast and evening hors d'oeuvres. High tea is served from 3 p.m. to 5 p.m. in the Marquis bar, and the lavish Sunday buffet brunch is among the town's most elegant, popular and expensive.

One-bedroom suites: $220-$250; two-bedroom suites: $260-$475; penthouse suites: $475-$660.

NIGHTLIFE

DOING THE SUBURBS

Y ou don't "do the town" in Los Angeles; L.A.'s "townness" has dissolved into its mighty suburbs. Therefore, you'll spend the evening driving through these 'burbs, looking for signs of vitality and action. Still, there's a lot going on across this vast metropolis. Whether you're a fast-track single looking for new friends, a jazz buff, a club aficionado or a fan of the classic neighborhood bar, you'll find what you're after somewhere in L.A. We must tell you, however, that the city's nightlife scene is extremely fickle and fractured. The hottest clubs tend to be moveable feasts, invading a venue for one or two nights a week and then, in a few months, moving on. Of course, we keep our information as current as possible, but for more up-to-the-minute listings, check the *L.A. Weekly*, the *Reader*, the *Los Angeles Times*'s "Calendar" section or *Los Angeles* magazine. Also, cover charges and hours change frequently, so check first, and remember that a 2 a.m. closing time usually means a 1:30 a.m. last call.

Unfortunately, the L.A. club-hopper is dependent on the automobile. Keep in mind California's tough drunk-driving laws; if you're going to be celebrating, hire a taxi or have one of your group be the evening's nondrinking "designated driver." Besides, in this health-conscious town, it's fashionable to stick to mineral water.

BARS

Angie's
11700 Wilshire Blvd., W.L.A.
477-1517
Open Mon.-Fri. 11 a.m.-midnight, Sat. 5 p.m.-midnight. All major cards.

The très chic and uniformly handsome pass away evenings at Angie's perfecting their poses in front of mirrored walls, even though, alas, casting directors and *GQ* photographers don't scout here. While waiting to be discovered, these immaculately suntanned creatures chitchat about their agents, their hairstylists and other such weighty topics, all the while eyeing the opposite sex. The decor fits the crowd: lots of rattan, potted palms, white stucco walls and, of course, mirrors. This is a terrifically amusing people-watching-people place.

Baja Cantina
311 Washington St., Marina del Rey
821-2250
Open Mon.-Sat. 11:30 a.m.-1 a.m., Sun. 10:30 a.m.-1 a.m. Cards: AE, MC, V.

This cluttered but comfortable bar provides a welcome respite from the mating frenzies going on, and on, at other Marina bars. True, its clientele has that same beach-chic look that dominates at El Torito and the other singles' spots. But this place is nicer for a relaxed drink and conversation in a cozy, plant-filled Mexican-style setting. Don't pass up the appetizers—they're made with the wonderful fresh tortillas prepared to order on a grill in the middle of the room.

The Bar at the Regent Beverly Wilshire
Regent Beverly Wilshire, 9500 Wilshire Blvd., Beverly Hills
275-5200
Open daily 11 a.m.-2 a.m. All major cards.

Tired of the scenes, the smooth operators, the pickup places? Then head to this class joint and lose yourself in one of the monstrous martinis (mixed to perfection, we might add). This spiffy new watering hole in the newly spruced-up Beverly Wilshire is the perfect hotel bar: elegant but not ostentatious, relaxed but not boring, lively but not irritatingly loud. Terrific appetizers are served during the after-work hours, and a skilled pianist plays all evening long. Dress up a bit, and by all means head across the lobby before or after your bar visit for an excellent meal in the dining room.

Barney's Beanery
8447 Santa Monica Blvd., W. Hollywood
654-2287
Open daily 6 a.m.-2 a.m. Cards: AE, MC, V.

The small, always-full bar adjacent to Barney's dining areas offers an unbeatable selection of beers (over 200), a friendly, somewhat gritty atmosphere, well-used pool tables, lots of rather worn dark wood and a display of an international collection of license plates. The regulars aren't always chic (and they're decidedly straight, which is unusual given the number of gay-oriented businesses in the area), but we like the refreshing honesty of the place.

Tom Bergin's
840 S. Fairfax Ave., Wilshire District
936-7151
Open Mon.-Fri. 11 a.m.-2 a.m., Sat. 4 p.m.-2 a.m. All major cards.

Bergin's is a cozy though much too dark pub whose button-down clientele is a mix of L.A.'s Irish Americans, local businesspeople and preppy college students. The substantial local Irish community has made Bergin's and nearby Molly Malone's its home away from home for many years. Bergin's highly touted Irish coffee is worthy of all the praise, and the dining room behind the bar serves decent pub fare. It gets particularly rowdy here when USC wins a football game.

Carlos 'n' Charlie's
8240 Sunset Blvd., W. Hollywood
656-8830
Open Mon.-Fri. 11 a.m.-2 a.m., Sat.-Sun. 5 p.m.-2 a.m. All major cards.

Mix a successful chain of Mexican restaurants with an easygoing California attitude and you get Carlos 'n' Charlie's. This import works as well as the originals, which are found in various cities in Mexico. The bar is generally crowded, active and glittery, and the kitchen maintains its good reputation. It's a comfortable spot for an evening or an after-theater drink, the kind of place that would make a good setting for an upscale beer commercial. The upstairs cabaret provides more action, hosting a variety of entertainment and dancing (the cover ranges from $7 to $10). The

club gets some name talent, and it's hard not to have a good time. The marquee outside announces a Joan Rivers workshop for would-be comedians, and La Joan herself performs once in a while.

Casey's Bar and Grill
613 S. Grand Ave., Downtown
629-2353
Open Mon.-Fri. 11 a.m.-11 p.m. All major cards.

The house is full weeknights during happy hour, when downtown's business sorts come to Casey's to shed the just-another-day-in-the-office doldrums. Amid a handsome, comfortable Irish-pub decor they talk shop and sports with co-workers and exchange small talk with new-found friends. Though it's convivial and lively at 6 p.m., by 9 p.m. most everyone has headed home.

Cassidy's Pub
500 S. Sepulveda Blvd., Manhattan Beach
372-7666
Open Mon.-Tues. & Thurs. 5 p.m.-2 a.m., Wed. & Fri. 4 p.m.-2 a.m., Sat.-Sun. 7 p.m.-2 a.m. Cards: AE, MC, V.

A young crowd hits Cassidy's to dance on the tiny dance floor and let the deejay put them through their paces. A well-known pickup place in the beach area, Cassidy's is worth a visit not for its uninteresting clientele, but for its lovely outdoor terrace, where you can sit with a friend before an open fire and enjoy a drink under the stars.

Cat and Fiddle Pub
6530 Sunset Blvd., Hollywood
468-3800
Open daily 11:30 a.m.-1:30 a.m. Cards: AE, MC, V.

The Cat and Fiddle's Hollywood neighborhood is full of clubs and ethnic restaurants, and the people who venture there like that kind of life. The place attracts a young, good-looking Hollywood crowd that loves its music and film lore but is remarkably unpretentious. Everyone seems to have a good time, whether inside shouting over the noise and the terrific jukebox, or outside in the stunning Spanish-style courtyard quietly nursing a pint of British ale. There's live jazz on Sundays, and a full menu for those who don't want to drink their dinner.

Chez Jay

1657 Ocean Ave., Santa Monica
395-1741
Open daily 11:30 a.m.-2 a.m. Cards: AE, MC, V.

After a hard day in the California sun, it's sometimes good to get away from it all. Chez Jay is a beach bar, more popular in the summer than in the winter, but with a year-round philosophy of "Live now, pay later." It's something of a hangout for writers and artists, a quiet place with sawdust on the floor and good American food served at cozy, red-vinyl booths. The eclectic jukebox plays tunes from the 1930s and '40s, along with such classics as Lou Reed's urban hit, "Take a Walk on the Wild Side." Owner Jay's friendliness is reflected in the ambience.

The Circle

926 Main St., Santa Monica
399-9948
Open Mon.-Wed. 2:30 p.m.-2 a.m., Thurs. noon-2 a.m., Fri.-Sun. 10 a.m.-2 a.m. No cards.

The Circle is where the real people of Santa Monica go to drink. It's a refreshing break from the sterile yuppie bars that plague Venice Beach's Main Street. There's nothing here but cheap drinks, a large 360-degree bar, pinball, pool, a great jukebox and plenty of friendly, laid-back folks.

Cocola

1410 Boyd St., Downtown
680-0756
Open daily 11:30 a.m.-2 a.m. Cards: AE, MC, V.

As downtown L.A.'s art scene grew bigger, trendier and more upscale, it was inevitable that a bar would emerge to cash in on the trend. Cocola, a bright, fluorescent oasis in L.A.'s murky loft district, sports trendy, industrial art on its walls and hip, attractive, upscale people at its bar. The food is simple, honest and good enough for a bar. On weekends, when the bar gets crowded, the parking

---

Chances are that your night on the town will mean a night in the car. If you plan on drinking, take a cab or have one of your group be the evening's "designated driver."

---

lot generally fills up, which means you have to forage for parking on the street.

Cutters

2425 Colorado Ave., Santa Monica
453-3588
Open Mon.-Thurs. 11 a.m.-midnight, Fri. 11 a.m.-12:30 a.m., Sat. noon-12:30 a.m., Sun. 4 p.m.-11 p.m. Cards: AE, MC, V.

The warehouses in this neighborhood are dark by the time Cutters lights up each night, and this place does light up. The kitchen has a good reputation and the well-stocked and brightly lit bar—the height of two basketball players—is a sight to behold. Cutters attracts a young, well-to-do, professional group of men and women who worry about car payments and corporate buyouts and who don't smoke cigarettes. About the only creativity here is on the walls, but Cutters is a clean, comfortable place with a graceful, art deco elegance to it. Located in a low-rise office and shopping complex called Colorado Place, Cutters supplies validated underground parking, so the elements won't ruin the paint on all the BMWs.

DC3

Santa Monica Airport, 31st St. entrance, Santa Monica
399-2323
Open Mon.-Wed. 11 a.m.-midnight, Thurs.-Sat. 11 a.m.-2 a.m. Cover $15 Fri.-Sat. All major cards.

What a spot! When we first drove into this bland office and shopping complex, we thought DC3 would be a bore. But soon enough there were treats for the eye—like the *Charles S. Jones,* an actual DC3 just hanging out in the Museum of Flying that's downstairs from this club/bar/restaurant—to keep us going. Take the nifty elevator up to DC3. The actual entrance to the bar is a huge anodized aluminum ball that has to be seen to be believed. You recognize immediately that you are in upscale territory. Even the bathrooms are architectural wonders. We prefer to leave the food to the trendies, who seem to adore it, but we're always happy to have a drink on the balcony overlooking the Santa Monica Airport runway. On Friday and Saturday there's dancing to a stirring mix of house, hip-hop and Top 40 tunes. Though the place is packed with all manner of wealthy vulgarity on those nights, we've found that if we restrict ourselves to gazing at inanimate objects, we have a pretty good time.

The Dresden Room
1760 N. Vermont Ave., Los Feliz
665-4294
Open daily 10 a.m.-2 p.m. Cards: AE, MC.

The Dresden Room is so unhip that it's naturally evolved into one of the hippest spot in town. The regulars tend to be older, polyester types who've been fixtures here since—well, for a long, long time. Serious drinkers all, they either pass time at the bar or in the plush booths ingesting the so-so Italian cuisine. We like to grab seats at the piano bar (except on Mondays), order a drink and swoon to Marty and Elayne belting out the oldies. Close your eyes, and you'll swear it's Frank himself singing. Start spreading the news. Make believe you're in New York; there are no windows here, so you'll never know the difference. Tuesday is open-mike night, where anything can happen and usually does.

Engine Co. No. 28
644 S. Figueroa St., Downtown
624-6996
Open Mon.-Fri. 11 a.m.-10 p.m., Sat. 5 p.m.-10 p.m., Sun. 4:30 p.m.-9 p.m. Cards: AE, MC, V.

On the day it opened, the Engine Company immediately became downtown's best bar. Granted, that's a pretty easy accomplishment, given downtown's pathetic lack of good watering holes, but this place would make the grade even in New York or San Francisco. It's a manly sort of place, full of polished dark wood, conservatively upholstered booths and lots of properly suited professional types. We prefer to visit a little later, when the considerable after-work crowd has thinned a bit and we can better hear the swell old standards on the stereo. The bartenders are as friendly as the drinks they pour.

The Ginger Man
369 N. Bedford Dr., Beverly Hills
273-7585
Open Mon.-Sat. 11:30 a.m.-1 a.m. Cards: AE, MC, V.

A New York bar, complete with an Upper East Side decor and an appropriately prosperous, professional clientele. This lively, handsome pub, owned by actor Carroll O'Connor, is a fun spot to meet old friends, make new ones or have a restorative and a decent hamburger or salad after a Beverly Hills shopping spree.

Grand Avenue Bar
The Biltmore, 506 S. Grand Ave.,
Downtown
624-1011
Open Mon.-Fri. 11:30 a.m.-10 p.m. All major cards.

This very civilized bar, located in a very civilized hotel, plays host to the downtown deal-making, happy-hour set that prefers a more sedate atmosphere than Casey's or Itchey Foot. It's tastefully done in browns that complement the tiled walls and marble tables, and live jazz brightens the mood and the dull business talk. The lovely buffet lunch is so popular that there's rarely room left over for nondining bar patrons, but it becomes a full-fledged bar at 4 p.m., when upscale hors d'oeuvres are served and vintage wine is poured by the glass. Like downtown itself, the bar is generally deserted after 9 p.m. The Biltmore now has another entirely worthy bar, an attractive piano lounge located in the former lobby.

Harry's Bar and American Grill
ABC Entertainment Center, 2020 Ave. of the Stars, Century City
277-2333
Open daily 11:30 a.m.-midnight. All major cards.

Sometimes, after we've been in Harry's awhile, we forget where we are. This replica of Harry's Bar in Florence is as charming as its cousins sprinkled throughout the world. There's the ubiquitous wood paneling, brass detailing and attractive clientele that appears to be successful, well groomed and well fed. This is practically the only spot for a nightcap after a show at the Shubert or a movie at one of the several plush theaters here. Harry's also serves a fine Italian meal. All in all, Harry's is a clean, well-lighted place.

Houlihan's Old Place
17150 Ventura Blvd., Encino
(818) 986-2100
Open Sun.-Wed. 11:30 a.m.-midnight, Thurs.-Sat. 11:30 a.m.-1:30 a.m. All major cards.

The "Alabama Slammer," one of Houlihan's house drinks, provides a good clue as to what it's like around here on weekends. If you visit on a weekend night, you'll have to shove your way through the young, randy crowd and search, most likely in vain, for a seat. Houlihan's has jumped on the sports-bar bandwagon and installed a big-screen TV for the hoot-and-holler pleasure of its customers. Monday (after Monday Night Football, in season) and Thursday through Saturday, a deejay spins Top 40 dance music. Tuesday is devoted to live mellow jazz. On Sunday, the sacred sports day, there are no distractions to interfere with the practice of the gridiron religion.

Itchey Foot Ristorante
801 W. Temple St., Downtown
680-0007
Open Mon.-Sat. 11 a.m.-9 p.m., Sun. 4 p.m.-8 p.m. Cards: CB, DC, MC, V.

Don't be put off by the awful name—this is a friendly, casually attractive bar just a few blocks away from the Music Center and downtown's burgeoning condo developments. It's a folksy place that's popular with both the downtown happy-hour set and the pre- and post-theater crowds. The atmosphere is comfortable, convivial and sometimes noisy; the adjoining restaurant serves so-so pastas, pizzas and steaks.

Molly Malone's Irish Pub
575 S. Fairfax Ave., Wilshire District
935-1577
Open daily 11:30 a.m.-2 a.m. Cards: MC, V.

For years this plain, dark neighborhood pub has attracted L.A.'s Irish Americans, who love the nondescript but very Irish decor, the good Irish music, the darts competitions, the Guinness on tap and the straightforward approach to drinking. There's no pretension and no hustling here—just a relaxed, folksy atmosphere with a clientele to match.

Martini Lounge
L.A. Nicola, 4326 Sunset Blvd., Silverlake
660-7217
Open nightly 5 p.m.-2 a.m. All major cards.

Adjacent to the popular, California-modern L.A. Nicola restaurant, the Martini Lounge caters to a well-dressed, sweaters-tied-around-the-neck yuppie crowd from Los Feliz and Silverlake. Cool jazz plays on the stereo, cool white walls hold contemporary art, and cool patrons discuss cool movies, money (which is always cool) and mergers (which can be cool, depending on your political orientation). The atmosphere is sophisticated, relaxed and conversation-inducing.

Next Door to Fellini's
6810 Melrose Ave., Hollywood
937-4657
Open daily 11 a.m.-2 a.m. Cards: AE, MC, V.

A fine spot for a drink after a visit to one of the Melrose-area small theaters. A band plays every night of the week (no cover), and reasonably priced drinks are served, so cheap dates take note. The long, handsome bar fills most of the narrow room (which adjoins Fellini's, a most forgettable restaurant); facing mirrored walls provide an illusion of space. Even on weeknights, Fellini's draws a fair-sized crowd, but the vibes are good and the bar service is always friendly. On the down side, the music is rather loud for our taste, and conversation can get a little rough. The crowd is a mixed bag of TV-, movie- and record-industry rank and file, thirtysomething tweedy types and neohippies. Big-name recording artists have been known to arrive unannounced and jam with the band.

The Polo Lounge
Beverly Hills Hotel, 9641 Sunset Blvd., Beverly Hills
276-2251
Open daily 7:30 a.m.-1:30 a.m. All major cards.

They're all here: old stars, expensive young women, unproductive producers, the old nouveaux riches, the new nouveaux poor and a crowd of voyeurs on hand to watch other voyeurs. The action at this Hollywood mecca is created and perpetuated by the sheer number of people who don't realize that there isn't any action, particularly, it seems, at precisely 6 p.m., when The Polo Lounge is the most eclectic center in town. Breakfast is a must for deal makers, and lunch on the outdoor patio is an event. And it's possible that the waiters who brought you tea instead of green peas, then took away your steak (which you've already returned three times because it's overcooked—the third time it is three times overcooked), and then cleared the table before you were finished simply didn't know any better. None of this really matters—these are only the small dramas of the grand life.

Rangoon Racquet Club
9474 Santa Monica Blvd., Beverly Hills
274-8926
Open daily 11:30 a.m.-2 a.m. All major cards.

This is a hustlers' bar; if the clientele (in their 30s to 50s) isn't hustling deals, they're hustling one another. Evidently there are a lot of hustlers around, because it's standing room only, with a decibel level so loud you couldn't hear a proposition, let alone a business deal. The handsome, well-dressed Beverly Hills crowd melds perfectly with the pretty decor (brick walls, potted palms, trellises) and the self-important service.

Rebecca's

2025 Pacific Ave., Venice
306-6266
Open Sun.-Thurs. 6 p.m.-midnight, Fri.-Sat. 6 p.m.-2 a.m. Cards: AE, MC, V.

Rebecca's—sister to the West Beach Café across the street and DC3 over at the Santa Monica Airport—is still one of the hottest bars (and restaurants) in town. It hosts a crowd that, although young, thinks nothing of spending $20 for an order of fajitas—a crowd firmly convinced of their right to have it all. The Frank Gehry–designed interior is as wild as the ambience: huge papier-maché crocodiles and an octopus float overhead, and the marble and metal surfaces serve as great conductors for the considerable noise level. To fit in here, you must be: 1) a 30ish executive man wearing Armani or Ralph Lauren and driving a BMW, Saab or Porsche; 2) a 30ish creative-type man (artist, designer) sporting a ponytail and an oversized black outfit; or 3) a very attractive, gainfully employed 20ish-to-30ish woman with carefully moussed hair, designer leathers and a pair of $150 pumps. They all come here to drink and to be seen, but mostly they come here to find mates who will complement their images, their lifestyles and their cars. Nebbish computer programmers and mild-mannered, bookish types need not apply.

Revolver

8851 Santa Monica Blvd., W. Hollywood
550-8851
Open Mon.-Thurs. 4 p.m.-2 a.m., Fri. 4 p.m.-4 a.m., Sat. 2 p.m.-4 a.m., Sun. 2 p.m.-2 a.m. No cards.

You get the feeling that this mostly male crowd was weaned on TV—they stand around mesmerized by the video shows on monitors throughout the club. The clientele is primarily those attractive, youngish clean-cut men that L.A. is so famous for. It's packed and has become more popular with chic young gays than the staid, more *GQ* types.

J. Sloane's

8623 Melrose Ave., W. Hollywood
659-0250
Open daily 11:30 a.m.-2 a.m. Cards: MC, V.

This is an honest-to-god, sawdust-on-the-floor, go-ahead-and-help-yourself-to-a-bag-of-popcorn kind of place. More suited to Eugene, Oregon, than West Hollywood, the clientele at Sloane's is straight, young and favoring plaid flannel over pink polos. The decor is as frantic as the crowd, with model ships, airplanes, movie posters and all sorts of oddities hanging from the high ceiling. There's a small, much-used dance floor with a deejay providing good music, while upstairs a frantic foosball game is generally in progress. The management has thoughtfully installed a blaring red siren that wails every few minutes to keep the crowd suitably energized.

Stanley's

13817 Ventura Blvd., Sherman Oaks
(818) 986-4623
Open daily 11:30 a.m.-2 a.m. Cards: AE, MC, V.

If the girl of your dreams has hair out to there, a leather miniskirt and serious fingernails, or the guy of your dreams has a blow-dried do, a gold-chain-drenched neck and an open-to-the-chest-hair shirt, then by all means rush right over to Stanley's, where you'll find the pickings fat. The handsome but neutral decor—white walls and blond wood—makes for a good people-watching backdrop. The adjacent restaurant serves the expected California-casual food, which is acceptable but no better.

Stepps on the Court

Wells Fargo Court, 330 S. Hope St., Downtown
626-0900
Open Mon.-Fri. 11 a.m.-11 p.m., Sat. 5 p.m.-11 p.m., Sun. 4 p.m.-9:30 p.m. All major cards.

If you're single, under 40, wear a Brooks Brothers uniform and work downtown, then you'll certainly want to check out the bar at Stepps after work. Both the restaurant and the bar were carefully designed to attract just such a crowd, and they have succeeded famously. There's a big-screen TV for the game of the moment, decent wines by the glass, a fabulous collection of single-malt scotches, the required high-noise level and plenty of good-looking professionals of both sexes. The restaurant serves moderately priced, trendy dishes that are decent, if not inspired.

Stratton's Grill
1037 Broxton Ave., Westwood
208-0488
Open Mon.-Fri. 11:30 a.m.-2 a.m., Sat.-Sun. 11 a.m.-2 a.m. Cards: AE, MC, V.

Stratton's Grill is the little brother of Stratton's, another Westwood Village restaurant, and the folks here do a good job of providing a watering hole for the moderation generation. There is also a reasonably priced menu that lists creative bar food. Stratton's Grill is a well-lit, coolly decorated place with a long bar as the featured centerpiece of the house. Handsome young men pour drinks, and attractive young women wait on fashionable young professionals from the banks and office towers that have sprung up in the village. The happy hour (weekdays from 5 p.m. to 7 p.m.) is one of Westwood's best, but there are no specials on drinks.

Tequila Willie's
3290 N. Sepulveda Blvd., Manhattan Beach
545-4569
Open daily 11 a.m.-2 a.m. All major cards.

Located in a Manhattan Beach mall, this frantically decorated bar is one of the hot spots for the young beach residents who cram into the place every evening. The clientele ranges from young office workers still dressed for work to ultra-cool dudes in T-shirts and jams. If you can't figure out what to talk about, there's always backgammon—and the decor. The clutter inspires less articulate individuals to carefully point out the best objects to their new friends. If all else fails, you can have a tolerable, inexpensive Mexican dinner here (it's part of the El Torito chain).

T.G.I. Friday's
13470 Maxella Ave., Marina del Rey
822-9052
Open Mon.-Thurs. 11:30 a.m.-2 a.m., Fri. 11:30 a.m.-midnight, Sat. 11:30 a.m.-2 a.m., Sun. 10 a.m.-2 a.m. All major cards.

This noisy, hectic, crowded place would fascinate anthropologists studying the tribal rites of the California singles scene. Pretty, healthy-looking people play the overnight mating game with other pretty, healthy-looking people—all ages, all sizes, all types. In all, it's an amusing and entertaining marketplace. Although food isn't the issue here, you'll find

a 23-page menu, complete with index, listing over 165 dishes, many of which are deep-fried. The decor is the predictable clutter of Americana and unattractive stuffed animals.

Tiki-Ti
4427 Sunset Blvd., Silverlake
669-9381
Open Wed.-Sun. 6 p.m.-2 a.m. No cards.

If Timothy Leary were Polynesian, his house would look something like the Tiki-Ti. This tiny, cluttered bar juxtaposes funky tropical motifs (primitive face masks) with '60s tackola (lava lamps and wave machines). And the drinks! No humdrum beer, wine or scotch here. No, Mike the barman, usually dressed in a garish Hawaiian shirt, serves up delicious and powerful tropical concoctions—the sort of drinks usually served with an umbrella. Go ahead, try a Ray's Mistake, "151" Rum Sizzle or Vicious Virgin. Or hand over your car keys to someone more responsible and try all three. Be aware that in typical tropical fashion, the Tiki-Ti seems to have a cavalier relationship with its posted hours. As a matter of fact, the locals refer to it as "that place that only opens when they feel like it." Still, it's a one-of-a-kind bar that's definitely worth a visit.

West Beach Café
60 N. Venice Blvd., Venice
823-5396
Open Mon. 6 p.m.-1:30 a.m., Tues.-Fri. 8 a.m.-1:30 a.m., Sat.-Sun. 10 a.m.-1:30 a.m. All major cards.

You'll find a fabulous collection of beers, Cognacs, wines by the glass, pretty women and handsome men affiliated in one way or another with the art world, and a scene that will seduce you into returning as often as possible. It's civilized but fun, and you're sure to meet someone interesting-looking and quite possibly worth talking to. But dress up a bit, as the look is ultra-casual chic at its best. The later it gets, the better it looks.

Ye Olde King's Head
116 Santa Monica Blvd., Santa Monica
451-1402
Open daily 11 a.m.-2 a.m. No cards.

For a minute we thought we took a wrong turn and went across the Channel instead of across town. British accents abound in this authentic English pub; also in abundance are pale-complexioned Watney's drinkers and darts (and, ahem, draughts) fanatics. Owners

Phillip and Ruth Elwell have worked hard to make this a real neighborhood pub for the local English and Irish expatriates as well as for Santa Monica's many young pub crawlers. They sponsor darts competitions, along with local cricket, rugby and soccer teams. It's predominantly male, with a good number of scruffy beach people during the week. In the bar, you can order Guinness, John Courage, Watney's and Bass on tap (and English rock on the jukebox); in the adjoining restaurant, you can order great fish and chips. The crowd gets thick on weekends, when a line usually forms outside after 9 p.m.

Yee Mee Loo
690 N. Spring St., Chinatown
624-4539
Open nightly 4 p.m.-1 a.m. No cards.
Imagine, if you will, a time machine disguised as a bar. Adjoined by a restaurant of the same name, this is one of the few bars in Chinatown. And what a bar it is . . . through a heavy iron door off a quiet street, you will enter a small dark place with a line of black bar stools that seat a cast of unusual characters. Behind the bar is a display of bottles and a chorus of smiling Buddha figures. Stay a while and everyone will seem like a happy Buddha.

It's hard to say what's changed at Yee Mee Loo in the past 40 years, but it's probably only the prices, which are still cheap. This place is a throwback to another age, a Raymond Chandleresque vision of 1940s Los Angeles, a place where cops and criminals feel at home with one another. Slip a quarter in the jukebox and hear the likes of Frank Sinatra, Billie Holiday and Vic Damone. But hurry down. At the time of this writing, Yee Mee Loo is battling the wrecking ball, and it's uncertain how far into the '90s it'll be around.

CABARETS

Cafe Largo
432 N. Fairfax Ave., Hollywood
852-1073
Open Tues.-Sat. 7 p.m.-2 a.m., Sun. 6 p.m.-midnight. Cover varies (2-drink minimum). Cards: AE, MC, V.
Former Lhasa Club impresario Jean Pierre Boccara took Lhasa's artsy and experimental booking policy and gave it a decidedly uptown twist. His new Largo presents an eclectic mix of folk, blues, rock 'n' roll, poetry and performance art. While dyed-in-the-wool hipsters are put off by its spanking-clean, hushed-tone fine dining ambience, the thirtysomething clientele with a yen for off-the-beaten-path entertainment feels right at home. The food, although a bit on the expensive side, is quite good (if nouvelle in portion), and there's a full bar to assist you in the fulfillment of the two-drink minimum.

La Cage aux Folles
643 N. La Cienega Blvd., W. Hollywood
657-1091
Open Sun.-Thurs. 7 p.m.-2 a.m., Fri.-Sat. 6 p.m.-2 a.m. Shows Sun.-Thurs. 9:15 p.m., Fri.-Sat. 8 p.m. & 11 p.m. Cover $7.50 with dinner, $12 with drinks (2-drink minimum). All major cards.
Female impersonators entertain a straight, touristy, voyeuristic crowd. The costumes rival Vegas's, although the quality of entertainment left us cold. The sound system overwhelms the starlets, but apparently the glitter makes audiences forget such technicalities. The best fun is the rambling mistress of ceremonies, who manages to approach the clever bitchiness immortalized in the film for which this place was named. The waiter/waitresses are great—it's all one big costume party featuring men who are as entertaining as the tinsel onstage.

> *Many Nightlife categories overlap—some bars offer live music, some music clubs also showcase comics, and so on. So please give this chapter a thorough look before heading out for a night on the town.*

Carlos 'n' Charlie's
See "Bars."

Gardenia
7066 Santa Monica Blvd., Hollywood
467-7444
Open Mon.-Sat. 6:30 p.m.-midnight (dinner until 10:30 p.m.). Shows Mon.-Sat. 9 p.m. Cover varies. Cards: AE, MC, V.

This supper club is beautiful to look at: subdued lighting, mirrors, gray-and-salmon coloring and white trees with tiny lights framing the stage area. After dinner, Gardenia turns into a watering hole for the smart set, with reasonably good jazz and cabaret entertainment. The food is nothing special, but you'll enjoy sharing dessert, drinks and music in an elegant setting that makes singles bars seem terribly adolescent.

The Queen Mary
12449 Ventura Blvd., Studio City
(818) 506-5619
Open Tues.-Sun. 11 a.m.-2 a.m. Showtimes vary. Cover $5. No cards.

Since the room was engulfed in darkness when we entered, we could not be certain that it was the queen of England who was sliding a five-dollar bill into the tiny, silver-spangled G-string of a handsome young dancer. In case it wasn't really she, we can only urge her to come with her family to celebrate her next birthday at this respectable establishment bearing her ancestor's name. She would surely adore these people, who wear dresses and hats that are little different from her own, and who remove them with great elegance. They show nothing so personal as would shock the queen, and their movements at the boldest consist of bestowing kisses on women who are bewitched by the beauty of their bodies. Wednesday through Sunday evenings, the stage is reserved for female-impersonator shows. It can get rather complicated—in this specialized world, where one changes one's sex as readily as a woman changes her dress,

If you plan on drinking on your night on the town, take a cab or have one of your group be the evening's "designated driver."

nothing is for sure, not even a name. Reservations are suggested.

The Rose Tattoo
665 N. Robertson Blvd., W. Hollywood
854-4455
Cabaret: open nightly 5:30 p.m.-2 a.m.; restaurant: open Tues.-Sat. 6:30 p.m.-11 p.m., Sun. 11 a.m.-3 p.m. & 6:30 p.m.-11 p.m. Shows continuous. Cover $5-$10. All major cards.

The Rose Tattoo is one of the most decent, charming places in the world. Well-bred gays adore the company of ladies, and owner Michel Yueall knows perfectly well that the presence of pretty women is an infallible sign of success for a gay club of high quality. Yueall welcomes them warmly, if not with the same interest, as he does the often beautiful men who gather here to meet one another and drink scotch at the small, closely spaced tables. In this room you will never see a vulgar gesture; at The Rose Tattoo, even the most flamboyant queens are straight. If you go to The Rose Tattoo only once in your life, go on Halloween evening. There, in the tent with crystal chandeliers and the stage (converted from the parking lot), you'll experience an unforgettable fashion show. The men wear extravagant dresses, and we bet that Escoffier would have died instantly had he seen, as we did, some celebrated L.A. French chefs in tutus and net stockings.

Verdi Ristorante di Musica
1519 Wilshire Blvd., Santa Monica
393-0706
Open Tues.-Sun. 5:30 p.m.-2 a.m. Shows continuous. No cover. All major cards.

Unless you consider it an outrage to present operatic arias with show tunes, you'll find Verdi to be great fun. It's primarily a dinner club, and its kitchen turns out so-so, expensive northern Italian dishes. We suggest coming for dessert, after-dinner drinks and stirring renditions of opera favorites and winning Broadway tunes from such old warhorses as *Man of La Mancha* and *My Fair Lady*. Verdi's decor is more elegant and contemporary than you might expect of an Italian music restaurant, and the atmosphere is refined and subdued. This place takes its music seriously: tuxedoed and gowned singers (who are often quite talented) perform onstage in front of a well-dressed audience that saves its chatter for between sets.

COMEDY & MAGIC

Comedy and Magic Club

1018 Hermosa Ave., Hermosa Beach
372-1193
Open nightly. Hours & showtimes vary. Cover $7-$15 (2-drink minimum). Cards: AE, MC, V.

This club keeps beach residents entertained with generally first-rate acts, including such big names as Jay Leno and Harry Anderson. The place is roomy, and you can get decent snack foods or a full-fledged dinner before the show. It's a popular, reasonably priced club whose weekend shows usually sell out (reservations are required). One of the best selling points here is higher-class comedy that doesn't reduce itself to the cheap, often vulgar thrills presented in many L.A. clubs. As a matter of fact, on Friday and Saturday afternoons the Comedy and Magic Club offers comedy for kids (call for times). It celebrates its own New Year's Eve in July, and it's a party not to be missed!

The Comedy Store

8433 W. Sunset Blvd., W. Hollywood
656-6225
Open nightly 7:30 p.m.-2 a.m. Showtimes vary. Cover $6-$14 (2-drink minimum). Cards: AE, MC, V.

The dreary interior is brightened by the hopeful talent seeking fame and fortune. Comic relief comes from a changing-nightly cast of stand-up performers, some of whom have already hit the big time and return to try out new material. The humor is usually topical, often with direct sexual overtones. Drinks are expensive.

Funny You Should Ask

Melrose Theater, 733 N. Seward St., Hollywood - 465-0070
Shows Sat. 10:30 p.m. Cover $12. No cards. ·

These talented young comedians have been performing improvisational comedy for several years around town, and now they're settled in the Melrose Theater. The cast—made up of TV and film writers and actors—has undergone relatively few changes of personnel, which is important since improvisational comedy can be a hit-or-miss affair. The actors build scenes from scratch based on audience suggestions. It requires solid ensemble work built through years of working together. So even on their weaker nights, these folks far outstrip most of the other improv groups around town. On good nights, they're positively inspired. No liquor is served.

Groundlings Theatre

7307 Melrose Ave., W. Hollywood
934-9700
Shows Fri.-Sat. 8 p.m. & 10 p.m., Sun. 7:30 p.m. Cover $8.50-$15. Cards: AE, MC, V.

The Groundlings is probably the best place in town for comedy. No tired, stand-up shtick here—this is a cozy professional little theater showcasing a talented troupe of performers. Many Groundlings have gone on to the big time, most notably Paul Rubens, a.k.a. Pee-Wee Herman. The main show on Friday and Saturday, which changes every few months, is generally a collection of funny set pieces with the occasional improv thrown in. The Sunday show features a different cast and different skits, but it's still funny; the late shows are more experimental. No liquor is served; the lobby snack bar sells junk food and sodas.

The Ice House

24 N. Mentor Ave., Pasadena
(818) 577-1894
Shows Mon.-Thurs. 8:30 p.m.; Fri. 8:30 p.m. & 10:30 p.m.; Sat. 7:30 p.m., 9:30 p.m. & 11:30 p.m.; Sun. 7 p.m. & 9 p.m. Cover $6.50-$8.50, $4.50 Sun. early show (2-drink minimum). Cards: MC, V.

A New York–style comedy club with exposed brick walls and a cozy, earthy ambience, The Ice House was a real ice warehouse in the 1920s. By the early '70s it had become an acclaimed comedy house featuring the likes of Steve Martin and Lily Tomlin. After some slow years it shut down; now it's back on the scene, showcasing fair-to-good stand-up comics and improv shows, with the likes of Roseanne Barr and Bobcat Goldthwaite as occasional surprise guests. The 7 p.m. Sunday show is amateur night, and performances can be painful. Fried snack foods are offered, and the two-drink minimum is loosely enforced.

Igby's

11637 W. Pico Blvd., W.L.A.
477-3553
*Hours vary. Shows Mon. & Wed. 7:30 p.m.,
Thurs.-Sat. showtimes vary. Cover $6.50-$10
(2-drink minimum). Cards: MC, V.*

A bit more casual (and therefore having a welcome looser spirit) than the long-established Improv and Comedy Store, Igby's is a fine place to hear hot young stand-up comics. The setting is intimate, the drink prices fair, and the talent almost always worth a listen. If you're ready to make your television debut, visit on Monday or Wednesday, when the cameras roll to tape Fox's *Comedy Express.*

The Improvisation

8162 Melrose Ave., W. Hollywood
651-2583
*Open daily noon-2 a.m. Shows Tues.-Thurs. 8
p.m. & 10:45 p.m.; Fri.-Sat. 7:30 p.m., 9:45
p.m. & 10:30 p.m.; Sun. 8 p.m. & 10:45 p.m.
Cover $7-$10 (2-drink minimum). Cards: MC,
V.*

Budd Friedman first found fame and fortune with his Improv Club in New York; once that took off, he moved to L.A. to open this place, a spacious brick-walled club that bears a strong resemblance to its New York brother. Friedman, obviously a frustrated stand-up comic himself, occasionally emcees the generally good shows that feature top local comics; many of today's top comedy superstars came out of one or both Improvs, and some of them stop by now and then for impromptu performances. Weekends get crowded with a touristy/date crowd. The later shows are usually better—they tend to be looser and more spontaneous. Drinks are quite expensive. You can get a simple dinner in the adjacent café.

L.A. Cabaret

17271 Ventura Blvd., Encino
(818) 501-3737
*Open nightly 6 p.m.-2 a.m. Shows Sun.-Fri. 8:30
p.m., Sat. 7:30 p.m. Cover $5-$8 (2-drink minimum). All major cards.*

This small cabaret, formerly the Laff Stop, is primarily a comedy club, though a few nights are reserved for musical entertainment. A string of stand-up comedians takes the stage nearly every night, and though the greats don't usually drop by to try out new acts, as at the Comedy Store or The Improv, the level of entertainment is nearly as high. The room is comfortable, and the drinks are good, if a tad expensive. On the down side, the audience has to endure a few too many bad comedians and MCs.

The Magic Castle

7001 Franklin Ave., Hollywood
851-3314
*Open nightly 5 p.m.-2 a.m. Shows continuous.
Members only; cover $7.50 with guest card. All
major cards.*

The Magic Castle has achieved quite a reputation. It's a weird and wonderful idea: and a great place to spend an entire evening trying to figure out how the professional magicians perform their sleight-of-hand tricks. The labyrinth of rooms in this fantastic converted mansion are all filled with experts plying their trades; the big room has a full-blown show. Watch out if you sit in the front row—you'll wind up onstage as part of the act. People dress up to come here, and many have dinner first. Don't. Our last dinner here was so bad we found ourselves wishing a magician would pop in and make it disappear. It's a members-only club, but it isn't too difficult to find someone who can get you a guest card.

Second City

214 Santa Monica Blvd., Santa Monica
451-0621
*Shows Tues.-Thurs. 8:30 p.m., Fri.-Sat. 8 p.m. &
10:30 p.m., Sun. 7:30 p.m. Cover $12.95-
$13.95. Cards: AE, MC, V.*

A great deal of optimism greeted Second City's arrival in Los Angeles. This, after all, was the group that gave birth to both *Saturday Night Live* and *SCTV*. The new group moved into the old Mayfair theater, an impressive Santa Monica landmark building. But sadly, Second City does not live up to its reputation, its building's architecture or its ticket price. The cast members are adept enough as actors, but the material—the show consists primarily of set pieces with a few improv bits thrown in—is flat and uninspired. Ditto for the food. An improv show goes on afterward; the best thing we can say about it is that it's free.

DANCING

No matter where you are in Los Angeles, you're probably no more than a few minutes away from a hopping, throbbing dance club. However, at the city's cutting edge, the clubs don't seem to stay at one address for more than a month or two. It is therefore wise to check the listings in the *L.A. Weekly* for these clubs-of-the-moment. Below are the more stable venues, which we can promise (more or less) will be pumping out dance music onto crowded floors for quite some time to come. Also, please note that the distinction between music clubs and dance clubs tends to blur—some of the following venues feature live music, and many music clubs listed later in this chapter boast great dance floors. Check those listings as well before planning your evening.

China Club
1600 N. Argyle Ave., Hollywood
469-1600
Open nightly 9 p.m.-2 a.m. Cover $10 Sun.-Thurs., $15 Fri.-Sat. Cards: AE, MC, V.

Don't let the low-rent neighborhood fool you. This China Club is nearly identical to its sister in New York. It caters to snazzy dressers who come to see and be seen, so get out your best threads. As you enter, your olfactory glands will be assaulted with more perfume than you've ever smelled in your life. Bump and grind on the spacious dance floor to the hard-driving rock 'n' roll dance music (live music Sunday through Wednesday), work your way up to the circular bar, and order decent dim sum treats at one of the side tables. You'll find youself surrounded by well-heeled Rolex-wearing men and actress/model types. Pretend the prices of the food and drink don't bother you and your presence may generate a little interest.

Coconut Teaszer
8117 Sunset Blvd., W. Hollywood
654-4773
Open Sun.-Thurs. 8 p.m.-2 a.m., Fri.-Sat. 6:30 p.m.-4 a.m. Cover $5 Fri.-Sat. Cards: MC, V.

With two dance floors and a wide variety of dance music, this spacious club recalls the funky days when the Sunset Strip was a long, wild stretch of dance-fevered nightspots. Weeknights, the new and improved Teaszer books the cream of L.A.'s rock scene and draws a young, dedicated and energetic crowd; Sunday nights are rock marathons featuring band after band in short, sharp succes-

sion. Black rocker gear seems to be de rigueur, with nary a primary color to be seen. Friday and Saturday nights are reserved for R & B and acoustic bands, and the crowd veers more toward the mainstream. There's outdoor seating to cool off from the breakneck dance pace, and large drinks for the same purpose.

Crush Bar
The Continental Club, 1743 N. Cahuenga Blvd., Hollywood
462-9156
Open Thurs.-Sat. 9 p.m.-2 a.m. Cover $5 Thurs., $7 Fri.-Sat. No cards.

Papa's got a brand-new bag in these nostalgic '90s, and the '60s Motown soul of the Crush sends out a freewheeling message: do what you want to do. A variety of deejays spin those golden oldies for a new generation of boppers. Frequented by a younger crowd, most of whom were watching cartoons when the music played here was originally recorded, the Crush maintains a feverish dance pace that rapidly turns it into a house of sweat. After an evening here, you'll have to rev up the little Pontiac GTO and take that miniskirt or those pleated trousers to the cleaners.

Florentine Gardens
5951 Hollywood Blvd., Hollywood
464-0706
Open Thurs. 8 p.m.-2 a.m., Fri. 8 p.m.-3 a.m., Sat. 8 p.m.-4 a.m., Sun. 8 p.m.-2 a.m. Cover $10. No cards.

This immense barn of a dance club is located in a typically bizarre Hollywood spot: it sits on garish Hollywood Boulevard between a triple-X-rated movie theater and a Salvation Army tabernacle. The sizable crowd is young (18 and over), dressed up and enthusiastic

FM Station
11700 Victory Blvd., N. Hollywood
(818) 769-2220
Open Sun.-Thurs. 8:30 p.m.-2 a.m., Fri.-Sat. 8:30 p.m.-4 a.m. Cover varies. Cards: MC, V.

It's hard to figure this place out. FM Station (named acronymically for Filthy McNasty, the proprietor of this unique establishment) is the spandex capital of the Valley. You'll see band after band of young men with long moussed hair cranking out the kind of ear-splitting music that everybody's parents hate. But then, in between sets, a kind of latter-day Saturday Night Fever takes hold, with deejays spinning the most danceable tunes imaginable. The place is full of bars and tables, and couches where you can rest, drink or order munchies. There's a great dance floor and a room in back where you can rest your ears and shoot a little pool.

Kingston 12
814 Santa Monica Blvd., Santa Monica
451-4423
Open Tues.-Sun. 8:30 p.m.-2 a.m. Cover $13 Fri.-Sat. No cards.

This is *the* place to go in L.A. when you're feeling *i-rae*. The crowd here is a mixed bag of hipsters, funksters, rastas and plain old westsiders. A fun-loving crowd, they come here to shake it on Kingston's enclosed dance floor to the deejay-spinned, steady stream of island music or to the solid roster of local and international reggae bands. At the time of this writing, Wednesday night is Bahama Mama Night, which is heavier on hip-hop. For the quintessential Jah-loving Kingston 12 experience, it's best to come on the weekend.

The Palace
1735 N. Vine St., Hollywood
462-3000
Open most nights. Hours vary; concerts usually start at 8 p.m.; dancing 10:30 p.m.-4 a.m. Cover $10-$15 for dancing; cover for concerts varies. Cards: AE.

Star Wars meets the twenties. The people who run this place look like they're hooked

up with NASA; earphones (probably to muffle the deafening sound), laser machines and monitoring screens are the tools of this dancing trade. The Palace does double-duty as both a concert hall and dance club. On concert nights, dancers move in after the concertgoers move out; Saturday nights are frequently reserved for dancing only, with the music beginning about 8 p.m. It's a great-looking place, a refurbished architectural gem modernized with a pretty good sound system and mind-boggling lights. The crowd tends to be 18-and-over sophisticates with carefully moussed hair and the latest fashions. One of the more fun clubs in town.

Peanuts
7969 Santa Monica Blvd., W. Hollywood
654-0280
Open nightly. Hours & cover vary. No cards.

Once a women-only disco, Peanuts now hosts different theme nights every night of the week. Some, such as the Monday night drag show, hew closely to the club's West Hollywood roots; others, such as Bordello on Thursday nights, pack in a huge crowd that is quite hetero. Still, with two bars, video games, pool, go-go dancers, a great sound system and all kinds of wild antics, there'll always be something to make you say, "I don't think we're in Kansas anymore."

Sasch
11345 Ventura Blvd., Studio City
(818) 769-5555
Open Tues.-Sun. 8 p.m.-2 a.m. Cover $5 Tues.-Thurs. & Sun. after 9 p.m., $7 Fri.-Sat. after 9 p.m. Cards: AE, MC, V.

Sasch is probably the most popular club in the Valley. The crowd, music and fashions aren't nearly as cutting-edge as at the hot clubs over the hill, but this won't stop you from having a good time dancing to the middle-of-the-road recorded and live music. Weekends, a good house band plays Top 40 songs; some of the better mainstream club bands in town are featured on other nights. It's a friendly, comfortable place, with lots of space, a good-sized dance floor, two bars and a game room with backgammon and a fireplace. It's best to arrive before 9 p.m. if you want to get a table. Don't expect to carry on more than the most basic of conversations—

the elaborate sound system is excellent but tremendously loud.

The Strand
1700 S. Pacific Coast Hwy., Redondo Beach
316-1700
Open nightly 4 p.m.-2 a.m. Cover varies. Cards: MC, V.

Formerly Annabelle's, The Strand has a reputation for attracting musical performers of the highest caliber—no mean feat for a South Bay club. The crowd is attractive, and there are often some great dancers. There are three bars, three dance floors and plenty of people to whoop it up with. The kitchen serves pretty good Californian cuisine.

Vertigo
1024 S. Grand Ave., Downtown
747-4849
Open Fri.-Sat. 10 p.m.-4:30 a.m. Cover $10. No cards.

The experience here begins at the door— and, for some, might also end there shortly afterward. Vertigo's New York–style door policy is one that we wish would've stayed in the Big Apple. Arrogant, aloof doormen— who consider themselves to be in a postion of extreme importance—keep many would-be guests waiting outside indefinitely, while others, by virtue of their being gorgeous females, famous, or friends with the doorman, scoot blithely past. After an hour, if you're lucky, you'll be "allowed" in, meaning you've somehow earned the right to part with $15 and join the very chic mass of people queezing their way up to a packed bar. Now the evening kicks into high gear. You dole out more money for drinks; then you have people turn down your offer to dance in favor of someone who owns more corporations or has more screen credits than you do. Just shrug, elbow your way up to the bar again and spend more money. If this is getting to be a grind, go out onto the balcony, take a breather, drink a drink, and start the process all over again. Are you having fun yet?

JAZZ

Alfonse's
10057 Riverside Dr., Toluca Lake
(818) 761-3511
Open nightly 4 p.m.-2 a.m. Shows nightly 9:30 p.m. No cover (2-drink minimum). All major cards.

Riverside Drive in suburban Toluca Lake is getting to be like West 52nd Street in New York City when such great jazz venues as Eddie Condon's and Jimmy Ryan's were open. A walk down the street in this unpretentious area of the San Fernando Valley leads you to discover the strains of jazz from three establishments, all of which are actually longtime restaurants that have added jazz to their menus. Alfonse's is one of them, and it does a pretty good job. For one thing, it's not a bad Italian restaurant—dimly lit, with red vinyl booths and hanging plants. The entertainment varies, and though it may not be bigname, it's certainly enjoyable. And there's something to be said for sitting with a bottle of fairly priced Chianti, listening to good music for unhurried hours.

At My Place
1026 Wilshire Blvd., Santa Monica
451-8596
Open nightly 7 p.m.-2 a.m. Showtimes & cover vary (1-drink minimum). Cards: MC, V.

This cavernous nightclub is dark and packed with serious and appreciative listeners. The murky atmosphere must be intended to further highlight the well-lit stage, where good music is presented nightly. Jazz and rhythm and blues are the headliners. There are several shows each evening, so call ahead for information.

The Baked Potato
3787 Cahuenga Blvd., Studio City
(818) 980-1615
Open nightly 7 p.m.-2 a.m. Shows nightly 10 p.m. & midnight. Cover $8-$10. Cards: AE, MC, V.

In this small, plain room, it's clear that more attention has been paid to the music than the decor. A casually dressed and unusually mixed crowd (Japanese, Anglo and black) arrives late to hear good local jazz and fusion bands.

Dinner of a sort is served—huge baked potatoes, stuffed with everything from cheese and spinach to steak with pizzaiola sauce—and it's inexpensive and actually quite tasty.

Birdland West

105 W. Broadway Ave., Long Beach
436-9341
Hours & showtimes vary. Cover $10-$17.50 (2-drink minimum). All major cards.

A fine club with excellent sound and a welcoming vibe, Birdland West is well worth the drive to Long Beach. It draws such first-rate talents as Les McCann and Eddie Harris, and the clientele treats the music with respect. Owner Al Williams is a respected drummer whose quintet comprises the house band. A full dinner menu is served, along with the usual cocktails, beer and wine.

Bon Appetit

1061 Broxton Ave., Westwood
208-3830
Open Mon.-Thurs. 11 a.m.-midnight; Fri. 11 a.m.-1 a.m.; Sat. 5 p.m.-1 a.m.; Sun. 5 p.m.-midnight. Shows Mon.-Thurs. 9 p.m. & 10 p.m., Fri.-Sat. 9 p.m. & 11 p.m., Sun. 8 p.m. & 10 p.m. Cover $6-$12 ($8.95 dinner minimum for early shows, 2-drink minimum for later shows). Cards: AE, MC, V.

This is the place to take transplanted New Yorkers for a taste of home. It seizes urban life with subtle determination and a sultry appeal. It's one of our favorite spots in the city—unpretentious, with good food and a progressive attitude. And unlike New York, the weather outside is almost always nice. Bon Appetit gets a lot of students from nearby UCLA, along with a pleasant mélange of professional types. The music, which ranges from solo vocalists to small combos, spills out onto the Westwood streets and attracts notice from the crowds who create a carnivallike atmosphere on most weekend nights.

Catalina Bar and Grill

1640 N. Cahuenga Blvd., Hollywood
466-2210
Open nightly 6 p.m.-2 a.m. Shows nightly 9 p.m. Cover varies (2-drink minimum). All major cards.

The neighborhood may look pretty grungy, but once you've stepped inside, all that disappears. This is a class joint. You'll find yourself bathed in soft, rose-colored light, while being served delicious, moderately priced Continental cuisine. Catalina offers a full bar, validated parking and, of course, its real attraction, some of biggest names in jazz onstage.

The Cinegrill

Hollywood Roosevelt Hotel,
7000 Hollywood Blvd., Hollywood
466-7000
Shows Tues.-Thurs. 9 p.m., Fri.-Sat. 8:30 p.m. & 10:30 p.m. Cover $10-$20 (2-drink minimum). All major cards.

Take a step back to the time when stepping out for the evening was in order. Grab your top hat and your cane, put on the ritz, and enter the glittery world of old-time Hollywood. Like the once-seedy Roosevelt itself, The Cinegrill has been restored to the glory of its Hollywood heyday, and the remodeling reeks of subdued charm. The Cinegrill recalls the era when first-class hotels offered the best talent in town; it headlines performers fresh from New York in shows that generally last about an hour. Hollywood Boulevard, however, is not the beauty queen it was back when there were people around who had voted for Teddy Roosevelt, for whom the hotel is named. The noted Walk of Fame is now home to a more seamy clientele, though local officials are trying to clean up the area. Any stepping out should therefore be done inside the attractive hotel, which also has a nice, expensive restaurant called Theodore's.

The Loa

3321 Pico Blvd., Santa Monica
829-1067
Open Thurs.-Sun. 7 p.m.-midnight. Shows Thurs.-Sat. 9 p.m. & 11 p.m., Sun. 8:30 p.m. & 10:30 p.m. Cover varies (2-drink minimum). All major cards.

By virtue of its unflinching dedication to booking only the hottest names in jazz, and despite its so-so acoustics, The Loa has quickly risen up L.A.'s jazz-club ladder, becoming probably the most talked-about new club in town. There's something about its soft, blue-lit, bare-walled ambience that makes it eminently comfortable for listening, and seeing, live jazz. The bar serves beer and wine, and the pizzas and appetizers aren't bad.

The Money Tree

10149 Riverside Dr., Toluca Lake
(818) 766-8348
Open Mon.-Sat. 11 a.m.-2 a.m. Shows Mon.-Sat. 9 p.m.-1:30 a.m. No cover. Cards: AE, MC, V.

The Money Tree has a devoted band of followers in and around Toluca Lake, but its reputation is beginning to spread beyond the neighbohood. Writers, camera operators, character actors and technicians from the many nearby studios come to this small, friendly (albeit too gloomy) bar/restaurant to hear good to very good jazz singers perform. Happily, there's no cover charge—something the management is quite proud of—so for the price of a drink or a steak dinner, you can relax for a few hours and listen to fine, old-fashioned jazz.

Nucleus Nuance

7267 Melrose Ave., W. Hollywood
939-8666
Open Mon.-Sat. 6 p.m.-2 a.m., Sun. 7 p.m.-2 a.m. Shows nightly 9:30 p.m., 11 p.m. & 12:30 a.m. $5 cover for tables in front room. Cards: AE, MC, V.

There's a positive beat at Nucleus Nuance that says it's all right to drop what you're doing, put on those natty clothes and go listen to the jazz or blues band featured that night. It has an open, sophisticated atmosphere, the kind of place where the saxophone and the wine flow freely. A long hallway leading to the main room is lined with photos of old-time Hollywood stars. A young to middle-age professional crowd hangs out here, and it can get intimate on weekends. Set off from the bar area, away from the band, the restaurant serves so-so food. We suggest you come instead for romance, dessert and liqueurs.

Vine Street Bar & Grill

1610 N. Vine St., Hollywood
463-4375
Open nightly 5 p.m.-midnight. Shows nightly 9:15 p.m. & 11:15 p.m. Cover $5-$25 (2-drink minimum). Cards: CB, DC, MC, V.

This elegant, costly club consistently offers the best in headline entertainment, with a crowd of aficionados that probably spent the hours before the show listening to well-worn recordings of that night's artist. There's something absolutely wonderful about being able to hear popular entertainers like Nina Simone in such a small club. It's like stumbling into a Chicago blues dive and coming across B. B. King playing tracks from his next album. Vine Street also serves northern Italian cuisine that is better than the standard supper-club fare, but it's expensive, and you have to pay the price of admission whether you're having dinner or just drinks at the bar. But you won't mind when you get a chance to listen to the likes of Joe Williams, Eartha Kitt and George Shearing working on new and old material in the intimate setting.

MUSIC CLUBS

Los Angeles has traditionally been a great place to hear live rock 'n' roll. There are dozens of venues, of every size, showcasing major stars and next year's stars. In this section, we've listed some of the better music nightclubs in town, but we haven't included the theaters and concert arenas, where you'll find the higher-end performers. Two of our favorites of these are the Wiltern and the Beverly theaters, both physically and acoustically beautiful halls that tend to attract more jazz, soul and progressive music than rock; of the outdoor arenas, the best are the Greek Theater, a delightful outdoor amphitheater, and the Universal Amphitheater, which offers every comfort but is somewhat sterile. Check the calendar and entertainment sections of L.A.'s daily and weekly papers for listings.

Al's Bar
305 S. Hewitt St., Downtown
625-9703
*Open Mon.-Fri. 6 p.m.-2 a.m., Sat.-Sun. 2 p.m.-
2 a.m. Cover varies. No cards.*

The downtown loft scene is the closest
thing L.A. has to New York's SoHo, and Al's
Bar sits smack in the middle of it all. Though
it's been revamped, it has maintained some of
its rough edges; Al's is usually crowded,
smoky, raw and loud. It is not for the faint of
heart. Dress is casual to downright poor, and
the bar serves cheap beer and wine. Friday
through Monday Al's presents live music, and
it has a good reputation for attracting some
first-class bands. Tuesday and Wednesday are
theater nights, where you'll find an eclectic,
way-out mix of dramatic goings-on. Thursday
is "no talent night," with a variety of off-the-
wall acts. Weekends sometimes get quite good
bands.

Bebop Records & Fine Art
18433 Sherman Way, Reseda
(818) 881-1654
Hours & showtimes vary. Cover $5. No cards.

What a treat for the kids! Bebop Records—a
combination record store, music club, performance space and art gallery—has no bar, so all
ages are admitted. What it does have are some
of the hottest performers playing their hearts
out in this tiny space before a youthful crowd
squeezed in between the record racks. It's like
having the band come into your dorm room
to play. Besides rock 'n' roll, Bebop hosts folk
and other more esoteric types of music, as well
as poetry readings and performance art. The
third Wednesday of each month is reserved for
open poetry readings, and the last Wednesday
of the month for open mike.

Club Lingerie
6507 W. Sunset Blvd., Hollywood
466-8557
*Open Mon.-Sat. 9 p.m.-2 a.m. Cover $5-$12. No
cards.*

While other clubs have come and gone,
Lingerie has managed to chart a course that
has kept it on the hot-spot list for a number
of years now. The bare-bones brick decor
transcends the cartoony motifs that have relegated other clubs to the has-been bin. It also
allows you to see the stage from just about
anywhere in the club. Lingerie has always

maintained a loyal group of yuppie Hollywood rockers, while its heads-up booking
policy, featuring the most happening bands in
town, helps hook in the errant hipsters who
would otherwise be out seeking newer thrills
at newer venues. We always enjoy the costume-party ambience; most seem more interested in what everyone else is wearing than
what the latest rock, reggae or R & B bands
have to play.

The Gaslight
1608 N. Cosmo St., Hollywood
466-8126
*Open daily 10 a.m.-2 a.m. Shows nightly 9 p.m.
Cover varies. No cards.*

You'll know immediately that you've entering a rock demimonde once you've entered
the long tunnel entrance of The Gaslight and
read the sign proclaiming, LIVE GIRLS TO-
TALLY NUDE ON STAGE (actually, the sign
refers to the theater next door). The Gaslight
has been around, in one incarnation or another, since the 1950s. Today it's a total
rocker hangout, with black motorcycle gear
the wardrobe of choice. The full bar serves
cheap drinks, and the stage hosts great local
talent of the loud-and-fast variety, so sensitive
eardrums beware.

Madame Wong's West
2900 Wilshire Blvd., W.L.A.
870-2244
*Open nightly 8:30 p.m.-2 a.m. Shows nightly 9
p.m. Cover $5-$8. Cards: AE, MC, V.*

An energetic, young thrift-shop-chic crowd
comes here to listen to hard-driving rock
bands, most of which are regulars on the L.A.
club circuit. The first floor is filled with video
games and an oversized screen broadcasting
MTV, all of which makes us think we've stum-
bled into the wrong place for vanguard music.
But upstairs, under the chandeliers (in disre-
pair), a mixed bag of groups, from the painfully bad to the promisingly talented, play and
play and play.

McCabe's Guitar Store
3101 Pico Blvd., Santa Monica
828-4497
*Shows Fri.-Sat. 8 p.m. & 10:30 p.m. Cover
$12.50-$15. All major cards.*

A throwback to the early '60s, McCabe's is
a place for all musical seasons: guitar/mando-

lin/banjo shop by day, folk music school by night, concert hall on Friday and Saturday. It is the only place of its type, and it showcases lesser-known artists from the Southern world of bluegrass, folk, blues and gospel—with the occasional big-name rock band thrown in. The small auditorium holds only 150, so all the seats are good, and the sound system is top-notch. No liquor license, but no one here seems to have any trouble whooping it up on tea and cookies.

The Palace

1735 N. Vine St., Hollywood
462-3000
Open most nights. Hours, showtimes & cover vary. Cards: AE.

The Palace attracts a higher level of performer than most clubs—usually upbeat rockers like the Stray Cats, Oingo Boingo, Joe Ely and Concrete Blonde. The handsomely renovated twenties theater has decent acoustics, but it's clearly a place more appropriate for partying than for serious listening. The few seats usually go to those who eat in the restaurant prior to the show, so most guests have to stand. After the shows, the concert hall turns into a dance hall for a fashionable college-age crowd.

The Palomino

6907 Lankershim Blvd., N. Hollywood
(818) 764-4010
Open daily 10 a.m., closing time varies. Showtimes & cover vary. Cards: AE, MC, V.

This country-western institution is struggling against the tide of all the newer, nicer, up-and-coming spots. The decor is tacky, the clientele raucous, and the beer ridiculously overpriced. However, The Palomino clings to its faded glory and continues to attract top country and rockabilly names, along with some lively rock bands. And so, in turn, the fans keep coming back for more. Thus, the legend lives on. Monday night is "talent" night, which has to be seen to be believed.

Raji's

6160 Hollywood Blvd., Hollywood
469-4552
Open Thurs.-Mon. 9 p.m.-2 a.m. Cover $7. No cards.

A favorite with L.A.'s hipsters, Raji's is the quintessential rock dive. Upstairs, you'll find a long bar serving cheap beer and wine and one of the best jukeboxes in town. The action doesn't really heat up, though, until you go underground. At the foot of the stairs there's a window through which cheap Indian dishes are sold. Hang a right and enter the cavernous performance area. Raji's is known for hosting some of the best rock bands in town. Expect high-decibel, high-energy fare—everything an up-and-coming rock band should be.

The Roxy

9009 W. Sunset Blvd., W. Hollywood
276-2222
Open most nights. Shows 8 p.m. Cover $10-$20 (2-drink minimum). Cards: AE, CB, MC, V.

More than a few years back now, The Roxy was probably the best pop nightclub in town; it hosted everyone from Bruce Springsteen to Jackson Browne to the Blasters. Then, unfortunately, it became home to a couple of long-running plays and stopped booking music. Now it's back in the music world, although thus far its bookings have been more or less limited to lesser-known local bands. We can only hope that this comfortable, well-designed club will start booking the quality names it used to.

The Troubadour

9081 Santa Monica Blvd., W. Hollywood
276-6168
Open nightly 8:30 p.m.-2 a.m. Showtimes vary. Cover $6-$10 (1- to 2-drink minimum). All major cards.

National fame was once The Troubadour's, back in the early '70s, when it was one of the premier spawning grounds for the burgeoning folk-rock movement; musicians The Troubadour helped launch include Elton John, Jackson Browne and Linda Ronstadt. But don't be misled by its reputation. This concert club, now rather run-down, plays host to dozens of mediocre heavy metal and garage-band rock groups. Much of the crowd sports black leather jackets, long, feathered hair (both sexes), tattoos and other such headbanger trappings. These days it's really only for tough-talking, malnourished rockers who wear skin-tight red leather pants and like ear-splitting, 30-minute guitar solos.

Whisky a Go-Go
8901 Sunset Blvd., W. Hollywood
652-4202
Open most nights. Hours & cover vary. No cards.

In the Sunset Strip's heyday, the Doors' Jim Morrison stripped down to his love beads and the band got banned from the Whisky. In those days it was one of L.A.'s most popular venues and the launching ground for many new bands. The Whisky boarded up its own doors a few years ago, but now the owners of the neighboring Roxy have breathed new life into the progressive club. Since there's no age limit, the crowd is young—and black leather and silver studs rule the night. The bands as well as the crowd are primarily New York Dolls–style glam rockers, so differentiating the sexes can get tricky.

See also Coconut Teaszer, The Strand, China Club and FM Station in "Dancing."

CHANEL

CHANEL BOUTIQUE: 301 NORTH RODEO DRIVE,

BEVERLY HILLS (213) 278-5500

©T&CO. 1990

Seven ways to say three words.
Diamond, emerald, ruby and sapphire rings from Tiffany.
Available at Tiffany & Co., at the Regent
Beverly Wilshire, Beverly Hills, 213-273-8880,
South Coast Plaza, 714-540-5330.

TIFFANY & CO.

SHOPS

INTRODUCTION

SHOPPING-MALL FEVER

S hopping-mall fever has taken over Los Angeles. It seems that most Angelenos no longer patronize neighborhood dress shops or haberdashers; they park their cars in the immense parking lots of the immense shopping centers sprinkled all over the Southern California landscape and make their purchases at one of the countless clone stores: Ann Taylor, Brookstone, The Limited, Laura Ashley, The Gap and Banana Republic, to name just a few of the better ones. This is by no means a purely American phenomenon—witness the incredible worldwide success of Italy's Benetton—but it seems to thrive especially well in our car culture.

Thankfully, you don't have to be a slave to the boring repetitiveness of malls. Also sprinkled throughout L.A.'s great sprawl are terrific one-of-a-kind shops that are worth seeking out: designer boutiques in Beverly Hills, antiques in Pasadena, camera gear in Hollywood, trendy fashions on Melrose Avenue and gourmet shops everywhere. These are the kinds of places we've outlined in the pages that follow, without neglecting the better chain stores, which have become almost essential to modern life.

Like it or not, shopping centers are here to stay. Every year or so, another behemoth opens somewhere in the Southland, while the established ones grow as fast as dividing amoebas. (Before long, the Glendale Galleria will be so big it will become its own city!) Here are some of the better malls:

- Beverly Center, La Cienega and Beverly boulevards, West Hollywood. This affront to architecture draws a more elite crowd than most shopping centers, and it has many worthwhile, upwardly mobile shops, including the Irvine Ranch Farmer's Market, Shauna Stein, Ice, Descamps, M. Gallery, Williams-Sonoma, Mondi and the first Conran's Habitat home-furnishings store on the West Coast. Some of the city's best films are screened at the Beverly Center's tiny Cineplex theaters, and there are a number of restaurants, of which Mandarin Cove, the Hard Rock Café and California Pizza Kitchen are among the best. We love the Beverly Center for its people- and fashion-watching shows.

- Brentwood Gardens, 11677 San Vicente Boulevard at Barrington, Brentwood. A glistening white entry on the shopping-mall scene, Brentwood Gardens is one of the westside's hottest fashion spots. The nearly 50 high-end, high-style retailers keep company with celebrities, who retreat to the "Gardens," away from Hollywood's glitz. Some top draws: Modasport, State of the Art, Artworks, Brentfair, By Theodore, Ron Herman and the very good Daily Grill restaurant.

- Century City Shopping Center, 10250 Santa Monica Boulevard, Century City. This shopping center has moved into the 21st century, thanks to a $36 million expansion. Once a part of 20th Century-Fox's back lot, the new "festival marketplace" is one of the city's only outdoor regional shopping centers, though there's plenty of shade from the overhead structures that let the sky shine through. An upscale configuration of shops (Rosenthal/Truitt, Cottura, Pottery Barn, Crate & Barrel) balances anchor stores Broadway and Bullock's. There's a fourteen-movie-screen complex, a fine Brentano's bookstore and a chichi fast-food arcade called the Marketplace.

- Fashion Island, Newport Center, 1045 Newport Center Drive, Newport Beach. The Versailles of shopping centers has recently undergone a face-lift in an attempt to keep up with its burgeoning neighbor, South Coast Plaza. With its lushly landscaped grounds, open-air Mediterranean appeal and updated mix of shops, this island of tranquility continues to attract crowd-weary celebrities and Orange County's elite. The center boasts a Neiman-Marcus, a new multiple-theater complex and some exceptional new shops, including Go Sport, Modasport, Fogal and Merletto lingerie. In the glamorous Atrium Court, you can find everything from a Dior dress to designer asparagus (at the ritzy farmer's market). And there's plenty of good food at such restaurants as Five Feet Too, California Pizza Kitchen and El Torito Grill.

- Galleria at South Bay, 1815 Hawthorne Boulevard, Redondo Beach. If you love the Westside Pavilion and the newer part of the Glendale Galleria, you'll feel right at home here. Same barrel skylight, same Nordstrom, same high-end fast food and pretty much the same shops. Except for the Service Center (with a U.S. post office, ticket outlet and wrap-and-ship store) and the valet parking, it's a clone mall.

- Glendale Galleria, Central Avenue at Wilson Street, Glendale. A monster mall that continues to spread, the Galleria started life as a cheesy suburban center, with Buffum's, J. C. Penny, Leeds and the like. But more recent additions have brought some worthwhile higher-end chains, including Nordstrom, Go Sport, Eddie Bauer, Natural Wonders and numerous shoe stores, from Badicci to G. H. Bass. Be sure to avoid the mall on weekends, when the crush of humanity is nearly unbearable.

- Marina Marketplace, 13455 Maxella Avenue, Marina del Rey. Many of these shops—State of the Art, Ralph Lauren Polo, Chanin's, Ecru—and restaurants/markets—Gelson's, Angeli, Chin Chin—are familiar to Angelenos, but the oceanside branches offer updates and extras. This Ecru carries a different stock than its Melrose brother shop—domestic and European clothing, accessories and shoes have been purchased with the westside customer in mind. State of the Art has more furniture and lighting than can be found in the Brentwood Gardens or Beverly Hills stores, and local designers are well represented. Never mind Marina Marketplace's predictable design and preponderance of pink and gray; the stellar mix of retail shops and restaurants hits the mark.

- South Coast Plaza, 3333 Bristol Avenue, Costa Mesa. Hordes of well-tanned nouveau riche women from Newport Beach and seemingly all of Orange County flock to this megamall, undoubtedly the classiest, cleanest and best-organized mall in the greater L.A. area. The selection (299 stores at last count) is simply unbeatable and includes two fabulous Big Apple imports you won't find elsewhere in L.A.: Rizzoli Books and Barney's New York. The breadth of upscale stores is amazing: Ralph Lauren, Abercrombie & Fitch, F.A.O. Schwarz, Aida Grey, Williams-Sonoma, not to mention eight major department stores, including Nordstrom and Saks Fifth Avenue. South Coast Plaza has earned tourist-attraction status with the U.S. Travel and Tour Administration, accommodating marathon shoppers with a fleet of shuttles that service over 40 major hotels in the area. To be avoided on weekends before Christmas.

- Westside Pavilion, 10800 W. Pico Boulevard, West Los Angeles. Something of a West L.A. landmark, the Westside Pavilion flags down motorists with its bright and busy facade (designed by the firm that created the look of the 1984 Olympic Games). There's a good collection of shops that you won't necessarily see in every other mall—from Guess for Kids (trendy kids' clothes) to Traveling Light (creative travel accessories). The Pavilion also has a handsome Nordstrom, good movie theaters and decent restaurants, including the Panda Inn. It's a baby boomer's dream, but weekend parking can be a nightmare.

Believe it or not, there are a few good shopping areas not enclosed by shopping-center walls. If you feel an urge to do that most un-L.A. thing—walk outdoors—park your car on Rodeo Drive in Beverly Hills, in Sunset Plaza on the Sunset Strip, on Melrose Avenue in West Hollywood, on Westwood Boulevard in Westwood Village, on Lake Street in Pasadena, on Colorado Boulevard in Old Town Pasadena, on Larchmont Boulevard in Hancock Park, on Montana Avenue in Santa Monica or on Main Street in Venice. You'll enjoy the fresh air, and you just might find a great little independent shop that you'd never find in a mall.

ANTIQUES & COLLECTIBLES

AMERICAN & MEXICAN

Blue Meringue
4475 Sunset Dr., Silverlake
666-8690
Open Mon.-Sat. 1 p.m.-6 p.m., or by appt.

A well-organized assortment of '50s and '60s collectible Americana, including vintage television sets, household appliances, lighting fixtures, designer and period furniture, glassware, California pottery, decorative objects, rugs, old cameras, toys, magazines and postcards. Everything is guaranteed to be in excellent working order.

Buddy's
7298 Melrose Ave., W. Hollywood
939-2419
Open Tues.-Sat. 11 a.m.-6 p.m.

Buddy's was the first store in L.A. to call attention to Bauer, the highly collectible pottery from California kitchens of the '30s. But Bauer is just the beginning of owner Buddy Wilson's brilliantly displayed colored-pottery collection; other familiar names are Fiesta, Catalina, Harlequin and Franciscan. To that he's added stunning American art pottery (primarily vases by Rookwood, Roseville, Teco, Fulper) and corresponding Craftsman furniture, produced between 1900 and 1918

(Gustav Stickley, Limberts and Roycroft). One of Melrose Avenue's real gems.

Cadillac Jack

318 N. La Brea Ave., Wilshire District
931-8864
Open Mon.-Sat. 11 a.m.-6 p.m.

Walking into Cadillac Jack is like visiting a Midwestern relative's home that's been frozen in post–World War II days. Owners Penny and Don Kolclough are devoted to twentieth-century American design; their collection includes cowboy furniture and accessories, wagon-wheel furniture, pistol- or horse-motif clocks, boot-motif lamps and Wallace rodeo-pattern restaurant china. One entire room displays Heywood Wakefield solid-birch furniture of the 1930s through the 1950s.

Fat Chance

7716 Melrose Ave., W. Hollywood
653-2287
Open daily noon-6 p.m.

Important designer furniture and accessories from the '50s and '60s, including that of Charles Eames, Herman Miller and George Nelson. After thirteen years on Melrose, Fat Chance is itself a fixture.

Federico

1522 Montana Ave., Santa Monica
458-4134
Open Mon.-Sat. 10 a.m.-6 p.m.

Hailing from Oaxaca, Mexico, owner Federico is an authority on American Indian and Mexican folk art, and he stocks his shop accordingly. There's a substantial collection of pre-Columbian, Colonial and contemporary Mexican textiles, Navajo textiles, beadwork, baskets and furniture. The store is also known for antique and contemporary jewelry by such masters of Mexican silver as William Spratling, Frederick Davis and Margot of Tasco.

Hemisphere

1426 Montana Ave., Santa Monica
458-6853
Open Mon.-Sat. 10 a.m.-6 p.m., Sun. noon-4 p.m.

If rustic elegance is your goal, Hemisphere can help you dress the part. This store showcases a rich mélange of home furnishings, art objects and collectible fashion from the American Southwest, Mexico, South America—all around the western world. Here authentic Navajo crushed-velvet "broomstick" skirts, Guatemalan shirts, hand-tooled belts, old trade beads, silver jewelry, boots and moccasins are right at home with Early California Monterey furniture, Afghan dhurries, Navajo rugs, pottery and a library of related books.

Jack Moore American Arts and Crafts

59 E. Colorado Blvd., Pasadena
(818) 577-7746
Open Wed.-Sat. noon-5 p.m.

Jack Moore devotes his store to two design styles near and dear to California's past: mission oak (also known as Craftsman), furniture found in many local bungalows from the years 1900 to 1920; and the hacienda style of 1920 to 1940, ranging from Spanish to Monterey to the newly collectible "motel cowboy" style. Add to that a smattering of paintings, tile-topped tables, California and art pottery, vintage Mexican serapes, a few late-ninteenth-century ranch artifacts and old Southern California books, maps and magazines.

Nonesuch Gallery

1211 Montana Ave., Santa Monica
393-1245
Open Mon.-Sat. 11 a.m.-5:30 p.m.

Perhaps "unerring eye" is too overused a phrase to apply to owner Gloria List. But she definitely has a gift for putting together art and antiques from west of the Mississippi into cleverly composed still lifes. Early California and modernist paintings and American Indian artifacts mix with cowboy relics, vintage Navajo and Mexican weavings (*santos* and *retablos*) and old jewelry.

Off the Wall

7325 Melrose Ave., W. Hollywood
930-1185
Open Mon.-Sat. 11 a.m.-6 p.m.

The name says it all. Off the Wall sells weird stuff, most of which happens to be vintage 1930 to 1950, according to co-owner Dennis Boses. In this carnival of kitsch, it's not uncommon to see a life-sized cow on display, next to restored jukeboxes, neon miscellanea, mechanical memorabilia, fantasy furniture, trains, planes and automobiles. As Boses says, everything here is "bigger than it should be, smaller than it should be or moves when you think it won't."

Territory

6907 Melrose Ave., Hollywood
937-4006
Open Mon.-Sat. 11 a.m.-6 p.m.

Territory maintains a lighthearted approach to what can be some pretty serious collectibles. Whenever we're there, we usually want to buy everything in sight: vintage Western jewelry, richly colored Pendleton blankets, Beacon blankets in rowdy cowboy motifs, Mexican pottery from the '20s to the '40s (sometimes complete table settings), Monterey-style furniture, Aspen wood lamps and contemporary Navajo folk art. For that big splurge, consider the gorgeous California Plein Aire paintings of the '20s and '30s.

ART DECO & ART NOUVEAU

Dazzles

13805 Ventura Blvd., Sherman Oaks
(818) 990-5488
Open Tues.-Sat. 11 a.m.-6 p.m., Sun. noon-5 p.m.

This sparkling, attractive little place reflects care and attention to detail. It has one of the largest selections of campy celluloid jewelry in the city; each colorful trifle is temptingly displayed in long neat rows. There's also a good assortment of picture frames, tubular chrome and lacquer tables, lighting fixtures and a few upholstered chairs. Everything is in mint condition, the prices are fair, and the service is first-rate.

Harvey's

7365 Melrose Ave., W. Hollywood
852-1271
Open Mon.-Sat. 10:30 a.m.-6 p.m.

Decomania practically oozes out the front door of this friendly, funky art deco department store, stocked with oodles of lamps, desk accessories, cigarette lighters, pictures, mirrors and furniture—including a bounty of rattan sofas and tables and chairs that were particularly popular in the '40s. Expect to pay Melrose prices. Some of the accessories may be in less-than-perfect condition, so perfectionists may choose to shop elsewhere.

Hans Korthoff Antiques

7406 Melrose Ave., W. Hollywood
658-6661
Open Mon.-Sat. 11 a.m.-5 p.m., Sun. 11 a.m.-4 p.m.

This narrow, well-kept shop stocks an attractive assortment of small, primarily art deco offerings. A fine place for such accessories as clocks, glassware, lighting fixtures, frames and small-scale furniture. There's a little bit of everything in a wide price range, and all the goods appear to be in fine condition.

Mid-Melrose Antiques

5651 Melrose Ave., Hollywood
463-3096
Open Mon.-Sat. noon-6 p.m.

Specializing in art nouveau, Mid-Melrose puts its accent on the theatrical. On our last visit, we just missed the eight-foot-tall male angel and the life-sized painting of an enraged gorilla. Whether you love it or hate it, this shop caters to Hollywood's taste for the dramatic and the magical, buffered by some serious eighteenth-century antiques.

Papillon Gallery

8111 Melrose Ave., W. Hollywood
655-4468
Open Tues.-Sat. 10:30 a.m.-6 p.m., Sun. noon-5 p.m.

Originally located in a velvet-carpeted Sherman Oaks showroom, this shop now displays more precious things in less space. It's still one of the most glamorous, alluring shops of its kind, specializing in decorative and fine arts from 1860 to 1960, with an emphasis on sculpture and paintings. Other must-see items include glass and ceramic objets d'art, period light fixtures and some furniture, deco silver coffee services, tiny enameled picture frames, crystal perfume bottles and—surprise—a wonderful collection of '40s-era gold jewelry.

Piccolo Pete's

13814 Ventura Blvd., Sherman Oaks
(818) 990-5421
Open Tues.-Sat. 11 a.m.-6 p.m., Sun. noon-5 p.m.

There's some art nouveau here, but the bulk of the merchandise is either art deco or in the art deco mode. The shop stocks plenty of furniture and light fixtures, including figural lamps. Upstairs you'll find goods from the '40s and '50s and colorful paintings and posters. The rear of the shop houses a substantial selection of California pottery. All the wares are in good condition.

Shapes Gallery

8444 Melrose Ave., W. Hollywood
653-0855
Open Mon.-Sat. 10:30 a.m.-6 p.m.

One of the last bastions for French furniture from 1925 to the late 1940s. Each extravagantly crafted console, desk, dining table, chair and daybed has been restored to its original luster. There are also some finely selected lamps, vases, art glass, architectural pieces and posters. In all, pieces are less expensive than those at Shapes's Beverly Hills brother, the Robert Zehil Gallery (2445 N. Rodeo Drive).

Thanks for the Memories

8319 Melrose Ave., W. Hollywood
852-9407
Open Mon.-Sat. 1:30 p.m.-6 p.m.

Requisite gray walls enhance a substantial assortment of restored black-and-chrome art deco furniture: a good assortment of upholstered chairs; a small but lovely array of Lalique; commercial, glass and crystal perfume bottles from the 1920s and 1930s; and a large collection of jewelry, including '20s vintage pieces, Mexican silver from the '40s and men's watches, cuff links and belt buckles.

Turner Dailey

7220 Beverly Blvd., Wilshire District
931-1185
Open Fri.-Sat. 11 a.m.-6 p.m., or by appt.

A spinoff of the well-established William and Victoria Dailey bookstore (8216 Melrose Avenue), Turner Dailey offers a finely edited collection of works on paper and paintings from 1900 to 1950. The emphasis is on California art and artists, the European avant-garde of the 1920s, typography and travel posters. The changing exhibitions alone are worth the visit.

Robert Zehil Gallery

445 N. Rodeo Dr., Beverly Hills
858-0824
Open Mon.-Sat. 11 a.m.-6 p.m.

This small jewel box of a shop yields exquisite art nouveau and art deco glass (Galle, Daum, G. Argy-Rousseau, Lalique) and sought-after ceramics by R. Buthaud. Much of the top-quality art deco furniture is

wrought iron by E. Brandt and R. Subes. The pricey merchandise ranges from $1,000 to $60,000; for a more reasonable range (and more furniture), try Zehil's Shapes Gallery (8444 Melrose Avenue). A number of books on the art nouveau and art deco periods are also available for sale.

BOOKS

Angel City Books

1641 Westwood Blvd., W.L.A.
477-4991
Open Tues.-Sat. 11 a.m.-6 p.m.

This choice antiquarian bookstore is tucked away on well-traveled Westwood Boulevard. First editions and fine reading copies of classics by Fitzgerald, Chandler, Hemingway, Faulkner, Wolfe and West are the emphasis here, but works by lesser known authors (many of whom played a part in Hollywood's early days) are also well represented. Co-owner Phil Syracopoulos, a ten-year veteran of the rare-book business, advises collectors on all levels and carries such related collectibles as old literary magazines, scripts and original author photographs.

Arcana Books on the Arts

1229 3rd St. Promenade, Santa Monica
458-1499
Open Tues.-Sat. 10 a.m.-6 p.m.

Arcana is an architectural setting for books on post-Impressionist art, architecture and photography (and exhibition catalogs), many of which are out of print or hard to find. This shop is well known in collectors' circles here and overseas. There are some fine values among the many long-lost literary and art gems waiting to be discovered—if not in the shop or showcase, then in the back room, available by special request.

William and Victoria Dailey

8216 Melrose Ave., W. Hollywood
658-8515
Open Tues.-Fri. 10 a.m.-6 p.m., Sat. 11 a.m.-5 p.m.

This small shop features rare books, art reference and illustrated books, as well as science and fine-press books. Nineteenth-through early-twentieth-century prints are also for sale. All in all, this place is aimed at serious collectors, who might also be interested in visiting the related Turner Dailey gallery (7220 Beverly Boulevard).

Golden Legend
7615 Sunset Blvd., Hollywood
850-5520
Open Mon.-Fri. 10 a.m.-5:30 p.m., Sat. 10 a.m.-4:30 p.m.

A user-friendly shop where exquisite leather-bound book sets, primarily from the turn of the century, are displayed next to deluxe illustrated books with original signed prints by such painters as Picasso and Miró. Rare books are neatly arranged on shelves under glass. Retreat to the reading room upstairs for one of the largest selections of out-of-print theater and dance books in the country. According to owner Gordon Hollis, "You don't have to be a book collector to browse here. Lookers are welcome."

Heritage Book Shop
8540 Melrose Ave., W. Hollywood
659-3674
Open Mon.-Fri. 9:30 a.m.-5:30 p.m., Sat. 10 a.m.-4:30 p.m. (Closed Mon. July-Sept.).

Heritage ranks among the country's finest bookstores of its kind, dealing in first editions, fine printings, Western Americana, early travel and rare and out-of-print books. There are also extensive autograph and manuscript departments and its own bindery. No specialty per se, but a vast selection in an attractive, comfortable setting.

George Houlé
7260 Beverly Blvd., Wilshire District
937-5858
Open Mon.-Fri. 10 a.m.-6 p.m., Sat. 10 a.m.-4 p.m.

George Houlé stocks a wide array of lovely leather-bound books from the eighteenth through twentieth centuries, as well as first editions. There's also one of the largest collections of framed autographs in the city—whether of authors, political figures or film stars. Most of the material on film is not on view, so request whatever piques your interest.

Elliot M. Katt Bookseller
8570 Melrose Ave., W. Hollywood
652-5178
Open Mon.-Sat. 11 a.m.-6 p.m.

Comfortably ensconced in a converted California bungalow, Elliot M. Katt is one of the few bookstores in the city that specializes in the performing arts, including cinema, theater, music and dance. The well-informed Katt calls his shop, where you're almost sure to spot someone from Hollywood's A-list, "a research library where the material is for sale." Mail order welcome; catalogs available upon request.

Michael R. Thompson
1001 N. Fairfax Ave., W. Hollywood
650-4887
Open Mon.-Sat. 10 a.m.-7 p.m., Sun. noon-5 p.m.

This comfortable, cluttered shop stocks what's possibly one of the largest selections of books on philosophy and history in the United States. It's a scholarly place that sells primarily to university libraries, but browsers are welcome. Since the books are in excellent condition, this emporium should not be overlooked by the inquisitive.

Zeitlin Periodicals Company
817 S. La Brea Ave., Wilshire District
933-7175
Open Mon.-Fri. 7 a.m.-5 p.m.

An estimated two million back issues of technical and scientific periodicals are in residence here—that's more than 40,000 titles. Zeitlin primarily serves learned society collectors, museums and educational institutions, but it's also a perfect way to browse away a lazy day.

CHINA

Pamela Barsky
511 N. Robertson Blvd., W. Hollywood
274-6988
Open Mon.-Sat. 10 a.m.-7 p.m., or by appt.

We know of just one place in Los Angeles that stocks a diverse supply of diner dinnerware from America's golden age of roadside dining (1940s to 1960s): Pamela Barsky's shop. The funkiest—and most collectible—"restaurant leftovers," as Barsky likes to call them, all have a logo or motif, such as Nino's Steak House (with cow heads around the rim), Donutland, Chevron service station and the legendary Brown Derby. Also stocked here are old sterling-silver spoons from obscure places, all reasonably priced. Complete sets of china are available, and special requests are welcome.

Foster-Ingersoll
805 N. La Cienega Blvd., W. Hollywood
652-7677
Open Mon.-Fri. 10 a.m.-5 p.m.

A small, civilized, well-staffed shop where—if you're persistent—you can find sets of old china. The focus is on new goods, but the owners try to ensure that ample old offerings are available. On several occasions we've spotted exquisite sets of hand-painted service plates and dessert plates, all of which sell quickly. We suggest you notify the owners of your china needs, as they continually buy sets of old dinnerware and will keep your requests in mind.

CLOCKS

California Clockmakers Guild
7971 Melrose Ave., W. Hollywood
653-1081
Open Mon.-Fri. 10:30 a.m.-5:30 p.m.

A pleasing assortment of primarily nineteenth-century wall clocks fashioned from wood, as well as a smaller selection of floor and mantel timepieces that are professionally installed if purchased here. The owners have been in business nearly 40 years, and all clocks come with a written one-year guarantee. The service is friendly and personalized, the atmosphere comfortable and relaxed.

Jacobsohn's
8304 W. 3rd St., W. Hollywood
655-6105
Open Tues.-Fri. 10 a.m.-5 p.m., Sat. 10 a.m.-4 p.m.

Jacobsohn's has the largest selection of antique clocks in the Southland—all sorts of sizes and shapes from England, France, Germany and America. Most of the clocks are fashioned from wood and brass, but you'll see crystal, marble and nearly every other conceivable material used as well. About 100 timepieces are on hand, and 80 percent are ticking and chiming. Try visiting on the hour for an unusual midmorning or afternoon concert.

FURNITURE

The Antique Guild
8800 Venice Blvd., Culver City
838-3131
Sat.-Thurs. 10 a.m.-6 p.m., Fri. 10 a.m.-9 p.m.

Once upon a time, this was *the* place to go for inexpensive antiques. Now about two-thirds of the antiques have been replaced by reproductions, including the company's own line of furniture, Guild Hall. Nonetheless, there is still plenty of old furniture at low to moderate prices, from pine trunks and armoires to oak dining room sets. The many other branches around town stock mostly reproductions.

The Antique Mart
809 N. La Cienega Blvd., W. Hollywood
652-1282
Open Mon.-Fri. 11 a.m.-noon & 1 p.m.-4 p.m., or by appt.

The kind of place grandma would have loved, The Antique Mart overflows with confused clutter. Tiny trifles are crammed into curio cabinets, and antique American and English furniture and paintings spill from nooks and crannies. Owner Alice Braunfeld has been in the business for more than 40 years. She doesn't say much, but she guarantees everything she sells, and the prices are realistic.

Baldacchino
919 N. La Cienega Blvd., W. Hollywood
657-6810
Open Mon.-Fri. 9 a.m.-5 p.m.

The small, elegant collection of eighteenth- and nineteenth-century French and Continental furniture—everything from period side chairs to dining tables—is a feast for the eyes. Antique crystal chandeliers twinkle from a sixteen-foot ceiling, an abundance of Oriental porcelain is on hand, and you'll also find one of the best selections of reproduction bouillotte lamps in the city.

J.F. Chen Antique Orientalia
8414 Melrose Ave., W. Hollywood
655-6310
Open Mon.-Fri. 10 a.m.-5 p.m.

The prices of the colorful and substantial array of Oriental porcelains, from cachepots to garden stools, won't give you heart failure.

So what if some of the goods aren't museum quality? Just drape a strand of ivy over a nick, and no one will ever know. There's also a fine selection of Oriental and Continental furniture and many neoclassical pieces, which the helpful staff can help you locate.

Connoisseur Antiques

8468 Melrose Pl., W. Hollywood
658-8432
Open Mon.-Fri. 9 a.m.-5 p.m.

This is the hall of mirrors, opulent, glittery and Hollywood-style. One of the largest collections of nineteenth-century crystal chandeliers in the country drips from the high ceiling; these in turn are reflected in a staggering assortment of Venetian mirrors. If you can tear your eyes away from this splendor in the glass, you'll find a good deal of eighteenth-century French furniture sitting amid signed terra-cotta statues from Italy and other accessories. If you're still not satiated, ask to see the shop's addendum at 8471 Melrose Avenue. Not for everybody, but certainly worthwhile if you're aiming for a drop-dead interior.

The Cricket

70 N. Venice Blvd., Venice
823-6512
Open Tues.-Sat. 10 a.m.-6 p.m.

This sun-filled shop, with large verdant plants and soft music wafting through the air, features primarily good-looking French and Italian provincial antiques, along with a few painted pieces from Austria. The prices aren't low, but the offerings are decidedly above-average in quality. This attractive store is the best of its kind in the area.

G.R. Durenberger

31531 Camino Capistrano, San Juan Capistrano
(714) 493-1283
Open Tues.-Sat. 10 a.m.-5 p.m.

You're apt to whiz right by this simple cottage (about one hour south of L.A.) that bears G. R. Durenberger's name. But once inside, you'll find five rooms brimming with lovely French and English provincial antiques and accessories. This new but equally charming location (the original building at 31431 Camino Capistrano is now the Center for the Study of Decorative Arts, worth a stopover itself) features a picturesque courtyard garden.

Durenberger enjoys a fine reputation, and the cognoscenti from the mansions of San Marino and Beverly Hills make the trek down here regularly (he takes a lucky few on an antiques tour of a European country once a year). Durenberger sums up his philosophy: "I buy things I like, and my look is not shiny or polished. I call it faded grandeur. My clients are conservative, well-established individuals who are not buying for investment or impression." If the shoe fits, don't pass up this exceptional shop.

Paul Ferrante

8464 Melrose Pl., W. Hollywood
653-4142
Open Mon.-Fri. 8:30 a.m.-4:30 p.m.

Known for its lighting fixtures, Paul Ferrante is always busy and bustling. The place brims with antique chandeliers, Chinese porcelains and French and English furniture. Well-heeled locals are dismayed if they can't find it here. Custom work is a specialty.

Richard Gould Antiques

216 26th St., Santa Monica
395-0724
Open Mon.-Fri. 10 a.m.-4 p.m.

Far from mighty Melrose Place is a two-room shop chock-full of English furniture and accessories that date from the late seventeenth through nineteenth centuries. The Gould family has been in the antiques business for more than 30 years, and their reputation is as solid as the many oak tables they feature. Chinese export porcelain is also in good supply, as is an assortment of early metalware. Good quality and realistic prices.

Bruce Graney & Company

Cal-Fair Plaza, 1 W. California Blvd., Pasadena
(818) 449-9547
Open Mon.-Sat. 10 a.m.-5 p.m.

Graney is known for its eighteenth- and nineteenth-century English furniture, and just about the most sophisticated carved-pine bookcases in town. A native of Pasadena, Graney stocks only furniture that is in superb condition, and considering the quality of the goods, the prices seem fair. Dining tables and chairs are usually in fine supply, and there's always a good assortment of bookcases, armoires and small tables.

Licorne
8432 Melrose Pl., W. Hollywood
852-4765
Open Mon.-Fri. 9 a.m.-5 p.m.

A large, austere showroom with good-quality French provincial furniture from the eighteenth and nineteenth centuries. Primarily big pieces, with stately designs and a sense of opulence.

La Maison Française
8420 Melrose Pl., W. Hollywood
653-6534
Open Mon.-Fri. 9 a.m.-5 p.m., Sat. by appt.

This sumptuous shop features château-quality European antiques, from Gothic and Renaissance tapestries to chandeliers and Baccarat crystal. Sometimes the owner's indifference can be annoying—perhaps decorators receive better treatment. If you're game, try the store's other outlet (8435 Melrose Avenue) for architectural elements, period mantles, fireplaces and flooring.

John J. Nelson
8472 Melrose Pl., W. Hollywood
652-2103
Open Mon.-Fri. 9 a.m.-5 p.m., Sat. by appt.

Each time we've visited, there's been a warm greeting and a helpful attitude from the sales staff. A good selection of eighteenth- and nineteenth-century French provincial furniture fills several rooms—lots of tables, buffets and armoires. The wares have a well-worn, old-money quality, both of which might be mandatory if you choose to shop here, since the prices reflect the quality of the merchandise.

The Pine Mine
7974 Melrose Ave., W. Hollywood
653-9726
Open Mon.-Tues. & Fri.-Sat. 11 a.m.-6 p.m., Wed.-Thurs. 9:30 a.m.-5:30 p.m.

An extraordinary amount of English and Irish country pine comes from this cozy shop. The majority of goods are plain, but the selection and variety are ample and include pieces with more decorative moldings. Everything is pine—from dressers to side tables, crocks to cupboards, boxes to benches—and the prices are reasonable.

Charles Pollock Antiques
8478 Melrose Pl., W. Hollywood
651-5852
Open Mon.-Fri. 9 a.m.-5 p.m.

In addition to the good selection of country English antiques and Scandinavian Biedermeier empire pieces, there's a smattering of Oriental furniture and porcelains. Large-scale pieces are usually featured.

Quatrain
700 N. La Cienega Blvd., W. Hollywood
652-0243
Open Mon.-Fri. 9 a.m.-5 p.m.

Fifteen pounds of potpourri are scattered in various antique porcelain and crystal bowls throughout the shop. If you think the scent of the stuff is bold, wait until you see the containers in which it's kept: a superb gathering of faintly exotic yet tasteful seventeenth- and eighteenth-century antiques, from Continental to Oriental, plus some of the most beautiful mirrors in town, which, like everything, are in mint condition. Manager Phillip M. Jelly Jr. sums up the owners' philosophy: "We like things a little unusual. You won't find boring British mahogany here."

Ralf's Antiques
807 N. La Cienega Blvd., W. Hollywood
659-1966
Open Mon.-Fri. 10 a.m.-5 p.m.

A sensible emporium. Ralf's has hardly any cute little curios to distract the eye (or cover scratches) from the good assortment of seventeenth- through nineteenth-century French and English provincial furniture. This isn't the shop for those with grand houses or ideas, since most of the pieces are moderately sized and could easily fit in with most decors. There are usually lots of lowboys, Windsor chairs, sideboards, cricket tables and armoires, as well as some antique silver and paintings. Fair prices and a helpful staff.

Tennant Galleries
725 N. La Cienega Blvd., W. Hollywood
659-3610
Open Mon.-Fri. 10:30 a.m.-5:30 p.m.

Consistently tasteful merchandise and fair prices. This shop is a treat, particularly if you collect eighteenth- and nineteenth-century country French and English furniture. There's also an exquisite assortment of eighteenth- and nineteenth-century European paintings, all offered with personal and friendly service.

West World Imports
171 E. California Blvd., Pasadena
(818) 449-8565
Open Mon.-Sat. 10 a.m.-5 p.m.

You'll enter this spacious shop through a brick-covered courtyard brimming with nineteenth-century charrettes (carts)—which is a prelude of things to come. Inside, there's a bountiful assortment of eighteenth- and nineteenth-century English and French provincial furniture in eight rooms. Proprietors Betty and Jim Wade keep an apartment in France, and Jim heads to Europe about every six weeks to round up the goods. The abundant stock is continually replenished, and there's always a roomful of antiques on sale.

Williams Antiques
1714 Euclid St., Santa Monica
450-2550
Open Mon.-Sat. 10 a.m.-5 p.m.

WIlliams is one of our favorite haunts for pine furniture, since the offerings are plentiful, the prices fair, the service caring, and the wares attractively displayed. The pine-only stock is primarily from the eighteenth and nineteenth centuries and is a refined lot. Cupboards and armoires seem to be emphasized, and any item purchased can later be traded in to finance future shopping sprees in this charming shop.

Richard Yeakel
1099 S. Coast Hwy., Laguna Beach
(714) 494-5526
Open Tues.-Fri. 9 a.m.-5 p.m., or by appt.

An outstanding shop. Actually, two shops: one showroom purveys Egyptian wares from 2000 B.C. and features, along with a staggering array of fifteenth-through-seventeenth-century furniture, artifacts from King Farouk's collection. The main store stocks three floors of superb eighteenth-century English and American furniture in addition to paintings and silver and much more. The variety is astounding, and goods are sometimes either loaned or sold to museums. The friendly, always professional staff enhances the shopping trip. Don't miss visiting this exquisite emporium.

JEWELRY

Kazanjian Jewels
9808 Wilshire Blvd., Ste. 300, Beverly Hills
278-0811
Open by appt. only.

Known for purchasing estate jewelry, the business is geared toward the wholesale trade, but there is a retail clientele as well. Call first and make an appointment; at that time, discuss your jewelry needs with a salesperson, and, with luck, a good selection of baubles will be on hand for you to survey.

Frances Klein
310 N. Rodeo Dr., Beverly Hills
273-0155
Open Mon.-Sat. 10:30 a.m.-5:30 p.m.

If your taste in jewelry tends toward the art nouveau and art deco periods, you'll have a field day with Klein's collection of estate and antique jewels. Her pieces are rare and beautiful, and many have been designed by such famous jewelers as Bulgari and Cartier.

Matinee
10 E. Holly St., Pasadena
(818) 578-1288
Open Wed.-Sat. 11:30 a.m.-5 p.m., Sun. 1 p.m.- 5 p.m.

This veritable treasure trove of vintage designer costume jewelry includes such names as Miriam Haskell, Schiaparelli, Eisenberg and Joseff of Hollywood (designer to matinee idols of the '30s and '40s), plus a superb collection of Bakelite and celluloid pieces and some old hats with a new twist. All of it works wonderfully with today's clothing. A dazzling selection at reasonable prices, considering the quality. Don't miss the goods in the window.

Morgan & Co.
908 Montana Ave., Santa Monica
458-0397
Open Tues.-Sat. 10 a.m.-5 p.m.
1131 Glendon Ave., Westwood
208-3377
Open Mon.-Sat. 10 a.m.-5 p.m.

The pretty little shop captures the contemporary charm of up-and-coming too-chic Montana Avenue. It primarily sells a pleasing assortment of unpretentious rings and other things, and plenty of restored men's watches from 1915 to 1950. If you're in search of something showier and costlier, head for the other branch in Westwood Village. Custom designs available at both locations.

David Orgell
320 N. Rodeo Dr., Beverly Hills
272-3355
Open Mon.-Sat. 10 a.m.-6 p.m.

Among the glittering selection of antique and estate jewels, located toward the rear of the shop, the offerings are expensive and exquisite. Usually on view are fine examples by Cartier, Tiffany and Fabergé. These are definitely top-drawer goods—the type you'll want to store in a safe. But while the baubles are beautiful, service can be sorry. At times we've been treated royally, on other occasions, ignored.

Regency Jewelry
8129 W. 3rd St., W. Hollywood
655-2573
Open Mon.-Sat. 10 a.m.-4 p.m.
12215 Ventura Blvd., Ste. 103, Studio City
(818) 761-9447
Open Mon.-Fri. 11 a.m.-6 p.m., Sat. 10 a.m.-5 p.m.

Hardly la crème de la crème, but there is a great deal of old jewelry (costume and fine) at fair prices (starting at $5). A friendly staff, a good jewelry-repair service and a certified appraiser are on the premises.

Slightly Crazed
7412 Melrose Ave., W. Hollywood
653-2165
Open Tues.-Sat. noon-6 p.m.

The specialty here is vintage watches and jewelry, including pieces by Joseff, Eisenberg, Weiss, Bakelite and semiprecious enamels by Vega. But we couldn't overlook the wide array of collectible art and California pottery, vintage appliances (blenders, toasters) and Bakelite flatware. Watch repair on the premises.

Le Vieux Paris
342 N. Rodeo Dr., Ste. 202, Beverly Hills
272-1884
9606 Santa Monica Blvd., Beverly Hills
276-9558
Open Mon.-Fri. 10 a.m.-5 p.m.

You can always count on this small shop on Rodeo Drive to carry a good assortment of antique and estate jewelry, as well as a few objets d'art; that's why it has such a loyal clientele.

Wanna Buy a Watch?
7410 Melrose Ave., W. Hollywood
653-0467
Open Mon.-Sat. 11 a.m.-6 p.m.

This place is the headquarters for stylized vintage timepieces from World War II to 1960. The riveting range includes everything from more affordable gold-filled models by Rolex and Cartier ($300 and up) to rare exotics by Patek Phillipe and Vacheron Constantin. Add to that Hamilton's new line of classic '40s look-alikes, and you'll begin to understand why this is where serious collectors and celebrities like to spend time and money.

MARKETS

Antiquarius
8840 Beverly Blvd., W. Hollywood
854-6381
Ground floor open Mon.-Sat. 11 a.m.-6 p.m.; second floor open Mon.-Sat. 11 a.m.-11 p.m., Sun. noon-11 p.m.

Collectively, the 40 like-minded merchants at Antiquarius are reminiscent of the Paris bookstalls that line the banks of the Seine. Over the years, the building has turned into a talked-about source for authentic, high-quality collectibles, particularly antique jewelry. There's a vast array of attractively priced jewels for everyday use, as well as some selected multidigit dazzlers. Along the way are unusual finds in contemporary jewelry, paintings, Victorian silver, Persian rugs, bronzes, crystal and kaleidoscopes. While all the shops deserve a brief visit, several are noteworthy. Excaliber: antique and estate jewelry and restored vintage alligator handbags. Frances Frazen: silver-handled makeup brushes and French art glass, circa 1900. Neil Lane: estate jewelry from the '20s to '40s with an emphasis on workmanship and beauty, as well as a number of signed pieces, including Cartier and Tiffany. Peskin's Jewelers: antique and period jewelry, gem lab and certified appraiser. Russian Antiques: art objects, icons and hand-painted miniature boxes. Second Time Around: vintage and contemporary watches, both new and used.

Holly Street Bazaar
16 E. Holly St., Pasadena
(818) 449-6919
Open daily 10:30 a.m.-5:30 p.m.

The emphasis at Holly Street, a small antiques mall, is clearly on the golden days of the '40s and '50s. Several dealers stock individual stalls with art deco, antique toys and cute salt and pepper shakers. This is Mecca for collectors of California pottery: lots of Bauer, Fiesta and Catalina, though not necessarily in pristine condition. We recommend comparison shopping among the booths; there is a surprising variety for such similar stock.

Westchester Faire
8655 S. Sepulveda Blvd., Westchester
670-4000
Open Mon.-Sat. 10 a.m.-6 p.m., Sun. noon-5 p.m.

You'll enter via the mall's upper level, where fifteen contemporary gift shops keep company with several fast-food outlets. The mall, located on the lower level (take the escalator), houses 52 stalls and a dizzying assortment of all sorts of collectibles, ranging from Depression-era glass, old toys and advertising and military memorabilia, to crystal, china and jewelry. A sharp eye may spy some true antique treasures, but for the most part the offerings are not geared for those who haunt Sotheby's. Nonetheless, this is a fine place with a twinkling landscape—and you never know what might turn up next week.

QUILTS

The Margaret Cavigga Quilt Collection
8648 Melrose Ave., W. Hollywood
659-3020
Open Mon.-Fri. 10 a.m.-5 p.m., or by appt.

Somewhat of a tradition on Melrose, chatty Margaret Cavigga stocks more than 400 quilts, old and new, circa 1805 through the present. She also writes and sells books on American antique quilts. Some of the older quilts are exquisite; new ones are attractive but not always of the highest quality. Prices can be pretty astonishing. A potpourri of American folk art includes samplers and hooked rugs, and there are also antique American hand-woven coverlets, Victorian doilies, laces

and linens, curtains, tablecloths and a selection, albeit small, of children's clothing and toys. Instant New England ambience.

Peace and Plenty
7320 Melrose Ave., W. Hollywood
937-3339
Open Mon.-Sat. 11 a.m.-6 p.m.

This homey shop has a serene atmosphere, good lighting and a highly selective cache of pre-1940 quilts, coverlets and folk art. Merchandise is displayed in gallery fashion, with most of the quilts suspended from white walls. All are in excellent condition and priced between $350 and $650. Among the other goodies: contemporary jewelry, folksy European pottery, picture frames, an eclectic assortment of paper items and cat-oriented gifts for feline lovers.

Ludy Strauss/The Quilt Gallery
1611 Montana Ave., Santa Monica
393-1148
Open Mon.-Sat. 11 a.m.-5 p.m., or by appt.

Strauss specializes in antique and Amish quilts, hooked rugs (one of the most impressive selections on the West Coast), American folk art and painting. Everything is geared from an artistic viewpoint—graphic patterns and bold colors in "versatile quilts that bridge shifts in decorating." All are in fine condition and available in a broad price range. In the folk art area, there are unusual weather vanes and carved wooden pieces that, as Strauss puts it, "say something about the culture or individuality of the maker."

SILVER

David Orgell
320 N. Rodeo Dr., Beverly Hills
272-3355
Open Mon.-Sat. 10 a.m.-6 p.m.

David Orgell once said that nothing announces status more quickly than Georgian silver dispersed throughout a home. If you share Orgell's philosophy, rush to the phone and make an appointment to visit the Georgian Room. Here you're apt to find sets of service plates by Paul Storr, along with a bounty of exquisite handcrafted items, many of which were made by well-known English silversmiths. Of course, you'll need more than status to pay for the privilege of owning such treasures. Less costly silver collectibles are located near the store's entrance; generally on hand are dazzling antique biscuit boxes, fish services, serving pieces, trays, tea sets and more. The more contemporary silver merchandise is less interesting.

BEAUTY & HEALTH

FACE & BODY CARE

The Face Place
8701 Santa Monica Blvd., W. Hollywood
855-1150
Open Tues.-Sat. 8 a.m-7 p.m.

Treatments at this well-established salon are based on modern, medically proven techniques rather than cosmetic methods. Instead of masks, massages or creams, clients here (half of whom are professional men) follow clinical programs designed for long-range results. A 75-minute facial using The Face Place's exclusive product line is $60; other services, such as lash and brow tinting, waxing, manicures and pedicures, are available at an additional charge.

Aida Grey
9549 Wilshire Blvd., Beverly Hills
276-2376
Open Mon.-Wed. 9 a.m.-5:30 p.m., Thurs.-Sat. 8:30 a.m.-5:30 p.m.

One of the gurus of skin care, Aida Grey now sells her own line of cosmetics and creams at her full-service salon. There are many devotees of her facials, but she also offers hair styling, makeup applications, manicures, pedicures, waxing, acupressure massage, lash tints, paraffin and scalp treatments and electrolysis. Services can be purchased individually, or you can indulge in the "Day of Beauty" package for $200.

Ole Henriksen of Demark Skin Care Center
Sunset Plaza, 8601 W. Sunset Blvd., W. Hollywood
854-7700
Open Tues.-Sat. 8:30 a.m.-5 p.m.

Using products and techniques developed in Denmark, this salon takes an almost holistic approach to skin care. The all-natural product line is based on botanical extracts. Ole Henriksen provides light acid peels for comprehensive rejuvenation, as well as full body waxing, lash and brow tinting, makeup, manicures, pedicures and complimentary nutritional guidance. A 75-minute standard facial runs $55.

Georgette Klinger
312 N. Rodeo Dr., Beverly Hills
274-6347
Open Mon.-Tues. & Thurs.-Fri. 9 a.m.-6 p.m., Wed. 9 a.m.-8:30 p.m., Sat. 8:30 a.m.-6 p.m.

With spa boutiques cropping up all over the country, this salon is devoted to retarding the aging process. After a two-hour workover and workout, you will emerge with the benefit of the well-trained staff's specialties, such as facials, scalp treatments, massages and so on. Prices range from $28 (for a vegetable peeling mask for men and women) to a full hedonistic day of beauty care for $260.

Nance Mitchell Company
330 N. Lapeer Dr., Beverly Hills
276-2722
Open Tues.-Fri. 10 a.m.-5 p.m.

Author/lecturer/skin-care specialist Nance Mitchell concentrates on antiaging education and treatment using two exclusive products for women and men: a nonabrasive enzyme exfoliator and a "Youth Lift" tightening mask. You can experience both by asking for the "Star Treatment," a one-hour session for $65. An authority on preventive and corrective skin care, Mitchell offers up-to-the-minute consultations on corporate image, nutrition, cosmetic surgery and total grooming. Geared to the international set, her products are designed to adapt to different climates.

Aida Thibiant Skin and Body Care Salon
449 N. Cañon Dr., Beverly Hills
278-7565
Open Mon. & Wed.-Sat. 9 a.m.-5:30 p.m., Tues. 9 a.m.-7 p.m.

Thibiant's French techniques and treatments are developed in her own laboratory and are designed to get skin in its best possible shape. All her products are free of lanolin, waxes and mineral oils and are perfect for people with problem, sensitive or allergic skin. In addition to facials, the salon offers body massages, a cellulite treatment, waxing, makeup application and the panthermal bath, which supposedly aids in weight loss and improves circulation. Add to the list the new "Trichology Clinic," a service that analyzes hair and scalp and prescribes an appropriate treatment.

Vera's Retreat in the Glen
2980 Beverly Glen Circle, Ste. 100, Bel Air
470-6362
Open Mon.-Tues. & Fri. 9 a.m.-4:45 p.m., Wed.-Thurs. 9 a.m.-7:15 p.m., Sat. 9 a.m.-3:30 p.m.

Just ten minutes from downtown Beverly Hills, Vera Brown's lavender-hued salon provides a pleasant dose of pampering at a reasonable cost. Here a half day or full day of services may include superb massages, waxing, electrolysis, makeup lessons, brow and lash tinting and some of the finest facials around, which use all-natural, aloe vera–based products. Vera's latest wonder is called "facial contouring," which involves an amazing little machine that seems to actually "iron" all the fine lines away, at least temporarily. Another branch in Tarzana.

FRAGRANCE

Crabtree & Evelyn
Century City Shopping Center,
10250 Santa Monica Blvd.
557-1705
Open Mon.-Fri. 10 a.m.-9 p.m., Sat. 10 a.m.-6 p.m., Sun. 11 a.m.-6 p.m.

We come here for English products in an old-London atmosphere: assorted soaps, shampoos, scented bath oils, hairbrushes and shaving supplies, as well as such edible goodies as cookies, preserves and exotic mustards. Any of the merchandise can be packed into an attractive gift basket. There are several Crabtree & Evelyn shops (in Long Beach, the Westside Pavilion, Sherman Oaks and elsewhere), and Crabtree & Evelyn products are also sold at The Soap Plant, Fred Segal Santa Monica and many other stores.

Homebody
8500 Melrose Ave., W. Hollywood
659-2917
Open Mon.-Sat. 10 a.m.-6 p.m.

Homebody may look out of place, tucked away in a pink-and-black, postmodern-gone-mad building, but it always enchants with its fragrant gift ideas. Owner Susan Fonarow is an aroma therapist who will custom-scent a full line of lotions and gels with your choice of essence.

Fred Segal Essentials
Fred Segal Scentiments
Fred Segal Santa Monica, 500 Broadway,
Santa Monica
458-3766
Open Mon.-Sat. 10 a.m.-7 p.m., Sun. noon-6 p.m.

Fred Segal is synonymous with the latest and the best, at prices to match. Essentials carries natural skin, hair-care and bathing products, including the entire line of hard-to-find Kiehls products, Alba Botanica, Dr. Hauschka and Dr. Geometti's seaweed products from Rome. We checked off our entire gift list upon discovering exotic toothbrushes and twenty-plus different toothpaste flavors from all over the world.

Neighboring Scentiments specializes in fragrance-related products for the home and body. Here you can have a fragrance named after yourself, blended to order and kept on file for future reference. Or choose from up to 150 unusual and imported perfumes. There are scented and aromatherapy candles from Rigaud and Manuel Canovas, soaps in whimsical shapes (fruits, hearts and cupids), potpourri, cosmetic and bath accessories and vintage hatboxes. Don't miss the showcase of antique-silver perfume bottles and men's grooming accessories. Custom gift baskets are available.

The Soap Plant
7400 Melrose Ave., W. Hollywood
651-5587
Open Mon.-Wed. 10:30 a.m.-11 p.m., Thurs.-Sat. 10:30 a.m.-midnight, Sun. 11 a.m.-8 p.m.

Where else but on Melrose would you find a psychedelic-colored new-wave soap shop? Actually, it's the gift items that are ultra-trendy (cactus-shape salt and pepper shakers, artsy books, Keith Haring T-shirts, wacky cigarette lighters, milk cow and Mexican ceramics); the soaps, perfumes and oils are by such trusted traditionalists as Caswell-Massey, Crabtree & Evelyn and Pears. La Luz de Jesus art gallery (upstairs), Zulu ethnic clothing and jewelry (next door) and Wacko cards (a few doors west) are all part of The Soap Plant's miniempire. This is eclectic L.A. at its best.

Tottenham Court

12206 Ventura Blvd., Studio City
(818) 761-6560
1231 Montana Ave., Santa Monica
394-3306
Open Mon.-Sat. 10 a.m.-6 p.m.
Designed to resemble an Edwardian chemist's shop, these stores are brimming with luxurious soaps, colognes, shaving accessories and bath sundries. Stocking primarily European merchandise, including Bronnley, Woods of Windsor, Trumper (perfumer to Her Majesty), Caswell-Massey and Crabtree & Evelyn. Gift baskets can include any of the shop's sterling-silver trifles and be shipped or delivered anywhere. Phone orders are welcome.

HAIR SALONS

Blades

801 Larrabee St., W. Hollywood
659-6693
Open Mon.-Fri. 11 a.m.-7:30 p.m., Sat. 10 a.m.-7 p.m.
One of West Hollywood's more stable institutions (over a decade old), Blades still leads the pack when it comes to short haircuts for men and women, still reasonably priced at $28 to $35. "We're the cutting edge that shapes the '90s," owner Harold Petersen says modestly. The upscale salon boasts lots of natural lighting ("perfect for color application") and a panoramic view of the Pacific Design Center and Santa Monica Boulevard.

Bruno & Soonie

404 N. Cañon Dr., Beverly Hills
275-8152
Open Tues.-Sat. 8 a.m.-6 p.m.
This shop is best known for its celebrity client roster. Years ago, Bruno and Soonie were two of the top stylists at Jon Peters.

When they opened their own shop, it was an overnight success—and still ranks among L.A.'s top salons. Stylists here have a knack for creating cosmopolitan yet individualized cuts. The atmosphere is remarkably relaxed.

Burton Way Salon

9020 Burton Way, Beverly Hills
274-5411
Open Tues.-Sat. 8:30 a.m.-5:30 p.m.
Despite its Beverly Hills address, this salon ranks high in personal service and feels more like it's located in the Italian countryside than amid urban sprawl. Known for their creativity in haircuts ($50), expert color by Londoner Jane Paddon and health-oriented manicures by Marni Alba, the staff all use top-notch products. Best of all, the back windows look out over the garden of adjoining Il Cielo restaurant.

Char Salon

9756 Wilshire Blvd., Beverly Hills
274-0808
Open Mon.-Wed. & Fri.-Sat. 9 a.m.-6 p.m., Thurs. 9 a.m.-8 p.m.
Large and usually peppered with celebrities, Char is best known for color application (particularly blond highlights) and the very latest haircuts ($50 to $60). Between beauty boosts (try Rene Furterer's one-hour relaxing scalp treatment, $40), you can grab a bite to eat at the salon's own café, which serves espresso, sandwiches, salads and sweets. Marja, the makeup artist for Victoria Principal, offers makeup lessons and preparty applications. It's not uncommon to see women in salon garb, their hair in perm rods, running out to check their meters.

Doyle-Wilson

8006 Melrose Ave., W. Hollywood
658-6987
Open Tues.-Wed. & Fri.-Sat. 9 a.m.-6 p.m., Thurs. 11 a.m.-7 p.m.
Low-key and coolly modern, Doyle-Wilson is the antithesis of the Beverly Hills salon. Haircuts here ($45) are on the leading edge—they look more natural and less overly "finished." "Our cuts do all the work and don't need a lot of styling," promises co-owner Alex Doyle.

Jose Eber
9426 Santa Monica Blvd., Beverly Hills
278-7646
Open Tues.-Sat. 9 a.m.-6 p.m.
Beverly Center, 121 N. La Cienega Blvd.,
W. Hollywood
855-1410
Open Mon.-Fri. 10 a.m.-9 p.m., Sat. 10 a.m.-6 p.m.

Jose "Shake your head, darling" Eber is the stylist to the stars, and unless your face has been on the cover of *People*, he won't even consider taking you. What he will do is conduct a "hair consultation," updating you on color, texture and style, for a mere $50. After that, one of his fleet of accomplished stylists in these two impossibly trendy salons will give you a skillful, chic cut for $45 to $60.

Allen Edwards Salon
345 N. Camden Dr., Beverly Hills
274-8575
Open Mon.-Wed. & Fri.-Sat. 9 a.m.-5 p.m., Thurs. 9 a.m.-7 p.m.

Award-winning stylist Allen Edwards has spent twenty years designing images for a demanding clientele: Mary Hart, Donna Mills, Cathy Lee Crosby and Dustin Hoffman among them. In this studiolike atmosphere (filtered lighting, polished concrete floors), you can stop in for a simple cut ($45 to $75) or be pampered from a long list of hair, makeup and manicure services, with special attention given to professional women. Other locations in Encino, Long Beach, Woodland Hills and Newport Beach.

Joseph Martin
Rodeo Collection, 421 N. Rodeo Dr.,
Beverly Hills
274-0109
Open Mon.-Sat. 8 a.m.-6 p.m.

A marble-floored, ivory-and-black enclave in the Rodeo Collection, Joseph Martin has an impressive number of English-trained stylists on staff—35 at last count. Each is highly specialized in his/her own field. In addition, there are such professional salon services as facials, electrolysis, makeup and manicures. An exclusive product line is formulated to Martin's specifications and sold at the counter. Valet parking.

Ménage à Trois
8822 Burton Way, Beverly Hills
278-4430
Open Tues.-Sat. 9 a.m.-4 p.m.

This spacious beige-and-chrome salon is highly recommended for mature women who want a cut that's stylish but not too trendy. Cuts start at $55. The able staff includes manicurists, who also provide pedicures and sculptured-nails services.

Micheal Villella
Sunset Plaza, 8616A Sunset Blvd.,
W. Hollywood
657-4756
Open Tues.-Sat. 9 a.m.-5 p.m.

Hair stylist/actor Micheal Villella's salon is practically a one-man show, tucked away in chic Sunset Plaza. Art-covered walls and jazz music contribute to the deco-moderne, gallerylike atmosphere. A choice spot for a soothing haircutting experience ($60 to $75), color or perm.

SPAS

The Ashram
2025 McKain Rd., Calabasas (mailing address: P.O. Box 8009), Calabasas
(818) 888-0232

Located in the hills of Calabasas, not far from Malibu, The Ashram (meaning "spiritual retreat") is not for the fainthearted. It's probably the toughest spa in the country. Director Anne-Marie Bennstrom has put together a Spartan regime that results in serious benefits—but not without pain. The day begins at 6:30 in the morning with yoga in a geodesic dome. Next comes a breakfast of fresh-squeezed orange juice, followed by a two-hour hike straight up a rugged mountain. Before lunch (typically a tiny serving of yogurt or cottage cheese, accompanied by a few slices of fresh fruit) is an hour of weight-lifting exercises and an hour of pool sports. Following lunch you can indulge in a one-and-a-half-hour rest period, only to look forward to calisthenics, an evening walk and more yoga. The only real luxury is the daily one-hour massage.

A salad-bar-type dinner is served at 7 p.m. and is usually followed by a lecture by Bennstrom on health-related topics. Spa loungers stay away! The Ashram is not the place to go if you want pampering. It is, however, an absorbing mind-body adventure that will be unlike anything you've ever experienced. Since there are only about eleven guests per week, a familylike relationship develops among guests and staff. All you need to bring is a bathing suit, shoes and cover-up; all other spa attire is provided. Since it costs $1,800 per person per week, most of the guests (male and female) are fairly affluent super-achievers. The waiting list generally hovers around the three-month mark, so book well in advance.

Cal-a-Vie
2249 Kilbirnie Dr., Vista (mailing address: 2249 Somerset Rd., Vista, CA 92084)
(619) 945-2055

Husband and wife William and Marlene Power spent five years researching the spas of Europe before founding Cal-a-Vie, a secluded 126-acre retreat that combines American fitness techniques with fabled European treatments. This three-year-old spa now ranks among the country's best. Designed on the order of a pristine French château, Cal-a-Vie accommodates up to 24 guests a week in individual cottages. A rousing early-morning hike is followed each day by a choice of aerobic circuit training, low-impact sessions, laps in the pool or any number of specialized workouts. Afternoons are devoted to relaxation and rejuvenation through such blissful treatments as a cocoon-style "sea wrap" to detoxify and restore the body's mineral balance, soothing hydrotherapy or a gentle aromatherapy massage using Eve Taylor's oils and botanical extracts. Diet is low in sodium, rich in carbohydrates and incorporates many fresh herbs. A favorite with the fiftysomething crowd, but also popular with young professionals, the spa hosts men's weeks, mother-daughter weeks and other special programs. The inclusive fee is as extravagant as the facilities: $3,500 per person per week, single occupancy.

La Costa
Costa del Mar Rd., Carlsbad
(619) 438-9111

A very country club–like atmosphere pervades La Costa, which is a luxury resort as well as a health spa. There are actually two spas here—one for men and one for women—but both are equally lavish. The grounds are gorgeous, and the spa building houses Roman pools, Swiss showers, steam rooms, massage and facial cubicles and a large beauty salon. The program begins with a medical evaluation and a meeting with a spa counselor, who helps you plan your schedule based on individual goals. A typical day begins at 7:30 a.m. with breakfast in your room, followed by a half-hour walk and a stretch class. What you do after this can be leisurely or stringent, depending on your goals. Choose from aerobics, aqua aerobics, dance, yoga, tennis (there are even grass courts) and golf. You can schedule beauty treatments and massages for any time during the day. The meals are delicious and appetizing; a typical day's calorie intake is a mere 800. Usually you'll find sophisticated, affluent couples here who are concerned enough about their health and appearance to devote a week to a strict diet, exercise and plenty of pampering. Most of the guests here wouldn't last a day at a place like The Ashram. There's a four-day minimum stay at $430 per day, single occupancy. (Basic resort hotel rates run $195 to $255.)

Jane Fonda's Laurel Springs Retreat
Star Rte., Santa Barbara
(805) 964-9646

Situated high above Santa Barbara on Jane Fonda's 122-acre ranch, the Laurel Springs Retreat has been attracting the country's elite since it opened in November 1988. Only four to six guests a week are booked into Fonda's exquisitely outfitted "home," furnished with Tiffany lamps, Appalachian mountain desks, Ralph Lauren sheets and handmade mattresses. Programs are geared to fitness—and we mean *fitness*—with an emphasis on education. The week begins with a complete fitness evaluation by exercise physiologist Daniel Kosich, Ph.D., who prescribes an individual training plan designed to keep guests in their target range. Trainers (one to two per group) spend every waking hour with guests, guiding them through diverse exercise options: a fully equipped gym and pool, aerobic circuit training, hiking in the Santa Barbara Mountains and bike riding in the wine country or on the beach. Videos are provided for guests while using the cardiovascular equipment, but we much preferred watching Fonda's Arabian horses in the orchards below. The 1,200-calorie-a-day diet of low-fat cuisine is offset by the luxury of a daily massage. Everything, including the whirlpool, sauna and laundry services, is included in the cost, which is a hefty $2,500 per person, single occupancy, per week; $2,000 per person, double occupancy. All profits from the retreat go to the Temescal Foundation., which supports Fonda's nearby performing-arts camp for underprivileged children.

The Golden Door

777 Deer Springs Rd., Escondido (mailing address: P.O. Box 1567, Escondido)
(619) 744-5777

Forty miles northeast of San Diego lies a peaceful replica of a Japanese country inn. The Golden Door, with its superb reputation for the perfect balance of exercise, diet, beauty treatments and serenity, is considered to be one of the best spas—if not *the* best—in the country. Credit is due to Deborah Szekely, who has been involved with health resorts for over 40 years. Many people who have never spent a week at The Golden Door think it a snobbish haven for the ultra-rich. But actually, once the 39 guests are checked in, they spend the next week in matching spa-supplied exercise garb, sans jewelry, makeup and fancy hairdos, so no one really knows (or cares) whether the woman next to her in exercise class is an heiress or an underemployed actress who has saved all her waitressing tips to come here.

The exercise-to-pampering ratio is perfect. The day begins at 6 a.m. with a hike. Back in your charming Japanese-decorated room you'll find a breakfast tray and the day's schedule. A typical day might include a stretch class, aerobics, an herbal wrap, water ballet, pool volleyball, a steam bath or sauna, a massage in your room, a choice of sports activities, yoga and a Japanese whirlpool bath. The newest treat is a body scrub with rose-scented clay and silicone beads, administered with silk mitts. The low-calorie, low-sodium, low-cholesterol gourmet menus are delicious, thanks to new chef Tracy Ritter, a petite New Yorker who has a remarkable skill for imparting flavor to low-calorie dishes. Diet or not, we would happily dine again on her rosemary grilled chicken, summer asparagus with red-beet vin-

aigrette and wonderfully light pastries. All you need to bring is a swimsuit, leotard and shoes—everything else is provided. There are men's and couples' weeks a few times a year, but most of the week-long sessions are for women only. This may be one of the best spas in the country, but at $3,500 per week, it's also one of the most expensive.

The Oaks at Ojai

122 E. Ojai Ave., Ojai
(805) 646-5573

Owned by fitness enthusiast Sheila Cluff (who also owns The Palms), The Oaks is extremely popular among Southern Californians who want to experience a week at a spa without having to spend a fortune. Located in downtown Ojai (an absolutely charming town), The Oaks caters to mature men and women, as well as to younger people who aren't on a strict exercise-and-diet regime but would like to begin one. The facilities are hardly luxurious, and the food is pretty dismal, but there's a warm, friendly atmosphere and a well-trained staff. The day begins with a walk through scenic Ojai, followed by a breakfast of fresh fruit and a minuscule bran muffin. For the rest of the day, it's up to the individual guests to decide how much exercise they want. A variety of classes run all day; they include stretch, aerobics, yoga and aqua aerobics. When we visited we noticed that the slimmer guests participated in almost all of the classes, while the plumper ones chose to gossip by the pool. Guests can follow a 750-calorie-per-day diet or tailor meals to their personal needs. We were amused to learn from the owner of a local drugstore how many candy bars he sells to Oaks guests who jog over for a quick fix. Two-night minimum; rates range from $105 to $165 per person per day.

The Palms

572 N. Indian Ave., Palm Springs
(619) 325-1111

Neither particularly strenuous nor particularly expensive, this is the perfect place for mature and older men and women who don't want to spend a fortune on a week of mild exercise and diet. The facilities aren't plush (in fact, they could use a little updating), but the atmosphere is comfortable and friendly. Guests participate in as many or as few exercise classes as they choose, and there's plenty of time to walk the couple of blocks to downtown Palm Springs for shopping. Beauty and health services are available at an extra charge and include massage, facials, hairstyling, manicures and cellulite treatments. Two-day minimum; rates range from $105 to $185 per person per day. There are special rates in the summer, if you're crazy enough to try to withstand the 100-degree-plus weather—though you may sweat the pounds off faster!

Rancho La Puerta
Tecate, Baja California, Mexico
(619) 744-4222, (800) 443-7565

Founder Deborah Szekely, who also started The Golden Door, opened "The Ranch" with her husband, Edward, in 1940. But this coed natural health resort is not at all like its super-elegant sister spa. The facilities themselves are modest, though there are six tennis courts, three swimming pools, a hot whirlpool, in-door and outdoor gyms and a Swedish massage center. It's up to each guest to decide how much exercise and how much pampering to include in his or her daily schedule. But unlike those at other unstructured spas, most of the guests are serious fitness enthusiasts who are here to push their fitness limits. The selection of exercise classes and sports activities is grand, and there are also beauty treatments, for a modest extra charge. The lacto-ovo-vegetarian diet is basically what it sounds like: 1,000 calories per day and includes a nice variety of milk products, nuts, grains, fish and eggs. There's also a virtuous liquid diet that features almond milk and gazpacho. The seven-day plans range from $1,000 to $1,650 per person, double occupancy. Very popular with young singles. Complimentary transportation to and from San Francisco International Airport on Saturday

BOOKS & STATIONERY

BOOKS

Acres of Books
240 Long Beach Blvd., Long Beach
437-6980
Open Tues.-Sat. 9:15 a.m.-5 p.m.

As the name suggests, Acres of Books is an enormous warehouse filled with thousands of used books. For those who love to spend hours browsing through a bookstore, it's easy to spend an entire afternoon here; what's more, you can probably pick up six or seven books for under $20. The sales staff is exceptionally helpful. Acres also carries a few new volumes—primarily coffee-table books.

Bodhi Tree Bookstore
8585 Melrose Ave., W. Hollywood
659-1733
Open daily 11 a.m.-11 p.m.

Organic, holistic, new age: all these terms apply to Bodhi Tree, a bookstore filled with good reads on holistic healing, meditation, psychology and the like. You will also find all sorts of natural, organic and/or holistic gifts, along with greeting cards, crystals, incense and a good selection of meditation and environmental music records. This is Mecca for those in search of self-enlightenment.

Book Soup
8818 W. Sunset Blvd., W. Hollywood
659-3110
Open daily 9 a.m.-midnight.

Book Soup is described by those who work there as "a store for art- and literature-loving residents and expatriates of other countries looking for home papers." Be that as it may, the recently expanded shop carries a particularly good collection of books on show business, music and cooking, as well as a fine selection of new and classic fiction and periodicals. Book Soup regularly hosts book signings by first-time and famous authors; Helmut Newton, Dominick Dunne, Ann Beattie and David Byrne are among them. Quiet by day and crowded by night (when shoppers wander over from Tower Records across the street), Book Soup is one of our favorite browsing bookstores in the city.

Brentano's
Century City Shopping Center,
10250 Santa Monica Blvd., Century City
785-0204
Open Mon.-Thurs. 10 a.m.-9 p.m., Fri.-Sat. 10 a.m.-11 p.m., Sun. 11 a.m.-9 p.m.

This is one of the largest and most respected bookstores in L.A., with a particularly good selection of gift books—and gifts of other sorts, for that matter, including electronic gadgets, Filofax accessories and Mont Blanc pens. Brentano's likes to call itself "a cross between an independent bookstore and a chain, with the benefits of both." Service is above average, considering its size and diversity.

A Change of Hobbit
1433 2nd St., Santa Monica
473-2873
Open Mon.-Fri. 10:30 a.m.-8 p.m., Sat.-Sun. 10:30 a.m.-6 p.m.

Paradise for lovers of science fiction, fantasy and horror tales, with salespeople who are well read on all subjects. Owner Sherry Gottlieb prefers to call her well-stocked shop "a library full of 'speculative fiction'"; whatever it's called, this collection of books has become immensely popular.

Chatterton's Bookshop
1818 N. Vermont Ave., Los Feliz
664-3882
Open Mon.-Sat. 10 a.m.-10 p.m., Sun. noon-9 p.m.

This is a bookstore for serious browsing. Classical music entertains the clientele of rather tousled intellectuals and assorted book lovers while they roam through the aisles of film and theater, literature, poetry, philosophy, children's books and gay books. Of particular note is the excellent selection of paperback fiction and classics, along with the good selection of fine-arts magazines.

La Cité des Livres
2306 Westwood Blvd., Westwood
475-0658
Open Tues.-Sat. 10 a.m.-6 p.m.

The best collection of French classics, contemporary literature and best-sellers in the city. It also stocks French Revolution materials, European travel guides and maps, bilingual dictionaries, cookbooks, comic novels, records and compact discs, magazines and foreign-language learning cassettes. The sales staff (and customers) are always enthusiastic about conversing in French with Francophiles and homesick expatriates.

Crown Books
7916 W. Sunset Blvd., W. Hollywood
851-9183
Open Mon.-Sat. 10 a.m.-9 p.m., Sun. 11 a.m.-5 p.m.

When it comes to prices, you can't beat Crown Books. Now that this chain store has locations literally all over the city, and the savings are so pronounced, many Angelenos won't go anywhere else to buy new books. The selection, however, is limited to the best-seller/how-to/cookbook offerings found at most chain bookshops.

B. Dalton Bookseller
6743 Hollywood Blvd., Hollywood
469-8191
Open Mon.-Thurs. 9:30 a.m.-9 p.m., Fri.-Sat. 9:30 a.m.-10 p.m., Sun. noon-7 p.m.

Though the B. Dalton chain is, as a rule, made up of typical shopping-mall best-seller stores, this branch, once the landmark Pickwick Books, must be commended for its breadth of selection. In two rooms of rather cluttered, musty shelves, you'll find titles in areas ranging from literature and computers to travel and cooking, with a little of everything in between thrown in. It's a perfect after-movie escape from the bizarre Hollywood Boulevard street life. There are many other B. Daltons around town.

Dangerous Visions
13563 Ventura Blvd., Sherman Oaks
(818) 986-6963
Open Tues.-Wed. & Sun. 11 a.m.-6 p.m., Thurs.-Sat. 11 a.m.-8 p.m.

Lydia Marano describes her collection of books as "speculative fiction." The mixture includes children's literature and science fiction/fantasy/horror books and magazines—appropriate either for children or for lovers of science-fiction. New, used and out of print.

Doubleday Book Shop

735 S. Figueroa St., Downtown
624-0897
Open Mon.-Fri. 10 a.m.-7 p.m., Sat. 10 a.m.-6 p.m.

Boasting a better-than-adequate selection of new titles, with an emphasis on business books, Doubleday also stocks good collections of books on Los Angeles, as well as travel books and classics. Best-sellers are usually displayed in the windows. One of the last survivors of the Doubleday Book chain, the shop is housed in an art deco–style building.

Dutton's Books

5146 Laurel Canyon Blvd., N. Hollywood
(818) 769-3866
11975 San Vicente Blvd., Brentwood
476-6263
Open Mon.-Fri. 9:30 a.m.-9 p.m., Sat. 9:30 a.m.-6 p.m., Sun. 11 a.m.-5 p.m.

Dutton's is an excellent all-purpose bookstore with a thorough stock, certainly among the finest in the city. Along with all the current fiction and nonfiction (including lots of paperbacks), there are used reference books of all kinds, art books, children's books, used and out-of-print books, rare leather-bound titles and posters and engravings. The staff is extremely helpful in finding and ordering out-of-stock books. A third branch is in Burbank.

Larry Edmunds Book Shop

6658 Hollywood Blvd., Hollywood
463-3273
Open Mon.-Sat. 10 a.m.-6 p.m.

Everyone in the "industry" (which sometimes feels like nearly everyone in L.A.) knows about Larry Edmunds's small shop—it's *the* place for new and out-of-print books on film, theater and related fields. Whether it's a scandalous biography of a matinee idol, a scholarly study of British films, a poster or a hard-to-find movie still you want, try Edmunds's store first.

Fowler Brothers

717 W. 7th St., Downtown
627-7846
Open Mon.-Fri. 9 a.m.-5:30 p.m., Sat. 9:30 a.m.-5 p.m.

Fowler Brothers is California's oldest bookstore, and even though it's changed locations four times since it first opened over a century ago, this family-run business has retained its old-time atmosphere. A recent expansion allowed for a less cramped feeling, but Fowler Brothers is admittedly "a vertical store." As far as we know, the store has the only children's-literature department in the downtown area. The travel, business and literature sections are excellent, as is the service.

Geographia

4000 Riverside Dr., Toluca Lake
(818) 848-1414
Open Mon.-Sat. 10 a.m.-6 p.m.

Wanderlust victims take note: Geographia is worth a considerable trek. If you don't have a trip planned to some exotic destination, you'll start making plans the minute you visit this shop. In addition to an outstanding collection of national and international travel guides, Geographia has a terrific collection of maps, atlases and globes, along with map accessories (compasses, magnifiers) and travel accessories (foreign-language study tapes, travel alarms).

Hennessy & Engalls Art & Architecture Books

1254 3rd St. Promenade, Santa Monica
458-9074
Open Mon.-Fri. 10 a.m.-6 p.m., Sat. 10 a.m.-5 p.m.

One of the largest bookstores on art and architecture in the world. Every aspect of the subject is on display: landscape architecture, interior design, photography, art technique, building types, world art, graphic design, monographs on artists, and the list goes on. Up to 4,000 books are on sale at any given time, and there's also a large selection of imported magazines and journals. Noted for excellent personal and prompt mail-order service worldwide. The first name on any arts-loving Angeleno's lips.

Herskovitz Hebrew Book Store

442 N. Fairfax Ave., W. Hollywood
852-9310
Open Sun.-Thurs. 9 a.m.-6 p.m., Fri. 9 a.m.-3:30 p.m.

For the last 50 years, Herskovitz has been the major supplier of religious books and icons to L.A.'s synagogues and Jewish homes. You can also find ethnic jewelry here.

Maps to Anywhere Travel Bookstore
1514 N. Hillhurst Ave., 2nd Fl., Los Feliz
660-2101
Open Mon.-Fri. 9 a.m.-6 p.m., Sat.-Sun. noon-4 p.m.

You'd drive by the humble building near the chaotic intersection of Hillhurst, Sunset, Hollywood and Fountain for ages (as we did), never knowing that up on the second floor lurks a tiny shop packed with an astounding collection of guidebooks, maps, language books and travel accessories. Owner Larry Doffing claims to have the largest collection of travel books and language aids in the entire country ("guaranteed, or your gas money back")—and after seeing the more than 3,500 guidebooks and 5,000 color maps, we're not about to argue his claim. Don't plan a trip *anywhere* without a visit here first.

Midnight Special Bookstore
1350 3rd St. Promenade, Santa Monica
393-2923
Open Mon.-Sat. 10:30 a.m.-6 p.m., Sun. noon-5 p.m.

Locals with a special interest in politics and social sciences hang out at this unique bookstore. An entire wall is covered with an extensive collection of magazines; the shop also sponsors evening programs that vary from poetry readings to talks with authors and discussions on current events.

The Mysterious Bookshop
8763 Beverly Blvd., W. Hollywood
659-2959
Open Mon.-Sat. 10 a.m.-6 p.m.

In the retail arm of New York's megamystery publisher, the extensive inventory of mysteries, true-crime and detective and spy thrillers includes rare and out-of-print books. (We spotted first editions by Raymond Chandler and Ross MacDonald on our last visit.) Manager and seasoned bookseller Sheldon MacArthur hosts frequent author appearances and offers a helpful search service.

Outer Limits
14513 Ventura Blvd., Sherman Oaks
(818) 995-0151
Open Mon.-Thurs. 11 a.m.-9 p.m., Fri.-Sat. 11 a.m.-11 p.m., Sun. noon-7 p.m.

Outer Limits is a well-edited "depository of twentieth-century pop culture," according to comanager Jesse Horsting, who, along with most of the staff, is involved in the creative end of publishing. As the Southern California home base for Titan, England's top comic book publisher/retailer, Outer Limits carries the latest in comic, science fiction and dark-fantasy literature. The shop's layout is sleek and uncluttered, and there are frequent book signings by new and well-known talents. You'll also find out-of-print and limited editions, original artwork, film and television memorabilia, special-interest videos, T-shirts and collectible toys. Special requests are welcome.

Scene of the Crime
3764 Wilshire Blvd., Mid-Wilshire
487-CLUE
Open Mon.-Sat. 10 a.m.-8 p.m.

Ruth and Al Winfeldt's well-known shop recently relocated from Sherman Oaks to the art deco landmark Wiltern Theater building. Their stock of 20,000 books includes imports and rare and out-of-print mysteries—from Smiley to Holmes, Simenon to Hammett.

The Scriptorium
427 N. Cañon Dr., Beverly Hills
275-6060
Open Tues.-Sat. 10 a.m.-6 p.m.

Collectors of old letters, manuscripts and documents can buy them, sell them or have them appraised here. The goods and services are not inexpensive, but you'll get the well-respected knowledge of owner Charles Sachs.

Sherlock's Home
4137 E. Anaheim St., Long Beach
494-2964
Open Tues.-Thurs. noon-6 p.m., Fri. noon-7 p.m., Sat. 11 a.m.-6 p.m.

This exceptionally warm and appealing shop is well worth a trip for fans of murder mysteries, spy thrillers and political-intrigue tales. Run by gregarious, mystery-loving Beth Caswell, Sherlock's Home has an outstanding selection of titles, including some hard-to-find imports from England. And books are just the beginning: antique Victorian clocks, marvelous hats (from British bobby hats to Holmesian caps), murder-mystery games, gargoyle bookends, pop-up haunted mansions and all kinds of similar amusements that make great gifts for mystery buffs. Phone and mail orders accepted. Ask to be included on the autograph and mystery-party list.

Sisterhood Bookstore
1351 Westwood Blvd., Westwood
477-7300
Open Mon.-Fri. 10 a.m.-8 p.m., Sat.-Sun. 10 a.m.-6 p.m.

The shelves of this shop are crammed with books on women's history, women's health and psychology and Third World women. There's also a men's and children's section featuring nonsexist literature. Sisterhood also stocks posters, jewelry, cards, T-shirts and records exclusively produced by and performed by women.

The Soap Plant
7400 Melrose Ave., W. Hollywood
651-5587
Open Mon.-Wed. 10:30 a.m.-11 p.m., Thurs.-Sat. 10:30 a.m.-midnight, Sun. 11 a.m.-8 p.m.

L.A.'s late-night hot spot for the best books on style, architecture and design is planted in the middle of a zany tchotchke paradise. Instant gift ideas guaranteed.

Thomas Brothers Maps & Bookstore
603 W. 7th St., Downtown
627-4018
Open Mon.-Sat. 10 a.m.-6 p.m.

To L.A. residents, a Thomas Brothers map book is a Bible, a Talmud, a Koran—the book that guides us through this confused land. Although you can find these map books at many places, you'll find the best selection here, along with every imaginable kind of map and a good selection of books, particularly guidebooks.

Vroman's Bookstore
695 E. Colorado Blvd., Pasadena
(818) 449-5320
Open Mon.-Thurs. & Sat. 9:30 a.m.-6 p.m., Fri. 9:30 a.m.-9 p.m., Sun. noon-5 p.m.

At the turn of the century, when wealthy Easterners who settled in Pasadena wanted to fill their bookshelves with impressive titles, A.C. Vroman catered to them by buying inexpensive sets of the classics and sending them to England for binding. The expensive-looking books soon gained Vroman a solid reputation among Pasadena's moneyed immigrants, and it's still considered one of the area's cultural assets. An excellent all-around bookstore.

Waldenbooks
Westside Pavilion, 10800 W. Pico Blvd., W.L.A.
474-6550
Open Mon.-Fri. 10 a.m.-9:30 p.m., Sat. 10 a.m.-7 p.m., Sun. 11 a.m.-6 p.m.

Nearly every shopping mall in Southern California has a branch of Waldenbooks. These small, well-organized stores stock all the latest fiction and nonfiction, along with some art books, gift items and a noteworthy assortment of videos and books on tape. Don't look for depth of selection, because you won't find it—but you will find helpful salespeople and a pleasant though unremarkable atmosphere. Waldenbooks does more special ordering and mail order than most other chains.

STATIONERY

Aahs!
14548 Ventura Blvd., Sherman Oaks
(818) 907-0300
Open Mon.-Thurs. 10 a.m.-9 p.m., Fri.-Sat. 10 a.m.-11 p.m., Sun. noon-6 p.m.

This is the headquarters for good-humored cards and the latest novelty gifts you never thought you needed. What's an inexpensive piece of jewelry, wacky wall clock or car-window accessory without a jigsaw puzzle card to go along with it? Aahs! stocks all the ingredients for a well-put-together package, including gift wrap, bows and standard greeting cards for more understated tastes. Other locations on Sunset Boulevard, Westwood Boulevard and Wilshire Boulevard in Santa Monica.

Robin Caroll
16930 Ventura Blvd., Encino
(818) 788-3396
Open Mon.-Sat. 10 a.m.-6 p.m.

The Francis Orr of the Valley, selling quality papers, unique, costly invitations and charming fill-in invitations for all occasions. The shop itself is warm and comfortable, with cozy sofas where you can leisurely sort through the numerous books of invitations and personalized stationery. Party-planning services are available.

Ann Fiedler Creations

10544 W. Pico Blvd., W.L.A.
838-1857
Open Mon.-Fri. 9 a.m.-5:30 p.m., Sat. 10 a.m.-3 p.m.

Handmade invitations, decorations, favors, odd accessories . . . you'll find whatever it takes to make your party a success. No matter what type of theme you opt for, Ann Fiedler will either carry or make (from bows to feathers to sequins) all the one-of-a-kind party accessories you can imagine. Fiedler also stocks attractive personalized stationery, as well as a few gift items..

Funnypapers

1953 N. Hillhurst Ave., Los Feliz
666-4006
Open Mon.-Fri. 10 a.m.-6:30 p.m., Sat. 10 a.m.-6 p.m., Sun. 11 a.m.-5 p.m.

A lively, cheery little shop with a very good selection of greeting cards for all occasions. You'll also find colorful wrapping papers, informal invitations and all kinds of fun, inexpensive gifts—from tiny silver frames and rubber stamps to inflatable dinosaurs and wild T-shirts.

Claudia Laub Studio

183 N. Martel Ave., Ste. 220,
Wilshire District
931-1710
Open Mon.-Fri. 9 a.m.-6 p.m.

Claudia Laub is our favorite source for truly exquisite custom invitations. In the business for fourteen years, designer Claudia Laub is dedicated to the disappearing art of hand-set type. Her work ranges from old-world elegance to modern looks on fine rag papers. You select from imported handmade papers, ribbons and raffia ties, and the studio staff fastidiously hand-colors designs and hand-lines envelopes. Greeting cards, calling cards, place cards, business packages, private menus and announcements are all available.

McManus and Morgan

2506 W. 7th St., Downtown
387-4433
Open Mon.-Fri. 8:30 a.m.-5:30 p.m., Sat. 10 a.m.-2 p.m.

No stationery store in L.A. can compete with McManus and Morgan's stock of specialty papers. There are lots of decorative Japanese and pressed flower papers for shoppers with exotic tastes; those interested in a classic look for French matting or creative framing will be swept away by the hand-marbleized imports from Europe. Many papers lend themselves to bookbinding or such decorative purposes as drawer linings, gift wraps and cards. Established in 1923, McManus and Morgan is light years ahead of other stores of its kind when it comes to selection. For calligraphers, artists and others who appreciate truly exceptional handmade papers, it's well worth a trip downtown.

Francis Orr

320 N. Camden Dr., Beverly Hills
271-6106
Open Mon.-Sat. 9 a.m.-5:30 p.m.

The emphasis here is on quality and tradition. There are books full of invitations and stationery that can be printed or engraved with just about any monogram you could imagine. One nice bonus here is that the sales staff is helpful and seems to know every rule of etiquette that applies to invitations and thank-yous. There's also a nice selection of leather desk blotters and accessories, desk-related antiques, preprinted invitations and Limoges china boxes.

Stampa Barbara

6903 Melrose Ave., Hollywood
931-7808
Open Mon.-Sat. 10 a.m.-6 p.m., Sun. noon-5 .

An offshoot of the original Stampa Barbara in, you guessed it, Santa Barbara, this store stocks an awesome inventory (over 25,000 at last count) of rubber stamps—everything from traditional holiday images to outrageous tongue-in-cheek joke designs. Ideas, too, are always in generous supply, and there are markers, blank cards, glitter glue and rainbow and metallic ink pads with which to embellish your handmade creations.

CHILDREN

BOOKS

Children's Book & Music Center
2500 Santa Monica Blvd., Santa Monica
829-0215
Open Mon.-Sat. 9 a.m.-5:30 p.m.
  If you have a child in your life, you're sure to spend more time (and money) than you should at this granddaddy of children's bookshops. The lavishly illustrated hardbacks by the front door will put you way over budget before you even get to the main shelves. (Luckily, many of these storybooks also come in paperback, which are kept in bins near the back.) A great source when you need a book on a specific topic: sibling rivalry, death of a grandparent, science projects for preschoolers, ethnic holidays, drawing space ships and so on. Best of all, the staff truly knows about every book and record in stock and will know what you're looking for even before you do—or they'll let you alone to browse for hours.

CLOTHES

American Rag Cie Youth
136 S. La Brea Ave., Wilshire District
965-1404
Open Mon.-Wed. 10:30 a.m.-9 p.m., Thurs.-Sat. 10:30 a.m.-10:30 p.m., Sun. noon-7 p.m.
  A spin-off of the nearby American Rag Compagnie for adults, this store specializes in the "sporty chic" look for children, which means classic colors (navy) and hip neutrals (khaki, brown and black) in new European and '50s vintage clothing. On our last visit, we came across richly detailed Tyrolean jackets, mini–riding pants, baggy jeans, quilted leather jackets, Wally Cleaver–style windbreakers, black-silk party dresses, trench coats, hats and '50s bow ties. Shoes range from thick-soled Dr. Martens to traditional English styles labeled "By Appointment to Her Majesty the Queen." There are even reproductions of '50s cowboy (and cowgirl) outfits, complete with chaps, skirts, vests and a tent for showing them all off in. Take note that it's open late some nights.

Animal Kracker
17324 Ventura Blvd., Encino
(818) 986-0264
Open Mon.-Sat. 10 a.m.-6 p.m.
  Lots of hand-painted items and out-of-the-ordinary accessories, including leather headbands, wooden fish barrettes and decorated socks. Clothing for boys runs from Gotcha surf duds to Christian Dior suits; for girls, from bright cotton pieces by Cut Loose to Jessica McClintock's frilly frocks. Owner Abby Faranesh is a former teacher who handpicks educational toys and a complete library of books. Newborn to preteens and juniors; shipping and complimentary gift wrap available.

Bartel Chapter IV
203 N. Larchmont Blvd., Larchmont Village
462-5310
Open Mon.-Sat. 10 a.m.-5 p.m.
  There's a delightful, international mix of children's clothes in this small Hancock Park shop, including J.G. Hook classics, Florence Eiseman knits, Sarah Prints' pajama-inspired play sets from Israel and related separates from Mexx of Holland. The baby stuff is particularly nice, with unusual sleepers, diaper sets and tiny T-shirts. A bookcase along one wall has a small but superb collection of children's books, including Beatrix Potter. There are some adorable stuffed animals from Gund, plus Brio trains, Ambi rattles and other small toys. The January and July sales are always excellent. Infant to size fourteen, boys and girls.

Bear Threads
1624 Montana Ave., Santa Monica
828-6246
Open Mon.-Sat. 10 a.m.-6 p.m., Sun. 10 a.m.-5 p.m.
  Never mind the name—Bear Threads is a merchandise-packed store with absolutely everything from European designer clothes to hand-knit sweaters. The store is devoted to cotton unisex looks, both foreign and domestic, and carries enough Oilily of the Netherlands to outfit Mom and the kids. There are also shoes, accessories, European periodicals and children's videos.

Bloomers for Kids

Sunset Plaza, 8646 Sunset Blvd.,
W. Hollywood
854-6901
Open Mon.-Sat. 10 a.m.-7 p.m., Sun. noon-5 p.m.

Modeled after a New York boutique, Bloomers for Kids coordinates trendy to sophisticated looks in head-to-toe presentations. A precious selection includes high-end European entries. Infant to size fourteen, boys and girls.

Chez Kids

16571 Ventura Blvd., Encino
(818) 783-5363
Open Mon.-Sat. 10 a.m.-5:30 p.m.

Mothers and others flock to Chez Kids for its exclusive Kotton Kelly line of preshrunk cotton basics in bright colors, which are reasonably priced and available in ten different styles. It also carries a good selection of American and European clothing, toys, gifts and accessories for infant to size seven for boys, to size fourteen for girls. The store wisely provides a play area, has complimentary "confetti" gift wrap, and takes special orders..

Costumes for Kids

7206 Melrose Ave., W. Hollywood
936-5437
Open Mon.-Fri. 9 a.m.-5:30 p.m., Sat. 11 a.m.-5 p.m.

As far as we know, this is the only costume shop in the country exclusively for children. Eighty percent of the costumes, all of which are of ready-to-wear clothing quality, are designed and made on the premises of comfortable, natural-fiber fabrics. The costumes range from characters from film favorites (*Batman* and *Ghostbusters*) to nursery-rhyme characters (Cinderella, Captain Hook, Peter Pan). Accessories include special-occasion flower garlands and "birthday headbands" for $15. Sizes two through twelve.

Dak

Malibu Country Mart, 3835 Cross Creek Rd., Malibu
456-9771
Open Mon.-Sat. 10:30 a.m.-5:30 p.m., Sun. 11:30 a.m.-5:30 p.m.

Learning to dress for the Malibu lifestyle comes early—and easily—at Dak. Mostly cotton, mostly European clothing by Petit Boy, Mousefeathers and Maugin keeps company

with unusual books and gifts: handcrafted mobiles, hand-painted accessories, quilts and dolls. Infant to size seven, boys and girls.

Lollipop Shop

137 S. Robertson Blvd., Beverly Hills
659-7501
Open Mon.-Sat. 9:30 a.m.-5:30 p.m.

This shop is anything but a place for the basics. Oriented to its celebrity clientele, the Lollipop Shop features pricey European imports, private-label and upper-end unique items. Custom orders, shipping and complimentary gift wrapping are available. Infant to preteen.

Malina's Children's Store

2913 Main St., Santa Monica
392-2611
Open Mon.-Sat. 10:30 a.m.-6 p.m., Sun. 11 a.m.-6 p.m.
11163 Santa Monica Blvd., W.L.A.
312-5347
Open Mon.-Sat. 10 a.m.-5:30 p.m.

European designer Malina Gerber lends dashes of unexpected wit to her mostly unisex, stylish children's staples. She was one of the first to dress babies in black.

Mon Petit Chou

203 N. Robertson Blvd., Beverly Hills
276-9910
Open Mon.-Fri. 9:30 a.m.-5:30 p.m., Sat. 10 a.m.-4:30 p.m.

The taste level here is of silver-spoon quality. It's an ideal place for well-heeled parents and grandparents to indulge in custom-designed linens and exclusive clothing, decorative nursery items, hand-smocked dresses, Victorian suits for boys, whimsical stuffed toys and heirloom-quality christening gowns. Newborn to 6 years old.

Pee Wee Segal

Fred Segal Melrose, 8106 Melrose Ave.,
W. Hollywood
651-3698
Open Mon.-Sat. 10 a.m.-7 p.m., Sun. noon-6 p.m.

This is one of the best sources in town for newborn and toddler-size trendyware, with such novelties as baby bandanas, mismatched outfits with their own suspenders, neon-colored cotton knits, picture frames covered with little plastic toys, designer bibs, socks, stuffed animals and a showcase of candy.

Pixie Town

400 N. Beverly Dr., Beverly Hills
272-6415
Open Mon.-Sat. 10 a.m.-5:30 p.m.

Beverly Hills babies have been getting their party and play clothes at Pixie Town for almost 50 years. The saleswomen are sticklers for good quality and perfect fit. American and European clothes and shoes in newborn through size fourteen.

Fred Segal Baby

Fred Segal Santa Monica, 500 Broadway, Santa Monica
451-5200
Open Mon.-Sat. 10 a.m.-7 p.m., Sun. noon-6 p.m.

A small store brimming with big ideas, this place carries costly European clothing (leather and velvet jackets), trendy imported shoes (real-leather cowboy boots), funky jewelry, decorated socks, books, toys, even furniture and strollers. The perfect place to find a novel gift for children aged 3 months to 4 years.

This Little Piggy & Co.

238 S. Beverly Dr., Beverly Hills
859-0914
Open Mon.-Sat. 10 a.m.-6 p.m.

This store does a booming business in layette items and baby gifts, but it also excels in European clothing for boys and girls (Fix of Sweden, Petit Faune of France, Bini of West Germany). Hand-decorated wearables by local artisans are always in demand and run from delicate beading for baby to daring rhinestones and sequins for a six-year-old. Christening gowns and wedding-party gear can be custom-designed. The staff will help plan your nursery while you order furniture and accessories such as hand-painted rocking chairs and step stools

---

FURNITURE

Baby Motives

8362 W. 3rd St., W. Hollywood
658-6015
Open Mon.-Fri. 10 a.m.-5:30 p.m., Sat. 10 a.m.-5 p.m., or by appt.

When you've decided on black and white for the baby's nursery, Baby Motives is the place to shop. Sure, they've got cribs, changing tables and rockers in predictable pastels,

but it's those hot, new, the-grandparents-will-hate-it colors that make this place special. This is a one-stop nursery store, with wallpapers, fabrics, custom bumper pads, linens, kicky-colored rubber pants and good decorating advice in addition to the excellent furniture selection—from traditionally styled cribs to postmodern convertibles designed to last well into junior high. This shop is especially strong on all the latest baby gadgets—owner and young mother Wendy Pennes says she selects them only if they're safe, stimulating and a good value. There's also a nice selection of children's books and clothing. Baby Motives boasts that it supplies everything but the baby.

Funiture

8451 Beverly Blvd., W. Hollywood
655-2711
Open Mon.-Sat. 10 a.m.-5 p.m.

The secret behind the success of architect Gary Gilbar's furniture for kids (and kids at heart) is a deft touch with a band saw. Headboards are done up like silhouettes of castles, dinosaurs or quarterbacks; shelves sprout palm fronds or look like little cottages. Rockers are hand-painted to match cribs. It's all great fun, and never *too* cute; the styles work for everything from newborn nurseries to teenagers' rooms. There are plenty of offbeat accessories: banana nightlights, Red Grooms posters, taxi toy boxes and so on. Everything is available in six colors or by custom order.

HAIR CARE

Merry-Go-Round

18633 Ventura Blvd., Tarzana
(818) 343-9000
Open Tues.-Sat. 10 a.m.-5:15 p.m.

No screaming kids at this salon, thanks to the cookies, video games and balloons provided to keep the young clients occupied. Haircuts start at $12 for boys and girls. Very-first haircuts receive a certificate. A hectic, high-energy, fun place. Parents' cuts, too.

Tipperary

9422 Dayton Way, Beverly Hills
274-0294
Open Tues.-Sat. 9:30 a.m.-5:30 p.m.

Tipperary is *the* place for the young set to go for shampoos, perms and the latest bobs for girls and spiked looks for boys. Cuts and blow-drys start at $16 for boys and $19 for girls. Adults in need of a cut can head upstairs to Tipperary North.

The Yellow Balloon

12114 Ventura Blvd., Studio City
(818) 760-7141
Open Mon.-Wed. & Fri. 9:30 a.m.-5:15 p.m., Thurs. 9:30 a.m.-6:30 p.m., Sat. 9 a.m.-5 p.m., Sun. noon-4 p.m.

The Yellow Balloon was the first L.A. salon to cater to kids. Babies, boys and girls get snipped and curled here for $9 to $15 (adults are $20). Those having their very first cut receive a special certificate and a lock of hair in an envelope. There are plenty of stuffed animals and video games to keep the kids amused, and they all walk out with balloons, lollipops and cookies.

TOYS

Allied Model Trains

4411 S. Sepulveda Blvd., Culver City
313-9353
Open Mon.-Thurs. & Sat. 10 a.m.-6 p.m., Fri. 10 a.m.-9 p.m.

In its new and improved location, Allied Model Trains could be the world's largest model-train store, stocking a vast assortment of model trains and everything there is to go with them. Allied does carry some inexpensive lines, though it specializes in some of the better and more costly trains, such as those by Lionel, Marklin and Athearn.

California Toys & Costume

752 S. Broadway, Downtown
622-0184
Open Mon.-Sat. 9:30 a.m.-7 p.m., Sun. 11 a.m.-6 p.m.

It's worth a drive downtown for this enormous selection of mass-produced toys, stuffed animals and model sets. You'll find everything imaginable, including educational toys, at competitive prices. Nothing is particularly unique, however. Now owned by Hollywood Toys & Costume, the store also stocks an extensive supply of costumes, masks, makeup and accessories for children and adults. Both rentals and sales.

The Doll Emporium

13035 Ventura Blvd., Studio City
(818) 506-7586
Open Thurs.-Sat. 11 a.m.-4:30 p.m.

One of the largest doll troves in the country. You'll find everything having to do with dolls here, including Barbie dolls, antique dolls, Alexander dolls, doll books and free doll appraisals.

Imaginarium

Century City Shopping Center,
10250 Santa Monica Blvd., Century City
785-0227
Open Mon.-Fri. 10 a.m.-9 p.m., Sat. 10 a.m.-6 p.m., Sun. 11 a.m.-6 p.m.

Imaginarium's motto, "A Toy Store Kids Can Handle," is true in more ways than one. Not only do kids adore this place, but they're also allowed—nay, encouraged—to handle every item in the place. Resembling a dream playroom more than an ordinary toy store, Imaginarium sells an unbeatable collection of toys and games that fascinate and amuse children while at the same time challenging and even educating them. An exemplary toy store.

Intellitoys

Beverly Center, 121 N. La Cienega Blvd.,
W. Hollywood
652-6141
Open Mon.-Fri. 10 a.m.-9 p.m., Sat. 10 a.m.-8 p.m., Sun. 11 a.m.-6 p.m.

Here we have toys for child prodigies, but this place is really more appealing to the adults who *claim* they're there to buy a gift for their kid—and end up spending an hour or so "trying them out." It's a sign of the times that children past the age of 6 will ignore the shelves of enticingly displayed games, toys, books and dolls and head straight for the back, where video games and kids' home computers are on display. There are amusing windup toys, imported educational toys and wonderful stuffed animals. Exemplary service.

Lakeshore Curriculum Materials Company

8888 Venice Blvd., W.L.A.
559-9630
Open Mon.-Fri. 9 a.m.-5:30 p.m., Sat. 9 a.m.-5 p.m.

It's an odd name for one of L.A.'s best-kept secrets. What first appears to be a dull assortment of teaching aids quickly turns out to be a broad collection of hard-to-find toys, supplies, furniture and books for children—not those trendy, overpriced, baby-yuppie baubles, but real things like bags of buttons, colored pipe cleaners, dollhouses that you won't be afraid to let your kids play with, costumes, dinosaur books, unusual building and counting toys and sturdy tricycles. There's also a large area in which kids can test drive toys, under parental supervision.

The Last Wound-Up
7374 Melrose Ave., W. Hollywood
653-6703
Open Mon.-Thurs. 11 a.m.-10 p.m., Fri.-Sat. 11 a.m.-midnight, Sun. noon-8 p.m.

Here you'll find every sort of enchanting windup toy, starting at $1.50. There are toys from all over the world, "tubbies" that perform in water and just generally ingenious designs (the Godzilla that hatches out of an egg was one of our favorites). Japanese windup toys from the '50s are prize finds.

Mostly Miniatures
13759 Ventura Blvd., Sherman Oaks
(818) 990-6713
Open Tues.-Sat. 10:30 a.m.-5 p.m., Sun. 1 p.m.-5 p.m.

Mostly Miniatures stocks dollhouses in all shapes and sizes, and everything that's related to the making and furnishing of them. This shop will also appeal to ambitious craftspeople; there are thousands of vignette ideas and teeny gifts to choose from. For those who'd rather not dirty their hands, custom dollhouse design and construction are offered.

Toys & Joys
7375 Melrose Ave., W. Hollywood
658-8697
Open Mon.-Thurs. 10 a.m.-11 p.m., Fri.-Sat. 10 a.m.-midnight, Sun. noon-9 p.m.

Cheryl and Sebastian Giefer have created the perfect toy store: exceptionally well-designed European imports line up next to adult art objects selected for their toylike character. Add to that Bauhaus-inspired mobiles of metal and fabric, musical instruments, an all black-and-white line for infants, fascinating books, games and gadgets, children's decorated T-shirts and shoes and funky jewelry for the whole family. You won't find a war toy or even a plastic gun in sight; what you will find are touchable displays that break the traditional toy-store mold. Open late at night, too.

The Very, Very Beast
233 Santa Monica Place, Santa Monica
394-0439
Open Mon.-Fri. 10 a.m.-9 p.m., Sat.-Sun. 11 a.m.-6 p.m.

This is the complete, aardvark-to-zebra animal shop, a wild kingdom carrying ceramic, pewter, crystal, glass and stuffed animals and animal books and stationery. You'll find pigs in every preposterous color. You can also find such witty creations as wolves in sheeps' clothing. There are more teddy bears than the law should allow. Dogs of every recognizable breed are available, including irresistible mutts, and there is a six-foot gorilla for big spenders.

CLOTHES & JEWELRY

ACCESSORIES

Faux Body Ornaments
7309 Melrose Ave., W. Hollywood
931-3763
Open Mon.-Sat. noon-8 p.m., Sun. 1 p.m.-6 p.m.

This full-service accessory salon is as well known for its overdone interior design as for its intriguing inventory. Faux works with 25 designers and a variety of materials to create artful, advanced statements in jewelry and accessories.

Gloves by Hammer of Hollywood
7210 Melrose Ave., W. Hollywood
938-0288
Open Mon.-Fri. 9 a.m.-5 p.m.

Hammer has worked in Tinseltown since 1946, providing all manner of gloves for moviestars and other glitterati: Marilyn Monroe wore Hammer's gloves, and Michael Jackson still does. It's worth a visit just to take a peek at the selection here: handcrafted gloves like these are almost a lost art. Be sure to see the top-drawer quality in spandex, English lace and satin. And, of course, custom designs are done.

House of Canes

5628 Vineland Ave., N. Hollywood
(818) 769-4007
Open Tues.-Fri. 10 a.m.-5 p.m., Sat. 10 a.m.-3 p.m.

Owner Mark Fontaine stocks over 10,000 canes, ranging from simple wooden walking sticks to elaborate creations embellished with ivory or jade. Popular traveling models are a cane that folds to twelve inches and a "shooting stick," the handle of which converts to a seat for sitting out long waits at Customs. Prices, as you might imagine, vary quite a bit—from $10.50 to $2,000.

L.A. Eyeworks

7407 Melrose Ave., W. Hollywood
653-8255
Open Mon.-Fri. 10 a.m.-noon & 1 p.m.-7 p.m., Sat. 10 a.m.-noon & 1 p.m.-6 p.m.

Home to off-the-wall window displays and the utmost in optical names and frames. On Saturdays, this place is so packed with Melrose Avenue trendies (and a famous face or two) that it locks the door to control the crowds. We wonder if it's worth the wait—the prices certainly aren't.

Maya

7614 Melrose Ave., W. Hollywood
655-2708
Open Mon.-Thurs. & Sat. 11 a.m.-7 p.m., Fri. 11 a.m.-9 p.m., Sun. noon-6 p.m.

Maya has sterling-silver and costume bracelets, brooches and an outstanding selection of bolo ties. But the best buys in this shop are earrings—there are over 5,000 pairs to choose from. Many are of ethnic origin, including beaded, American Indian and Balinese styles.

Oliver Peoples

8642 Sunset Blvd., W. Hollywood
657-2553
Open Mon.-Fri. 10 a.m.-7 p.m., Sat. 10 a.m.-6 p.m.

This cutting-edge boutique is giving L.A. Eyeworks a run for its money. The owners acquired a cache of optical treasures from the art deco and art nouveau eras and have used it as a basis for a collection of classically inspired eyewear fashions. Two of its best-sellers are frames that combine tortoiseshell eye pieces and temples with a wire bridge; and clip-on sunglasses circa the 1930s. Prices, for many budgets, are prohibitive.

Patina Millinery

119 N. La Brea Ave., Wilshire District
931-6931
Open Wed.-Sat. noon-6 p.m.

Jodi Bentsen and Katrin Noon share fine-arts backgrounds and a love of textiles, ribbons and trims. After training privately with traditional milliners, they opened Patina, a charming shop in which their creations showcase the vintage feathers, buttons, buckles, taffeta bows and silk flowers they've collected over the years. Like the shop itself, the hats are labors of love, made completely from scratch. The partners have also designed and gathered a small collection of easy-wearing, one-of-a-kind clothing pieces, scarves, "country primitive" jewelry and such architectural details as vintage lighting fixtures, picture frames and old latticework. Custom hat designs and mail order available.

Rosenthal/Truitt

8648 Sunset Blvd., W. Hollywood
659-5470
Open Mon.-Sat. 10 a.m.-6 p.m., Sun. noon-5 p.m.

This cozy den for men's fine furnishings harkens back to eighteenth- and nineteenth-century England. Traditionalists will love such well-bred notions as cashmere socks, leather-bound books and antique cuff links. Another branch in the Century City Shopping Center.

So Much & Company

8669 W. Sunset Blvd., W. Hollywood
652-4291
Open Mon.-Sat. 10 a.m.-5:30 p.m.

It's amazing how many one-of-a-kind items are packed into this tiny boutique: everything from gold, silver and brass jewelry to extraordinary picture frames, belts, hair accessories, hand-knit sweaters, leather purses, baby clothes, beaded earrings and much more

CASUAL CLOTHES (MEN & WOMEN)

Banana Republic

9669 Santa Monica Blvd., Beverly Hills
858-7900
Open Mon.-Sat. 10 a.m.-6:30 p.m., Sun. noon-6 p.m.

For all the Walter Mittys of the world, a browse in Banana Republic is the next best thing to actually being there. Where? The tropics, jungles, cobblestone villages, deserted beaches—any place you'd need snazzy but serviceable ensembles (make no mistake, Banana Republic turns out ensembled travelers). This is a good place for khaki in every configuration, comfortable cotton shirts and vests with no less than a dozen pockets. The store is an excursion in browsing: all kinds of safari props, old steamer trunks, hundreds of hats overhead and great old music from Bob and Bing's *Road* pictures lend a truly adventurous air. Four other Los Angeles–area locations, plus one in South Coast Plaza.

Eddie Bauer
Woodland Hills Promenade,
285 Promenade Mall, Woodland Hills
(818) 884-5255
Open Mon.-Fri. 10 a.m.-9 p.m., Sat. 10 a.m.-6 p.m., Sun. noon-5 p.m.

Seattle-based Eddie Bauer is an excellent chain that sells high-quality clothing and equipment for the outdoor life. Nothing is particularly fashionable, but there are great basics in both men's and women's sportswear: khaki pants, flannel shirts, cotton turtlenecks, sturdy shoes and lightweight but warm jackets. There's also a wide selection of well-made Eddie Bauer–label backpacks and small traveling items for both campers and jet-setters: money bags, insect repellents, binoculars and so on. Other locations in Santa Monica, Costa Mesa, Beverly Center and Glendale Galleria.

Benetton
7409 Melrose Ave., W. Hollywood
852-0775
Open Mon.-Sat. 11 a.m.-8 p.m., Sun. noon-7 p.m.

In the winter most of the garments are wool; in the spring and summer, cotton. But no matter what the season, these young, colorful unisex separates are always fun to mix and match. Sweaters are the specialty—bold, dynamic cardigans, pullovers, vests, turtlenecks and sweater dresses. Under the brotherhood banner of its United Colors and United Contrasts advertising campaigns, Italy's Benetton has been a huge American retail success story: there are nearly 30 stores in Southern California, including many in shopping malls.

Camp Beverly Hills
9640 Santa Monica Blvd., Beverly Hills
274-8317
Open Mon.-Sat. 10 a.m.-6:30 p.m., Sun. noon-5 p.m.

A candy-pink eclectic store that's just plain fun, particularly for kids. There are lots of funky, "preworn" jeans, cotton shirts, ethnic-print T-shirts, Hawaiian shirts and accessories. For the label-conscious, about one-quarter of the inventory is printed with the store's campy (but highly touristy) logo.

CP Shades
2937 Main St., Santa Monica
392-0949
Open Mon.-Wed. & Fri. 11 a.m.-7 p.m., Thurs. 11 a.m.-9 p.m., Sat. 11 p.m.-6 p.m., Sun. noon-5 p.m.

Quintessentially Californian, CP Shades puts comfort above all else. Soft, quality cotton knits, elastic waists and loose cuts result in sportswear so relaxed you'll feel like living in it. Since eliminating the middle man and selling only direct from its own stores, CP Shades has relaxed its prices, too: a T-shirt that used to sell for $50 now ranges from $18 to $38. The wide assortment of cropped turtlenecks, long cardigans, skirts of all lengths, shorts and pants, all in muted solids and stripes, will keep you in comfortable chic. Also in Beverly Hills. Catalog available.

Mark Fox
7326 Melrose Ave., W. Hollywood
936-1619
Open Mon. noon-7 p.m., Tues.-Thurs. 11 a.m.-7 p.m., Fri.-Sat. 11 a.m.-8 p.m., Sun. noon-6 p.m.

This is a good place to find vintage (new and used) leather jackets, Western shirts and boots in the John Wayne vein. For a price, Fox will create custom designs in boots, belts, jewelry and motorcycle accessories. A favorite haunt of Bruce Springsteen.

The Gap
1931 Wilshire Blvd., Santa Monica
453-4551
Open Mon.-Fri. 10 a.m.-9 p.m., Sat. 10 a.m.-6 p.m., Sun. 11 a.m.-6 p.m.

The Gap used to be your basic cheesy mall store, à la Miller's Outpost, but several years ago it was transformed into *the* great place for colorful, all-American playclothes for men and women. The only vestiges of the old days are the shelves of Levi's jeans in every size and color; the rest of the merchandise, all Gap-labeled, is made up of fun and attractive cotton shirts, pleated twill trousers and shorts, bold cotton sweaters, basic T-shirts, sweats, colorful socks and belts and faded denim jackets, all at reasonable prices. Except for the occasional wool sweater, everything here is made of sturdy cotton. This store is one of the biggest and best. There are branches literally all over the city, including smaller branches on Lake Street in Pasadena, Melrose, Main Street in Santa Monica.

Livestock

708 N. Heliotrope Dr., Silverlake
662-8886
Open Tues.-Sat. 11 a.m.-7 p.m., Sun. 11 a.m.-5 p.m.

Judy Kameon seeks out relatively unknown L.A. designers who excel in bold clothing and accessories with a sense of humor. A few examples: Lisa Weger's bra tops with cups that look like eyes, flowerpot hats and J.M. Reva's "junk" jewelry. This store is a must if you're dining at Café Mambo (across the street), but we get a kick out of Livestock anytime.

Na Na

631 Santa Monica Blvd., Santa Monica
393-7811
Open Mon.-Sat. 10:30 a.m.-7 p.m., Sun. 11 a.m.-6 p.m.

The new-wave accoutrements here are more sensibly priced than those you'll find in Melrose Avenue boutiques. All the merchandise is brand-new, and much of it is imported from England. Na Na is known for its stock of clunky Dr. Marten shoes with air-cushioned soles. There are bins of underwear, cotton socks, skinny ties and colored tights. There are also studded bracelets, imported records, English music magazines, miniskirts and, of course, skin-tight black jeans.

Paradise Found

7617 Melrose Ave., W. Hollywood
852-9894
Open daily 11 a.m.-7 p.m.

Outfitting ourselves for the islands is easier now that this Honolulu-based manufacturer has found its way to the mainland. Prints range from the ever-popular parrot and orchid designs to reproductions of such classics as "scenic hibiscus" or old postcard motifs. There are

Tahitian tie-dyed pareos, short and long sarongs, sun dresses and the ubiquitous aloha shirts ($38). Everything is moderately priced and can be customized—movie mogul Jerry Weintraub ordered a single pair of drawstring "baggies" in four different prints.

Fred Segal Melrose

8106 Melrose Ave., W. Hollywood
651-4129
Open Mon.-Wed. & Fri.-Sat. 10 a.m.-7 p.m., Thurs. 10 a.m.-8 p.m.

Walk into Fred Segal Melrose on any given day and you'll come out with a new understanding of that *California feeling.* It's the sights and sounds of trends in motion: Fred Segal, L.A.'s perpetually tanned retailer. Now owned by nephew Ron Herman, the separate boutiques that comprise the store are united by a red, white and blue color scheme and a star-spangled banner of customers. The "jeans bar" is a raging success, a survivor of Segal's first store a couple of decades ago. Tucked into every nook and cranny is a highly edited and generally costly selection of unusual goods—merchants here have a sure sense of what's hot and hip. You'll find avant-garde menswear, a designer-eyewear counter and a flashy array of T-shirts.

Fred Segal Santa Monica

500 Broadway, Santa Monica
393-4477
Open Mon.-Sat. 10 a.m.-7 p.m., Sun. noon-6 p.m.

The latest emporium (opened in 1985) for the Fred Segal brand of fashion is bigger (and some say better) than the Melrose Avenue outpost. The 35,000-square-foot store has everything you ever wanted in a new-age mall. The charged atmosphere includes a sometimes jarring disc jockey, and the red, white and blue color scheme persists. You may feel compelled to go in all different directions at once, but don't forget to break for a flavor-packed muffin at Mrs. Beasley's, one of four good (and pricey) eateries on the premises.

Sweats & Surf

Galleria at South Bay, 1815 Hawthorne Blvd., Redondo Beach
542-6543
Open Mon.-Fri. 10 a.m.-9 p.m., Sat. 10 a.m.-7 p.m., Sun. 11 a.m.-6 p.m.

This quintessential California beach store in a quintessential California beach town is the place for neon-shade T-shirts, shorts and swim trunks to put together with boogie boards, wetsuits, backpacks and sunglasses. And no true unstudied beach ensemble is complete without color-coordinated thongs (in hot yellow, pink or blue). Good selection of sweats for kids.

Vacationville
7372 Melrose Ave., W. Hollywood
653-6683
Open Mon. 11 a.m.-10 p.m., Tues.-Sun. 11 a.m.-midnight.

Come here for the best presentation of printed T-shirts in town, including lots of L.A.-oriented creations. Customized designs available.

Wilkes Sport
Beverly Center, 121 N. La Cienega Blvd., W. Hollywood
659-8725
Open Mon.-Fri. 10 a.m.-9 p.m., Sat. 10 a.m.-8 p.m., Sun. 11 a.m.-6 p.m.

A spin-off of the award-winning Wilkes Bashford line. The 100 percent private-label collection consists of knit-based casual and career sportswear, shoes and accessories for the thirtysomething crowd. Other locations in Century City Shopping Center and Beverly Hills.

JEWELRY

Butler & Wilson
8644 W. Sunset Blvd., W. Hollywood
657-1990
Open Mon.-Sat. 10 a.m.-6 p.m.

This is the English counterpart to Kenneth Jay Lane, but for a younger set. Direct from London come faux gems with a flamboyant following: devoted fans include Elton John, Little Richard, Jerry Hall and Princess Di. The design team also styles oversized glittery accessories for Giorgio Armani and Calvin Klein.

Cartier
370 N. Rodeo Dr., Beverly Hills
275-4272
Open Mon.-Fri. 10 a.m.-5:30 p.m., Sat. 10 a.m.-5 p.m.

There are some truly gorgeous pieces of jewelry here, the best of which are designed from original Louis Cartier drawings and

made by hand in Paris. Unfortunately, many of the sportier designs have been widely copied. The store established its reputation with its watches and now offers two popular perfumes. Don't miss the cases in the back, where you'll find a (relatively) reasonably priced sterling-silver collection. The leather goods are excellent in quality, rather boring in style and astronomical in price.

Fred Joaillier
401 N. Rodeo Dr., Beverly Hills
278-3733
Open Mon.-Sat. 10 a.m.-6 p.m.

Joaillier's reputation precedes him. This is not Cartier or Tiffany; it's strictly California glitter here, not the least of which is the Force 10 collection of jewelry, which mixes eighteen-karat gold with stainless-steel nautical cable. Elegant, polite and terribly expensive, the place perfectly encapsulates the ostentatious wealth that flourishes in this resort-mentality town.

Kenneth Jay Lane
441 N. Rodeo Dr., Beverly Hills
273-9588
Open Mon.-Sat. 10 a.m.-6 p.m.

As a leading designer of faux jewels, Lane has made a name for himself with couture designers and the jet set. His stunning gemstone look-alikes have starred on fashion runways and TV's now-defunct *Dynasty*.

Laykin et Cie
9634 Wilshire Blvd., Beverly Hills
278-1168
Open Mon.-Sat. 10 a.m.-5:30 p.m.

This small jewelry boutique on the ground floor of I. Magnin features tasteful pieces in eighteen-karat gold and platinum, as well as precious and semiprecious stones. The styles are as conservative and as discreetly handsome and elegant as I. Magnin's merchandise—with elegant prices to match.

M Gallery
8649 W. Sunset Blvd., W. Hollywood
652-4964
Open Mon.-Sat. 10 a.m.-6 p.m.

A small but dramatic showcase for up-to-the-minute jewelry design, from the traditional to the outrageous. Some choice designers: Robert Lee Morris, Katherine Post and Londoner Tom Binns. Another branch in the Beverly Center.

Tiffany & Company

9502 Wilshire Blvd., Beverly Hills
273-8880
Open Mon.-Sat. 10 a.m.-5:15 p.m.

No Beverly Hills shopping expedition is complete without a trip to this West Coast branch of the Fifth Avenue classic. Tiffany carries exquisite formal and sporty jewelry, designed by such artists as Paloma Picasso and Elsa Peretti, plus beautiful gift items made of silver, crystal and china, clocks, stationery, leather goods, scarves and its own Tiffany fragrance. Browse through the entire store—you'll have plenty of time for it while you're waiting for one of the slow-motion salespeople to get around to helping you.

Van Cleef & Arpels

300 N. Rodeo Dr., Beverly Hills
276-1161
Open Mon.-Fri. 10 a.m.-5 p.m.

No fun little trinkets here—just major pieces of jewelry with major price tags. The collections are rather conventional, but the workmanship and the quality of the stones are exceptional.

MENSWEAR

Bijan

420 N. Rodeo Dr., Beverly Hills
273-6544
Open by appt. only (fragrance department open Mon.-Sat. 10 a.m.-6 p.m.).

You've seen this pearly-toothed character popping out of billboards and leaping flamboyantly across the pages of fashionable magazines as part of an ad campaign for the Bijan fragrance line. You can experience Bijan live in his exclusive boutique—if you are either wealthy or clever enough to receive an appointment. If you do, you'll find an opulent display of fur (a cap is about $7,000), leather, silk, cashmere, and Bijan's "classic" wool suits, priced at $3,000 to $3,500. Bijan shoes and fragrances are also sold here, and the boutique can custom-design any item.

Brooks Brothers

604 S. Figueroa St., Downtown
620-9500
Open Mon.-Sat. 9 a.m.-6 p.m.

Brooks Brothers is an American institution, but we were still amazed not to find an abundance of young preps trying on the cotton trousers, tweed jackets, leather loafers and oxford shirts. Instead, most of the shoppers are middle-age and older gentlemen who began dressing this way long before it became stylish. What is surprising is the number of women buying the crested cotton shirts (invented here) and men's tie-back boxer shorts, both more reasonably priced than equivalent women's merchandise. As we went to press, Brooks Brothers announced its new line of more contemporary (if such a thing is possible here), stylish clothing, particularly for women. Other locations in Century City and Fashion Island in Costa Mesa.

Carroll & Company

466 N. Rodeo Dr., Beverly Hills
273-9060
Open Mon.-Fri. 8 a.m.-6 p.m., Sat. 9:30 a.m.-6 p.m.

Carroll & Company started dressing Beverly Hills men 40 years ago—and what it's selling now isn't too different from what it was selling then. If you're a nice, conservative gentleman who's looking for a nice pair of shoes or a nice camel hair jacket, you'll find a nice salesman to help. Boring, but some good values (for Rodeo Drive) nonetheless.

Chanins

Beverly Center, 121 N. La Cienega Blvd., W. Hollywood
652-2626
Open Mon.-Fri. 10 a.m.-9 p.m., Sat. 10 a.m.-8 p.m., Sun. 11 a.m.-6 p.m.

Targeted to fashion-aware men for whom price and pragmatic styling are a consideration. The broad-ranging, at times inconsistent, inventory is in sync with California lifestyles and includes representatives from Nancy Heller, Hugo Boss, Axis and Katherine Hamnett. There are several other branches, including one in Westwood Village and in a number of shopping malls.

Clacton & Frinton

731 N. La Cienega Blvd., W. Hollywood
652-2957
Open Mon.-Sat. 10 a.m.-6 p.m.

"The Englishman in the Tropics Look" is how Michael and Hilary Anderson describe their summer line. What this shop actually features is traditional English styling spiced with '40s and '50s Americana: the results are modish jackets and baggy pleated trousers.

The Andersons design and manufacture 90 percent of their merchandise, using imported cottons and woolens. There is also some womenswear.

Sami Dinar
9677 Brighton Way, Beverly Hills
275-2044
Open Mon.-Sat. 9:30 a.m.-6:30 p.m.
The shop's chichi location belies its amiable atmosphere. An impeccable dresser, Sami Dinar has a sharp eye for European and American design, plus a penchant for a relaxed but elegant look and personal service. His small store is packed with "subdued yet different" offerings: double-breasted suits by Canali, hand-loomed sweaters by Marienbad, deco-inspired ties by Modules, colorful patterned socks by Laura Pearson, sterling-silver accessories, butter-soft leather coats and luxurious bathrobes.

Ecru
7428 Melrose Ave., W. Hollywood
653-8761
Open Mon.-Sat. 11 a.m.-7 p.m., Sun. noon-6 p.m.
The outside of this monumental store (with ECRU spelled out in 30-foot-high metal letters) attracts as much attention as its contents. Ecru is really three stores under the single banner of brilliant design: men's and women's European and American clothing, Ecru couture and Ecru shoes from an international designer roster. For men, expect to find Bill Robinson, Compagnia Della Pelli and Hilton.

G.B. Harb & Son
3359 Wilshire Blvd., Mid-Wilshire
386-5496
Open Mon.-Wed. & Fri. 10 a.m.-6 p.m., Thurs. 10 a.m.-9 p.m., Sat. 10 a.m.-4:30 p.m.
George Harb's shops are temples to conservatism—à la Brooks Brothers and Carroll & Company—but the styles and fabrics are more elegant here than at its famous competitors. There's a marvelous choice of beautiful Egyptian pima cotton and oxford shirts, sober suits, handsome cashmere and wool sports coats, accessories and colorful, casual menswear, all at very high prices. But you'll get your money's worth in the impeccable fabrics and tailoring that manages to be classic without being boxy or dull, along with friendly, help-

ful service. Other stores include one in South Coast Plaza, a small one in downtown's Seventh Street Marketplace and a shop on Larchmont Boulevard in Hancock Park, which features equally conservative, handsome and expensive womenswear.

Fred Hayman Beverly Hills
273 N. Rodeo Dr., Beverly Hills
271-3000
Open Mon.-Sat. 10 a.m.-6 p.m.
One needs new trousers less often than one needs a drink. And for this reason, Fred Hayman Beverly Hills (formerly Giorgio) is a precious address. It is, in fact, one of those rare clothing stores in the world that has a bar for its customers. You may profit from this ruse if you stop here awhile to survey this quasi-historic place (one of the first stores on Rodeo Drive, which makes Hayman a true veteran), where most of the Hollywood stars have left their autographs both on photographs and memorable checks. Hayman's latest women's fragrance, "273" (as in 273 Rodeo Drive), promises not to go the much-commercialized route of its predecessor, Giorgio, because it's only available here. To dress from this high-profile salon is always an adventure; one can leave outfitted head to foot in true elegance or walk away garishly disguised as a nouveau riche. The racks remind us of an enormous tossed salad, where the best shows up next to the worst. In the women's department, there are unbelievable Academy Award–quality dresses, and, despite the appalling prices of such luxuries, you can find some items of good taste. The majority of the menswear is imported from Italy and chosen with a discerning eye. And if you are willing to pay $900 for a sports coat that is 50 percent wool and 50 percent cashmere (which would cost half the price in Milan), you'll have no problem finding something.

Jaeger
9699 Wilshire Blvd., Beverly Hills
276-1062
Open Mon.-Sat. 10 a.m.-6 p.m.
Fine English sportswear that's simple, elegant and well cut. The fabrics—tweed, flannel, camel hair, cashmere—are top of the line and more appropriate for the conservative and traditional than the young and trendy, though

this is still more stylish than Carroll & Company and Brooks Brothers.

Maxfield

8825 Melrose Ave., W. Hollywood
274-8800
Open Mon.-Sat. 11 a.m.-7 p.m.

Maxfield is the place to outfit yourself for dinner at DC3 or an opening at MOCA, especially if you wear black. This minimalist, gallerylike enclave showcases au courant clothing from European, American and Japanese designers; of special note is Armani for Men and the Yohji Yamamoto boutique. Personal and high-fashion accessories, many of which are purchased by elitists purely for conversation's sake, are in fine form.

Modern Objects

4355 Melrose Ave., Silverlake
669-8309
Open Mon.-Sat. 11 a.m.-7 p.m., Sun. noon-4 p.m.

Restaurateur Mario Tamayo (of Cha Cha Cha and Café Mambo fame) and designing partner Jef Huereque specialize in sporty elegance for men. That translates as '40s-inspired suits, red-satin boxers, full-cut trousers, panne velvet or brocade vests, antique silk pocket squares, neckwear, French-cuffed shirts and artful sterling-silver cuff links.

Mr. Guy

369 N. Rodeo Dr., Beverly Hills
275-4143
Open Mon.-Sat. 9:30 a.m.-6 p.m.

Both a stylish, affluent young man and an older, more conservative gentleman could walk into Mr. Guy and readily outfit themselves from head to toe. Suits and slacks are beautifully cut and can be altered on the premises. The ties and silk and cotton shirts range from plain, solid colors to the contemporary prints of Japanese and European designers. There's also a good selection of quality shoes and tuxedos.

New Man

9628 Wilshire Blvd., Beverly Hills
859-0916
Open Mon.-Sat. 10 a.m.-6 p.m.

New Man is a French line of contemporary, well-fitting lightweight cotton and denim sportswear, but the jeans, jackets and shirts really have that oh-so-casual California look. There are numerous shades and styles to choose from. Women's styles and sizes are also available.

Polo Ralph Lauren

444 N. Rodeo Dr., Beverly Hills
281-7200
Open Mon.-Sat. 10 a.m.-6 p.m.

Although Ralph Lauren first achieved success by designing women's clothing, he really hit his stride in menswear. Traditional English haberdashery, with its strong traditions and rich vocabulary, has afforded him a broad range for restatement and interpretation. He has extended this motif from the clothing to the Polo shop as a whole. In the entryway, slowly circling wooden fans and bleached-wooden benches surrounded by potted palms vaguely suggest a British colonial outpost in, say, the Bahamas—an impression that evaporates the instant you cross the shop's threshold. Upon leaving the foyer, lined with tall mahogany cases displaying vanity kits, jewelry and other antique personal items, you enter the men's department, where you are surrounded by the paraphernalia of traditional masculine pursuits: carved wooden walking sticks, trophies, mounted game heads, equestrian equipment. And man's best friend, a symbol of the landed gentry and of general bonhomie, is everywhere in effigy—carved wooden dogs, bronze dogs, dog-headed canes and framed photos and paintings of dogs. The clothing is equally masculine—traditional and English-tailored, yet with a dash of MGM. The same goes for the shoes and accessories, which are executed in the finest leathers. For quality this high and for what is truly investment dressing, the prices are not exorbitant. Boys' and women's clothing is also sold, and the entire second floor is devoted to Lauren's home furnishings. Polite service and a mahogany bar on the top floor, where you can contemplate your choices over a cappuccino, complete the gentlemen's-club atmosphere.

Raffles

16921 Ventura Blvd., Encino
(818) 905-8205
Open Mon.-Sat. 10 a.m.-6 p.m., or by appt.

Raffles for men has probably one of the most impressive collections of Hugo Boss in the country, as well as a full line of Axis, Reds, Falke by Jeff Sayre and Basco. Sweaters—a hard-to-find item in Los Angeles—are plentiful in styles by all of the aforementioned, as well as Nani Bon and Laura Pearson (who also designs conversation-piece socks).

Studio
1615 Montana Ave., Santa Monica
394-2673
Open Tues.-Sat. 10 a.m.-6 p.m.

Literally off the beaten track (tucked into an alley off Montana), Studio is the kind of store you're glad you went out of your way to find. By design, this tiny cubicle is filled with colorful clothing by Clacton & Frinton (a westside exclusive) in wonderful contrast to elegant shaving accessories and leather travel kits by Italy's G. Lorenzi. The "jewel box" assortment includes eyeglasses by L.A. Eyeworks, Trumpers traditional English scents and sterling-silver jewelry from Santa Fe.

Theodore Man
451 N. Rodeo Dr., Beverly Hills
274-8029
Open Mon.-Sat. 10 a.m.-6 p.m.

Specializing in the slouchy, dressed-down look, Theodore Man presents lots of cotton, lots of linen and lots of easy-on-the-eye colors. Think of the sportier pages of *GQ*, and you'll get the picture. Prices are a little higher than average.

Traffic
Beverly Center, 121 N. La Cienega Blvd., W. Hollywood
659-4313
Open Mon.-Fri. 10 a.m.-9 p.m., Sat. 10 a.m.-8 p.m., Sun. 11 a.m.-6 p.m.

Clothing here is described as slightly off-center. Traffic is apt to carry tuxedos with a twist, unique European color mixes and local talent exclusives. Outstanding customer service.

Weathervane for Men
1132 Montana Ave., Santa Monica
395-0397
Open Tues.-Sat. 10 a.m.-6 p.m., Sun. noon-4 p.m.

A well-chosen mix of fine-quality, contemporary clothing reminiscent of the old Jerry Magnin store. There are no serious suitings

here, just tasteful classics with a twist by Andrew Fezza, Jhane Barnes, Axis and Zanella.

DISCOUNT

Rick Pallack
4554 Sherman Oaks Ave., Sherman Oaks
(818) 789-7000
Open Mon.-Fri. 10 a.m.-8 p.m., Sat. 10 a.m.-6 p.m., Sun. 11 a.m.-5 p.m.

High-fashion European and American clothing at below-retail prices. Designerwear often spotted here includes clothing by Hugo Boss, Daniel Schagen and Zanella. Rick's selection is so good, in fact, that he is no longer thought of as a discount merchant. Winner of awards for his service and quality, Pallack wardrobes many of Hollywood's leading men.

Sacks Fashion Outlet (S.F.O.)
652 N. La Brea Ave., Hollywood
930-2313
Open Mon.-Fri. 10 a.m.-8 p.m., Sat. 10 a.m.-7 p.m., Sun. 11 a.m.-6 p.m.

David Sacks has become perhaps L.A.'s best, and best-known, discount-sportswear merchant. The emphasis is on natural fabrics, and the selection of all-cotton dress shirts (often less than $15) is superb. There are also cotton, wool and silk sweaters, handsome ties (often under $10), attractive sports coats (under $100), cotton polo shirts, casual jackets, and leather and suede jackets and skirts. What sets Sacks apart from other discounters is a brand-name lineup which rivals that of better department stores, at ridiculously low prices. We find the selection varies so much that it takes regular visits to hit the jackpot. There are several other locations, including Studio City, Tarzana, West Los Angeles and West Hollywood.

LARGE SIZES

Beverly Hills Big and Tall
9687 Wilshire Blvd., Beverly Hills
274-9468
Open Mon.-Sat. 9:30 a.m.-6 p.m., Thurs. 9:30 a.m.-8 p.m., Sun. noon-5 p.m.

The only shop in Beverly Hills dedicated exclusively to big and tall men, this shop features suits and sports coats by Perry Ellis, Lanvin and Hickey-Freeman.

SHIRTS

Jack Varney
214 N. Beverly Dr., Beverly Hills
278-4500
Open Mon.-Fri. 10 a.m.-6 p.m., Sat. 10 a.m.-5 p.m.

Whether you're after a classic tuxedo shirt, a sports shirt or a dress shirt, Jack Varney will custom-tailor one that fits perfectly. Varney uses fine materials and works very quickly.

SHOES

Bally of Switzerland (for men)
340 N. Rodeo Dr., Beverly Hills
271-0666
Open Mon.-Sat. 10 a.m.-6 p.m.

Their comfort and excellent leather have made Bally shoes a favorite of men all over the world—at least men who prefer the slimmer lines of European shoes over more solid-looking American classics. We find some of the designs, especially the loafers, to be unattractive, but there are enough fashionable styles to make even the trendiest young men happy.

Bally of Switzerland (for women)
409 N. Rodeo Dr., Beverly Hills
275-0902
Open Mon.-Sat. 10 a.m.-6 p.m.

Mostly classic (though some are rather dated) shoes, handbags and leather jackets of excellent quality. Unfortunately, they're sold by very pushy salespeople. This always-busy shop is small, but the range of styles and colors is large.

Bootz
2654 Main St., Santa Monica
396-2466
Open Mon.-Sat. 10 a.m.-11 p.m., Sun. 10 a.m.-7 p.m.

Owned by a Texan, Bootz does a rousing business in top-notch Western boots (Justin, Nocona, Tony Lama, Larry Mahan), as well as handmade belts, boot straps, tips and heel plates. Exotic skins range from neon-green-marked lizard to sea bass. Bootz also carries one of the largest selections of shoe boots in L.A. Regular patrons include Billy Crystal, Martin Sheen and Kelly McGillis. One other location in Beverly Hills.

Church's English Shoes
9633 Brighton Way, Beverly Hills
275-1981
Open Mon.-Sat. 9 a.m.-6 p.m.

Excellent quality has given these classic English men's shoes the fine reputation they deserve. Styles and prices are rather middle-of-the-road—not too old, not too new, not too low and not too high. Actually, most of Church's customers are more interested in comfort and quality (which are ample) than in designs (which are rather clunky).

Charles Jourdan
9654 Wilshire Blvd., Beverly Hills
273-3507
Open Mon.-Sat. 10 a.m.-6 p.m.

Just about every department store in the city carries some of Jourdan's ever-popular pumps, but if you want to see *all* the styles and *all* the colors (along with some attractive hats, gloves, jewelry, watches, scarves, hair accessories, belts, handbags and sunglasses), you really should pay a visit to this large chrome-and-glass shop. The prices aren't nearly as shocking as Frizon's and Pfister's, and the styles are about as tasteful and classic as you can get. The store also offers shoes for men and, like every designer name in town, its own fragrance.

Nordstrom
Westside Pavilion, 10830 Pico Blvd., W.L.A.
470-6155
Open Mon.-Sat. 10 a.m.-9:30 p.m., Sun. 11 a.m.-6 p.m.

When you're in the market for, say, a pair of red pumps, come to Nordstrom, where'll you'll find twenty or more styles to choose from: from moderately priced Bandolinos and frisky Esprits on up to more sedate Anne Kleins, magnificent Italian Sesto Meuccis and Ferragamos, and to-die-for Andrea Pfister lizard. Nordstrom has by far the best women's shoe department of all the department stores—and it's one of the only places in town where women with size ten (and bigger) feet can find truly fashionable shoes. The men's selection is simpler, although there are plenty of handsome styles from Cole-Haan, Ralph Lauren, Timberland and Nordstrom's own shoemakers. The children's shoe department is also excellent. And where else does a tuxedoed pianist play Sondheim while you slip on the borrowed peds? Nice touch. Nordstrom is also located in the Glendale Galleria, South Coast Plaza, Topanga Plaza and the Galleria at South Bay.

Le Petit Jean

368 N. Beverly Dr., Beverly Hills
858-3843
Open Mon.-Sat. 10 a.m.-6 p.m.
Westside Pavilion, 10830 Pico Blvd., W.L.A.
475-7856
Open Mon.-Fri. 10 a.m.-9 p.m., Sat.-Sun. 10 a.m.-6 p.m.

Le Petit Jean's line of women's shoes is attractive, fashionable, well made and extremely reasonably priced. The shoes are made in Mexico, and with the peso devaluations of the last few years, the prices have stayed quite low—usually about $50 a pair for the full line of colorful pumps. Definitely worth a visit.

Privilege

1470 Brighton Way, Beverly Hills
276-8116
Open Mon.-Sat. 10 a.m.-6:30 p.m.

The best shop to buy quality, fashion-forward women's shoes at reasonable prices. Ninety percent of the stock is made specially for the store in Italy, France or Spain. There are always terrific sandals, flats, boots and pumps. Like seemingly every other halfway-successful L.A. store, Privilege has begun cloning itself and can be found at many higher-end shopping centers, including the Beverly Center and Westside Pavilion.

The Shoe and Clothing Connection

17404 Ventura Blvd., Encino
(818) 784-2810
Open Mon.-Thurs. & Sat. 10 a.m.-6 p.m., Fri. 10 a.m.-9 p.m., Sun. noon-5 p.m.

A fabulous collection of men's and women's shoes and clothing from American and European makers. The selection and service alone make a trip to the Valley worthwhile, and the sales are outstanding.

VINTAGE CLOTHES

Aaardvark's

7579 Melrose Ave., W. Hollywood
655-6769
Open daily 11 a.m.-9 p.m.

L.A.'s answer to New York City's Antique Boutique, Aaardvark's carries primarily used clothing, and it looks it. If you don't mind more than a little wear and tear, you'll have a field day going through the stacks and racks of leather jackets, beaded sweaters, bowling shirts and '50s dresses.

American Rag Cie

150 S. La Brea Ave., Wilshire District
935-3154
Open Mon.-Sat. 10:30 a.m.-10:30 p.m., Sun. noon-7 p.m.

The largest used-clothing store in Los Angeles, this place appeals to more than just those hard-core rag pickers who delight in eccentric dressing. It's a great browse spot and trip down memory lane: band uniforms from Carthage, Texas, tie-dyed T-shirts, out-to-there crinolines and Jackie Kennedy coats. An entire section is devoted to black and white clothing: tuxes and such for men (jackets and pants sold separately) and little black dresses for women. American Rag imports much of its used clothing, sometimes in great quantity, as with the overcoats and khaki jackets. There are also some new designer items and a miniboutique that features haberdashery menswear by New Republic. This is a head-to-toe store with affordably priced new hats, shoes, gloves, jewelry and patterned socks.

American Rag Cie Youth

See "Children."

Brenda Cain

1617 Montana Ave., Santa Monica
393-3298
Open Mon.-Sat. 11 a.m.-6 p.m.

When other vintage clothing stores have fallen with the changing times, Cain's sure sense of style will keep this small shop buzzing. Her Hawaiian shirts are carefully chosen and in excellent condition. She makes vests and pillows from '40s-era tablecloths and skirts from old floral-print rayon. The store is also notable for ties and collectible salt and pepper shakers. Besides clothing, you'll find exquisite antique linens, watches, Bakelite and costume jewelry and Victorian gold and sterling silver.

Cinema Glamour Shop

343 N. La Brea Ave., Hollywood
933-5289
Open Mon.-Fri. 10 a.m.-4 p.m.

The clothes found here are donated by actors and actresses, and the proceeds go to the Motion Picture and Television Fund. Most of the items are slightly worn contemporary sportswear pieces, but if you're lucky, you'll visit when it receives a shipment of new clothing from designers or stores that have gone out of business. On our last visit, there was an excellent selection of new chiffon dresses for women and sports coats for men.

The Junk Store
11900 Wilshire Blvd., W.L.A.
479-7413
Open Mon.-Fri. noon-6 p.m., Sat. 11 a.m.-6 p.m.
This junk store is a good westside source for vintage Hawaiian shirts and a full range of accessories: hats, scarves, hankies, cuff links, ties and so on. Purists might be disappointed to find a new line of rayon and cotton sportswear by Cactus Club. Prices are somewhere between Aaardvark's and Montana Avenue shops.

Leathers and Treasures
7511 Melrose Ave., W. Hollywood
655-7541
Open Mon. 11 a.m.-8 p.m., Tues.-Sat. 11 a.m.-9 p.m.
A flea market with four walls. It offers a vast selection of vintage leather jackets from biker to bomber styles, cowboy boots, Mexican silver, rhinestone jewelry and satin-covered shoes to color-coordinate with your '40s ball gown.

Out of the Past
515 Wilshire Blvd., Santa Monica
394-5544
Open daily 1 p.m.-7 p.m.
Specializing in formalwear and jewelry from the '40s and '50s, Out of the Past rents and sells new and period tuxedos and dinner jackets. This is the place to come when you suddenly find yourself in need of tails or a strapless dress. Same-day service.

Repeat Performance
7264 Melrose Ave., W. Hollywood
938-0609
Open Mon.-Sat. 11 a.m.-6 p.m.
Of all the Melrose Avenue vintage-clothing stores, this one stocks the most well-preserved items, which explains why customers have to ring a buzzer for admittance. In the back room, there are garments and accessories that date back to the late 1800s. But the best buys

are the Western Americana wear for men and women, including vintage hand-painted skirts from Mexico, '50s gabardine men's shirts and costume jewelry.

A Star Is Worn
7303 Melrose Ave., W. Hollywood
939-4922
Open Mon. noon-7 p.m., Tues.-Sat. 11 a.m.-7 p.m., Sun. noon-5 p.m.
Beats us as to why, but celebrity cast-offs are hot sellers here. It's probably the only place in town where you can buy one of Cher's sequin-covered bras, for about $500. You can also find clothes formerly worn by Belinda Carlisle, Catherine Oxenberg and Prince. Whether you want to own them is another thing.

Time After Time
7425 Melrose Ave., W. Hollywood
653-8463
Open Mon.-Sat. 11 a.m.-6 p.m.
This boutique specializes in wardrobes from the golden era of cinematography. On any visit, there could be gems once worn by Marilyn Monroe, Claudette Colbert, Errol Flynn or Tyrone Power, as well as Victorian wedding dresses and petticoats, ball gowns from all eras and lots of beaded garments from the twenties. The prices don't cater to bargain hunters; these clothes are for those who truly appreciate the romantic, sometimes dramatic styles of days gone by.

WESTERNWEAR

King's Western Wear
6455 Van Nuys Blvd., Van Nuys
(818) 785-2586
Open Mon.-Thurs. & Sat. 9:30 a.m.-6 p.m., Fri. 9:30 a.m.-8 p.m.
Literally a westernwear department store, this place is paradise for cowboys and anyone else in a yahoo mood. There's a king-size selection of Stetson and Resistol hats ($35 and up), Acme boots for men and women ($79 and up), fancy buckles, tooled leather belts, authentic Western suits, embroidered shirts, square-dancing outfits, saddles and kids' clothing.

Western Frontier Establishment

Farmer's Market, 150 S. Fairfax Ave.,
Wilshire District
934-0146
Open Mon.-Sat. 9 a.m.-6:30 p.m., Sun. 10 a.m.-5 p.m.

Before moccasins were sold all over Paris, visiting Europeans flocked to this small store to choose from its 200-plus styles. Now they come for a fine selection of leather jackets by Avirex, Robert Comstock and Schott. Lots of Western paraphernalia, too, as well as Native American crafts.

WOMENSWEAR

Abbruzzese

1706 S. Catalina Ave., Redondo Beach
540-9406
Open Mon.-Sat. 10 a.m.-6 p.m.

This store has expanded its delicious assortment of lingerie to embrace a total sportswear concept. Everything for sophisticated lifestyles is here—from plush-velour running suits by L.A.'s own Christine Albers ($400) to tailored jackets and trousers by Bogner and Crisca. In addition to lingerie and casual clothes, you can also find shoes, fragrance, accessories and even sportswear-inspired eveningwear. Excellent personal service.

Laise Adzer

Beverly Center, 121 N. La Cienega Blvd.,
W. Hollywood
659-2813
Open Mon.-Fri. 10 a.m.-9 p.m., Sat. 10 a.m.-8 p.m., Sun. 11 a.m.-6 p.m.

The look here is big and loose: soft, earthtone ensembles with a definite Moroccan/Middle Eastern feel. The full skirts, billowy pants, fringed shawls and roomy tops in nubby cotton and rayon all coordinate well. The perfect accessories are wide, jewel-studded belts and heavy jewelry, which the shops also sell. Prices seem high for what you get, though. Several other branches, including one on Rodeo Drive and in the Century City Shopping Center.

Laura Ashley

Century City Shopping Center, 10250
Santa Monica Blvd., Century City
553-0807
Open Mon.-Fri. 10 a.m.-9 p.m., Sat. 10 a.m.-6 p.m., Sun. 11 a.m.-6 p.m.
Beverly Center, 121 N. La Cienega Blvd.,
W. Hollywood
854-0490
Open Mon.-Fri. 10 a.m.-9 p.m., Sat. 10 a.m.-8 p.m., Sun. 11 a.m.-6 p.m.

Everything's frilly, flowered, feminine and flounced—and strictly for those who want to look like maidens ready for an afternoon in the country. Since many of these little-girl dresses don't have waistbands, they make wonderful maternity dresses. Laura Ashley also sells picture frames, address books and other gift items covered with its famous floral print cottons. The same fabrics are also available by the yard and are used by its decorators for draperies, bedspreads and wall coverings. The look can be oppressively cute if overdone, but the fabrics do lend themselves to creating a lovely baby's nursery.

Le Chat

329 Manhattan Beach Blvd., Manhattan Beach
545-4551
Open Mon.-Sat. 10 a.m.-6 p.m., Sun. noon-5 p.m.

This highly personal little shop is filled with soft dressing ideas and one-of-a-kind finds. The selection of casually elegant clothing includes sportswear by up-and-coming English designer Bryan Emerson, silk knits from San Francisco's Catherine Bacon and private-label jewelry, scarves and belts. Definitely worth a trip to Manhattan Beach for its highly specialized approach.

Ecru

7428 Melrose Ave., W. Hollywood
653-8761
Open Mon.-Sat. 11 a.m.-7 p.m., Sun. 11 a.m.-6 p.m.

Probably the most inspired collection of women's clothing and accessories on Melrose. If the striking storefront doesn't stop you in your tracks, the merchandise will: clothing by Selwyn/Peck, Gordon Henderson, Marina

Spadafora, Sara Sturgeon; couture offerings by Michel Hardy, Costume National, Martine Sitbon, David Fielden; shoes and hats by Philippe Model; and jewelry extraordinaire. Ecru is a real star along L.A.'s shopping highway.

The Esprit Store
8941 Santa Monica Blvd., W. Hollywood
659-9797
Open Mon.-Fri. 10 a.m.-8 p.m., Sat. 10 a.m.-6 p.m., Sun. 11 a.m.-6 p.m.

No mere department store's paltry selection of Esprit goodies will do after you've seen this bowling alley turned super-store filled with nothing but Esprit. Famous for spirited sportswear (in colors that your mother always said clashed), the stock is set off against a high-tech black interior (including black shopping carts to encourage you to buy more than you can carry). From T-shirts and belts to shoes and coats, there's an entire lifestyle waiting here, including Esprit bedding in co-ordinating bold graphics. And to get them on the fashion track early, there's a large children's department—it's marketed as a unisex collection, but few little boys would be duped into it.

Charles Gallay
8711 Sunset Blvd., W. Hollywood
858-8711
Open Mon.-Sat. 9:30 a.m.-6 p.m.

A monument to minimalism, Charles Gallay's store is the antithesis of his ex-wife Madeleine's store across the street. Among the seriously stylish contents: clothing by Azzedine Alaia, Romeo Gigli, Callaghan, Giorgio di Sant'Angelo, Norma Kamali and Isaia; shoes by Maud Frizon, Stephane Kelian and Robert Clergerie; and artful jewelry by Stephen Dweck and Tom Binns.

Madeleine Gallay
8710 W. Sunset Blvd., W. Hollywood
657-9888
Open Mon.-Sat. 10 a.m.-6 p.m.

A rose by any other name is Madeleine Gallay (ex-wife of Charles Gallay, proprietor of the Gallay store directly across the street). Visit both stores and you'll agree: Charles and Madeleine have dramatically different fashion tastes. The romantic theme, from an eccentric English rose garden just outside to the petal-pink walls inside, runs throughout the shop. Unconventional European designers include Rifat Ozbek, Sybilla and John Galliano. The lighthearted (and costly) accessories are a real treat.

Greta
141 S. Beverly Dr., Beverly Hills
274-9217
Open Mon.-Sat. 10 a.m.-6 p.m.

Those closed-minded individuals who are convinced that life (at least *fashionable* life) does not exist south of Wilshire Boulevard are missing out on a wonderful shop. Although Greta does a terrific job of buying better European sportswear (Jenny, Byblos, Studio Ferrè), some of this shop's best items come from her own drawing board. An equally enticing evening selection (Vicky Tiel, Carolyne Roehm and Eva Chung, plus Greta's own) is now available at Greta Night, 157 S. Beverly Drive.

Ice
Beverly Center, 121 N. La Cienega Blvd., W. Hollywood
657-4845
Open Mon.-Fri. 10 a.m.-9 p.m., Sat. 10 a.m.-8 p.m., Sun. 11 a.m.-6 p.m.

The mix is the message at Ice. Owner Juliana Claridge is one of L.A.'s most innovative retailers, stocking her store with a fire-and-ice assortment for the fashion-aware customer, from $20 T-shirts to suits by the influential Jean-Paul Gaultier. The designer roster covers the world and includes local and emerging talent. Uncommon accessories make the clothes work.

Jaeger
9699 Wilshire Blvd., Beverly Hills
276-1062
Open Mon.-Sat. 10 a.m.-6 p.m.

Nothing high-fashion or trendy in this classic English shop, but if you're after an impeccably tailored camel-hair blazer or a soft and beautiful cashmere sweater to wear with either standard wool trousers or black-leather pants, you'll find them at Jaeger.

Betsey Johnson

7311 Melrose Ave., W. Hollywood
931-4490
218B Main St., Venice
452-7911
Open Mon.-Sat. noon-7 p.m., Sun. 1 p.m.-6 p.m.

Betsey Johnson is a love-her-or-hate-her designer who has been doing pretty much the same thing for twenty years. Her styles are young, flattering, sexy . . . but predictable. Since everything has a Johnson label, the stock seems a little thin: one line, one season. To her credit, Johnson has always had a wacky way with knits. You'll find lots of stretchy lycra shapes and eye-popping prints. Off-season sales can provide real steals.

Jôna

12532 Ventura Blvd., Studio City
(818) 762-5662
1013 Swarthmore Ave., Pacific Palisades
459-4800
1325 Montana Ave., Santa Monica
458-0071
Open Mon.-Sat. 10 a.m.-6 p.m.

This store's motto, "At Jôna we put you together," couldn't be more appropriate. If you usually like to browse without a salesperson's assistance, this is not the place for you. But if you're after a total look, Jôna is a sure bet. Hardly any of the merchandise is actually on the floor; instead, members of the sales staff bring elegant silk and linen ensembles and dramatic cocktail dresses out from the seemingly endless stockroom and work patiently with each customer (as well they should, given the lofty prices). Most shoppers walk out with a complete wardrobe: clothing, shoes and accessories.

Eleanor Keeshan

8625 W. Sunset Blvd., W. Hollywood
657-2443
Open Mon.-Sat. 10 a.m.-6 p.m.

A well-established store for designs by Donna Karan, Valentino, Calvin Klein, Ungaro, Anne Klein II and Gianfranco Ferrè, as well as local luminaries Nancy Heller and Michelle Lamy. Very good for ladies who are no longer in their twenties but who still like to dress with a little youthful pizzazz. The large eveningwear collection covers a broad price range and includes both imported couture and domestic dresses.

The Limited

Beverly Center, 121 La Cienega Blvd.,
W. Hollywood
652-2423
Open Mon.-Fri. 10 a.m.-9 p.m., Sat. 10 a.m.-8 p.m., Sun. 11 a.m.-6 p.m.

The Limited is one of Wall Street's biggest success stories, and it's easy to see why. This chain store sells its own lines of stylish sportswear at reasonable prices. Look to Outback Red for romantic, English-inspired sweaters, embellished rayon blouses, jeans, jodhpurs and riding jackets. Forenza is a pseudo-Italian line of fun, active pieces, bright colors, short skirts and baggy jeans. The styles, fits and fabrics are good for the prices (you can usually find a sweater or pair of jeans for $35 or less). Carefully thought-out accessories—belts, socks, costume jewelry—round out the collection. New at the Beverly Center Limited are lingerie and children's departments. Many other locations, mostly in the better malls. (Also in the Beverly Center is its sister store, The Limited Express, which carries a line of clothes—fairly similar in price range—that is more casual and colorful.)

Maxfield

8825 Melrose Ave., W. Hollywood
275-7007
Open Mon.-Sat. 11 a.m.-7 p.m.

Fast-trackers flock to this imposing steel-and-concrete structure for the latest from Romeo Gigli, Jean-Paul Gaultier and Commes des Garçons. If you're serious about making a multidigit purchase, a painfully stylish and generally helpful salesperson will offer you a glass of Champagne. At Maxfield it's customary to hear salespeople being paged by such callers as Geena Davis or Nancy Reagan (really—we heard it ourselves!). All in all, this is one of the world's most fascinating stores.

Mister Frank

8801 Santa Monica Blvd., W. Hollywood
657-1023
Open Mon. 11 a.m.-6 p.m., Tues.-Sat. 10 a.m.-6 p.m.

In the '60s, Santa Monica Boulevard was what Melrose Avenue is today. Like the street, Mister Frank is no longer leading the fashion pack. But if television's *L.A. Law* has you making a case for power suits, look no further than Mister Frank, where Eleanor Brenner

274

and Thalia suits are purchased for actresses Susan Dey and Jill Eikenberry.

Modasport

Brentwood Gardens, 142 S. Barrington Ave., Brentwood
207-5514
Open Mon.-Wed. & Fri.-Sat. 11 a.m.-7 p.m., Thurs. 11 a.m.-9 p.m.
9458 Brighton Way, Beverly Hills
271-5718
2924 Beverly Glen Circle, Bel Air
475-3665
Open Mon.-Sat. 10 a.m.-6 p.m.

One of L.A.'s upper-league retailers, Modasport never ceases to inspire with a highly edited collection of stellar design talent, both local and imported. If the tight security at the Beverly Hills store is too much for you, retreat to the nearby Rodeo Collection for Modasport Footwear and Modasport Encore eveningwear.

Mr. G

356 N. Bedford Dr., Beverly Hills
272-7529
Open Mon.-Sat. 9:30 a.m.-6 p.m.

Another vestige of the days when store names were preceded by miss or mister. The best finds here are the hand-knit sweaters, but this small, friendly womenswear boutique also has terrific French and Italian sportswear and suit coordinates (Zanella, Le Painty) in mostly menswear fabrics. There are also some good-looking suede and leather pieces.

Polo Ralph Lauren

444 N. Rodeo Dr., Beverly Hills
281-7200
Open Mon.-Sat. 10 a.m.-6 p.m.

Not just a clothing and home-furnishings shop, Polo is a consumer experience, a theme park, a supplier of ready-made heritages. The interior, rather like a condensed stately private home, is replete with the trappings of the good life and old money—old Wasp money, to be precise. Tall mahogany cases hold antique bracelets and cameos; walls sport old school portraits and trophies. Under the sway of the atmosphere, patrons begin to discuss hunt balls or their last visit to Liberty in London; everyone wants to participate. An equal but not really predominant element in the scenario is the clothing. Lauren's

womenswear collection, exceedingly well made from high-quality materials, comprises, for the most part, reinterpretations of classic designs, counterparts to his traditional men's styles. Dressmakers' dummies sport extremely tailored menswear-style tweed and gabardine suits; hand-knit sweaters, handkerchief-linen blouses, corduroy dirndls, jodhpurs, jeans and khakis fill the floor-to-ceiling shelves. Equally traditional in style and beautifully crafted in fine leathers are the shoes and accessories. The saleswomen are courteous and helpful, and won't neglect you after having shown you into one of the well-appointed dressing rooms. And to spare you the sight of all that filthy lucre changing hands, the cash registers are discreetly hidden in little curtained alcoves.

Profils du Monde

9567 Wilshire Blvd., Beverly Hills
276-9416
Open Mon.-Fri. 10 a.m.-6 p.m., Sat. 10 a.m.-5 p.m.

When only authentic ethnic will do, Profils du Monde lets you select from imported laces, lamés, brocades, beaded chiffons and jeweled silks, then custom-designs a gown, coat, shoulder wrap or sarong skirt of your choice. This couture salon provided the showy, exotic fabrics for the costumes in the movie *The King and I* and regularly creates exotic garb for weddings and bar mitzvahs.

Raffles

17554 Ventura Blvd., Encino
(818) 501-6782
Open Mon.-Sat. 10 a.m.-6 p.m., or by appt.

A good San Fernando Valley source for upper-crust American and European designer labels: tailored clothes, such as Zanella slacks and silk blouses, as well as the spice of a wardrobe by Michael Kors, Go Silk, Ronaldus Shamask and Byblos. Thorough attention is paid to all accessories, from footwear to jewelry.

Torie Steele Boutiques

414 N. Rodeo Dr., Beverly Hills
271-5150
Open Mon.-Sat. 10 a.m.-6 p.m.

As its Rodeo Drive address indicates, this is a posh setting for world-class Italian design. Pieces by Valentino, Gianfranco Ferrè, Armani, Krizia, Fendi and Genny, as well as

Texas retailer Steele's own designs, hang in individual boutiques. Cappuccino and wine bar.

Shauna Stein

Beverly Center, 121 N. La Cienega Blvd.,
W. Hollywood
652-5511
Open Mon.-Fri. 10 a.m.-9 p.m., Sat. 10 a.m.-8 p.m., Sun. 11 a.m.-6 p.m.

Exquisite taste, not trends, is the driving force behind Shauna Stein's style outpost. In assembling known and unknown European and American designers, she encourages customers to contrast the modern with the classic. Stein combines some of the most prestigious names in fashion: Romeo Gigli, Callaghan, Moschino, Rifat Ozbek and Norma Kamali. Her motto: "Buy Better, Buy Less."

Suite 101

270 N. Cañon Dr., Beverly Hills
276-7143
Open Mon.-Sat. 10 a.m.-5:30 p.m.

Most of this salon's couture merchandise is kept in the back, so personal attention by salespeople is requisite. The stock turns over quite quickly—one week a saleswoman will show you wonderful Galanos and Bill Blass gowns, and the next week, Valentino suits.

Ann Taylor

357 N. Camden Dr., Beverly Hills
858-7840
Open Mon.-Sat. 10 a.m.-6 p.m.

Long popular among young-thinking women in New York and Boston, Ann Taylor has captured the shopping dollars of many a West Coast sophisticate. Many of the clean, tailored styles (most designed specially for the store) manage to be current and classic at the same time, and the prices are moderate given the quality of the fabrics and designs. There is everything from cocktail dresses to leather coats. You'll also find terrific collections of Joan and David shoes, and great accessories: leather gloves, wool hats, fashionable belts and cheery socks. There are Ann Taylors scattered around the city; although they carry much of the same merchandise, the stock varies somewhat according to location. The Century City shop, for example, has more

clothing for professionals, whereas the Westwood shop caters to student tastes and budgets. The Beverly Hills store is the largest and carries the most inclusive range.

Theodore

453 N. Rodeo Dr., Beverly Hills
276-9691
Open Mon.-Sat. 10 a.m.-6 p.m.

A sporty yet sophisticated lineup of foreign and domestic designer clothing. Beware of overzealous salesclerks who obviously work on commission. Adding to the atmosphere is the scent of Spoiled, owner Herb Fink's new fragrance. For a newer installment of the store, visit By Theodore in Brentwood Gardens.

DESIGNER

Agnes B.

100 N. Robertson Blvd., W. Hollywood
271-9643
Open Mon.-Sat. 11 a.m.-7 p.m., Sun. noon-6 p.m.

This French designer's store is a triple treat: womenswear, Agnes B. Homme and Agnes B. Enfant, all interconnected with a pervasive penchant for light and open space. Agnes B. is known for her expressive ways with classics. The striped fisherman's T-shirts that have been in demand for more than ten years are here, next to signature snap-front cardigans, linen suits and leather accessories.

Giorgio Armani

436 N. Rodeo Dr., Beverly Hills
271-5555
Open Mon.-Sat. 10 a.m.-6 p.m.

This is a stunning store by all accounts, the biggest retailing effort by the kingpin of Italian design and the most talked-about store to hit Rodeo Drive in years. The interior—lacquered surfaces, gold-leaf panels, glass and steel—is as dazzling as the lineup of menswear, womenswear, shoes, luggage, accessories, tuxedos, underwear and cashmere items.

Chanel

301 N. Rodeo Dr., Beverly Hills
278-5500
Open Mon.-Sat. 10 a.m.-6 p.m.

Named the most expensive store in Los Angeles by a local magazine, the Chanel boutique is a gleaming interplay of crystal, black lacquer, marble and mirrors. The entire Chanel line is here: ready-to-wear, cosmetics, fragrances and, yes, those famous satin hair bows, a mere $290 each.

Grau
7520 Melrose Ave., W. Hollywood
651-0487
Open Mon.-Sat. 11 a.m.-8 p.m., Sun. noon-6 p.m.

Claudia Grau is a self-professed "fabricholic" who designs colorfully concocted women's clothing, hats and jewelry—all with a very eclectic style. Such regional fabrics as Guatemalan hand-wovens are a shop specialty. Daryl Hannah and Cher both shop here (though probably not together).

Hermès
343 N. Rodeo Dr., Beverly Hills
278-6440
Open Mon.-Sat. 10 a.m.-6 p.m.

Designed to capture the spirit of the 150-year-old house of leather in Paris, the Hermès boutique presents its celebrated handbags, luggage, attaché cases, belts, equestrian-theme silk scarves and ties, ready-to-wear for men and women and fragrances.

Karl Logan
138 Santa Monica Place, Santa Monica
451-5583
Open Mon.-Fri. 10 a.m.-9 p.m., Sat. 10 a.m.-6 p.m., Sun. 11 a.m.-6 p.m.

Tongue-in-chic looks in suits, dresses and separates from California's award-winning designer. The clothes are a comfortable blend of feminine and man-tailored elements, with just enough wit to make them fun to wear, as well. Logan's easygoing menswear collection is offered, too.

Max Studio
2712 Main St., Santa Monica
396-3963
Open Mon.-Sat. 11 a.m.-7 p.m., Sun. 11 a.m.-5 p.m.

This studio is an architectural showcase for L.A. designer Leon Max's cutting edge in comfortwear: stretchy bicycle shorts, cropped tops and little black dresses are big here. Accessories reflect Max's uncomplicated formula.

Claude Montana
469 N. Rodeo Dr., Beverly Hills
273-7925
Open Mon.-Sat. 10 a.m.-6 p.m.

Montana caters to those men and women with a commanding personal style. An expert at molding clothes, especially leather, to the body, his sculpted creations are adored by those who like to make dramatic entrances.

Parachute
844 N. La Brea Ave., Hollywood
461-8822
Open Mon.-Sat. noon-8 p.m., Sun. noon-5 p.m.
456 N. Camden Dr., Beverly Hills
273-0501
Open Mon.-Sat. 11 a.m.-7 p.m.

This cavernous concrete-and-steel store is not as radical as it looks. Once inside, you'll discover a men's and women's hybrid-clothing collection that's rather refined. Trousers and suits are known for their exceptional fabrics, which are cut by a talented Montreal-based husband-and-wife team

Sonia Rykiel
415 N. Rodeo Dr., Beverly Hills
273-0753
Open Mon.-Sat. 10 a.m.-6 p.m.

This polished presentation of wardrobe options is ideally suited for the young executive-class woman. Even the sportswear is chic here.

Traction Avenue
Beverly Center, 121 N. La Cienega Blvd., W. Hollywood
652-6052
Open Mon.-Fri. 10 a.m.-9 p.m., Sat. 10 a.m.-8 p.m., Sun. 11 a.m.-6 p.m.

A hot and spicy mix of cross-cultural references from French-born, L.A.-based designer Michele Lamy. Her creations include supple knits and contoured cuts in little dresses, big-shouldered jackets, tight-fitting tops and bicycle pants. Shocking-bright color is characteristic of Lamy's designs.

Tyler Trafficante
7290 Beverly Blvd., Wilshire District
931-9678
Open Mon.-Fri. 11 a.m.-7 p.m., Sat. noon-6 p.m., or by appt.

Since its opening in the spring of 1989, Australian-born designer Richard Tyler's art deco (by way of London) salon has been attracting rock stars, visiting Europeans, Hancock Park and Beverly Hills professionals and anyone who loves quality and cutting-edge design. Appealing to both men and women, Tyler's tailored clothing ranges from a retro-influenced classic suit to a jacket with exaggerated details in a show-stopping shade of purple. Off-the-rack women's suits start at $950. Custom designs are available.

Ungaro
17 N. Rodeo Dr., Beverly Hills
273-1080
Open Mon.-Sat. 10 a.m.-6 p.m.

Silk fabrics, seductive fits, draped dresses and brilliant floral prints are the hallmarks of Parisian designer Emanuel Ungaro. Widely considered to be the master of the female form, Ungaro and his daring designs are not for the timid.

DISCOUNT

A Chic Conspiracy
350 S. La Cienega Blvd., W. Hollywood
657-1177
Open Mon.-Sat. 10 a.m.-6 p.m., Sun. noon-6 p.m.

You'll find designer clothes here that you'll never see in any other discount store. That's because its once-worn and never-worn stock comes from the closets of movie studios and wealthy women who never wear anything twice. Prices are more than fair, and the clothes are in excellent condition. A worthwhile shop.

Importique
17145 Ventura Blvd., Encino
(818) 990-4733
Open Mon.-Sat. 10:15 a.m.-6:30 p.m., Sun. noon-5 p.m.

Westsiders used to make a special trip over the hill to bargain-hunt in this pleasant boutique. Unfortunately, the merchandise isn't what it used to be; worthwhile designer pieces are difficult to find among the racks of uninteresting silk dresses and wool pants.

Loehmann's
6220 W. 3rd St., Wilshire District
933-5675
Open Mon.-Fri. 9:30 a.m.-9 p.m., Sat. 9:30 a.m.-7 p.m., Sun. noon-6 p.m.

If you can't stand sales, hate the thought of a million women crammed into one dressing room and like to browse at a leisurely pace, forget Loehmann's. But if you have the patience to carefully look through rack after rack of clothing (much of it outdated and tacky), you will be rewarded with some wonderful bargains. On our last visit, we spied Anne Klein II trenchcoats, Perry Ellis blouses, Bill Blass dresses and Giorgio Sant'Angelo pieces at a fraction of what they sell for elsewhere. Loehmann's receives daily deliveries.

Jerry Piller's
937 E. Colorado Blvd., Pasadena
(818) 796-9559
Open Mon.-Thurs. 10:30 a.m.-6 p.m., Fri.-Sat. 10:30 a.m.-6:30 p.m.

Many first-timers walk out shaking their heads at the sheer wonder of so many women, so many garments and so many shoes. Your purse, no matter how small, will be taken from you at the door; you'll be asked to remove your shoes before entering that department. For these inconveniences, you will be rewarded with the most crowded racks we have ever seen, which are filled with fairly hideous clothing. But if you have an iron will and an inherent optimism you'll leave with some very handsome designerwear bought for nearly nothing. There's also a large menswear department.

The Place & Co.
8820 S. Sepulveda Blvd., Culver City
645-1539
Open Mon.-Sat. 10 a.m.-5:30 p.m.

Considered the cream of L.A.'s resale crop, The Place has an outstanding selection of new and slightly used designer clothing at terrific prices. Socialites and celebrities now regularly hand their seldom-worn suits and gowns over to owner Joyce Brock, who prices them within reason, considering the quality. On our last visit, we spied a Chanel suit marked at $425; Armani matching jacket and pants for $325; and an Ungaro dress for $395. Most everything is current and in mint condition. The Place's close proximity to LAX makes it a worthwhile shopping layover.

Sacks Fashion Outlet
652 N. La Brea Ave., Hollywood
930-2313
Open Mon.-Fri. 10 a.m.-8 p.m., Sat. 10 a.m.-7 p.m., Sun. 11 a.m.-6 p.m.

David Sacks is a nut for first-rate natural fabrics, and he has a good eye for stylish bargains. The sales at SFO are among the best in town, taking down the everyday prices, which are already well below the going rates. We've spotted fashions by California designers and well-known staples of Melrose boutiques at substantially lower prices, and there are usually terrific buys on leather jackets and accessories. Don't miss the kids' discount outlet next door. There are several other locations, including Studio City, Tarzana, West L.A. and West Hollywood, where hours may vary.

FURS

Somper-Lowell Furs
301 N. Cañon Dr., Beverly Hills
274-5395
Open Mon.-Wed. & Fri. 9:30 a.m.-6 p.m., Thurs. 9:30 a.m.-8 p.m., Sat. 10 a.m.-6 p.m.
In spite of the negative publicity surrounding this segment of the fashion industry, Somper-Lowell is known around the world for its designer fur collections. Fox, mink, chinchilla, lynx and sable—whatever type of fur you're looking for, you should be able to find it here. If there isn't a Juilano Teso, Bob Mackie or Valentino to your liking, Merrill Lowell or one of his able designers will craft a custom model.

LARGE SIZES

The Forgotten Woman
9683 Wilshire Blvd., Beverly Hills
859-8829
Open Mon.-Wed. & Fri.-Sat. 10 a.m.-6 p.m., Thurs. 10 a.m.-7 p.m.
Quite popular up and down the East Coast, this shop specializes in sportswear, gowns, dresses and coats for women who wear larger sizes.

LINGERIE

Fogal
439 N. Rodeo Dr., Beverly Hills
273-6425
Open Mon.-Sat. 10 a.m.-6 p.m.
This European hosiery line has a leg up on most ready-made counterparts. There are 150 luxurious, high-style looks (in 105 colors), plus sheer body stockings and other delicate intimates. There's nothing like the sheer indulgence of a pair of cashmere tights to pick up your day.

Frederick's of Hollywood
6608 Hollywood Blvd., Hollywood
466-8506
Open Mon.-Thurs. 10 a.m.-8 p.m., Fri. 10 a.m.-9 p.m., Sat. 10 a.m.-6 p.m., Sun. noon-5 p.m.
The fame of this Hollywood landmark is probably only second to that of Mann's Chinese Theatre. This large, shockingly purple building is *the* place for risqué lingerie. Surprisingly, the merchandise here is more tacky and suggestive than kinky, and the adorable saleswomen are quite unlike the lithe, corset-clad creatures you'll find at Trashy Lingerie. Also surprising is that many well-heeled women frequent Frederick's to purchase undergarments in sizes and styles that simply aren't available in department stores or other lingerie shops.

Eleanor Keeshan
8625 W. Sunset Blvd., W. Hollywood
657-2443
Open Mon.-Sat. 10 a.m.-6 p.m.
Without a doubt, this is one of the finest lingerie selections around. Keeshan generally has a good number of pieces by Jonquil, Natori, Gemma and Jeune Europe. There are always lots of pretty, sexy nightgowns, robes, teddies, undergarments and loungewear.

Lisa Norman Lingerie
1134 Montana Ave., Santa Monica
451-2026
Open Mon.-Sat. 10 a.m.-6 p.m.
Norman's exquisite lingerie is just a touch sexier and more youthful than Eleanor Keeshan's, though we think the range of robes, foundations and gowns is overrated. What Norman can't find at home or abroad, she designs herself, notably classic tailored silks.

Lili St. Cyr
8104 Santa Monica Blvd., W. Hollywood
656-6885
Open Mon.-Fri. 9:30 a.m.-5 p.m., Sat. 9:30 a.m.-4 p.m.
This shop's namesake, the grande dame of striptease, has long since retired. But her provocative bathtub act of the '50s will not soon be forgotten. Enter her private world to find boudoir ensembles, merry widows and garter stockings. Madonna restocks her wardrobe of black bustiers here.

Trashy Lingerie
402 N. La Cienega Blvd., W. Hollywood
652-4543
Open Mon.-Sat. 10 a.m.-7 p.m.
  Don't be intimidated by this shop's name—many of the styles are merely provocative and seductive. Owner Mitch Shrier not only car-ries every style of teddy, negligee, panty and the like, but has them in every color and size imaginable. You'll understand why you're charged a small "membership fee" before en-tering—it's to keep out voyeurs who want to catch a glimpse of the saleswomen, who are decked out in the store's merchandise.

DEPARTMENT STORES

The Broadway
Century City Shopping Center, 10250
Santa Monica Blvd., Century City
277-1234
Open Mon.-Sat. 10 a.m.-9 p.m., Sun. 11 a.m.-7 p.m.
  At some point during the last few years, the owners of this department-store chain must have decided that the Broadway's image needed an overhaul. Thus, what was once a mediocre store has become a surprisingly at-tractive and well-stocked place to shop. On the whole, merchandise isn't as expensive as at Bullock's, but the Broadway does have departments, such as V.I.P. Sportswear, where you can find working wardrobes by the likes of Adrienne Vittadini, Dana Buchman, Paul Stanley and Tahari. The Century City location has particularly spacious cosmetic and cookware departments. Many other locations, including in the Glendale Galleria, and an especially well-stocked store at the Beverly Center.

Bullock's
Beverly Center, 121 N. La Cienega Blvd.,
W. Hollywood
854-6655
Open Mon.-Sat. 10 a.m.-9 p.m., Sun. 10 p.m.-7 p.m.
  Bullock's is everything you expect a depart-ment store to be—nothing more and nothing less. You won't find any innovative and spec-tacular departments (such as the Kiehl section at Neiman's or the children's department at Saks), but you will find a good selection of merchandise in all the standard departments, from housewares to clothing, shoes to linge-rie. There are a number of Bullock's stores in the Los Angeles area, and they do tend to carry slightly different merchandise (varies depend-ing on neighborhood); the Pasadena branch, for instance, has an air of old-money refine-ment, and the new store in downtown's Sev-enth Street Marketplace boasts exceptionally good service and excellent clothing for work-ing men and women. Bullock's is beginning to follow Nordstrom's lead on the service front. Its "B.B.A." (Bullock's by Appoint-ment), a private shopping-consultant service, is a winner. There's even a concierge at the South Coast Plaza branch and at other se-lected locations. Other Bullock's stores in-clude the Westwood, the Sherman Oaks Galleria and the Century City branches.

Bullocks Wilshire (I. Magnin)
3050 Wilshire Blvd., Mid-Wilshire
382-6161
Open Mon.-Wed. & Fri.-Sat. 10 a.m.-6 p.m., Thurs. 10 a.m.-8 p.m., Sun. noon-5 p.m.
  We're sad to say that by the time you read these lines, Bullocks Wilshire will most likely have become an I. Magnin. We're sad, be-cause BW is one of L.A.'s most beloved insti-tutions. In recent years, a visit here was like a trip through time: from the glorious art deco building to the ever-popular tea room (where fashions were modeled daily) to the shoppers themselves (darling little ladies who smell of powder and carry patent-leather pocket-books). We always felt as though we were in a place that time forgot. True, some of the merchandise was a bit dated, but the crystal and china, stationery, bridal and better-dresses departments were better than at any other department store. I. Magnin promises to preserve the building—and the marvelous tea room—but we still don't think it'll be the same. There's a Bullocks Wilshire in the Woodland Hills Promenade and Fashion Is-land, Newport Beach, both of which are de-cades newer and not nearly as fun as the mother store.

I. Magnin

9634 Wilshire Blvd., Beverly Hills
271-2131
Open Mon.-Wed. & Fri.-Sat. 10 a.m.-6 p.m.,
Thurs. 10 a.m.-8 p.m., Sun. noon-5 p.m.

The merchandise is usually so similar to that at Saks that it's easy to forget which store you're in—especially when you're shopping for womenswear, cosmetics, handbags and junior sportswear. However, I. Magnin's Gift Gallery and lingerie department are better stocked than those of its neighbors. There's an I. Magnin in Sherman Oaks, with a smaller selection and less expensive merchandise, and I. Magnins in South Coast Plaza, the Mid-Wishire district and Pasadena. The Beverly Hills store is an elegant though somewhat staid store frequented by L.A. and Orange County's old-money families.

The May Company

6067 Wilshire Blvd., Wilshire District
938-4211
Open Mon.-Fri. 10 a.m.-9 p.m., Sat. 10 a.m.-8 p.m., Sun. 11 a.m.-7 p.m.

Few people shop at The May Company *occasionally.* Either you buy just about everything here (and it does have just about everything) and swear that you're saving loads of money, or else you simply refuse to walk through the doors of this rather faded Los Angeles landmark, because it's not on the level of Neiman-Marcus, Saks, I. Magnin and Bullock's. If you wouldn't dream of buying a handbag without designer initials on it, or sheets without a signature splashed in the corner, skip The May Company altogether—not because it doesn't carry designer items (it does), but because you'll be uncomfortable with the low prices on the tags. The service is friendly once you find someone to help you. Newer locations include the Westside Pavilion, Northridge and downtown's Seventh Street Marketplace.

Neiman-Marcus

9700 Wilshire Blvd., Beverly Hills
550-5900
Open Mon.-Sat. 10 a.m.-6 p.m.

Neiman-Marcus is like no other single department store in the world—but at the same time, it's a little bit like many of the world's most renowned. Take the avant-gardeness of Henri Bendel's, the boutiquey layout of Bloomingdale's and Galeries Lafayette, the unhurried, pleasant atmosphere of Bergdorf's, the variety (well, almost) of Harrod's and the ostentatious overindulgence of this store's nouveau-riche home state, Texas, and you've got Neiman-Marcus. Though this famous department store has been nicknamed "Needless Markup," you won't find merchandise here that's more expensive than elsewhere—it's just that Neiman carries some more exclusive and pricey items. The standard departments (womenswear, menswear, childrenswear, cosmetics, lingerie and housewares) are quite boring but reasonably well stocked; the best departments are the small ones that feature Kiehl's pharmaceutical products, Fendi furs, and handbags and sportswear by Donna Karan. Special mention should be made, too, of Neiman's huge women's shoe department (with the best of Frizon, Pfister and Jourdan) and sinful fine-chocolate counter. There's another Neiman-Marcus in Newport Beach's Fashion Island.

Nordstrom

Westside Pavilion, 10830 Pico Blvd., W.L.A.
470-6155
Open Mon.-Sat. 10 a.m.-9:30 p.m., Sun. 11 a.m.-6 p.m.

Seattle-based Nordstrom started out as a shoe store, expanded into men's, women's and children's clothing and has taken California by storm. Nordstrom doesn't get distracted with housewares, food, furniture and the like; it offers only things you put on your body, from shoes and clothes to jewelry and cosmetics. Two key qualities have brought Nordstrom its tremendous success: unrivalled selection and near-perfect service. Salespeople are exceptionally helpful without being pushy; don't be surprised if you receive a personal thank-you note from the salesperson who helped you put together that great new outfit. The return policy here is legendary: if you are unhappy with your merchandise, at any time or for any reason, it will be cheerfully accepted for return, no questions asked. The selection is exceptional—in fact, it's almost too much to absorb. There is an incredible array of women's shoes in every imaginable style, color and size (size elevens know to come here); a good offering of classic men's shoes; trendy clothes for young men and beautiful, more conservative clothes for grown-up men; children's clothes in all price ranges; and many departments of womenswear, from the fun play clothes in the Brass Plum to the classic sportswear in The Individualist to such fashion contemporaries as Karl Logan, Michele Lamy and Vaako leather in Savvy. Nordstrom recently expanded its designer roster to include such international stars as Ungaro, Gianfranco Ferrè, Patrick Kelly, Isaac Mizrahi and Umberto Ginocchietti in addition to mainstays Ralph Lauren, Liz Claiborne, Esprit, Cole Haan and Cricketeer. If you're looking for a particular item—say, a white blouse or a red jacket—try Nordstrom first: you're sure to find it in several styles and at several prices. Hat buyers receive the added bonus of a Nordstrom-labeled hat box. Other locations include the Glendale Galleria, South Coast Plaza, the Galleria at South Bay and Topanga Plaza.

Robinson's
9900 Wilshire Blvd., Beverly Hills
275-5464
Open Mon.-Fri. 10 a.m.-9 p.m., Sat. 10 a.m.-6 p.m., Sun. noon-5 p.m.

Now that Robinson's is owned by May Company, the merchandise assortment is not what it was a few years ago. The recently remodeled men's department is still strong, carrying such labels as Ralph Lauren, Perry Ellis Portfolio and Liz Claiborne. We found Mary Ann Restivo and Anne Klein in the designer women's area, and the store carries Giorgio Armani for both men and women.

The Pacesetter shop caters to contemporary clotheshorses with such names as Leon Max and Christian de Castelnau. The home-furnishings department features Waterford and Baccarat crystal. There's a restaurant (on the fourth level), a café and a better-than-average candy counter. In general, the pervasive laziness and who-cares? attitude of the staff is annoying. A tip: visit in person and skip the seemingly impossible task of getting someone to answer the phone. Other locations include Santa Monica, downtown L.A., Sherman Oaks Galleria, Woodland Hills Promenade, South Coast Plaza and most major shopping centers.

Saks Fifth Avenue
9600 Wilshire Blvd., Beverly Hills
275-4211
Open Mon.-Wed. & Fri.-Sat. 10 a.m.-6 p.m., Thurs. 10 a.m.-8:30 p.m.

Those on the inside track know Saks as *the* designer department store. In addition to all the major European and American designers, Saks is home to a Chanel boutique and an exclusive Adolfo boutique. Designer collections are even launched in the children's department, the latest of which was Taki, designed by the wife of the president of Anne Klein. Saks also excels in layette and related maternity items. A good source for hats, fine and antique jewelry, small leather goods and cosmetics. By all means attend Saks's sales, which are usually exceptional. The pleasant café on the fifth level features an espresso bar.

FLOWERS

Broadway Florists
218 W. 5th St., Downtown
626-5516
Open daily 8:30 a.m.-6 p.m.

Broadway is one of the biggest and friendliest florists in town. The Stathatos family has been running this business for more than 70 years, and despite its large size, the service remains remarkably personal. Broadway does the flowers for many of the major weddings and society affairs in town and has been decorating the Academy Awards for years; the

designs are more classic than avant-garde, and they are truly beautiful. The downtown shop is located in a pretty grim neighborhood, so it does a great deal of telephone business.

Campo Dei Fiori
646 N. Martel Ave., Hollywood
655-9966
Open Mon.-Thurs. 9 a.m.-9 p.m., Fri.-Sat. 9 a.m.-10 p.m., Sun. 10 a.m.-8 p.m.

Fast-trackers who shop at Ecru buy their flowers at Campo Dei Fiori, just off Melrose Avenue. Stepping into this shop is a complete visual experience, from the stark, architectural surroundings to the stylized arrangements wrapped in unusual papers and tied with raffia. Flowers are of the uncommon and hard-to-get variety—here's where you'll find imported French ivory tulips at $15 each. There's a superb selection of vases in the modernist vein: materials are lightweight concrete, glass, terra cotta and black slate. You'll also find cacti at competitive prices.

Canyon Blooms
654-6965
Open Mon.-Sat. 10 a.m.-4 p.m.

Operating via telephone out of his Laurel Canyon home, Rick Holloway combines fresh-cut blooms with potted flowers and exotic clump grasses in imaginative re-creations of natural settings. The moss-and-raffia "pond basket" features polished black stones that appear to float in water, and a handle entwined with ivy and orchids. Baskets can be personalized with a gift of your choosing (a string of pears? a special bottle of wine?). Floral baskets (not including gifts) start at $75; pond baskets begin at $100 with 24 hours' notice.

The Flower Basket
12244 Ventura Blvd., Studio City
(818) 985-1055
Open Mon.-Sat. 9 a.m.-5 p.m.

A large, homey shop that designs exotic arrangements in baskets, bottles and Oriental bowls. Most of the flowers are imported from Holland or France. Since The Flower Basket makes up numerous custom orders, it doesn't keep a lot of flowers in stock for walk-in customers, so always call ahead to see what sort of selection there is.

Jef's ... an Affair with Flowers
8621 Wilshire Blvd., Beverly Hills
659-8634
Open Mon.-Sat. 8 a.m.-5:30 p.m.

Simply put, Jef is a floral designer extraordinaire. Every arrangement he does, whether it's a gift to be delivered or one of 200 centerpieces for a huge party, is a true original. Not only does he give his utmost attention to the flowers themselves but to every other aesthetic detail for a party as well. He has earned his excellent reputation. When a local magazine did a blind test to determine which L.A. florist's roses lasted the longest, Jef's came in first place. Centerpieces and gift baskets for all occasions, from weddings and dinner parties to get-well bouquets, are creative and beautiful.

Stanley R. Kersten Flowers and Service
734 S. San Julian St., Downtown
622-2261
Open Mon.-Sat. 8 a.m.-4 p.m.

Located in the Los Angeles flower mart, Kersten always has the freshest and most exotic arrangements. Recommended if you like a very airy floral design with lots of long twigs. Popular among Beverly Hills hostesses.

Los Angeles Flower Market
754 Wall St., Downtown
622-1966
Open Mon.-Sat. dawn-2 p.m.

There are incredible bargains available to anyone with cold cash (though wholesalers do most of their selling to the trade). Taken as a whole, the street offers more, fresher, better and cheaper than any ten florists in town: elegant lilies, stately pink ginger and halyconia and bundles of country-fresh delphiniums and protea. Prices are one-third to one-half of those in neighborhood florists. Besides exotic flowers, the stalls sell such workhorse flowers as mums and roses, indoor plants, dried greenery (such as curly bamboo), silk flowers and willow baskets. Both sides of the street are lined with stalls that sometimes spill onto the sidewalk. Savvy shoppers know to arrive as early as possible, to make snap decisions and to wear rubber-soled shoes (there's muck everywhere).

My Son the Florist
119 N. La Brea Ave., Wilshire District
935-2912
Open Mon.-Fri. 9 a.m.-5 p.m.

A great all-purpose florist for contemporary tastes. My Son the Florist designs romantic nosegays, rosegays, English garden bouquets, sprawling arrangements of delicate seasonal flowers and angular, geometric designs using Hala leaves, corkscrew willow and bold singular blooms—all with equal aplomb. My Son the Florist furnishes nearby Campanile restaurant with its impressive floral designs and is reasonably priced. One of our favorites.

Silver Birches
180 E. California Blvd., Pasadena
(818) 796-1431
Open Mon.-Sat. 8:30 a.m.-5 p.m.

Silver Birches is a first-rate florist that approaches floral arranging as creating pieces of art. Designs are done according to the specifications of the top-drawer clientele, to make a statement, from exotic to English garden to classic. Moss, rocks, branches and other natural or unusual materials are often combined

with high-quality flowers in containers designed specially for the shop.

The Solarium
2922 Beverly Glen Circle, Bel Air
274-7900
Open Mon.-Sat. 9 a.m.-5 p.m.

This is a full-service florist housed in spacious white surroundings that encourage a leisurely stroll. The Solarium creates uncluttered and striking arrangements with rare imported tropical and European flowers. It specializes in custom wedding parties and event planning.

FOOD

BAKERIES

Viktor Benes Continental Pastries
8718 W. 3rd St., W. Hollywood
276-0488
Open Mon.-Sat. 6 a.m.-6 p.m.

At 5:59 a.m., men and women from nearby neighborhoods are waiting outside Benes's door to buy loaves of bread and delicious cheese danish. The Parisian cream cakes and alligators (pecan coffee cake) are also worth getting out of a warm bed for.

La Brea Bakery
624 S. La Brea Ave., Wilshire District
938-1447
Open daily 8 a.m.-4 p.m.

Campanile coproprietor (and former Spago pastry chef) Nancy Silverton bakes and sells the most talked-about breads in town, right here on La Brea. Arrive early (most everything sells out by early afternoon) to partake of the fabulous rye currant (we love it toasted), Greek olive, walnut, whole-grain and more. Many of L.A.'s best restaurants serve these hearty, healthy breads; there are special shapes for when you really want to wow your friends.

The Buttery
2906 Main St., Santa Monica
399-3000
Open Mon. 7 a.m.-noon, Tues.-Sun. 7 a.m.-6 p.m.

Before chocolate-chip cookie and croissant stores started springing up on every L.A. cor-

ner, people would line up outside The Buttery, waiting to buy its soft, chewy cookies, buttery croissants, cakes and breads. The lines are now gone, but these cookies and croissants are still better than 90 percent of those you'll find elsewhere.

Café Maxwell
777 Deep Valley Dr., Rolling Hills Estates
541-2600
Open Tues.-Sun. 7 a.m.-6 p.m.

Some of the best pastries (most notably, croissants) in the area can be found in this charming little shop. It's under the reign of opinionated co-owner Rosalie Shenkarow, formerly with Le Bel Age hotel. But even if her welcome may be off-putting, your spirits won't be dampened when you taste the heavenly concoctions she's created. You can also sample a light lunch on the patio or order quiches, fresh pasta and other delights packed in a basket to go.

Cake and Art
8709 Santa Monica Blvd., W. Hollywood
657-8694
Open Mon.-Sat. 10 a.m.-6 p.m.

Celebrating the birthday of a dog-lover money-lover or hamburger-lover? Cake and Art will produce a cake in the shape of *any thing*. This shop has been catering to show-biz types for thirteen years. For the twentieth anniversary of *Star Trek*, Cake and Art fashioned a giant-sized Starship *Enterpise* to feed 500, complete with smoke and laser lights. I may not send your gourmet friends running for seconds, but some of these cakes are sure to get a laugh. Prices range from $15 to $5,000.

La Conversation
2118 Hillhurst Ave., Los Feliz
666-9000
Open Mon.-Thurs. 7:30 a.m.-7 p.m., Fri. 7:30 a.m.-10 p.m., Sat. 8 a.m.-10 p.m., Sun. 8:30 a.m.-2:30 p.m.

When you try one of La Conversation's wonderful croissants, you too will become a regular patron, even if you don't live in the area. People come from all over for the fresh-daily buttery croissants, the marvelous Italian-cheese-and-spinach torte, the rich chocolate cake and the many unusual and delicious cookies and minitarts. If it's not too crowded (weekends are) and you have some time to kill, have an espresso and a croissant at one of the tables squeezed into a corner of this tiny shop.

La Crème de la Crème
3562 Sepulveda Blvd., Manhattan Beach
416-9199
Open Mon.-Thurs. 7 a.m.-7 p.m., Fri.-Sat. 7 a.m.-8 p.m., Sun. 8 a.m.-6 p.m.

This charming little place serves excellent pastries and light luncheon foods, all prepared on the premises and served indoors or on the small patio adjacent to the Manhattan Village cinema. Try the excellent pain almond that nearly melts in your mouth, the delicate pain raisin, any of the delicious tarts and the extraordinary cakes (strawberry charlotte, Black Forest cherry cake and exquisite fruit tarts, among others, are also served by the slice). The pastas and layered tortes are also quite good.

Emil's Swiss Pastry
1751 Ensley Ave., Century City
277-1114
Open Tues.-Sat. 7 a.m.-5:30 p.m.

With their flaky crusts, rich custards and assorted fresh fruits, Emil's tarts are among the most attractive and delicious we've found in the city. Baked fruit tarts have such tempting fillings as prune, apricot and Italian plum. A popular party request is Emil's fresh-fruit sponge cake, the layers of which are filled with whipped cream and custard, bananas, grapes and whole strawberries, encased in a clear plastic "collar." The rest of Emil's cakes, cookies and pastries are slightly above average, but rather conventional and banal.

Il Fornaio
301 N. Beverly Dr., Beverly Hills
550-8330
Open Mon.-Sat. 7:30 a.m.-7 p.m., Sun. 8:30 a.m.-7 p.m.

Now a full-fledged café, Il Fornaio is famous for its lively European-style breakfasts. There are over 25 varieties of handmade Italian bread, including focaccia on weekends. After breakfast, you can take home freshly prepared pasta sauces and pastas from Santa Monica's Pasta Etc.

Hansen Cakes
193 S. Beverly Dr., Beverly Hills
272-0474
Open Tues.-Fri. 10 a.m.-6 p.m., Sat. 9 a.m.-5 p.m.

Something of an L.A. legend, Hansen creates an exquisite-looking but flavorless cake in almost any shape (for more daring shapes, go to Cake and Art). Downstairs is a whole roomful of wedding cakes that will take your breath away. There's a larger Hansen in the Wilshire District and another in Tarzana.

L.A. Desserts
113 N. Robertson Blvd., Beverly Hills
273-5537
Open Mon.-Sat. 10 a.m.-5 p.m.

This aromatic bakery, a sister to the superchic Ivy restaurant next door, is one of our favorites. L.A. Desserts makes *everything* by hand, including wonderful chocolate-chip cookies with hazelnuts and almonds, New England anadama bread with a touch of homemade molasses and a sugar-free fresh raspberry pie with an old-fashioned latticework top. The white-chocolate lemon cakes decorated with flowers and berries from the owner's garden are breathtaking ($25). Another real treat is the fudgy-chocolate "baby cakes," so rich they serve two people ($7). It's best to order in advance, though there's usually a dazzling assortment on hand.

Miss Grace Lemon Cake Co.
422 N. Cañon Dr., Beverly Hills
274-2879
Open Mon.-Sat. 10 a.m.-5:30 p.m.

Of the conventional (but still tasty) bundt cakes in assorted flavors, the best are the lemon and chocolate. Skip the carrot cake altogether, but do allow yourself at least a taste of the chocolate-chip cookies. Several other locations.

Mrs. Beasley's
19572 Ventura Blvd., Tarzana
(818) 344-7845
Open Mon.-Fri. 10 a.m.-6 p.m., Sat. 10 a.m.-5 p.m.

Mrs. Beasley's bakes the way you remember baking used to be. Each gift basket or tin is filled with a luscious assortment of plump minimuffins or tea cakes, heavenly cookies and brownies that manage to be both light and rich at the same time. Phone orders can be sent anywhere in the United States or delivered throughout Los Angeles. Other locations at Fred Segal Santa Monica and Fred Segal Melrose.

Nicolosi's
17540 Ventura Blvd., Encino
(818) 789-0922
Open Tues.-Sat. 9 a.m.-6 p.m., Sun. 9 a.m.-3 p.m.

Very popular among Valleyites for traditional Italian and French pastries and desserts, the best of which are the cannoli, rum cakes, napoleons and gâteaux Saint-Honorés. It's best to get to Nicolosi's early—by midafternoon, all the best pastries are long gone.

Old Town Bakery
166 W. Colorado Blvd., Pasadena
(818) 792-7943
Open Sun.-Thurs. 9 a.m.-11 p.m., Fri.-Sat. 9 a.m.-midnight.

Besides being a pleasant spot for a European-style pastry and espresso, Old Town Bakery excels in imaginative, freshly baked offerings to take home. There are homey fresh-fruit pies with latticework tops, presentation desserts like the chocolate-and-vanilla striped "zebra cake" and such fresh-daily breads as olive spiral, potato-onion, pumpkin and rosemary. The triangular bittersweet-chocolate terrine decorated with gold leaf makes a stunning birthday cake. There are also great gift-basket possibilities. Everything is reasonably priced.

Pioneer Boulangerie
2012 Main St., Santa Monica
399-7771
Open daily 7 a.m.-9:30 p.m.

This deli, restaurant and bakery is jammed on Sunday mornings and at lunchtime when the weather is warm. Though most of its pastries are less than satisfactory, the sourdough and French breads, for which Pioneer is most famous, are always fresh.

Michel Richard
310 S. Robertson Blvd., Beverly Hills
275-5707
Open Mon.-Sat. 9 a.m.-7 p.m.

Michel Richard's cakes and pastries are true works of art. Nowhere else will you find such exquisite desserts. Some of the cakes (such as the chocolate mousse with raspberries, covered with marzipan) are a little too rich and gooey but nonetheless appealing to sugar addicts. Take note that Richard himself no longer owns this store, though it remains first-rate; the Valley store bearing his name also no longer belongs to him, but its pastries are disappointing.

Snookie's Cookies
1753 Victory Blvd., Glendale
(818) 502-2013
Open Mon.-Fri. 10 a.m.-6 p.m., Sat. 10 a.m.-3 p.m.

Snookie and husband Don's chocolate-chip cookies are some of the best we've tasted: warm, moist, chock-full of chips and not overly sweet. Better yet, they'll deliver warm cookies and milk on ice just about anywhere in L.A. or Orange County.

Sweet Lady Jane
8360 Melrose Ave., W. Hollywood
653-7145
Open Mon.-Sat. 8:30 a.m.-11:30 p.m.

Everything at this European-style café and bakery, from simple scones and brownies to dreamy and complicated desserts, is made from the freshest ingredients. Sweet Lady Jane is acclaimed for its cheesecakes and lemon-meringue tarts and can put together beautiful gift baskets. Don't miss the English fruitcakes with "royal icing" during the holidays. A welcome addition to Melrose Avenue.

Weby's Bakery
12131 Ventura Blvd., Studio City
(818) 769-6062
Open Mon.-Sat. 7 a.m.-7 p.m., Sun. 7 a.m.-6 p.m.

Weby's has been a Valley institution for nearly 25 years now. Though many of the cookies and layer cakes are tasteless, the bagels, breads, coffee cakes, strudels and chocolate-chip rolls are fabulous. Weby's specializes in French-style seven-inch cakes with fresh fruit and whipped cream ($7 to $14.50). The bakery is always crowded in the morning, and by midafternoon the display cases are almost empty.

CATERERS

Along Came Mary
5265 W. Pico Blvd., Wilshire District
931-9082

Mary Micucci is famous for her full-scale catered extravangazas, primarily for the movie industry. She and staff take care of every detail—from the food and service to the decor, transportation and theme-attired serving staff. Renowned for its custom themes (Caribbean-style parties are a current favorite), Along Came Mary offers a diverse selection of dishes, including regional American and international cuisine. Location choices of unique event sites—from yachts to museums and mansions—are a specialty.

Jeanson's
8760 Venice Blvd., Culver City
204-5085

Located in the recently restored Helms Building in Culver City, Jeanson's is not only a good caterer but a fine spot to hold your gathering, whether you're planning a luncheon for 25 or a blow-out for 400. They'll do it all: cook the food (pretty elegant stuff), rent all necessary supplies, provide an experienced serving staff, arrange the flowers and hire the musicians and photographers. The on-site party facilities—including a delightful patio—are simple but quite attractive.

Julienne
2649 Mission St., San Marino
(818) 441-2299
Open Mon., Wed. & Fri. 8 a.m.-6 p.m., Tues. & Thurs. 8 a.m.-9 p.m., Sat. 8 a.m.-5 p.m.

Pasadenans haven't succeeded in keeping their favorite caterer a secret—once they invited their westside friends to their Julienne-catered weddings and parties, the word was out. Now Sue Campoy and her able crew cook for the many people—from San Marino to Santa Monica—who have become addicted to her deeply satisfying French country cooking. Before you decide on a menu, visit the romantic takeout shop/café to sample the many treats for lunch, tea or dinner.

Sheila Mack Gourmet Cooking
1116 N. Crescent Heights Blvd.,
W. Hollywood
656-5897

If you're looking for a caterer/party designer who specializes in real food with a French or Mediterranean twist, Sheila is the one to call. Her recipes are well respected, particularly such dishes as torte di ricotta, Brie in brioche with apricots, roast leg of lamb provençale, veal medallions with a grapefruit-reduction sauce and yucca-root fries. Her "chocolate essence" brownies are famous—and rightfully so.

Parties Plus
3455 S. La Cienega Blvd., Culver City
838-3800

When Julie and Michael Loshin noticed the parties they were frequenting lacked pizzazz, they hired a set designer and a chef and formed their own party production/catering company, specializing in the spectacular. Full-service in every sense of the term, Parties Plus has organized such productions as the NFL Superbowl XXI gala for 3,500 guests, myriad fund-raisers, corporate events, film-industry bashes and deluxe private dinner parties. Executive chef Robert Wilson has gained notoriety with coverage in such magazines as *Food & Wine* and *Bon Appétit*. Definitely one of L.A.'s premier party planners.

Rococo
6734 Valjean Ave., Van Nuys
(818) 909-0990

If you follow the society columns in the *Los Angeles Times*, you'll know of Rococo. Though its small parties are always well done, Rococo is most famous for catering gala affairs for the record industry, movie studios and many of L.A.'s biggest charity and society events. Its repertoire is more classic than inventive, but the food is first-rate no matter what the menu.

CAVIAR

Caspian Caviar
204 S. Beverly Dr., Beverly Hills
274-4909
Open Mon.-Fri. 9:30 a.m.-5 p.m., Sat. 10 a.m.-2 p.m.

Only the finest imported Iranian and Russian caviar is sold at this shop, which supplies many restaurants in town. This isn't a place for browsing; you can call for information and a price list, and deliveries are made seven days a week. The pride of the house is Caspian imperial caviar, from osetra sturgeon; before the Iranian revolution it was reserved just for the Shah and for his gifts to other heads of state. All the caviars are hand-packed here, so quality is assured.

CHEESE

The Cheese Store
419 N. Beverly Dr., Beverly Hills
278-2855
Open Mon.-Sat. 9:30 a.m.-6 p.m.
Virtually every cheese available in America can be found at this wonderful shop, which stocks more than 400 types of cheese: chèvres from France and California, Parmesans and buffalo mozzarellas from Italy, Stiltons from Britain and more, much more. Certainly the best cheese shop in Los Angeles.

Say Cheese
2800 Hyperion Ave., Silverlake
665-0545
Open Tues.-Sun. 10 a.m.-6:30 p.m.
A remarkable selection of cheeses from around the world are crammed into the deli cases in this tiny Silverlake shop, one of the few decent cheese shops in L.A. The men and women who run the place are exceptionally friendly, and they're happy to let you taste the cheeses before you buy. You'll also find a few fancy French wines, good deli meats, sun-dried tomatoes, porcini mushrooms, chocolate truffles from the Bay Area's peerless Cocolat, coffee beans, imported grocery items, candies, coffee grinders, espresso machines and teapots. Say Cheese also carries Fortnum and Mason English teas and preserves.

Trader Joe's
10850 National Blvd., W.L.A.
474-9299
Open daily 9 a.m.-9 p.m.
The selection of cheeses is varied, the prices unbeatable. The offerings change regularly, depending on the store's latest finds, but you'll generally find the more popular cheeses from Britain, France, Denmark, Switzerland and the United States. An added discount for buying whole wheels is available. There are several other locations, including Sherman Oaks, West Hollywood and Pasadena.

Wally's
2107 Westwood Blvd., Westwood
475-0606
Open daily 10 a.m.-7 p.m.
Not only is Wally's one of the finest wine shops in the city, it is also the best place on the westside to find a large selection of excellent cheeses. Triple crèmes and double crèmes are particularly in evidence. There's no better accompaniment to your cheese than breads from La Brea Bakery, which are available at Wally's. Gift baskets and delivery available.

COFFEE

Graffeo Coffee Roasting Company
315 N. Beverly Dr., Beverly Hills
273-4232
Open Mon.-Sat. 9 a.m.-5:30 p.m.
As far as we're concerned, there's only one coffee merchant in town: Graffeo. Now that this San Francisco institution has come south, you need look no further for great coffee. The store is simplicity itself, just a counter, a few burlap coffee bags, a giant roaster behind glass walls and an intoxicating aroma. The selection is simple: just three varieties. Buy the light roast if you like an American-style brew, the dark if you like it European-style (including espresso), and the Swiss water-process decaf if you've given up caffeine. Graffeo's high-quality beans and skillful roasting make for a superb cup of coffee. If you don't want to deal with Beverly Hills parking, take advantage of Graffeo's booming mail-order business.

CONFECTIONS

Confection Connection
18660 Ventura Blvd., Tarzana
(818) 881-9991
Open Mon.-Sat. 10 a.m.-6 p.m.
Here you'll find more than 500 varieties of imported and domestic chocolates and can-

dies, including everything from giant blackberry truffles, chocolate cordials and white-chocolate seashells to chocolate-dipped popcorn and fruits. For kids of all ages there are old-fashioned suckers, giant jawbreakers and licorice ropes; for the diet-conscious, a large selection of low-calorie and sugar-free confections.

Edelweiss Chocolates
444 N. Cañon Dr., Beverly Hills
275-0341
Open Mon.-Fri. 9:30 a.m.-5:30 p.m., Sat. 10 a.m.-5:30 p.m.
Since 1940, this shop has been known for its handmade chocolates. There's a variety of truffles and chocolate-covered fruits, but the best candies in the shop (and perhaps the best candies in L.A.) are the chocolate-covered marshmallows. Attractive and delicious gift baskets, party favors and holiday candies are also available.

Jo's Candies
213 Manhattan Beach Blvd.,
Manhattan Beach
545-1138
Open Mon.-Fri. 9:30 a.m.-6 p.m., Sat. 9:30 a.m.-5 p.m.
For almost 45 years, Jo's Candies has been a closely guarded secret in Manhattan Beach—and for good reason. This "candy cottage" has won international awards for its truffles (Grand Marnier and Chambourd are popular flavorings), while the peanut-butter creams, bordeauxs, caramels and English toffee also win raves. This is the only place we know of to get semisweet-chocolate-covered graham crackers—and they're absolutely divine.

Littlejohn's English Toffee House
Farmer's Market, 6333 W. 3rd St.,
Wilshire District
936-5379
Open Mon.-Sat. 9 a.m.-6:30 p.m., Sun. 10 a.m.-5 p.m.
English toffee–lovers come from miles around for this exceptional chocolate-and-almond-covered crunchycandy. Lately Littlejohn's sells as many caramel apples and pounds of fudge (nine kinds in all) as it does buttery, fresh-daily toffee.

Teuscher Chocolates of Switzerland
9548 Brighton Way, Beverly Hills
276-2776
Open Mon.-Thurs. 10 a.m.-9 p.m., Fri.-Sat. 10 a.m.-10 p.m.
These are without a doubt the most beautiful boxes of chocolates you'll find in the city. They're also the most expensive. The chocolates are imported weekly from Zurich and aren't quite as sweet as those made by domestic confectioners. A few varieties can be a bit dull, but we must profess a weakness for the white-chocolate and Champagne truffles, not to mention the truffles with nuts.

GOURMET TO GO

Cheese and Pasta
1415 Montana Ave., Santa Monica
394-2131
Open Mon.-Sat. 10 a.m.-7 p.m., Sun. 10 a.m.-5:30 p.m.
Perhaps not quite sophisticated enough for true gourmets, but well appreciated by those looking to pick up an à la carte salad or a quick, freshly prepared meal, Cheese and Pasta prides itself on its premier selection of European cheeses, including world-class Bucheron flown in weekly. There are seventeen different three-course boxed meals to go. Our recommendations for the picnic-bound: curried chicken salad, dilled cucumber salad, chicken-liver pâté and La Brea Bakery breads (available Wednesday through Saturday). Catering services available.

Hugo's
8401 Santa Monica Blvd., W. Hollywood
654-4088
Open Mon.-Fri. 6 a.m.-11 p.m., Sat.-Sun. 7 a.m.-midnight.
For some, Hugo's is an informal but intelligent restaurant—the pumpkin pancakes and pasta Mama get rave reviews. For other's, it's a gourmet pitstop before a beach or Hollywood Bowl outing. Hugo's takeout counter presents an array of excellent pasta sauces, salads, hot entrées, baguettes and desserts; pâtés, terrines and picnic baskets to order are available. The prices are as high as the quality.

The Kitchen for Exploring Foods
1434 W. Colorado Blvd., Pasadena
(818) 793-7218
Open Tues.-Fri. noon-6 p.m., Sat. 10:30 a.m.-6 p.m.

This full-service caterer features a daily selection of innovative gourmet foods, including salads, sandwiches, soups, fresh breads and delectable desserts. Bring in a platter and the staff will display your order to your liking; with advance notice, The Kitchen will pack a complete lunch or dinner from dozens of choices. Cooking classes and culinary accessories, too.

Le Marmiton
1327 Montana Ave., Santa Monica
393-7716
Open Tues.-Sat. 9:30 a.m.-7 p.m.

Accomplished French chefs prepare fine salads and appetizers, entrées (both fresh and frozen) and pastries—everything you need to fool your friends into thinking you studied at La Varenne. The dishes tend toward the Provençale and the classic instead of the nouvelle. Rye country bread and chocolate Grand Marnier truffles are a speciality. There are also some good French cheeses. Prices are high but not unreasonable.

Netty's
See "Cafés" in the Quick Bites chapter.

Pasta, Etc.
8650 W. Sunset Blvd., W. Hollywood
854-0094
Open Mon.-Sat. 9 a.m.-10:30 p.m.

Lenore Breslauer's selection of pastas, salads, hot entrées, cheeses, wines and desserts is so tempting that the option of sitting down to enjoy a meal here is difficult to resist. The expanded antipasto bar includes hot pasta specialties, including "power pasta," a low-calorie, oil-free dish of fresh tomatoes, chicken breast, basil and capers. Breslauer also packs a rustic gift basket full of homemade delights, starting at $60.

Pasta, Pasta, Pasta
8134 W. 3rd St., W. Hollywood
653-2051
Open Mon.-Fri. 10 a.m.-7 p.m., Sat. 10 a.m.-6 p.m.

If you bring in your own serving dish, Pasta, Pasta, Pasta will fill it with any number of ready-to-heat pasta entrées. There are four kinds of lasagne, including duck and vegetarian, plus pasta salads and fresh and prepared tortellini and ravioli.

The Pasta Shoppe
1964 Hillhurst Ave., Los Feliz
668-0458
Open Mon.-Fri. 10:30 a.m.-6:30 p.m., Sat. 9:30 a.m.-5:30 p.m.

An outstanding array of fresh-daily pasta colors the showcase here. We could easily build a meal around such flavors as jalapeño-pepper, lemon-basil, mushroom, rosemary, carrot, garlic, tomato or black squid ink. The pasta is cut to order, with five noodle varieties to choose from, and there are delicious cream and pesto sauces to complement the noodles. A real gourmet find.

Le Petit Four
8654 Sunset Blvd., W. Hollywood
652-3863
Open Mon.-Sat. 9 a.m.-11 p.m., Sun. 9 a.m.-6 p.m.

There's no question that these pastries are wonderful (especially the fruit tarts and miniature petits fours), but you'll be missing out on some gourmet treats if you don't try the quiches, feuilletés, pâtés, Belgian chocolates, hors d'oeuvres, cold salads and grocery products from Fauchon. There are a few tables in the back if you can't wait till you get home. Charming service by young Frenchwomen.

MARKETS

ETHNIC MARKETS

Alpine Market
Alpine Village, 833 W. Torrance Blvd., Torrance
321-5660
Open daily 11 a.m.-7 p.m.

The Bavarian smells here are irresistible: smoked meats, fresh cheeses, potato salads and black breads. Over 50 kinds of meats can be ordered at the counter, including kitchen-made sausages, Hungarian bacon and salami and Black Forest hams; the bakery is stocked with freshly baked, diet-defeating Continental pastries; and the liquor department is a year-round Oktoberfest, with dozens of imported beers as well as German wines. The Alpine Market's own brewery is next door.

Bay Cities Importing
1517 Lincoln Blvd., Santa Monica
395-8279
Open Mon.-Sat. 8 a.m.-7 p.m., Sun. 8 a.m.-6 p.m.

Even if you've never cooked a day in your life, this place will make you want to run home and whip up some pasta al pesto. It's a large deli/market that sells almost every food product Italy imports: spices, pastas, dozens of olive oils, wines, sweets, coffees and cans of everything from tomato sauce to anchovies. A large deli counter sells meats, sausages, pasta salads, cheeses from around the world and excellent sandwiches to go. Some French and Middle Eastern imported delicacies are also offered, along with delicious French and Italian breads from local bakeries and first-rate fresh pasta.

Bezjian's Grocery
4725 Santa Monica Blvd., Hollywood
663-1503
Open Mon.-Sat. 10 a.m.-7 p.m., Sun. 10 a.m.-4 p.m.

This friendly market is a gold mine of foodstuffs for both Middle Eastern and Indian cooking. For Indian cooks, there are unusual chutneys, freshly prepared garam masalas (mixture of ground spices), tandoori pastes, chickpea flour and ghee (clarified butter). For Middle Eastern cooks, there is a deli counter stocked with four kinds of feta and plumb olives, cold-case shelves piled with frozen spanakopita, tyropita and moussaka, and fresh hummus and baba ghanooj for spreading on the great Middle Eastern breads. Rounding out the stock are cooking utensils and cookbooks.

Bharat Bazaar
11510 W. Washington Blvd., Culver City
398-6766
Open Mon. & Wed.-Sat. 11 a.m.-7 p.m., Sun. 11 a.m.-6 p.m.

No devotee of Indian cooking could fail to be delighted with the incredible offerings here. The shelves are packed with jars of chutneys (called pickles on most labels), including lime, tamarind and mango. There are ready-made sauces from every part of India, as well as everything you need to start from scratch. Flours include graham and chickpea. The fairly large shop is run by a friendly, helpful staff.

Domingo's Italian Grocery and Delicatessen
17548 Ventura Blvd., Encino
(818) 981-4466
Open Tues.-Sat. 9 a.m.-6 p.m., Sun. 10 a.m.-4 p.m.

Counters and aisles are crammed with Italian breads, fresh pasta, homemade sauces, olive oil, vinegars, imported hams, sausages, cheeses and Italian wines. Don't even attempt to find what you're looking for without assistance—there are just too many goods packed into this small shop. Patience is the key word here; someone will eventually climb up to the top shelf and get the tomato sauce you've been waiting for.

Enbun
Japanese Village Plaza, 1st St. & Central Ave., Little Toyko
680-3280
Open Mon.-Sat. 9 a.m.-6:30 p.m., Sun. 10 a.m.-6 p.m.

This charming grocery has sleek architectural lines and a full assortment of Japanese foods, which are displayed with the unerring eye of an artist. In the produce department, persimmons and lady apples are piled with care. The fish counter sells the freshest cuts for sashimi. The cold cases are filled with packages of fishcake rolls and pickled vegetables. Bakery items include mochigashi (rice cakes filled with bean paste) and anpan (bread rolls filled with bean paste). There are also plenty of sakes, beers and imported rice crackers in this most browsable of markets.

Gianfranco
11363 Santa Monica Blvd., W.L.A.
477-7777
Open Mon.-Sat. 9:30 a.m.-11 p.m.

This spacious, modern and tempting deli sells everthing Italian, from wine to panettone (a light yeast cake), cheese to olive oil. There's an entire wall lined with boxes of Perugina chocolates, and glass cases full of cold meats, good antipasti, homemade pastas, wonderful cheeses and warming trays with such dishes as polenta, sausages, stuffed shells and meatballs.

Most of it, except the lackluster pastries, is tasty and reasonably priced. Gianfranco also serves lunch and dinner.

Liborio Market
864 S. Vermont Ave., Mid-Wilshire
386-1458
Open daily 8 a.m.-8 p.m.

This neighborhood market (whose neighbors are Mexican, Salvadoran and Guatemalan) is filled with hard-to-find ingredients necessary for many south-of-the-border recipes. There are manioc and plantain flours, guava pastes for dessert pastries, ready-to-use canned black beans, banana leaves for wrapping chicken dishes, and such odd tubers as malanga. Check out the frozen section for Cuban tamales, the soda section for unusual imports, the canned goods for fiery salsas and the spice section for packets of red achiote paste for Yucatecan-style cooking. Not much English is spoken here, so it pays to know what you want—and to experiment.

El Mercado
3425 E. 1st St., E.L.A.
268-3451
Open Mon.-Thurs. 10 a.m.-8 p.m., Fri.-Sun. 9 a.m.-9 p.m.

A true Mexican market, not a tourist spot, El Mercado is the closest thing we have to Guadalaraja's La Libertad or Mexico City's La Merced. This place is raucous, messy and full of life. Vendors call to you—gently—to buy their wares. In the center of this three-story building is a grocery filled with chiles, chayotes (a vegetable of the melon and gourd family), plantains and packaged spices. All around it, small stalls sell Mexican cheeses and sour creams, chorizo, Mexican chocolate, an addictive caramel sauce called cajeta de Celaya, teas, piñatas, clay cookware (much cheaper than in Olvera Street shops), meats and fish. Kids love to watch the tortilleria in action: huge machines turn out fresh, hot corn tortillas. Upstairs, there are several fast-food restaurants and wonderful mariachi music.

New Meiji Market
1620 W. Redondo Beach Blvd., Gardena
323-7696
Open Mon.-Sat. 8 a.m.-9 p.m., Sun. 8 a.m.-8 p.m.

For any serious cook of Asian cuisines, a visit here is a died-and-gone-to-heaven experience. Although primarily a Japanese market, there is plenty to captivate cooks of Chinese, Korean, Filipino and Southeast Asian dishes. In this huge market there are whole aisles devoted to soy sauces, and to noodles and rice crackers (200 kinds). The cold cases feature Filipino lumpia wrappers and Mandarin pancakes, both ready to fill at home. The produce section is worth a drive in itself: Chinese broccoli, winter melon, Japanese pears and more. The meat counter offers cuts you can't buy from Western-style butchers, including beef cut for sukiyaki and shabu shabu and thinly sliced rib-eye steak for Korean barbecue. At the fish counter are giant clams, fresh tuna and blue mackerel.

GOURMET MARKETS

Ashford Market
1627 Montana Ave., Santa Monica
458-1562
Open Mon.-Sat. 7 a.m.-6:30 p.m., Sun. 8 a.m.-2 p.m.

Several swell shops make up this market. Closest to the Montana door is Il Fornaio, which has fresh pasta sauces and a good assortment of breads and pastries, the most popular of which are the bran muffins, blueberry muffins and cannèlla (cinnamon twists). There's a flower shop that's small but filled with stunning posies. Then there's Tanaka's, which makes buying fresh produce as visually satisfying as a visit to an art gallery. The people there may not be able to spell the names of the exotic fruits and vegetables, but they sure can display them with panache. And, finally, there's L.A. Gourmet, which offers a typically trendy takeout menu of salads, soups and snacks.

Bristol Farms
606 Fair Oaks Ave., S. Pasadena
(818) 441-5450
Open Mon.-Sat. 9 a.m.-9 p.m., Sun. 10 a.m.-7 p.m.
837 Silver Spur Rd., Rolling Hills Estates
541-9157
Open Mon.-Sat. 9 a.m.-8 p.m., Sun. 10 a.m.-7 p.m.

Bristol Farms is simply a marvel: pristine produce, excellent California wines, homemade sausages, home-smoked meats, myriad cheeses, fresh pasta, prepared sauces, a sushi chef to filet the fresh fish of your choice, dozens of coffees, fresh breads and pastries, gourmet-to-go entrées, a small café, quality cookbooks and utensils and the finest domestic and imported groceries (spices, soups, soy sauces, you name it). This grocery store is pure entertainment; we can while away hours here, wandering the aisles, sipping the free coffee and nibbling at the many free food samples. Pasadena's Bristol Farms ranks high on our list for selection, service and just plain fun. The Rolling Hills Estates store, the first Bristol Farms, is a smaller-scale jewel of a market. Prices reflect the high quality of the products.

Chalet Gourmet

7880 W. Sunset Blvd., W. Hollywood
874-6301
Open daily 9 a.m.-9 p.m.

Chalet Gourmet is, along with Jurgensen's, the granddaddy of L.A. gourmet markets, and it recently purchased the once-impressive Irvine Ranch Market in the Beverly Center. In recent years Chalet Gourmet has seemed a little drab and passé, but new management is in the process of updating. There is the expected array of first-rate meats, fish and cheese, along with good baked goods, gourmet takeout, decent produce and high-end grocery items, as well as a vast wine department, gift baskets and Hollywood Bowl boxed meals, with free delivery in the surrounding area.

Gelson's Market

Marina Marketplace, 13455 Maxella Ave., Marina del Rey
306-2952
Open daily 8 a.m.-10 p.m.

L.A.'s venerable gourmet market is grander than ever in its new Marina Marketplace location. There's a first-rate bakery and small espresso bar, premarinated fish, Oriental entrées fresh from the wok, sushi, complete catering and eight different "Elite Complete Meals to Go," stylishy packed in double-deck boxes. Other locations include the Century City Shopping Center and the Valley.

Grand Central Public Market

317 S. Broadway, Downtown
624-2378
Open Mon.-Sat. 9 a.m.-6 p.m., Sun. 10 a.m.-5 p.m.

Grand Central's face-lift has transformed it into an approachable emporium for middle-class folks who find the shabby, hectic life on Broadway a bit nerve-racking. Inside, the huge marketplace is like Disneyland for food groupies. The meat stalls are filled with lamb heads, bull testicles, pig tails and more. The produce stands feature cacti, chayotes, a dozen or more kinds of fresh chiles, and bargains on ripe bananas, pears and the like. At the apothecary near the Hill Street entrance are jars filled with both herbs for cooking and for curing all your ills. Several stalls feature dried chiles, nuts, coconuts, fruits, rice and beans, all sold in bulk so you can buy just the amount you need. It pays to comparison shop among the stalls, because prices can vary considerably, and to have a shopping list before you leave home—impulse buyers run amok here.

Irvine Ranch Market

Beverly Center, 142 S. San Vicente Blvd., W. Hollywood
657-1931
Open Mon.-Sat. 9 a.m.-10 p.m., Sun. 9 a.m.-9 p.m.

On the ground floor of this battleship-as-shopping-mall, you'll find the once-legendary Irvine Ranch Market. The new owner, Chalet Gourmet, is in the midst of revamping and upgrading, particularly the meat, fish and cheese departments. The market is still known for its exceptional choice of vegetables, fresh herbs and exotic fruits, an array that stretches as far as the eye can see. In general, the quality is above average, but prices can be exorbitant. There is a good choice of French, Italian and California wines. Try to avoid this place on Saturday or during the after-work hours, when it is jammed with every yuppie in town. Customer service is good; purchases are sent directly by elevator to a pickup point in the parking garage.

Jurgensen's

842 E. California Blvd., Pasadena
(818) 792-3121
Open Mon.-Sat. 8 a.m.-7 p.m.

The newly refurbished Jurgensen's is a full-service, fine-foods market with a meat department, deli, cappuccino bar, bakery and hot foods to go. Most produce is organically grown; the selection of gourmet-food items and fine wines hails from all over the world. There are elaborate gift baskets to order and delivery that's as specialized as a pack-the-fridge-for-you service. There's another location in Beverly Hills as well as a smaller gourmet gift and wine store in the Jonathan Club downtown.

Trader Joe's
610 S. Arroyo Pkwy., Pasadena
(818) 356-9066
Open daily 9 a.m.-9 p.m.

Illustrious founder Joe Coulombe has a certain prescience (and a good business sense), and several years ago he saw a trend developing. He noticed that young urban Americans were getting more education and were traveling more, and therefore developing tastes for the finer things in life—but they didn't yet have the money to pay for them. So he had the very good idea to offer good wines, cheeses, high-ticket grocery items and tasty, natural frozen foods, all at prices a graduate student could afford. He struck gold—not only did graduate students flock to his store, but soon much of Los Angeles was making Trader Joe's a regular stop. Consequently, new stores continue to open all around the city, and more items are added to the store's line. The selection of domestic and imported cheeses is excellent, as is the selection of wines, both respected California boutique wines and wines from around the world—at well-below-retail prices. Trader Joe's–brand nuts, dried fruits, vitamins, granola cereals, blue-corn tortilla chips, locally baked goods and imported coffees are admirable. There are surprisingly delicious frozen foods, from fresh-frozen jumbo tiger shrimp to pizzas to spring rolls and such imports as jars of crabmeat from Thailand, tins of Roma tomatoes and "colossal" stuffed olives. This Pasadena location is spacious and pleasant; other locations include 10850 National Boulevard, West L.A. (474-9299), 7304 Santa Monica Boulevard, West Hollywood (851-9772) and 14119 Riverside Drive, Sherman Oaks (818-501-9349).

WINE

Briggs Wines & Spirits
13038 San Vicente Blvd., Brentwood
476-1223
Open Mon.-Sat. 9 a.m.-7 p.m., Sun. 11 a.m.-5 p.m.

Briggs stocks thousands of bottles of wines that are neatly arranged alphabetically and by varietal type. This shop is especially recommended for its large selection of ports and California boutique wines from some of the smaller growers. It is also happy to special order, with a six-bottle minimum.

L.A. Wine Co.
4935 McConnell Ave., Mar Vista
306-9463
Open Mon.-Sat. 10 a.m.-6 p.m., Sun. noon-5 p.m.

The prices are about the lowest in town at the L.A. Wine Co., a hard-to-find garagelike shop that stocks an excellent selection of California wines, including the smaller labels. There are also imports from France, Italy and Germany, though the specialty is clearly California. The staff is helpful and extremely knowledgeable, and you would do well to attend to their advice.

Red Carpet Wine & Spirits Merchants
400 E. Glenoaks Blvd., Glendale
(818) 247-5544
Open daily 9 a.m.-11 p.m.

This spacious 5,500-square-foot store, complete with a redwood-paneled wine room where classes and tastings are held, carries rare and premium wines from all over the world, including ones from the best German, Italian and French estates, as well as those from such small California wineries as Chalone, Quail Ridge and Long. Red Carpet also stocks exotic beers and liqueurs. Free delivery with orders over $75.

Trader Joe's
610 S. Arroyo Pkwy., Pasadena
(818) 356-9066
Open daily 9 a.m.-9 p.m.

Trader Joe's is absolutely indispensable to wine-lovers on a budget—or any wine-lover, for that matter. Veteran wine buyer Bob Berning has a special talent for buying up overstocks and the tail ends of lots from good wineries all over the world, and there's always a large selection of drinkable wines priced under $5. Try the Trader Joe's label for table wine; it's bottled by some of the best California and French wineries and is dirt cheap. In addition, there's a full stock of California boutique wines, priced below retail, and a vast assortment of imported and domestic sparkling wines. This Trader Joe's is the oldest and the nicest; there are several other locations, including 10850 National Boulevard, West L.A. (474-9299); 7304 Santa Monica Boulevard, West Hollywood (851-9772); and 14119 Riverside Drive, Sherman Oaks (818-501-9349).

Wally's
2107 Westwood Blvd., Westwood
475-0606
10152 Riverside Dr., Toluca Lake
(818) 505-6454
Open Mon.-Sat. 10 a.m.-8 p.m., Sun. 10 a.m.-6 p.m.
Wally's is the crème de la crème of L.A.'s wines-and-spirits stores. This airy shop in blond-wood tones has a remarkable selection of Cognacs, grappas, single-malt scotches, vintage ports and imported beers. The sales staff is extremely knowledgeable and particularly helpful in party planning, quantity buying and sending gift baskets filled with wines, Champagnes, imported chocolates, cheeses and crackers.

Wine House
2311 Cotner Ave., W.L.A.
479-3731
Open Mon.-Sat. 10 a.m.-7 p.m., Sun. noon-6 p.m.
No charming boutique atmosphere here, just acres of wines from around the world, including a huge selection of always-changing special bargains. For those who are serious about their wines, the Wine House is a beloved home away from home. Special classes and tastings are held frequently.

The Wine Merchant
9701 Santa Monica Blvd., Beverly Hills
278-7322
Open Mon.-Sat. 9:30 a.m.-6:30 p.m.
A full-service wine shop, The Wine Merchant stocks a spectacular selection of popular and rare vintages and offers wine-appreciation classes and regular wine tastings to introduce new vintages. It also rents out 58-degree wine lockers so you can store that Bordeaux, which won't be perfected until the year 2000.

The Wine Shop
223 N. Larchmont Blvd., Larchmont Village
466-1220
Open Mon.-Sat. 10 a.m.-7 p.m.
This narrow, crowded shop doesn't have thousands of bottles, but it does have an excellent selection of California wines, hard-to-find premium Champagnes from small production houses and boutique beers from remote breweries. You'll also be impressed with the choice ports, Cognacs, Armagnacs and single-malt scotches and imported wines in every price range. Thankfully, the salespeople are knowledgeable and helpful. The small grocery area in back is stocked gourmet items such as with pâtés, cheeses, caviar, smoked salmon and imported delicacies. Prices are fair, and the specials are always good deals.

GIFTS

Abercrombie & Fitch
Beverly Center, 121 N. La Cienega Blvd., W. Hollywood
652-4761
Open Mon.-Fri. 10 a.m.-9 p.m., Sat. 10 a.m.-8 p.m., Sun. 11 a.m.-6 p.m.
All of the objects here have one thing in common: they effuse the aura of old money. Musts for some, ridiculous to many, the stock includes everything from wooden-duck decoys to $2,500 croquet sets to overpriced safari suits.

Asiaphile
7975 Melrose Ave., W. Hollywood
653-4744
Open Mon.-Sat. 11 a.m.-6 p.m.
The ancient Japanese art of imbuing otherwise common objects—combs, brushes, knives—with an uncommon beauty comes alive here. Washi boxes, made of woven strips of handmade Japanese paper that are painstakingly coated with 60 applications of vermilion lacquer, are a wonder. So is a polished box made from stone. Other beautiful and intri-

guing items: bamboo-handled brushes, contemporary matte-black and white glazed porcelain tableware and Noguchi paper lamps.

Brookstone
Beverly Center, 121 N. La Cienega Blvd., W. Hollywood
659-9491
Open Mon.-Fri. 10 a.m.-9 p.m., Sat. 10 a.m.-8 p.m., Sun. 11 a.m.-6 p.m.

This gadget store, high on concept, employs the gimmick of a showroom atmosphere, where only floor samples fill the space; customers note their choices on clipboards, and an eager staff fills the orders from a behind-the-scenes stockroom. You'll find exceptionally giftable items: high-tech and well-thought-out tools for the garden, garage, car, closet, bathroom and kitchen, even some unique games.

Casa de Sousa
19 Olvera St., Downtown
626-7076
Open daily 10 a.m.-9 p.m.

A tradition on Olvera Street, Casa de Sousa imports its folk art directly from Mexican and Central American sources, so prices are extremely reasonable. Vases with a soft, polished luster from Oaxaca are $49.50, and decorative plates and serving platters range from $4.95 to $10. There are rustic signed metal wall pieces with "tree of life" motifs from Haiti ($49.50) and wonderful Guatemalan fabric cocktail napkins (packaged by the dozen, at $4.95).

Craft and Folk Art Museum Shop
5800 Wilshire Blvd., Wilshire District
937-9099
Open Tues.-Sun. 11 a.m.-5 p.m.

This nonprofit shop of the Craft and Folk Art Museum offers contemporary and ethnic folk art at reasonable prices. The selection of jewelry (from avant-garde to whimsical) is particularly good; there are also beautiful ceramics and glassware. a good choice of art books and a novel collection of postcards and cards. It's nearly impossible to resist a purchase in this friendly and enticing shop. Most of the offerings are from local craftspeople.

The Folk Tree
217 S. Fair Oaks Ave., Pasadena
(818) 795-8733
Open Mon.-Wed. & Fri.-Sat. 10 a.m.-6 p.m., Thurs. 10 a.m.-8 p.m., Sun. noon-5 p.m.

Nicely displayed in a series of small rooms, the primarily Hispanic folk crafts here are a mix of mainstream and bizarre. Hand-blown glasses, serapes, primitive pots and tin-framed mirrors are set off by fantasy wooden figures and religious antiques. You'll also find clothes and jewelry from around the world, including Indonesian batiked shawls and Guatemalan fabrics by the yard. The spacious back room, which looks onto a charming yard, is set up as a small art gallery where four themed shows are held each year. The Folk Tree is appealing to both the serious collector and the casual browser. The neighboring Folk Tree Collection is a new branch that carries an eclectic mix of contemporary and antique Southwest furniture, crafts and collectibles.

Freehand Gallery
8413 W. 3rd St., W. Hollywood
655-2607
Open Mon.-Sat. 11 a.m.-6 p.m.

Carol Sauvion has amassed a unique collection of beautiful handmade clothing, jewelry, ceramics, glassware and gift items. Everything's one of a kind, and she has an excellent eye for unusual yet eminently tasteful crafts, all made by local artisans. You're sure to find something for anyone in this bright, attractive shop, from charming little $15 earrings to beautiful ceramic vases to handsome, avant-garde clothing.

Geary's North
437 N. Beverly Dr., Beverly Hills
273-4741
Open Mon. 9:30 a.m.-9 p.m., Tues.-Fri. 9:30 a.m.-6 p.m., Sat. 10 a.m.-5:30 p.m.

Much less stodgy than its mother shop down the street, Geary's North stocks trendy, colorful ceramics, the popular Lladro Spanish porcelain, framed graphics, pillows and other decorative accessories, instead of the traditional crystal, china and silver gifts offered at Geary's. Prices are within reason, and the selection is sometimes unusual.

Hammacher Schlemmer

309 N. Rodeo Dr., Beverly Hills
859-7255
Open Mon.-Sat. 10 a.m.-6 p.m.

Known for its high-tech gadgetry and non-essential (but oh-so-clever) gift items, this is the famous catalog company's only West Coast retail store. HS likes to tout its wares as "the best," "the smallest" and "the only"—as in the best home exercise bicycle, the smallest copy machine and the only automatic vinaigrette mixer. While there are some purely gimmicky items here, the store's (and the catalog's) strength lies in its high-quality practical items. We love the cordless upright vacuum, the electronic cat door through which only your code key–wearing kitty may pass (we're not kidding) and the Russian military wristwatch.

Heaven

Beverly Center, 121 N. La Cienega Blvd., W. Hollywood
657-3565
Open Mon.-Thurs. 9:30 a.m.-9:30 p.m., Fri.-Sat. 9:30 a.m.-11 p.m., Sun. 11 a.m.-8 p.m.

Young at heart, overpriced and extremely successful, Heaven is filled with the silliest stock in town: monster makeup, rubber snakes, plastic Kewpie dolls, T-shirts emblazoned with the Shirelles, Captain Video and Heckel and Jeckel, and a great selection of penny candy (needless to say, penny candy is no longer a penny), from red hots and jawbreakers to cigarette-shape bubble gum. Other stores on Melrose and in Beverly Hills.

Jadis

2701 Main St., Santa Monica
396-3477
Open daily noon-5 p.m., or by appt.

An unusual shop with an equally unusual collection of "pseudo-scientific" objects, perpetual-motion machines, authentic 1930s telephones, Teslar coils and other fascinating oddities. Any of these make great movie-prop rentals or gifts for entertainment's sake. Everything is in perfect condition. The adjacent shop, Paris 1900, sells lovely white-lace Victorian-era clothing for women via mail order or by appointment.

Koala Blue

7366 Melrose Ave., W. Hollywood
655-3596
Open Mon.-Sat. 11 a.m.-7 p.m., Sun. 11 a.m.-6 p.m.

This shop knows how to sell itself, over and over again. The brainchild of Australian princess Olivia Newton-John, this store is pretty much a Johnny-one-note. Almost everything here has the name "Koala Blue" printed on it, along with the shop's cutesy logo (naturally, a koala bear). Still, there's something to be said for a boutique that stocks Aussie cookbooks, cookies, cakes, candies, wine, beer (Fosters) and pleasantly casual (if self-serving) clothes.

Lavender & Lace

656 N. Larchmont Blvd., Larchmont Village
856-4846
Open Tues.-Fri. 10:30 a.m.-6:30 p.m., Sat. 10 a.m.-5 p.m.

A treat for anyone yearning for the gentler graces of yesteryear. Owner J.J. Jenkins and her husband, John Waterson, modeled the shop after the French country flea markets she frequented while studying fashion design in Paris. Her penchant for flowers comes through in the starched bed linens, pillows with vintage crocheted borders, tapestry-covered hatboxes, tea runners, tablecloths and lace curtains. Use your imagination, and you might hear strains of the hustle and bustle of a French flea market as you shop here.

Lawry's California Center

570 W. Ave. 26, E.L.A.
224-6800
Open daily 10:30 a.m.-9 p.m.

Clearly dedicated to the art of gift giving, Lawry's is seemingly set up for impulse buying during a lunch-and-tour visit. The gift shops are extensive enough to warrant a trip on their own, especially before Christmas. These shops are dedicated to the good life, the *Sunset* magazine life. You'll find everything it takes to pull off home entertaining with style: terrific paper goods, barbecue and patio items, stunning tureens, lavish platters and bright tablecloths. There's also great ethnic clothing, toys, cute stationery and cards and lots of kitchen gadgets.

Lehr and Black

345 N. Cañon Dr., Beverly Hills
278-8200
Open Mon.-Fri. 10 a.m-6 p.m., Sat. 10 a.m.-5 p.m.

This store is well known for its handmade invitations, party accessories and some unusual gifts and home accessories. Items range from crystal, silver and antique pieces to less costly Lucite boxes and picture frames. There's everything you'll need for hosting a party, and wonderful gifts (such as a sweets basket), which can be delivered anywhere in L.A.

New Stone Age

8407 W. 3rd St., W. Hollywood
658-5969
Open Mon.-Sat. 11 a.m.-6 p.m.

This gallery/store does a good job of accommodating the burgeoning American crafts movement. The focus is on artists who "push the limits" of traditional craft materials. Among the unconventional finds: hand-forged wrought-iron candlesticks, folk art, small-scale furniture, art glass, conversation-sparking jewelry and other inspired gift ideas. Prices range from $5 to several hundred.

Pierre Deux

428 N. Rodeo Dr., Beverly Hills
550-7265
Open Mon.-Sat. 9:30 a.m.-5:30 p.m.

With branches all over the world, this beautiful provincial garden offers country florals printed on anything and everything. The frames, notebooks, calendars, shoulder bags that remind us of traveling cosmetic carryalls, clothes and fabrics are all nestled into a rustic store with a cozy atmosphere. Worth spoiling a little girl are the pinafore-style dresses and huggable cloth dolls.

The Pleasure Chest

7733 Santa Monica Blvd., W. Hollywood
659-7970
Open Mon.-Thurs. & Sun. 10 a.m.-midnight, Fri.-Sat. 10 a.m.-1 a.m.

Sex is out of the closet and onto the shelves of this elegant, modern erotic-items supermarket. Here you can find the largest selection of carnal merchandise anywhere in the country. Lingerie, chastity belts, massage oils, enema kits, chains, leather restraints—even edible panties—are all here, waiting to satisfy your every fantasy (or nightmare, depending on your preference). Plain brown wrappers and mail-order catalogs are available for the timid.

The Price of His Toys

9601 Santa Monica Blvd., Beverly Hills
274-9955
Open Mon.-Sat. 10 a.m.-6 p.m.

No man has *everything*, despite the old adage, and if you know one who is sorely in need of a sterling-silver Monopoly game, gourmet high-speed cooking oven or a perfect replica of a Testarossa, visit The Price of His Toys. Naturally, the price tags on these frivolities lean toward the astonishing, but it's well worth it to delight the boy inside the man.

Sadie

167 S. Crescent Heights Blvd.,
W. Hollywood
655-0689
Open Mon.-Fri. 10:30 a.m.-6 p.m., Sat. 10:30 a.m.-5 p.m.

This personal wood-shingled shop stocks an unusual assortment of gifts—from such chic kitchen items as raspberry vinegar to old-fashioned toys, art cards, toiletries, jewelry and children's books. The selection of cookware, baskets and gourmet grocery items is particularly nice, and there's a deli counter with good takeout sandwiches. Service is attentive.

The Sharper Image

601 Wilshire Blvd., Downtown
622-2351
Open Mon.-Sat. 10 a.m.-6 p.m., Sun. noon-5 p.m.
Galleria at South Bay, 1815 Hawthorne Blvd., Redondo Beach
542-8775
Open Mon.-Fri. 10 a.m.-9 p.m., Sat. 11 a.m.-7 p.m., Sun. 11 a.m.-6 p.m.

There's something about all the high-tech gadgets here that makes customers—probably more browsers than buyers—laugh out loud. Why would anyone need such a fancy phone? Or a device to detect whether your phone is being bugged? Or a sonic massager? Need has nothing to do with the things for sale here. They are all icing-on-the-cake items, toys for adults, wonderful conversation starters. Imagine toting the beverage-dispensing cushion to the Rose Bowl (the spigot, we're sorry to inform you, is between your legs). From sound soothers to exercise and tanning machines, you'll wish you had them all—just not bought with *your* money.

The Soap Plant/Wacko
7400 Melrose Ave., W. Hollywood
651-5587
Open Mon.-Wed. 10:30 a.m.-11 p.m., Thurs.-Sat. 10:30 a.m.-midnight, Sun. 11 a.m.-8 p.m.

Located just steps from each other, these same-owner shops are quintessential Melrose. Both are tributes to the owner's oddball tastes: he seems to stock what he likes, the public be damned. Mexican Day of the Dead skulls sidle up to magic-shop trinkets, avant-garde greeting cards, soaps, trendy toys, scents and a quirky but delightful book section.

Sonrisa
8214 Melrose Ave., W. Hollywood
651-1090
Open Tues.-Sun. 10 a.m.-6 p.m.

Sonrisa is alive with color, displaying some of the best Mexi-L.A. and Southwestern arts and crafts in the city. Owner Peggy Byrnes combines fine art by local Hispanic artists with handcrafted furniture from Taos, New Mexico, and contemporary local folk art. A Melrose must.

Tidepool Gallery
22762 W. Pacific Coast Hwy., Malibu
456-2551
Open Tues.-Sat. 10 a.m.-5:30 p.m., Sun. noon-5:30 p.m.

As with searching for the Grail, the rewards here are well worth the perseverance. Located up the coast a ways, this charming shop is filled with exquisite seashell treasures. The rare, exotic, beautiful specimens are sold in their natural states, as well as recycled into tasteful jewelry and items for the home. The gracious shopkeepers also help make the trip worthwhile.

Twigs
1401 Montana Ave., Santa Monica
451-9934
Open Mon.-Sat. 10 a.m.-6 p.m.

A warm, rustic shop filled with wreaths, boxes, baskets, crystal, toys and collectibles. There are also silk flowers and antique and brass pieces that make wonderful gifts for people with English-style or traditionally decorated homes.

Uncle Jer's
4447 Sunset Blvd., Los Feliz
662-6710
Open Mon.-Fri. 11 a.m.-7 p.m., 10 a.m.-5 p.m., noon-5 p.m.

Eccentric, eclectic, intriguing—all these words apply to Uncle Jer's, a terrific little shop in an oddball neighborhood in southern Los Feliz, near the Vista Theatre and Blue Meringue. There are three main components to Uncle Jer's stock: ethnic arts and crafts from the Far East, Africa, Latin America and beyond (religious artifacts from Tibet, hand-painted ceramic objects, decorative wall sculptures); imported womenswear, ranging from the latest Parisian popular styles to lots of batiked garments to clothing made from beautiful Central American fabrics; and a silly collection of cheap toys, novelties and party gags. A good source for an unusual, reasonably priced gift.

Wild Blue
7220 Melrose Ave., W. Hollywood
939-8434
Open Mon.-Sat. 11 a.m.-6 p.m., Sun. noon-5 p.m.

Artists with a sense of humor sell their wares here. The ceramics are a hoot: a platter shaped like a swimming pool, laughing-dog boxes, a plate lined with 3-D chile peppers. A Wild Blue "TV" pin (it flashes a digital message such as LIVING COLOR or STAY TUNED) makes an offbeat gift, along with one of the store's funky cards. There are also some exquisite vases, perfume bottles, hand-tinted photographs and serious original jewelry.

Wilder Place
7975 Melrose Ave., W. Hollywood
655-9072
Open Mon.-Sat. 10 a.m.-6 p.m.

The most marvelous array of gifts and household objets d'art are squeezed into this closet-size shop. The selection leans toward the handmade and the unusual; on our last visit, we were captivated by the dinosaur candlesticks, plasticized fish pins, white-birch and steel picture frames and American flag crib quilt. Wilder Place carries talented jewelry-artist Lisa Jenk's line of desk and tabletop accessories and lots of clocks, lamps and vases.

Everything is chosen with a tasteful, discerning eye, from the fun and inexpensive to the pricey and ultra contemporary.

Zero Minus Plus
Fred Segal Santa Monica, 500 Broadway, Santa Monica
395-5718
Open Mon.-Sat. 10 a.m.-7 p.m., Sun. noon-6 p.m.

When it comes to decorative home accessories, this is one of L.A.'s top retailers. Savvy shoppers flock here to find high-end tabletop wares by Swid Powell, Sabattini and Salvatore Polizzi, local art glass and pottery, hand-painted table linens (at $30 a place mat), vases and candlesticks. The highly selective buyers for Zero Minus Plus also excel at greeting cards, stationery, gift wrap, desk sets, elegant little gifts for men, blank journals, photo albums and picture frames. And an unusual claim to fame:: this store is o:ne of the largest suppliers of Filofax agenda accessories in the city.

HOME

CHINA & CRYSTAL

Cottura
7215 Melrose Ave., W. Hollywood
933-1928
Open Mon.-Sat. 11 a.m.-6 p.m., Sun. noon-5 p.m.
Century City Shopping Center,
10250 Santa Monica Blvd., Century City
277-3828
Open Mon.-Fri. 10 a.m.-9 p.m., Sat. 10 a.m.-6 p.m., Sun. 11 a.m.-6 p.m.

This breathtaking little shop sells vibrant hand-painted ceramics from Italy, Spain and Portugal. There are many colorful, unique dinnerware patterns; quality ranges from rustic to fine. You'll find everything from egg cups to urns in ceramic, as well as handmade and hand-painted Venetian glass. Prices are reasonable.

Geary's
351 N. Beverly Dr., Beverly Hills
273-4741
Open Mon. 9:30 a.m.-9 p.m., Tues.-Fri. 9:30 a.m.-6 p.m., Sat. 10 a.m.-5:30 p.m.

Stocking the most extensive collection of china, crystal and silver in town, Geary's is the oldest specialty shop in Beverly Hills, with two enormous floors of Wedgwood, Lalique, Baccarat, Royal Crown Derby, Spode, Wallace and Villeroy & Boch, to name just a few. We wouldn't advise shopping here on Saturday (it's a madhouse); instead, come during the week (particularly on Monday evening). You'll find a most helpful and courteous sales staff. Geary's does a booming business in bridal registry and mail order.

David Orgell
320 N. Rodeo Dr., Beverly Hills
272-3355
Open Mon.-Sat. 10 a.m.-6 p.m.

Crystal, silver, china, antiques and such specialties as old English silver, estate jewelry, rare gifts and collector's items are the stock-in-trade here. Everything is well displayed, and the prices are most reasonable. Excellent sales are occasionally held. Service can be lacking, particularly for gift registries. Several other locations, including Farmer's Market.

Tesoro
319 S. Robertson Blvd., W. Hollywood
273-9890
Open Mon.-Fri. 9 a.m.-6 p.m.

Tesoro has a reputation for prompting contemporary design wizards into creating home accessories as art for his store. The store is a showcase for tabletop wares, imported linens, jewelry and objects *extraordinaire*. A great place for wedding and housewarming gifts.

Villery & Boch Creation
338 N. Rodeo Dr., Beverly Hills
858-6522
Open Mon.-Sat. 10 a.m.-6 p.m.

At this new branch of the prestigious European-based ceramics giant, collectors will find many more patterns and unusual pieces than have previously been available in L.A. The latest arrival is Paloma Picasso's Bijou: crystal and bone-china giftware ringed in gold and embedded with semiprecious orbs of black onyx, green agate or red carnelian. There are sensuously shaped bowls, vases, goblets, covered boxes, candle holders and ashtrays.

FABRIC

Elegance
8350 Beverly Blvd., W. Hollywood
655-8656
11618 Exposition Blvd., W.L.A.
858-0261
Open Mon.-Sat. 10 a.m.-6 p.m.

Devotees of the French magazine *Elegance* will rejoice in its local incarnation. These two shops (the first Elegance walk-in shops in the country) sell virtually every fabric, button and trim in the magazine's editorial pages, making this the best coordinated of the upscale-yardage shops. There are two collections a year, and at season's end, these silks, linens and woolens are marked down 50 percent.

Left Bank Fabric Company
8354 W. 3rd St., W. Hollywood
655-7289
3415 Newport Blvd., Newport Beach
(714) 675-9165
Open Mon.-Tues. & Thurs.-Sat. 10 a.m.-6 p.m., Wed. 10 a.m.-9 p.m.

Half the customers at this upscale shop don't know how to sew—but they know a dressmaker who'll use these fabrics to whip up knock-'em-dead suits and dinner dresses. Much of the stock comes from Europe or designer cutting rooms (Albert Nipon, Calvin Klein, YSL, Oscar de la Renta): silk charmeuse, wispy, thin lamés, soft cashmeres and more. Expensive but worth it. Another location in Tarzana.

Oriental Silk Import and Export Co.
8377 Beverly Blvd., W. Hollywood
651-2323
Open Mon.-Sat. 9 a.m.-6 p.m.

This cluttered, musty shop has excellent prices on silk of average to good quality. The selection of prints and brocades is particularly nice (most are $9.95 per yard, though sales often bring the prices down much lower). There's also a good selection of Chinese cotton T-shirts and little embroidered silk blouses; the Chinese vases and knickknacks are forgettable.

Princess Fabrics
6745 Van Nuys Blvd., Van Nuys
(818) 781-2622
Open Mon.-Sat. 10 a.m.-6 p.m., Sun. noon-5 p.m.

Silks, woolens, cottons, knits, drapery and upholstery fabrics are sold here at reasonable prices. If you have the patience to go through masses of rather unorganized materials, you'll be rewarded with some excellent buys. Princess also stocks craft supplies.

FURNISHINGS

American Lighting Co.
8327 Melrose Ave., W. Hollywood
653-8555
Open Mon.-Sat. 10 a.m.-6 p.m., Sun. noon-5 p.m.

Since 1943 American has been offering all types of lighting. During the last few years, it has expanded its stock of contemporary, transitional, crystal, recessed and track lighting. Fixtures here tend to be on the overdone side. Prices are competitive. If you don't find what you want here, visit the neighboring Lighthouse.

Celia's
468 S. Robertson Blvd., W. Hollywood
276-2039
Open Mon.-Fri. 9 a.m.-5 p.m.

This showroom specializes in designing unique custom area rugs and manufactures them in its local factory. There are more than 150 stock designs to choose from, including floral prints and striking bordered patterns, and all can be done in a variety of colors. Prices are reasonable.

Civilization
8921 Venice Blvd., Culver City
202-8883
Open Mon.-Sat. 10 a.m.-7 p.m., Sun. 11 a.m.-6 p.m.

Civilization devotes most of its 25,000 square feet of space to contemporary, domestically designed and produced furniture, lighting and accessories. Forty percent of the offerings are one-of-a-kind and limited-production pieces by local artists and architects. Co-owners Jay Dunton and Rick Green have collected such cutting-edge designs as cast-aluminum tables, hand-finished chairs, table-top mosaics of tiles set in colored concrete, polished-steel end tables and coffee tables of broken stone. Dunton and Green plan to add a "museum" shop for housewares and art-inspired collectibles.

Conran's
Beverly Center, 121 N. La Cienega Blvd., W. Hollywood
659-1444
Open Mon.-Fri. 10 a.m.-9 p.m., Sat. 10 a.m.-8 p.m., Sun. 11 a.m.-6 p.m.
This L.A. branch of the wildly popular London-based store features 50,000 square feet of contemporary and country-simple home furnishings. Conran's strength lies in straightforward design, function and affordability in products that range from soap dishes to leather sofas. Among the L.A. firsts: European wooden and metal garden furniture (carried year-round), art deco–inspired armoires from Italy and solid-maple bedroom furniture.

Danica
9244 Wilshire Blvd., Beverly Hills
274-0613
Open Mon.-Sat. 10 a.m.-6 p.m., Sun. noon-5 p.m.
Lots of big, bold, modern Scandinavian furniture, especially in chrome, glass and teak. Especially popular are the modular couches, wall units and dining sets. Prices tend to be on the high side.

Domestic
7385 Beverly Blvd., Wilshire District
936-8206
Open Mon.-Fri. 10 a.m.-6 p.m., Sat. 11 a.m.-5 p.m.
An innovative furniture-production house and a sterling addition to L.A.'s design landscape, Domestic sells moderately priced pieces with severe lines and homey appeal. All of the furniture is a mix of solid maple or cherry and plywood veneer with a clear matte-lacquer finish. The timeless designs range from ladder-back dining chairs to a two-poster queen-size bed with a massive molded-plywood headboard.

Fantasy Lites
7126 Melrose Ave., W. Hollywood
933-7244
Open Mon.-Fri. 9 a.m.-5:30 p.m., Sat. 9 a.m.-5 p.m.
If you love beaded Tiffany lamp shades, Wayne Cline's collection of antique-replica lamps and newer glass models will thrill you. Cline uses gorgeous colors, and if you can't find a creation of his that suits your home, he'll be happy to custom-design one for you. Many of the lamps and much of the lighting you see in movies and on TV were supplied by Fantasy Lites.

Harry
148 S. La Brea Ave., Wilshire District
938-3344
Open Mon.-Sat. 11 a.m.-6 p.m., Sun. noon-5 p.m.
Kitsch is a well-worn term, but one that applies ruthlessly to this used-and-revamped furniture emporium. In this warehouselike atmosphere, Harry offers cast-off atrocities from the '40s, '50s and '60s to well-heeled rubes who harbor the mistaken notion that this stuff is hip. Those decades saw the execution of beautiful, revolutionary design in furniture and housewares, the very simplicity of which lent itself to some fairly hideous knock-offs. Harry has a lot of these, and what he can't find he creates—like bentwood Eames chairs desecrated with cowhide and paint, or geometrical sofas, each section reupholstered in differently colored garish vinyls or drab, recycled '40s and '50s fabrics in colors like puce and lime. Among the miscellany are dishes, lamps and large examples of advertising art. Once in a while a really good piece or two will show up, like the moderne armoires from England we once spied, which seemed like bargains compared to the rest of the overpriced merchandise here.

Indigo Seas
123 N. Robertson Blvd., W. Hollywood
550-8758
Open Mon.-Sat. 10 a.m.-6 p.m.
A distillation of the design business co-owner Lynn von Kersting shares with Michael Smith, Indigo Seas surrounds you with a sense of history, whether it be the colonial Carib-

bean, the deep South or glamorous old Hollywood. Among the antiques, imports and architectural treasures making up the romantic-traditional inventory: dark-green folding "regatta" chairs, wicker furniture with '40s chintz cushions, Victorian iron doorstops, vintage watering cans and Jamaican flatware.

Kreiss Ports of Call Imports

8619 Melrose Ave., W. Hollywood
657-3990
Open Mon.-Fri. 9 a.m.-5 p.m.

Definitely a California look, though a somewhat dated one. Everything's oversized and overstuffed and made of either wicker or duck canvas. The furniture and accessories are trendy but at the same time extremely attractive and well made. The decorating service is excellent. There are other locations, though the West Hollywood branch is the largest. These showrooms are open to the public, but you must buy through a designer.

Bobi Leonard

2727 Main St., Santa Monica
399-3251
Open Mon.-Sat. 10 a.m.-7 p.m., Sun. 11 a.m.-7 p.m.

Bobi Leonard was big in the early '80s. A visit to her large Main Street shop reveals her carefully formulated taste in vases, baskets, silk flowers—everything from trinkets to custom furniture.

Lexington Place

552 S. Lake Ave., Pasadena
(818) 793-0077
Open Mon.-Sat. 10 a.m.-5:30 p.m.

Few shops manage to pull off the true charms of the country look as successfully as Lexington Place does. The skillful blend of antiques and reproductions, wicker, pine, twigs, quilts and decoys is irresistible. In addition to off-the-floor furniture and accessories, the shop has a decorating service for advice, upholstery and draperies; if you prefer to seek inspiration yourself, there is a strong collection of books on Americana. Nice things for seasonal tables: for Easter, a basket of wooden robin's eggs; for Thanksgiving, a hand-carved Puritan family; for Christmas, beautiful wreaths.

Polo Ralph Lauren

444 N. Rodeo Dr., Beverly Hills
281-7200
Open Mon.-Sat. 10 a.m.-6 p.m.

Once upon a time, in a universe not too far away, existed the tiny kingdom of Pololand, where landed gentry and captains of industry rode to hounds and played croquet with their elegant ladies on the vast lawns of Long Island estates. They took tea in front of dancing fires in dark, book-lined studies, an Irish setter curled up at their feet. And when their handsome, ruddy-cheeked children returned from Ivy League colleges or English universities, they engaged in earnest discussions of their futures over crystal-laden dinner tables, the flicker of candlelight reflected in fine china and silver. Everything was either very well made and/or very old: the houses, the furniture, the clothing, the money.

Today, if you have a substantial amount of *new* money, you can re-create your own personal Pololand. On the second floor of the Polo shop you'll find everything you need, from Edwardian-style rattan bedsteads and woolly throws to fine bed linens and dark paisley comforters. There are even two tableaux vivants of complete bedrooms, all cozy with plump, ruffled pillows and four-poster beds, to serve as models. England and Europe have been virtually emptied of naive animal paintings, vintage ceramics and sundry other antique doodads that will lend just the right touch of authenticity. And if photographs of your own relatives don't look quite right, heck, just throw them out. Here you can buy photos, in frames appropriately tarnished with age, of really great-looking families, all decked out in tweeds or leaning against expensive old cars. These ready-made heirlooms and prêt-à-porter heritages can remedy almost all accidents of birth and upbringing.

Rapport

435 N. La Brea Ave., Hollywood
930-1500
Open Tues.-Sat. 9:30 a.m.-5 p.m.

Popular among young couples who want to furnish their entire house in a contemporary yet affordable way. Prices are always discounted, and there's an enormous inventory, but nothing in the way of cutting-edge design.

We've never found anything that's wowed us here.

Umbrello
8607 Melrose Ave., W. Hollywood
655-6447
Open Mon.-Fri. 9 a.m.-5:30 p.m., Sat.-Sun. 10 a.m.-6 p.m.

Southwest style with a vengeance—and a high price tag. This is where West Hollywood meets Taos, a breathtaking collection of the traditional and the trendy: overscale pine lodgepole beds and sofas covered in gorgeous Guatemalan cotton stripes, Santa Fe–designed chairs, Zapotec rugs from Oaxaca, *equipales* (pigskin patio furniture), *trasteros* (antique cupboards) and primitive Tarahumara pots. There are many one-of-a-kind items, and everything seems larger than life. To complete the Southwestern look (which we find quite tiresome), there are such accessories as hand-woven Guatemalan place mats and napkins, chunky hand-blown Mexican glass, lodgepole ladders and Native American ultra-stylized *kachinas* and hand-painted wooden snakes. There are two prices on everything, retail and to-the-trade, so by all means bring your designer. No sense paying $900 for a hand-painted snake when you can get it for $600.

HOUSEWARES & KITCHENWARE

All American Home Center
7201 E. Firestone Blvd., Downey
927-8666
Open Mon.-Sat. 8 a.m.-9 p.m., Sun. 8 a.m.-6 p.m.

Downey may not be on your beaten path, but if you're contemplating any sort of home improvement, this place is worth a special trip. It's set apart from the normal home-improvement centers by its immense size—21 departments spread over four acres, with an extra six acres of parking—and by that raritiy of rarities these days, independent family ownership. So instead of the confused impersonality of such dreaded chains as Builder's Emporium, you get first-rate professional service. And you get a selection that blows most home-improvement stores out of the water, with more than 90,000 items in stock at any given time. Whether you're contemplating buying a new garden hose or adding a new master bathroom, All American will get you what you need.

Armstrong Home and Garden Place
11321 Pico Blvd., W.L.A.
477-8023
Open Mon.-Thurs. 7:30 a.m.-7:30 p.m., Fri. 7:30 a.m.-9 p.m., Sat. 7:30 a.m.-6 p.m., Sun. 9:30 a.m.-6 p.m.

So much more than just a place to buy landscape rock, hardware and paint, Armstrong is an all-things-to-all-people store, a great place to find all kinds of housewares. With a stop for free coffee, a good browse here will take at least an hour. The indoor plant section is extensive and staffed by knowledgeable workers. The basket selection is too tempting. Don't miss the rag rugs, slick T-shirts, great kitchen gadgets, checkered toothbrushes, clever shower curtains and, of course, shiny black pebbles to grow paperwhite narcissi in.

Avery Services
905 E. 2nd St., Downtown
624-7832
Open Mon.-Fri. 8 a.m.-5 p.m., Sat. 8 a.m.-1 p.m.

Many of L.A.'s headlining restaurants are serviced by Avery Services, the largest restaurant-supply store on the West Coast. Thankfully, Avery Services is also open to those who cook for pleasure—and what a pleasure it is to discover everything from Waring blenders to Wolf ranges, at wholesale prices. Those with smaller budgets can pick up barbecue tools, measuring cups and professional cookware among the many major brands represented.

Esprit de Cuisine
Orangewood Shopping Center,
143 W. California Blvd., Pasadena
(818) 793-8855
Open Mon.-Sat. 10 a.m.-6 p.m., Sun. noon-5 p.m.

This homey gourmet cookware shop is certainly among the finest in town. Hanging from the ceiling and stocked on the shelves are Calphalon cookware, Fitz & Floyd accessories, French porcelain, table linens, cookie cutters, gourmet teas and coffees, cookbooks, Atlas pasta machines and all sorts of kitchen gadgets, from the novel to the just-plain-useful. The staff will be happy to let you browse at your leisure and can help you create themed gift baskets.

Home Economics

The Marketplace, 6487 E. Pacific Coast Hwy., Long Beach
430-3967
Open Mon.-Fri. 10 a.m.-7 p.m., Sat. 10 a.m.-6 p.m., Sun. noon-5 p.m.

A bright, contemporary store with more than the typical kitchenware. Of course, there are Chinese sauté pans, colorful kitchen linens, classic stemware, Southwestern table settings and gadgets, gadgets and more gadgets. But you'll also find all kinds of unusual merchandise, from the elegant (beautiful hand-painted Italian dishes), to the practical (Lucite salad bowls), to the zany (chile-pepper earrings). Picnic tote bags, barbecue supplies and paper goods, too.

Landis Department Store

157 N. Larchmont Blvd., Larchmont Village
464-9939
Open Mon.-Sat. 9 a.m.-6 p.m.

If, as a kid, you spent your Saturday afternoons roaming the aisles of the local five-and-dime, clutching your allowance and looking for something to spend it on, you'll find Landis an authentic, charming trip down memory lane. Sure, just about everything can also be found at Thrifty or Woolworth's, but there's no joy in buying notions, housewares, school supplies, toys, cards, socks and such at those places. Landis, with its old wooden counters, creaky shelves and post office in the back, is staffed with small-town help. No '50s revival could match it for authentic, low-key appeal.

Montana Mercantile

1500 Montana Ave., Santa Monica
451-1418
Open Mon.-Fri. 10 a.m.-6:30 p.m., Sat. 10 a.m.-6 p.m.

This gourmet cookware store and cooking school is slick as can be. The emphasis is on high-end serving pieces, plates, bakeware and glasses. But Montana Mercantile is also be-coming known for its artware, jewelry, personal accessories and luxurious bathrobes.

Pottery Barn

Century City Shopping Center, 10250 Santa Monica Blvd., Century City
552-0170
Open Mon.-Fri. 10 a.m.-9 p.m., Sat. 10 a.m.-6 p.m., Sun. 11 a.m.-6 p.m.

These cheerful stores carry the latest in kitchen gadgets and accessories, as well as stoneware, earthenware, stainless steel and casual furniture. Most of the merchandise is brightly colored and très modern, but the prices aren't as high as high style generally commands. There are several other locations around town, along with a thriving catalog business.

Salutations Ltd.

11640 San Vicente Blvd., Brentwood
820-6127
Open Mon.-Sat. 10 a.m.-6 p.m.

A great westside source for colorful tableware, home furnishings, linens, infant clothing, personal accessories and custom gift baskets. Owner Carey Appel combines the respected and the one of a kind with elegant presentation and warm personal service. A few of her choice finds: hand-painted tablecloths in the post-Impressionist vein, bath salts in terra-cotta pots and iridescent-glass fruits.

Williams-Sonoma

317 N. Beverly Dr., Beverly Hills
274-9127
Open Mon.-Sat. 10 a.m.-5:30 p.m.

Straight from the pages of the popular and successful mail-order catalog, this clean-lined store is loaded with kitchen classics and brand-new gadgets, many of which only a professional chef (or a very imaginative amateur) would know what to do with. There is a beautiful mix of functional equipment, decorative accessories, kitchen furniture, handsome tableware and hard-to-find food items. You'll also find lots of copper, brass, all-white and hand-painted dinnerware and an excellent selection of dish towels, napkins and tablecloths. There are several other locations around the city: the Beverly Center, South Coast Plaza, Palos Verdes and on Lake Street in Pasadena.

LINENS

Descamps

Beverly Center, 121 N. La Cienega Blvd.,
W. Hollywood
659-3820
*Open Mon.-Fri. 10 a.m.-9 p.m., Sat. 10 a.m.-8
p.m., Sun. 11 a.m.-6 p.m.*

This French firm is known for fine-quality
linens and distinctive border prints, with
prices well below those of Frette and Pratesi.
Descamps recently introduced a new French
Revolution bicentennial pattern featuring
cameos and ornamental medallions. The store
also stocks kimono-style terry bathrobes,
complementary French toiletries and exquisite baby items, and will custom-make coordinating accessories.

Frette

449 N. Rodeo Dr., Beverly Hills
273-8540
Open Mon.-Sat. 10 a.m.-5:30 p.m.

These exquisite linens are unequaled in
quality and design, except perhaps by Pratesi.
Its handmade, hand-embroidered beauties for
the bed, body, bath and table are sold at
absolutely breathtaking prices. Frette specializes in woven jacquards.

Pratesi

9024 Burton Way, Beverly Hills
274-7661
Open Mon.-Sat. 10 a.m.-6 p.m.

The finest linens in town are on Pratesi's
shelves. These Italian sheets, towels, blankets,
tablecloths and quilts are woven to Pratesi's
specifications; the cashmere blankets are exceptionally beautiful. Prices, as you might expect, are numbing.

Scandia Down

310 N. Camden Dr., Beverly Hills
274-6925
*Open Mon.-Sat. 10 a.m.-6 p.m., Sun. noon-5
p.m.*

Nothing is as heavenly as cuddling up in an
enormous down comforter, and here they're
not only exceptionally soft and puffy but beautiful and practical as well. Separate cotton
covers are made for the comforters so you can
get two or three colors or patterns and create
completely different looks. Prices are reasonable.

NURSERIES

S.B. Nickerson Nursery

3948 Sepulveda Blvd., Culver City
390-3347
*Open Mon.-Fri. 7:30 a.m.-4 p.m., Sat. 7:30
a.m.-11 a.m.*

The operative word here is *cheap*. So cheap
you'll forget your neighborhood nursery and
willingly make the drive out to Culver City—
for plants priced 40 to 50 percent less than
those in retail nurseries. Even Joan Collins
shops here, landscapist in tow. These are not
sad, cast-off plants but healthy shrubs and
trees grown at Nickerson's own facility in
Fallbrook. Everything is sold at wholesale-to-
the-public prices, except for the small selection of indoor plants. The selection is
enormous: bougainvillea vines, red-leaf bananas, bamboo, eucalyptus, tree ferns, ficus
and much, much more. Five-gallon plants,
which cost about $15 at most nurseries, are
about $8.75 here; fifteen-gallon plants, usu-
ally $75, are only $47.50. The nursery will
deliver free of charge for purchases over $50.

Sassafras Nursery

275 N. Topanga Canyon Blvd., Topanga
Canyon
455-1933
Open daily 9 a.m.-5:30 p.m.

Sassafras is everything you'd imagine a nursery in Topanga Canyon to be: country-style,
casual, cluttered. If you're into the English-
country-garden look, this place is a source for
both inspiration and such unusual plants as
black pansies, cattails, lotuses, water lilies and
Irish moss. New at Sassafras are organic vegetables, old-fashioned sweet peas, copper
arches covered with climbing roses and
wrought-iron furniture. For gifts, there are
exquisite baskets filled with plants and flowers.
Stop by for holiday surprises, including tiny
pumpkins and twiggy wreaths. Inside the shed
are indoor plants and exotic cut flowers. For
really grand schemes, a landscaping service is
available.

IMAGE & SOUND

PHOTOGRAPHY

ABC Photo
9136 Sepulveda Blvd., Westchester
645-8992
*Open Mon.-Fri. 10 a.m.-7 p.m., Sat. 10:30 a.m.-
6 p.m., Sun. 11 a.m.-5 p.m.*

Expert underwater photographer Alan Bro-
der provides an extensive list of services, including photography classes, and new and
used equipment for sale or rent—from the
Nikon Action Touch all-weather camera to
complete underwater systems.

Frank's Highland Park Camera
5715 N. Figueroa St., Highland Park
255-0123
*Open Mon.-Thurs. & Sat. 9:30 a.m.-6 p.m., Fri.
9:30 a.m.-8 p.m.*

This noteworthy shop is a bit out of the way
(off the Pasadena Freeway just north of downtown), but it's worth the effort to seek it out.
The selection isn't as vast as at L.A.'s camera
supermarkets, but there's plenty of top-name
gear, including professional medium format
cameras, at very low prices. The shop's catalog
is justly acclaimed as one of the best discount
camera catalogs in the country.

Freestyle Photo Supplies
5124 W. Sunset Blvd., Hollywood
660-3460
*Open Mon.-Fri. 9 a.m.-5:30 p.m., Sat. 10 a.m.-
3:45 p.m.*

Amateur photographers on a budget flock
to Freestyle for camera supplies and equipment at bargain prices. There seem to be
enough outdated and current film, tanks, en-
largers, processing equipment and paper here
to stock every home darkroom in L.A.

Olympic Camera
828 W. Olympic Blvd., Downtown
746-0575
Open Mon.-Sat. 9:30 a.m.-6 p.m.

Olympic is one of the better camera stores
in town. It's friendly and incredibly well

stocked, with a full range of photographic
equipment for amateurs as well as professionals, from pocket cameras to industrial-quality
movie cameras. The selection of used equipment is quite good. Prices are excellent both
in the store and through its booming mail-
order business. Additional branches around
town.

Pan Pacific Camera
825 N. La Brea Ave., Hollywood
933-5888
*Open Mon.-Fri. 9 a.m.-6 p.m., Sat. 9 a.m.-5
p.m.*

A longtime favorite of L.A.'s professional
and amateur photographers. All the best
names in photographic equipment are represented, and you'll find everything a photographer could possibly want, from lens caps to
elaborate professional lighting systems. Prices
are competitive, and the staff well informed.

Samy's Camera
7122 Beverly Blvd., Wilshire District
938-2420
Open Mon.-Sat. 9 a.m.-6 p.m.

This large, well-established store carries a
large stock of new and used cameras from all
the name manufacturers, along with stereo
and video equipment, binoculars and all sorts
of electronic equipment. It's a hectic, cluttered place, but the prices are low and the sales
good.

RECORDED MUSIC

A-1 Record Finders
5639 Melrose Ave., Hollywood
732-6737
*Open Mon.-Tues. & Thurs.-Fri. noon-6 p.m., or
by appt.*

Every record junkie should keep this phone
number on file. If the nice people at A-1 don't
have the rare, out-of-print record you want in
stock, they'll find it and sell it to you for a very
reasonable price. From Chet Atkins to Frank

Zappa, the hardest-to-find discs can be tracked down via A-1's national search service. There are no tapes or CDs here, strictly records at all speeds, and particularly nostalgia, movie soundtracks, rock, pop, classical and jazz. A-1 keeps a customer "want list" and maintains a worldwide mailing service. Store hours are not very regular; it's best to call before you visit.

Aron's Record Shop
1150 N. Highland Ave., Hollywood
469-4700
Open Mon.-Thurs. 10 a.m.-10 p.m., Fri.-Sat. 10 a.m.-midnight, Sun. noon-8 p.m.

Lovers of rock, jazz and classical music can be seen digging through Aron's used-record bins day and night. They come to this newly expanded shop in the heart of Hollywood for the superb selection and, even more, for the excellent condition of the albums. There's also a good choice of new and used cassettes and CDs and new rock, jazz, folk, classical, soul and reggae albums; the import section is particularly strong. One of the best record stores in town.

Bebop Records & Fine Art
18433 Sherman Way, Reseda
(818) 881-1654
Open Mon.-Sat. 1:30 p.m.-6 p.m. & for evening performances.

This tiny place is a young, hip hangout, for more reasons than its fine assortment of used records (folk, jazz, pop, rock, classical, you name it) and extremely reasonable prices. Bebop features performances (musical, theatrical, poetry readings) by local and traveling artists four to five nights a week and regular rotating contemporary art. More than a record store, Bebop is fast becoming the social center of the community.

Bleecker Bob's
7663 Melrose Ave., W. Hollywood
852-9444
Open daily noon-midnight.

New Yorkers know Bleecker Bob's in Greenwich Village as the best in rare, alternative and new music, hard-to-find recordings and oldies. British imports are a specialty. Now Bleecker Bob's has branched out and is attracting a comparable following among

Hollywood's new wavers. If you can't visit the store, call to be placed on the hugely successful mail-order list.

Disc Connection
10970 W. Pico Blvd., W.L.A.
208-7211
Open Mon.-Thurs. & Sat. 11 a.m.-7 p.m., Fri. 11 a.m.-9 p.m., Sun. noon-6 p.m.

This small shop boasts excellent prices on hard-to-find movie soundtracks, Broadway shows, rock, jazz and nostalgia, both on vinyl and CDs. The selection is remarkably in-depth. A friendly place with helpful salespeople and exceptional sales.

Off the Record
2621 Wilshire Blvd., Santa Monica
829-7379
Open daily 10 a.m.-10 p.m.

Off the Record divides its inventory between recorded music and videotape rentals and sales. There are a noteworthy number of rare, mainly rock, cassettes and a newly expanded section of used CDs in addition to the top 200 new albums. The shop will "search the world" to fill special orders. The equally large video section stocks many titles that can't be found in chain outlets.

Pooh-Bah Records
1101 E. Walnut St., Pasadena
(818) 449-3359
Open Mon.-Sat. 11 a.m.-9 p.m., Sun. 11 a.m.-7 p.m.

This friendly, well-established store stocks an unusually good selection of old rhythm and blues and cutting-edge contemporary jazz. There's a sizable CD department (up to 7,000 titles) and a good assortment of used CDs. You'll also find an excellent selection of albums and singles from independent and alternative labels, and the used-record department is comparable to that of any other used record store in the L.A. area.

The Record Trader
7321 Reseda Blvd., Reseda
(818) 708-0632
Open Mon.-Sat. 10 a.m.-9 p.m., Sun. 11 a.m.-6 p.m.

Besides bins and bins of used records, The Record Trader gets ahold of many new releases before anyone else has them. The new and used selection covers the gamut, from rock and jazz to country and gospel. The imports section is sizable and complemented by some 78s. Watch for the blockbuster parking-lot sale once a year.

Rhino Records
1720 Westwood Blvd., Westwood
474-8685
Open Mon.-Sat. 10 a.m.-11 p.m., Sun. 11 a.m.-10 p.m.
This legendary store recently tripled in size, an improvement Rhino management likens to being born again. It seems like Rhino has always been there for serious lovers of rock, jazz, blues, folk, bluegrass and reggae who are looking for good additions to their collections. Chances are they'll find it among the newly expanded inventory of new and used records, CDs, cassettes, independent labels and imports. And now Rhino also carries books and magazines. Excellent prices and an extremely knowledgeable staff.

Rockaway Records
2390 N. Glendale Blvd., Silverlake
664-7778
Open daily 10 a.m.-9:30 p.m.
Although Rockaway has small but choice collections of classical, jazz and country, its strong suit is rock 'n' roll. The bins have the best discount cutouts in town—not just from lesser-known talents, like most stores, but from major stars as well. The choice of new records is limited, but the used and cutout CDs, rare albums and rock memorabilia are unbeatable. A great browsing store and a must for any rock 'n' roll collector.

Tower Records
8801 W. Sunset Blvd., W. Hollywood
657-7300
Open Sun.-Thurs. 9 a.m.-midnight, Fri.-Sat. 9 a.m.-1 a.m.
The be-all and end-all of record stores, Tower puts all other chain record stores to shame. This branch, L.A.'s main store, is a huge, teeming place on the Sunset Strip with thousands of CDs, tapes and records in every category, from gospel to punk, Vivaldi to Ellington. Both the classical annex (657-3910) and the video store (657-3344) across

Sunset are thoroughly stocked and run by intelligent, helpful salespeople. The staff at the main store is less helpful, though that's probably because of the constant crush of customers, who come to Tower to find that special record or just pass the evening browsing. Prices are average to low, and the collection of singles from the '50s, '60s and '70s alone is worth a visit.

STEREO & VIDEO EQUIPMENT

ABC Premiums
7266 Beverly Blvd., Wilshire District
938-2724
Open Mon.-Fri. 10 a.m.-8 p.m., Sat. 10 a.m.-7 p.m., Sun. 11 a.m.-5 p.m.
ABC is an excellent discount store for anything you plug in or use batteries with. The selection of TVs is better than that of stereo equipment, but both departments carry good name brands at very low prices. Know what you want before you go in—service is minimal, as is often the case in discount houses. But ABC is considerably friendlier than its hectic neighboring competitor, Adray's.

Beverly Stereo
8413 Beverly Blvd., W. Hollywood
651-3523
Open Mon.-Sat. 10 a.m.-6 p.m.
The selection is not large at this long-established shop, but the components and systems offered are high in quality—from terrifyingly priced handmade equipment to more middle-of-the-road audiophile lines like Bang & Olufsen. Check the selection of the used components in back, which are thoroughly restored and can be great buys. Good selection of Original Master Recordings and video discs.

The Federated Group
7060 W. Sunset Blvd., Hollywood
871-0895
Open Mon. & Thurs.-Fri. noon-8 p.m., Sat. 10 a.m.-9 p.m., Sun. noon-5 p.m.
The best of the chain stereo-video stores that bombard local media with hyperactive

advertising (and Federated's ads have certainly been the most hyperactive). It's large and, for the most part, clean. But this is not to say it's the best stereo place in town. The salespeople can be pushy, the wait at the counter can be unbearable, and the selection is not as wide as you would think, considering the vastness of the place. But The Federated does carry some good lines, and sales can be outstanding. Excellent prices on blank video and audio tape. This McDonald's of stereo stores has many other branches around the area.

Christopher Hansen

646 N. Robertson Blvd., W. Hollywood
858-8112
Open Mon.-Sat. 10 a.m.-6 p.m.

The music "designers" at this small shop create outstanding, unusual home or professional music systems from such elite components as Magnepan, Mark Levinson, Audio Research and Goldmund. You can spend anywhere from $1,500 to $250,000, assured you'll have the finest stereo equipment your money can buy. Christopher Hansen's clients come from all over the world—even from cities as far away as Jakarta, Indonesia, and Tokyo. One former staff member designed a $100,000 stereo bed (as in king-size)—a little Christmas gift from Paul McCartney to Stevie Wonder. A serious stereo store for true lovers of music or electronics.

Paris Audio

12401 Wilshire Blvd., W.L.A.
820-2578
Open Mon. & Thurs. 11 a.m.-8 p.m., Tues.-Wed. & Fri. 11 a.m.-7 p.m., Sat. 11 a.m.-6 p.m., Sun. noon-5 p.m.

If you're looking for that ultimate stereo system, by all means visit Paris Audio. It sells some of the best available—Bang & Olufsen, Nakamichi, NAD, KEF—and is one of few stores that specializes in custom system design and installation. All this, of course, comes at a premium. But can you put a price on perfection? Paris Audio's exceptionally competent staff will custom-design a home stereo system or home theater system with surround sound for anywhere from $2,000 to $200,000. For those who are passionate about their music, Paris Audio is a must. Member of the American Society of Interior Designers.

Rogersound Laboratories

8381 Canoga Ave., Canoga Park
(818) 882-4600
Open Mon.-Fri. 11 a.m.-9 p.m., Sat.-Sun. 10 a.m.-6 p.m.

For overall selection and prices, Rogersound Labs (seven in all) are considered to be Southern California's number-one audio/video dealer. Sound rooms for demonstrations combined with noncommissioned salespeople make buying a system a truly pleasant, pressure-free experience. You'll find all the latest in quality audio/video components, big-screen TVs, audio/video furniture and the company's own RSL line of speakers, all competitively priced. When cost is no object, don't miss the Upscale Audio department in the Canoga Park store, which carries the absolute ultimate in home audio equipment.

VIDEO SALES & RENTALS

Rocket Video

633 N. La Brea Ave., Hollywood
965-1102
Open Sun.-Thurs. 11 a.m.-10 p.m., Fri.-Sat. 11 a.m.-11 p.m.

Rocket Video is a refreshing change of pace from the chain video stores that stock mainstream movies. Besides all the typical video fare, the cordial people at Rocket seek out hard-to-find classic and foreign titles. A favorite among Hollywood's artsy-movie addicts.

Vidiots

302 Pico Blvd., Santa Monica
392-8508
Open Sun.-Thurs. 11 a.m.-11 p.m., Fri.-Sat. 11 a.m.-midnight.

Vidiots is a small, funky, refreshingly unslick little shop known for its excellent selection of rare and foreign movies and its books on movies, screenwriting and scripts. The cozy espresso oar and mini-café help ease the agony of decision making, as do occasional presentations by independent filmmakers and performance artists. Vidiots will even "deliver your vidoes with a $10 purchase from the café. A hot number in every L.A. videophile's Rolodex.

LEATHER & LUGGAGE

Bottega Veneta
457 N. Rodeo Dr., Beverly Hills
858-6533
Open Mon.-Sat. 10 a.m.-6 p.m.
These Italian artisans get our vote for the most attractive leather goods. Their shoes and handbags are done in the softest leathers imaginable in a variety of subtle shades. The luggage and briefcases are handsome and un-tainted with pretentious initials. Naturally, such refinement doesn't come cheap—the signature woven-leather bags start at $300.

Céline
460 N. Rodeo Dr., Beverly Hills
273-1243
Open Mon.-Sat. 10 a.m.-6 p.m.
Yes, it's quite expensive, but the quality of the leather is superb. The purses are well regarded by women who like to carry classic handbags and don't mind the rather obvious gold-signature fasteners. Though Céline's loafers might not be as popular as Gucci's, those who have discovered them swear by their comfort and durability.

Gucci
347 N. Rodeo Dr., Beverly Hills
278-3451
Open Mon.-Sat. 10 a.m.-6 p.m.
We thought maybe they were giving the Gs away. The boutique was loaded with foreign customers, all buying up Gucci classics with no evidence of being offended by the prices. Apparently Gucci has found its natural habitat in Los Angeles; even the meter maids tote the clichéd fabric bags. This branch is a cross between Milan high-tech and space-shuttle decor; the shoe department is dominated by space pod seating that looks more appropriate for the astronaut program. No matter that we were treated without courtesy—Gucci is doing a land-office business without us.

Hermès
343 N. Rodeo Dr., Beverly Hills
278-6440
Open Mon.-Sat. 10 a.m.-6 p.m.
This Parisian import carries exquisitely made leather handbags (including the famous Grace Kelly bag), wallets, briefcases and luggage. Styles are classic, not outdated, and its logo is tastefully and unobtrusively imprinted on the goods. This shop also sells Hermès's lovely silk scarves, watches, accessories and fragrances.

The Leather Club
9555 Santa Monica Blvd., Beverly Hills
274-9331
Open Mon.-Sat. 10:30 a.m.-6:30 p.m.
You won't find a store within the city limits that has more leather and suede apparel. This ten-year-old shop sells everything from lip-stick-red leather jeans to Jean-Paul Gaultier–inspired epaulets. From the large assortment of skins, you can have custom-tailored practically anything you desire. Linda Evans, Anthony Quinn and Aaron Spelling are regulars.

North Beach Leather
8500 Sunset Blvd., W. Hollywood
652-3224
Open Mon.-Sat. 10 a.m.-6 p.m.
Mostly Sunset Boulevard–L.A. rocker stuff here: leather bowling jackets, fringed skirts and skin-tight jeans. More wearable items include tuxedo-inspired coatdresses and trench coats. Before Versace, Armani and Montana began featuring leather garments in their collections, and when one couldn't find leather trousers, skirts and dresses *just anywhere*, North Beach had the L.A. monopoly. What was once among the trendiest, most innovative and costliest in design has become only semifashionable, rarely daring and rather reasonable in price.

H. Savinar Luggage
4625 W. Washington Blvd., Wilshire District
938-2501
Open Mon.-Fri. 8 a.m.-5:30 p.m., Sat. 9 a.m.-5:30 p.m.
A huge mainstream selection of luggage, business accessories and small leather goods are sold here at prices well below retail. Knowledgeable Angelenos know that this is *the* place in town to buy luggage. It carries all the popular mid-range lines, including Tumi,

Andiamo, Boyt, Lark, Hartmann and Ventura. Another branch in Canoga Park.

Louis Vuitton
307 N. Rodeo Dr., Beverly Hills
859-0457
Open Mon.-Sat. 10 a.m.-6 p.m.
Gold LVs are splashed across every inch of not-very-soft leather in this pretentious shop.

At one time we saw one out of three Beverly Hills ladies with a Vuitton bag on her arm, but fortunately, they're fewer and farther between now. The only thing about this collection that has managed to change over the years is the cost (which continues to climb), not the styling, which is as conventional as ever. We will admit a fondness, however, for the more classic nonmonogrammed leather items.

RENT-A-. . .

CAR

Luxury Line
8747 Wilshire Blvd., Beverly Hills
657-1218
Open Mon.-Fri. 7:30 a.m.-7 p.m., Sat.-Sun. 7:30 a.m.-4 p.m.
You name it, the Luxury Line (a division of Budget) has it: everything from Ford Escorts and family vans to Jaguars, Rolls-Royces, Ferraris and late-model convertibles. All are available by the day or the week.

National Car Rental's Emerald Club
LAX, 9419 Airport Blvd., Inglewood
(800) CAR-RENT
Open daily 24 hours.
Join the Emerald Club of National Car Rental (with a $50 initiation fee), and any number of unforgettable cars from the '50s and '60s are yours for hire. The classic convertible lineup includes Corvettes, Chevrolet Impalas, Ford Galaxies, Cadillacs, Buicks and Eldorados, all magnificently restored. A must for classic-car–lovers and tourists looking for a topless L.A. experience.

Rent-a-Wreck
12333 W. Pico Blvd., W.L.A.
478-0676, (800) 423-0676
Open Mon.-Fri. 7 a.m.-7 p.m., Sat.-Sun. 8 a.m.-4 p.m.
Never mind the name: Rent-a-Wreck stresses quality and professional service. This location is the company's oldest—some survivors of the original early '60s fleet can still be taken for a spin. The specialty here is vintage Mustang convertibles, but inventory ranges from new and slightly used Toyotas and Nissans to such classic American standards as Valiants or Buick Skylarks. There are even some pickup trucks, station wagons and vans available.

COMPUTER

Ganton Temporary Computer
1201 S. Flower St., Downtown
(818) 842-6866
Open Mon.-Fri. 8:30 a.m.-5:30 p.m.
Most major brands of personal computers, including IBM, MacIntosh and the Toshiba laptop, are rented by the day, week or month. Pickup and delivery are included in the rental fees, which vary depending on the equipment selected (laptops go for $125 to $235 a week).

COSTUME

Glendale Center Theatre Costume Shoppe
324 N. Orange St., 2nd Fl., Glendale
(818) 244-8481
Open Mon.-Sat. 9:30 a.m.-6 p.m.
This costumer is noteworthy for its breadth of selection, uncomplicated rental procedures and prices (costumes from $35 to $75). One whole department is devoted to Joker, Invisible Man and other classic horror characters.

There's an extensive collection of Ben Nye theatrical makeup and some dazzling ornate masks.

Somewhere in Time
98 E. Colorado Blvd., Pasadena
(818) 792-7503
Open Mon.-Sat. 10 a.m.-6 p.m.

The custom costumes here range from Carmen Miranda to unicorns; the specialty is spectacular masks, including suede troll ones. The full rental stock of costumes and accessories ranges from $45 to $250. Also prop rentals and party set-up services.

Western Costume
5335 Melrose Ave., Hollywood
469-1451
Open Mon.-Fri. 7 a.m.-9 p.m.

This vast warehouse has become a Hollywood institution. For almost three-quarters of a century, it's been renting costumes to movie studios and to the public. Chances are very good that no matter who or what you want to disguise yourself as, you'll find the appropriate costume here, whether it's a Southern belle or a gorilla. Costumes aren't always in good condition, however, and service can be less than friendly.

DESIGNER EVENING DRESS

Dressed to Kill
8762 Holloway Dr., W. Hollywood
652-4334
Open Tues.-Fri. 11 a.m.-7 p.m., Sat. 10 a.m.-6 p.m.

This shop is a bonanza for fulfilling sartorial fantasies, if only for an evening. Dressed to Kill specializes in haute couture for rent: the latest in cocktail dresses to ball gowns from Patrick Kelly, Bob Mackie, Giorgio di Sant'Angelo, Ungaro, Dior—over 300 styles in all. Dress rentals range from $50 to $350 per night. For an additional charge, the shop will outfit you with a matching handbag and jewelry. Call ahead to book an appointment and/or reserve a specific designer look.

FUR

Auntie Mame
1102 S. La Cienega Blvd., Wilshire District
652-8430
Open Tues.-Sat. noon-5 p.m.

You can rent almost every kind of fur from Auntie Mame, which also sells, cleans and repairs furs. Most of the furs rent for $50 a night, and flat fees are arranged for weekend rentals. The size selection is limited..

LIMOUSINE

Fleetwood Limousine
208-0209

A well-established, reputable firm with a full line of limousines and discreet drivers.

V.I.P. Limousine Service
273-1505

V.I.P.'s fleet of Cadillac formal limousines, Lincoln and Cadillac Presidential stretches (complete with color TVs and bar service), luxury sedans and even fifteen-passenger vans is on call 24 hours a day.

PARTY

Abbey Rents
1001 N. La Brea Ave., Hollywood
466-9582
Open Mon.-Fri. 8:30 a.m.-5:30 p.m., Sat. 8:30 a.m.-5 p.m.

The biggest and best party-rental store in town. Abbey will provide you with everything you need, from tables, chairs and silverware to dance floors, lighting systems and heaters.

TUXEDO

Tuxedo Center
7360 Sunset Blvd., Hollywood
874-4200
Open Mon.-Fri. 9 a.m.-7 p.m., Sat. 9 a.m.-6 p.m.

Tuxes in every size and style, including those made by the best designers, can be rented here. The selection is unbeatable, the prices competitive, and the service good.

SPORTING GOODS

Adventure 16

11161 W. Pico Blvd., W.L.A.
473-4574
Open Mon.-Fri. 10 a.m.-9 p.m., Sat. 10 a.m.-6 p.m., Sun. noon-5 p.m.

Even if you've never camped out a day in your life, Adventure 16, a.k.a. A-16, will have you yearning for a hardy hike. Catering to camping families, backpackers and world-wide travelers, A-16 sells everything from the latest in high-tech clothing to hiking boots, from single-burner stoves to freeze-dried food and water-purification tablets. Best of all, the staff—all denizens of the great outdoors—has an excellent base of expertise with which to help you plot your every move. The travel-book section is one of the city's best; A-16 takes special orders, and it offers equipment rental, laundry and repair, free classes and special events.

Big 5 Sporting Goods

6601 Wilshire Blvd., Wilshire District
651-2909
Open Mon.-Fri. 10 a.m.-9 p.m., Sat. 9 a.m.-9 p.m., Sun. 10 a.m.-6 p.m.

Big 5 is an ever-growing chain of reputed discount–sporting goods stores, though most of its prices don't seem too low to us. It does, however, have a sort of ongoing sale—you can check the Thursday and Saturday *L.A. Times* to find out the current (and often very good) bargains. The selection is fair but not of a very high quality; service is pleasant but not terribly well informed. The merchandise assortment ranges from ski goods to tennis and exercise equipment to a large selection of athletic shoes for every sport. There are several other locations, including one in Santa Monica.

Roger Dunn Golf Shop

4744 Lankershim Blvd., N. Hollywood
(818) 763-3622
Open Mon.-Fri. 9 a.m.-7 p.m., Sat. 9 a.m.-6 p.m., Sun. 10 a.m.-5 p.m.

A large, very well-stocked shop with everything for the golfer. The service is intelligent and friendly. Prices are reasonable; during sales, they are very low.

Lords of the Fly

12227 Wilshire Blvd., W.L.A.
820-7546
Open Mon.-Sat. 10 a.m.-6 p.m.

These people truly understand the obsessional nature of fly-fishing. The tiny shop serves as a sort of men's club for die-hard fly-fishermen (are there any other kind?)—a place they can go to heft rods, take fly-tying classes, hear about undiscovered streams and talk endlessly about fly fishing with fellow addicts.

I. Martin Imports

8330 Beverly Blvd., W. Hollywood
653-6900
Open Mon. 10 a.m.-8 p.m., Tues.-Fri. 10 a.m.-7 p.m., Sat. 9 a.m.-6 p.m., Sun. 11 a.m.-5 p.m.

I. Martin is crammed with bikes—they are literally stacked to the ceiling. There's every kind of ten-, twelve- and eighteen-speed bike, from such makers as Diamond Back, Specialized, Bottecchia, Trek and Bianchi. Prices range from $100 for a tiny bike with training wheels to more than $2,000 for a top-of-the-line racing bike. Full service department.

MDR Bike

2472 Lincoln Blvd., Marina del Rey
306-7843
Open Mon.-Fri. 11 a.m.-8 p.m., Sat. 10 a.m.-6 p.m., Sun. 11 a.m.-5 p.m.

In addition to a full range of bikes, cycling ware and accessories, MDR Bike offers services we never dreamed possible: complete restorations of vintage models and sentimental favorites, custom-design and paint work and professional "fittings" for improved performance. There's a sizzling selection of Spandex clothing, gloves with gel-padded palms and "soft-shell" Giro helmets with interchangeable brightly colored tops.

The Merchant of Tennis

1118 S. La Cienega Blvd., Wilshire District
855-1946
Open Mon.-Sat. 10 a.m.-6 p.m.

You have to be buzzed in to this spare, modern tennis shop, as if it were an elite jewelry store. But the only valuables here are rows of men's and women's tennis clothes and dozens of rackets. The clothing selection, although it includes four top names, is limited, but there's a fine collection of expensive graphite rackets. Time on the court behind the shop is rented out to the public and is used for lessons given by the shop's three full-time pros seven days a week.

The Racket Doctor
3214 Glendale Blvd., Atwater
663-6601
Open Tues.-Sat. 10 a.m.-6 p.m.

Atwater may not be the first place that springs to mind when you think of tennis, but it should be. The Racket Doctor has one of the largest selections of tennis rackets in the Western United States—virtually every popular racket made can be found here, from graphite to ceramic. And, best of all, the prices are perhaps the lowest in the country. (To get on the national mail-order list, call 663-2950.) The selection of tennis shoes and clothing is equally well priced.

R.E.I. Co-op
405 W. Torrance Blvd., Carson (off the 110 Fwy.)
538-2429
Open Mon.-Tues. & Sat. 9:30 a.m.-6 p.m., Wed.-Fri. 9:30 a.m.-9 p.m., Sun. noon-5 p.m.

Plaid flannel shirts and hiking boots will never go out of style with the clientele at Seattle-based R.E.I. (Recreational Equipment Incorporated). The great outdoors is the specialty here—camping, fishing, snowshoeing, backpacking and so on. R.E.I. sells and rents everything you could possibly need for these wholesome recreations, and at very modest prices. For $10 you can join the co-op, and you'll receive a yearly dividend usually equal to 10 percent of your year's purchases. However, nonmembers are welcome customers. The staff is exceptionally knowledgeable and honest.

The Scoreboard
Farmer's Market, 3rd St. & Fairfax Ave., Wilshire District
930-1291
Open Mon.-Sat. 9 a.m.-6:30 p.m., Sun. 10 a.m.-6 p.m.

The Scoreboard sells everything for the armchair athlete: pennants, caps, T-shirts, even trash cans and beer mugs, all emblazoned with logos from pro and college baseball, football, hockey and basketball teams. Die-hard fans will also find personalized bats and balls with players' signatures on them. Much of this stuff is hard to find outside of the teams' hometowns. Other outlets in Beverly Hills, Studio City and Woodland Hills.

Sports Chalet
920 Foothill Blvd., La Cañada
(818) 790-9800
Open Mon.-Fri. 9:30 a.m.-9 p.m., Sat. 9 a.m.-6 p.m., Sun. 10 a.m.-5 p.m.

This is it—nirvana for every kind of athlete. Located in the Verdugo foothills of La Cañada, Sports Chalet is well worth the drive. It sprawls across three buildings; the biggest (and it's huge) sells everything and anything (except ski equipment) for the sports-minded—runners, climbers, tennis players, divers, baseball players, you name it. The second building, also large, stocks absolutely everything for the downhill and cross-country skier, with a tremendous selection of clothing. A third building, a converted gas station, rents it all: skis, scuba gear, tennis rackets, camping equipment, boats, mountaineering gear and so on. Prices are moderate, sales are great, and the staff is friendly and helpful. Just about the only sporting goods store you need to know about in L.A.

Val Surf
4810 Whitsett Ave., N. Hollywood
(818) 769-6977
Open Mon.-Fri. 10 a.m.-8 p.m., Sat. 10 a.m.-6 p.m., Sun. 10 a.m.-5 p.m.

This colorful shop was the first to bring the burgeoning '60s surf craze inland to the Valley (while the Beach Boys were spreading the word nationwide). While other surf shops have come and gone, Val Surf is still a trendsetter in Southern California casualwear and a good place to get neon-bright trunks, T-shirts, Hawaiian shirts, Vuarnets, thongs, bikinis and junior sportswear. There are more than 80 surfboards, from small tri-fin wave carvers to classic longboards. You'll also find Churchill fins, Boogie boards, wet suits and all sorts of ocean-sports paraphernalia, as well as a professional snow-skiing shop. Other locations in Woodland Hills and Thousand Oaks.

TOBACCONISTS

The Cigar Warehouse
15141 Ventura Blvd., Sherman Oaks
(818) 784-1391
1632 Westwood Blvd., W.L.A.
475-4325
Open Mon.-Sat. 8 a.m.-6 p.m.

Without a doubt the best place in town to buy the world's best cigars. You name it, they've got it, and at discounted prices. The house brands, especially the Honduran Bravo, are very good values. There's a lesser but still good choice of pipe tobaccos as well, along with beautiful pipes (including bargain-priced seconds), humidors and smoking accessories. The show-biz crowd makes up a large percentage of the Cigar Warehouse's business. For "cigars to the stars" outside California, call (800) 426-8924.

WHERE TO FIND . . .

AN ANTIQUES RESTORER

Antique Services
7349 Hinds Ave., N. Hollywood
(818) 765-1265
Open Mon.-Fri. 9:30 a.m.-4 p.m.

For more than 30 years this European-trained staff has been repairing and restoring antique and period furniture; they are experts in veneer and inlay repairs.

A BABYSITTER

The Baby Sitters Guild
P.O. Box 3018, S. Pasadena
469-8246, (818) 441-4293

Founded by artist Gene Hanner to provide employment for older women, the Guild provides babysitters who range in age from 25 to 70, on call 24 hours a day. The rate is $6 an hour, with a four-hour minimum.

A CHIMNEY SWEEP

The Chimney Sweeper
(818) 994-4800

They'll repair, clean, inspect, rebuild and custom-fit your chimney with spark arresters, as well as install fireplaces and clean heating and air-duct systems.

CLEANERS

Effrey's
8917 Melrose Ave., W. Hollywood
858-7400
Open Mon.-Fri. 5:30 a.m.-5:30 p.m., Sat. 5:30 a.m.-1 p.m.

Penny-pinchers should steer clear of Effrey's, which is quite possibly the most expensive dry cleaners in the state. But those looking for a cleaners they can *really* trust for that hand-tailored suit or Dior gown can rest assured that their investment clothing will receive flawless care. Everything, including the ironing, is done lovingly by hand, and garments often return looking better than new. Pickup and delivery with a $25 minimum.

Leroy's Cleaners
9107 W. Olympic Blvd., Beverly Hills
273-6266
Open Mon.-Fri. 7 a.m.-5 p.m., Sat. 8 a.m.-6 p.m.

Well above average when it comes to silk and wool garments; not quite as trustworthy for suedes and leathers. A definite plus: pickup and delivery service is offered throughout Beverly Hills, West Hollywood and even to the Valley.

Premier Leather Cleaners
3098 N. California St., Burbank
(818) 842-2151
Open Mon.-Fri. 7 a.m.-6 p.m., Sat. 9 a.m.-4 p.m.

If you have a suede or leather garment that needs to be cleaned, repaired or refinished, it's worth driving to Premier, which has been doing excellent work since 1946. Premier also specializes in wedding gowns, hats, pillows and beaded and jeweled dresses.

V.I.P. Wardrobe Maintenance
11701 Wilshire Blvd., W.L.A.
479-4707
Open Mon.-Fri. 7 a.m.-7 p.m., Sat. 9 a.m.-5 p.m.

For the care and cleaning of investment-quality clothing, see Vicki Messersmith. For more than ten years, she's handled everything from Armani suits to Bette Midler's mermaid costume. Alterations and restoration work available. Pickup and delivery, too.

A DRESSMAKER

Salah
8340 1/2 Beverly Blvd., W. Hollywood
653-2862
Hours vary.

Have an exact mental picture of the party frock you're seeking, but can't find it anywhere? Salah Saad will design and manufacture exactly what you're looking for, and it'll fit like a dream. These dresses aren't cheap, but they're less expensive than true haute couture, and you'll have a one of a kind.

A DRUGSTORE

Rexall Drugs
8490 Beverly Blvd., W. Hollywood
653-4616
Open daily 8:30 a.m.-10:45 p.m.

Los Angeles has countless other drugstores and a number of other Rexalls, but the Beverly Boulevard store is the biggest and best of them all. It carries everything a drugstore should, and more: cosmetics, tobacco, books, toys, appliances, magazines, candy sold by the pound, gift-wrapping materials, art supplies, office supplies—and, oh yes—a pharmacy.

A FIVE-AND-DIME

Landis Department Store
157 N. Larchmont Blvd., Larchmont Village
464-9939
Open Mon.-Sat. 9 a.m.-6 p.m.

Sadly, the five-and-dime seems to be going the way of the telegraph. A few, however, are still hanging on in the L.A. area, and Landis is the best of the lot. It's all here: creaky wooden shelves, a one-window post office in the back, a staff right out of *Mayberry R.F.D.* and all those little essentials, from notions and school supplies to stockings and the kind of knickknacky gifts that 8-year-olds buy their parents for Christmas. A good antidote for the K-Mart blues.

A FIX-IT

Residential Services
1801 Ave. of the Stars, Century City
277-0770, (818) 787-7775
Open daily 24 hours.

Wes Carlson has been operating this complete home-service referral system for 25 years. From painting to window cleaning, sprinkler installation, roofing or remodeling, Wes will match you with the right person for the job, and he'll follow up to make sure it was done right.

A FRAMER

Artifact
2502 Main St., Santa Monica
399-7300
Open Mon.-Sat. 10 a.m.-6 p.m.

This store once framed the letters, menus and related memorabilia of an entire love affair. Scarves, marathon runners' vests and a Keith Haring doodle on the back of a menu have all found their way into Artifact's frames. Owner Phyllis Doppelt and staff get personally involved in coordinating hand-painted borders, marbled papers, gold-leaf finishes, even hand-cast plaster molds of architectural details.

Art Services

8221 Melrose Ave., W. Hollywood
653-9033
Open Mon.-Fri. 9 a.m.-5:30 p.m., Sat. 10 a.m.-4 p.m.

Art Services will custom-frame anything, no matter what its shape or size. The people here do an excellent job.

A MESSENGER

Bare Minimum

(818) 784-2485
Open Mon.-Fri. 10 a.m.-9 p.m., Sat. 11 a.m.-11 p.m.

Send in a luscious lady or gorgeous guy to deliver a special message, and they won't stay dressed for long. In no time at all, they'll strip right down to the proverbial bare minimum, whether it's in a restaurant, office or at a party. Embarrassment guaranteed. Service available daily from 7 a.m. to midnight.

Eastern Onion

942-2222, (714) 670-1212,
(818) 442-4333
Open Mon.-Fri. 8 a.m.-8 p.m., Sat. 9 a.m.-5 p.m., Sun. 10 a.m.-4 p.m.

No matter what kind of message you want relayed, there's a talented performer here to do it . . . everything from singing Christmas trees and gorillas to dancing birthday cakes and belly dancers. Make sure you okay the message first, since they can be on the raunchy side. Gag gifts, balloon bouquets and gift baskets are available, too. Services available daily from 8 a.m. to midnight.

Shelly Balloon & Associates

2845 S. Robertson Blvd., Culver City
272-UPUP
Open Mon.-Sat. 10 a.m.-6 p.m.

Personalized hand-painted balloons are delivered anywhere in the city; $69.95 will get you seven Mylar (metallic) or one Mylar and eighteen regular balloons, personalized both for the occasion and for the recipient. Also party planning, promotions and advertising specialties.

A NEWSSTAND

Al's Newsstand

370 N. Fairfax Ave., Wilshire District
935-8525
Open daily 6 a.m.-midnight.

If you can't find it at Al's, you probably won't find it anywhere in town. His wide selection of newspapers, paperbacks and esoteric magazines covers every subject, every taste.

World Book and News

1652 N. Cahuenga Blvd., Hollywood
465-4352
Open daily 24 hours.

No matter what the hour, there's always a crowd at this Hollywood institution—from tourists to moviegoers to oddballs who've wandered off nearby Hollywood Boulevard. The selection is excellent.

See also "At Your Service" in the Basics chapter.

PARTY SUPPLIES

Michael's

733 S. San Julian St., Downtown
689-4830
Open Mon.-Sat. 9 a.m.-6 p.m., Sun. 11 a.m.-5 p.m.

Anything and everything for prepping a party: plastic or paper garlands, a bright assortment of solid-color paper plates and napkins, hats, invitations, favors, plastic serving containers and tins, invitations and costume supplies.

A PET HOTEL

Pet Set Inn

14423 S. Crenshaw Blvd., Gardena
644-2938
Open Mon.-Fri. 7:45 a.m.-6 p.m., Sat. 8 a.m.-4 p.m., Sun. 2 p.m.-4 p.m., or by appt.

Special attention is given to each dog and cat. Facilities include individual sleeping quarters with connecting outside private patios and thermostatic heat. There's a grooming parlor on the premises and a veterinarian next door. Pickup and delivery and 24-hour emergency service.

Van Nuys Pet Hotel
7004 Hayvenhurst Ave., Van Nuys
(818) 787-7232
*Open Mon. & Fri. 8 a.m.-6 p.m., Tues.-Thurs.
8 a.m.-5 p.m.*

Valley cats and dogs can live it up in individual patio apartments, complete with air conditioning and heating. All guests are groomed daily. Reasonable rates include breakfast, snacks, dinner and dessert.

Velvet Harbor
7009 Willoughby Ave., Hollywood
874-9817
*Open Mon.-Tues. & Thurs.-Fri. noon-6 p.m.,
Sat. noon-4 p.m.*

There are accommodations for about 30 cats in this friendly home. They're kept in their cages for the first day; once they've adjusted to the new environment, they're allowed out to exercise.

A PHOTOGRAPHER

Lawrence Lesser Photographers
19582 Ventura Blvd., Tarzana
(818) 881-3102
Open Tues.-Fri. 9:30 a.m.-5:30 p.m.

Lawrence Lesser and his talented staff can capture any special moment with photography or video. They are always in demand for social events, family functions and portrait sittings.

Mitchell Rose Photography
7274 W. Sunset Blvd., Hollywood
850-0229
Open Mon-Fri. 10 a.m.-6 p.m.

You can come to Mitchell Rose's small portrait studio, or he'll come to you—to your wedding, your office function or wherever you need a professional picture taken. Rose is a no-frills, hard-working photographer whose work is consistently good and whose prices are more than fair. Makeup and hairstyling services available.

A TAILOR

Richard Lim's High Society Tailors
2974 Wilshire Blvd., Mid-Wilshire
382-0148
Open Mon.-Sat. 10 a.m.-6 p.m.

Lim's individual designs for each client make him unique. With fabrics from around the world, he custom-tailors suits, tuxedos, slacks, sports coats and shirts. There's a definite emphasis on individuality, and special attention is given to physique, profession and style of living. Lim also does alterations.

A VETERINARIAN

West Los Angeles Veterinary Medical Group
1818 S. Sepulveda Blvd., W.L.A.
473-2951
Open daily 8 a.m.-11 p.m.

These veterinarians have an outstanding reputation. Aside from their regular office hours, there's a vet on call 24 hours a day, seven days a week.

A WATCH REPAIRER

C.R. Clark & Company Watchmakers
427 N. Cañon Dr., Beverly Hills
275-9141
Open Mon.-Fri. 9 a.m.-5 p.m., Sat. 9 a.m.-1 p.m.

Excellent, reasonably priced and efficient, Clark will repair almost any type of watch to factory specifications.

SIGHTS

AMUSEMENTS

Gene Autry Western Heritage Museum
4700 Zoo Dr., Griffith Park
667-2000
Open Tues.-Sun. 10 a.m.-5 p.m. Adults $4.75, seniors & students $3, children 2-12 $2, children under 2 free.

Skillfully blending "scholarship and showmanship," the Gene Autry Western Heritage Museum is dedicated to preserving the real and imaginary history of the Wild West. The permanent collection is housed in seven themed galleries called "Spirits," covering everything from extraordinary saddles (Spirit of the Cowboy) to the important *Mountain of the Holy Cross* painting by Thomas Moran (Spirit of Romance) to a charming Hopalong Cassidy children's room (Spirit of Imagination). There's a special exhibition gallery, a sculpture court surrounded by Guy Deel's *Spirits of the West* master mural and two theaters, one for regularly scheduled favorite Western films and live performances, the other for a spectacular presentation that brings the many "Spirits of the American West" to life. Guided tours are available by reservation. Don't miss the gift shop stocked with everything from Stetson hats to Native American contemporary jewelry and pottery. The Golden Spur indoor/outdoor restaurant serves fried chicken and other chuck wagon–style meals.

Cabrillo Marine Museum
3720 Stephen White Dr., San Pedro
548-7562
Open Tues.-Fri. noon-5 p.m., Sat.-Sun. 10 a.m.-5 p.m. Admission free (parking $4).

The Cabrillo Marine Museum makes it possible to explore Los Angeles Harbor, the Channel Islands, offshore kelp beds, sandy beaches and mud flats without getting your feet wet. In addition to the artificial ocean habitats, there are 34 saltwater aquariums showcasing sea creatures as they would appear naturally, a multimedia show and hands-on exhibits that are perfect for children. Call for information on field trips such as whale-watching and Channel Islands tours.

California Museum of Science and Industry
700 State Dr., South-Central L.A.
744-7400
Open daily 10 a.m.-5 p.m. Admission free.

This is one of our favorite Los Angeles museums. The chick hatchery and simulated-earthquake exhibits attract curious flocks of schoolchildren (the latter is an especially valuable teaching tool after a Southland shaker), not to mention the fascinating hands-on experiences with computers, the behind-the-scenes glimpse at a McDonald's restaurant, the chance to operate a bicycle factory of the future, the economics "arcade," the basics on electricity and magnetism and, in the Kinsey Hall of Health, a workshop that lets you make "lifestyle choices" about alcohol, tobacco, cocaine and marijuana—and shows how your choices affect your body. Throughout the museum, scientific theories are made accessible and understandable, using plenty of moving parts and interactive displays. Don't miss the IMAX theater (call for showtimes and ticket prices), a showcase for incredibly vivid short films shown on a five-story-high screen.

Disneyland
1313 Harbor Blvd., off I-5 Fwy., Anaheim
(714) 999-4565
Summer (June 19-Labor Day): open daily 9 a.m.-midnight; spring, fall & winter: open Mon.-Fri. 10 a.m.-6 p.m., Sat.-Sun. 9 a.m.-midnight. Adults $23.50, children 3-11 $18.50; senior discounts available. No cards.

If you want to get a close look at Middle America—well fed, outgoing, accompanied by children—Disneyland is a people-watching spectacle that will keep you entertained for hours. Here, masses of people, both American and foreign, don Mickey Mouse ears without a trace of embarrassment. They climb with delight into little trains and shudder in the Haunted House—which is, by the way, one of the best rides, followed closely by Star Tours and Pirates of the Caribbean. Other popular attractions include Michael Jackson's *Captain EO* film, Splash Mountain and Space

Mountain. In spite of intolerably long lines, visitors seem to know the secret of some magic potion that allows adults to have fun like a bunch of kids, immersing themselves in the atmosphere completely and trustingly. Even if one is past the age at which a roller-coaster ride is the biggest thrill imaginable, in this pristine environment, surrounded by so much friendliness and contagious excitement, it's hard not to resist the spirit and revisit one's childhood for an afternoon. And the clockwork efficiency with which the Disney army runs the park is unbelievable: a dropped cigarette butt is whisked away in a matter of seconds. Despite the stress to the park caused by millions of visitors daily, it remains flawlessly clean; every doorknob shines as if it were brand new.. Disneyland is a required trip for those with children over the age of 3.

Griffith Observatory

2800 E. Observatory Rd., Griffith Park
664-1191, (818) 997-3624
Spring & summer: open daily 12:30 p.m.-10 p.m.; fall & winter: open Tues.-Fri. 2 p.m.-10 p.m., Sat.-Sun. 12:30 p.m.-10 p.m. Admission free.

Nestled in the Los Feliz hills, the Griffith Observatory is a classic example of '30s public-monument architecture. The old-fashioned alcoves house space-age astronomical and scientific displays. You'll find information on everything from cosmic rays to the Mayan calendar to black holes. The various star shows are always as enjoyable as they are educational. The narrators are personal and engaging, and they help solve some of the mysteries of the skies. Laserium is a dramatic laser light show geared around a changing repertoire of music. The observatory grounds are lovely, and on a clear day you can see—as James Dean did in *Rebel Without a Cause*—from the mountains to the sea.

Hollywood Wax Museum

6767 Hollywood Blvd., Hollywood
462-8860
Open Sun.-Thurs. 10 a.m.-midnight, Fri.-Sat. 10 a.m.-2 a.m. Adults $7, seniors $6, children 6-12 $5, children under 6 free.

If you've been dying to see the *Last Supper* next to Marilyn Monroe, Ronald Reagan, Michael Douglas and Magic Johnson, this is your chance. What the wax museum lacks in realism, it more than makes up for in bad taste. Come if you must, compelled by curiosity or masochism. Traveling-circus sideshows do a better job.

Knott's Berry Farm

8039 Beach Blvd., Buena Park
(714) 827-1776
Summer (Memorial Day-Labor Day): open Mon.-Thurs. 10 a.m.-10 p.m., Fri.-Sun. 10 a.m.-midnight; winter: open Mon.-Fri. 10 a.m.-6 p.m., Sat. 10 a.m.-10 p.m., Sun. 10 a.m.-7 p.m. Adults $19.95, children 3-11 $15.95, children under 3 free. Cards: AE, MC, V.

Knott's has grown from a simple, re-created ghost town to a sprawling major entertainment center, with thrill-seeker rides and heavily promoted evening concerts that attract fresh-faced teenagers. The latest attractions include one of the longest manmade rapids rides in California; Fiesta Village, with its "Montezooma's Revenge" roller coaster; and XK1, a participatory flight ride. But some of the original charm can still be found behind the standard amusement-park glitz. Camp Snoopy features an old-fashioned mule-powered carousel, and the Calico Mine ride relives a Western train ride, complete with holdup. People come from all over just for the humble, hearty and good chicken dinners at the gigantic restaurant, and the simple fruit preserves are as tasty as they were 50 years ago. The fantasy element here isn't as much in evidence as at Disneyland, making it both a little less enchanting and a little less deceiving.

Los Angeles Children's Museum

Los Angeles Mall, 310 N. Main St.,
Downtown
687-8800
June-Sept.: open Mon.-Fri. 11 a.m.-4:30 p.m., Sat.-Sun. 10 a.m.-5 p.m. Oct.-May: open Wed.-Thurs. 2 p.m.-4 p.m., Sat.-Sun. 10 a.m.-5 p.m. Admission $4, children under 2 free.

You can bring children here to let them dress up like firemen, play in Sticky City, make instant wall shadows, crawl through a tunnel, create recycled artworks, record their own voices, do a TV newscast, ride a street sweeper and measure their height next to a full-size photo of Kareem Abdul-Jabbar. The multi-tiered labyrinthine place is filled with screaming children looking like little pagans with their brightly painted faces. It is controlled educational chaos, staffed with museum teachers who have the patience of many Jobs. Everything is meant to be touched and felt, and, amazingly enough, everything is intact— the kids seem to have great respect for the property. Special birthday parties can be arranged. Our favorite place in L.A. for young children.

Los Angeles County Museum of Natural History

900 Exposition Blvd., South-Central L.A.
744-DINO
Open Tues.-Sun. 10 a.m.-5 p.m. Adults $3, students, seniors & children 12-17 $1.50, children 5-12 75 cents, children under 5 free. Admission free first Tuesday of each month.

This is a comfortable, old-fashioned institution, complete with a charming, coffered-ceilinged marble rotunda. The cultural exhibits have musical soundtracks to get you into the spirit of things. There's something for everybody here: a fossil room that's a great monument to L.A.'s mammoth and mastodon forebears; a contemporary gem and mineral hall with a most impressive display of gems in their natural states; an American history hall with a charming, nostalgic view of the past; and a hall of mammals, one of those classic natural-habitat simulations with peaceful beasts captured in immortal stasis. The gift shop is a very nice place to buy a little history— natural or otherwise.

Museum of Flying

Santa Monica Airport, 2800 Airport Ave.,
Santa Monica
392-8822
Open Thurs.-Sun. 10 a.m.-6 p.m. Adults $4, seniors $3, juniors $2, children $1.

Located on the north side of the Santa Monica Airport, the Museum of Flying has one of the most complete aviation and aeronautical libraries in the country. There are exhibits on both commercial and aerospace aviation. Flight-ready examples of historically significant aircraft include the *New Orleans*, the first airplane to fly around the world, an authentic Spitfire and the Douglas DC3. Of special interest is an extensive collection detailing the history of the Douglas Aircraft Company. If you feel the need to come out of the romantic aeronautical past and into the scene-making, hustling '90s, the hyper-trendy restaurant DC3 is adjacent to the museum.

Olvera Street

Between Alameda, Main, Macy &
Los Angeles sts., Downtown
628-7833 (Olvera Candle Shop)
Open daily; hours vary.

L.A.'s own permanent Mexican marketplace, Olvera Street is a perennial source of quality finds and bona fide buys. Start off by sampling the hand-shaped tortillas, some of the best in the city, at La Luz Del Dia (near the bandstand, 628-7494). In the jumble of *puestos* (small shops) running down the center, look for Mexican bingo games ($2.95), huge loofah sponges ($3.73) and exotic candy made from cactus, pumpkin or caramelized goat's milk. One stall stocks kitchen goods: wedding cake molds ($6.89 for a set of eight), wooden "chocolate whippers" ($2.65) and dipping irons for making traditional fritters called buñuelos ($5.96). Casa de Souza (on the second level, 626-7076), one of Olvera Street's oldest establishments, imports folk art directly from Mexican and Central American sources: vases with a soft, polished luster from Oaxaca, decorative plates and serving platters, rustic signed metal wall pieces with "tree of life" motifs from Haiti, and wonderful Guatemalan fabric cocktail napkins. Artes de Mexico (620-9782) specializes in Taxco sterling silver jewelry and also stocks a fine selection of Guatemalan fabrics sold (inexpensively) by the yard. Finally, visit the Olvera Candle Shop for candles, candle holders and candle-making supplies. Olvera Street is a short walk from Union Station (800 N. Alameda Street), the stunning mission-style train station and landmark.

See also "Old Los Angeles" in "Excursions."

George C. Page Museum & La Brea Tar Pits

5801 Wilshire Blvd., Wilshire District
936-2230
Open Tues.-Sun. 10 a.m.-5 p.m. Adults $3, seniors & students $1.50, children 5-12 75 cents, children under 5 free.

Hidden away in this office-building neighborhood near the Los Angeles County

Musuem of Art, the La Brea Tar Pits provide a glimpse of our primordial roots. After wandering around the peaceful, tar-scented Hancock County Park, where you may see excavations in progress, head into the George C. Page Museum, a tribute to the animals that once roamed Wilshire Boulevard. You'll discover a saber-toothed cat that changes from a skeleton to a realistic hologram image, a miniature tar pit that simulates the sensation of being pulled into the mire, a paleontology lab where you can watch scientists at work piecing together the past, an impressive wall of wolf skulls, several audio-visual presentations and a storeroom of drawers filled with fossil bones. But the most chilling vestige of the past is the restored skeleton of a woman who died 9,000 years ago in the asphalt pits. Tar-pit jokes aside, this place is definitely worth a visit.

Queen Mary
Pier J, Long Beach
435-3511
Open daily 10 a.m.-6 p.m. Adults $14.95, children $7.95. All major cards.

This aging dowager retains her elegant charm, even though the decks are sprinkled with earnest, polyester-clad tourists sporting first-class admission passes. You can spend an afternoon here witnessing the excitement of lifeboat drills, nautical knot tying, semaphore flag signaling and a simulation of the ship under way. But the most fascinating sights are the subtle personal traces of long-gone sophisticated travelers. Delicate bone china waits in a tea service, the operating table in the infirmary is ready, the chapel is appropriately silent, the oar machine in the exercise room looks just used, and eveningwear awaits its owners in the first-class suite. We were especially amused by the peach-tinted mirrors, meant to disguise any possible seasickness affecting the wealthy travelers who once crossed the Atlantic in luxurious splendor. The art deco bar and formal dining room are monuments to period decor, and it looks more than incongruous to see informally attired contemporary families in such a glamorous setting. As a concession to the present, the ship is filled with gift shops and modern food services. Don't pass up a visit to the neighboring *Spruce Goose*; admission is free with your Queen Mary pass.

Will Rogers State Historic Park
14253 W. Sunset Blvd., Pacific Palisades
454-8212
Open daily 9 a.m.-7 p.m. Parking $3.

You can learn all about Will Rogers's life here, including his prowess as a roper, his spontaneity as a political/social observer and his enthusiasm for flying. All of this and more is covered in a biographical film, followed by a guided (or audio) tour of his pelt-strewn ranch house. The grounds are impressive; the polo field, roping corral and stables are open for roaming. If you choose not to hike around the ranch, you can watch young riders learn the tricks of the horse-show trade, coached by young equestrian experts. Equestrian Day, filled with special events, is held every year in the fall.

Santa Monica Heritage Museum
2612 Main St., Santa Monica
392-8537
Open Thurs.-Sat. 11 a.m.-4 p.m., Sun. noon-4 p.m. Admission free.

The rooms on the first floor of this historic mansion are devoted to different eras of Santa Monica's colorful past; exhibits on the second floor chronicle the history of California. A tiny gift store offers old-fashioned candy and items that correspond to temporary exhibitions, such as Victorian quilts, folk art or '50s housewares.

Six Flags Magic Mountain
Magic Mountain Pkwy. at I-5 Fwy., Valencia
(818) 992-0884
Summer (Memorial Day-Labor Day): open daily 10 a.m., closing hours vary; winter: open Sat.-Sun. & holidays 10 a.m.-6 p.m. Adults $21, adults over 55 & children under 48 inches $11. Cards: AE, MC, V.

A classic American amusement park. There's no magical fantasyland here, just first-rate thrill-seeker rides, concerts featuring an occasional top-name pop act, slower-paced amusements for young children and lots of junk food. The best attractions are the major rides: the world's largest dual-track wooden roller coaster, a loop-the-loop roller coaster, the Roaring Rapids, a fast-and-wet white-water raft ride, and Tidal Wave, which plummets you into two and a half tons of water. This is a good park for children; the six-acre Bugs Bunny World features an excellent petting zoo, pint-size vehicular rides and a scaled-down racetrack with tiny race cars.

Spruce Goose
Pier J, Long Beach
435-3511
Open daily 10 a.m.-6 p.m. Adults $14.95, children $7.95. All major cards.

It's quite eerie and surreal to walk out of the sunlight and into this dark hangar housing the dramatically lit *Spruce Goose*, Howard Hughes's monstrous flying boat. That first view of the wooden plane, which has the wingspan of a football field and the design of a potbellied whale, will take your breath away. Nothing else is as impressive as that first look, but the exhibits are interesting nonetheless—especially the inside of the plane and the audio-visual exhibits that explain both the facts and the myths of Howard Hughes's eccentric life and the realization of his impossible dream. Your ticket also includes admission to the neighboring *Queen Mary*.

Universal Studios
100 Universal City Plaza (Lankershim Blvd. at the 101 Fwy.), Studio City
(818) 508-9600
Tour times vary with the season. Adults $21, seniors & children 3-11 $15.50, children under 3 free. Cards: MC, V.

This is one of the greatest masochistic shows Hollywood has ever produced. For nearly six hours, the movie industry gives away all its secrets, empties its bag of tricks and destroys all our illusions and dreams. "Earthquake—The Big One" is the newest attraction; what's most frightening, particularly after the big San Francisco quake of 1989, is not the ride itself but the idea that a catastrophic nightmare has become sheer amusement for the masses. The shark from *Jaws* makes a lunge as harmless as that of a tadpole. The crossing in the Red Sea is nothing more than a footpath. The *Psycho* villa is an empty facade. The 30-foot-high King Kong is an impressive creation, but you never forget you're on a soundstage. *Star Trek* loses its magic, and we are ultimately like children,

sadly triumphant after breaking a toy to discover how it worked.

Venice Gondola Charters
4016 Lyceum Ave., Venice
823-5505
Tour times vary.

For $65, you and your significant other can board an authentic replica of a Venetian gondola and cruise through the maze of channels in Marina del Rey and Venice, complete with taped Italian music and a black-and-white-clad gondolier. The price also includes Champagne during the tranquil, hour-long journey. For the hopelessly romantic and those who don't mind a rather ludicrous substitute for the real thing.

Watts Towers and Art Center
1765 E. 107th St., Watts
569-8181
Towers open Sat. 10 a.m.-3 p.m.; Art Center open Tues.-Sat. 8 a.m.-5 p.m. Adults $2, children $1.50.

Rising out of a bleak suburban landscape in Watts is this whimsical creation of childlike charm and innocence. Simon Rodia, a barely literate Italian immigrant, came to L.A. with a dream, and this latter-day da Vinci created the towers over a 33-year period with no aesthetic, architectural or engineering background. He created his folk art sculpture on ranch land alongside the railroad tracks, so Red Car passengers would see his work. A naïf creation, the sculpture is a fantasy of found art: shells, ceramics, glass, tools and rocks are imbedded and imprinted into a honeycomb of walls and organic, spiraling towers, a cross between an Islamic mosque, a pueblo and a sand castle. The metal framework is eroding, and the glorious towers are encased by scaffolding as artisans painstakingly restore and renovate the structure (expected to take until 1992 or longer). Until the renovation is complete, you'll have to content yourself with viewing the towers from a short distance. But by all means, visit the adjacent Watts Towers Art Center, a lively community center that shows African-American and Third World art and hosts workshops and two major festivals a year. Ignore the overblown stories about

Watts's crime problems and make a pilgrimage to this inspirational place.

Whale Watch
Sport Fishing Pier, 233 N. Harbor Dr.,
Redondo Beach
372-3566
Tours times & prices vary.
   A three-and-a-half-hour boat ride will take you about two miles offshore in the hopes of spotting whales migrating toward Baja. Your hosts take it all very seriously, and soon the whole crowd joins in the effort to help find one of these magnificent mammals. We were fortunate enough to see a mother whale and her calf making the leisurely voyage south. The ride is refreshing, although a bit choppy at times. But the best part is the return trip, where you can see the entire dramatic panorama of Los Angeles, with snow-peaked mountains in the distance. It can be one of those stunning moments that makes you realize why people settled here in the first place.

ART GALLERIES & MUSEUMS

GALLERIES

CONTEMPORARY ART

Ace Gallery
5514 Wilshire Blvd., Wilshire District
935-4411
Open Tues.-Sat. 9 a.m.-6 p.m.
   The Ace Gallery has survived a somewhat checkered past and 29 years of history to remain an important force in the L.A. art circuit. Its latest colossal space (equaling the size of MOCA) allows owner Douglas Christmas to mount exhibitions of museum-quality works by such international artists as Robert Rauschenberg, Richard Serra and Bruce Nauman.

Asher/Faure Gallery
612 N. Almont Dr., W. Hollywood
271-3665
Open Tues.-Sat. 11 a.m.-5 p.m.
   Directed by Patricia Faure (and co-owned by Betty Asher, one of the grande dames of the Los Angeles art scene), this recently renovated space exhibits a variety of established international and California artists, including Robert Graham, Robert Yarber, Jack Goldstein, Bruce Cohen, Laura Lasworth, Craig Kauffman and others.

Jan Baum Gallery
170 S. La Brea Ave., Wilshire District
932-0170
Open Tues.-Sat. 10 a.m.-5:30 p.m.
   Along an increasingly fashionable stretch of La Brea (now home to City Restaurant and American Rag Cie), Jan Baum has organized an entire building devoted to the visual arts, which houses one other gallery, an art consultancy, a bookstore featuring artists' books and a small, chic restaurant. The Baum Gallery focuses on emerging and established international artists, with some of the work having sources in the primitive. To that end, there is a small collection of masks and sculpture from Africa and Indonesia.

Blum/Helman
916 Colorado Ave., Santa Monica
451-0955
Open Tues.-Fri. 10 a.m.-6 p.m., Sat. 11 a.m.-5 p.m.
   Located in what is quickly becoming the hub of the closely watched art scene in Los Angeles, Blum/Helman is the second L.A. gallery to be directed by the near-to-legendary art dealer Irving Blum. After his stewardship of the extremely farsighted and influential Ferus Gallery in L.A. during the '60s, Blum moved to New York, partnering with Joseph Helman. Blum/Helman in New York is one of the premier contemporary art galleries in

the world, with a roster of artists that includes Ellsworth Kelly, Robert Moskowitz, Bryan Hunt and Richard Tuttle. The gallery is also well known for selling important pictures by such major American artists as Frank Stella, Roy Lichtenstein, Jasper Johns and Andy Warhol.

The Santa Monica gallery, although relatively small, is smartly designed and features the same high standards of works found in New York. Future exhibitions will focus on artists in the gallery stable, as well as periodic historical and group exhibitions, which this gallery puts on with considerable dash and style.

Cirrus Gallery
542 S. Alameda St., Downtown
680-3473
Open Tues.-Sat. 11 a.m.-5 p.m.

Owner Jean Milant was one of the first westside dealers to move into the once-uncharted reaches of downtown Los Angeles. Combining an active fine-arts press, which has published such established California artists as John Baldessari, Ed Ruscha, Billy Al Bengston and Peter Alexander, with a large gallery highlighting younger and hitherto unknown California artists, Cirrus is one of the few noteworthy galleries currently active downtown. Strictly industrial setting.

James Corcoran Gallery
1327 5th St., Santa Monica
451-4666
Open Tues.-Fri. 10 a.m.-5 p.m., Sat. 11 a.m.-5 p.m.

Corcoran is one of the leading galleries in Los Angeles. The expansive, well-appointed space in Santa Monica has exhibited such important American and European figures as Joseph Cornell, James Rosenquist, Francesco Clemente, Mimo Paladino and Sandro Chia, as well as representing a solid group of established and popular local artists: Billy Al Bengston, Peter Alexander, Ed Ruscha, Joe Goode and Charles Arnoldi. However, Corcoran's real, if not altogether public, métier is the sale of major paintings by Franz Klein, Willem de Kooning, Clyfford Still, Sam Francis and other abstract expressionists and postwar masters.

Rosamund Felsen Gallery
669 N. La Cienega Blvd., W. Hollywood
652-9172
Open Tues.-Sat. 10 a.m.-5 p.m.

Rosamund Felsen handles a top-notch stable of young L.A. talents, two of the most important being Richard Jackson and Chris Burden, whose reputations in international circles far exceed their reputations at home (a pity). Consistently interesting exhibitions in a relatively small but well-lighted and open space.

Future Perfect and Associates
318 Omar St., Downtown
620-1608
Open Tues.-Sat. 11 a.m.-5 p.m., or by appt.

A high-funk setting for works on paper, limited-edition serigraphs and fine-art photography, Future Perfect showcases cutting-edge artists as diverse as Carlos Almaras, Bob Zoell and Jeffrey Vallance and such well-known names as Dennis Hopper and Bravo. The "non-neutral" surroundings include Road Warrioresque furniture, a coffee bar, books and videos.

Gallery of Functional Art
2429 Main St., Santa Monica
450-2827
Open Tues.-Fri. 10 a.m.-7 p.m., Sat. 11 a.m.-7 p.m., Sun. noon-7 p.m.

Under Frank Gehry's roof in the Edgemar mini-mall, Lois Lambert's Gallery of Functional Art showcases the bright lights of L.A.'s design, craft and art communities. Art furniture is the primary focus, with selective shows of incredible vessels and jewelry. Exhibitions change every two months; top draws include artists David Gale, Gregg Fleishman, Eugenia Butler, Anne Kelly, Chris Colicott, Phil Garner and John Bok.

Kiyo Higashi Gallery
8332 Melrose Ave., W. Hollywood
655-2482
Open Tues.-Sat. 11 a.m.-6 p.m.

Owner Kiyo Higashi is passionate about the abstract, and her minimalist approach is reflected in a stable of mainly L.A. artists—such pivotal painters as Guy Williams and New Mexico's Larry Bell (he designed the gallery space) hang with such newer names as William

Dwyer, Perry Araeipour and Penelope Krebs. Also expect to find sculpture and constructions in this young, as yet noncommercial gallery.

Fred Hoffman Gallery
912 Colorado Ave., Santa Monica
394-4199
Open Tues.-Fri. 9:30 a.m.-5:30 p.m., Sat. 10 a.m.-5 p.m.

Scholar, adviser and curator Fred Hoffman opened his gallery in the fall of 1986 after operating New City Editions, a small gallery and fine-art publishing concern in Venice. Although he will continue to publish editions of Charles Arnoldi, Frank Gehry, Jean-Michel Basquiat and others, Hoffman's rather vast gallery affords him an opportunity to also show such strong New York artists as Glenn Goldberg, Barbara Kruger and Ross Bleckner, along with California's John Miller and John McCracken and Europe's Sophie Calle, A. R. Penck and Ulrich Ruckriem. The gallery has also undertaken a large-scale exhibition of the seminal American sculptor Richard Serra, whose massive abstract steel forms leave a profound impression upon the viewer.

Hunsaker/Schlesinger Gallery
812 N. La Cienega Blvd., W. Hollywood
657-2557
Open Tues.-Sat. 11 a.m.-5 p.m.

Joyce Hunsaker and Laura Schlesinger, two art consultants who had the courage and the intelligence to open a gallery, exhibit a wide range of material featuring young California artists as well as the historical works of such eminent figures as Milton Avery. Prints, photographs and multiples are included in the inventory, along with paintings and sculpture. It's a small but effective gallery environment with information and advice pleasantly rendered.

Michael Kohn
313 N. Robertson Blvd., W. Hollywood
271-8505
Open Tues.-Sat. 10 a.m.-6 p.m.

Well-informed and personable almost to a fault, Michael Kohn has built his reputation on emerging and recognized New York artists (Joan Nelson, Kevin Larmon, Mark Innerst,

Kenny Scharf, Keith Haring) both in solo and more than normally provocative group or theme shows. Most recently, the gallery has begun to foster the work of such L.A. unknowns as Cindy Bernard and Jamey Bair.

Kurland/Summers Gallery
8742A Melrose Ave., W. Hollywood
659-7098
Open Tues.-Sat. 11 a.m.-6 p.m., or by appt.

Art glass is the focus here, both blown and constructed and combined with nonglass elements. Kurland/Summers shows off the fragile work of American and international talents (Dan Dailey, Richard Jolley, Christopher Lee, John Luebtow and Richard Marquis, among them) with theatrical flair. Look for a new exhibition about every six weeks.

L.A. Louver Gallery
55 N. Venice Blvd., Venice
822-4955
Open Tues.-Sat. 1 p.m.-5 p.m.
77 Market St., Venice
822-4955
Open Tues.-Sat. noon-5 p.m.

L.A. Louver was one of the first L.A. galleries to show important international art; now it's a vital part of the thriving westside art community. Near the West Beach Café, Rebecca's and 72 Market Street, Louver shows a renowned group of American and European artists, including David Hockney, Ed Moses, Domenico Bianchi, Edward Kienholz, Leon Kossof and Wallace Berman. Thankfully, Louver is blessed with a parking lot in this typical (meaning crowded) Venice neighborhood. A genial, well-run environment with British émigré Peter Goulds as owner/director, Louver recently spawned another location in New York's Soho.

Margo Leavin Gallery
812 N. Robertson Blvd., W. Hollywood
273-0604
817 N. Hilldale Ave., W. Hollywood
273-0603
Open Tues.-Sat. 11 a.m.-5 p.m.

One of the most powerful and respected dealers in town, Margo Leavin focuses much of her attention on blue-chip American artists, such as Jasper Johns, Willem de Kooning and

Claes Oldenburg. An established power in the West Coast art world, Leavin deserves credit for raising the standard of contemporary art in Los Angeles and for providing a venue in which to see the great and near-great contemporary masters from the East Coast. This is not to say the gallery shows only acknowledged masters; it also represents three very interesting L.A.-based artists, John Baldessari, Jill Giegrich and Mark Lere. The second space, just a short walk away on Hilldale, is a clean, open rectangle replete with the newly fabricated installation of the Oldenburg *Knife* on the building's facade.

Burnett Miller Gallery
964 N. La Brea Ave., Hollywood
874-4757
Open Tues.-Sat. 10 a.m.-5:30 p.m.

Formerly a curator at the La Jolla Museum of Contemporary Art, Miller shows conceptual-based art that encompasses strong European influences, such as the minimalist work of Ettore Spalletti and the spiritual leanings of Wolfgang Laib. Two other artists of note are L.A.-based Charles Ray, with his installation-oriented pieces, and Nancy Spero, whose work, when it avoids a rather strident feminism, can be wonderfully hermetic and intriguing.

Herbert Palmer Gallery
802 N. La Cienega Blvd., W. Hollywood
854-0096
Open Tues.-Fri. 10 a.m.-6 p.m., Sat. 11 a.m.-5 p.m.

Holding no regular exhibition schedule, but one or two small shows yearly, Palmer, a long-standing veteran of L.A.'s art community, does not run a gallery per se, as there is no consistent exhibition program or stable of artists. Yet he does offer a fine, select group of well-known artists' work.

Pence Gallery
908 Colorado Ave., Santa Monica
393-0069
Open Tues.-Fri. 10 a.m.-5:30 p.m., Sat. 11 a.m.-5 p.m.

Pence Gallery is known for its stellar lineup of multiples by Sam Francis, David Hockney, Ed Ruscha and others. You'll usually find two different shows going on in the front and main

galleries. The roster of emerging and mid-career artists includes Sabina Ott and Ann Preston from L.A. and New Yorkers David Levinthal and Paul Laster.

Saxon-Lee Gallery
7525 Beverly Blvd., Wilshire District
933-5282
Open Tues.-Sat. 10 a.m.-5:30 p.m., or by appt.

Collectors know co-owners Dan Saxon and Candace Lee for their spirited tastes in abstract, figurative and representational art. The spacious gallery is home to a wide spectrum of work (paintings, sculptures, drawings, ceramics, art furniture) by Mac Adams, Rose-Lynn Fisher, Gronk, Red Grooms, Judy Rifka and Peter Shire, among others. There's an outdoor sculpture court, a private viewing room and an upstairs loft space. Evenings, the main gallery becomes a 100-seat theater for performances, lectures and musical events.

Thomas Solomon's Garage
822 1/5 N. Hayworth Ave., W. Hollywood
653-8980
Open Wed.-Sat. 1 p.m.-7 p.m., Sun. noon-5 p.m.

Selling art from a two-car garage is fresh and appropriate for L.A., especially when it's masterminded by Thomas Solomon, son of New York art dealer Holly Solomon. In keeping within the experimental context, no show runs longer than two weeks—quick takes include many first, solo and group shows by new talents (Michael Gonzalez) or new bodies of work created especially for the "garage" (Willi Wegman). Contemporary and controversial, it's a must-visit for collectors on the cutting edge.

Jan Turner
8000 Melrose Ave., W. Hollywood
655-2694
Open Tues.-Fri. 10 a.m.-5:30 p.m., Sat. 11 a.m.-5:30 p.m.

This is one of the most elegant gallery spaces in L.A. The building's facade is enough of an eye-catcher to warrant further investigation. Jan Turner exhibits a variety of established artists, including L.A. sculptors John Frame and Tony Delap and painters Carlos Almarez, Astrid Preston, John Alexander and Ole Fischer.

Daniel Weinberg Gallery
2032 Broadway, Santa Monica
453-0180
Open Tues.-Sat. 11 a.m.-5 p.m.

A pioneering art dealer, Weinberg came to Santa Monica from San Francisco by way of West Hollywood. Exhibiting major new and established American artists in the westside's emerging art center, this latest gallery continues to break new ground while remaining true to its rather rigorous aesthetic vision. Featuring such artists as Richard Artschwager, Saint Clair Cemin, Jeff Koons, Sol Lewitt, Robert Mangold, Meyier Vaisman, Terry Winters and Christopher Wool, Weinberg offers a perennially challenging exhibition roster.

PHOTOGRAPHY

G. Ray Hawkins
7224 Melrose Ave., W. Hollywood
550-1504
Open Tues.-Sat. noon-5 p.m.

One of the oldest and most respected fine-art photography galleries in the country, G. Ray Hawkins exhibits both vintage and contemporary work. The stellar roster includes Ansel Adams, Bruce Davidson, Judy Coleman, Margaret Bourke-White, Herb Ritts, Helmut Newton, and Jo Ann Callis.

Susan Spiritus Gallery
South Coast Plaza, 3333 Bear St., Ste. 330, Costa Mesa
(714) 549-7550
Open Mon.-Fri. 10 a.m.-9 p.m., Sat. 10 a.m.-6 p.m., Sun. noon-5 p.m.

Located in South Coast Plaza's Crystal Court, Susan Spiritus shows contemporary fine-art photography by the likes of André Kertész, Ansel Adams and Yousuf Karsh. Such up-and-comers as Mark Matthews and Larry Vogel are also represented. There's a strong emphasis on French photography and hand-painted and -colored work.

PRINTS & GRAPHICS

Cirrus Editions
542 S. Alameda St., Downtown
680-3473
Open Tues.-Sat. 11 a.m.-5 p.m.

Cirrus publishes work primarily by California artists, although it also produces works on paper from New York artists. Recent editions include John Baldessari, Lita Albuquerque, Lari Pittman and Mark Lere.

Gemini G.E.L.
8365 Melrose Ave., W. Hollywood
651-0513
Open Mon.-Fri. 9:30 a.m.-5:30 p.m., Sat. 11 a.m.-5 p.m.

Internationally recognized as a leading fine-arts publisher, Gemini G.E.L. has published works by such noted artists as Jasper Johns, Robert Rauschenberg, Philip Guston, Ellsworth Kelly, Mark di Suvero and others. The beautifully designed workshop and gallery was created by one of L.A.'s hottest architects, Frank Gehry. The gallery exhibits only current editions, yet the bulk of the material published over the years is available for inspection upon request. Gemini G.E.L. is a tremendous asset for Los Angeles, as it publishes the world's finest artists working today.

Emma-Louise Hayley
7201 Melrose Ave., Ste. 205, Hollywood
965-9320
Open by appt. only.

Through an extensive network of sources all over Europe, Londoner Emma-Louise Hayley is introducing L.A. designers and collectors to an extraordinary range of decorative antique prints. Her showroom of "classical and curious" prints from the eighteenth and nineteenth centuries encompasses fine architecturals, illustrations of Parisian deco costumes, floating botanical studies, surrealistic citrus fruit and other antiquarian finds for classical and contemporary interiors. Framing that complements the period and style of the print is available.

Marilyn Pink Master Prints and Drawings
4129 Sepulveda Blvd., Culver City
391-3883
Open Mon.-Fri. 9 a.m.-5 p.m., Sat. 10 a.m.-3 p.m.
509 Avondale Ave., Brentwood
395-1465
Open by appt. only.

At her Culver City gallery and private home in Brentwood, Marilyn Pink offers the largest selection in Los Angeles of prints, graphics and drawings from the fifteenth through the twentieth centuries. It isn't a fine-arts press like Gemini G.E.L. or Cirrus but rather two showcases with a fine, select body of work. Bulging print drawers and countertops strewn with material are the trademarks of this noted dealer and lecturer. There's a congenial, un-hurried atmosphere and a knowledgeable staff, not the least of whom is Pink herself.

PUBLIC & ALTERNATIVE GALLERIES

Japanese-American Cultural and Community Center
244 S. San Pedro St., Little Tokyo
628-2725
Open Tues.-Sun. noon-5 p.m.
Regularly rotating exhibitions are offered in the gallery tucked inside this cultural center. In addition, an 828-seat theater offers numer-ous programs related to Japanese culture, in-cluding performances by Japan's Kabuki Theatre Group. There is also a library special-izing in Japanese cultural information.

LACE
1804 Industrial St., Downtown
624-5650
Open Tues.-Sat. 11 a.m.-5 p.m., Sun. noon-5 p.m.
This nonprofit space features performance and conceptual art, installations and exhibi-tions of paintings and sculpture by relatively unknown L.A. artists. Los Angeles Contem-porary Exhibitions (LACE) is more experi-mental than most galleries in town. Results are sometimes disappointing, yet it's a valuable alternative environment for L.A.'s younger artists. There's a video screening room and a well-stocked bookstore. The annual art auc-tion is LACE's biggest fund-raiser and always promises some great deals on art.

Los Angeles Municipal Art Gallery
Barnsdall Park, 4804 Hollywood Blvd.,
Los Feliz
485-4581
Open Tues.-Sun. 12:30 p.m.-5 p.m.
This city-sponsored gallery mounts exhibi-tions that include a variety of media, from paintings and sculptures to graphics and ce-ramics, all by Southern California contempo-rary artists. The Junior Arts Center (485-4474) consists of a gallery space, classes and special events designed to increase kids'

awareness of art. While you're on the grounds, visit the Hollyhock House, designed by Frank Lloyd Wright.

MUSEUMS

Bowers Museum
2002 N. Main St., Santa Ana
(714) 972-1900
Hours vary.
With its lovely grounds and tranquil court-yard, this mission-style museum is the historic centerpiece of a cultural redevelopment plan by the city of Santa Ana. The Bowers Museum focuses on cultural arts of the Americas and Pacific Rim, with special collections of pre-Columbian, Native American, African, Amer-ican and Southern Californian decorative arts. Due to renovation and expansion (a new wing will house the museum's far-reaching travel-ing exhibition program), the exhibition pro-gram is inactive through 1991. Call for scheduled cultural festivals and educational programs.

Craft and Folk Art Museum
Wilshire Blvd. & Fairfax Ave. (May Co.
bldg., 4th Fl.), Wilshire District
937-5544
Open Tues.-Sun. 11 a.m.-5 p.m. Admission free.
In its temporary home on the fourth floor of the landmark May Company building, the Craft and Folk Art Museum is awaiting con-struction of a new museum tower, part of a mixed-use project by L.A.'s noted architec-ture/development firm, The Ratkovich Com-pany. Since opening in 1973, the museum's growth has paralleled Angelenos' interest in the decorative arts, crafts and folk art. Every-thing from African-American folk art and ver-nacular architecture to British crafts and designs and art jewelry has found its way into these galleries. The celebrated museum shop continues to operate for the time being at 5800 Wilshire Boulevard, while a satellite shop in the May Company sells exhibition publications and cards. The museum also op-erates a small library on the mezzanine. This institution has always been a lively, rewarding place to visit; we expect it won't let us down in the future.

The J. Paul Getty Museum
17985 W. Pacific Coast Hwy., Malibu
458-2003
Open Tues.-Sun. 10 a.m.-5 p.m. Admission free; parking reservations required.

This Romanesque villa off the Pacific Coast (with splendid grounds and gardens) looks slightly out of place without the Bay of Naples in its rightful location. As one of seven operating entities of the J. Paul Getty Trust (a private foundation devoted to the visual arts, with an endowment of $3 billion), it is an institution to be reckoned with. The museum is as much fiction as fact; if they can't have the original, they enthusiastically replicate it. On the first floor, you'll find endless Greek and Roman antiquities in lavish inlaid-marble vestibules and wings. There is a gloomy gallery upstairs of oversized paintings, and rooms filled with French, Dutch and Italian works from the early fourteenth through the late nineteenth centuries. More recent acquisitions that have upgraded the entire collection include fifteenth- and sixteenth-century works by Bouts, Mantegna, Pontormo and Masaccio. Drawings, sculptures, illuminated manuscripts, photographs and decorative arts round things out. But the drama here lies in the overwhelming display of seventeenth- and eighteenth-century French furniture. We find it amusing that so many visitors pass by one corner cupboard, apparently unaware that it was acquired for the premium price of $2 million. The Getty has a charming tea garden that serves a good, light al fresco lunch amid the lovely pools and fountains, as well as a bookstore. We have to admit that the place has class; you'll find one of the most elegant parking garages we've ever seen, as well as chic gray-marble restrooms and solid-marble stairways. Add the spectacular setting to the lovely house and fine art, and a visit to the Getty is mandatory during any trip to L.A.

The Huntington Library Art Collections and Botanical Gardens
1151 Oxford Rd., San Marino
(818) 405-2275
Open Tues.-Sun. 1 p.m.-4:30 p.m. Suggested donation $2. Advance reservations required on Sun.

Henry Huntington certainly had few delusions of grandeur—he simply built his own petit Versailles in San Marino. His former home, now converted to an art gallery, is a modest Georgian palace filled with an interesting collection of eighteenth- and nineteenth-century oil paintings—including Gainsborough's *Blue Boy*—furniture and decorative accessories. The library houses an impressive 600,000 books, many of which are first editions. Educational display cases give visitors the chance to see letters from George Washington, illuminated books of hours, a Gutenberg Bible and Chaucer's *Canterbury Tales*. But the charming gardens are what make your visit here worthwhile. You can tour the world with trips to the jungle or the desert, stopping along the way in the Zen, Shakespeare and rose gardens. Visitors can spend the whole afternoon wandering around the 150 acres of carefully landscaped grounds. You'll want to wander, too, enjoying this touch of civilized European life paradoxically located in sunny, relaxed Southern California.

Long Beach Museum of Art
2300 E. Ocean Blvd., Long Beach
439-2119
Open Wed. & Fri.-Sun. noon-5 p.m., Thurs. noon-8 p.m. Admission free.

Behind this humble California-bungalow facade lurks one of the most dynamic and youthful museums in Southern California. The minimalist decor is the perfect partner for the contemporary and often avant-garde art, with a strong bent toward video. Shows change often, and the museum closes during installations, so be sure to call first. The view of the Pacific is stunning, the grounds are tranquil, and the bookstore/gallery is filled with treasures to take home. Our only regret is that there isn't more to this conservancy of 21st-century art.

Los Angeles County Museum of Art
5905 Wilshire Blvd., Wilshire District
857-6000, 857-6111
Open Tues.-Fri. 10 a.m.-5 p.m., Sat.-Sun. 10 a.m.-6 p.m. Adults $3, seniors & students $1.50, children 5-12 75 cents. Special exhibition prices vary.

The L.A. County Museum of Art complex consists of five incongruent buildings surrounding a central court: the visually stunning Anderson Building, with its stepped facade and abundance of glass brick; the monstrous trio of original LACMA buildings, circa 1964; and the latest addition, an architectural eyesore known as the Pavilion for Japanese Art. Most of the museum's permanent holdings are housed in the Ahmanson Building; the collection of pre-Columbian Mexican art is especially noteworthy, as are the Gilbert collection of mosaics and monumental silver and an important Indian and Southeast Asian art collection. LACMA also houses American and European paintings, sculpture and decorative arts and one of the nation's largest holdings of costumes and textiles. Providing you get past its atrocious exterior and wander inside the Pavilion for Japanese Art, you'll find the internationally renowned Shin'enkan collection of Japanese paintings, as well as a restaurant serving Japanese tea.

As for the rest of the museum, there is an outstanding special exhibition roster, wonderful film retrospectives at the Bing Theater, a rather institutional gift shop, an outdoor food stand and a quite decent indoor/outdoor café for self-service salads, sandwiches and complete meals.

Museum of Contemporary Art

California Plaza, 250 S. Grand Ave., Downtown
621-2766
152 N. Central Ave. (Temporary Contemporary), Downtown
621-2766
Open Tues.-Wed. & Fri.-Sun. 11 a.m.-6 p.m., Thurs. 11 a.m.-8 p.m. Adults $4, seniors & students $2, children under 12 free; admission free Thurs. 5 p.m.-8 p.m.

Following its auspicious launch in 1986, the Museum of Contemporary Art (MOCA) has come a long way in terms of the kinds of exhibitions and media and performing events it has programmed. The museum structure, designed by Arata Isozaki, is a triumph, with its beautifully proportioned and abundantly skylit galleries. MOCA has also retained its first temporary location, an old police warehouse that was sensitively overhauled by Frank Gehry in 1983 and that is referred to as either the TC or the Temporary Contemporary.

The donation of 64 minimalist and neoexpressionist works from the collection of the late Barry Lowen, together with an acquisition from Count Giuseppe Panza di Biumo, forms the cornerstone of MOCA's permanent collection. The museum paid $11 million for Panza's brilliantly uneven group of works by such figures as Mark Rothko, Franz Kline and Robert Rauschenberg. The permanent collection was recently buoyed by two noteworthy gifts: paintings, sculptures and drawings from the Rita and Taft Schreiber collection, including important works by Jackson Pollock, Piet Mondrian and Alberto Giacometti, and some 200 vintage and contemporary prints from the estate of L.A. photographer Max Yavno.

Critically acclaimed exhibitions at MOCA's California Plaza facility and the TC have included a show titled "The Architecture of Frank Gehry," and an Anselm Kiefer show. As part of its provocative program for the creation of new art, MOCA produces *The Territory of Art*, a radio series with commissioned performances by artists from a diversity of disciplines. The MOCA store is a destination in itself, packed with art books, colorful toys and eye-popping, artist-crafted ceramics, jewelry and housewares. At the TC store, the offerings are even more offbeat. An outdoor lunch of tasty Italian sandwiches, salads and desserts can be had at the Il Panino café at the California Plaza building. Be sure to get your parking validated to avoid the exorbitant charge.

Museum of Neon Art

704 Traction Ave., Downtown
617-1580
Open Tues.-Sat. 11 a.m.-5 p.m. Admission $2.50.

Behind the unassuming gray cinder-block facade lies a celebration of everything that moves and lights up. The garage space is filled with marvelous artworks that are a putterer's paradise and an electrician's nightmare. The neon artworks range from the representational to the ridiculous, but they're all fun. Special exhibitions change every three months. Classes in neon design and technique are taught by artist Lili Lakich. Be sure to inquire about the neon night cruises that take you on a double-decker bus tour of the city's dazzlers (call for tour times and ticket prices).

Newport Harbor Art Museum

850 San Clemente Dr., Newport Beach
(714) 759-1122
Open Tues.-Sun. 10 a.m.-5 p.m. Adults $3, seniors, students & military $2, children 6-17 $1, children under 6 free.

This reputable museum has an ambitious exhibition program with more than eight shows a year focused on late-twentieth-century California and international art. The social life of Newport's rich and powerful (a very large group indeed) seems to revolve around the openings and fund-raisers at this museum, which has benefited from their prosperity. We can assure you it's worth the trip to see any of the museum's traveling shows, which in the past have included retrospectives of artworks by Chris Burden, L.A. Pop Art in the '60s and the sculpture of Englishman Tony Cragg. The museum is closed between exhibitions; call before visiting.

See also "Orange County" in Out of Los Angeles.

Pacific Asia Museum
46 N. Los Robles Ave., Pasadena
(818) 449-2742
Open Wed.-Sun. noon-5 p.m. Adults $3; seniors & students $1.50; children under 12 free.

This is the only museum in Southern California to focus on the arts of the Pacific Rim countries and Asia. Housed in the historic Grace Nicholson Building, it's authentically outfitted with a Chinese roof, tiles and bronze dragons. The second-floor gift shop offers one-of-a-kind kimonos, ikat clothing from Indonesia, contemporary and antique jewelry, toys, masks, cooking utensils and more.

Santa Monica Museum of Art
2437 Main St., Santa Monica
399-0433
Open Wed.-Thurs. 11 a.m.-8 p.m., Fri.-Sun. 11 a.m.-6 p.m. Suggested donation $3; seniors, students & artists $1.

The former Edgemar Farms egg-processing plant has hatched a gem of a museum, surrounded by a new-age mini-mall (called Edgemar), admirably designed by Frank Gehry. Still in the early stages of development, the Santa Monica Museum of Art (SMMOA) has no permanent collection. It promises a host of performances and projects by lesser-known artists in new and unconventional contexts.

Norton Simon Museum
411 W. Colorado Blvd., Pasadena
(818) 449-6840
Open Thurs.-Sun. noon-6 p.m. Adults $3; seniors & students $1.50, children under 12 free.

Contrary to rumor, Los Angeles does acknowledge that civilization existed before its stucco sprawl became the locus of American

trendiness. If you want proof, drive over to the Norton Simon in Pasadena, where you'll see a wonderful collection of masterpieces. After the Burghers of Calais by Rodin greet you at the gates, you'll view a broadly representative inventory of art, with particularly good collections of the Impressionists, Degas, Picasso's works on paper and Renaissance and eighteenth- and nineteenth-century European works. The Galka Scheyer Collection of the Blue Four (Kandinsky, Klee, Feininger and Jawlensky) is superb. Some of the works are oddly displayed, with pieces from different epochs complementing and reinforcing one another. It may be a bit jarring to the traditionalist, but, after all, this is California, and they play by new rules here.

Skirball Museum
Hebrew Union College, 3077 University Ave., South-Central L.A.
749-3424
Open Tues.-Fri. 11 a.m.-4 p.m., Sun. 10 a.m.-5 p.m. Admission free.

This little museum is housed in Hebrew Union College, bordering the USC campus. It is filled with Judaica, from a reconstruction of an archaeology dig in the Near East and a room filled with Torah-based religious decorative arts to a gallery of paintings and a special exhibit about the five senses as reflected in Jewish ritual art. There are a few special exhibitions a year, with corresponding lectures and special events. It's an interesting place to get a sense of the past and to admire the richness of Jewish religious and folk culture.

Southwest Museum
234 Museum Dr., Highland Park
221-2163
Open Tues.-Sun. 11 a.m.-5 p.m., Sun. 1 p.m.-5 p.m. Adults $3, seniors & students $1.50, children 7-18 $1, children under 6 free.

On a clear day, this hillside museum offers a commanding view of the mountains. The Southwest Museum is one of the city's treasures, as every local schoolchild knows. It showcases Native American arts and crafts, and gives visitors a glimpse of what California and its neighboring states were like before the Spanish and American colonizations. The pottery and basketry collections are especially good, as is the intriguing exhibit on the Plains Indians, with detailed explanations of cosmology, clothing and war rites. Rotating special exhibitions feature everything from contemporary photography to prehistoric pottery. The gift shop is a favorite of collecting cognoscenti, and the Braun Research Library houses one of the finest collections of material on Native American cultures in the world. While you're in the neighborhood, another must-stop is the Casa de Adobe (a block away on Figueroa Street), a fascinating re-creation of an early nineteenth-century dwelling.

EXCURSIONS

The Beaches

Each L.A. beach has its own character—some have a teen-party ambience, some are surfing beaches and some attract the bizarre. At the northernmost end of the county are the Malibu-area beaches, starting with County Line, a great surfing spot. Then (moving south) comes Zuma Beach, where Valley teens congregate, and the private Malibu Colony, home to crowd-shy celebrities. Next stop is Santa Monica, L.A.'s great public beach; on hot summer days tens of thousands stake out their spots on Santa Monica's huge expanse of sand, even if the water is polluted. Try to make friends with a member of one of the private beach clubs (the Jonathan Club and the Beach Club are two big ones); their parking and club facilities make the crowds much more bearable.

Then comes Venice, a beach like no other. Venice typifies the hyperbole of Los Angeles, at once seductive, exhilarating, intriguing, entertaining and completely devoid of substance. But you don't come to Venice for depth. You come for the string-bikinied nymphs who whiz by on roller skates, the street performers, the skateboard jockeys, the sunbathers, the bodybuilders, the rap masters and the galaxy of people who take all of this in without a trace of surprise. The soundtrack to this show is a cacophony of competing portable stereos. Your first response to the Venice visual assault is to realize that you are overdressed, no matter how little you may be wearing. The bazaar stalls are a good source for a throw-away pair of sunglasses; most have the look of an eccentric neighbor's garage sale. And scattered through all this are the most bourgeois-looking people, out for their Sunday stroll.

South of Venice, in airplane-strafed Playa del Rey, is the broad, usually crowd-free expanse of Dockweiller State Beach, a popular spot for picnics, parties and big touch-football games—and the only county beach that allows beach fires. Manhattan Beach, farther down the line, is where the pretty people come out for volleyball, running, bicycling, Frisbee and flirting. A desperate parking situation keeps these beaches from getting too crowded with outsiders. Neighboring Hermosa Beach and Redondo Beach are similar to Manhattan, although the houses and residents are slightly seedier.

We heartily recommend taking a leisurely bike ride along well-marked paths from Santa Monica to any of the South Bay beaches. It's a great way to absorb the California experience—and to earn your lunch!

Chinatown

Broadway & Hill, north of 1st St., Downtown

Although only a tiny enclave of Orientalisms, the maze of shops is of interest. If you've had enough of the Chinese slippers, rice bowls, cotton T-shirts and souvenirs, you can find respectable dim sum to sample a taste of the Orient. This Chinatown is actually L.A.'s third, being created by Anglo developers after the first and second were moved to make way for large developments.

Griffith Park

Vermont Ave. N. of Los Feliz Blvd., Los Feliz
666-2703
Open daily 5 a.m.-10 p.m.

This gigantic park has something for everyone, just as a Los Angeles public park ought to. There's the zoo, housing more than 2,000 creatures living in simulated natural habitats. There are the Griffith Park Observatory and Planetarium, with the expected science-student–quality star show that is not without charm. The Laserium light-and-music show attracts both families and teen dates, and the Greek Theatre presents top-name pop musicians in a lovely outdoor arena. For young children, there are pony rides, a small-scale choo-choo train complete with overalled engineer, a classic old carousel and Travel Town, a marvelous collection of antique trains. If you tire of life in the fast lane, cool out in peaceful, woody Ferndell; if you aren't having luck spotting celebrities, come bird-watch in the bird sanctuary. And, as expected, there are facilities for ballplayers, cricketers, soccer players, golfers, tennis nuts, hikers and swimmers. And for the less athletic, there are dozens of picnic areas. A truly great city park.

The Mountains

If you've had enough of the hordes of hip Angelenos in Beverly Hills or Venice, try escaping to one of Los Angeles's two mountain ranges for some solitude and (at least partially) clean air. The Santa Monica Mountains, home to deer, coyotes, chaparral and reclusive canyon dwellers, cut across Los Angeles from Hollywood to Malibu, separating the L.A. basin from the San Fernando Valley. You should at least take a drive along Mulholland, the windy, sometimes rutted road that runs the length of this range—the views are often breathtaking. If you're more outdoors-inclined, there are thousands of acres of trails, wildlife and streams at Point Mugu State Park, in the west end of the Santa Monicas; at Will Rogers State Park, in Pacific Palisades; and at Topanga State Park.

The San Gabriel Mountains, part of the huge Angeles National Forest, rise above northeast Los Angeles, Pasadena and the San Gabriel Valley. Here you'll find contrasts typical of Los Angeles—waterfalls and fern glens just around the corner from dry hills of scrub and chaparral. The miles of trails and parkland are reached through the Angeles Crest Highway; we recommend you check with the Red Box Ranger Station on the highway for information before exploring this wonderful natural expanse.

Old Los Angeles

Though efforts to preserve early Los Angeles have been sadly inadequate, some of its early history can be found. Two Franciscan missions remain in the L.A. area from the Spanish colonial period, and they are worth seeing. The San Gabriel Mission, 537 West Mission Drive in San Gabriel, was established in 1771 as the fourth in the chain of Junípero Serra's California missions. The current church dates from about 1805 and looks much like the very first design. The San Fernando Mission, 15151 San Fernando Mission Boulevard in Mission Hills, was founded in 1797. The charming adobe buildings surround a green courtyard; the church, destroyed in the 1971 earthquake, has been rebuilt as an exact copy of its former self. Bypass the dull exterior and look at the beautiful Spanish detail work inside.

Adobe houses, Spanish architecture, and the oldest residence in Los Angeles (Avila Adobe, 1818) are the landmarks of early central Los Angeles, at Olvera and Main streets in downtown. This area is interesting architecturally, especially the Plaza Church, built for the tiny pueblo of Los Angeles in 1822, and the Pico House Hotel. But contemporary life takes its toll, and Olvera Street has become a commercial bazaar with shops selling curios, Mexican clothes and mediocre Mexican food.

Believe it or not, cultured people did live here before postwar stucco tracts usurped the old ranchos. For a look at some lovely turn-of-the-century architecture, drive through old Pasadena, especially down Grand and Orange Grove, which are lined with imposing mansions; down Carroll Avenue in Angelino Heights near downtown, home of beautifully restored Victorian houses; through the old West Adams district south of Mid-Wilshire, which was once a wealthy community; and through Ocean Park and Venice, where Victorian charmers are tucked in between modern condos. If you're interested in touring some California Victorians, visit Heritage Square, 3800 North Homes Street, Highland Park, 485-2433.

THE GREAT OUTDOORS

One would hardly be experiencing Southern California completely if one were to stay inside restaurants, nightclubs and galleries all the time. Although we are certainly fond of such civilized activities, we do subscribe to the "when in Rome" cliché. So when in California, do as the sun-drenched Californians do: get outside and go sailing, bicycling, hiking, golfing or hang gliding. With that in mind, we've drawn up a list of places that will supply you with the equipment, lessons and/or facilities needed to become fully initiated into active Los Angeles life.

BALLOONING

Balloon Adventures
P.O. Box 1201, Malibu
(818) 888-0576
Open daily dawn-dusk.
The Balloon Adventures hot-air balloon pilot will take you on a quiet, majestic soar. Sunrise flights ($110 per person) leave from Moorpark, Lancaster or Perris Valley; sunset rides ($150 per person) start at Camarillo. You must book in advance, and if you want to arrange a special flight (as did the couple who were wed aloft), all sorts of charters and parties are available.

BICYCLING

Westside Beaches
Excellent bike paths follow the coastline from Santa Monica to South Bay; riding from beach to beach is one of the best possible ways to spend a sunny Saturday. Although there are no formal shops with regular hours, several ad hoc bike-rental operations can usually be found in Venice Beach parking lots on weekends and summer weekdays.

Woody's Bicycle World
3157 Los Feliz Blvd., Los Feliz
661-6665
Open Mon.-Sat. 9 a.m.-6 p.m., Sun. 9 a.m.-4 p.m.
One of the very few places in L.A. (surprisingly) to rent bikes, Woody's is located near Griffith Park, which has some fine bike lanes.

Mountain and ten-speed bikes rent for $10 to $15 a day. The shop is friendly, and the bikes are in decent shape.

GOLFING

Arroyo Seco Golf Courses
1055 Lohman Ln., S. Pasadena
255-1506
Summer: open daily 7 a.m.-10 p.m.
These two three-par courses (nine holes each) aren't the most challenging in Los Angeles, but the price is certainly right: $3.75 per person for nine holes, $5.25 for eighteen ($6 after 6 p.m. and on weekends). The courses are just a short drive from downtown L.A. Women, juniors and senior citizens are given daytime discounts.

Griffith Park Golf Course
4730 Crystal Springs Dr., Griffith Park
663-2555
Open daily dawn-dusk.
You won't be able to get into this popular public course on weekends without a reservation card, but it isn't too hard to get a starting time on weekdays (call the office for information on a reservation card). There are two eighteen-hole courses here, and both are challenging. On weekdays, the greens fee is $9.50 per person; on weekends, $13.50.

Industry Hills Golf Course
1 Industry Hills Pkwy., City of Industry
(818) 810-GOLF
Open daily 6 a.m.-dusk.
A huge Sheraton "resort" and convention-center hotel surrounds these two eighteen-

hole courses, which are beautiful, well designed and expensive: $40 per person Monday to Thursday, $45 Friday to Sunday (fees include an electric golf cart). Located 30 minutes east of downtown L.A., the courses are quite a drive away for those living west of Pasadena. But if you're an avid golfer and don't have any club-member friends, it may be worth the drive and the cost; it's one of the best public courses in the country.

HANG GLIDING

Windsports International
16145 Victory Blvd., Van Nuys
(818) 988-0111
Open Tues.-Fri. 10 a.m.-6 p.m., Sat. 9 a.m.-noon.

With the help of this friendly organization, you can act out humanity's oldest fantasy: to fly like a bird. Windsports teaches hang gliding at three levels: beginner, novice and intermediate. In twelve to fifteen lessons you can become an advanced hang-glider pilot, or you can take just one lesson—you'll still experience that indescribable thrill of flying, even though it'll just be off a small sand hill. There's also a tandem high-altitude program that soars up to 2,000 feet..

HIKING

Wilderness Institute
23018 Ventura Blvd., Ste. 202, Woodland Hills
(818) 887-7834
Open Mon.-Fri. 9 a.m.-6 p.m. (Outdoor Center, 28118 Agoura Rd., Agoura, 818-991-7327, open Sat. 10 a.m.-4 p.m.).

Operating in national park sites throughout the Santa Monica Mountains, this "outdoor school" offers sunset and Sunday-brunch hikes, full-moon hikes and half-day geology hikes for about $15 to $20 per person. Other notable programs include periodic storytelling under the stars, weekend Mojave Desert explorations and other adventure outings, plus classes in wilderness survival, mountaineering and cultural history for the whole family. Call for a free catalog.

HORSEBACK RIDING

Los Angeles Equestrian Center
480 Riverside Dr., Burbank
(818) 840-9063
Open daily; hours vary.

This large equestrian center is one of the best in the country, with two regulation polo arenas, a polo school, a beautiful indoor arena and a pavilion with horsey shops, including a premium saddlery. Events include Grand Prix horse shows, rodeos and professional polo, a trendy way to spend a Saturday night with friends. Cafe Polo serves lunch, dinner and an excellent Champagne Sunday brunch—dress ranges from blue jeans to black tie. For the recreational rider, there are a variety of lessons, good rental horses and more than 250 miles of trails throughout Griffith Park. Horses rent for $12 an hour.

Sunset Ranch Hollywood Stable
3400 N. Beachwood Dr., Hollywood
464-9612
Open daily 9 a.m.-5 p.m.

One of the most exhilarating ways to get a great view of Los Angeles (on a seemingly rare clear day) is to rent one of Sunset Ranch's horses and ride through the trails high in the Hollywood Hills (just below the Hollywood sign). The horses are well trained and the ranch hands are friendly; you don't need a guide and are free to explore the hills on your own. A not-to-be-missed experience is the guided Friday-night dinner trip: you set out at dusk, ride for nearly two hours over the mountain to Burbank, have dinner in a Mexican restaurant, and ride back by the light of the moon ($25 per person). If the weather is good, it can be a truly magical experience—except for the terrible Mexican food. Horses are $15 an hour, and a refundable $10 deposit is required.

SAILING & BOATING

Blue Water Charter Concepts
4051 Glencoe Ave., Ste. 7, Marina del Rey
823-2676
Open Mon.-Fri. 9 a.m.-5 p.m.

For an elegant Catalina trip, a surprise birthday party or a quiet moonlight cruise, call Blue Water Charter Concepts. It has a fleet of twenty luxury motor yachts (from 85 to 115 feet) and will arrange almost any sort of charter imaginable. The company is particularly proud of its gourmet catering department. The cost varies considerably, depending on the yacht, the time at sea and the staff required.

Rent-a-Sail
13560 Mindanao Way, Marina del Rey
822-1868
13719 Fiji Way, Marina del Rey
822-2516
Open daily 10 a.m.-sundown.

These two shops rent a variety of boats, from Hobie Cats to sloops to power boats; with the smaller boats you can explore the Marina, with the larger you can cruise the Santa Monica coastline. Fourteen-foot sailboats rent for $14 an hour, 21-foot sailboats for $20, and fifteen-foot power boats for $28. Sailing lessons are also available for $28 an hour ($38 for two people), plus rental fees.

SKIING

Mt. Waterman
817 Lynn Haven Ln., La Canada (Angeles Crest Hwy., 43 miles NE of L.A.)
(818) 790-2002

One of the closer ski slopes, Mt. Waterman is only an hour's drive from Los Angeles. It's a small place—just a few chairs—and the runs are fairly simple, though there are a couple of challengers. But the drive is right and the slopes are usually well groomed and uncrowded. Call before going; it sometimes closes when the weather gets unseasonably warm.

Snow Summit
880 Summit Blvd., off Hwy. 38, Big Bear Lake
(714) 866-5766

Probably the best local skiing (and snow boarding) spot, which unfortunately means the crowds can get oppressive, especially now that advance tickets are sold through Ticketron and Teletron. There's a limit to the number of tickets sold, however, and the midweek crowd is kept quite manageable. Snow Summit isn't as close to L.A. as Mt. Baldy or Mt.

Waterman (about a two-hour drive), but that means the snow is better. There are ten chair lifts, plenty of manmade snow and runs for all levels, rentals, lessons and a child-care center. Call for prices on full-day, half-day and night-skiing tickets. Try to avoid the weekends.

Snow Valley
Hwy. 18, east of Running Springs
(714) 867-2751

The largest local ski area, with thirteen lifts and plenty of runs, Snow Valley is also one of the most expensive—full-day tickets are $33, half-day $25 and night skiing $20. During dry spells the many snow machines keep the packed-powder level up. There's a newly re-modeled bar and restaurant, rentals, lessons and an all-day kids' program that includes lunch (for ages 5 through 10, $30). Very crowded on weekends.

TENNIS

Griffith Park Tennis Courts
3401 Riverside Dr. (Los Feliz Ave. entrance), Griffith Park
662-7772
Open daily 7 a.m.-10 p.m.

There's usually a wait for these well-maintained courts during prime time; if you buy a reservation card from the city, however, you can book courts in advance. Courts are free weekdays before 4 p.m.; other times, they're $4 an hour. Also try the other park facility, a pretty, woodsy setting that can be reached from the Vermont Avenue entrance.

The Merchant of Tennis
1118 S. La Cienega Blvd., Wilshire District
855-1946
Open Mon.-Sat. 9 a.m.-6 p.m. (courts available daily 24 hours).

This successful tennis shop has two fine courts, one for singles and one for doubles. The cost ranges from $7 to $11, depending on when you play. Since there are only two courts, reservations are critical; you can drop by and pay in advance or give them a charge-card number over the phone. The Merchant of Tennis's professional instructors rank among the best in Southern California.

The Racquet Centre

10933 Ventura Blvd., Studio City
(818) 760-2303
Open Mon.-Fri. 6 a.m.-midnight, Sat.-Sun. 7 a.m.-midnight.

The Racquet Centre has probably the best facilities of any public courts in town. It has the feel of a private club; there are twenty first-class tennis courts, eleven racquetball courts, paddle tennis courts, ball machines, good locker rooms and a well-stocked shop. Tennis courts are $5 to $9, depending on time of day; racquetball courts run $6 to $12. You can become a member for $42 a year, which entitles you to reserve courts. Otherwise you take your chances.

The Tennis Place

5880 W. 3rd St., Wilshire District
931-1715
Open daily 7 a.m.-11 p.m.

These courts, adjacent to the huge Park La Brea apartment complex, do a booming business. There are sixteen lighted courts in good condition; the cost is $12 per court hour before 4 p.m. and $14 after 4 p.m. and on weekends. Reservations are advised. A $70 yearly membership fee entitles you to a $5 discount on court fees and other privileges. The Tennis Place will arrange games and offers professional instruction.

WATERSKIING

Endo's Waterski Werks

5612 E. 2nd St., Long Beach (Naples Island)
434-1816
Hours vary with the season.

Endo's rents (and sells) waterskis and accessories to the suntanned young residents and visitors of Belmont Shore and Naples, two charming beach communities hidden away in Long Beach. Ski rentals start at $8 a day; lessons (highly recommended for first-timers) can be arranged.

LANDMARKS

Los Angeles is rich with both history and architectural achievements, its fly-by-night reputation notwithstanding. We'll leave it up to the historians and architectural critics to provide you with detailed information on L.A.'s landmarks and architecture. But we've provided a list of some of the city's most acclaimed structures, some of which are open for visiting and some of which can be viewed only from the street. For more information, try the Los Angeles Conservancy, 623-2489.

AVILA ADOBE, 10 E. Olvera Street, Downtown, 628-1274. Oldest surviving house in Los Angeles, built in 1818.

BONNIE BRAE STREET, two blocks south of Wilshire Boulevard, Wilshire District. Neighborhood of beautiful Victorian homes.

BRADBURY BUILDING, 304 S. Broadway Street, Downtown. A stunning, well-preserved office building built in 1893, with a skylit central atrium, wrought-iron stairways and caged elevators.

BULLOCKS WILSHIRE, 3050 Wilshire Boulevard, Wilshire District. An art deco classic; one of L.A.'s finest buildings. By the time you read this, I. Magnin will have taken over the property, but it'll always be Bullocks Wilshire to us.

CARROLL AVENUE, at Kensington Avenue, Angelino Heights (near Echo Park). These Victorian jewels are being restored one by one.

DOHENY MANSION, 8 Chester Place, Downtown, 746-0450. An imposing turn-of-the-century mansion at Mount Saint Mary's College.

ENNIS-BROWN HOUSE, 2607 Glendower Avenue, Los Feliz. A hilltop

Mayan-style concrete-block house designed by Frank Lloyd Wright.

GAMBLE HOUSE, 4 Westmoreland Place, Pasadena, (818) 793-3334. The Craftsman era is epitomized in this Greene and Greene masterpiece. The house is open to the public; call for information.

HERITAGE SQUARE, 3800 N. Homes Street, Highland Park, 485-2433. The Cultural Heritage Board of Los Angeles has saved about a dozen of these beautiful Queen Anne/Eastlake–style homes from the wrecker's ball. Several are open to the public.

HOLLYHOCK HOUSE, 4800 Hollywood Boulevard (Barnsdall Park), Hollywood, 662-7272. This Frank Lloyd Wright classic is the centerpiece of the Barnsdall Art Center. Tours are held several days a week (call for times).

HOLLYWOOD SIGN, Durand Drive off Beachwood Drive, Hollywood. You'll have to hike awhile to get a close-up look at this world-famous landmark.

LOS ANGELES CENTRAL LIBRARY, 630 W. 5th Street, Downtown, 626-7461. Although tragically damaged by fire in the mid-1980s, the exterior remains as beautiful as ever. An aesthetic gem, mixing Roman, Mediterranean, Byzantine, Islamic and Egyptian sources.

LOS ANGELES CITY HALL, 200 N. Spring Street, Downtown. Designed by Albert C. Martin, one of L.A.'s premier early architects, this 28-story building was once a sky-scraping marvel that towered above the rest of the city. Although far surpassed in height, it is still lovely, and its observation decks provide good views.

LUMMIS HOME, 200 E. Avenue 43, Highland Park, 222-0546. It took Charles Lummis twelve years to build this marvelous house made of boulders found in the nearby arroyo.

MILLION DOLLAR THEATRE, 307 S. Broadway Street, Downtown, 642-6272. A spectacular theater, this was L.A.'s first glamorous movie palace and is now a rundown neighborhood movie theater.

NEUTRA HOUSES, Silverlake Boulevard, Silverlake. Richard Neutra's clean lines and architectural purity can be seen in the International-style houses he built facing the Silverlake Reservoir. There are several between 2200 and 2300 Silverlake Boulevard.

PACIFIC DESIGN CENTER, 8687 Melrose Avenue, West Hollywood. This striking glass building houses L.A.'s cutting-edge products in home design and decor. Two huge, brightly colored additions recently joined the Blue Whale.

PAN-PACIFIC AUDITORIUM, 7600 W. Beverly Boulevard, Wilshire District, 938-7070. The handsome, streamlined moderne building is looking sadder and sadder (a recent fire struck the last blow); ambitious renovation plans offer a glimmer of hope of salvaging what's left, but nothing's firm.

PICO HOUSE, 430 N. Main Street, Downtown, 628-1274. The first three-story masonry building in L.A., the Pico House has been lovingly restored. The Pueblo de Los Angeles State Historical Park conducts tours; call for information.

SAINT VINCENT DE PAUL CHURCH (Roman Catholic), 612 W. Adams Boulevard, South-Central Los Angeles, 749-8950. Across from USC, this church is one of L.A.'s loveliest.

UNION PASSENGER TERMINAL, 800 N. Alameda Street, Downtown, 624-0171. The set for countless movies. The main terminal is enormous and very beautiful.

WRIGLEY HOUSE, 391 S. Orange Grove Boulevard, Pasadena. A stately mansion typical of those built in Pasadena by wealthy turn-of-the-century industrialists.

TOURS

For many, a visit to Movieland is not complete without an inside tour of a television or film studio. In addition to The Burbank Studios, several other studios and stations are worth a call: ABC Television Studios, 557-4100; CBS Television Studios, 852-2345; Walt Disney Studios, (818) 560-1000; Fox Television Station, 856-1000; Lorimar Studios, 280-8000; NBC Television Studios, (818) 840-3537; Paramount Studios, 468-5575; Sunset-Gower Studio, 467-1001; Warner Hollywood Studios, 850-2500. (For Universal Studios, see "Amusements.")

The Burbank Studios
4000 Warner Blvd., Burbank
(818) 954-1744
Tours weekdays 10 a.m. & 2 p.m. by reservation only. Children must be 10 or older. Admission $22.

If you want a behind-the-scenes look at how Hollywood *really* works, not a stunt-filled, amusement-park–style tour, call up The Burbank Studios (home to Warner Brothers and Columbia Pictures) and make reservations for this fascinating tour—the most intensive of any in the L.A. area. The group is limited to twelve; you'll walk throughout the huge lot (sometimes assisted by an electric cart), going through the property department, unused sound stages, empty Western streets, construction departments and all the day-to-day operations behind moviemaking. On occasion, tours are allowed on the set to watch live filming in progress.

Grave Line Tours
P.O. Box 931694, Hollywood
876-0920, 876-4286
Tours daily at noon. Admission $30 per body.

Call it tacky and tasteless, but Grave Line Tours is easily Hollywood's hottest novelty. This two-hour tour of Tinseltown's most morbid and scandal-ridden sites departs from Hollywood Boulevard and Orchid Avenue (near Mann's Chinese Theater), spiriting you and six others away in a Cadillac hearse. "Director of Undertakings" Greg Smith really camps it up, with a taped narration that covers every sordid detail (including music and sound effects). You'll see the "last-breath" locations of luminaries John Belushi, Janis Joplin, Sal Mineo, Montgomery Clift and Superman's George Reeves, to name a few. Each "mourner" receives maps to "Cemeteries of the Stars" to explore later. Among tours, this is one, uh, to die for.

Gray Line Tours
6541 Hollywood Blvd., Hollywood
856-5900
Open daily 7 a.m.-8 p.m.

Strictly for tourists. Most of Gray Line's tours go to the attractions (Disneyland, Knott's). There are a few other bus tours: a Tijuana shopping spree, a Hollywood/Beverly Hills/movie-star tour and a general city tour that hits everything from Mann's Chinese Theatre to the Hollywood Bowl. The all-day city tour is $34 and the two-hour movie-star tour is $25.

Hollywood on Location
8644 Wilshire Blvd., Beverly Hills
659-9165
Open Mon.-Fri. 9:30 a.m.-4:30 p.m.

Every weekday morning at 9:30, Hollywood on Location publishes a list of locations of the TV series and movies filming around L.A. that day and through the night (until dawn the next day). This list, which names each production and its stars, also tells the exact address, shooting times and the stunts and special effects planned for each location site. Typically, 40 locations are listed, most within ten miles of the Hollywood on Location office. You'll also get a set of large, detailed maps showing you how to find each location. You can start any time up to 4:30 p.m., driving to as many locations as interest you. The $29 fee includes the list and maps.

It's a must for the hopelessly star-struck who can't get into Spago—and it's worthwhile for those who just want a look at how Hollywood works.

L.A. Party Bus
6253 Hollywood Blvd., Hollywood
467-4697
Tours evenings & weekends; times & prices vary.

When the whim strikes (and no more regularly than that), owner Cash Oshman conducts a "tour" of L.A.'s hottest nightclubs in one of four conspicuous artist-designed buses: an Egyptian sphinx, Groucho Marx, a "gobot transformer" and a dragon. The predetermined schedule lets partygoers get on or off as they please, and drinks are allowed on the bus, which saves you from the perils of driving under the influence. Another novel idea is Oshman's Art Hop, a day-long excursion in which passengers stop at artists' lofts and galleries and encounter impromptu performance pieces. Needless to say, no two Party Bus extravaganzas are the same. The attention-getting buses are also available for private tours and parties.

Los Angeles Conservancy Tours
433 S. Spring St., Ste. 1024, Downtown
623-CITY
Hours vary. Tours $5.

These very nice people will quickly disprove the rumor that Los Angeles has no history. Every Saturday morning at 10, enthusiastic docents lead residents as well as tourists on seven downtown walking tours. The Pershing Square tour takes you to and through such landmarks as the Oviatt Building, The Biltmore hotel, the Bradbury and Edison buildings and Grand Central Market. The Broadway Theaters tour explores the once-glorious theater district, with forays into the Orpheum, United Artists and Los Angeles theaters, all dating from the teens and twen-

ties. Highlights of the Palaces of Finance tour include the Banco Popular, the Design Center, the Palm Court of the Alexandria Hotel and the Los Angeles Theater Center. And the Mecca for Merchants tour visits the old Seventh Street beauties, including the palatial Fine Arts Building, the Los Angeles Athletic Club and the 818 and Roosevelt buildings. There are also periodic tours through L.A.'s most historic and beautiful homes and neighborhoods; check with the Conservancy for details.

El Pueblo de Los Angeles Historic Park
130 Paseo de la Plaza, Downtown
628-1274
Tours Tues.-Sat. 10 a.m., 11 a.m., noon & 1 p.m. Admission free.

For a look at the early Spanish and Indian days of Los Angeles, when it was a tiny, dusty village, come down to Olvera Street for this delightful walking tour. You'll see many of the old buildings, including the Pico House and the Avila Adobe. There's no charge, and reservations are necessary for large groups.

Ultimate Dimensions in Dining
18540 Chase St., Ste. 8, Northridge
(818) 349-1895
Open 9 a.m.-midnight. Price varies. Cards: AE, MC, V.

Here's a winning idea for gastronomic explorers: Ultimate Dimensions in Dining will custom-design a progressive dinner at three different award-winning L.A. or Orange County restaurants. An intimate party of two goes by limo; groups numbering up to 80 travel by van, sampling, for example, a preselected appetizer at Jimmy's, an entrée at Citrus and dessert at L'Ermitage. Champagne and nibbles are served en route and beverages with each course are included in the cost.

OUT OF LOS ANGELES

BIG BEAR & LAKE ARROWHEAD

THE MAGIC MOUNTAINS

Less than a two-hour drive from the heart of Los Angeles, Big Bear offers a rustic breath of fresh air. The community feels sort of like a gold rush town—slightly tacky and thrown together quickly, with an informal, friendly mountain aesthetic. The setting is lovely, not unlike a mini Lake Tahoe: a clear blue lake surrounded by pine-topped mountains. Winter weekends are overrun with skiers headed for the three local mountains, Snow Summit, Goldmine and Snow Forest. And it's just as busy in summer, when city people come up here to fish, waterski, hike and just plain relax in the clear air and open spaces.

Not far from Big Bear is Lake Arrowhead, a privately owned lake and moneyed weekend retreat. Many well-to-do Angelenos own second homes here, some right on the water with private docks. If you can't make friends with one of these lucky home owners, you can rent a house or stay at the Lake Arrowhead Hilton Lodge (see "Hotels"). Arrowhead lacks the down-home charm of Big Bear, but it does boast an exceptionally beautiful lake and plenty of clean mountain air.

RESTAURANTS

12/20 George & Sigi's Knusperhauschen

829 W. Big Bear Blvd., Big Bear City
(714) 585-8640
CONTINENTAL
Open Mon.-Wed. & Fri.-Sun. 5 p.m.-9 p.m. Cards: MC, V.

It's hard to take this Hansel and Gretel cottage too seriously. The exterior is reminiscent of a Christmas gumdrop house; the interior is a cozy clutter of stained glass, oil paintings and private booths. If you are lucky enough to have Sigi serve you, your evening will certainly be a success. This lovely lady in alpine dress takes care of her customers with lots of motherly love. She helps make this place as warm, authentic and friendly as it is, as does her husband-chef, George. (The couple emigrated to these mountains from Latvia in 1957.) George takes his work seriously, and his expertise crosses an international boundary with such specials as beef Wellington, an Italian-style paella and stuffed pheasant. Dinners here are generous and, as Sigi says, smothered (with good tastes and a lot of care). You may be among the fortunate to taste the chicken-mushroom soup flavored with sour cream, the homemade Burgundy salad dressing and one of the many Schnitzels. George's repertoire is vast: chicken Kiev, goulash, Schnitzel Oscar (which we normally avoid but which is wonderful here), Sauerbraten, braised oxtails and more—and it's all good. So are the desserts, especially the chocolate-mocha layer cake and the orange charlotte. We suggest you skip the wines and try some of the wonderful German beers. The finishing touch to such a large and good dinner is the reasonable bill; a huge dinner with beer will run about $50 for two.

11/20 The Iron Squirrel

646 Pineknot, Big Bear City
(714) 866-9121
FRENCH
Open Mon.-Sat. 5:30 p.m.-9 p.m., Sun. 10 a.m.-1 p.m. & 5:30 p.m.-9 p.m. Cards: AE, MC, V.

This is a family place with surprisingly good country cooking. The pine-paneled mountain decor includes enormous grapevine wreaths and simple, homey touches. Although the cuisine is not what we would call inspired, it is authentic and good. Joyce and Paul Ortuno greet you, while their uncle Roger runs the kitchen with Basque enthusiasm. Entrées come with soup and salad, making this place a good value; if you still want a starter, try the lovely thyme-studded pâté. Most everything we've tried has been good (though nothing is exceptional): hearty paella, rack of lamb with garlic, veal normande with plump apples, roast chicken and more simple French classics. Desserts are rich, sweet and satisfying. There are two wine lists; ask for the California version, and you will be able to choose from excellent vintages at reasonable prices. About $55 for two, with a simple wine.

QUICK BITES & NIGHTLIFE

Blue Ox
441 W. Big Bear Blvd., Big Bear City
(714) 585-7886
Open Sun.-Thurs. 11 a.m.-3 p.m. & 5 p.m.-9 p.m., Fri.-Sat. 11 a.m.-3 p.m. & 5 p.m.-9 p.m. (bar open 11 a.m.-midnight). Cards: MC, V.

A good place for a family dinner, the Blue Ox is filled with antique farm equipment, sweet miniature-print wallpaper and peanut shells on the floors. The storybook menu is a little precious for our tastes, but you can get Paul Bunyan–size portions, and the food is pretty good. Stick to the beef—it comes in a variety of preparations from steaks to ribs. The fish tends to have been frozen, but the chicken is basic and generally tasty. Dinner will run about $45 for two for plentiful, simple fare.

Boo Bear's Den
572 Pine Knot, Big Bear Lake
(714) 866-2932
Open Mon.-Thurs. 7 a.m.-11 p.m., Fri. 7 a.m.-1 a.m., Sat. 6 a.m.-1 a.m., Sun. 6 a.m.-11 p.m. Cards: MC, V.

Don't let the foolish name put you off— Boo Bear's is a good, unpretentious café well located in the heart of Big Bear's "downtown" shopping area. Sit on the enclosed patio and stick to the simpler fare (omelets, burgers, sandwiches), and you'll have a relaxed, pleasant meal. Breakfast for two will run about $12, lunch a couple of dollars more.

Chad's Place
40740 W. Big Bear Blvd., Big Bear Lake
(714) 866-2161
Open daily 10 a.m.-2 a.m. Cards: MC, V.

This genuine cowboy bar may be a bit rustic for some visitors. But you'll definitely get the flavor of this mountain village when you come here to drink beer, play pool, listen to good bar bands, watch sports, catch up on the latest local gossip or observe the macho men and mountain women warm up in winter and cool down in summer. It's a Big Bear landmark and a pleasant, low-key place to hang out. Sand-wiches and snacks are served by friendly, seasoned veterans. About $25 for two.

Heidi's
Lake Arrowhead Village, Lake Arrowhead
(714) 336-1511
Open Sun.-Fri. 7 a.m.-3 p.m., Sat. 7 a.m.-9 p.m. All major cards.

Heidi's is about as authentically Bavarian as Frontierland is Western, but it does combine a comfortable, if kitschy, setting with excellent service and good, hearty food. On a cold mountain day, a bowl of rich, homemade chicken soup and a hot open-face sandwich will revive you in no time at all. Breakfasts are also hefty and tasty. About $15 for lunch for two.

Maggio's Pizza
Interlaken Shopping Center, 42160 Big Bear Blvd., Big Bear Lake
(714) 866-8815
Open Sun.-Thurs. 11 a.m.-9 p.m., Fri.-Sat. 11 a.m.-10 p.m. No cards.

Maggio's is considered by many to be the best pizza joint in Big Bear, and we're not about to argue. The ingredients are fresh and tasty, the pizzas and calzones are generous, the atmosphere is friendly, and the prices are low. You can eat in or take out. A pizza-and-beer dinner for two will run about $16.

HOTELS

In Big Bear, a good alternative to staying in a hotel or inn is to rent a condo or cabin. Well-established rental agencies include Big Bear Reservation Service (714-866-5878), Sleepy Forest Rentals (714-866-7567) and Blue Skies Reservations (714-866-7415). In Lake Arrowhead, houses—including some right on the water—can be rented through Arrowhead Property Management (714-337-2403).

Big Bear Inn
42200 Moonridge Rd., Big Bear Lake, 92315
(714) 866-3471

You'll need a fairly high tolerance of kitsch to properly enjoy a stay at the Big Bear Inn. Fortunately, the lapses into tastelessness are more than compensated for by the hotel's excellent comfort and good amenities. Built by a developer of Greek luxury hotels, the Big Bear Inn has a grandiose, rather silly lobby decked out in marble and crystal and an overall decor that's too fussy for relaxed Big Bear. But the place is certainly impressive: a formal Italian garden, an ornate, heavily draped dining room (serving costly Continental fare), an art nouveau bar, five acres of forest and a health club and pool are among the amenities here. Each of the 80 rooms is decorated differently, and they're all warmed with fireplaces, down comforters, antiques and color TVs. A complimentary shuttle service will take you to the ski slopes, golf course and lake.

Singles & doubles: $55-$105 midweek, $75-$130 weekend; suite: $150-$375 midweek, $200-$450 weekend.

Gold Mountain Manor

1117 Anita, Big Bear City, 92314
(714) 585-6997

Originally built in the twenties as part of the ritzy (but long-gone) Peter Pan Club, Gold Mountain Manor was restored a few years back and is now a fine bed-and-breakfast inn. The decor and antique furnishings are handsome, the rooms are charming and comfortable and the hosts are helpful. Romantics should request the Gable Room, with a beautiful walnut bed and the Franklin stove that helped keep Clark Gable and Carole Lombard warm during their Big Bear honeymoon. The room rate includes breakfast, afternoon wine and hors d'oeuvres and the use of the Big Bear Athletic Club.

Doubles: $75-$135 midweek, $75-$150 weekend.

Knickerbocker Mansion

P.O. Box 3661, Big Bear Lake, 92315
(714) 866-8221

A historic (built in 1917) bed-and-breakfast with lots of rustic mountain charm, this 4,000-square-foot log cabin features stone fireplaces and brass kerosene lanterns; the five spacious, rather basic rooms in the main house share two bathrooms. If you want more privacy, request either the room or the suite in the separate Carriage House, each of which has a private bathroom, lots of quiet and plenty of romance (the suite features an *Out of Africa* decor). Breakfasts feature lovely homemade pastries, such as peach or apple cobblers. The setting is quite picturesque, with the imposing mansion presiding over two and a half acres of mountain land.

Rooms: $85-$95; suite: $150.

Krausmeier Haus Bavarian Village

1351 E. Midway Blvd., Big Bear Lake, 92315
(714) 585-2886

Located about five miles from Big Bear City and four miles from the lake itself, this little chalet complex shares the landscape with Baldwin Lake, horse breeders and the mountains. Its seclusion ensures tranquility—as do the absence of TVs and telephones—and its location makes sunset walks a must. The decor borders on the Spartan-bachelor style, but people don't come here to spend much time admiring the indoor scenery. You can reserve a large two-bedroom chalet with fireplace or a simple room in the central lodge. During the weekends, reservations are essential; it's usually booked from January through March. The complex is perfectly situated for skiing, hiking and fishing, and after a day out in the mountain air you'll appreciate the inn's outdoor Jacuzzi. Our only complaint is the paper-thin walls in some of the rooms.

Lodge rooms: $49-$69; studio chalets: $65-$86; chalets with kitchens: $75-$113.

Lake Arrowhead Hilton Resort

Hwy. 18, Lake Arrowhead Village, 92352
(800) 223-3307

This sprawling resort won't give you the feeling of quiet, peaceful charm that a mountain cabin or bed-and-breakfast will, but it has lots of amenities and is a great place for families. Enthusiastic staff members run all-day kids' programs, so the little monsters can spend their days swimming, ice skating, playing games and making new friends while you catch up on your R & R. The Hilton also boasts a private beach (a vital necessity, since Lake Arrowhead is privately owned and has no public beach), a heated pool, an affiliation with a large health club, a couple of restaurants and a location within walking distance of Lake Arrowhead Village's shops and restau-

rants. The rooms are pretty basic; we prefer the suites, which have loft bedrooms, sleeper sofas downstairs, kitchens and, in some cases, fireplaces.
Doubles: $159-$199; suites: $225-$245. Midweek packages available.

SPORTS

Big Bear's busiest season is winter, when the nearby ski mountains attract thousands of snow-starved Southern Californians. The biggest and best ski area is Snow Summit (714-

866-4621), which is so popular that on weekends its lift tickets often sell out in advance (through Ticketron). We try to avoid the weekend crowds, instead sneaking away for an occasional weekday on Snow Summit's slopes. Cross-country skiers can rent gear at Steve's U-Rent, 42039 Big Bear Boulevard, (714) 866-8888; the Forest Service (714-866-3487) will provide you with trail maps.
Hikers and bikers can get trail information from the Forest Service; rental bikes (and all sorts of sports equipment) are available at Barry's Sports Rentals, 42131 Big Bear Boulevard, (714) 866-6441.

CATALINA

ACROSS THE SEA

Besides the sentimental song that immortalized the 26-mile distance from the mainland to Catalina, this sleepy island doesn't have much claim to its fame. Its pace is slow, and it's low on luxury—the town is dusty, the nine-hole public golf course is a little shabby, and the accommodations can be quite rustic. But that's part of Catalina's charm. Prosperous people from Brentwood and Pasadena come here for a change from their well-manicured lawns and lives; they love the island's lack of pretension and sophistication. This is a great place to escape the smog and traffic and ease into a leisurely state of mind, where the biggest decisions you'll be faced with are whether to have pancakes or waffles for breakfast and whether to get up and go snorkeling or just stay sleeping on the beach.
If you can stay in Catalina for more than a day, try to get out of Avalon: hike into the back country, take a boat ride around the island, stopping for a picnic at one of the lovely inlets, or go exploring with Catalina Safari Tours (510-2800), whose trained naturalists lead snorkeling adventures and van and hiking trips in search of buffalo, bald eagles, deer and island fox. Outside of town the island is virtually undeveloped (cars are not allowed on about 80 percent of it); wild

buffalo and mountain goats are the primary citizens.
If you don't have your own boat or plane, or a friend who does, you'll have to use a means of public transportation to get to the island. Catalina Cruises makes the two-hour trip several times daily ($24.30 round trip); call (800) 888-5939 for information; Catalina Express (519-1212) offers a bit faster, somewhat classier ferry ride for $27.70 round-trip. Or you can fly over, either by plane (Catalina Flying Boats, 595-5080; Island Express, 491-5550) or by helicopter (Helitrans, 548-1314). Be prepared for crowds and higher room rates in season, which runs from June 1 to mid-September.
For more information on things to see and do in Catalina, call the Tourist Information Center at 510-2000.

RESTAURANTS

Armstrong's Fish Market & Seafood Restaurant
306 Crescent Ave., Avalon
510-0113
Seafood
Open Mon.-Thurs. 11:30 a.m.-9 p.m., Fri. 11:30 a.m.-10 p.m., Sat. 11 a.m.-10 p.m., Sun. 11 a.m.-9 p.m. Cards: MC, V.
We can't in fairness give Armstrong's a rating, because when we stopped in during our last Catalina trip it was closed for remod-

eling after suffering storm damage. But we can tell you that the setting is marvelous (right on the water), the decor simple and welcoming, the fresh-fish dinners a bargain (swordfish, mahi mahi and local red snapper in the $10 to $13 range), and the style of cooking refreshingly unfussy, relying heavily on the mesquite grill. We can also tell you that the local abalone steak is a highly regarded treat that locals say is well worth the $21.95 investment. And from the displays at the fish-market side of the business, it's clear that freshness is a priority here. Two will spend about $55 for dinner with wine.

11/20   Cafe Prego
603 Crescent Ave., Avalon
510-1218
ITALIAN
Open in season: Sun.-Thurs. 5 p.m.-9 p.m., Fri.-Sat. 5 p.m.-10 p.m.; off-season: Sun.-Mon. & Thurs. 5 p.m.-9 p.m., Fri.-Sat. 5 p.m.-10 p.m. Cards: AE, MC, V.

An intimate, engaging little place on the waterfront with lots of warmth, homey service and decent food. Pastas can be good, especially the rigatoni with ham and broccoli in a fine cream sauce, the thick, cheesy lasagne and the linguine with a hearty (and heavy) clam sauce. Salads are banal, but the minestrone soup is respectable. Also tasty are the scampi, the swordfish in a wine sauce and the cheesecake. None of it is especially memorable, but it's pleasant enough food in a very comfortable setting—and it's one of your best bets on Catalina. About $45 for two, with a simple wine.

9/20   Channel House
205 Crescent Ave., Avalon
510-1617
AMERICAN/SEAFOOD
Open daily 11 a.m.-2 p.m. & 5:30 p.m.-10:30 p.m. Cards: MC, V.

Most tourists run right from the ferry to the Channel House for an al fresco lunch on the attractive terrace, with a perfect view of the harbor and their ferry heading back to the mainland. After an extensive renovation, the indoors is spry and cheery, with a welcoming ambience. Lunch is limited to salads and sandwiches; the burgers are the most popular with the well-fed clientele, which also loves the oversized, exotic drinks. Dinner is fairly classic and pretty boring, featuring local and imported (and sometimes frozen-tasting) seafood with silly names: Au Go to Halibut, Shrimp Boats Are a-Comin' and so on. There are also a few steaks, chops and chicken. All of it is uninspired and unsatisfying, though filling. It's a shame that the lovely setting and decor are not matched with decent food. About $8 per person for lunch and $20 for dinner, without drinks.

11/20   Ristorante Villa Portofino
111 Crescent Ave., Avalon
510-0555
ITALIAN
Open Sun.-Thurs. 5:30 p.m.-9 p.m., Fri.-Sat. 5:30 p.m.-10 p.m. Cards: AE, MC, V.

One of Catalina's classier dinner joints, Villa Portofino combines a romantic pink-and-white decor with a highly appealing northern Italian menu, and the result is a continual crowd—make sure to make reservations early for a weekend dinner. All the classics are here—carpaccio, insalata mista, spaghetti alla checca, tortellini in a Parmesan-cream sauce, calamari steak, veal scaloppine—and they're admirably prepared, at least by Catalina standards. Portions are as hearty as the flavors are full; though your meal won't be subtle, it ought to be quite enjoyable. From $55 to $70 for dinner for two, with wine.

QUICK BITES

Antonio's Pizzeria
114 Sumner Ave., Avalon
510-0060
Open Sun.-Thurs. 11:30 a.m.-midnight, Fri.-Sat. 11:30 a.m.-1 a.m. Cards: MC, V.

There's a lot of college spirit in this vintage '50s dinerette. Countertop jukebox selectors dish out classic rock, while a silent bison and moose watch over the young clientele drinking Corona and Moosehead beer. The decor is late fraternity house, with beer signs, posters, red-and-white-checked tablecloths, sawdust-strewn floors, clutter and some interesting local color. Cheerful people dole out acceptable (but not better) pizzas, meatball heroes, pastas and generous, messy Italian sandwiches. There's a take-out counter on the street for quick getaways. This is one of the most appealing places on the island. But steer clear of the new waterfront branch, a dismal tourist trap if there ever was one. About $15 for pizza and a beer for two.

Catalina Cookie Co.
101 Marilla, Avalon
510-2447
Open Sun.-Thurs. 10 a.m.-10 p.m., Fri.-Sat. 10 a.m.-11 p.m. No cards.

This tiny shop in the El Encanto arcade bakes wonderful cookies daily that weigh in at about 55 cents apiece. You won't be disappointed by the oatmeal raisin, chocolate chip, peanut butter, oatmeal chocolate chip or fabulous piña colada macaroons.

Lani's Pancake Cottage
118 Catalina St., Avalon
510-0726
Open daily 7 a.m.-1:30 p.m. (closed in winter). No cards.

Everyone comes to this simple, crowded, rather dingy coffee shop for one of the 22 omelets (green chile, olives, and chili con carne, to name a few). The chef will prepare your own personal "mess," a combination of whatever pleases you. There are also nine pancake choices (macadamia nut, chocolate chip, fruit, and a pancake sandwich) and 27 varieties of luncheon sandwiches. It will cost two of you about $13 for a hearty breakfast, and the same for an honest, home-cooked lunch.

Runway Cafe
Catalina Airport, 1 Airport Rd., Avalon
510-2196
Open daily 7:30 a.m.-5 p.m. No cards.

If you want a true Catalina experience, come here for a buffalo burger, buffalo omelet or buffalo chili. In fact, a good number of L.A. businesspeople with their own small planes sometimes hop over here for a quick buffalo-burger lunch. The buffalo doesn't actually taste too different from regular hamburger, but it's fun to try it. The nonbuffalo dishes are entirely forgettable. About $15 for lunch for two, with a beer.

HOTELS

Garden House Inn
3rd & Clarissa, Avalon, 90704
510-0356

We like everything about the Garden House Inn: its small size (just seven rooms), its quiet location (in town but away from clogged Crescent Avenue), its decor (a 1920s house furnished with handsome antiques and lovely shades of rose) and the comfort of its rooms (with queen-size beds and private baths; some have bay views, private terraces and sitting areas). The price includes a cold breakfast buffet and afternoon wine and cheese. An admirable bed-and-breakfast inn.

Doubles: $125-$225. Rates depend on the season.

Glenmore Plaza Hotel
120 Sumner Ave., Avalon, 90704
510-0017

Built in 1891, the Glenmore Plaza is a charming pink-and-green Victorian hotel. The bright, clean and spacious rooms have white wicker furniture, ceiling fans, pickled-pine armoires and comfortable queen- and king-size beds; many have whirlpool baths. Try the Clark Gable cupola, with its fabulous views and oversized round bed in the circular bedroom, or the Amelia Earhart suite, with its own Jacuzzi. There's no pool, but the beach is practically across the street.

Rooms: $105-$325. Rates depend on the season.

Hotel St. Lauren
Metropole & Beacon, Avalon, 90704
510-2299

A relative newcomer to Catalina, the Hotel St. Lauren looks as if it's been around for a century or so—until you notice such small details as the aluminum windows. The Victorian-seaside-resort theme may not have been flawlessly executed, but with rooms starting at just $45, who can complain? Dollar for dollar, the upper-floor "minisuites" constitute one of the best bargains in town: $145 gets you a spacious room for four, with a king-size bed, a sleeper sofa, a terrace and a great ocean view. Room rates include a modest Continental breakfast.

Rooms: $45-$145.

 Inn on Mt. Ada
207 Wrigley Rd., Avalon, 90704
510-2030

Although the innkeepers call their landmark the Inn on Mt. Ada, everyone else calls it the Wrigley Mansion, which is how it's been known since it was built by the chewing-gum magnate in 1921. Usually bed-and-breakfasts are on the more modestly priced end of the hotel scale, but this posh six-room inn is certainly Catalina's most expensive inn. It's terribly luxe, with period antiques and good-sized rooms, all of which have views of either Avalon and the bay or the Pacific and San Pedro. Extras include a full breakfast, served in the dining room each morning, wine and hors d'oeuvres in the early evening, and unlimited cab rides to and from town and the beach (both of which are a half mile away). And now the dining room is serving a full-blown romantics' dinner, which we haven't been able to try yet but which we hear good reports about. The Grand Suite, once Mr. Wrigley's personal quarters, features a fireplace in the bedroom, a large living room and a private balcony. There's a two-night minimum on weekends—which are usually booked a full year in advance.

Doubles & suites: $220-$440 (no seasonal variation).

ORANGE COUNTY

FUN, FUN, FUN

In just a couple of short decades, Orange County has been transformed from a region marked by sprawling farms and sleepy suburbs to one of the fastest-growing and wealthiest regions of the country. Housing developments are as plentiful here as Day-Glo skateboards. High-tech and service businesses attract sun-struck workers—and business travelers—from across the country. The wealthy have taken over the beachfront homes that, before the boom, belonged to retired schoolteachers and people of moderate means who had found their escape from the city. Tourists continue to come and go in record numbers. For good reason: when the Beach Boys sang about "Fun, Fun, Fun" and "California Girls," they were singing about Orange County's beaches: Sunset Beach, Huntington, Newport, Laguna and Doheny, where surfers "shred" waves, volleyball players spike balls in the sun, and vacationers soak up the easygoing Southern California beach lifestyle.

We couldn't begin to cover all that Orange County has to offer, so we've focused on the two destinations that attract the most visitors, Laguna and Newport/Irvine, with occasional forays north and south. Though there are a number of lovely beaches, we must confess to a preference: for our money, Laguna is Orange County's vacation paradise, with more charm per square inch than any place south of Carmel (except in the thick of July and August, when the crowds and traffic are thick). Take a room for the weekend or a week in one of the sweet bed-and-breakfasts or ocean-view hotels—you'll return home from the incredibly lovely setting and small-town atmosphere feeling renewed, relaxed and refreshed.

8/20   Gustaf Anders
South Coast Plaza Village, 3810 S. Plaza Dr., Santa Ana
(714) 668-1737
CONTINENTAL/SCANDINAVIAN
Open Mon.-Sat. 11:30 a.m.-midnight. All major cards.

The fellow at the piano seemed to think himself the very reincarnation of Jerry Lee Lewis. For a while, he managed to stay put on his piano bench as he punched out mildly embarrassing versions of "Whole Lotta Shakin' Goin' On" and "Breathless." But when he got around to "Great Balls of Fire," the poor fellow just lost all control. He began seated on the piano bench, then quickly rose to standing on the bench, bent over the keyboard, his bum sticking way out into the ether. Finally, he leaped from the piano bench and started running around the bar and the restaurant, a man possessed by an antic demon spirit, singing out a wretched a cappella version of the song. He actually stopped in front of diners, their sautéed rabbit liver in a peppery Cognac sauce poised on the end of their forks, about to enter their gaping maws, to utter rough-hewn "Great Balls" lyrics before dashing off to ruin someone else's dinner. We had heard for years of Gustaf Anders, generally regarded to be the finest restaurant to ever grace the fertile shores of San Diego. People spoke of its Scandinavian/Continental cuisine in reverential terms; it was proof that there really was civilization south of San Juan Capistrano. Then Gustaf Anders headed for a curious mall in Santa Ana that's home to more than its fair share of upscale restaurants. The place is strangely empty even on weeekends— apparently San Diego's best isn't impressing Orange County.

While the Jerry Lee clone sang, we ate dry-as-parchment roast rack of lamb with chanterelles, and gummily breaded sweetbreads in a Madeira peppercorn sauce. We tried a curious plate of herring (pickled inhouse), served with a shot of akvavit. We liked the akvavit, and we liked the herring. But for $10, we hardly got enough to provide a real taste. In Scandinavia, herring is eaten by the kilo; here it was served by the milligram. We didn't think much of the soggy chunks of Parmesan served with olives and pickled peppers that tasted only lightly marinated. (We asked our waitress where the Parmesan was from. She replied, "Italy.") We were also a bit mixed concerning the smoked eel and scrambled eggs on toast—an interesting idea that would have worked better if you didn't have to work so hard to avoid the bones in the eel. We left decidedly underwhelmed. But we were impressed by the fellow at the piano. In terms of upscale restaurants, he was definitely something new. We wonder if he does Elvis impersonations on Saturdays. Dinner for two, with wine, costs about $80.

⟨16⟩ **Antoine**
4500 MacArthur Blvd., Newport Beach
(714) 476-2001
FRENCH
Open Tues.-Sat. 6 p.m.-10 p.m. All major cards.

With each visit to Antoine, we are more impressed. It's not the decor that strikes us; the three long dining rooms are elegant in a drawing-room sort of way, mirrored and mauved, but entirely predictable. Nor is it the service, which is entirely adequate (though we find the staff down the road at the Ritz-Carlton to be a shade more poised). No, what impresses us is the menu and its execution. The style and subtlety at Antoine is not matched anywhere else in Orange County. It is a restaurant that knows its mind. Completely. Much of this is due to Gérard Vié of Les Trois Marches in Versailles, who was an early, if not the first, proponent of nouvelle cuisine. Vié develops the menus, blending the traditional and the modern so intelligently that the edge between is blurred. The kitchen is directed by chef de cuisine Dominique Chavanon, whose daily specials may be a bit bolder than the regular menu but are just as well balanced.

Classic French cuisine civilizes food, conquers it, often to the point of unrecognizability. But Vié's food reveals itself. An appetizer of tuna tartare may be finely chopped, but sweet bell peppers give it texture; the fresh peas in a cream soup can be tasted through a fine whiff of curry. Dishes can be marvelously rich and clean at the same time. A thick turbot filet, stuffed with an airy filling of mushrooms and chives and then wrapped in a veined cabbage leaf, has an entirely appropriate robust meatiness; huge, barely browned sea scallops take on the clean earthiness of the bed of lentils beneath. The dish of squab set over Cassis-tinted spinach, the legs wrapped like miniature mummies with threads of potato, teeters on the baroque—teeters, but never topples. Antoine is not a restaurant of contrasts and collisions, but rather one of nuances. This is what sets it above the rest of Orange County's restaurants. The dessert list is tempting, but somehow we have often been disappointed. More effort seems to be put into such froths as a gratin of raspberries or a sorbet surrounded by passion-fruit coulis than is warranted—the results are wishy-washy. You won't be disappointed by the wine list, however, particularly when it comes to French vintages. A good bottle will push the bill into the stratosphere; with a modest choice, dinner for two should run about $120.

12/20   Bangkok 3

101 Palm St., Balboa
(714) 673-6521
THAI
Open Sun. & Tues.-Thurs. 6 p.m.-10 p.m., Fri.-Sat. 6 p.m.-11 p.m. All major cards.

In this all-white, stylishly designed little place you will find all sorts of chic young people from Newport and Laguna who come here to eat good food in a setting that complements their fashion sense and air of sophistication. But the real reason to visit this lovely place is the owner, a genuine delight. He and his family have three Bangkok restaurants, all of which are handsome and offer authentic and delicious Thai standards: savory spring rolls with a spicy dipping sauce, marvelous mee krob, hot sausage salad, a dish of whole pompano (a silvery fish, battered and fried)— the owner will come over and cut it for you— and a beef satay with a not-too-sweet peanut sauce. Desserts are simple, and sometimes incorporate experiments with avocado or coconut ice cream. It's a gracious, friendly place imparting good will and good food. A Bangkok 3 dinner for two, with wine, costs about $60.

12/20   Bistango

The Atrium, 19100 Von Karman Ave., Irvine
(714) 752-0968
ITALIAN
Open Mon.-Thurs. 11:30 a.m.-3 p.m. & 5:30 p.m.-10:30 p.m., Fri. 11:30 a.m.-3 p.m. & 5:30 p.m.-11 p.m., Sat. 5:30 p.m.-11 p.m. All major cards.

Bistango is a lovely place for lunch, as businesspeople in the surrounding Koll Center know. Daylight filters through the stepped-glass atrium that forms the building's center, while the fountain makes relaxing tinkling noises and the food—lightened-up Italian, from pizzas to pastas to grilled fish—delights without dazzling. At night, the restaurant can seem somewhat cold and lonely, even when filled with people and the music from a tinkling piano, a fate that stems from the fact that this is a restaurant smack in the middle of an office tower, albeit a particularly attractive one.

Nonetheless, even at dinner we've had some good meals at Bistango. The pastas are inventive and highly colored, from the popular chicken-and-leek ravioli in a neon-orange sauce of sun-dried tomatoes to the tricolor gnocchi with Gorgonzola. Appetizers are among the best in the county's Italian (or, more accurately, Italianate) restaurants; look for the superb crabcakes with pink grapefruit. Entrées include a rather plain osso buco—a new offering that adds a rustic note to the menu—and, as one would expect in an Orange County office tower, many a fish, the best of which is the grilled mahi mahi with spicy black-bean sauce. A number of dishes appear on the menu marked with hearts—including a pungent pizza, the best of the bunch, with grilled eggplant, olive-oil-brushed peppers and goat cheese—indicating dishes light on saturated fats and cholesterol. Dinner for two, with wine, costs about $70.

9/20   Las Brisas

361 Cliff Dr., Laguna Beach
(714) 497-5434
CALIFORNIAN/MEXICAN/SEAFOOD
Open Mon.-Thurs. 8 a.m.-10:30 a.m., 11 a.m.-3:30 p.m. & 5 p.m.-10 p.m., Fri. 8 a.m.-10:30 a.m., 11 a.m.-3:30 p.m. & 5 p.m.-11 p.m., Sat. 8 a.m.-10:30 a.m., 11 a.m.-3:30 p.m. & 4:30 p.m.-11 p.m., Sun. 9 a.m.-3 p.m. & 4 p.m.-10 p.m. (extended summer hours vary). All major cards.

What this comfortable cliffside restaurant lacks in tastes for the tongue it makes up for in feasts for the eyes. Spectacular ocean views from most tables (but do try for a window), California girls and boys rubbing tanned shoulders at the patio bar and superb art just one door away combine for an exhilarating lunchtime experience. We enjoy a late-morning visit to one of the exhibitions of American art at the Laguna Art Museum next door, followed by a long lunch spent gazing across the rose garden to the "American Riviera" vista beyond.

Las Brisas serves an array of salads, but they're generally the kind of overblown iceberg-lettuce affairs that come in deep-fried taco-shell bowls. We've been much happier with the fish, such as the sea bass filet in a tangy sauce that's as much French as it is Mexican, served with a terrific chile-spiked square of scalloped potatoes. The calamar de mojo de ajo, a perfectly tender squid steak, lightly dipped in egg batter and sautéed, is finished with a sauce of tomatoes, peppers, capers and onions. Specials seem to lean toward the overly rich, such as one frequent offering of butter-laden blackened pieces of mixed fish served on a cream-sauced fettuccine. A nice extra and a beloved standby is the basket of homemade cornbread and sweet little white rolls. The on-again, off-again daily breakfast buffet is a hearty, savory start to a big day, but it hasn't yet caught on with customers—call to find out whether breakfast is on that month or off. Dinner for two, including wine, runs about $50.

11/20 Carmelo's

3520 E. Pacific Coast Hwy., Corona del Mar
(714) 675-1922
ITALIAN
Open Sun.-Thurs. 5:30 p.m.-10:30 p.m., Fri.-Sat. 5:30 p.m.-11:30 p.m. All major cards.

For a long time, we passed Carmelo's by. With its neon sign and brick-enclosed patio, it looked like a place where the waiters would wear black suits and set fire to things beside your table, where you'd get serenaded whether you liked it or not, and where the breathlessly described house specialty would turn out to be fettuccine Alfredo. As a matter of fact, the waiters do wear black suits at Carmelo's, some things do get flamed, and there's even a strolling guitarist. But the menu, a surprisingly varied one, tells a more interesting story. Alongside such Frenchified northern dishes as veal Pavarotti in cream sauce, there is a great tomato sauce. More than one tomato sauce, in fact. The sauce on the mussels appetizer is light and garlicky with a note of anise, while veal comes in a fresh-tasting but more familiar thick tomato sauce. We were also pleased to find that Italian dishes are not as overloaded as they so often are in Orange County. Saltimbocca is the original recipe: white veal scaloppine wrapped around prosciutto and fresh sage. The veal Parmigiana is a restrained and elegant one: thin-sliced veal alternating with thin-sliced eggplant. Alongside filet Rossini topped with goose-liver pâté is elegantly simple vermicelli tossed in olive oil and basil with lots of garlic and some chopped raw tomatoes. Many dishes are hearty and peasanty, such as rabbit stewed in red wine with onions and served with polenta. In the Italian tradition, there's little for dessert be-

sides zabaglione. Dinner for two, with wine, runs about $60.

9/20 John Dominis

2901 W. Coast Hwy., Newport Beach
(714) 650-5112
SEAFOOD
Open Mon.-Thurs. 6 p.m.-10 p.m., Fri.-Sat. 6 p.m.-10:30 p.m., Sun. 10 a.m.-2:30 p.m. & 5:30 p.m.-10 p.m. Cards: AE, MC, V.

Put on your Hawaiian shirt, prepare for a wait and plan to spend a good piece of change when you come to John Dominis. Dominis is one of Hawaii's most acclaimed eateries, legendary for its fresh seafood, and it fits right in on Newport's waterfront next door to the Chart House, which Dominis resembles more than it would like to. When you check in at the front desk for your reservation, you're given a sort of claim check and dispatched to the upstairs, where it is hoped you will buy a few drinks before your table is "ready." While you drink and admire the view (admittedly in great comfort), you can amuse yourself by watching the dolled-up singles on patrol. You'll then be escorted downstairs to the dramatic dining room, a huge, grottolike place with beautiful rock ponds, gurgling waterfalls and enough teak to outfit Noah's Ark. With luck, you'll get a window table, where you're sure to pass a quite pleasant evening, served reasonably good seafood by a "Hi, my name is Chad" waiter.

We cannot fault the quality of the fish, as fresh as it is expensive, but we can fault the kitchen for tending to overcook it. Such delicate fish as the opakapaka we sampled one night loses all flavor when left on the stove just a minute too long. Still, the menu's breadth is remarkable (especially the selection of Hawaiian fish), and among some very good choices, our favorite is the fabulous cold appetizer assortment for two, which includes lovely sashimi, smoked salmon and fresh oysters, among other seafaring delicacies. The salads and chowders are also delicious, as are the desserts (albeit in an overdone, all-American way). If you're watching your budget, watch what you order; such dishes as cioppino ($26) and fresh tiger prawns ($30 and up) can send your bill rocketing, but a carefully ordered dinner for two, with wine, will run about $90.

12/20   Five Crowns
3801 E. Coast Hwy., Corona del Mar
(714) 760-0331
AMERICAN
*Open Mon.-Sat. 5 p.m.-11 p.m., Sun. 10:30
a.m-3 p.m. & 4 p.m.-11 p.m.. All major cards.*

This copy of a twelfth-century English inn looks as out of place along Coast Highway as the Matterhorn would along Interstate 5. But that's not to say it lacks charm. Inside it's quite cozy and comforting, with stone walls, fireplaces, high-backed chairs, Villeroy and Boch china and cheery young waitresses dressed up like tavern maids. A Lawry's restaurant, Five Crowns serves up chops, roasts, prime rib and seafood, all with the consistency of preparation and quality of ingredients the chain is known for. But Five Crowns takes it a step further, producing food that is often better than good. Care is evident in all the details: the marvelous wine list and knowledgeable sommelier, the intelligent presentation and the well-thought-out starters and accompaniments. Soups are always good, and the house salad (Bibb lettuce, walnuts, bacon, Gruyère and garlicky croutons) is delicious, with a light herb dressing; other salads include an endive-duck in a mustard dressing and a hearts of romaine in an excellent Stilton dressing. But the real reason to come here is the meat, which is always well prepared and of fine quality. The prime rib is as good as at L.A.'s Lawry's, the chops and steaks are marvelous, and the roast spring lamb provençale with garlic and herbs (in season) is absolute perfection. On the other hand, the ambitious seafood dishes are often overcooked and clumsy. But if you order carefully, you can have a terrific meal here. About $80 for two, with wine.

Five Feet
328 Glenneyre, Laguna Beach
(714) 497-4955
CHINESE
*Open Sun.-Thurs. 5 p.m.-10 p.m., Fri. 11:30
a.m.-2 p.m. & 5 p.m.-11 p.m., Sat. 5 p.m.-11
p.m. Cards: AE, MC, V.*

Yes, the name of this restaurant is Five Feet (the sign out front actually reads: 5'0"). The waiters give mutually contradictory explanations for the name, but a good enough reason is that we are in artsy Laguna Beach, in a restaurant with a spare and whimsical decor (exposed bricks and beams set off by a droll

mural). As for what's served here, another sign is more forthcoming: CHINESE CUISINE EUROPEAN STYLE. And that is precisely what you get: Chinese dishes (sometimes using somewhat European ingredients), listed on a menu that changes every six or eight weeks (like that of an ambitious French restaurant), served with forks instead of chopsticks. One dish that's a constant on the menu is a whole braised catfish, and with good reason—it's usually the best thing available, an irresistibly sweet and delicate catfish. One version has a mildly peppery sauce; another has a garlic sauce that's just as good. There are always a few dim sum selections as well, such as steamed shu mai filled with shrimp, pork, black mushrooms and cabbage, or potstickers filled with pork, cabbage and Chinese chives. Some of the dishes are familiar Chinese standards, like duck with homemade plum sauce, but there are also such Sino-European experiments as scallops in a grapefruit-mustard sauce or a boneless quail stuffed with rice in a peach–and–Grand Marnier sauce. We could as easily be in an avant garde California cuisine place, but for a certain knowing Chinese quality in the sauce, an ironic dash of soy . . . or something. Dinner for two, with wine, runs about $75.

Five Feet Too
Fashion Island, 1145 Newport
Center Dr., Newport Beach
(714) 640-5250
CHINESE
*Open Sun.-Thurs. 11:30 a.m.-2:30 p.m. & 5:30
p.m.-10:30 p.m., Fri.-Sat. 11:30 a.m.-2:30 p.m.
& 5:30 p.m.-11:30 p.m. Cards: AE, MC, V.*

A bigger, sleeker, cooler clone of chef/owner Michael Kang's Five Feet, Five Feet Too is an ambitious restaurant: it's trying to be hip and urban in an upscale shopping center. It makes the leap on design alone; the smooth metals and concrete, the mauves and blues and grays, and the sly but perfectly corporate art are all right in line with what you'll see at a trillion L.A. restaurants. And the menu, best described as contemporary Chinese, is a sassier, brassier version of Chinois on Main's. This is a completely unique restaurant for the area, and the novelty keeps them coming in.

The open kitchen, where a half dozen or so stir-frying chefs whirl like cyclones, sends out plates that look like miniature views of Hong Kong: teeming, dense, multicolored, futuristic. Special entrées—usually stir-fried meats or fish with an elaborate number of extras—can include monkfish with a rice-wine-and-lychee sauce set on sautéed endive, with a sashimied plum here, a curlicue of carved cucumber there. Or a delicious combination of mahi mahi and opakapaka in spicy black-bean sauce, accompanied by yellowed fried rice. Or, as an appetizer, tempura-fried soft-shell crab with two sauces, set off with snips of purple basil. Nothing is spared; this is cooking by accretion. The regular menu sticks to more recognizably Chinese dishes, such as kung pao shrimp, chicken and scallops and vegetarian mu shu. All are good choices. But where all these dishes have a flying-by-the-seat-of-the-pants sense of adventure to them, the desserts are pedestrian. A lime cheesecake is topped with a gelatinous layer of berries, and a cookie-crusted chocolate mousse cake is spineless, hardly able to hold its own shape. We generally opt instead for the ice creams or sorbets, particularly the pineapple. Dinner for two, with wine from a surprisingly, idiosyncratically good wine list, ends up at about $90.

11/20 Gemmell's

3000 Bristol St., Costa Mesa
(714) 751-1074
FRENCH
Open Mon.-Fri. 11:30 a.m.-2:30 p.m. & 6 p.m.-10:30 p.m., Sat. 6 p.m.-10:30 p.m. All major cards.

The sign outside reads, CUISINE UNIQUE, which tells us nothing, but the building has the look of a house that has been around for a while. Though its staff is fairly young, Gemmell's for some reason has chosen the style of a settled, even ancient, institution. It feels like the dining room in an old family property that is being kept up out of family pride, still elegant in its gracious and understated way, yet somehow creaky. The waiter announces that "Byron"—Byron Gemmell, the chef—has prepared such and such a dish today with the air of referring to a cantankerous old virtuoso whose whims we are privileged to hear. The restaurant has recently changed owners, but Gemmell remains (though the menu has been stripped of its pricier offerings).

The words *cuisine unique* ominously suggest beef tartare in kiwi cups, but the kitchen is as old-fashioned as the look of the building. The sauces are not thickened with flour, one nod to current fashion, but there's a lot that is positively, unquestionably antique: serving meat on a bed of spinach, making lots of little vegetable mousses, sprinkling the fancy salad with truffle shavings, for example. Fortunately, a sense of tradition is a chef's best friend, and the cooking here is disciplined and skillful. When Gemmell combines meat with fruit, he does so in the most restrained and tasteful manner. The raspberry in the chicken with raspberry shows up only as a pleasant tartness and subtle aroma in the meaty sauce. Pork noisettes come with baked pear slices in a meat glaze flavored with pear eau-de-vie in a similarly chaste style. One of our favorite appetizers is the wonderfully buttery foie gras slices wrapped in a lightly browned cabbage leaf. But the finest is certainly the salmon, smoked on the premises; it has a very pleasing texture and an impressive smokiness. We could easily make a meal of it. As for making meals, figure on $80 for two (with wine) at dinner.

12/20 JW's

Anaheim Marriott Hotel, 700 W.
Convention Way, Anaheim
(714) 750-8000
FRENCH/CONTINENTAL
Open Mon.-Thurs. 6 p.m.-9:30 p.m., Fri.-Sat.. 6 p.m.-10:30 p.m. All major cards.

At first glance, nothing could be less like Disneyland's Swiss Family Robinson home than JW's, a block away at the Anaheim Marriott. Still, for all the sobriety of sixteen-foot ceilings, old paintings lining the walls and touches of nineteenth-century-manor architecture, this is a fantasy structure, as is the Disneyland treehouse. There must be fifteen tiny rooms or quasi-rooms, all connected on slightly different floor elevations, suggesting a warren of playhouse hidey-holes, and all decorated in a respectable, homey manner appropriate to the Swiss Family Robinson. Together with a hushed sound level and fairly unobtrusive service, the design works—we feel like we're home, while at the same time being conveniently close to the warmth of the human herd.

The emphasis here is on the classical: fresh herbs, concentrated meat juices and lots of cream and butter are the predominating flavors. JW's specializes in seafood and game, and while a new menu has been introduced, many of the best dishes from the past have survived the cut. We've found some delightful seafood dishes: for instance, the giant prawns in a garlicky cream sauce with ground red peppers, the sole stuffed with salmon mousse in beurre blanc and the lobster in a rather tangy Champagne-cream sauce with wild mushrooms. The game, however, can be a bit on the mild side. The venison is said to be domestic, rather than the bland lettuce-fed New Zealand venison, but we still found it too tame. The breast of pheasant is also far from gamey, though the sauce of cream, Armagnac and mustard was exquisite. It is this occasional excessive caution about strong flavors that is JW's only real flaw. Among the notable desserts are a number of unusual sorbets (passion fruit, wild grape) and an exceptionally chocolatey mousse. Following dinner there is a most civilized selection of drinks: vintage port, old Calvados and, above all, a smashing dry oloroso sherry (Gran Corregidor). JW's is a special-occasion place (yes, gentlemen are requested to wear jackets). Dinner for two, with wine, runs about $100.

11/20 Kachina

222 Forest Ave., Laguna Beach
(714) 497-5546
SOUTHWESTERN
Open Sun.-Thurs. 5:30 p.m.-10 p.m., Fri.-Sat. 5:30 p.m.-11 p.m. Cards: AE, MC, V.

Tucked in a half basement a few steps below Laguna Beach's cute Forest Avenue, the one-room Kachina glows with desert colors. Bright-painted reliefs hang like contemporary Navajo jewelry on the walls; the tables are set with mixed colors of Fiestaware. Despite the fact that things Southwestern have slipped in fashion, Kachina manages a level of sophistication that is hard to find in the south county. The food is stylish, too. One of the best appetizers, the saddlebag, is an ingenious corn crêpe folded over roast duck with a barbecue sauce roughened with chile powder. And the quesadillas are always a sage bet. Ingredients change frequently—from Jack cheese and big Gulf shrimp to goat cheese and roasted red peppers—on the appetizer pizza. The differ-

ent combinations of mole and chile sauces, blue and yellow corn flours and fire-roasted vegetables, wrapped around, poured over or simmered with duck and salmon and sirloin, most often work. One of the kitchen's best, corn-flour fettuccine with a spicy sauce of roasted tomatoes, tastes something like polenta, only subtler. (Specials often feature fish, such as charbroiled salmon or corn-floured soft-shell crab.) But on occasion the chefs, David Wilhelm and Thomas Tran, lose it, galloping off into the sunset with such over-wrought dishes as bacon-wrapped beef filet with goat cheese, pasilla chile and roasted peppers in smoked pinto-bean sauce. While such food can seem strained, one has to applaud their cheek; the half-open kitchen is about as big as one of the restaurant's bleached wood tables. Kachina can get noisy, to put it mildly. Dinner for two, with wine, runs about $80.

Kitayama (14)

101 Bay View Pl., Newport Beach
(714) 725-0777
JAPANESE
Open Mon.-Fri. 11:15 a.m.-2 p.m. & 6 p.m.-11 p.m., Sat.-Sun. 5 p.m.-11 p.m. Cards: AE, MC, V.

If we were to take a visitor to see some of Orange County's most handsome landscapes, we'd head to this calm and contemporary Japanese restaurant, and just let the meal unfold. Many of the area's chefs can take pride in their presentation, but Kitayama's Yoshio Shirari creates miniature worlds. The restaurant itself blends the traditional with the contemporary: tatami mats upholster the booths, wicker chairs surround tables. Some waitresses wear kimonos, others, black pants and white shirts. During the day, full-length windows offer views of a meticulous garden lighted by sunlight seeping through skylights; at night, the lighting is not so elegant, but the calm of the place remains unchanged. There is a sleek sushi bar, complete with performing chef, but somehow we prefer being surprised by the miniature culinary landscapes at the tables.

If you can afford it, a meal composed entirely of sashimi and sushi is a disciplined form of gluttony. An order of hamachi (yellowtail tuna) arrives in a luminous blue bowl mounded with crushed ice. Fat triangular slices of filet are set like dominoes to one side, while a half grapefruit holds transparent slices of the fish cut to mimic the fruit's sections. Maguro, a deep-pink tuna, is poised in a gazebolike basket. But we have come to expect this display from raw fish; it's the cooked entrées at Kitayama that surprise. They too come in a succession of handmade platters and bowls and baskets, each cone of red ginger or carved and crab-stuffed shiitake mushroom suited to its container. At lunch, a wonderful dish called udon (thick wheat noodles served on a bed of ice with a sesame-seed-paste dipping sauce) is served, as are deep-fried croquettes of butterflied shrimp ringed with tiny side dishes of tofu cake and steamed spinach salad. But the dinner entrées are more rarified. The seafood salad is a bright-green cabbage roll filled with cubes of squid. What is called beef stew in the English translation consists of three butter-soft strips of beef blanketed with a smooth potato sauce—the most elegant form of meat and potatoes imaginable. We've ordered dessert hoping for more perfect compositions, but the only offerings, ice creams in such soothing flavors as green tea and ginger, are succinct things. They are, perhaps, in their way, a Zen lesson in simplicity. Dinner for two, with wine, costs about $80.

11/20 Marrakesh
1100 W. Coast Hwy., Newport Beach
(714) 645-8384
MOROCCAN
Open Mon.-Thurs. 6 p.m.-10 p.m., Fri.-Sun. 5:30 p.m.-11 p.m. All major cards.

This is perhaps the best of Southern California's Moroccan-chain restaurants (including the other, less consistent Marrakesh in Studio City), surpassed only by West L.A.'s outstanding Koutoubia. Under a ceiling the color of an evening sky sits a series of tent rooms done in desert tones, with long, low couches and inlaid tables. The soft-spoken Moroccan waiters describe the set feast, a main-course choice of chicken, lamb, rabbit or fish, and explain Moroccan dining customs, such as the ritual hand washing to begin the meal and the serving of men first, which they take very seriously—when a woman among us reached first for the proffered bread, the basket was sharply yanked away by an unsmiling waiter.

Nearly every dish is delicious. The lamb-based harira soup is rich and spicy, but not too

hot. The salad of three marinated vegetables (eggplant, zucchini and marvelous carrots) is perfectly prepared and full of flavor. The b'stilla is incomparable, with a light phyllo crust and tender, moist chicken. The main courses can be overcooked (particularly the fish), but the lemon chicken is delicate and the red snapper is served in a zesty tomato sauce with olives and peppers. By now you will be uncomfortably full (portions are huge), but try to save room for the couscous; the semolina is rich, moist and perfectly cooked, topped with meltingly tender lamb, carrots, raisins and zucchini. This orgy of food is topped off with moist little baklava triangles, sweet mint tea, a basket of fruit and nuts and, all things considered, a reasonable check: $65 for two, with a decent Moroccan red wine.

10/20 McCormick & Schmick's
2000 Main St., Irvine
(714) 756-0505
SEAFOOD
Open Mon.-Fri. 11 a.m.-11 p.m., Sat.-Sun. 5 p.m.-11 p.m. All major cards.

If it weren't for the valet parking and the wraparound parking structure, McCormick & Schmick's wouldn't feel like Orange County. The dark paneling, the steamy bar, the leaded glass and the nonstop hissing from the grills in the open kitchen—this must be some drizzly point north, not Irvine. In fact, the McCormick and Schmick's chain of (several) restaurants originates in the Pacific Northwest. The northern coziness perhaps explains why this multiroomed restaurant always appears to be crowded. And perhaps explains as well why we forgive the occasional slipups in the food. A piece of thresher shark, coated with a mildly spicy peanut sauce, can be wonderfully meaty one day, rubbery the next. A filet of blackened ahi, coated with dry Cajun spices (and when was that ever a good idea?), is not rare inside. But when the fish is good, it is very, very good; the company owns its own fisheries, and ingredients are always first-rate. We've had excellent grilled razor clams dusted with bread crumbs, grilled steelhead salmon and firm crabcakes that the most skeptical Easterners have enjoyed. And then there are the impeccable oysters, the tiny Olympias with their sweet-salty taste, the huge, blowsy Gulfs, the metallic Chiloés from Chile—the best selection around. For the full impact of these flavors, they are best compared on the combination plate; ask the waiter to identify them all and describe the different flavors—he or she probably will be able to do it, for if there's one thing about McCormick, it knows fish. Dinner for two, with wine, costs about $75.

 Morell's

Irvine Hilton and Towers,
17900 Jamboree Blvd., Irvine
(714) 863-3111
CALIFORNIAN
Open Mon.-Thurs. 11:30 a.m.-2 p.m. & 6:30 p.m.-10 p.m., Fri. 11:30 a.m.-2 p.m. & 6 p.m.-10 p.m., Sat. 6 p.m.-10 p.m. All major cards.

Just the idea of another hotel restaurant can put most of us in a stupor. More tasteful pink wall coverings, more somber wine lists and more swordfish-salmon-rabbit-or-tenderloin entrées. All this sobriety can make a traveler rush for the nearest Carl's Jr. So, yes, Morell's is a hotel restaurant, and while it has its soporific moments (particularly when the string quartet arrives), it is in fact one of Orange County's more sophisticated places. The executive chef, Michael Watren, and the chef de cuisine, Thomas Selzer, actually have creative streaks, and they have been known to come up with gently surprising variations on the swordfish-etc. litany.

While the menu shifts occasionally, staples include an excellent salmon en papillote that is all innocence, the filet steamed in its own moisture along with black olives and herbs. Venison is treated lightly, served rare in a reduction of juices. In fact, virtually all of Morell's sauces are reductions—no big news elsewhere, but a flavor victory for the hotel restaurant. The menu can be witty. A spinach salad is a takeoff on the Italian insalata caprese of mozzarella, basil and tomato, with spinach leaves replacing the basil; the cheese is cut into tiny cubes to mimic the tiny croutons. Other salads are arranged like froufrou Easter bonnets, just for fun. The side dishes have personality: a cool mound of angel-hair pasta touched with mango, a cooked apple slice, a gratin of carrots, steamed whole baby beets. The bread basket includes a spunky sourdough specked with green peppercorns and rye with a fine texture. The room, of course, conforms precisely with regulation hotel-restaurant decor: pinky-peach walls, soft light-

ing, paintings of irises by Billy Al Bengston. However, to get there, one must pass through the hotel lobby, crossing a river (in lobby lingo, a fountain) and passing the gift shop. Dinner for two, with wine, runs about $100.

 Pascal

Plaza Newport, 1000 N. Bristol St.,
Newport Beach
(714) 752-0107
FRENCH
Open Mon.-Fri. 11:30 a.m.-2:30 p.m. & 6 p.m.-10 p.m., Sat. 6 p.m.-10 p.m. Cards: AE, MC, V.

Pascal Olhats, the chef and owner of this charming restaurant, is a quiet man, almost shy, but his food speaks loud and clear. It is southern French cooking with great polish, the robustness of olives and rosemary tempered by Olhats's careful, classical training. One doesn't find this high-quality level often, but the loyal clientele Olhats has earned proves that it is sorely desired. That may sound like a lot of hyperbole for a restaurant in a strip mall a few miles south of the San Diego Freeway, not to mention a fairly informal one, with walls of white-painted brick and Provençal-print tablecloths. But Pascal is well worth praising.

Ohlats keeps the food as approachable as his decor; a bowl of mussels may come with an elegant saffron-laced broth, but they are piled casually high. No posturing here. Fish is flatout excellent. Olhats's signature dish is sea bass with thyme, which he modifies gently throughout the year, at one time napping the cooked-to-butter filet with a tomato coulis, the next, with a serious Champagne sauce. There are other fish of note, such as a swordfish steak done au poivre, the cracked black peppercorns joined by green ones and a julienne of red peppers, or poached salmon ringed with mussels. Recently Olhats prepared an appetizer of fresh Dutch sardines, their mica skins glistening with a second skin of olive oil. Richer, more robust dishes—rack of lamb, tiny quartered quail on a crunchy potato pancake, sweetbreads with mushrooms—are dense with flavor. Once we were disappointed by the chicken breast dressed with olives, capers and tomatoes, but only because it was merely good. A fixed-price dinner showcases the simplest and best of the chef's work; a dessert tray does the same. The latter may include a poached pear dripping chocolate, strawberries iced with meringue, a sliver of chocolate terrine and a custardlike lemon tart. Dinner for two, with wine, runs about $90.

 Pavilion
Four Seasons Hotel, 690 Newport Center Dr., Newport Beach
(714) 759-0808

CALIFORNIAN
Open Mon.-Fri. 6:30 a.m.-10:30 a.m., 11:30 a.m.-2 p.m. & 6 p.m.-9:30 p.m., Sat. 6 p.m.-10:30 p.m., Sun. 10 a.m.-1:30 p.m. & 6 p.m.-10:30 p.m. All major cards.

It looks like a hotel dining room (all those pinky warm colors and paintings and framed prints that lean toward the floral), and it acts like a hotel dining room (a well-trained staff and a constant changing of forks and knives), but once the food is served at Pavilion, it doesn't taste like a hotel dining room. The kitchen, now headed by chef Bill Bracken, has done away with the heavy, the buttery, the dense and the flamboyant. A typical sight: an appetizer of ravioli, the pasta as translucent as a wonton skin, revealing the dill-flecked morsel of salmon inside, set in a just-warm "sauce" of salmon broth. Call this cuisine transparent. Even the most avowed trencherman couldn't leave Pavilion with clogged arteries. How about the salad of split heads of limestone lettuce in a bleu d'Auvergne cheese dressing? Sounds rich, right? But the dressing is a delicate, zabaglione-like froth that almost vanishes into the lettuce. How about lobster medallions with wild-mushroom ravioli and truffles? Sorry, the bright rounds of lobster float in a truffle-darkened stock (no cream to be seen) that tastes as much of the creature as the meat does. The peas in the center aren't even cooked—just warmed by the hot plate. The kitchen never underestimates the power of a perfect ingredient. Why mess with a fresh pea? Why mask a good lobster stock with cream? Pavilion is not about spa cuisine at all; rather, it has developed an approach to lighter foods that is unique for Orange County.

The menu changes—evolves, actually—every eight or nine months, but perennial offerings include a moist slip of swordfish steak in a Merlot sauce, an appetizer of lobster and wild-mushroom strudel, sea bass roasted with herbs and a rack of lamb that, yes, is wondrously light. The innovative, refreshing desserts are some of the finest around: an apple tart, the apples barely cooked (of course) and the puff pastry thin but fine, topped with a tiny scoop of prune and Armagnac ice cream, and a chocolate torte that will prove once and for all that this is most certainly not spa cuisine. Dinner for two, with wine, runs about $110.

 Prego
18420 Von Karman Ave., Irvine
(714) 553-1333

ITALIAN
Open Mon. 11:30 a.m.-10:30 p.m., Tues.-Thurs. 11:30 a.m.-11 p.m., Fri. 11:30 a.m.-midnight, Sat. 5 p.m.-midnight, Sun. 5 p.m.-10 p.m. All major cards.

Close your eyes and you're in . . . well, pretty nearly Italy, but more precisely, Beverly Hills. The menu at the Irvine Prego is indistinguishable from the one at the Beverly Hills Prego, with its light, appealing pizzas, simple grilled meats and unusual pastas. Open your eyes, though, and you'll know you're definitely not in Beverly Hills. This Prego is not a closed-in building on a shopping block but a striking tile-roof Tuscan villa with a lawn and even a bit of garden around it. Beautifully done in mustard and rust, it's spacious and airy with tall windows on three sides. There's even a bit of outdoor dining, that greatest of luxuries in this neck of the woods. Understandably, at lunchtime Prego jumps with business types descending on it from the surrounding office-building hive.

The food includes all the Prego favorites, including breadsticks that actually taste good and pizzas, the best of which may be the simplest and on the face of it the most hackneyed: pizza Margherita, topped with tomato and cheese. With its fresh tomato sauce and fresh basil and sage, we can't imagine a more attractive pizza. Fresh herbs are used frequently here. Grilled lamb chops are brushed with butter and sprinkled with sage and rosemary, and grilled chicken is marinated in garlic and rosemary. Prego does best with simple dishes (the dry-aged rib-eye steak is tastier than anything you can find at most steakhouses); avoid, however, the fettuccine integrale and the whole-wheat pasta, unless your doctor prescribes it. Otherwise, anything you order is certain to be among the most distinguished Italian food in Orange County. Dinner for two, with wine, runs about $65.

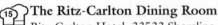

Rex of Newport
2106 W. Ocean Front, Newport Beach
(714) 675-2566

SEAFOOD

Open Sun.-Fri. 5:30 p.m.-9:30 p.m., Sat. 5:30 p.m.-10 p.m. All major cards.

There are people who have always gone to Rex for the decor, which is in the masculine, gaslight-era style of fancy steak and/or seafood places; its bar is famous for some rather misty, Renoiresque nude paintings. Rex's newest room lightens this style with a dose of satin wallpaper and painted chandeliers, with a bracing subtext of art deco, and the result is curiously romantic. The new room seems full of couples sliding close and cuddling. Which is all well and good, but we want to know what's to eat. Seafood, of course, and even a steak. There are no surprises; you could write the menu yourself. Seafood cocktails with horseradish cocktail sauce. Oysters Rockefeller. Clams (or oysters, for that matter) casino—which are more interesting than usual because of an aggressive dose of garlic. The most appealing appetizer is the crisp, sweet fried soft-shell crabs, much better than the mushy, faintly bitter soft shells usually found in California. Entrées are simple treatments of remarkably good ingredients: swordfish steak, live lobster with drawn butter, abalone with hollandaise (practically the universal sauce at Rex). And Rex's few red meat dishes are also good—pepper steak is tender and beefy, and rack of lamb is moist and lamby. Desserts include a good buttery chocolate mousse with a little mint in it, and a tart cheesecake. Dinner for two, with wine, costs about $95.

The Ritz-Carlton Dining Room
Ritz-Carlton Hotel, 33533 Shoreline Dr., Laguna Niguel
(714) 240-5008

FRENCH

Open nightly 6 p.m.-11 p.m. All major cards.

It's a shame, the common criticism goes, that the Dining Room doesn't share some of the hotel's great ocean views. But the point of the restaurant is not California cliffs or hang gliders; the point is that this is a classic restaurant, where the tables are set a perfect distance apart, the lighting is like honey, and the lines of gold leaf in the moldings hint of some past grandeur on the Continent. No, the fact that the restaurant does not have a view is not an oversight, for the dining experience here is not intended to reflect the peculiarities of the Southern California coast, but rather a timeless international brand of good taste. And it's not for want of imagination that the Dining Room is generically named.

Finding fault to find with the restaurant, which is overseen by the hotel's steely executive chef, Christian Rassinoux, is next to impossible. The service is impeccable (crumbs dutifully disappear between courses), the choreography of fish knives well rehearsed, the presentation of wine straightforward and smooth. The food is a lightened, elegant variation of what we will call international nouvelle, usually predictable and always precisely executed. One pays dearly for the entrées (probably the most expensive in the county), but they are superb. The sautéed and sliced filet of rabbit, set on dark wild mushrooms, seems to cut itself—the meat doesn't so much resemble rabbit as sea bass. An equally tender filet of beef tenderloin is thinly crusted with a gratin of turnips and napped with a port sauce; it may sound heavy, but it's simply rich, like chocolate truffle. In fact, none of the food here is cloying. Overlapping slices of salmon are touched with a lime-butter sauce that actually tastes of lime. Make sure to sample the daily special appetizers, with which the chef de cuisine can experiment a bit; these dishes, such as filet of ahi laid across a pickup-stick pile of green beans, often have a spiciness totally lacking in the rest of the menu. Even the desserts (unless you orders the soufflé, which is often bland no matter how much Kahlúa or white chocolate it is threatened with) are highly refined and pure—more works of art than sugar hits. The best dessert is the Pernod parfait, a soft rectangle of licorice-flavored ice cream in a softer pool of vanilla sauce, edged with a mix of berries. Of course, the wine list cannot be faulted; it does not brook the second-rate. But don't look for the idiosyncratic bottle. The list relies on pedigree—all the first and second growths, all the blue-blood Napa Cabs. In fact, if there is fault to find with the Dining Room, it is that it is perfectly, even brilliantly, cautious. Passion is sublimated in favor of precision, which makes for a delicious meal—though not one that knifes deep into memory. Dinner for two, with wine, costs $130 or more.

12/20 Scott's Seafood Grill and Bar

3300 Bristol St., Costa Mesa
(714) 979-2400
SEAFOOD
Open Mon.-Fri. 11 a.m.-2:30 p.m. & 5 p.m.-11 p.m., Sat. 11 a.m.-3 p.m. & 5 p.m.-11 p.m., Sun. 11 a.m.-3 p.m. All major cards.

The original Scott's may be in San Francisco, but this skylighted, cream-colored, French-doored restaurant looks more like a Newport Beach designer's idea of Southern California living. It's beautifully appointed, with a copper-lined kitchen, mounds of ice punctuated with oysters and two bars. But the biggest plus is the location: Scott's is within walking distance of the Orange County Performing Arts Center and the South Coast Repertory Theatre. The food is convenient, too: simple fish entrées, the occasional pasta, the ubiquitous pizza. In short, nothing really significant, but all of it fresh and tasty.

The seafood changes daily according to what chef Ernest Pinata has ordered: grilled swordfish with polenta (good), sea bass with a sharp lemon-caper butter (better), halibut with strawberry beurre blanc (no comment). What Scott's specializes in is different fish with interchangeable sauces—nothing to confound the mouth and mind before the opera. Nonfish offerings are often more engaging, from the simplest appetizers of oysters or smoked salmon to the excellent pastas spiked with shellfish. The salads, arranged at a curve of the open kitchen as part of the entertainment for drinkers at the bar, are particularly good, ranging from a delicious mix of tangy greens, such as oakleaf and arugula set with a round of goat cheese, to a refreshing spinach with citrus. And the sugar rush from desserts, such as the ridiculously large zabaglione ice cream–filled truffle or the butter-pecan ice cream, will keep you awake through the dreariest third act. The wine list, mostly California whites, is decent and well priced. Dinner for two, with wine, runs about $80.

10/20 Tavern by the Sea

2007 S. Coast Hwy., Laguna Beach
(714) 497-6568
CALIFORNIAN/CONTINENTAL
Open Sun.-Thurs. 5 p.m.-midnight, Fri.-Sat. 5 p.m.-1 a.m. Card: AE, MC, V.

You wouldn't think of stopping at the Tavern for its food. All you can see when you stick your head in is a busy bar complete with TV set. However, we noticed that the dining rooms upstairs do not for the most part have good views of the big screen and are populated by a better-dressed group. Curiosity got the better of us. Our first appetizer was the atrociously named "griddled calamari," which turned out to be remarkably good: calamari steaks in rather garlicky breading topped with strips of poached leek and chunks of artichoke, bell pepper and raw tomato. Then came homemade angel-hair pasta with scallops and a chervil mustard sauce, and a salad of mâche, frisée and radicchio topped with chunks of sweetbreads wrapped in bacon, all in a tarragon-mustard vinaigrette. We wondered how much of this Mediterranean-eclectic fare they move on Monday nights. Or rather, it seemed Mediterranean, an illusion that continued through a thick grilled veal chop with olive-flavored butter and sun-dried tomatoes. Then we discovered the respectable (and strikingly hot) blackened fish and a red-bean and ham soup that added a Cajun variable to the equation. There is eclecticism and there is eclecticism, and this is the sensible kind, where foreign styles are mastered and made to serve a central vision. By the time we were ready for dessert, the selection had dwindled to homemade ice cream and chocolate cake, but we were sure we'd seen more interesting items offered to other tables, and we'd bet they are of the same quality as the rest of the meal. All in all, surprising finesse and sophistication for a Laguna hangout. Dinner for two, with wine, runs about $70.

11/20 El Torito Grill

951 Newport Center Dr., Newport Beach
(714) 640-2875
SOUTHWESTERN
Open Sun.-Thurs. 11 a.m.-10 p.m., Fri.-Sat. 11 a.m.-11 p.m. All major cards.

The El Torito Grill is owned by the El Torito chain, but you'd never know it from looking. The walls aren't crowded with Mexican baroque motifs; they're whitewashed and decorated in a spare, semi-Navajo style, and there isn't a stick of wrought iron in the place. As for the food, about all it has in common with El Torito is the plain, hot table salsa. In fact, this is not a Mexican restaurant at all—it's a Southwestern place, meaning it does a lot of mesquite grilling. And it makes its own flour tortillas (the giant stamping device and revolving griddle are among the attractions of the display kitchen). As a Southwestern restaurant—the only one in this part of Orange County—the ET Grill seeks out the unusual, generally with good results. The mesquite-roasted meats come with tasty, though sometimes faintly stringy, sweet-potato chips. There are tiny blue-corn duck tamalitos in a surprisingly rich and hot sauce, and a corn-flour pasta that tastes intriguingly like fettuccine Alfredo with a bit of corn flavor and red-pepper bite. The best dessert is a banana deep-fried in a tortilla and served with syrup. In the end, the simplest things are the most memorable: the refritos made with rich, faintly tart black beans, and, in particular, the plain frijoles de olla, far more flavorful than the standard refried beans. The ET Grill is reasonably priced for its Fashion Island location and its good food; dinner for two, with a couple of beers each, runs about $40.

13 **The Towers**
Surf and Sand Hotel, 1555 S. Coast Hwy., Laguna Beach
(714) 497-4477
CALIFORNIAN
Open Mon.-Thurs. 7 a.m.-2:30 p.m. & 5:30 p.m.-10 p.m., Fri.-Sat. 7 a.m.-2:30 p.m. & 5:30 p.m.-11 p.m., Sun. 11 a.m.-3 p.m. & 5:30 p.m.-10 p.m. All major cards.
The Towers can get by on its looks alone. Set like a green lozenge of a jewel on the ninth floor of the Surf and Sand Hotel, inside it is all faceted glass and mirrors, like an art deco jewel box. And this box has one great view: the curve of Laguna's bay to the north, the rounding coast to the south, and ocean and more ocean straight ahead. At night when the lights go down, the ocean fades to black and there's only what's left on the hexagonal plates. In the past it wasn't much to look at, but a new chef recently arrived, and the outlook is decidedly good.

Jackson Kenworth, who comes to The Towers via Paris's La Varenne and L.A.'s Citrus, has an elegant, lustrously clear style; he never nudges the diner in the ribs, but rather gestures with a slight nod. A pale and delicate melon soup washed with ginger is sweet, yes, but also surprisingly cleansing. An endive salad is tinted a bright rose with beet vinaigrette, but the flavor is subtle. Perhaps because this is a hotel restaurant, or perhaps because Kenworth prefers to err on the side of the tasteful, main courses are straightforward. It's no surprise to find a sautéed salmon filet napped with Champagne sauce—this sauce, however, is as light as a reduction and barely flavored with leeks. The rack of lamb is simply prepared and is one of the best in the county. The fanned breast of roast duck is no news, except that the bird has been basted and basted to velvet, and the accompanying stir-fried julienne of vegetables carries a hint of soy—a well-behaved hit that does not overwhelm. There are occasional bon mots: a spinach salad with clever circles of croutons filled with barely baked quail-egg yolks, or a strange dish of sautéed scallops surrounding riced potatoes cooked into a buttery "risotto." As for desserts, we have not yet tried anything chocolate here, being seduced instead by such things as mango mousse cake or peach gratinée, all pretty in a little-girl way. But it seems that something simple and adult (and thoroughly chocolate) might do Kenworth's sophisticated food the most honor. The wine list includes some marvelous French bottles and any number of good California ones, but there are few priced in the mid-range. Dinner for two, with wine, costs about $100.

12/20 **Tutto Mare**
Fashion Island, 545 Newport Center Dr., Newport Beach
(714) 640-6333
ITALIAN
Open Mon.-Thurs. 11:30 a.m.-11 p.m., Fri.-Sat. 11:30 p.m.-midnight, Sun. 5 p.m.-10 p.m. All major cards.
We must admit that we get a little confused sometimes. Tutto Mare, Bistango, Prego—these upbeat Italianate restaurants can start to run together in one's mind, and the menus certainly do. Tutto Mare has the same sleek clientele, the same rustic offerings of arugula

and grilled fish, the same bustling energy as its cousin restaurants. It does, however, differ in one striking way: the menu is short and to the point, and that means seafood and pasta. Pasta is definitely the thing to order here. They offer just the right combination of rustic and refined: the simplest rigatoni with a tart-fresh tomato sauce, fettuccine weighed down with a rich lamb ragoût, fussy black and white triangles of pasta filled with sea bass. The most interesting is the variation of gnocchi, here served as discs of semolina and ground sea bass—terrific if you needs some babying. But the best pasta is the green raviolini with spinach and ricotta in brown butter with snips of fried sage and plenty of Parmesan. This last dish is a spin-off of one featured at Prego a few miles inland, which is no coincidence; Tim Dobravolskis is executive chef of both. Following the memorable pastas, the second courses don't seem too necessary. There are an odd dish of grilled prawns set in lemony white beans and a whole baked fish (the species depends on the market) that, when it's cooked just right (which is generally the case), can be memorable. However, Tutto Mare has increasingly been serving exceptional specials, such as pink scallops in the shell, that do justice to the restaurant's name. Skip dessert; we've had a soggy apricot tart and a dry tiramisu, though the ricotta torte can, on a good day, throw some sparks. Two will spend about $70 for dinner with wine.

11/20 Yankee Tavern

333 Bayside Dr., Newport Beach
(714) 675-5333
AMERICAN
Open Mon.-Sat. 5 p.m.-1 a.m., Sun. 4 p.m.-10 p.m. Cards: MC, V.

The restaurant's name, the Kennebunkport stew on the menu, the staff in nautical navy blazers . . . on first sight, Yankee Tavern appears to be a theme restaurant in the time-honored Southern California tradition. In fact, Yankee Tavern is at heart a moderately priced place that serves the food we'd like to think our mothers made, from meatloaf to pot roast to chicken pot pie. It would be a neighborhood restaurant if it weren't for the valet parking—though in Newport, that seems to be the norm. That Kennebunkport stew is one of the best items on the menu, crawling with crab claws, shrimp, mussels, clams, snapper,

you name it, in a light tomato-based broth. The chicken pot pie, filled with big chunks of chicken in a cream sauce and topped with an unexpectedly fine crust that not a lot of mothers could make, serves about two people. Meat dishes, such as pot roast, are bargains, if not culinary successes. The vegetables, however, are just like Mom's; skip the tasteless carrots and the bland succotash. Desserts are sweet and big. Loaded with raisins, then soaked with an eggy brandy sauce, the bread pudding is almost preternaturally dense. It's great. About $60 for dinner for two, with wine.

QUICK BITES

Belisle's

12001 Harbor Blvd., Garden Grove
(714) 750-6560
Open daily 24 hours. Cards: MC, V.

Just a mile south of Disneyland, Belisle's could qualify as an attraction on its own—call it Paul Bunyanland. The food is Midwestern with a smattering from the great American ethnic melting pot, and everything is huge, we mean huge: pies a foot high, meat overflowing off the plate, iced tea in quart-sized glasses. The Texas-style breakfast, which includes a 24-ounce steak, a dozen eggs any style, a stack of hot cakes and country-fried potatoes, is generally split by two or more people, though some of the customers here look as if they could handle it on their own. The rooms, decorated with old farm tools, are plain and homey—during the day Belisle's is a family place with a lot of overflow from Disneyland; at night, it's a truck stop. Lunch for two runs about $15.

Bennie the Bum's Diner

238 Laguna Ave., Laguna Beach
(714) 497-4786
Open daily 24 hours. No cards.

Bennie the Bum's wants very much to be a classic diner. The menu tells you all you'd ever want to know, and then some, about the evolution of the American diner, and the place is crammed with antique touches: Coke posters, jukebox extensions at every table, a worn-out old Hamilton Beach mixer and a gum-snapping pink-and-turquoise art deco design. It may be a little self-conscious, but the old-fashioned American fare is more than convincing—the coffee's decent, for one thing. The BLT is a model, the pies are fresh, and the milk shakes are of the classic foamy variety. A sampling of Laguna types can be seen here at all hours, particularly the very odd hours, like 3 a.m. Lunch for two is about $10.

Burrell's Rib Cage

305 N. Hesperian St., Santa Ana
(714) 835-9936
1701 E. McFadden Ave., Santa Ana
(714) 541-3073
Open Sun.-Thurs. 10:30 a.m.-8 p.m., Fri.-Sat. 10:30 a.m.-10 p.m. No cards.

Deep in Santa Ana thrives a barbecue worthy of the stars. Fred Burrell, whose terrific ribs, sweet-potato pies and black-eyed peas have been served backstage at Michael Jackson concerts, makes one mean soul barbecue. Not one fiery spice has been tamed in his sauce, which seems to seep permanently into the eater's fingers. The two Rib Cages are oases of authenticity. There are a few tables, but most get take-out. About $18 for a barbecue feast for two.

Café Casse-Croûte

656 S. Brookhurst St., Anaheim
(714) 774-8013
Open daily 6 a.m.-2 p.m. No cards.

For the regulars, this is not only a place to get rib-sticking French Canadian breakfasts and lunches but a homey place to gather and speak the old language. The food is reason enough to come, though, at least when the weather's not too hot—this is food designed to stoke your internal fires against the Canadian winter. Most of the substantial meat dishes are flavored with the usual French sausage spices (allspice, cinnamon, clove) and covered with gravy. A good example is tourtière, the national dish of Quebec, which is a sort of meatloaf pie. The two most exotic items are ketchup maison, a sort of celery and apple chutney (with the same spices), and sugar pie, an amazing thing filled with an intense, slightly caramelized maple-sugar filling that takes over your mouth for at least 30 seconds following each bite. Breakfast is lumberjack-sized; the blueberry pancakes are particularly good. Lunch for two runs about $10.

Café Zinc

350 Ocean Ave., Laguna Beach
(714) 494-6302
Open Tues.-Sat. 7:30 a.m.-6 p.m., Sun. 7:30 a.m.-4 p.m. No cards.

Don't even try to get a table on a Sunday morning at this tiny, sophisticated sidewalk café; Laguna regulars will have staked them out, in order to nurse big bowls of café au lait and creamy, almost chocolatey cappuccinos, to pick at bran muffins loaded with nuts and scones loaded with currants and to spoon soft-boiled eggs from egg cups. Don't even think about coming back for lunch; the zinc-topped tables will be full again with pizzette (small pizzas topped with chèvre and pesto or eggplant and olives) loyalists. Maybe, just maybe, late in the day, some counter space will free up, and you can sit down to an espresso with a big pecan cookie, or the rice pudding oozing raspberry purée. Breakfast or lunch for two runs about $8.

The Cottage

308 N. Coast Hwy., Laguna Beach
(714) 494-3023
Open Sun.-Thurs. 7 a.m.-10 p.m., Fri.-Sat. 7 a.m.-11 p.m. Cards: AE, MC, V.

This welcoming bungalow is extremely popular on weekends; tourists, surfers, families and hungry locals wait in line together. Recycled antiques, a cheery atmosphere and sweet service make The Cottage a good bet for breakfast or an inexpensive lunch. The egg dishes are good (especially the corned beef hash with poached eggs—but decline the hollandaise), as are the pancakes and light french toast. Lunches are run-of-the-mill burgers and those California specialties with avocado and sprouts, while dinners are surprisingly good when the kitchen sticks to simple grilled fish and chicken. Breakfast or lunch for two runs about $15, dinner about $50.

The Crab Cooker

2200 Newport Blvd., Balboa
(714) 673-0100
Open Sun.-Thurs. 11 a.m.-9 p.m., Fri.-Sat. 11 a.m.-10 p.m. No cards.

If you're with your mother-in-law, baby-sitter, three kids, nephew and little sister, park the station wagon outside and join the other local families who love The Crab Cooker. If you like the echoes of children, happy or otherwise, as an accompaniment to Chopin's preludes, then you will be entranced by the noisy ambience and unpretentious fun of this simple restaurant housed in a converted twenties bank building. The decor is as unusual as is the bikini-clad clientele, with mismatched chairs, baroque oil paintings, paper plates, marlin trophies and the original bank vault in which the seafood is kept chilled. The food is plain and simple: a tasty clam chowder (improved with Tabasco sauce), good grilled seafood kebabs, popular broiled king crab and broiled fish. There's no wine to speak of, but beer does the job nicely. A seafood lunch runs about $20 for two, dinner about twice that.

Farmers Market at Atrium Court

The Atruim at Fashion Island,
401 Newport Center Dr., Newport Beach
(714) 760-0403
Open daily 8 a.m.-9 p.m. Cards: AE, MC, V.

The Farmers Market is a social center, a carnival, a way of life. At its center is a fountain surrounded by a first ring of chairs and tables (and a grand piano), then a second ring of food stands: La Salsa (tacos made with blue-corn tortillas), a salad bar and a surprisingly good hot dog cart, among them. A third ring is specialty-food and -drink suppliers: a wine and beer bar, an espresso bar, a sushi bar, a frozen yogurt bar, a huge cheese counter, several bakery/pastry counters (Il Fornaio has the best bread) and fancy fishmongers with live-lobster tanks. Ready-to-eat food is available from a number of places in this tier, as well as in the second ring—ask at the salad bar for tableware to eat with. And finally, surrounding all, there is aisle after aisle of rare produce, wines, condiments and canned goods. Everything converges on the fountain area and the crowd of people that is always sitting or milling around in it.

Grand Finale

13882 Newport Ave., Tustin
(714) 669-9310
Open Mon. 10 a.m.-3 p.m., Tues.-Sat. 10 a.m.-5:30 p.m. No cards.

The only shortcoming of this superb bakery is the absence of tables. Just one look in the

glass case, where pastry chef Paula Rice's cakes beckon with their ribbons and flowers, makes us nearly mad for a fork and plate. While Rice's classic French training is clearly evident, she has modified her recipes a bit to suit California tastes—lightening the génoise, for instance, or substituting bing cherries for liqueur in the Black Forest cake. The lemon tart, decorated at center with baby ivy leaves, is up there near perfection. About $17 for two.

Ho Sum Bistro

3112 Newport Blvd., Newport Beach
(714) 675-0896
Open Mon.-Thurs. 11 a.m.-10 p.m., Fri.-Sat. 11 a.m.-11 p.m., Sun. 4 p.m.-9 p.m. Cards: MC, V.

In its bright and shiny storefront setting, Ho Sum Bistro turns the dim sum idea into something delightfully Californian—a surfer in a Mao jacket. The series of small dishes, most of them updated with chicken and fish instead of pork and beef, includes some tasty noodle representatives, such as tai tai mein, with thick spaghettilike wheat noodles in spicy peanut sauce, and Marco Polo, with a gutsy dressing of ground chicken, ginger, garlic and a punch of chili. This really is a bistro, with an excellent, well-priced selection of California wines by the glass—up to twenty offerings a day. Dinner for two, with wine, costs about $25.

Khai Hoan

14390 Brookhurst St., Garden Grove
(714) 531-4965
Open Mon.-Thurs. 9 a.m.-10 p.m., Fri.-Sat. 9 a.m.-midnight, Sun. 9 a.m.-11 p.m. Cards: MC, V.

Orange County has more than 100 Vietnamese restaurants, the largest concentration in the country. And all of them are the real thing—the food hasn't been steamrollered to fit American tastes, and you can be sure of some real adventures. Khai Hoan looks like a large Chinese restaurant, all done up in gilt wallpaper and brass chandeliers, but you can tell it's Vietnamese because of the battery of bottled sauces: vinegar, plum, sweetish garlic and hot pepper as well as soy, plus the famous pungent fish sauce called nuoc mam, served in a bowl with carrot shreds floating in it. The huge menu is one of the most extensive in Garden Grove's Little Saigon, and the quality of the food is high. There are the ubiquitous noodle soups served in what look to be mixing bowls, broken rice dishes that are a favorite peasant food and elaborate preparations of steamed snapper. Any given evening, the room will be filled with smoke as people cook bo nuong vi—thin slices of raw beef grilled on table braziers. The young waiters are happy to lead non-Vietnamese diners through the menu. A many-course dinner for two will be about $20.

Newport Oyster Bar & Grill

2100 W. Ocean Front, Newport Beach
(714) 675-9977
Open Sun.-Thurs. 11:30 a.m.-10:30 p.m., Fri.-Sat. 11:30 a.m.-11:30 p.m. All major cards.

This is the informal sister of the very formal Rex, with the standard utilitarian oyster-bar look (hexagonal tile floors, wood paneling, a railroad-flat shape), and it benefits from using Rex's excellent seafood suppliers. It's a standard oyster bar with the expected fresh shellfish (the raw clams and oysters are generally better than the baked or sautéed dishes). The red and white chowders are unusually good; best of all is the creamy oyster stew, dotted with plump little oyster pillows. There are also straight broiled-fish dishes, a couple of pastas and occasional specials (crabcakes, for one). The only desserts are variations of fresh cheesecake. Reservations are not accepted, and there can be a long wait. If that's the case, we like to order food to go and eat on the sand. Prices vary according to the seafood market, but expect dinner for two to run about $25, oyster-bar snacks about half that.

Nui Ngu

10528 McFadden Ave., Garden Grove
(714) 775-1108
Open Sun. & Tues.-Thurs. 9 a.m.-6 p.m., Fri.-Sat. 9 a.m.-8 p.m. No cards.

Restaurants like Nui Ngu, the Vietnamese equivalent of the American coffee shop, populate this area, now called Little Saigon. Nui Ngu, however, is unique, serving a distinctive menu of Central Vietnamese dishes. Try the utterly exotic bahn bat loc, transparent rice tortellini filled with unshelled shrimp, and the refreshing soups, such as bun bo hue, a spicy

beef-and-noodle variety. A meal for two will be about $15.

Partner's Bistro

448 S. Coast Hwy., Laguna Beach
(714) 497-4441
Open Mon.-Thurs. 11:30 a.m.-2:30 p.m. & 6 p.m.-9:30 p.m., Fri. 11:30 a.m.-2:30 p.m. & 6 p.m.-10:30 p.m., Sat. 11:30 a.m.-3 p.m. & 6 p.m.-10:30 p.m., Sun. 10:30 p.m.-3 p.m. & 5:30 p.m.-9 p.m. Cards: AE, MC, V.

This popular, attractive bistro has an old-fashioned hunt-club decor, including bare brick walls and wooden floors, which don't help the noise level any. It's a pleasant spot to lunch on salads and sandwiches, but we wish the food were more exciting. Best bets are the spinach salad and the grilled fish. Cinnamon coffee and tea blends are faultless. Dinner for two, with wine, will run about $50.

The Place Across the Street from the Hotel Laguna

440 S. Coast Hwy., Laguna Beach
(714) 497-2625
Open Sun.-Thurs. 11 a.m.-10 p.m., Fri.-Sat. 10 a.m.-11 p.m. All major cards.

The blank view of the rather dreary Hotel Laguna is certainly less intriguing than its name may imply. But this crowded little café has an outdoor patio that's perfect for people-watching. The decor inside is cutesy arts and crafts, with macramé wall hangings and plenty of plants and caged birds. The menu is basic: pastas, salads and sandwiches, all of which are passable but not impressive. Best bets are the tasty chili, delicious homebaked bread and overstuffed omelets. A meal here, for two, costs in the neighborhood of $20.

Ruby's

1 Balboa Pier, Newport Beach
(714) 675-RUBY
Open daily 7 a.m.-9 p.m. Cards: AE, MC, V.

You might go to Ruby's for the food, which is quite good—slightly tarted-up versions of old-fashioned burger-stand fare, namely burgers, sandwiches, chili and a few fountain treats—but the real reason is to be at the end of Balboa Pier in a solid, enduring art moderne eatery that looks like it hasn't changed in 40 years. It's a delicious time warp, restored in accurate detail as a gum-snapping '40s lunch counter complete with Speedball

Graphics lettering on the signs, swing music on the lo-fi loudspeakers and appropriate uniforms for the help. In good weather, the thing to do is eat on the upstairs deck, which looks a little like an industrial rooftop with a great ocean view. We shamelessly love the greasy burgers and the tuna-salad sandwich, which falls apart in your hands just about as fast as you can eat it. Lunch for two is $10.

Tlaquepaque
11 W. Santa Fe Ave., Placentia
(714) 528-8515
Open daily 6 a.m.-10 p.m. Cards: MC, V.
The reason to come to Tlaquepaque is the mariachi band that plays on Friday and Saturday nights and at Sunday brunch (reservations are essential—the place gets packed). No livelier show can be imagined than this cocky, clowning crew with their infectious music, imitation-Motown steps and penchant for serenading blond señoritas. They're the real thing, and so is the audience, a number of whom get out on the floor and dance. In fact, the restaurant is all but empty when the band isn't playing. And it's no mystery why: the food is pretty awful, though the carnitas and the goat stew (birria) are above average, and there's a good, earthy red sauce for the beef enchilada and the special burrito. Dinner for two, with drinks will fall somewhere in the neighborhood of $20 to $25. (Note: At showtimes, drinks must be paid for on the spot. Bring cash.)

Tortilla Flats
1740 S. Coast Hwy., Laguna Beach
(714) 494-6588
Open Mon.-Sat. 11:30 a.m.-10 p.m., Sun. 10 a.m.-10 p.m. Cards: AE, MC, V.
This is a great place to come for brunch, although the sleepy clientele looks somewhat stunned by the rousing mariachi music that reverberates off the walls. There is a cheerful, sunny terrace annex downstairs, a main room filled with plants and wall paintings, an upstairs cantina and a lovely outdoor patio with a clear view of the ocean. Brunch offers nearly a dozen Mexican-style egg dishes, along with the standard taco basics. Lunch and dinner are a bit more ambitious, featuring the complete range of typical upscale-Mexican entrées. Brunch runs about $20 for two, lunch and

dinner slightly more (not counting the price of the good margaritas).

Wahoo's Fish Taco
1862 Placentia Ave., Costa Mesa
(714) 631-3433
Open Mon.-Sat. 11 a.m.-10 p.m., Sun. 11 a.m.-9 p.m. No cards.
Looking for Southern California's indigenous cuisine? Wahoo's is one of the bigger and more ambitious of the Baja-inspired surfer joints (and certainly the cleanest), where the regional specialty is the fish taco. The owner of this stucco bunker of a building, Win Lam, was born in Brazil and speaks five languages, including Southern California surf. He brings in a different fish every day to stuff his corn-tortilla tacos, big burritos and French-roll sandwiches; a blackboard lists rock cod, swordfish, snapper and even the Baja wahoo. For those who don't want to swim, there are pork carnitas and grilled chicken, and for those watching their health, Win Lam promises that no lard is used in cooking. A fun dinner for two, with beer or wine, runs about $12.

HOTELS

 ### The Carriage House
1322 Catalina St., Laguna Beach, 92651
(714) 494-8945
This little bed-and-breakfast inn is the most charming in Laguna. The New England–style gray-shingled house has two stories of apartment suites, all decorated with grandmother's hand-me-down antiques, lace curtains and a feminine touch. Each suite opens onto the outdoor courtyard, a lush garden overflowing with flowering plants, a fountain, trees and two friendly cats, who act as sleepy guardians atop the only comfortable patio furniture. Guests share breakfast—including home-baked pastries prepared by innkeeper Dee Taylor—in the cozy dining room. As lovely as the main house is, we suggest you splurge on the cottage. At $150 a night, you will have a most adorable little house, complete with white picket fence, flower garden, amusing veneered antiques, kitchen, living room, par-

lor, old-fashioned bathroom and lovely bed-room. It is a romantic, storybook hideaway all in peach and rose. The Carriage House is just up the street from the ocean and within walking distance of town.
Suites: $80-$125; cottage: $150.

Casa Laguna
2510 S. Coast Hwy., Laguna Beach, 92651
(714) 494-2996
It's more of a small hotel, really, but Casa Laguna considers itself a bed-and-breakfast. This is fair enough, for it does have many bed-and-breakfast qualities: every room is different, all are old-fashioned and romantic, and guests are provided with a good breakfast and personalized service. It's located just a short walk from the beach and is equipped with a pool for those who don't like sand. If you want an ocean view and lots of space, get one of the lovely suites, whose only failing is some noise from Coast Highway. If you prefer quiet, take one of the balcony rooms, which are set back off the street but still have wonderful ocean views, or splurge on the Cottage, a peaceful, charming home away from home replete with fireplace, large ocean-view deck, kitchen and beautiful leaded glass windows.
Rooms & suites: $85-$155; cottage: $195.

Doryman's Inn
2102 W. Ocean Front,
Newport Beach, 92663
(714) 675-7300
Without a doubt, our favorite small hotel in Orange County. Doryman's is actually a bed-and-breakfast, not a hotel, but its comfort, opulence, style and personal service put it out of the typical bed-and-breakfast league. Although the handsome tile-roofed building was built in 1921, its plush decor is more reminiscent of the gaslight era. The ten rooms all have gas fireplaces (with bedside controls), marble window seats, beautiful antiques and marble bathrooms with sunken tubs, skylights and telephones. Some feature ocean views, some Jacuzzi tubs; guests in all rooms can take advantage of the rooftop sundeck and Jacuzzi, as well as the generous breakfast served on a lovely tiled patio. Its location, across the street

from the beach and the Newport Pier boardwalk, is perfect for exploring Newport on foot—but, unfortunately, this location can sometimes mean an unpleasant degree of weekend late-night noise from partying kids and hot-rodders on the street outside. On the ground floor is Rex, an admirable restaurant with a similar gaslight-era decor.
Doubles: $150-$275.

Eiler's Inn
741 S. Coast Hwy., Laguna Beach, 92651
(714) 494-3004
A delightful bed-and-breakfast built around a courtyard, where guests congregate for breakfast and evening wine and cheese. The rooms, tastefully decorated with antiques, have that pleasant nostalgic fragrance associated with a great-aunt's old home. Fresh flowers, touching extras (shells filled with bonbons) and a pleasant management make this one of the most welcoming places to stay in Laguna. You will be greeted with a bottle of Champagne to get your visit off to a good start. Each room is different; we can recommend "Crescent Bay" and "Woods Cove." The beach is two blocks away.
Singles & doubles: $95-$125; suite: $170.

Four Seasons Hotel Newport Beach
690 Newport Center Dr.,
Newport Beach, 92660
(714) 759-0808
Newport's most beautiful hotel belongs to the prestigious Four Seasons chain, which has also just opened a grand Los Angeles hotel. Done in particularly attractive '80s hotel pastels, with plenty of marble and fabulous fresh flowers, the Four Seasons is located next to Fashion Island and near Balboa Island, making it a good spot for both vacationers and business travelers. The 294 rooms are quite large; all have balconies, views and tasteful furnishings, including the ubiquitous TV-in-the-armoire. There's a complete exercise club stocked with Lifecycles, exercise equipment, saunas, a whirlpool and a heated swimming pool. The Four Seasons vies with the Meridien

for the best-big-hotel-in-the-Newport/Irvine-area title.

Singles: $185-$235; doubles: $210-$260; suites: $300-$1,700.

Hotel Meridien

4500 MacArthur Blvd.,
Newport Beach, 92660
(714) 476-2001

Service is the watchword at the French-owned Meridien—everyone here, from the bellhops to the maids to the concierges, is remarkably gracious and helpful. There are many things that make the Meridien one of our Orange County favorites: the outstanding restaurants, from the gourmet Antoine to the lighter-fare Bistro Terrasse; the third-floor pool and sundeck, complete with cabanas, food service and charming beachboys to serve you cold drinks; the shuttle to the Meridien's lovely little private beach in Laguna; and the bargain-basement weekend deals, which range from $94 to $249 a night (the more expensive packages include some meals and extras). It's perfectly located for the business visitor to Newport's financial center, and its location across from John Wayne Airport means a constant influx of Air France flight crews (and, unfortunately, a wee bit of airport noise, though it isn't intrusive). The spacious rooms, which are well equipped with all the upscale-hotel amenities, are done in the same pleasant neutrals as the lobby.

Singles: $160; doubles: $180; suites: $265-$500; weekend packages: $94-$249.

The Hyatt Newporter

1107 Jamboree Rd., Newport Beach, 92660
(714) 644-1700

Remodeling continues to take place at the sprawling Newporter, and it's looking better and better. All traces of the old Hawaiian-jungle theme are gone; the 410 rooms are now done in shades of peach, blue, mauve and rose (like every other contemporary hotel in Southern California). The new wing has 104 rooms, and there's a new third outdoor pool and a second Jacuzzi. Since this is a convention resort, expect to see lots of badge-wearing guests rushing to their next meeting—and

don't expect a homey feeling or much personal service. But you can expect good facilities, comfortable rooms and lovely views from the hotel's bay side. The small health club features Lifecycles and Universal weights. The weekend-package rate is a bargain.

Singles: $105-$165; doubles: $150-$180; suites: $275-$395; villas: $525-$595; weekend package: $95.

Irvine Hilton & Towers

17900 Jamboree Rd., Irvine, 92714
(714) 863-3111

A very good business hotel located near John Wayne Airport and the business hub of Newport/Irvine—and close to South Coast Plaza for those who'd rather go shopping than talk shop. The fairly spacious rooms are light and airy, with rattan furniture and TVs hidden in white-oak armoires; some of the better rooms have such extras as pure silk and cotton comforters and sheets. Service is friendly, meeting facilities are excellent, and the two restaurants, Morell's and Le Café, are admirable. You'll have to drive to the beach, but there is a large pool. Ask about the weekend packages, which can be very good deals.

Singles: $118-$148; doubles: $133-$163; suites: $275-$1,200.

Newport Beach Marriott

9000 Newport Center Dr.,
Newport Beach, 92660
(714) 640-4000

This enormous hotel leads a double life: during the week it is filled with serious-looking corporate business types; on the weekends an army of fitness fans mobs the lobby, carrying tennis racquets, golf clubs and beach bags. Surprisingly, this nine-story, 300-room chain hotel manages to be reasonably warm despite its large size. The dull but spacious rooms done in relaxing desert tones are comfortable enough oases—just fine for recovering after day of playing in the California sun, relaxing by the pool or investing in the shoppers' paradise in the adjacent Fashion Island. Ask about special weekend packages—rates can be quite low.

Singles: $144-$149; doubles: $164-$169; suites: $250; weekend package: $250 (for two nights, including two breakfasts and one dinner).

The Ritz-Carlton
33533 Shoreline Dr., Laguna Niguel, 92677
(714) 240-2000

Cynics cackled with glee when the opulent Ritz-Carlton opened in the boonies of Orange County, in that no-man's-land just north of Dana Point, far from the monied Newport-Irvine-Laguna triangle. "They'll never fill this place up at $250 a night," they said. "The locals will never put on ties and spend $130 at dinner here." And indeed, that seemed to be the Ritz's fate in the early days. But word of its beauty, its luxury and its facilities spread, and now there's never an empty room. The setting is lovely, on a lonely bluff between Coast Highway and the ocean, with an adjacent golf course and two miles of state-owned beach. The Ritz may not be convenient to central Newport, but then this isn't a business hotel. It's a self-contained escape from the workaday world, a true resort where you can play golf or tennis, swim in the ocean or the pools, work out in the gym, relax in the saunas and whirlpools and on the massage table, walk the beach, read a book in the lounge while enjoying the incredible view, linger over a lovely high tea, or have one of the best meals in Orange County in the Dining Room. And there's more—two less formal restaurants, a nightspot with live music, upscale shops and so on. The architecture (Mediterranean-inspired) and the carefully manicured grounds are worth a visit in themselves. Not all of the large, antiques-decorated rooms have ocean views; it's worth the extra money to request one that does. Big spenders can join the Ritz-Carlton Club, which features a private concierge, open bar and a round-the-clock buffet.
Doubles: $185-$350; suites: $650-$2,000.

Surf and Sand Hotel
1555 S. Coast Hwy., Laguna Beach, 92651
(714) 497-4477

We wouldn't exactly describe the Surf and Sand's exterior as architecturally inspired, but it does have something no other Laguna inn has—a great location perched right over the waves. And though the exterior may be banal, the interior has been renovated and redecorated, much to the hotel's betterment. The 160 rooms are now larger, with more spacious bathrooms, and the inviting, soothing decor features light colors and well-made rattan furniture. Most of the rooms have spectacular ocean views and private balconies. Amenities include a pleasant pool and two restaurants, the casual Boardwalk and the very elegant Towers, which has a great view, a terrific bar and first-rate food. The beachfront location, comfort and good service mean that the Surf and Sand is booked solid in the summer, so make sure to reserve early (and keep in mind that some rooms have three-night minimums in summer).
Doubles: $170-$210; suites: $350-$475.

NIGHTLIFE

The Beach House
619 Sleepy Hollow Ln., Laguna Beach
(714) 494-9707
Open Sun.-Thurs. 8 a.m.-11 p.m., Fri.-Sat. 8 a.m.-midnight. Cards: AE, MC, V.

The best thing going for this homey restaurant/bar is the superb view. It's a perfect location to watch the sun setting into the Pacific while enjoying the fresh air, the passable seafood menu, the generous Ramos fizzes and the pleasant service. We like it best as a place to meet for a quiet drink at the end of the day; the bar provides the perfect perch for people- (and seagull-) watching and enjoying the reflection of glorious summer sunsets.

Las Brisas
361 Cliff Dr., Laguna Beach
(714) 497-5434
Open daily 11:30 a.m.-midnight. All major cards.

Although this is a full-fledged restaurant (some people who have nothing better to do wait here for over an hour for Sunday brunch), we suggest you skip the food and instead languish outdoors on the bright blue-and-white patio. The view is dramatic: the Pacific floats below the cliffside pathway, and there is quite a social scene here on the weekends. There's no better place in Laguna to sip a margarita and watch the sunset, surrounded by sunburned tourists.

Club Postnuclear

775 Laguna Canyon Rd., Laguna Beach
(714) 497-3881
Open Fri.-Sat. 9 p.m.-2 a.m. Cover $7.50 before 10 p.m., $10 after 10 p.m. No cards.

Laguna's young and hip keep Club Postnuclear hopping every weekend, when deejays crank the fashionable dance music (rock, hip-hop, soul). The lack of a liquor license means that the crowd includes a good number of teens between 18 and 21, but some oldtimers in their 20s and 30s stop in regularly, too. The club also serves as an occasional live-music venue during the week, hosting moderately popular rock bands on tour through Southern California.

The Club Room

The Ritz-Carlton, 33533 Shoreline Dr., Laguna Niguel
(714) 240-2000
Open Sun.-Thurs. 6:30 p.m.-12:30 a.m., Fri.-Sat. 6:30 p.m.-1:45 p.m. (live music from 8 p.m. on). No cover. All major cards.

This may be the only beach-adjacent bar in Southern California that dares to have a dress code: no denim, jackets for men and, God forbid, no neon volleyball shorts and tank tops. While we're a bit annoyed at the Ritz's unwillingness to fit into the local community (where you're as likely to see a suit and tie as you are a snowstorm), we must admit that this policy gives The Club Room a considerable touch of class. In a handsome, Ralph Lauren-esque setting, a prosperous-looking crowd of all ages drinks, chats, relaxes and dances to the jazzy-pop live music, which is neither too square to offend younger ears nor too hard-pounding to frighten away their parents.

The Coach House

33157 Camino Capistrano,
San Juan Capistrano
(714) 496-8930
Showtimes vary. Tickets $10-$25. Cards: MC, V.

San Juan Capistrano is a little out of the way for the average Orange County resident or visitor, but it's worth the drive for fans of good rock 'n' roll. The Coach House books outstanding local and national bands—such noteworthy talents as David Lindley, Billy Vera &

the Beaters, Maria McKee, Ziggy Marley and T-Bone Burnette. Nearly every show is worth a visit. Simple dinners are available in this friendly music club, which serves alcohol but does not have a two-drink minimum.

Bobby McGee's

353 E. Coast Hwy., Newport Beach
(714) 673-5380
Open nightly 5 p.m.-2 a.m. All major cards.

Still a Newport hot spot, this relentlessly cheerful spot is where attractive young singles meet other attractive young singles. It's so popular, in fact, that it quickly reaches fire-regulation capacity on weekend nights. So come early if you want to share some of the incredible pent-up energy found on the dance floor, in the bar and even in the restaurant, where highly gregarious young waiters and waitresses put on a costume show that rivals the circus. Be forewarned: rumor has it that young women stalk middle-management executives, screening out those who drive "UCs" (undesirable cars).

The Saloon

446 S. Coast Hwy., Laguna Beach
(714) 494-5469
Open Sun.-Thurs. noon-11 p.m., Fri.-Sat. noon-2 a.m. Cards: MC, V.

A true drinking bar, the Saloon attracts a lively cadre of regulars, not hustling singles. The tiny, narrow room is filled with a handsome wood bar and a couple of minuscule tables; the lack of seats discourages lingering. A friendly and fun spot for a quick drink and a conversation about local news.

Studio Cafe

100 Main St., Balboa
(714) 675-7760
Open Mon.-Thurs. 11:30 a.m.-1:30 a.m., Fri.-Sat. 11 a.m.-1:30 a.m., Sun. 10 a.m.-1:30 a.m. Cards: AE, MC, V.

Located at the tip of the Balboa peninsula, the Studio Cafe is immensely popular with good-looking beachy sorts in their 20s and 30s who come here for the jazz and for one another. The small bistro with bentwood chairs, stained glass and an active bar is packed on weekends with young people who seem to care less about the music than hustling one another and relaxing with their exotic drinks.

The Towers

Surf and Sand Hotel, 1555 S. Coast Hwy.,
Laguna Beach
(714) 497-4477
Open daily 8 a.m.-1 a.m. All major cards.

Once you can see where you're going without walking into a mirror or etched-glass panel, you can settle into one of the tasteful banquettes or sieges to experience the piano bar here. We say *experience*, because the decor is so dramatic that it takes a few minutes to adjust and remember that you are in Laguna, not Paris, Monte Carlo or New York. The bar is small and elegant, with a fireplace and a glass-topped baby grand, at which customers hover in close conversation. Making the setting all the more dramatic is the bar's perch over the Pacific, making for a fabulous view. For a predinner Champagne or late nightcap, this is one of the most sensational-looking bars we've run into.

SIGHTS

Laguna Art Museum

307 Cliff Dr., Laguna Beach
(714) 494-6531
Open Tues.-Sun. 11 a.m.-5 p.m. Adults $2, students & seniors $1, children under 12 free.

This bright museum has generally excellent changing exhibitions, often of works by contemporary California artists. We last caught an admirable show of Granville Redman, one of America's premier landscape painters. Our favorite temporary show, however, was a display of paper-bag art created by elementary school children.

Mission San Juan Capistrano

32086 Camino Capistrano,
San Juan Capistrano
(714) 493-1424
Open daily 7:30 a.m.-5 p.m. Adults $2, children under 12 $1.

A few months after a bewigged gang of rebels signed the Declaration of Independence, Padre Junípero Serra founded this fascinating link in the California mission chain. Its small, dark, richly evocative chapel is the oldest in-use building in California; later came the beautiful Great Stone Church. To get the most out of your visit, take the time to wander the entire property, including the serene gardens. If there are more than fifteen of you, make sure to take the excellent docent-led tour; otherwise you'll take a self-guided tour. The legendary swallows are still returning to the mission each March 19, if in rather diminished numbers (due, it is thought, to the dramatic increase in development in southern Orange County).

Newport Harbor Art Museum

850 San Clemente Dr., Newport Beach
(714) 759-1122
Open Tues.-Sun. 10 a.m.-5 p.m. Adults $3, students & seniors $2, children $1.

A reputable museum with an ambitious exhibition program of several shows a year focused on late-twentieth-century and California art. The enthusiastic curator hunts for unshown and often unknown California artists to introduce to the Orange County public. An intelligent collection that is worth seeing. Please also see "Museums" in the Sights chapter.

Upper Newport Bay Ecological Reserve

Back Bay Dr. (off Jamboree Rd.),
Newport Beach

Perhaps our favorite place in the Newport-Laguna area. Its serenity is broken only by singing birds and duck discussions—or by an occasional motorist. We suggest you walk around the perimeter of this marshland to observe the waterfowl and learn from the bird-watchers who are visiting old friends. Be sure to take binoculars to get a better view of the egrets, mallards, rails and teals. The silence here is a welcome respite, and you can get some needed between-meal exercise walking around this rustic reserve.

Glenn E. Vedder Ecological Reserve

S. Coast Hwy., Laguna Beach

When you've had enough of the art galleries and shopping in Laguna, strike out for the coast and take this pleasant pathway parallel to Coast Highway that borders the cliffs overlooking the ocean. There are several access points to the rocky shore below, but the view is even more dramatic from above. Gardens, exotic plants and fellow strollers provide a pleasant diversion and an interesting pastime, particularly around sunset.

PALM SPRINGS

XANADU INCARNATE

The letter from the Palm Springs Convention Center began on a cheery note: "Greetings from the land of warm sunshine, snowcapped mountains, fresh desert air, crisp starlit evenings and swaying palm trees!"—in other words, just what you'd expect from a convention and visitors bureau. But the reality of Palm Springs is a quite a different thing to those who head there from the east to defrost and from the west to bake. Palm Springs is a state of mind more than a place, though the place can't be ignored. It's a curiosity—Las Vegas without the gambling, the Sahara without the exoticism, the beach without the ocean. Some people love it, some people don't love it—but not many are neutral when it comes to Palm Springs.

Even the journey to Palm Springs has an undeniably mythical quality to it. Driving east on Interstate 10 (which is actually called the Christopher Columbus Trans-Continental Highway, a term used by no living being in the world), coming out of San Bernardino and passing through Yucaipa, you'll encounter miles of windmills twirling in the desert emptiness. These strange totems are rumored by the doomsayers to be slowing the earth's rotation, which will eventually send us careening into the sun (and we're worried about smog?). You'll also discover the fattening joys of Hadley's, a hyperbolic dried-fruit and nut stand, where busloads of Japanese tourists stop for a requisite date shake on their way to a day of crazy shopping along Palm Springs' Palm Canyon Drive. Near Hadley's, the famous life-sized dinosaur models stand guard outside Cabazon's Wheel Inn, a truck stop where the pies come topped with whipped cream and the truckers all seem to have beards and ponytails (remember when truckers used to beat up people who looked like that?). And you'll pass the vast Morongo Indian Bingo Hall, where hundreds of believers in the great god Bingo sit with dozens of cards in front of them, fluorescent markers poised, waiting for B17 to come up. In fact, the trip is much like Dorothy's trip to the Emerald City; when you finally get to Palm Springs, you know you're not in Kansas anymore.

When people refer to Palm Springs, they actually mean a good-sized chunk of the Coachella Valley surrounding Mayor Sonny Bono's little town. Basically speaking, the Palm Springs area can be conveniently defined as those towns adjacent to Route 111 as it travels south of Interstate 10, from the Cabazon exit in the west to the Indio exit in the east. In between, you'll pass through the resort towns: first Palm Springs itself, then Cathedral City, Rancho Mirage, Palm Desert, Indian Wells and La Quinta. When you find yourself at streets with names like Bob Hope, Gerald Ford and Frank Sinatra drives, on your way past the Betty Ford Clinic, you'll know you've come to the right part of the world.

Palm Springs is a curiosity because it is, when you get right down to it, as inhospitable a plot of desert as you'll ever come across. And yet we love the place—though not wisely and too well. It's an area with history, albeit much of it little known and poorly kept. As with Los Angeles itself, history is of little interest to those who go to Palm Springs to take the waters, sit in the sun and play golf and tennis. Few know, for instance, that the area was practically unheard of before the turn of the century. What's called Palm Springs must certainly have looked rather odd back in 1907, when a squadron from the U.S. Army Camel Corps, surveying the Mojave Desert, came upon a series of natural hot springs, looking for all the world like oases out of *The Arabian Nights.*

Contributing Editor Deborah Sroloff, who's been going to Palm Springs since she was a small child, sums up the appeal of the place by saying, "It's a great place to do absolutely nothing. That's the point of Palm Springs. People who go there to shop and keep busy aren't using Palm Springs properly. The absence of activities is its greatest advantage. Since condos have kitchens, you don't even have to go to the bother of going to a restaurant. You can simply open a bag of potato chips, mix up some dip, sit by the pool and turn into a lizard. It's one of the best escapes in the world."

For others, it's an escape to a land of endless golf and tennis (sports that true Palm Springians play year-round, no matter how hot the weather). Interestingly, thanks to the number of golf courses built here over the past half century, it's one of the few places in the world where the average temperature is actually decreasing. Palm Springs is cooler now (though it certainly wouldn't be considered *cool*) than it was 50 years ago. For those who don't want to sit by the pool turning into oversized Pop Tarts, it's a land where you can empty your mind delving into the zen of tennis, golf, hiking, biking and nature-watching. Despite the seeming barrenness of the desert, for many this is Xanadu incarnate.

And for those who crave more urban pursuits, it's not a wasteland. There is shopping, of course, along North Palm Canyon Drive and nearby El Paseo, in a wide assortment of stores, primarily branches of posh places in Beverly Hills and West Palm Beach. There are cultural activities, centered around the Desert Musuem and the Bob Hope Cultural Center. There are plenty of (air-conditioned) movie theaters. And for those who can't stay still, even in the soothing desert sun, there are places to see and things to do. There are even restaurants to dine in, though your chances of dining well are, as a rule, limited (and we're being kind).

RESTAURANTS

Even the chains don't seem to be quite up to par in Palm Springs. Is it our imagination, or is the onion-ring brick served at the Palm Springs branch of Tony Roma's even oilier than it is at other Tony Roma's? And why is the salad bar at the Palm Desert Chart House so much skimpier than the norm? It speaks volumes that when Sonny Bono's deep-fried Italian cooking couldn't make it in L.A., he moved his operation to Indian Avenue, where he not only wound up with a hit restaurant but was elected mayor for his trouble. We've rarely eaten more overcooked enchiladas than the ones we've tried at Las Casuelas Nuevas, or worse pasta than at Tutti Gusti's in Palm Desert, or less-inspired Continental cooking than Eveleen's. The general rule concerning Palm Springs is that if you want to eat well, go to the market, take the food back to your

condo, and cook it yourself; you certainly couldn't do worse than many of the restaurants, and you'll have no one to blame but yourself. Still, despite all this caviling, we've found some pretty good food in Palm Springs—and in a few places, some very good food. You just have to know which sand dune to look behind.

12/20 Ajeti's House of Lamb

68784 Grove St., Cathedral City
(619) 328-7518
ALBANIAN
Open Tues.-Sat. 11:30 a.m.-2:30 p.m. & 5:30 p.m.-10 p.m. Cards: AE, MC, V.

Finding an Albanian restaurant anywhere in America is quite a surprise; finding one in the desert (it's a branch of another Ajeti's in Hermosa Beach) is astonishing. This bustling storefront restaurant describes itself, quite properly, as "A Curious Adventure." And indeed it is—and not one for those who don't love lamb. Shkodra is roast leg of lamb slow-cooked for six hours; the Tirana Treat is a baked lamb shoulder; the Toska Experience combines shkodra with a spiced-lamb dish called elbasan. With the Lamb Combo, you get a variety of lamb dishes along with cabbage, beans, vegetable soup, salad, sautéed vegetables, yogurt, brown rice and pita bread. There actually are several chicken and vegetarian dishes as well, but lamb is the name of the game. Dinner for two, with beer, costs about $40.

11/20 Las Casuelas

368 N. Palm Canyon Dr., Palm Springs
(619) 325-3213
MEXICAN
Open Mon.-Fri. 10:30 a.m.-10 p.m., Sat.-Sun. 10:30 a.m.-11 p.m. Cards: MC, V.

Tourists may flock to the more glamorous and popular Nuevas and Terraza branches of Las Casuelas, but the original branch in the heart of Palm Springs is where locals go who are more interested in enjoying a good Mexican dinner than a lively social scene. It doesn't look like much, and it doesn't serve margaritas (just wine and a great selection of beers), but the small kitchen turns out respectable Mexican home cooking (far better than the slop served at the trendier Casuelas branches), with an emphasis on such Cal-Mex standards as enchiladas, burritos, tostadas and tacos. It's all as tasty and satisfying as it is simple and inexpensive—a Palm Springs institution undoubtedly worth a visit. Also owned by the Delgado family is the nearby Las Casuelas Terraza (222 South Palm Canyon Drive, 619-325-2794), one of the busiest restaurants in town. Its menu and quality level are almost identical to those of the third branch, Las Casuelas Nuevas—which means it serves garden-variety Mexican food. About $20 for dinner for two, with beer.

9/20   Las Casuelas Nuevas
70050 Hwy. 111, Rancho Mirage
(619) 328-8844
Mexican
Open Mon.-Fri. 11 a.m.-10 p.m., Sat. 4 p.m.-10 p.m., Sun. 10 a.m.-10 p.m. Cards: AE, MC, V.

After you check in with the befuddled hostess at the hopelessly mobbed reception desk, you'll find yourself facing a potential two-hour wait on weekends. If your idea of a good time is getting plowed on margaritas, while being serenaded by mariachis, chances are you won't mind the wait. Eventually, you'll find yourself being waited on by an enthusiastic team of overburdened young women, who proudly serve food that can be both pretty good and pretty bad. You'll also be entertained by the attractive, tanned crowd, many of whom seem to know one another from L.A. Las Cas (as its legions of loyal fans call it) is qutie a handsome place, with a pleasant outdoor terrace and a honeycomb of rooms decorated in early casa. All the standards are offered here: chiles rellenos, tostadas, chimichangas, quesadillas, burritos, enchiladas and, of course, combination plates. Some of the house specialties, notably the fish and steak, can be failures. But all in all, and particularly considering the incredible numbers of people served here in the season, Las Cas serves decent Cal-Mex food—decent, as we say in the trade, "for Palm Springs." Dinner for two, with margaritas, will run about $30 if you order reasonably.

 Cuistot
73111 El Paseo, Palm Desert
(619) 340-1000
CALIFORNIAN/FRENCH
Open Tues.-Sat. 11:30 a.m.-2:30 p.m. & 6 p.m.-10 p.m., Sun. 6 p.m.-10 p.m. All major cards.

At Cuistot, in the midst of the El Paseo shopping district just above Highway 111, Californian/French cuisine has traveled surprisingly well from Los Angeles, thanks no doubt to chef Bernard Dervieux, a student of both Bocuse and Vergé who wound up in the desert by way of the Grand Champions Hotel. Dervieux does his work in what is basically an extended storefront, a double-sized space with a noisy dining room on one side and a quiet dining room on the other. By Palm Springs standards, the menu is downright audacious. The dinner appetizers dash madly from tuna sashimi with a daikon and Napa cabbage salad, through crabcakes with a mâche and baby-frisée salad, to salmon cured in the style of Bocuse (with lemon, herbs and olive oil), all the way to lobster-filled ravioli in a truffle sauce. Main courses are similarly eclectic: Chinese-style duck in a black-currant-and-apricot sauce, sautéed veal chops with wild mushrooms and roasted garlic, wild salmon in a ginger-and-chervil sauce. The dishes can be remarkably flavorful and refined, though we've noticed a penchant for sweetening things that may be a concession to desert taste buds. Still, we can offer Cuistot the high accolade of stating that it would do just fine in Santa Monica, which is no small praise for a restaurant in the middle of the desert. Dinner for two, with wine, costs about $110.

12/20   Cunard's
78045 Calle Cadiz, La Quinta
(619) 564-4443
FRENCH/CONTINENTAL
Open daily 5 p.m.-10 p.m. All major cards.

Cunard's, which sits at the eastern end of the Coachella Valley, close to the La Quinta Resort, serves grand food in a grand setting, complete with blazing fireplaces, books lining the shelves, bric-a-brac galore and service from a bygone era. The restaurant is built within a massive 1930s villa, a former home on three and a half acres that's been transformed into one of the desert's finest Continental restaurants. Cunard's is named for owner Robert Cunard, a restaurateur who ran places in Northern California and Honolulu before settling in Palm Springs. He's brought the desert the sort of classically romantic restaurant you go to to eat cornmeal blini with a dollop of beluga caviar, corn chowder garnished with shrimp and lobster, charred chilis filled with a quartet of cheeses, a wide assortment of pastas, salmon cooked in parchment, grilled duck with a pear-and-ginger sauce, free-range chicken with a peach-and-pecan chutney. In other words, food with one foot in the past and one in the present, well prepared and, we should add, significantly priced. One does not eat cheaply at this end of the Valley—being 45 minutes east of Palm Springs proper doesn't lower prices one bit. Dinner for two, with wine, will set you back $130 or so.

9/20   Dar Maghreb
42300 Bob Hope Dr., Rancho Mirage
(619) 568-9486
MOROCCAN
Open nightly 6 p.m.-11 p.m. Cards: DC, MC, V.

Unless you're in the mood for playing Arabian Nights, you'd be better off eating in your condo, for Dar Maghreb demands an excess of involvement from anyone who isn't primed for an evening of fun, fun, fun. Be ready to settle in for the evening—you've arrived at an event, not just a dinner. You'll be seated at low couches in one of the ornate Moroccan-palace rooms, surrounded by businessmen from Banning, weekend tourists and lively birthday-party groups. Although the food isn't overwhelming, it's a pleasant experience to share with a group with a good sense of humor. The meal starts with a ritualistic cleansing of the hands, essential since you'll be eating with your fingers. A good lentil soup arrives first, followed by marinated vegetables and cucumber with yogurt. Onward to the best item on the fixed-price menu, b'stilla, that sweet, nutty pie filled with bite-sized pieces of chicken. The main course (choice of squab, quail, rabbit, lemon chicken and three different lambs) is served with a couscous that can be too moist and lacking in its native spiciness. If you're not comatose after all that, you'll finish your feast with baklava, fruit, nuts, dates and refreshing mint tea. During the evening, belly dancers entertain and encourage guests to slip tips into their scanty costumes. Also costumed, but more conservatively, are the exceedingly kind waiters. German wines are recommended to accompany the slightly sweet, heavy food, advice we

heartily endorse. About $40 per person, with wine.

8/20   Eveleen's
664 N. Palm Canyon Dr., Palm Springs
(619) 325-4766
FRENCH/CONTINENTAL
Open Wed.-Sun. 6 p.m.-10 p.m. Cards: AE, MC, V.

"We never advertise," Eveleen's owner told us a couple of years ago. "All our customers come to us through referrals and recommendations." Since we had found the restaurant because of a full-page ad in a local magazine, we thought this a bad start to our meal. And sure enough, things got worse from there. Eveleen herself came over to our table to explain her specials, one of which she called "Jackson Pollock," a dish of pollock fish that was shredded like pasta and served in cucumber nests. Like much modern art, it was not a dish one easily warmed to—tasteless slivers of fish sitting in cucumber nests atop a nearly frozen sauce. If Jackson Pollock were alive, he could have sued. Eveleen also told us she had found a recipe in Spain for "baked steak tartare in a pastry shell." What arrived would have caused a revolution—overcooked hamburger in greasy pastry accompanied by bone-dry mashed potatoes, a genuinely inedible dish. Clearly, we've had very bad luck at Eveleen's, though trusted friends assure us they've had fine meals here. Dinner for two, with wine, is about $100.

11/20   Kiyosaku
456 N. Palm Canyon Dr., Palm Springs
(619) 327-6601
JAPANESE/SUSHI
Open Mon.-Tues. & Thurs.-Sat. 11:30 a.m.-2 p.m. & 5:30 p.m.-10:30 p.m., Sun. 5:30 p.m.-10:30 p.m. Cards: MC, V.

Kiyosaku reopened after a devastating fire that left it little more than a shell. Luckily, though the building was totaled, the spirit of the place remained intact. This popular but unpretentious Japanese restaurant occupies a space that once belonged to a Norwegian smorgasbord, which explained the pseudo-log cabin walls that were the restaurant's hallmark before it went up in flames. Otherwise this was and is a straightforward, respectable Japanese restaurant, complete with minimalist decor and a small sushi bar.

The menu lists all the standards (yakitori, chicken teriyaki, tempura) and a few more unusual dishes, such as salmon yaki (salmon cooked in butter), asparagus beef (thin layers of beef rolled around asparagus) and a Japanese bouillabaisse. The bouillabaisse is wan and bland, but everything else here is very good, particularly the beef teriyaki (which practically melts in your mouth), the fresh, tasty sushi and the boat dinner, a Japanese extravaganza for two that includes delicious shrimp and vegetable tempura, scallops, flavorful crab and clams, and chicken and beef kushi kebabs. Dinner comes to about $60 for two, with sake or Japanese beer.

10/20 The Nest

75188 Hwy. 111, Indian Wells
(619) 346-2314
ITALIAN/CONTINENTAL
Open nightly 5:30 p.m.-10:30 p.m. Cards: MC, V.

The Nest serves an odd mixture of Italian and French, with a little Swiss thrown in just for fun. Diners sit in a cluttered room filled with marble-topped bistro tables, Cinzano umbrellas hanging from the ceiling, French memorabilia, Swiss posters and Italian flags. The menu is equally eclectic, running from linguine with clam sauce to mahi mahi to beef bourguignonne. The kitchen seems most comfortable with the Italian dishes, particularly the house specialty of cannelloni stuffed with veal and spinach. Fresh fish, generally prepared à la meunière, is also a good bet, for those who aren't bored to death by the idea of the stuff. Portions are hearty; dinners are served with monstrous kettles of watery minestrone soup (the opposite of the old Woody Allen joke about how the food was terrible and the portions were so small). The wine list is all but nonexistent, but a carafe of house red is drinkable, more or less, and suits this homey, and homely, cuisine. The price is about $40 for two, with wine.

Otani—A Garden Restaurant

1000 Tahquitz Way, Palm Springs
(619) 327-6700
JAPANESE
Open Tues.-Fri. 11 a.m.-3 p.m. & 5 p.m.-11 p.m., Sat.-Sun. 5 p.m.-11 p.m. All major cards.

Otani looks for all the world like a shogun's palace—this truly is the proverbial mackerel in the middle of the Mojave. The high ceiling gives the effect of a Japanese gymnasium, with an assortment of activity areas scattered throughout the expanse: a sushi bar here, a tempura bar there, a yakitori bar in between, with teppanyaki tables shoring up the back wall and private dining rooms off in one corner. It's interesting to note that even though the floor is made of slate and the surfaces are marble and granite, Otani is still fairly quiet; the noise gets lost somewhere in that high ceiling. You can sit in any of the individual areas, or you can sit in the dining room and order dishes from either or both rooms, definitely a winning strategy. The salmon-skin salad is wonderful, with a good deal of salmon adhering to the skin. The California rolls are among the finest we've tasted, plump with avocado and crab. Along with all the usual tempura items are tempura calamari, lobster tail, garlic, jumbo clams and potatoes, a sort of Japanese-style french fry. The yakitoris—grilled skewers of tiny quail eggs wrapped in bacon, chicken chunks interspersed with green onions, beef intertwined with asparagus—alone are worth the trip. For dessert, the kitchen makes a messy thing out of vanilla ice cream, fudge cake and chocolate sauce—just a little reminder that you are still in Palm Springs. Dinner for two, with sake, is $70.

12/20 Ristorante Mamma Gina

73705 El Paseo, Palm Desert
(619) 568-9898
ITALIAN
Open nightly 6 p.m.-11 p.m. All major cards.

Palm Desert isn't so much a city as a string of very smart shopping malls that flow one into the other. Parking, as you can imagine, is quite convenient in Palm Desert, but restaurants have never really been the town's strong suit—at least not until Ristorante Mamma Gina opened. The first truly significant thing about Mamma Gina is that it's a branch (in fact, the only branch) of a restaurant in Florence. As in Florence, Italy. The second truly significant thing is that the food is actually very good. And in an area where Italian food generally means pizza and spaghetti with red sauce, this is no small accomplishment. The menu compromised little in its journey from Florence to Palm Desert, though the man at the front desk had forgotten all about the warmth found in Italian restaurants—we were not happy with his little tale about how he had no reservation for us (which we had made and reconfirmed) because our hotel had canceled it; an odd thing to say, given that our hotel had no inkling of our dining plans. Though the setting isn't overly Italian, the kitchen turns out such Tuscan specialties as deep-fried mozzarella, spinach sautéed in the Florentine manner (with lots of garlic), wonderful deep-fried artichokes, air-dried beef (bresaola) from the village of Valtellina, squid-ink-blackened ravioli stuffed with lobster, outstanding marrow-filled osso buco in a rich meat sauce, carpaccio topped with arugula and slices of Reggiano Parmesan and, of course, bistecca alla fiorentina, that grilled chunk of marvelous beef that is the triumph of Florentine cooking. The gelato is made on the premises, which is definitely unique. Mamma Gina has done more than its share of moving the desert's Italian food from lasagne to gamberoni. Dinner for two, with wine, costs about $100.

⑭ The Ritz-Carlton Dining Room
68900 Frank Sinatra Dr.,
Rancho Mirage
(619) 321-8282
FRENCH
Open nightly 6 p.m.-10 p.m. All major cards.
  Along with upping the ante in terms of the quality of Palm Springs hotels, The Ritz-Carlton has also done quite a bit for the state of the desert's restaurants—thanks to the Dining Room, the food scene has taken a quantum leap toward bona fide seriousness, even high respectability. An assortment of restaurants can be found in The Ritz-Carlton, all under the aegis of executive chef Jean-Pierre Dubray, from the cafés that feed guests at the pool and the tennis courts, to the Lobby Lounge, which offers a traditional English afternoon tea, and ultimately to the generically named Dining Room, which serves exceedingly tony meals to the hotel's guests (who have first preference for reservations) and Palm Springians (who often have to book a table two weeks or more in advance). As Palm Springs food goes, this is serious stuff, served in an atmosphere of great formality; tennis togs simply won't do. The menu features all the right culinary buzzwords—wild mushrooms, zucchini flowers, field greens, free-range chicken and young Californian vegetables, all of which come together in some

very impressive dishes: a delicate appetizer mousse of zucchini, red pepper and cauliflower; an assortment of smoked salmon, eel and sturgeon; a fricassée of crayfish and scallops (with baby carrots and chive butter, no less); a cassoulet of escargots, wild mushrooms, basil and garlic; a breathtaking lobster casserole with morels and asparagus; roasted air-dried duck, served with a sweet but not cloying sauce of pineapple, orange and ginger. The prices are high, though not as high as they might be in L.A. The experience is remarkable. And the influence should be significant—duck à l'orange soda pop may never be an acceptable dish in Palm Springs restaurants again. Dinner for two, with wine, costs a serious $135 or so, but it's money well spent.

12/20 Shame on the Moon
68-805 Hwy. 111, Cathedral City
(619) 324-5515
CONTINENTAL
Open Mon.-Sat. 11:30 a.m.-2:30 p.m. & 6 p.m.-10 p.m. Cards: AE, MC, V.
  Basically a small but attractively decorated storefront restaurant on one of Palm Springs's less attractive streets, Shame on the Moon serves California-tinged Continental cuisine. Shame on the Moon (a name taken, perhaps, from a Bob Seger song?) is popular with the younger members of the local gay community, who imbue the place with a pleasantly hip air. Service is chatty and friendly, a nice break from the stuffy tuxedoed formality that afflicts so many Coachella Valley restaurants. The food is functional, simple and quite tasty: baked Brie with almonds and apples, pasta primavera, lemon chicken, veal in a mustard sauce. There aren't a lot of surprises here—except that the food is good, and you'll feel as if you're eating in a real restaurant, rather than a tourist-town tiger pit. Dinner for two, with wine, costs about $60.

11/20 Le Vallauris
385 W. Tahquitz-McCallum Way,
Palm Springs
(619) 325-5059
FRENCH
Open Sun.-Thurs. 11:30 a.m.-2:30 p.m. & 6 p.m.-9 p.m., Fri.-Sat. 11:30 a.m.-2:30 p.m. & 6 p.m.-10 p.m. All major cards.
  Le Vallauris continues to look like a slightly shabby private club, despite the fact that it

hasn't been one for quite some time. The original concept failed, and democracy triumphed—now all can come to watch the just-retired clientele greeting one another, enjoying the still-attractive dining room and the attentive, professional service. The blackboard menu changes daily according to the chef's whims and market availability; you can often find onion soup, escargots, spinach salad and variations on duck and veal. We've been disappointed here with a sort of conservative nouvelle cuisine that's well intentioned but tends to be poorly presented and unevenly prepared. At worst, you'll enjoy the lovely ambience and the good wine list—until you're shocked back to reality by the bill. About $140 for dinner for two, with wine.

8/20 Wally's Desert Turtle

71775 Hwy. 111, Rancho Mirage
(619) 568-9321
FRENCH
Open nightly 6 p.m.-11 p.m.; fashion show lunch Fri. 11 a.m.-1 p.m. (except in summer). Cards: AE, MC, V.

If you're really dying to spend a desert evening in an ostentatious, nouveau-riche decor, being served by tuxedoed young men who try to pass themselves off as waiters, then here's your chance. There seems to be more of a caste system here than in Calcutta; if you're an unknown, you'll be shuttled off to outer Siberia—a dark, tranquil annex that's actually not the worst of places to sit. The desirables and the known chatter gaily among themselves, seeing and being seen in the main room, which is decorated in the distinctive style of a garish resort hotel. In either case, you'll pay upward of $65 apiece for the opportunity to eat food that's second-rate at best. True, there are one or two decent items, such as the tasty puréed mussel and fennel soup. And there are dishes whose worst crime is that they're boring—for example, veal Oscar, sweetbreads à l'orange and veal with morels. But we've been served far too many mistakes to justify the high prices. As is so often the case at mediocre restaurants, the desserts can be delicious—but a chocolate-marble mousse, no matter how good, cannot salvage a bad meal. If you decide not to arrive in your Rolls, the valet will make a statement regarding your social status by parking your car across the street. Count on $130 or more for dinner for two, with wine.

QUICK BITES

Bit of Country

418 S. Indian Ave., Palm Springs
(619) 325-5154
Open daily 5:45 a.m.-3 p.m. No cards.

What could be finer than to sit on Bit of Country's sunny, cheerful patio on a quiet desert morning having some decadent strawberry french toast with your morning paper? You won't be the only one with that good idea, so expect a wait on the weekends. The food is hearty and homey coffee-shop fare, and most all of it is good, particularly the home-baked biscuits served with pan gravy or jam. Breakfast will run about $12 for two, lunch slightly more.

Elmer's Pancake and Steak House

1030 E. Palm Canyon Dr., Palm Springs
(619) 327-8419
Open daily 7 a.m.-10 p.m. Cards: MC, V.

Everyone who loves pancakes and waffles wanders over to Elmer's for a generous, inexpensive home-cooked breakfast. It's an early-morning cultural event, and by 8:30 a.m. on weekends the place is jammed with folks that could be mistaken for a group at a Midwestern church social. But a chance to get at the date-nut pancakes, blueberry waffles, strawberry crêpes, Oregon-cheese blintzes and ten specialty omelets makes it worth the wait. You can also get lunch or dinner, but breakfast here is your best bet. About $12 to $14 for breakfast for two.

Louise's Pantry

124 S. Palm Canyon Dr., Palm Springs
(619) 325-5124
Open daily 7 a.m.-9:45 p.m. No cards.

Like Las Cas, Louise's is one of Palm Springs's great traditions. It doesn't look like much—a small, homey, yellow coffee shop—but it dishes up good cooking that's just like Mom's. In fact, there's a fleet of Moms serving you, advising you and making sure you clean your plate. You'll get decent, reliable, simple food, all presented in an honest but uninspiring environment. No liquor, but plenty of tea and coffee. Breakfast will run about $12 for two, lunch a bit more.

Nate's Delicatessen

100 S. Indian Ave., Palm Springs
(619) 325-3506
Open daily 7:30 a.m.-8:30 p.m. Cards: MC, V.
Nate's is classic deli. It has the requisite plain, coffee-shop decor, and its huge menu lists all the standards, from corned beef to kreplach to chopped liver. Locals and tourists alike love Nate's, and they have good reason: it's just about the only deli game in town. Fans of the Carnegie will find the food lackluster, but the portions are generous and service is unusually friendly. About $16 for lunch for two.

The Wheel Inn

I-10, Cabazon exit
(619) 849-7012
Open daily 24 hours. No cards.
There's hardly a traveler in the West who hasn't seen the dinosaurs along Interstate 10 in Cabazon. Along with Hadley's (a dried-fruit haven) and the Morongo Indian Bingo Hall, the dinosaurs are the most significant landmarks along this notably blank stretch of road. They were built by Claude Bell, owner of The Wheel Inn, the truck stop that stands slightly to the left of Claude's dinosaurs. One of them is a brontosaurus named Dinny, which is reputed to be the largest faux dinosaur in America; it's even been featured in Coke commercials, rock videos and *Pee-Wee's Big Adventure*. Next to the brontosaurus stands a rather fearsome tyrannosaurus rex. A woolly mammoth is planned for the future. In the great tradition of America's roadside attractions, the dinosaurs are actually bait to lure you in to The Wheel Inn, which is known far and wide as a quintessential California truck stop. It's not as massive as Little Wyoming, America, a truck stop so immense it has its own post office. But The Wheel Inn does feature all the necessary amenities of truck-stop life—a large tool section, a sizable display of turquoise belt buckles, a great country-western jukebox, sassy waitresses and relentlessly filling food, served 24 hours a day. For us, seeing the dinosaurs is really just a convenient excuse for going to The Wheel Inn for its truly awesome desserts. Every one of them—coconut cream, banana cream, rhubarb and raisin pies; berry, cherry, peach and apple cobblers; strawberry shortcakes of prehistoric dimensions; egg custards; bread puddings—is homemade. The dinosaurs outside look as if they got so big eating The Wheel Inn's pies.

HOTELS

Please note that the prices quoted below are for rooms and suites in-season, which runs roughly from Thanksgiving to the end of April (though each hotel defines "in-season" a bit differently). Almost every hotel in the desert lowers its rates considerably (sometimes more than half) in the off-season, which is why the early fall and late spring are many savvy travelers' favorite times to visit Palm Springs.

 Doubletree Resort

155 S. Vellardo Rd., Vista Chino at Landau, Palm Springs, 92263
(619) 322-7000
How curious—a desert resort opened by a cruise line. Yet that's exactly what the former Desert Princess is, a 345-acre all-suite resort with an eleven-lake, eighteen-hole golf course and ten tennis courts, home to the Bernie Kopell Celebrity Tennis Classic. Most of the rooms face the golf course, though golf isn't the driving force here; this is actually more a convention resort, with a dozen meeting rooms encompassing more than 15,000 feet of meeting space, including the 7,500-square-foot Royal Ballroom. Although Doubletree purchased the place in 1989, the decor and food are still strikingly reminiscent of what you might find aboard a Princess cruise ship, except chances are good you'll won't get seasick.

Suites: $280-$750. Rates drop off-season.

 Hyatt Grand Champions

44600 Indian Wells Ln.,
Indian Wells, 92210
(619) 341-1000
The name is actually a bit of an understatement, for just about everything done at this all-suite grand resort is done in a championship way. The tennis stadium, for instance, seats 10,500 spectators. Of the other twelve tennis courts, players have a choice of grass, clay or hard. There are two eighteen-hole golf courses, designed by Ted Robinson. There's even a restaurant with a menu created by Wolfgang Puck. Rooms range from large,

pleasant split-level parlor suites all the way up to two-bedroom garden villas. The only downside is that Grand Champions is far from Palm Springs proper, which may disappoint those who prefer shopping to golf.

Suites: $250-$1,200. Rates drop off-season.

La Mancha Private Pool Villas and Court Club

444 Avenida Caballeros,
Palm Springs, 92262
(619) 323-1773

At La Mancha, owner Ken Irwin has created an exclusive, rather plastic club that springs up like an oasis in a vacant lot in the middle of the desert (actually, it's just a short walk to downtown Palm Springs). Quiet and private—so much so that it's impossible to get in or out of the gates without permission—La Mancha is marked by oversized villas done in a Hollywoodish decor. They may not be to everyone's liking, but there's no denying the sheer opulence of the place. Each Mediterranean villa comes complete with a theater-style video-screening room, a private pool with a European-style wave generator, a Jacuzzi and a sunken tennis court (to keep errant breezes from ruining your serve). Other villas make do with just a private Jacuzzi or pool. If Palm Springs' restaurants don't thrill you, you can arrange to have dinner prepared for you in the comfort of your own villa. La Mancha is just across the street from the new Palm Springs Convention Center, so it's an excellent place to unwind after a long day of speeches and seminars.

Villas: one bedroom, $200-$600; two bedrooms, $270-$695; three bedrooms, $345-$765. Rates drop considerably off-season.

Marriott's Rancho Las Palmas Resort

41000 Bob Hope Dr.,
Rancho Mirage, 92270
(619) 568-2727

Marriott's Rancho Las Palmas is a modern-day re-creation of a Spanish village, a reasonably successful attempt on the part of the Marriott Corporation to disguise that distinctive Marriott look. Guests are housed in attractive hacienda-ettes circling the 27-hole golf course. But despite the San Miguel de Allende look of the place, all the resort amenities one could wish for are in place: 25 tennis courts (with video monitors to help you improve your game), two pools, hydrotherapy baths, terraces, restaurants, meeting rooms and friendly people—everything but privacy. With 465 rooms, it's nearly impossible to ensure intimacy for those who want to really get away from it all. But as large hotels go, the Marriott is among the desert's finest, simply in terms of its comfort, design and facilities.

Singles & doubles: $240-$260; suites: $475. Rates drop off-season.

Maxim's

285 N. Palm Canyon Dr.,
Palm Springs, 92262
(619) 322-9000

Maxim's looks more than anything like a desert-style update of a Mayan temple, except for the oddity of its location at the busiest intersection in downtown Palm Springs. It's part of the elegant new Desert Fashion Plaza, which makes it a great choice for diehard shoppers; you don't even have to step out onto the street to drop until you shop. Maxim's is an all-suite hotel—the basic room is actually a 600-square-foot miniapartment, complete with balcony, living room, dining area, bar, marble bath, bedroom with a king-size bed, and contemporary furnishings that are (somewhat surprisingly) both tasteful and comfortable. You'll have to go elsewhere for tennis and golf, but there's a large pool and a complete health spa (weight room, sauna, Jacuzzi and aerobics classes). And Maxim's does have all the advantages of being in the heart of town, which means there are loads of restaurants, shops, movie theaters and amusements (including the Desert Museum) just a short stroll away from your room.

Suites: $150-$450. Rates drop off-season.

Palm Springs Spa Hotel

100 N. Indian Ave., Palm Springs,
92262
(619) 325-1461

We love the Palm Springs Spa for purely sentimental reasons—it's a grand reminder of what Palm Springs used to be like in the days before the inclusive megaresort hotel; and it reminds us as well that there really is a spring somewhere beneath Palm Springs. Objectively speaking, the Spa Hotel is large and functional; the architecture is a classic example of '60s commercial design, complete with metal sculptures/fountains theoretically bringing mineral waters up from the underground springs. Most guests don't spend much time indoors; they're out on the tennis courts, in lounge chairs around the pool, taking the waters or using the spa. There's a definite Miami Beach look to the crowd; many of the visitors are silver-haired and (too?) friendly. Upon arrival, you're directed to the sauna, steam bath, eucalyptus-inhalation room, mineral Jacuzzi baths and cooling room, and then to meet your masseuse or masseur. Hotel guests get a discount on the spa facilities (which are open to the public).

Doubles: $135-$205; suites: $205-$900. Rates drop off-season.

Pepper Tree Inn

645 N. Indian Ave., Palm Springs, 92262

(619) 325-9124

The Pepper Tree calls itself a bed-and-breakfast, one of the few to be found in Palm Springs. Unlike the traditional bed-and-breakfast, however, this is not an old house converted into an inn. Most of the Pepper Tree's rooms are in one of Palm Springs' oldest motels; many of the modest but comfortable rooms, in fact, feature both kitchens and fireplaces, amenities not found in newer resort hotels. Rooms in the newer addition are a little brighter and more contemporary, if a bit less charming. Located just a few blocks from downtown Palm Springs, the Pepper Tree has an excellent location-to-price (and comfort-to-price) ratio—this is probably the best budget inn in town. Extras include a simple but generous breakfast, a pool, Jacuzzi and laundry room for extended stays.

Doubles: $60-$80. Rates drop off-season.

La Quinta Golf and Tennis Resort

49499 Eisenhower Dr., La Quinta, 92253

(619) 564-4111

Almost certainly the most elegant establishment in the eastern Coachella Valley, La Quinta Golf and Tennis Resort looks like a set from the old Zane Grey Theater. Restored to its original 1926 rustic elegance, the Spanish/Southwestern architecture is reminiscent of similar establishments in Taos or Santa Barbara, making the other, newer desert resorts seem almost pretentious by contrast. Guests stay in Spanish-style cottages scattered across the grounds. Many of the villas are draped with flowering vines, and pathways are bordered with bright poppies, petunias and pansies. A 36-hole championship golf course winds through the Santa Rosa mountain baseline, and the seventeen-court tennis facility is the home of one of the top men's professional tournaments. With its casual dining room and bar (adjacent to the oversized pool and whirlpool), this complex has been a haven for Hollywood stars for decades; the hotel toasts one famous guest, Frank Capra (he wrote eight films here), with a meeting room named in his honor. The drive from Palm Springs proper to La Quinta is a long one (close to 45 minutes), but once there, you won't want to leave.

Doubles: $195-$370; suites: $850-$1,800. Rates drop off-season.

The Ritz-Carlton

68900 Frank Sinatra Dr., Rancho Mirage, 92270

(619) 321-8282

Approaching The Ritz-Carlton in Rancho Mirage, driving up the manicured drive from Highway 111 and its endless sweep of chain restaurants and shopping malls, one has the ineluctable sense of being on the Yellow Brick Road to Oz. You are, after all, in the middle of an inhospitable desert, which you can see in all its dryness between the greens of the golf courses, made verdant by water piped in from the Colorado River. In a landscape filled with excessively ornate architectural nonsense—steakhouses that seem to grow out of the bare rock and discos complete with erupting volcanos—The Ritz-Carlton stands out as being almost unreal. It sits atop a 625-foot-high plateau in the rugged hills of the Santa Rosa Mountains, in the midst of a 310-acre wildlife sanctuary, where bighorn sheep can be seen roaming free. It looks like a slightly smaller version of the palace at Versailles. And this doesn't end when you walk through the vaulted marble portico. Outside, the temperature may linger in the low 100s. Inside, all is cool and agonizingly tasteful. Fine nineteenth-century art and sculptures line the halls. Polished wood and oiled leather abound. The couches in the lobby are so comfortable that we had to keep reminding ourselves that we also had a room to lounge in. The pool is large enough for a small armada, with a sweeping view of the valley beyond.

In a resort town with a number of good hotels but very few grand ones, The Ritz-Carlton stands out as the city's first truly deluxe model. Tennis courts, featuring an assortment of playable surfaces, are everywhere. You can walk from the hotel's manicured grounds to facilities that allow you to take Jeep rides or horseback-riding excursions through the wilderness. And, as befits a truly first-class hotel, there are worlds within worlds at The Ritz-Carlton. On one of the upper stories, separated from the rest of the hotel by its own elevator key, is The Ritz-Carlton Club, a private floor built around a central lounge, where hors d'oeuvres and cocktails are served (at no extra charge) all day and night. The club also has its own concierge and rooms equipped with VCRs. And the restaurants are exceptionally good. All in all, The Ritz-Carlton is so grand that descending the hill into Palm Springs can be something of a letdown. Gucci and Louis Vuitton seem plain by comparison.

Singles & doubles: $255-$375; suites: $550-$1,600. Rates drop off-season.

 **Two Bunch Palms**
67425 Two Bunch Palms Trail, Desert Hot Springs, 92240
(619) 329-8791
No casual visitors are allowed into Two Bunch Palms. No children are permitted. Although tourist-rich Palm Springs is only a twenty-minute drive away, few gawkers make their way to the far less hospitable reaches of Desert Hot Springs to linger outside the guarded gate. Two Bunch remains one of the desert's great secrets, a place more people have heard about than actually been to. And with only 44 villas and no golf course (though there are tennis courts), the clientele is understandably select. Many go to Two Bunch to get away from the ubiquitous Industry chat at Morton's and Spago. In the pools at Two Bunch, you don't hear agents from CAA screaming about how they want a percentage of the gross, not the net. You hear nothing

but the wind in the tamarisk trees and the beating of your own financially successful heart. There's no room service and no social director putting together a luau night. At Two Bunch, you're blissfully on your own. You can loosen up those tight limbs with obscure massage techniques ($60 per massage)—techniques with names like trager, jin shin do and aromatherapy—and you can luxuriate in a Roman-Celtic brush down or milk-and-honey facial. Al Capone built the place back in the late twenties, and you can stay in the main house he built, where his initials are engraved on a desk and a bullet hole is engraved in a mirror.

Doubles & suites: $98-$340. Rates do not vary seasonally.

NIGHTLIFE

Cecil's
Smoketree Shopping Center, Sunrise Ave. & Hwy. 111, Palm Springs
(619) 320-4202
Open Thurs.-Sun. 8 p.m.-2 a.m. Cover varies. All major cards.

America's comedy mania has reached the desert, and Cecil's has jumped right in to satisfy the giggling hordes with two stand-up comedy nights, on Thursday and Sunday. As with all comedy clubs, you take your chances: some of the performers can be great, some can be annoying as hell. Friday and Saturday nights are devoted to dance fever, in two adjacent rooms—one showcases live rock, pop and soul oldies, the other recorded Top 40 tunes. Once your eyes adjust to the dim lighting, you'll be able to appreciate the great fashion show. But you won't be able to hold much of a conversation over the blaring music. Despite the noise level, there's an attempt at elegance, with tuxedoed hosts and cocktail waitresses in slinky gowns.

SIGHTS

Date Shopping
No visit to Palm Springs is complete without paying proper homage to the date palms that gave the area its name. The area is thick

with palm trees, and from those palm trees come dates—particularly medjool dates, which are among the best in the world. Highway 111 is lined with date shops as you head east from Palm Springs, the best of which are Shields Date Gardens (80225 Highway 111, Indio; 619-347-0996), Jensen's Date & Citrus Gardens (80653 Highway 111, Indio; 619-347-3897) and the self-proclaimed "world-famous" Hadley's Fruit Orchards (Interstate 10, Cabazon; 800-472-5672), which is easy to find—just look for several dozen tourist buses parked in front.

Joshua Tree National Monument

I-10, Mecca
Open daily dawn-dusk. Admission free.

A wonderful day can be spent driving through Joshua Tree National Monument, an untouched expanse of high and low desert that is reached by taking Interstate 10 half an hour east of Palm Springs, getting off at the Twentynine Palms/Mecca exit. In the spring, the desert turns into a sea of wildflowers and blossoming Joshua trees, a gnarly cactus of unsurpassed beauty.

Living Desert Reserve

47900 S. Portola Ave., Palm Desert
(619) 346-5694
Open daily 9 a.m.-5 p.m. (closed in summer). Adults $5, children $2.

The Living Desert Reserve is one of our favorite desert escapes. In a single winter morning here, you'll be introduced to an aviary oasis, a variety of botanical gardens, several sleepy owls, clever educational exhibits, caged coyotes, one and a half miles of spectacular desert trails with snow-peaked mountains in the distance, red-tailed hawks, a family of longhorned mountain goats on their own little mountain, Cahuilla Indian history and slender male gazelles, looking quite festive wearing green garden hoses to protect their horns from damage in their inevitable tusslings with other males. You can spend happy hours here learning to appreciate the riches of desert life, in a natural habitat that makes the surrounding half-million-dollar condos look dramatically inappropriate by

contrast. Wear sturdy walking shoes, and if you're sun-sensitive, be sure to bring a hat.

Palm Springs Aerial Tramway

Hwy. 111 & Tramway Rd., Palm Springs
(619) 325-1391
Open in winter: Mon.-Fri. 10 a.m.-7:30 p.m., Sat.-Sun. 7:30 a.m.-9:15 p.m.; summer: Mon.-Fri. 10 a.m.-8:30 p.m., Sat.-Sun. 8:30 a.m.-10:15 p.m. Admission $14.95 adults, $9.95 children.

Two Swiss-made trams travel 12,800 feet in about fifteen minutes, depositing you in a tranquil mountain wilderness (once you make it past the tacky tourist concession stand). In winter, the snow-covered valley is splendid for cross-country skiing, snowshoe hiking and sledding. In summer, the refreshing coolness is perfect for hiking and picnics. If you're really desperate for something to do, the Miss Aerial Tramway competition is held every June; dogsled races are staged in March. You make the 5,873-foot vertical ascent accompanied by Vivaldi; the descent, by an enthusiastic Kenny Rogers. The Erector Set towers that support this tramway, the longest in the world, are surprisingly delicate-looking. The tram is no bargain, but it will give you a breath of cool mountain air and a clear perspective on Palm Springs a full mile below.

Palm Springs Desert Museum

101 Museum Dr., Palm Springs
(619) 325-7186
Open Tues.-Sun. 10 a.m.-4 p.m. Adults $4, children 6-17 $2, children under 6 free.

The ultra-contemporary architecture of the Desert Museum makes it look more like a modern hotel than a museum, which is appropriate for the well-endowed state of the arts here. The lobby is breezy and impressive, complete with Hiltonesque chandeliers. The exhibitions change frequently, and the permanent collection is rotated twice a year. You can tour the museum and view the natural-history dioramas that dramatize desert life, visit the Annenberg Theater to catch a lecture, film or concert, or see any of the traveling shows. There are two sculpture gardens and a gift shop, and all the wings bear famous names, including such unlikely artistic marriages as Sinatra and Disney.

SAN DIEGO

CALIFORNIA DREAMLAND

Real estate values have been shooting up in San Diego and its neighboring communities for good reason: everyone wants to live here. Who wouldn't? Its year-round sunshine is tempered by the cool Pacific, and within its boundaries are lovely beaches, beautiful back country and easy access to Mexico. It also has big-city advantages—a reasonable level of sophistication in hotels, restaurants, shops and "culture"—yet it isn't so big that you have to deal with terrible traffic and spreading urban blight. San Diego is a wonderful city as well for the vacationing athlete, particularly one who likes to surf, windsurf, run, walk on the beach or just throw a Frisbee around on the beach. It's also great for deep-sea fishing, sailing and hunting for authentic Mexican food and shopping bargains just over the nearby border. And, of course, there's the zoo, one of the country's best.

Another one of San Diego's must-sees is the new, much acclaimed Horton Plaza, a colorful, zany architectural gem that has helped immensely to revitalize downtown. Its design alone is worth a look, and the good shops and restaurants make it a mandatory stop. The recently restored surrounding area, dubbed the Gaslamp District, has a welcome touch of old-time charm. And the newly constructed, convention center is also breathing new life to the area by inspiring the construction of new hotels, restaurants and shops.

RESTAURANTS

10/20 Anthony's Star of the Sea Room
1360 N. Harbor Dr., San Diego
(619) 232-7408
SEAFOOD
Open nightly 5:30 p.m.-10:30 p.m. Cards: AE, MC, V.

It's been said of the better restaurants south of Los Angeles that it's more important for them to look good than to serve good food, and Anthony's is certainly a case in point. It looks great—a grand old waterfront palace filled with tuxedoed help and offering a marvelous view of San Diego's less-than-marvelous harbor. (This isn't San Francisco or Hong Kong, no matter which way you look at it.) But once you push past the opulent setting and the fussy service, you're left with food that is only a notch above the stuff usually found on fishermen's wharfs, at prices many notches above. Dishes tend to be dreadfully mucked up. Coquilles Veronique, for instance, features either scampi or crabs' legs cluttered with a white lobster sauce and grapes. The Far Eastern curry buries otherwise decent morsels of lobster, crab and shrimp beneath layers of chutney, coconut, peanuts, chives and hard-cooked egg. Petrale sole is stuffed with the same lobster, crab and shrimp, a trio of ingredients that are venerated here like the Three Horsemen of the Sea. Cooking like this makes the mild vulgarity of mesquite grilling seem positively pristine—smoky but at least clean-tasting. At least Anthony's is consistent; even if you dine here at five-year intervals, you are practically guaranteed that each experience will hardly differ from the last. Dinner for two, with wine, will cost a little over $100.

12/20 El Bizcocho
Rancho Bernardo Inn, 17550 Bernardo Oaks Dr., Rancho Bernardo
(619) 487-1611
FRENCH
Open Mon.-Thurs. 6 p.m.-10 p.m., Fri.-Sat. 6 p.m.-10:30 p.m., Sun. 10:30 a.m.-2:30 p.m. & 6 p.m.-10 p.m. All major cards.

El Bizcocho roughly translates as "hardtack," which is a plywoodlike biscuit carried by vaqueros and sailors on long journeys. But believe us, nothing as lowly as that would ever be allowed through the back door here. The cuisine is strictly of the haute French variety, although the restaurant's young chef, Thomas Dowling, manages to put some fresh spins on his dishes. We especially liked the terrine de volaille au basilac et poivrons rouges, a terrine of layered chicken, bell pepper, fresh basil and goat cheese, and a lovely dish of scallops with leeks, tarragon and anise baked in parchment. Lamb dishes, particularly the roast rack with fresh herbs, are very good, as are the beef dishes. And for those watching their waistlines, there's a cuisine minceur menu as well. Topping all this is an astounding wine list replete with 700 vintages. The must-have dessert is the wonderful hot chocolate soufflé. El Bizcocho is heroically scaled, and the elegant, romantic, mission-style room offers views of both the San Pasquale Mountains and an impeccably manicured golf course. The service is flawless. Dinner for two, with wine, can run from $100 to $120.

12/20 Chez Loma

1132 Loma Ave., Coronado
(619) 435-0661
FRENCH
Open Tues.-Fri. 11 a.m.-2 p.m. & 5:30 p.m.-10 p.m., Sat.-Sun. 5:30 p.m.-10 p.m. Cards: AE, MC, V.

Chez Loma, on Coronado Island just around the corner from the grand Hotel del Coronado (where the Duke of Windsor met the woman who caused him to give up the throne), is of that school of restaurants, found mostly around San Francisco, that are usually quartered in Victorian houses. The food is in the born-again French motif—not quite as light as nouvelle cuisine, not nearly as heavy as classic French. There are escargots niçoise, for instance—snails served provençale-style, simmered in white wine, garlic, tomatoes and herbs. In the brochette de St-Jacques, scallops and cucumbers are skewered and grilled, then served with a dipping sauce of garlic and saffron. The fine poulet braisé au Madeira, a half chicken in a sauce of Madeira wine and vermouth, is about as adventurous as the cooking gets at Chez Loma. The best thing here, aside from the marvelous goat-cheese dressing served on the salad, is the duck, perfectly crispy on the outside, moist on the inside and served with poivre vert (Madagascar green peppercorns) or à la Montmorency (with a sweet cherry port sauce and lingonberries). Dinner for two, with wine, costs about $70.

12/20 La Costa

Calle 7A No. 150, Tijuana
(011-5266) 85-31-24
MEXICAN/SEAFOOD
Open daily 11 a.m.-10 p.m. Cards: MC, V.

Although most gringos' perception of Mexican cooking doesn't even include seafood, it's everywhere in Mexico. After all, Mexico has thousands of miles of marvelous coastline that's teeming with it. And La Costa serves some of the best Mexican seafood we've ever encountered. Judging from the crowds that surge in and out of La Costa, its reputation is far from underground. Just around the corner from Tijuana's Jai Alai Frontón, La Costa offers its menu in both Spanish and English, but it never condescends to its many American customers—the food is always authentic, no matter what. The seafood is often rather bold in its presentation and a bit zany in its description. For instance, you can have your lobster (langosta) prepared in any of eight styles—"Watergate," "Hawaiian," "Seville," "New Burg" (sic) and so on. Oysters (ostiones) are prepared diabla ("she devil") and crilloa ("Creole Indian"). Ordering a meal at La Costa is a culinary crap shoot: you choose a likely sounding dish and hope for the best. But don't worry: it's hard to miss. Meals always begin with an appetizer of fried fish chunks, followed by a peppery fish soup. This is wisely followed by a seafood cocktail (go for the ceviche) and a choice of twenty fried-fish dishes, eighteen shrimp dishes and even frogs' legs (cooked "to taste"). Even if you don't order dessert, you'll be brought a cup of Kahlúa and cream. It's that kind of place. Dinner for two, with beer, will cost less than $30.

9/20 Crown and Coronet Rooms

Hotel del Coronado, 1500 Orange Ave., Coronado
(619) 435-6611
CONTINENTAL
Open Sun.-Fri. 7 a.m.-10 p.m., Sat. 7 a.m.-11 p.m. All major cards.

In an age of good hotel restaurants—places like The Dining Room at the Regent Beverly Wilshire and Checkers at the eponymous inn—the restaurants of the venerable Hotel del Coronado are a throwback to the great American tradition of mediocre (and worse) hotel cooking. Like the del Coronado itself, they *look* magnificent, especially the 33-foot-high ceiling in the Crown Room (which looks like the inside of a crown and is supposed to be the largest all-wooden edge-supported dome in the world—a claim we wouldn't dare question). But we will question the food, which is the sort of stuff we used to eat, somewhat begrudgingly, back in the '50s: dreadful rainbow trout in a bad amandine sauce, cooked to the point of absolute muck; wilted Cobb salad; cooked-forever prime rib served with rubbery Yorkshire pudding and a gravy that's mostly salt; and calf's liver à la lyonnaise that could double for shoe leather. The brunches are monstrously popular—don't even think of showing up without a reservation, made weeks in advance. Eating here is a tradition with many San Diegans; the food never changes, and they probably haven't noticed what it tastes like in years. Dinner for two, with wine, costs about $80.

 Dobson's
956 Broadway Circle, San Diego
(619) 231-6771
FRENCH
Open Mon.-Fri. 11 a.m.-3 p.m. & 5:30 p.m.-11 p.m., Sat. 5:30 p.m.-11 p.m. Cards: AE, MC, V.
The first San Diego restaurant to pretend it's in San Francisco, Dobson's offers the same clubby, masculine atmosphere as that city's Jack's and Tadich Grill. A pioneer of sorts, it opened before the revitalization brought nighttime crowds back to downtown San Diego. The gamble paid off for restaurateur Paul Dobson (a weekend matador of some repute in Baja bullrings); the restaurant quickly became the "in" spot for politicians, socialites and visiting celebrities, including the many opera and ballet principals who often drop by after performances. Amid all the see-and-be-seen bustle that goes on here, the fact that Dobson's is an excellent French restaurant often goes overlooked. But it is exacly that, with a chef in the kitchen who previously ran a two-star restaurant in the south of France, and a menu that changes daily. It's a good place for sweetbreads, which the kitchen takes in fascinating directions, such as a treatment that includes sautéed melon, chanterelles and saffron sauce. Portions tend to be heroic. A puff-pastry lid tops a good pint of suave mussel bisque; gardens of tender-crisp vegetables and browned potatoes accompany

the sautés of veal and lamb in wine sauces; and chunks of crisp, snappy sourdough—flown in daily from San Francisco—arrive throughout the meal. A favorite Dobson's starter is a sauté of chicken livers in a smooth Madeira sauce, but any of the cream soups make good alternatives. Seafood entrées run the gamut from simple grills to elaborately sauced presentations. Dobson's clientele tends to treat dessert with suspicion, preferring another taste of wine from the excellent by-the-glass list over the simple cakes and pastries offered. Dinner with wine will run about $90 to $110 for two.

11/20 La Especial
Avenida Revolución 718, Tijuana
(011-5266) 85-66-54
MEXICAN
Open daily 9 a.m.-10 p.m. Cards: MC, V.
La Especial may be truly special, but it's also mighty hard to find. One story below the main street in Tijuana, it sits on the edge of a large marketplace that's the perfect place to buy a serape, a bullwhip or an onyx ashtray while waiting in the usually long line. What you wait in line for is a chance to sit at plain wooden tables and eat some of the world's most straightforward Mexican cuisine—the equivalent of Mexican home cooking. As at many Mexican restaurants, the basic concept here is the combination plate, on which you can mix every imaginable permutation of tacos, tamales, enchiladas, quesadillas, tostadas and chiles rellenos, prepared as well here as they are anywhere. The chile relleno, for instance, too often a pathetic creation made from an anemic chile and some miserable excuse for cheese, is in this case long and elegant, stuffed with a tangy queso de Oaxaca, then breaded and fried to a turn. There are huevos rancheros served with a breathtaking salsa, exquisite baked pork and a guacamole with chunks of avocado, not a predigested purée. On the table are small ramekins of pickled carrots and jalapeños. The carrots are hot; the jalapeños are downright deadly. Dinner for two, with beer, will cost less than $25.

 La Fonda Roberto's
300 3rd Ave., Chula Vista
(619) 585-3017
MEXICAN
Open Mon.-Sat. 11 a.m.-10 p.m. Cards: MC, V.

This place would have all the glamour of a '50s coffee shop were it not for the murals of scenes from daily life in Oaxaca, Mexico, that brighten one of the dining room's walls. The family that runs the place is from Oaxaca, and when they moved north to this blue-collar suburb they brought with them a taste of Mexican home cooking. This is not the place to go for a double-knit burrito or any of the other synthetic dishes served at most of Southern California's "Mexican" hash houses.

The meal may start with a complimentary snack of tiny fresh tortillas folded around a spicy pork stew, which is served to occupy your time while your bottle of wine is opened and allowed to breathe (take that as a hint that the service is classy). Crepas de flor de calabaza (squash flowers) and cuitlacoche (savory corn fungus) also make good starters, and lead into full-bodied soups or carefully dressed romaine salads. The wildest entrée, and one that shouldn't be missed, is the chile en nogada, a kind of chile relleno filled with sweetened, minced meat and covered with a creamy sauce of nuts and candied fruits. Puntas de filete al chipotle dresses chunks of filet mignon with a subtly potent sauce; mole poblano is an excellent version of the classic chicken stewed in a sauce of peppers and chocolate; and mixiote de carnero features lamb slowly steamed in its own juices. For dessert there's flan, of course; try the one made with goat's milk, accompanied by excellent Mexican coffee. With wine, two will spend about $30 for dinner.

12/20 Le Fontainebleau
Westgate Plaza Hotel, 1055 2nd Ave.,
San Diego
(619) 238-1818
CONTINENTAL
Open Mon.-Fri. 11:45 a.m.-2 p.m. & 6:30 p.m.-10 p.m., Sat. 6 p.m.-10 p.m., Sun. 10 a.m.-2 p.m. & 6:30 p.m.-10 p.m. All major cards.

The Westgate Plaza Hotel appears as though it were decorated by a consortium of Louis (the kind with Roman numerals following their names) who had been transported into the '60s via Miami Beach. And Marie Antoinette would feel right at home in the hotel's restaurant, Le Fontainebleau. But all the ormolu, brocade, swag-draped mirrors and Old Master repros are actually kind of campy—and the restaurant is actually very good. It's fancy French, but not too fussy, and

while you could probably recite the menu by rote, there are some concessions to modernity and the food is beautifully prepared from fresh, best-of-the-market ingredients. The Caesar salad was lightly dressed with just a hint of anchovy, the grilled salmon with spinach pasta topped with clam sauce was cooked to moist crispness, and the asparagus on the side retained both its color and snap. Desserts are wonderfully retro—crêpes forêt noir flambées, pastries as ornate as the Victor Emmanuel—and the service is attentive without being cloying or condescending. On alternating nights, there is either a pianist or harpist playing in the dining room; if you want to be soothed rather than surprised, Le Fontainebleau isn't a bad bet. Dinner for two, with wine, will run about $80 to $100.

12/20 Il Fornaio
301 Del Mar Plaza, 1555 Camino del Mar,
Del Mar
(619) 755-8876
ITALIAN
Open Mon.-Thurs. 7 a.m.-11 p.m., Fri. 7 a.m.-midnight, Sat. 8 a.m.-midnight, Sun. 8 a.m.-11 p.m. Cards: AE, MC, V.

You find the darndest restaurants in malls these days, and in this case, it's a glitzy, fairly authentic Italian trattoria. Granted, this is no ordinary mall—it's a chic, Mediterranean-moderne one overlooking the ocean—and the restaurant, while part of a chain, is a very good one. Il Fornaio is the latest spawn of restaurateur Larry Mindel, who was the co-founder of the spectacularly successful Spectrum Foods (Prego, Ciao, MacArthur Park) and who is currently reorganizing the Italian-based Il Fornaio chain of restaurants and bakeries. His newest baby is just what this area has been crying out for—a place to see and be seen against a stunning backdrop. The restaurant is chockablock with sleek design elements, including hand-washed walls, lots of Carrara marble, mahogany and a panoramic mural of Pompeii; the European bar is perfect for sitting and sipping a cool Campari and soda.

The Tuscan-inspired menu is well chosen, and there's a real commitment here to using fresh, local produce—the herbs are grown in an on-site garden. It's difficult to restrain yourself from gorging on the poppy-seed-flecked bread and mixed breadsticks (there's a take-out bakery on the premises), and equally difficult to make decisions from a menu on which everything sounds wonderful. Among the best dishes are the luna piena, a dome-shape oven-roasted loaf of focaccia stuffed with cheese and covered with smoked prosciutto, and the filone di mozzarella, consisting of freshly made mozzarella rolled with prosciutto, ricotta, arugula and toasted pinenuts. Pizzas are delicious, too, as are the pastas (especially the mezzelune alla erbe amare, half-moon raviolis folded around ricotta, bitter herbs and sage, and glazed in browned butter). The roast chicken is crisp and tasty; we also like the zesty sausages with stewed peppers and grilled polenta and the wonderful version of pot roast marinated in a rich Barbaresco wine with herbs, a ragoût of grilled vegetables and polenta. As befits a restaurant named after an oven, desserts (most notably the raisin-studded bread pudding) are divine. Il Fornaio has also become the hottest spot in the area—on our visits, the place has been packed to the rafters. Prices are surprisingly gentle: two can expect to spend about $50 for dinner, including wine.

12/20 George's at the Cove

1250 Prospect St., La Jolla
(619) 454-4244
SEAFOOD/AMERICAN
Open Sun.-Thurs. 11:30 a.m.-10 p.m., Fri.-Sat. 11:30 a.m.-11 p.m. (café upstairs open daily 11:30 a.m.-2 a.m.). Cards: AE, MC, V.

Those in the know argue that George's is the best restaurant in La Jolla—and after a few visits, it's hard to argue with them. This is that rarest of establishments—a restaurant that both looks good and serves good food. George's has a fabulous view of the stunning La Jolla cove, with the waves lapping the shore and swimmers and divers bobbing about. It's a comfortable, rather preppy-looking place, done in warm tones of beige and green (a good variation on the standard pink and peach). The food is reminiscent of the food at 72 Market Street in L.A.: good grilled dishes, with a particular emphasis on seafood—so much fresh seafood, in fact, that a separate seafood menu is printed daily. At our last visit here, there were opa, ahi, ulua, onaga, tombo and opakapaka, all freshly arrived from Hawaii; silver salmon and baby coho salmon from Washington State; coral scallops from New Zealand; and local soupfin shark and sword-

fish. Sea scallops are sautéed and served on bok choy topped with a pecan butter sauce and a julienne of sun-dried tomatoes, which is one of the best things in the universe; sea scallops are also grilled with lime butter and served on Maui onions cooked in Cabernet. All this goes for prices less shocking than you might expect. Dinner for two, with wine, costs about $70.

⒀ La Gran Tapa

611 B St., San Diego
(619) 234-8272
SPANISH
Open Mon.-Fri. 11 a.m.-11 p.m., Sat. 6 p.m.-11 p.m. Cards: AE, MC, V.

La Gran Tapa is San Diego's most prominent entry in the current tapas-and-grazing craze, but don't be fooled: most dishes are substantial, two will make a meal, and any more will run the bill right out of sight. Modeled after several of Madrid's most noted *tascas* (as the wily Madrileños call their popular tapas bars), the place has become a hangout for downtown types and patrons of nearby theaters. The by-the-glass wine list and huge selection of light dishes make this especially popular for late-night diners. The soups are almost unreasonably good, especially the meaty black bean and the creamy brew of crab and peppers. For truly modest snacks, try the spiced lamb skewers or the tortilla, the classic baked omelet served at room temperature in a puddle of fresh tomato sauce. Skip the Caesar salad in favor of the simpler romaine salad, and then proceed on to the empanada of the day, which may be filled with either wild mushrooms or spiced pork hashed with pungent cured olives. Other good bets are eggs baked with artichoke hearts and chorizo; crisply fried baby squid; a whole baby octopus braised in olive oil and paprika; a crumbed, deep-fried round of Brie; boquerónes (fried mouthfuls of marinated shark); snails cooked in red wine seasoned with cured ham; or whatever else the menu, which changes several times a week, may list. For the stodgy, there are some sandwiches and an excellent burger, which are accompanied by crisp, hot, homemade potato chips. We have made a dozen trips to La Gran Tapa and have yet to be disappointed. However, desserts tend to be dull, except for the pecan-walnut-chocolate tart. This handsome bistro is quite a lively hangout, and the site of one of San Diego's most enjoyable dining experiences. A light dinner for two, with a glass of wine, will run about $40.

11/20 Grant Grill

U.S. Grant Hotel, 326 Broadway,
San Diego
(619) 239-6808
FRENCH/AMERICAN
Open Mon.-Fri. 11:30 a.m.-2 p.m. & 5:30 p.m.-11:30 p.m., Sat. 5:30 p.m.-11:30 p.m. All major cards.

If San Diego can be said to have a landmark restaurant, the Grant Grill is it. A quintessentially male, clubby establishment, this room banned women during the lunch hour until the late '60s, and the bankers, politicians and power brokers for whom it was a second home liked it that way. The current Grill is actually a new restaurant, having reopened in 1986 after the hotel's four-year, $80-million renovation. The room looks better than ever—the deep, well-spaced banquettes are comfortable oases for private conversations—but countenances sank and eyebrows rose when the kitchen's first offerings were sampled. Nothing was good, not even the famous turtle soup for which the Grill had been known.

The situation has improved since then; the Grill has regained some of its former expertise with roast meats and simple grilled steaks and seafoods. A rather self-conscious, coy Frenchness remains on the menu (for example, crayfish sausage in an unbearably salty sauce), but it is easily ignored. The Grill was always famous for its Cobb salad, which is once again excellent. The old-fashioned goodness of the roast of the day, wheeled to your table on a silver serving cart and carved to order, can bring tears to the eyes; it is likely to be served with a crisp vegetable and creamy gratin dauphinoise (potatoes baked in cream, a French touch for which the kitchen can be applauded). Roast baby chicken, roast duck, roast lamb, roast beef—these are all reliable. The lobster in vanilla sauce, on the other hand, is a Pandora's box that the curious will be sorry they opened. Luxury is the watchword here, from the tiny complimentary hors d'oeuvres that arrive with drinks to the elaborate cheese and dessert carts presented after dinner. The cheese selection outshines the desserts, so by all means say cheese, but be

careful of the ports—their price tags may cause you to miss your child's next tuition payment. Dinner for two, with wine, will run from $100 to $125.

Marius

Le Meridien, 2000 2nd St., Coronado
(619) 435-3000
FRENCH
Open Tues.-Sun. 6 p.m.-11 p.m. All major cards.

Marius is the best dining news to come down the Coronado pike in a hog's age—especially when you consider that its main local competition is the dreadful Prince of Wales and Crown rooms at the del Coronado. The restaurant is quite beautiful, done in soft, creamy tones with a country-French feel, intimate and softly lit. And while the chef here, Patrick Glennon, is a young American, he served a long apprenticeship in Provence before landing in this kitchen.

The Le Meridien hotel chain has long been dedicated to serving top-notch cuisine in its restaurants, and Marius upholds that tradition. While the dégustation menu, which changes daily, is the best way to go, the regular menu is no slouch. The soups are lovely, especially the delicate lobster broth with local vegetables and the heady mussel soup, rich with saffron. There's a gorgeous salad of sweet Pacific crab in an apple sauce, and the escargots with Swiss chard in a red-wine sauce is a rich riot of musky flavors. The lowly monkfish is served grandly, with fresh basil and a crisp potato galette, and the sea bass sautéed with black-olive purée, fruit and cacao sauce is an exotic, almost erotic delight. There's a marvelous Black Angus steak sautéed in an intoxicating rum-and-vanilla sauce, and the roasted duckling breast with lavender honey and lemon is as good as it sounds. Marius's freshly baked breads are heavenly, particularly the raisin-studded variety, which, when slathered with sweet butter, makes for quite an elegant meal in and of itself. Desserts do not disappoint; it's heartrending to have to choose between the light, bright gratin of exotic fruits washed with a coconut sabayon, the chocolate marquise with pistachio cream and the dreamy roasted pineapple with ginger, which is flambéed with hot white rum. But any of these choices will be good ones. Dinner for two, with wine, will run about $100 to $120.

10/20 McCormick & Schmick's

4190 Mission Blvd., Pacific Beach
(619) 581-3938
SEAFOOD
Open Mon.-Fri. 11:30 a.m.-2:30 p.m. & 5 p.m.-10:30 p.m., Sat. 5 p.m.-10:30 p.m., Sun. 10 a.m.-2 p.m. All major cards.

McCormick & Schmick's is a slick concept restaurant—the eponymous owners operate nine eateries in the Pacific Northwest and Denver, all of which serve more snap in the scene than in the food. The encyclopedic daily selection of fresh fish is prepared in myriad fashions; accompanying the fish is the usual gang of salads, pastas and soups. Best bets are the sea-fresh oysters and clams and such simple preparations as grilled or pan-fried fish. Stay away from the heavy, flavorless crabcakes and the oddly bland pastas—and the desserts aren't worth bothering with, either. But the atmosphere is lively, particularly around the bar, the wine list is very well chosen, and there's a nightclub upstairs called Mick's P.B. featuring live music nightly by local bands. Dinner for two, with wine, runs from $60 to $80.

12/20 Mille Fleurs

6009 Paseo Delicias, Rancho Santa Fe
(619) 756-3085
FRENCH
Open daily 11:30 a.m.-2:30 p.m. & 6 p.m.-10 p.m. Cards: AE, MC, V.

For the longest time, Mille Fleurs was just a typical luxury restaurant catering to the immensely rich (but not terribly demanding) residents of this chic rural community. But in early 1985 the place was taken over by Bertrand Hug, a consummate French restaurateur, who installed a quality chef in the kitchen and introduced Rancho Santa Fe to the joys of contemporary French cooking. It's expensive but not out of line, especially considering the neighborhood in which this handsome re-creation of a Moorish villa is located. Hug tries to keep his patrons in touch with whatever is new in cooking, without leading them into nouvelle excesses. To this end he changes the menu daily, although the garnishes tend to remain the same, particularly the wildly popular potato baskets filled with a selection of fresh, simply prepared vegetables. Guests have been observed fighting over scraps of leftover potato.

The cooking is always serious, running to such dishes as a filet of turbot encrusted with fresh herbs, veal kidneys in an elegant Cognac sauce, Norwegian salmon in a honey-mustard sauce spiked with chives (an interesting blend of flavors that was quite successful) and an entrecôte of aged Angus beef in a Roquefort sauce flavored with tarragon. First courses tend to take a breezy note—cream of mustard soup garnished with ginger and veal sausage, and a spinach salad crowned with ravioli filled with a veal mousse. The luxury of a terrine of foie gras paired with a salad of red cabbage in raspberry vinaigrette was stunning. The wine list is lengthy, and the service staff has been drilled so that it marches with the precision of a Marine Corps band. Desserts tend toward the rich and racy; try the vanilla Bavarian cream that voluptuously conceals a ball of chocolate mousse. Trays of petit fours and other sweets arrive with coffee. Dinner for two, with a modest wine, will be about $110 to $140.

11/20 Old Town Mexican Café y Cantina

2489 San Diego Ave., Old Town
(619) 297-4330
MEXICAN
Open daily 11 a.m.-11 p.m. Cards: AE, MC, V.

The Old Town Mexican Café, on the edge of San Diego's touristy replica of days gone by, may be a better place to drink and meet young singles than to eat, but it's actually not so bad—especially when you consider that fresh tortillas are pounded out in a window in front of the café; that the salsa is very hot and very good, not at all watered down for the gringo clientele; and that the food is reasonably authentic. (It had better be, with the Mexican border practically down the street.) Particularly good is the house specialty, pork carnitas—deep-fried chopped pork served with tortillas, cilantro, onion, slices of avocado, tomato, peppers and beans. The meat is exceptional, very juicy, yet with a crust that crunches when you bite into it. On the side are good nachos and excellent quesadillas. However, the chiles rellenos and enchiladas aren't always up to snuff, and in the past the red snapper Veracruz and shrimp in garlic sauce have seemed to tax the abilities of the kitchen. Actually, the food that works best at the Old Town is the food that you can eat with a margarita or a Mexican beer while watching a football game on the oversized video-beam TV—in other words, food that can be consumed while yelling a lot. Dinner for two, with beer, costs about $40.

12/20 Pacifica Grill
McClintock Plaza, 1202 Kettner Blvd., San Diego
(619) 696-9226
AMERICAN/CALIFORNIAN
Open Mon.-Fri. 11:30 a.m.-2:30 p.m. & 5:30 p.m.-10 p.m., Sat. 5:30 p.m.-10:30 p.m., Sun. 5 p.m.-10 p.m. Cards: AE, MC, V.
The Pacifica Grill belongs to that small coterie of newish, cutting-edge restaurants that's attempting to transform San Diego from a haven for dining dullards to a real food town. In other words, and with little cruelty implied, Pacifica Grill pretends it is a San Francisco restaurant, which is exactly the course of action taken by most of San Diego's better new eateries. A tenant of a strikingly remodeled warehouse, this restaurant has cleverly showcased its contemporary approach to cooking in a most attractive package. The high ceilings and vast approaches to the dining room provide a sense of spaciousness to an area that nonetheless seems intimate.

The menu changes with the market, though the emphasis is clearly placed on seafood and meat that can be grilled over mesquite and served either plain or painted with a lively sauce or mellow beurre blanc. There was a tendency for a while to play with Cajun dishes; now the emphasis is on Southwestern cuisine, but in any case, the kitchen remains addicted to peppers of all kinds. Grilled seafood is always a good bet (the almost-raw grilled salmon is lovely), as are the special crabcakes (flavored with buttermilk) and the grilled liver in a sauce of shallots and Zinfandel. The pastas can also be quite satisfying; one of the kitchen's favorite tricks is to throw a cream sauce into brilliant relief by adding a splash of hot seasoning. San Diego's young sophisticates come here for a crunchy-topped crème brûlée and an espresso after the theater. Dinner for two, with a glass of wine, runs about $70.

13 Rainwater's
McClintock Plaza, 1202 Kettner Blvd., San Diego
(619) 233-5757
AMERICAN
Open Mon.-Thurs. 11:30 a.m.-midnight, Fri. 11:30 a.m.-1 a.m., Sat. 5 p.m.-1 a.m., Sun. 5 p.m.-10 p.m. All major cards.
Located in an old Bekins storage building next to the historic Santa Fe train station—and upstairs from the above-reviewed Pacifica Grill—Rainwater's is an excellent copy of the Chicago-style chophouse. The decor is handsome and clubby, service is excellent, and the food is terrific, which is why Rainwater's was an immediate success. A decanter of crystalline water sits on every table, and the sourdough bread and cornsticks are a perfect foil for the restaurant's signature black-bean soup, a zesty potage that is closer to a chili than a broth. The steaks and chops are all prime, dry-aged Chicago beef, served in huge portions and cooked to perfection. And while the seafood dishes here are very good, the meat is really the name of the game. The side dishes are terrific, especially the gloriously old-fashioned creamed corn (which we could eat for breakfast, lunch and dinner) and the crispy frizzes of potatoes and onions. Desserts are divine, particularly the apple and pecan pies, and owner Laurel Rainwater has an admirably stocked and reasonably priced wine cellar. Dinner for two, with wine, will run about $80 to $100.

12/20 Remington's
2100 Jimmy Durante Blvd., Del Mar
(619) 755-5103
AMERICAN
Open nightly 5 p.m.-11 p.m. Cards: AE, MC, V.
If you've been to the Palm in New York, you've been to Remington's, except that the ceilings here are too low and the rather plain decor revolves around artwork by American master Frederick Remington. But otherwise, it's the same old story: prime beef and seafood served in portions that would make Gargantua blush, brought to the table by waiters who have been trained to believe that more is better, and who encourage parties of two to order meals that would feed a small village. There is no denying, however, that the kitchen knows how to select the best, most

tender aged steaks and grill them to the point of absolute perfection. The same goes for veal and lamb chops, and fish steaks cut so thickly that they acquire a fine crust at the precise moment their interiors are done. Maine lobsters are offered by the pound, usually starting at a four-pound minimum; this lobster also goes into a simple but superior bisque that gets a shot of brandy at the table. Caution is the operative word when ordering starters and side dishes. The heart-of-lettuce salad, topped with a generous handful of crumbled blue cheese, will feed two with ease, though the waiters will try to deny this. Vegetables come from nearby Chino Ranch, a Southern California landmark that grows only the best (try the corn in season). Fried silver-dollar potatoes and onion rings also make happy accompaniments to the steaks. A good rule of thumb is to order no more than one vegetable and one potato dish for every two or three guests. After all this food, you might not be able to cope with dessert, but Remington's does have some excellent, if very rich, pastries from a local baker. The place, by the way, is within wagering distance of Del Mar Racetrack, so it's jammed from late July to mid-September. Dinner for two, with wine, ranges from $110 to $150.

11/20 Top o' the Cove

1216 Prospect St., La Jolla
(619) 454-7779
CONTINENTAL
Open Mon.-Sat. 11:30 a.m.-2 p.m. & 5:30 p.m.-10:30 p.m., Sun. 5:30 p.m.-10:30 p.m. All major cards.

The Top o' the Cove can be traced back to what, in Southern Californian terms, is the last Ice Age—to 1897, when the house in which this venerable restaurant sits was built. At the time, the house had a name (as did most houses in quaint little La Jolla): "Ripple." Some 35 years ago it turned into Top o' the Cove, and it soon became La Jolla's place to meet people, admire the view and eat food that is rarely less than good, though not often inspired. It's the sort of honest standby that has built its solid reputation by serving dishes we've all eaten before and don't have to pay a lot of attention to, because we're really here for the view. So you can order such things as medallions of beef with forest mushrooms,

shallots and Madeira wine; tournedos of beef in a béarnaise sauce; or filet of sole Richelieu (sautéed in bread crumbs with the slightest hint of vermouth and truffles). This is La Jolla's place to be seen, something akin to Chasen's gone south. Dinner for two, with wine, costs about $110.

QUICK BITES

Hob Nob Hill

2271 1st Ave., San Diego
(619) 239-8176
Open Sun.-Fri. 7 a.m.-9 p.m. Cards: MC, V.

In Los Angeles, the "in" place to go for breakfast is Duke's. In San Diego, the "in" place is Hob Nob Hill. Hob Nob Hill hasn't always been known as Hob Nob Hill. When it opened as a fourteen-seat diner in 1944, it was called the Juniper Café. It then became the Melody Grill, Dorothy's Oven and finally (by now seating 120) Hob Nob Hill—one of the few restaurants in the world closed on Saturdays (so the family that owns the place can have a day to spend together). This is one of those wonderful places to return to now and again, a place that seems completely anachronistic, a working tribute to the joys of culinary Americana. The breakfast menu, for instance, is rich with such delights as the "Three Musketeers"—a trio of buttermilk pancakes, light and quite scrumptious, rolled around a slice of ham, a sausage and a dollop of sour cream. There are golden pecan waffles, eggs Florentine and tall or short stacks of wonderful Canadian blueberry hotcakes. Also offered are homemade pastries and sweet rolls of every description, served warm, fresh and reassuringly good. They come with jams served in orange halves. Hearty, homey lunches and dinners are served as well, but it's breakfast that people speak of when they speak of Hob Nob Hill. Breakfast for two costs less than $20.

John's Waffle Shop

7906 Girard Ave., La Jolla
(619) 454-7371
Open Mon.-Sat. 7 a.m.-3 p.m., Sun. 8 a.m.-3 p.m. No cards.

This La Jolla landmark, akin to Louise's Pantry in Palm Springs and Esau's in Santa

Barbara, is the type of divey little café every town should have. It's old and funky, with just a counter and a cluster of tables, and you'll often as not find business sorts elbow to elbow with the homeless. But the waffles are sublime—made to order in an old-fashioned waffle iron, crispy and golden outside, light and fluffy inside. John's also serves homemade Belgian waffles, and the crusty fried potatoes could send a spud-lover into paroxysms of joy. Other items are on the menu (sandwiches, eggs, some Mexican dishes), but ordering them would be like going to Lourdes for the scenery. Breakfast for two runs about $10.

HOTELS

Britt House
406 Maple St., San Diego, 92103
(619) 234-2926

Britt House, a popular destination for honeymooners and nostalgia addicts, seems a little grand to be placed in the bed-and-breakfast category, but that's how this charming little place categorizes itself. Housed in a Victorian mansion in the city's Banker's Hill District, Britt House isn't far from the museums, zoo and theaters in nearby Balboa Park, as well as downtown and the airport. Every room is different; some are quite large, several boast the intriguing nooks and crannies so beloved by Victorian architects, and all have been carefully and thoughtfully decorated with period pieces. Although this is by no means a full-service hotel, the service is very personal, which is one reason why Britt House counts many repeat visitors among its clientele. Another is breakfast, which, rather than the Danish pastry and coffee served at some such hostelries, is prepared to order and includes homemade breads and muffins, fresh juices and other tasty treats. The price of the room also includes afternoon tea.
Doubles: $95-$110.

Hotel del Coronado
1500 Orange Ave., Coronado, 92118
(619) 435-6611

Now into its second century, the Hotel del Coronado remains the dowdy dowager of San Diego County hostelries. The world's largest wooden structure also remains the area's most recognized landmark, and despite its shabbiness, it continues to play its generations-old role as a favorite honeymoon hideaway and weekend retreat. The Victorian architecture recalls the extravagance of that age so well that the hotel conducts daily walking tours of the premises. The turret rooms supposedly house ghosts (but certainly not in summer, when these rooms can be unbearably stuffy), and the lobby bar provides a superb vantage point for people-watching, provided that you like watching conventioneers and sloppily dressed tourists.

This full-scale resort is really a self-contained community; you'll never have to leave the hotel. The main building abounds in shops, the two restaurants are acceptable if far from great, and the Ocean Terrace Room features live music and dancing nightly. The hotel has its own tennis courts and immense pool, though in season, swimmers will want to head for the marvelous Pacific-fronting beach just steps from the lobby. Since it was built during a more gracious era, the rooms are out-sized by contemporary standards, and are comfortable enough. However, some of the appointments appear to be remnants from bygone days—nostalgia buffs who don't place a premium on luxury should be happy as clams here. Avoid the new tower, which has none of the Del's Victorian charm.

Singles & doubles: $115-$220; suites $275-$435.

Hotel Inter-Continental
333 W. Harbor Dr., San Diego, 92101
(619) 234-1500

The Inter-Continental proves that a hotel is not born with a soul, but rather develops one over time. It was hailed as a pinnacle of glamour and modern luxury when it opened in the spring of 1984, but it has failed to attract much of a local following for its restaurants and ballrooms. The sweeping lobbies and public rooms are unquestionably grand and monumental, but there is something cold about these rooms; it might be called a kind of international impersonality. In any case there is nothing about the Inter-Continental that says San Diego, and guests who don't glance out the windows could just as easily think they're in Bahrain or Bangkok. What lies outside those windows is what gives the hotel much of its attractiveness for business and pleasure travelers. The heart of the city is a few blocks away; the soul, in terms of San Diego Bay and its marinas and docks, is at the hotel's side door. All rooms have balconies that look down on the city's many sights (west-facing rooms survey Coronado and the Pacific), and this is just as well, because the balconies make the smallish rooms seem that much larger. The furnishings, it must be said, are new and quite fine, and service is of similar lofty quality. It isn't on the beach, but the Inter-Continental has two lovely pools.

Singles: $130-$170; doubles: $150-$190; suites: $360-$620.

 ### Kingston Hotel
1055 1st Ave., San Diego, 92101
(619) 232-6141

The new Kingston Hotel, which actually began life back in 1968 as The Executive, was built as a sister hotel to the Westgate Plaza by C. Arnholt Smith, the legendary, luckless local financier. Having only 100 rooms, it was meant to be a more intimate version of the grandiose Westgate. Now owned by Malcolm Kingston, a British-born, California-based developer, the Kingston has been completely and luxuriously refurbished, heavy on the marble, wood paneling and antiques. There are excellent business facilities here, including the Grand Terrace Meeting Room that has a retractable roof, which affords a fine view of the harbor. The staff is friendly, helpful and professional. There is also a fully equipped health club and spa, The Cuyamaca Club, located on the seventh floor of the adjacent Executive Office Complex, available for use by guests. The Kingston's new restaurant, Malcolm's First Avenue, features regional American cuisine and has a good pedigree—it is under the aegis of a partner in L.A.'s renowned Citrus restaurant. Afternoon tea is served daily on the second floor, and the Kingston offers another pleasant surprise: the 88-seat Kingston Playhouse, which has been offering some first-rate productions, including John Patrick Shanley's *Italian-American Reconciliation* and Joe Orton's *What the Butler Saw*. Good package deals that combine a room and theater tickets are usually offered,

along with other intriguing packages. This place is a more than welcome—and inexpensive—addition to the downtown hotel scene.
Doubles: $95; suites: $105-$150.

 ### Le Meridien
2000 2nd St., Coronado, 92118
(619) 435-3000

This recently opened resort is quite a stunner—and should give the tired, old del Coronado a real jolt. (Maybe it'll shame the Del's management into giving the grande dame the face-lift and overhaul she so richly deserves.) Located on sixteen San Diego Bay waterfront acres, the hotel is at the foot of the Coronado Bay Bridge and next to a lovely twenty-acre park and beach. The lobby and public areas are beautifully decorated in a tropical mode, with sun-washed pastel walls and oversized wicker furniture. There are 300 guest rooms and seven executive suites, as well as a 28-unit villa complex, tastefully decorated with Berber carpets and lithographs by major artists, with its own private pool and spa—definitely worth the splurge. But the other guest rooms aren't exactly shabby. Each one has a terrace, minibar, three telephone extensions and even the dread bathroom scale for those masochists who like to weigh themselves when they're on vacation. There are extensive meeting and banquet facilities, as well as a fully equipped business center. For the more hedonistic, you can't do much better than six lighted tennis courts, three swimming pools, two spas and bicycles for hire. There are other recreations that can be arranged, such as golf (at a championship course across the street), yachting, sportfishing and moped rentals. Le Meridien also has a fully equipped gym and a Clarins Institut de Beauté, offering facials, massages and other beauty services.

The grounds are simply gorgeous—a tropical paradise with waterfalls, burbling streams, lagoons stocked with fat koi, and ponds that are home to a variety of ducks, swans and geese. The hotel's premier restaurant, Marius, is excellent, featuring Provençal cuisine, and there's also a more casual brasserie, L'Escale, overlooking the bay, that serves breakfast, lunch, dinner and afternoon tea.

Singles & doubles: $155-$215; suites & villas: $350-$595.

Sheraton Grand
1590 Harbor Island Dr., San Diego, 92101
(619) 291-6400

The Sheraton Grand, once known as the Sheraton Harbor Island West, appeals primarily to the business trade, since it is no more than two minutes from the airport and five minutes from downtown. A fairly recent $15-million face-lift was designed to make it attractive to the luxury and leisure crowds as well, a market that may also be attracted to the quality of service and the small (200-room) size of the hotel. The Sheraton Grand features the largest rooms of any hotel in the city; luxuriously furnished, they include balconies that offer sweeping views of either San Diego Bay or the yacht harbor that fronts the north side of the building. Amenities include a full-time concierge service, a piano bar, a swimming pool and 24-hour room service. The pretty dining room, Merlano, serves Italian cuisine.

Singles: $125-$150; doubles: $135-$170; suites: $325.

 The U.S. Grant Hotel
326 Broadway, San Diego, 92101
(619) 232-3420

The Grant, traditionally known as San Diego's most prestigious hotel, lost much of its luster in the '60s and '70s and nearly became just another dreary relic of downtown America. Then came an $80-million restoration, completed at the end of 1985, that left the place grander than it had been when it was opened by the son of President Ulysses S. Grant in 1910. A magnificent central lobby has become a mid-afternoon gathering spot for the city's socialites, who enjoy the tea served by liveried waiters. The bar swings with jazz on Sunday afternoons and with conversation most nights. The Grant Grill, once the premier downtown dining spot, has been glamorously restored, and the food isn't bad. The Garden Room, also rather grand and formal, bursts with truckloads of fresh flowers, but we'd rather eat the daisies than what's on the menu. However, since the Grant is at the very heart of downtown (most locals feel it *is* the heart), there are plenty of good eateries nearby, including several in the new, architecturally acclaimed Horton Plaza, just across the street. All cultural, business and financial institutions are within easy walking distance (San Diego enjoys a compact, convenient downtown). Some of the choicest suites in town can be found here; the average rooms have been tastefully furnished and offer all the latest luxuries. Services include on-site parking, a concierge service and a generally well-trained staff. No pool.

Singles: $130; doubles: $145-$155; suites: $170-$1,700.

 La Valencia
1132 Prospect St., La Jolla, 92037
(619) 454-0771

Marion Davies, Ramon Navarro and other stars of silent films flocked to La Jolla's pink palace when it was new, and this refined retreat continues to be a favorite with both the Hollywood crowd and the jet set. It's a quiet, dignified place; visitors are tempted to speak in whispers when they cross through the front lobby. The rear lobby, a magnificent room that ends in an immense picture window framing La Jolla Cove, inspires quite a different sort of reaction: awe, a sense of well-being, and the hope that time will stand still and that La V (as La Jollans call this favorite institution) will never change.

Most rooms offer a view of the water, and most will seem a little antiquated—though by no means uncomfortable—when compared to those in the modern glass palaces rising in downtowns across the country. Service is extremely personalized, as befits a place that numbers so many repeat visitors, including a fair percentage who check in for months at a time. Businesspeople will find the hotel a little far from downtown San Diego, but La Valencia was built for pleasure, not business. The beach is a two-minute walk away, and there is both a pool and a Jacuzzi. The tiny (ten-table) Sky Room, in the hotel's tower, serves ambitious, well-prepared contemporary cooking and is a favorite of romantics. La Jolla's old guard continues to call the small but lively Whaling Bar its own; to command a table here on short notice is to prove that one belongs to the elite of this wealthy coastal community.

Singles: $108-$128; doubles: $118-$138; suites: $175-$310.

Westgate Plaza Hotel

1055 2nd Ave., San Diego, 92101
(619) 238-1818

Built by a wheeler-dealer whose fortune crumbled in one of San Diego's most celebrated financial scandals, the Westgate, while maintaining its position as one of the city's premier luxury hotels, looks like a rather glamorous whorehouse; if famed haute-Miami-schlock architect Morris Lapidus had married Ivana Trump, this is what their architectural progeny would look like. Very few surfaces are untouched by gold leaf, mirrors or flocking, and if there's ever a chandelier shortage in the world, this is where they're being stockpiled. But to be fair, the service is smooth, gracious and professional, and the ornate lobby is oddly comfortable to hang out in, as is the nuttily retro Plaza Bar. The rooms, while not overly large, are quite handsomely appointed and are equipped with all the little luxuries expected of a contemporary deluxe hotel. This is not a hotel for sunbathers, however, since there is neither pool nor beach. The Westgate's restaurant, Le Fontainebleau, is a bit more restrained in the design department than the hotel's other public rooms, and its French cuisine is surprisingly good.

Singles: $124-$144; doubles: $134-$154; suites: $275-$500.

SIGHTS

AMUSEMENTS

Balboa Park

Park Blvd., San Diego
(619) 239-0512

San Diego's greatest treasure is Balboa Park, home of the San Diego Zoo, the Old Globe Theatre, several fine museums and every imaginable recreational facility: 2 golf courses, 25 tennis courts, an Olympic-size pool, an archery range, a miniature railroad, a merry-go-round and hundreds of manicured and natural acres for hiking, running and picnics. Many of the park's extravagant Spanish-Moorish buildings date from the world's fairs held here in 1915 and 1935; the subtropical landscaping surrounding these structures is particularly lovely.

Old Town State Historic Park

Bordered by Juan, Twiggs, Congress & Calhoun sts., near the intersection of I-5 & I-8.

Visiting Old Town isn't as hokey as you might think—it's sort of an expanded version of L.A.'s Olvera Street, and it really is rich with history. In 1769, Father Junípero Serra founded San Diego Alcala, California's first mission, on a hill overlooking Old Town (it has since been moved several miles to the east). Anyone familiar with California's history knows of the bloody religious, cultural and imperialistic battles that ensued, and shortly after the United States finally emerged victorious in its 1846 war against Mexico, San Diego was officially named a U.S. city, with Old Town its hub.

Old Town is divided into several areas: California Plaza, which is where most of the historic buildings, stables and residences are located; Bazaar del Mundo, which most closely resembles Olvera Street and features a number of shops, restaurants and crafts exhibits; Squibob Square, a Victorian shopping area; Heritage Park, an area of restored Victorian houses (home to commercial tenants); and Presidio Park. There are kiosks with maps on them to guide you along. Wandering through Old Town is a terrific way to spend a day.

San Diego Wild Animal Park

15500 San Pasqual Valley Rd. (I-15 Hwy. to Via Rancho Pkwy., then follow the signs), Escondido
(619) 234-6541

Open daily 9 a.m.-4 p.m. Adults $12.95, children $6.20.

This glorious park is an 1,800-acre adjunct to the San Diego Zoo, and the same care, planning and beauty that make the zoo one of the world's best are also part and parcel of this park. Five natural habitats have been simulated—Asian Plains, Asian Swamps and North, South and East Africa—in this preserve, and, as is the credo of the zoo, the Wild Animal Park is dedicated to the protection and propogation of endangered species.

Since the park is so large, it's wise to take advantage of the Wgasa Bushline Monorail, a 50-minute, five-mile journey. More than 3,000 animals from nearly 300 species inhabit the grounds, offering not only wonderful photo opportunities but also a chance for us to see these marvelous creatures—lions, tigers, elephants, zebras, cheetahs, you name it—in something very close to their native environments. There are also hiking trails, exotic rare flora, observation decks and a petting zoo, as well as Nairobi Village, which features performers executing tribal dances, and the Congo Fishing Village.

San Diego Zoo
Balboa Park, 2920 Zoo Dr., San Diego
(619) 231-1515
Open daily 9 a.m.-4 p.m. Adults $8.50, children $2.50. Cards: MC, V.

The zoo is San Diego's Disneyland, attracting visitors from all over the world. Its fame and reputation as one of world's best zoos (if not *the* best) is well deserved. The 100 acres are more than any first-time visitor can take in one day; we recommend the 40-minute guided bus tour before venturing out on your own. It will help you get your bearings, prolong the life of your feet and help you decide which parts of the zoo you most want to see. Don't miss the fascinating (if somewhat creepy) Reptile House, the charming sea lion shows and the Great Apes Grotto, where junior King Kongs strut their stuff. And if you have children in tow, you must visit the remarkable Children's Zoo, which was built to the scale of a four-year-old and which allows kids to make eye contact (and often pet) baby elephants, giraffes, monkeys, pigs and chicks. New exhibits include Tiger River—an imitation rain forest housing prehistoric-looking water dragons, grand cats and a world-class jungle of exotic greenery—and the Sun Bear area.

Sea World
1720 S. Shores Rd., Mission Bay
(619) 222-6363
Open daily 9 a.m.-6 p.m. Adults $21, children 3-11 $15.50, children under 3 free. All major cards.

Sea World puts on shows that rival anything Hollywood and Busby Berkeley ever dreamed up. The headliners are the killer whales, who show off incredible intelligence and ability to displace water. (Despite 1989's tragic incident in which a supremacy battle between two of the killer whales caused the death of Baby Shamu's mother, Kandu, the shows are as popular as ever.) The dolphins also wow audiences, not only with their intelligence but with their remarkable precision feats, including spins, dives and back flips. These shows, combined with the exceptionally beautiful grounds, the breadth of marine life on display, the unbeatable children's play facilities and the speedy hydrofoil boat tour of Mission Bay, make Sea World our favorite amusement park in California. It's a particularly nice place for children, who can pet and feed the pilot whales, seals, dolphins and walruses, wade through the tide pools and play in the creative playground. Adults will be intrigued by the remarkable marine life on display—from rare, brightly colored fish to several species of live sharks. Sea World allows nature to dazzle us more than any roller coaster ever could.

BEACHES

Coronado Beach
Marilyn Monroe, Jack Lemmon and Tony Curtis made this beach famous by romping along it in *Some Like It Hot*, but some may find it a little too hot—this beach is very, very popular, and gets quite crowded during the season's peak. The del Coronado looms dramatically behind it, and if you can avoid the hordes, it's a nice beach indeed.

Imperial Beach
A good surfing and swimming beach in the South Bay, Imperial Beach is lively and reasonably clean. The pier recently reopened, and in July, the U.S. Open Sand Castle Competition—the one you see covered every year on the evening news—takes place there.

La Jolla Cove
Simply beautiful. This cove is sheltered by a palisade thick with palms, and when the tide is low, there are caves and tide pools to explore, and seal watchers can sometimes spot their favorite mammals resting on the rocks offshore.

Mission Beach
Though Mission Bay is quite crowded during the summer, it is most pleasant to walk or bicycle along its boardwalk.

Silver Strand State Beach
This Coronado beach doesn't get quite as crowded as the more popular Coronado

Beach does, which makes it more desirable as far as we're concerned. It's admirably clean, kids love to play in the tiny, harmless waves, and there's ample parking.

Torree Pines State Beach

Del Mar is one of Southern California's most stunning areas, and the beach there is beautiful. Large, clean and featuring barbecue facilities, Torrey Pines is a good family beach.

Tourmaline & Windansea Beaches

If your idea of haute couture comes from the houses of Body Glove, SideOut and Surf Fetish, then these are the beaches for you. Great surfing and, for those who don't indulge in the sport, great people-watching.

TIJUANA

You can get to Tijuana by trolley if you're so inclined, though why anyone would want to is beyond us. Aside from being a nice idea, the ride is endless, with stops every few blocks, and there's a persistent view of nothing; borders are not fabled for their scenic beauty. Our favorite gambit is to drive to the Mexican border, park on the American side in one of the many lots and walk across. You can then either take a taxi into town or just keep walking—it takes about twenty minutes, and you'll pass one of the world's great velvet-painting markets on the way.

Once in Tijuana, you'll find yourself on Avenida Revolución, which is basically one long bazaar and not nearly as bizarre as it once was. Gone are the donkey shows and the red-light districts. These days, sinning in Tijuana consists of betting on jai alai at the Frontón in the middle of town, or betting on the horses and the greyhounds just outside of town at the Agua Caliente Racetrack. And Tijuana is filled with modern shopping centers as well, especially in the newly constructed Rió Tijuana area, a modern facility that looks like every shopping mall we've ever been to in the United States, leaving the commonly asked question of why one should go there hanging pregnantly in the air.

As far as restaurants go, it's a good idea to avoid drinking the water. Aside from that, you can get an excellent taste of authentic Mexican cooking at La Especial in the marketplace just off Revolución (everyone in town knows

where it is; you'll know you're there when you see a long line in front of a friendly-looking little restaurant), and authentic Mexican seafood cooking at La Costa (right across the street from the Jai Alai Palace), which serves some of the best lobsters we've ever eaten. There are also a number of Chinese restaurants in Tijuana, probably left over from the 1940s, when it was a major port of call for soldiers and sailors who found Chinese food to be a good cheap meal. They serve the old-style Chinese-American (Chinese-Mexican?) cuisine built around chop suey, chow mein and egg foo yung. You may want to try one for the sakê of history—and to listen to Chinese people speaking Spanish.

SPORTS

DIVING, FISHING & BOATING

Many of the hotels in San Diego and its environs can schedule boating and diving excursions, but if the one you're staying in can't, try contacting any of the several local Diving Locker shops around town or Ocean Enterprises (619-565-6054).

HANG GLIDING

San Diego's dramatic topography—mountains, oceans, cliffs, beaches—makes hang gliding here a peak experience. Gliding (for the experienced or those wishing to take lessons) can be set up through the Hang Gliding Center (619-450-9008) or Flight Realities (619-455-6036).

JET SKIING

Rentals are available through Jet Ski Rentals (619-422-2829).

SAILING

If you BYOB (Brought Your Own Boat), try the Kona Kai Club (1551 Shelter Island Drive, 619-222-1191) or the Sunroad Resort Marina (955 Harbor Island Drive East, 619-574-0736). If you're looking to rent, try the Mission Bay Sports Center (1010 Santa Clara Place, 619-488-1004); several hotels, including the Catamaran, the Bahia and the del Coronado, also rent boats.

WINDSURFING

Again, several hotels provide windsurfing rentals and lessons (the Bahia and the Catamaran, for two). Also, try California Pacific Sailing Sports (2211 Pacific Beach Drive,

619-270-3211) and Windsport (844 W. Mission Bay Drive, 619-488-0612).

YACHT CHARTERS

Rentals are available through Hornblower Dining Yachts (P.O. Box 1140, Coronado, 619-435-2211) and Finest City Yacht Charters (4027 Kendall Street, 619-483-2727).

SANTA BARBARA

CALIFORNIA'S SHANGRI-LA

Every weekend, countless Angelenos come north and fill up Santa Barbara's hotels, motels and bed-and-breakfasts—and there's every reason why you should do the same. We don't normally recommend such crowd-following, but we can't help it in this case: Santa Barbara is just irresistible. The setting is idyllic, the weather is perfect ten months of the year, the Spanish and Victorian architecture is exceptionally handsome, and the restaurants are several notches above the standard resort-town tourist traps. For the aesthete, there's the commendable Santa Barbara Museum of Art; for the spiritualist, there's the peaceful Santa Barbara Mission; and for the athlete, there's tennis, swimming, scuba diving, bicycling, windsurfing and much more. Because of all that, rooms can be hard to find, especially from April to October, so book early—and be forewarned that most hotels have two-night minimums on weekends.

RESTAURANTS

 Brigitte's
1327 State St., Santa Barbara
(805) 966-9676
CALIFORNIAN
Open Mon.-Sat. 11 a.m.-2:30 p.m. & 5 p.m.-10 p.m., Sun. 5 p.m.-10 p.m. Cards: MC, V.
With the success of Brigitte's, Brigitte Guehr and her husband, Norbert Schulz (Norbert's owner and chef), have demon-

strated exceptional talent for restaurateuring. Both of their restaurants are among the best of their kind in California—Norbert's kind being the serious French restaurant, and Brigitte's the lively Franco-Italo-Californian bistro. And now this enterprising team has another winner, a terrific seafood café called Oysters (see review following). This tiny storefront has a modest bistro decor: brick walls, colorful flags overhead, a handful of tables in front with views of State Street promenaders, a small, friendly bar, and a few tables in back near the minuscule open kitchen. Unfortunately, reservations are not accepted, and there's usually a considerable wait on weekends.

While you wait, you can try one of the local wines by the glass and stare longingly at the plates passing you by: aromatic pizza bread topped with smoked salmon and golden caviar, lovely salads, pretty (but sometimes disappointing) pizzas with lamb sausage or lobster, elegant fresh fish, lamb and chicken entrées, and the house's most popular dessert, Chocolate Surprise—white- and dark-chocolate mousse dipped in chocolate and served with a raspberry sauce. Everything we've tried, except the aforementioned pizza, has been both delicious and an exceptional value: from a simple salad of butter lettuce and local shrimp for $3.50 to delicate angel-hair pasta with bay scallops and a robust goat cheese–walnut pesto for $7.75. At $9.95, the rare, flavorful lamb with an eggplant-oregano sauce or the tender New York steak with a vibrant red pepper coulis and smooth aïoli is like a gift from the angels. Accompany your meal with one of the reasonably priced local wines, and you'll feel as if you're in on one of California's finest culinary secrets. About $60 for a complete three-course dinner for two, with wine and cappuccinos; less for a light meal.

12/20   Brophy Bros. Clam Bar & Restaurant

The Breakwater, Cabrillo St., Santa Barbara
(805) 966-4418
SEAFOOD
Open daily 11 a.m.-10 p.m. Cards: MC, V.

Some time ago, a bit of a stir was caused when a local restaurant writer, in addressing the subject of the highest-grossing restaurants in the state, mentioned that Brophy Bros. came in at number one, with annual gross receipts in excess of $10 million. This was an interesting fact, since Brophy Bros. is nothing more than a counter with a dozen seats, and maybe another dozen tables scattered inside and out. Be that as it may, Brophy Bros. is about as good a seafood restaurant as we've got in these parts. It sits on the breakwater between Point Castillo and Stearns Wharf, on the second story of a fishing-supply shop. As restaurants go, it's noisy, somewhat chaotic and almost out of control. They call it a clam bar, though it could just as easily be an oyster bar or a shrimp bar (back in Baltimore, they call places like this "raw bars"). The chow is nothing new: clams and oysters on the half shell, peel-and-eat shrimp, steamed clams, steamed mussels, oysters Rockefeller (not a bad rendition at all), clams casino (an old dish that's actually kind of wonderful, in a bready way), beer-boiled shrimp, fine New England–style clam chowder, cioppino, tuna and crab melts and fried-clam sandwiches (ah, the cholesterol of it . . .). It may be the usual fare, but it's better than usual, served in a terrific setting, with Santa Barbara on one side of you and the Pacific on the other. Dinner for two, with wine, costs about $30.

12/20   Café Vallarta

626 E. Haley St., Santa Barbara
(805) 564-8494
MEXICAN
Open Tues.-Sun. 11:30 a.m.-2:30 p.m. & 5:30 p.m.-9:30 p.m. Cards: MC, V.

Not surprisingly, this mission town is thick with Mexican restaurants; it's one of the few American cities where burritos are more beloved than burgers. Of the dozens of enchilada-and-tostada eateries around, Café Vallarta stands out for its unusual degree of authenticity and its winning way with Mexican-style seafood. Instead of boring old chicken enchiladas and beef fajitas, you'll be offered the house's award-winning caldo de mariscos, a marvelous, slightly tangy Mexican bouillabaisse; such classics as mole poblano and conchinita pibil; fajitas made with calamari; camarones al mojo de ajo (with garlic galore); and an unusual but tasty tostada made with black beans and tart ceviche. Dishes are served with tasty black beans instead of the refried version, and desserts go beyond flan to chocolate pâté and, for the brave of palate, avocado-lime cheesecake. There's a fetching collection of local wines, along with beer, fruit liquados and espresso. You can dine inside, in the cheerful blue-and-white dining areas, or on the simple outside patio. Our only gripe is with the service, which can be as slow as a hot Cozumel afternoon. About $20 for lunch for two, with beer; dinner with beer runs about $40.

11/20   Cold Spring Tavern

5995 Stagecoach Rd., San Marcos Pass, Santa Barbara
(805) 967-0066
AMERICAN
Open daily 11 a.m.-3 p.m. & 5 p.m.-9:30 p.m. Cards: MC, V.

Hard to believe here in Lotus land, but this place is a genuine, bona fide, card-carrying roadhouse. For more than a century, the Cold Spring Tavern has been a rest stop for those heading north from Santa Barbara, and you can feel the history in every wind-loosened shutter, resounding from every creaky board. The place is one of those fine California treats, a bit of history down an old road, far from the freeway and from the noise of the madding crowd. The creek is still there, running more or less clean. And in the evening wind, you can still hear the rumblings of the old stagecoaches, which carried passengers over this pass long before the automobile was a glimmer in Henry Ford's eye. Though the place still looks venerable, the food has changed quite a bit with the years, to the point that this modest-looking inn has one of the most unique menus in the state: mushroom caps stuffed with venison sausage, rabbit pâté baked with pistachios and pine nuts, marinated and boned Santa Ynez rabbit, charbroiled Carolina quail moistened with roasted bell-pepper butter, even the occasional Cajun dish. But for a taste of what the food was probably like back in the real roadhouse days, go for the house chili, which is chili as chili should be—strongly flavored, full of meat, thick with onions and cheese. We also love the buffalo burger, a dish left over from back when the buffalo really did roam. Dinner for two, with wine, costs about $60.

16 Downey's
1305 State St., Santa Barbara
(805) 966-5006

AMERICAN
Open Tues.-Thurs. & Sun. 5:30 p.m.-9 p.m., Fri.-Sat. 5:30 p.m.-9:30 p.m. Cards: MC, V.

For residents of the Los Angeles/Orange County area, there can be few greater pleasures than a weekend in Santa Barbara. Just 90 minutes from downtown L.A., Santa Barbara has retained much of its small-town charm despite a growing influx of tourists. The Spanish-style architecture, broad, clean beaches and wide range of luxury hotels and bed-and-breakfast establishments make it a perfect weekend hideaway. But for folks who like to eat well, Santa Barbara's greatest attraction may be its restaurants—everything from the funky Mexican food at La Super-Rica to the sophisticated French fare at Norbert's. Every time we go to Santa Barbara, we try to have dinner at both Norbert's and Downey's, and until recently, we always preferred Norbert's. But chef John Downey has continued to polish his skills, and it is now difficult to choose which of the two serves the city's best food. We first encountered Downey several years ago at Penelope's, then the city's most elegant and formal restaurant. We found the ambience a bit stuffy and the food disappointing. Not surprisingly, Penelope's soon closed (the building now houses Michael's Waterside Inn), and Downey went on to open his own, much more modest restaurant on State Street, Santa Barbara's main drag. The restaurant is small, informal and comfortable, and, surprisingly, the food was very good from day one . . . and it's gotten progressively better.

Our favorite appetizers include mussels with sweet corn, served in a chile vinaigrette; home-cured prosciutto with local figs; and a grilled squab salad with mushrooms, chicory

and garlic. Downey has a nice, light touch with fish, and we can recommend his striped bass with a tomato/tarragon vinaigrette; local swordfish with grilled onions, in a roasted pepper sauce; and any of his various salmon preparations. Other good main courses include the squab with garlic and hot mustard greens, grilled duck with a summer-fruit chutney and coriander sauce, and grilled lamb loin with eggplant, peppers and rosemary. Alas, desserts are not as good as the rest of the items on the menu, so we sometimes order two appetizers and skip dessert. Dinner for two, with wine, costs about $135.

8/20   El Encanto Dining Room
El Encanto Hotel, 1900 Lausen Rd., Santa Barbara
(805) 687-5000

FRENCH
Open daily 8 a.m.-10 p.m. All major cards.

Permit us to offer a story about dining at the Dining Room at the El Encanto Hotel. Some time ago, we were invited to celebrate Bastille Day there with Julia Child. Arriving at the hotel, which sits high above Santa Barbara, we were struck by the absence of valet-parking attendants and bellboys to pick up our luggage. We parked ourselves, lugged our luggage into the hotel, then lugged our luggage to our room; no one offered to help. The reception that preceded the dinner featured a grand display of French cheeses, all of which were sealed; in front of them sat trays of cubed white and orange cheese, apparently from the local supermarket. At dinner, we were served a dreadful version of chicken consommé flavored with what we were told was a truffle but tasted like a piece of rubber. Sometime later we were served a chicken that had seen better days, hidden under a mucilaginous sauce. At the end of the meal, a chef appeared. He was introduced. No one said a word. No one applauded. No one even looked up. It was, we should add, just about an average meal at El Encanto. Two will spend more than $100 for dinner with wine.

12/20   Michael's Waterside Inn
50 Los Patos Way, Montecito
(805) 969-0307

FRENCH
Open Mon. & Wed.-Sun. 11:30 a.m.-2 p.m. & 6:30 p.m.-10 p.m. All major cards.

Some time ago, feeling exceedingly plump, we took ourselves to a spa called The Oaks in Ojai to shed a few extra pounds. After two days of eating boiled this and that, we were hollow-eyed with hunger and half-crazed with boredom. And so, following a dinner of boiled millet with zucchini or some such thing, we snuck off to Santa Barbara to eat some real food at Michael's Waterside Inn. This lovely old house on a bird sanctuary is a cousin of the Roux Brothers' fabled Le Gavroche and Waterside Inn restaurants in England, both of which were way stations for chef Michael Hutchings on his way to Santa Barbara. The cooking is approximately half classic French, half nouvelle French, with bits of California cuisine sprinkled in for good measure. Thus, you find tournedos of beef garnished with slices of avocado and an avocado terrine; sweetbreads with local oranges and basil; and duck with local olives, garlic and morels. Hutchings is actually at his best, though, when he's just being Hutchings, creating dishes without portfolio, such as his fine grilled-quail salad and his very British roast lamb. All in all, the setting, the service and the menu are quite conservative, too staid perhaps, and the food is a bit boring—particularly compared to the far more adventurous dishes created at nearby Norbert's and Downey's. But still, after too much diet food, it was a pleasure to revel in all that lovely cream and butter. It was also the reason we went home weighing more than when we arrived, though we didn't regret it much at all. Dinner for two, with wine, runs about $130.

Norbert's

920 De la Vina St., Santa Barbara
(805) 965-6012
FRENCH
Open Mon. & Thurs.-Sun. 5:30 p.m.-10 p.m. Cards: AE, MC, V.

Norbert Schulz and Brigitte Guehr—partners, parents and (for eighteen years) loving companions—provide one of Southern California's most pleasant dining experiences. Their small, thirteen-table restaurant is a converted old home, and it feels like an old home—warm, comfortable, pleasant . . . well, homey. Their excellent French food is lighter than one might expect of a German chef; clearly they have been influenced more by the demands and products of their adopted state than by those of their home country. Schulz, raised in a small town near Stuttgart, began his apprenticeship at 15 and worked in several spa hotels in Germany—meeting Brigitte at one such hotel, where she was an apprentice. In 1975, they came to the United States and spent a couple of years at Scandia, he in the kitchen, she as the venerable restaurant's first woman captain. At Norbert's, he's still in the kitchen, of course, and she now runs the front of the house, with much grace and efficiency.

Norbert's menu is small—usually just four appetizers and four main courses—but it changes nightly, and there are also two set menus, a seven-course "signature dinner" and a four-course "fitness dinner." A la carte appetizers might include a real delicacy—Santa Barbara abalone, in a salad with sesame dressing—as well as grilled venison with wild rice and huckleberry risotto or shrimp with chile-flavored pasta. Main courses might include breast of Muscovy duck with a pecan flan; boneless quail with morel mushrooms, foie gras and a Cabernet sauce; medallions of swordfish with a roasted-bell-pepper sauce; and sole with lobster mousse and basil. One recent signature dinner began with grilled filet of sturgeon with a fennel, orange and persimmon salad, followed by angel-hair pasta with black truffles; then came a squab soufflé, Champagne sorbet, medallions of venison with poppyseed-potato noodles, cheese and a dessert of cherries poached with cinnamon and wine, served with gingerbread ice cream. You can mix and match from among the various menus, substituting an à la carte dish for something on one of the set menus, for example. The wine list here is complete and reasonable, with most of the finer California Cabernets and Chardonnays represented, including the extremely hard-to-find Stony Hill Chardonnay. Dinner for two, with wine, can range from $125 to $165.

Oysters

9 W. Victoria St., Santa Barbara
(805) 962-9888
SEAFOOD
Open Mon.-Thurs. 11:30 a.m.-2:30 p.m. & 5 p.m.-9:30 p.m., Fri.-Sat. 11:30 a.m.-2:30 p.m. & 5 p.m.-10 p.m., Sun. 5 p.m.-9:30 p.m. Cards: MC, V.

Brigitte Guehr and Norbert Schulz weren't content to have just two excellent, popular restaurants. No, they saw that Santa Barbara was curiously lacking good, contemporary seafood restaurants and stepped right in to fill the void. The result is Oysters, an informal, open-kitchen café with a cool, quiet outdoor patio that makes an idyllic lunch spot. In good seafood-house fashion, the fresh-fish dishes change daily depending on the market; the offerings of the day (salmon, ono, swordfish, yellowtail) are expertly grilled, poached or baked in puff pastry. To live up to its name, Oysters also serves fresh, briny oysters in all forms, from shooters to oyster stew. And the kitchen does a good job of combining shellfish with pasta, as in the delicious fettuccine with lobster, scallops, tomato and pine nuts. Service is prompt and professional, and the wine list has plenty of good whites for under $20. About $60 for dinner for two, with wine.

13 The Palace Cafe

8 E. Cota St., Santa Barbara
(805) 966-3133
CAJUN/CARIBBEAN
Open Sun.-Thurs. 5:30 p.m.-10 p.m., Fri.-Sat. 5:30 p.m.-11 p.m. (desserts & drinks served 1 hour after closing). Cards: AE, MC, V.

In a town noted for friendly, laid-back restaurants, The Palace is certainly the friendliest and most laid-back. From the moment you walk in, you're part of the family; your waiter may just pull up a chair and sit down while he tells you how wonderful the specials are. Before you know it, you're swapping stories with the waiters and your fellow diners. It's a homey, aw-shucks kind of place, with a New Orleans–style lamppost in the window, old-fashioned jazz on the stereo, New Orleans jazz posters on the walls and impeccably authentic and delicious Cajun food on the tables (including *real* redfish). And now, perhaps in honor of the beach-town location, the kitchen is turning out some tasty Caribbean-style dishes as well. It's all good, starting with the marvelous corn and nut muffins that greet you. The more noteworthy of the new Caribbean dishes include rich Bahamian conch chowder, coconut shrimp and sole Martinique. The seafood gumbo is rich and strongly flavored, the crab claws cooked in "popcorn" batter are delicate and sweet, and the blackened filet mignon is seared perfectly: the inside rare, the outside spicy but not mouth-numbing. Other dishes can be blind-

ingly hot, however, like the mixed sauté of vegetables. Try not to burn off all your taste buds—you'll need them to appreciate the Louisiana bread-pudding soufflé with whisky sauce or the incredibly light and delicious sweet potato–pecan pie with chantilly. About $70 for two, with a local wine.

14 Pane e Vino

1482 E. Valley Rd., Montecito
(805) 969-9274
ITALIAN
Open daily 11:30 a.m.-10 p.m. No cards.

The Santa Barbara area is blessed with many good restaurants, but it's long been lacking in authentic Italian fare. It *was* lacking, that is, until this friendly group of Italians immediately raised Santa Barbara's Italian-food consciousness several levels. If you've been to L.A.'s Prego or San Francisco's Il Fornaio—or for that matter if you've been to Italy—you'll feel right at home in this inviting little trattoria, with its open kitchen, counter heaped with crusty Tuscan bread, tile-and-woodwork bistro decor and comfortable outdoor patio. Order one of the reasonably priced Chiantis, tear into the excellent bread and contemplate the menu, a minicatalog of the joys of Italian food. We can't imagine there's a disappointment to be found, not based on the dishes we've tried. The rich, herby brodetto crostini (bread soup) with tomato, the flavorful insalata mista with baby greens and leeks, the heavenly seafood risotto, the savory tortelloni with butter and sage, the gorgeous grilled veal chop with rosemary, the frothy cappuccino, the cool gelati . . . excuse us, but we've got to cut this review short and hurry back to Montecito. A first-rate Italian dinner for two, with wine, will run a fair $45 to $60.

12/20 Paradise Cafe

702 Anacapa St., Santa Barbara
(805) 962-4416
AMERICAN
Open Mon.-Sat. 11 a.m.-11 p.m., Sun. 8:30 a.m.-11 p.m. Cards: AE, MC, V.

A wonderfully unpretentious place, the Paradise Cafe is located off State Street's beaten path and is therefore filled with locals instead of tourists. The funky old building, with its simple '40s decor, comprises a straightforward bar, an outdoor patio and a split-level dining room; in good weather, the patio is always full at lunch and Sunday breakfast. The food is generously served and exceptionally good: interesting omelets and eggs (including a very tasty dish of scrambled eggs, black beans, salsa and cheese wrapped in a tortilla), a terrific hamburger and perfectly cooked oak-grilled steaks, chops and fish. Our favorite place in Santa Barbara for all-American classics. About $20 for lunch or Sunday brunch for two; about $50 for dinner for two, with a local wine.

11/20 The Ranch House
102 Besant Rd., Ojai
(805) 646-2360
CONTINENTAL/CALIFORNIAN
Open Wed.-Fri. 6 p.m.-8:30 p.m., seatings Sat. 6 p.m. & 8:30 p.m., Sun. 1 p.m., 3:30 p.m., 6 p.m. & 7:30 p.m. Cards: AE, MC, V.

For years and years, The Ranch House has been *the* place to dine in this neck of the woods, on the outskirts of the peaceful, pretty town of Ojai some 40 minutes from Santa Barbara. Back in its early, vegetarian days, it was a pioneer of sorts, one of the first to combine the lighter approach of French nouvelle cuisine with the local bounty of California. Sadly, those pioneering days are long gone. So are the vegetarian days—red meat can be found in abundance on today's Ranch House menu. What hasn't changed is the wonderfully romantic setting: the old inn, the babbling brook, the trees, the herb and vegetable gardens, the chamber music. Combine all that with the superb wine list, and you're bound to have a swell time—as long as you don't expect much of the food. In recent years, our meals here have been totally unmemorable, notable for an overall degree of blandness. Filet of sole Florentine is a boring dish no matter how you slice it, and here it was more tasteless than usual. The vegetables may have been plucked from this very garden, but after being subjected to assiduous overcooking, they might as well have been frozen. And the acclaimed homemade bread was served in slices that would make an anorexic happy; when we asked for more, we were given just two more microslices. To top it off, we've experienced abrupt service, a far cry from the warmth of its earlier days. If you're visiting Ojai and are in the mood for a little romance, The Ranch House will deliver the goods, but the tired food is not worth going out of your way for. Dinner for two, with wine, will run about $90.

12/20 Soho
21 W. Victoria St., Santa Barbara
(805) 965-5497
CALIFORNIAN
Open Mon.-Sat. 11:30 a.m.-2:30 p.m. & 5:30 p.m.-10:30 p.m. (light dishes served until midnight). Cards: MC, V.

At the time of this writing there is no more hip restaurant scene to make than Soho, tucked in one side of the ornate Victoria Street Theatre just off State Street. It's young, it's stylish, it's ebulliently friendly, and it's moderately priced: no wonder there's always a wait on weekends. The only thing we can't figure out is the name—the homey, converted-Victorian-house atmosphere is straight out of Berkeley, not New York, and the food is resolutely Californian, which is to say an eclectic jumble of this and that. It's good food, too, full of youthful enthusiasm and appealing flavors. In addition to the regular menu, a blackboard lists the appetizer-sized specials of the day (also served for late supper), ranging from crisp, tasty crabcakes to thick fried potatoes with a dollop of sour cream and a sprinkle of caviar. The house's pride and joy is the rotelle pasta with grilled prawns, jalapeños, cilantro, apples, cuminos, light cream and Brie. It may sound like a confused mess, but it actually tastes terrific, its ingredients blended with the necessary degree of restraint. Traditionalists can opt for the fresh ravioli paired with such good things as prosciutto, olive oil, garlic and Roma tomatoes. Also worth trying is the tender lamb on a bed of mildly spiced couscous. With a glass of Chardonnay each, you'll spend about $20 per person for dinner.

15 Stonehouse
San Ysidro Ranch, 900 San Ysidro Ln., Montecito
(805) 969-5046
FRENCH
Open Mon.-Sat. 8 a.m.-10:30 a.m., noon-2 p.m. & 6:30 p.m.-9:30 p.m., Sun. 10:30 a.m.-2 p.m. & 6 p.m.-9 p.m. All major cards.

A serious French restaurant in a ranchhouse setting may be stretching the imagination, but it works at the San Ysidro Ranch. Windows look out on the jungle of oak trees and bougainvillea, rough white-stone walls contrast with fine linens and silver, and a pianist in the adjacent bar adds a sophisticated touch. For many years called Plow & Angel, this dining room has had its culinary ups and downs; we've had a couple of pleasant but unremarkable meals here in recent years. But we paid a visit just before press time to sample the work of new chef Mark Ehrler, and left mightily impressed. The meal was far from flawless, but the evening's best dishes were well worth a ranking of 17/20. If the San Ysidro Ranch can hang on to this talented man longer than its previous chefs, Norbert's and Downey's will find themselves with a considerable rival on their hands.

Let's forget for the moment the grilled eggplant soup (a pleasant cream soup seemingly untainted by grilled eggplant) and the crème brûlée (featuring a soggy, mealy brown-sugar topping that hadn't been brûléed long enough). Instead, we'd rather dwell on two lobster dishes that had us reeling with pleasure. The first was a lobster ratatouille that combined sophistication with earthy Provençal flavor: a round "cake" of slightly chilled, finely chopped ratatouille surrounded by generous chunks of sweet lobster mixed with full-bodied tomatoes. The second was an entrée of lobster risotto worthy of the lobster hall of fame. On a pool of heavenly lobster-saffron sauce sat risotto of unimpeachable creaminess and taste; atop the risotto was a fan of tender, richly flavored lobster slices. Less breathtaking, but still delicious and expertly prepared, was the steamed halibut on a bed of sun-dried-tomato sauce ringed with fresh pasta squares. This dish may have been completely free of cream, butter and oil, but it still managed to be hearty, satisfying and bursting with flavor. And the chocolate soufflé was a dream. The wine list is pricey but respectable. The latticed patio provides a lovely setting for an al fresco weekend brunch. Dinner for two, with wine, will cost about $110.

QUICK BITES

The Bakery
129 E. Anapumu St., Santa Barbara
(805) 962-2089
Open daily 7 a.m.-9 p.m. Cards: MC, V.

Across the street from one of Santa Barbara's most visited tourist sites, the historic county courthouse, stands The Bakery, one of the most popular and most overrated bakery/cafés in town. Customers line up early on the broad porch outside this white-on-white café. True, the omelets are fluffy and the quiches rich. But the baguettes can have too-soft crusts, the Marie Callender pies can be overly sweet, and the croissants can be so soggy they pull apart like taffy. A better bet is the all-American, raisin-studded bran muffins.

Charlotte
742 State St., Santa Barbara
(805) 966-1221
Open Mon.-Thurs. 8:30 a.m.-9:30 p.m., Fri.-Sat. 8:30 a.m.-10:30 p.m., Sun. 9:30 a.m.-10:30 p.m. Cards: MC, V.

Charming French owner Patrick Leseq has created a first-rate café that serves both exquisite pastries and simple, delicious meals. Leseq, a passionate wine- lover, also offers a small but quite interesting collection of wines and holds occasional tastings of vintages from local vineyards and France's great châteaux. The place is nothing much to look at, though the pink walls and French music add a bit of charm. But we come here for the heavenly food, not the decor: crisp croissants, incredible breads, creamy quiches and cheesy feuilletés all make lovely breakfasts and lunches. Dinners are delicious (lamb couscous, fresh fish) and quite reasonably priced. Charlotte is also a great spot for a cappuccino and a flaky pastry or sinful chocolate dessert. About $20 for a light lunch for two with a glass of wine.

Esau's Coffee Shop
403 State St., Santa Barbara
(805) 965-4416
Open daily 6 a.m.-8 p.m. No cards.

Esau's looks like a beach-town café built on the back lot at The Burbank Studios. It's funky, nutty, homemade, too casual for words. And it works just fine. Aside from a few sandwiches, nothing is served here but breakfast dishes, most with more or less classic roots. The eggs are divided into three realms: the Basics, which translate as two eggs, any style, with ham (cut from the shank in-house), bacon, country sausage, cube steak, tri-tip steak (there's sort of a tri-tip fad going on in SB) and made-here corned beef hash; the Omelets, which are made with three eggs, and fall into the usual categories, including Western, Vegetarian, Mexican and Italian; the Scrambled category, which follows pretty much the same schemata as the Omelets, along with a few variations, such as the holy combination of salami and eggs. Accompanying each egg dish are homemade buttermilk biscuits, homemade jam, homemade salsa and a choice of home fries, grits, rice, cottage cheese, fruit salad or tomatoes. Breakfast is a good time for pancakes: buttermilk, wheat-germ and blueberry. As an added fillip, there's a fine dish called Irish Pizza, which is basically an order of nachos using potatoes instead of tortilla chips. The coffee is good and strong. The biscuits come with country gravy. We knew they would. Breakfast for two, with coffee, costs about $12.

Joe's Cafe
512 State St., Santa Barbara
(805) 966-4638
Open Sun.-Thurs. 11 a.m.-11 p.m., Fri.-Sat. 11 a.m.-12:30 a.m. Cards: AE, MC, V.

One of the most popular bars in town (see "Nightlife"), Joe's is a no-frills locals' hangout. It's a masculine, Brooklyn-style pub with dark wood, a great old jukebox, deafening noise level and simple, heavy bar-and-grill fare, from sandwiches and mama-mia-style pastas to good charbroiled steaks. The food is entirely forgettable, but the portions are large, the free accompaniments (soup, salad, onion rings) quite numerous, the prices low. And the people-watching is unbeatable. About $9 per person for lunch with a beer; $13 to $20 for dinner without drinks.

McConnell's Ice Cream
1213 State St., Santa Barbara
(805) 965-5400
Open Sun.-Thurs. 11 a.m.-11 p.m., Fri.-Sat. 11 a.m.-midnight. No cards.

One of the country's finest ice cream makers is based right here in Santa Barbara. McConnell's all-natural ice creams are very, very rich and very, very good. You can take your sundae or double waffle cone out for a stroll on State Street or eat at one of the small tables in this cheery shop. There are also good sorbets, shakes and cappuccinos. Don't miss the freezer-full of discounted "not-up-to-standards" cartons.

Mousse Odile
18 E. Cota St., Santa Barbara
(805) 962-5393
Open Mon.-Sat. 8 a.m.-2:30 p.m. & 5:30 p.m.-9:30 p.m. All major cards.

Mousse Odile serves a taste of its famous chocolate mousse with every dish, an unspoken reminder that chef/owner Odile Mathieu started out catering creamy mousses for the crème de la crème of Santa Barbara society. But there are other French delights that make this simple restaurant a fine spot for a casual breakfast or lunch. Fresh fruit and crème anglaise top marvelous waffles. Delicate roules enfold a béchamel sauce rich with Gruyère. Quiches hold custardy seafood or ham-and-cheese fillings. And there are fine, simple dinners, such as leg of lamb, couscous, boeuf bourguignon, along with a small but appealing wine list. Breakfast and lunch will run under $10 per person; dinner about $55 for two, with wine.

La Super-Rica
622 N. Milpas St., Santa Barbara
(805) 963-4940
Open daily 11 a.m.-8 p.m. No cards.

Until Julia Child's regular patronage brought much attention to this incomparable Mexican café, in-the-know Santa Barbarans were able to keep it to themselves. Now the word is out, and we cannot encourage you enough to rush right over for the best soft tacos you'll ever have—fresh, hot corn tortillas, made right there, topped with grilled chicken, pork, beef or chorizo. You must also try the frijoles, an addictive dish of beans, sausage, bacon and chiles. These soul-satisfying foods are best eaten with a Mexican beer on the rustic covered patio. About $12 for two, with beer.

Tutti's
1209 Coast Village Rd., Montecito
(805) 969-5809
Open Sun.-Mon. & Wed.-Thurs. 7 a.m.-9 p.m., Tues. 7 a.m.-3 p.m., Fri.-Sat. 7 a.m.-10 p.m. Cards: MC, V.

Sleekly modern and stylish, Tutti's is many things to prosperous Montecitans: a gourmet grocery store, an upscale deli, a wine and cappuccino bar and a fun place for a simple breakfast, lunch or dinner. It's quite handsome, if typically trendy, with gleaming deli cases, an open kitchen, stacks of packaged food and wine, and a narrow marble bar counter facing the window to the street, where you can have a meal or a drink while watching Montecito pass by. (Order the wine by the glass carefully—just because they've opened it doesn't mean it's ready to drink.) Dinners are on the expensive side, but breakfast and lunch are more reasonable. None of the food is exceptional, but it's all pleasant, especially the croissants, the breads and the salads. Tutti's also packs a good picnic lunch. About $15 for breakfast for two; $28 for lunch for two, with a glass of wine.

The Zia Café
421 N. Milpas St., Santa Barbara
(805) 962-5391
Open Tues.-Sat. 11:30 a.m.-2:30 p.m. & 5 p.m.-10 p.m., Sun. 5:30 p.m.-9 p.m. Cards: AE, MC, V.

The way Zia touts itself as preparing the fine cuisine of New Mexico, we expected to find a modest version of St. Estèphe. Instead, we found an attractive but humble little place that serves spicy-spicy variations on Mexican basics—enchiladas, tacos and tamales are about the only offerings here. New Mexico enters into the picture with the blue-corn tortillas, the delicious, slightly sweet sopapillas (kind of a cross between bread and a tortilla) and the substitution of posole for rice. Some of it is quite good (the chicken blue-corn taco), some of it is bad (the beef blue-corn taco, with beef that tastes like Taco Helper), and some of it tasty but dauntingly hot (the good tamales in red and green chile sauces). About $10 per person for lunch, with a Corona; dinner is a bit more.

HOTELS

Bath Street Inn
1720 Bath St., Santa Barbara, 93101
(805) 682-9680

Several years ago Nancy Stover, Susan Brown and Barbara Davis turned this once-faded Victorian home into one of Santa Barbara's most gracious and comfortable bed-and-breakfast inns. Each of the seven rooms has its own bathroom—from the period bath with a claw-footed tub in the spacious Par-

tridge Room to the minuscule shower-sink-toilet tucked under an eave in the Balcony Room. All the rooms are attractive and commendably quiet; extras include a handsome communal living room and a third-floor library and TV room. A fine breakfast is served in the lovely, flower-filled garden: homemade granola, nut breads and sweet rolls, warm croissants, fresh fruit (baked apples, strawberries and cream) and juice from the garden's orange trees. Other amenities include plenty of free bikes, complimentary wine and cheese in the evening, and the company of two outdoor cats.

Rooms: $90-$115 (discounts offered off-season weekdays).

Bayberry Inn
111 W. Valerio St., Santa Barbara, 93101
(805) 682-3199

Though rather fussy, the Bayberry Inn hardly lacks charm. The living room features a grand piano, ornate antiques and a much-used fireplace; the seven bedrooms all have canopy beds and private baths, and most have fireplaces. Located near central State Street, this very comfortable bed-and-breakfast is within walking distance of some of Santa Barbara's best shops and restaurants. A quiet and dignified (yet friendly) inn.

Rooms: $75-$125 (discounts offered off-season weekdays).

The Cheshire Cat
36 W. Valerio St., Santa Barbara, 93101
(805) 569-1610

Santa Barbara's newest bed-and-breakfast is also its loveliest—and most expensive. A dozen storybook-charming Laura Ashley-style rooms are spread between two neighboring stately Victorian homes, which share a serene garden and large Jacuzzi. The rooms have queen- or king-sized beds and private baths; some have fireplaces, sitting rooms, Jacuzzis and private patios. Public areas include a fireplace-warmed sitting room and a rather stately dining room; breakfast can also be enjoyed on the patio outside. A good breakfast, afternoon wine, complimentary bicycles, evening chocolates . . . nothing is lacking, except a needed bit of personality (when we spent a weekend here, we were greeted and served by teenage employees; if owners and/or managers existed, they kept a low profile).

Rooms: $119-$179 (weekends and summer), $79-$119 (off-season weekdays).

El Encanto Hotel
1900 Lausen Rd., Santa Barbara, 93103
(805) 687-5000

As the name implies, there is enchantment to be found at this hotel, which is actually a collection of cottages in the hills above Santa Barbara. Unfortunately, the enchantment stems from the gorgeous setting and view, not the accommodations. Though not without charm, the genteelly rustic cottages have become tired and shabby, radiating a motel feeling. Service can be a bit slipshod, and the dining room isn't nearly as good as its reputation would lead you to believe. On the up side, some of the rooms have fireplaces and kitchens, and the grounds are home to a tennis court and pool. And if the weather is cooperative, which it usually is, you can sit on the Astroturfed terrace just before sunset and soak in the kind of Pacific view that inspires countless frozen Midwesterners to move to California.

Cottages: $100-$325.

Four Seasons Biltmore
1260 Channel Dr., Santa Barbara, 93108
(805) 969-2261

Now that Four Seasons has put its stamp on this grande dame of Santa Barbara resort hotels, the decor, atmosphere and style of the place have shot up considerably. Unfortunately, so have the prices. What you get for your $300 or more a night is an architectural stunner of a Spanish-Mediterranean resort spread across 21 acres of superb gardens, a magnificent oceanfront setting, handsome, impeccably equipped rooms, professional service and loads of amenities: tennis courts, two swimming pools, golf- and polo-club privileges and an adjacent beach club. Try to get one of the small cottages, which are especially

charming. The lavish weekend brunch is one of *the* scenes to make in Santa Barbara.

Singles & doubles: $265-$350; suites: $400-$1,595. Special packages offered.

Miramar Hotel
1555 S. Jameson Ln., Santa Barbara, 93108
(805) 969-2203

In some ways this sprawling resort, in business since 1887, reminds us of a Bulgarian seaside resort where workers from the grain cooperative are rewarded wtih a vacation if they've had a productive year. There is nothing luxurious about the amenities at the Miramar: the rooms are large but plain, with threadbare towels and beds that are likely to be lumpy. But for one of the most spectacularly sited resorts in Southern California, the price is right. No other resort hotel in the vicinity has its own private beach (one of the best in California). There are four tennis courts and two swimming pools, large convention facilities and a snack shop in an old railway car. Reserve a beachfront room, if one is available, or a two- or three-bedroom cottage—some of these are quite charming, with fireplaces and full kitchens. (The most modern cottages, unfortunately, are also the noisiest, as they are set close to the freeway.) Don't bother to visit the dining room; cook your own breakfast and go into Santa Barbara for dinner.

Singles, doubles & cottages: $65-$125.

The Montecito Inn
1295 Coast Village Rd., Montecito, 93108
(805) 969-7854

The Montecito Inn must have been incredibly charming when it opened its doors in 1928—an intimate hideaway for Hollywood's greats, built by two of the greatest: Charlie Chaplin and Fatty Arbuckle. In 1981, a new owner decided to spend lavishly and completely restore it, hoping to recapture the look and feeling of its youth. As handsome as the remake is, there are two drawbacks the new management cannot decorate away: the Inn's close proximity to busy Highway 101 and the lack of air conditioning. If the ceiling fans provide enough air—and act as a noise screen for the freeway traffic—you'll enjoy everything else, particularly the gracious service. The tiled, arch-ceilinged lobby is lined with rose-velvet love seats and mirror-topped tables for taking tea or the complimentary Continental breakfast. The rooms are small by today's hotel standards, done in subdued Pierre Deux fabrics with modern bathrooms, each with unique Mexican tile. The pool is the size of a goldfish pond, but there is a Jacuzzi for relaxing and Nautilus equipment in the adjoining spa or free bicycles for those who insist on exercise. Off the lobby is the Montecito Café, which combines a lovely Mediterranean decor with tasty, moderately priced Californian cuisine.

Singles & doubles: $85-$135; suites: $185.

The Oaks at Ojai

See "Spas" under "Beauty & Health" in Shops.

 ## Ojai Valley Inn & Country Club
Country Club Dr., Ojai, 93023
(805) 646-5511

Vista International breathed new life into this longtime golf-oriented resort, and the results of its massive renovation and new construction are winning. More than 200 commodious, handsome rooms in some eleven buildings and cottages are scattered about the oak-dotted grounds. Also on the 200 rolling acres are an exceptionally attractive eighteen-hole golf course, an eight-court tennis center, a children's playground, sports fields for softball, volleyball, horseshoes and such, two pools, a health center complete with saunas, spas and workout equipment, walking/jogging trails, several restaurants, a lounge and a snack bar. As you can see, you'd have to make a real effort to be bored here. A short drive away is the picturesque, sleepy town of Ojai, a fine place for an afternoon shopping stroll and a meal in one of the appealing restaurants. Also nearby is Wheeler Hot Springs, where you can take the cure in steaming tubs of Ojai's legendary mineral water, submit to a rejuvenating massage, and relax over an excellent Sunday brunch.

Singles & doubles: $160-$200; suites: $295-$480.

 ## San Ysidro Ranch
900 San Ysidro Ln., Montecito, 93108
(805) 969-5046

This is one of the few places in America in the Relais et Châteaux chain of quality French hotels, and it deserves the affiliation. On a picture-perfect site in the verdant foothills of Montecito, the 105-year-old ranch has history (Churchill wrote his memoirs here), romance (Laurence Olivier and Vivian Leigh were married in the garden, and Jack and Jackie honeymooned here) and bushels of rustic charm. When the ranch was owned by actor Ronald Colman in the '30s, it was a weekend playground for Hollywood's heroes, but after his demise, it followed suit. Finally a former president of New York's Plaza Hotel bought the property and spruced it up for today's movie moguls, who aren't put off by the outrageously high prices. It's now fallen into the extremely capable hands of Claude Rouas, who also owns Napa Valley's superb Auberge de Soleil. The unpretentious simplicity is irresistible; we adore the little and not-so-little cottages decorated with fashionably homey furniture. The fragrance of the gardens and underbrush is as seductive as the privacy ensured by the supremely comfortable bungalows; many have fireplaces, some have Jacuzzis, and most allow well-behaved dogs, which is virtually unheard of in American hotels. Amenities include tennis courts, a small pool and children's wading pool with stunning views over the eucalyptus trees to the Pacific, golf privileges at the nearby Montecito Country Club, horses for riding the miles of mountain trails, and the terrific Stonehouse restaurant.

Cottages & cottage rooms: $160-$285 without Jacuzzi; $350-$425 with Jacuzzi.

 ## Villa Rosa
15 Chapala St., Santa Barbara, 93101
(805) 966-0851

This pale-pink palazzo, a converted Spanish-style home, is one of the most contemporary and tastefully decorated bed-and-breakfast inns in Santa Barbara. True, the others have old-fashioned charm and a little more personality, but the Villa

Rosa has sophistication and a handsome Southwestern interior in monochromatic grays and dusty beiges. No matter that the walls are paper-thin; you'll get to know your neighbors well enough in the Jacuzzi or relaxing around the pool in the beautiful courtyard, where wine and cheese are served in the late afternoon and a croissant breakfast is served each morning. The location is perfect for a stroll on the beach (around the corner) or to admire the Moreton Bay fig tree nearby, a huge landmark planted in 1877. The best rooms overlook the pool away from the sounds of traffic. One of our favorite inns in Santa Barbara.

Doubles: $80-$150 (midweek), $90-$185 (weekends).

NIGHTLIFE

Acapulco

1114 State St., Santa Barbara
(805) 963-3469
Open daily 11 a.m.-midnight. Cards: AE, MC, V.

This popular tourist spot concocts 31 different flavors of margaritas, which are served outdoors under the umbrella-shaded patio, in the spacious bar or in the jungle room, which is painted in the naïf style of Rousseau. It's always packed here but remains a pleasant place to watch afternoon shoppers in the little paseo or to spend an evening when the tempo and clientele pick up.

The Grill

1279 Coast Village Rd., Montecito
(805) 969-5959
Open daily 11 a.m.-1:30 a.m. Cards: AE, MC, V.

If you've had enough of the party-hearty collegiate/surfer scene around State Street, head Montecito way to this intimate, cozy bar, a civilized watering hole for an upscale 30-to-50-something crowd. Live music—an eclectic mix of blues, jazz and pop—kicks in every night about nine, and it's always worth a listen. To sweeten the deal, there's no cover charge. Our favorite Santa Barbara nightspot.

Joe's Cafe

512 State St., Santa Barbara
(805) 966-4638
Open Sun.-Thurs. 11 a.m.-11 p.m., Fri.-Sat. 11 a.m.-12:30 a.m. Cards: AE, MC, V.

On Friday and Saturday nights this place is a madhouse—randy young Santa Barbarans cram in three-deep at the bar, most of them looking for bitchin' babes and rad dudes. While they prowl, they try to talk to their many friends by shouting over the incredible noise level. It's considerably quieter during the day and in the afternoon, when you'll see a more relaxed crowd of seasoned Joe's veterans. A Santa Barbara landmark that is great for inexpensive drinks, local color and studying the native language of the California beach scene.

Zelo

630 State St., Santa Barbara
(805) 966-5792
Open 5:30 p.m.-1:45 a.m. Cover varies. Cards: MC, V.

For the last few years Zelo has held claim to the title of hippest nightclub in town—but keep in mind that this town is not exactly cluttered with hip nightclubs. Also keep in mind that Zelo's is a fashionable restaurant that serves too-cool Californian cuisine and turns on the recorded dance music at 9:30 each night for a young, self-consciously trendy crowd. Bands keep the crowd dancing twice a month; the rest of the time the tunes are deejay-spun rock, soul, hip-hop and the like.

SIGHTS

In addition to the worthy sights listed below, Santa Barbara boasts a wealth of outdoor activities, encouraged by the seemingly constant sunshine and the sparkling sea. Good beaches abound: surfers will want to head for Rincon Point, Carpinteria and the surf breaks near U.C. Santa Barbara; windsurfers for West Beach; and swimmers, sunbathers and strollers for any stretch of sand. And though it may be touristy, you ought to walk to the end of Stearns Wharf (where State Street meets the beach) for a superb view of the coastline and

413

a paper-plate meal of clam chowder and lobster at the Santa Barbara Shellfish Company.

For brochures detailing the area's many sports and activites (deep-sea fishing, sailing, horseback riding, bicycling, tennis, golf . . .), contact the Convention and Visitors Bureau, (805) 965-3021.

Santa Barbara Botanic Garden

1212 Mission Canyon Rd., Santa Barbara
(805) 682-4726
Open daily 8 a.m.-sunset. Admission free.

There's more to Santa Barbara's environment than sand, sun and red tile. There's also a staggering variety of native flora. For proof of this, spend an hour or so wandering the trails through the 65 peaceful acres of this marvelous botanic garden. You won't see many tourists, but you will see everything from vivid wildflowers to dramatic cacti, from spiky palm trees to cool redwoods.

Santa Barbara Historical Society

126 E. De la Guerra St., Santa Barbara
(805) 966-1601
Open Tues.-Sat. 10 a.m.-5 p.m., Sun. noon-5 p.m. Admission free.

This dedicated group of heritage-preservers runs a small, intriguing museum dedicated to the Santa Barbara of days gone by. It also offers docent-led trips along the city's Red Tile Walking Tour, a must for admirers of Spanish architecture. (The walking tour can also be self-guided; for a map call the Tourist Information Center, 965-3021.)

Santa Barbara Mission

2201 Upper Laguna St., Santa Barbara
(805) 682-4149
Open daily 9 a.m.-5 p.m. Adults $1, children under 16 free.

The Santa Barbara Mission, first built in 1786, is proof that Southern California has a more venerable history than its reputation would suggest. The tenth mission founded by the Spanish Franciscans, this "Queen of the Missions" is one of the loveliest, and is in the best condition. You can study dioramas of Franciscan life, wander in the gardens where the missionaries taught the native Chumash Indians, attend a service in the Indian-built chapel and walk among the gravestones of those buried there. Throughout are good examples of Spanish colonial architecture (on which the best architecture in town is modeled) and eighteenth- and nineteenth-century Spanish-Mexican art.

Santa Barbara Museum of Art

1130 State St., Santa Barbara
(805) 963-4364
Open Tues.-Wed. & Fri.-Sat. 11 a.m.-5 p.m., Thurs. 11 a.m.-9 p.m., Sun. noon-5 p.m. Admission free.

Thank goodness for the benefactors who keep this museum filled with their own highly personal collections. This provincial yet admirable museum may give visitors a sense of dizziness from the eclectic nature of the bequests; impressive American Hudson River school oils are hung next to modest Greek and Roman antiquities. The best, however, is the doll collection, with everything from African queens to Quaker matrons (check first—it's shown on a rotating basis). Traveling exhibitions in this well-endowed museum tend to be quite exciting and dynamic. It also sponsors art tours throughout the world and presents lectures frequently; in fact, it has thoughtfully provided a luncheon art lecture to accommodate local businesspeople during their lunch hours.

Santa Ynez Valley

An increasingly popular activity for Santa Barbara visitors is a pleasant day trip through the burgeoning wine country nestled into the Santa Ynez Valley, about a 90-minute drive inland. Wine-lovers (and nature-lovers) owe it to themselves to explore these country roads, home to such admirable wineries as Au Bon Climat, Firestone and Zaca Mesa. On the way back over the San Marcos Pass, you can stop in for an atmospheric dinner at Cold Spring Tavern (see "Restaurants"). For a map of the wine country, call the Santa Barbara Tourist Information Center, (805) 965-3021.

CITYLORE

HISTORY & LEGEND

Hopi legend tells of a lost civilization populated by what they called the Lizard People, who lived some 5,000 years ago. The Lizard People, it seems, built a number of underground cities—thirteen to be exact—one of which is said to be located under downtown Los Angeles (most of the ancient Indian settlements in Southern California do correspond to today's large population centers). The network of tunnels making up this city is purportedly shaped like a lizard, its head falling under what is now Dodger Stadium. According to the legend, these tunnels contain gold tablets that chronicle the history of the race. In the 1930s, an engineer named W. Warren Shufelt was convinced of the lost city's existence and set about finding it. He drilled a huge shaft and came up empty, which prompted howls of public derision. What keeps this story alive, besides the prospect of bringing down the astronomical tunneling costs of the Metrorail project, is that from time to time unexplained tunnels have in fact been discovered beneath downtown L.A.

In 1846 the United States and Mexico—with much exchange of gunfire—were squabbling over who would keep the Southwestern states. To his chagrin, Pio Pico, the last governor of Alta California, found that the Californios didn't care a bit—they accepted American rule with the same indifference that they had treated the Mexican government. That is, until Lt. Archibald Gillespie was appointed commander of Southern California. After he instituted a series of Draconian laws, the normally easygoing Angelenos took up the rebel call. Under Gen. José Maria Flores, they booted Gillespie out of the city, sparking a briefly successful insurgency that spread north to Santa Barbara and south to San Diego, keeping California (for a time) under Mexico's wing. Los Angeles and its citizens were not to figure prominently in a war again until World War II.

In October 1871, a white Angeleno mob descended on the center of the Chinese community, the Calle de los Negros, and massacred some twenty innocent Chinese residents. The police did nothing. A grand jury was convened and handed down indictments. A few of the attackers drew jail sentences, and it appeared that in the end justice would prevail, thanks in part to the efforts of presiding Judge Robert M. Widney, one of L.A.'s biggest real estate promoters. Possibly more interested in boosting land sales than keeping abreast of the finer points of the law, Widney overlooked a few legal technicalities in the indictments, and they were overturned on appeal. Still convinced that he possessed a great appreciation of the lofty pursuit of knowledge, Widney went on, in 1880, to help found the University of Southern California.

Sometime around 1885, Angeleno Daeida Hartell Wilcox took the train back to Ohio to visit relatives. En route, she met a woman who talked about her country estate in Illinois called Hollywood. Daeida loved the sound of the name. So when she returned to the 120-acre ranch she and her husband, H.H. Wilcox, owned in northwest Los Angeles, she named it Hollywood. Little did she know how that appealing name would go on to label so much more than a neighborhood: movies, glamour, celebrities, fame, the good life.

At about three in the morning on February 25, 1942, war fever hit home in Los Angeles. A few days earlier, a Japanese submarine had opened fire on a oil installation farther up the coast. Now, an unidentified aircraft was picked up on radar. Shortly thereafter, something was spotted wafting over Santa Monica. The city erupted in a frenzy of antiaircraft fire. Although the expected Japanese air raid failed to materialize, L.A. still managed to chalk up five fatalities that night—three people were killed in car accidents as panicky motorists attempted to navigate the city streets during the blackout; two more succumbed to cardiac arrest. Property damage that night was also high, thanks to some of the 1,400 U.S. antiaircraft shells that arced their way back downward onto peoples' homes. Steven Spielberg fictionalized the fateful night in his overblown movie, *1941*.

SEX & SCANDAL

To be sure, the Roaring Twenties found no shortage of hucksters and con men in booming Los Angeles. None, however, were quite as gifted as Chauncey C. (C.C.) Julian, founder of Julian Petroleum, which was affectionately known as Julian Pete. Julian came to L.A. a poor gambler, but had a demonstrable gift for advertising, salesmanship and, when necessary, bribery. But it was his talent for manipulating the stock market, particularly oversubscribing shares of his own oil company, that brought him his fortune. He used this money to live life to the hilt, partying constantly and often leaving outrageous tips, all the while dodging investigations from every law-enforcement agency from the local cops to the FBI. The boom was finally lowered on May 7, 1927. Trading was suspended on Julian stock, and his investment pyramid came crashing down. To the consternation of some 40,000 investors, Julian Petroleum was oversubscribed to the tune of $150,000,000, an even more staggering sum in that day. Although the affairs of C.C. Julian had parted company with legal business practice years before, the only one connected with the scandal to serve time was, ironically, the district attorney, who had accepted bribes to help throw the trial.

Sister Aimee Semple McPherson, the tambourine-tapping, marimba-playing evangelist, came to L.A. poor in material goods but rich in spirit. It wasn't long before she found herself surrounded by a loyal flock eager to hear her upbeat, flashy presentations of the Lord's message—and eager to make substantial faith offerings. She was able to start her own radio station and the still-extant Angelus Temple, off Sunset Boulevard in Echo Park. On May 18, 1926, while swimming at the beach, McPherson vanished. An exhaustive search yielded nothing; Sister Aimee, it appeared, had drowned. Then, miraculously, a month later she came stumbling out of the desert into a small Mexican town, spinning a wild tale about two people who had kidnapped her and taken her to Mexico. The faithful rejoiced, the cynical grew suspicious. The latter had trouble believing Sister Aimee could trudge across the desert without getting so much as a sunburn. Although an investigation into the affair went nowhere, the story persisted, with plenty of evidence to back it up, that Sister Aimee, yielding to a little weakness of the flesh, had been shacking up in Carmel with her radio-station engineer. She continued her ministry for a time, but gradually lost her following.

Hollywood's spiciest scandal to date splashed into the headlines in 1930 with the lurid revelations of the goings-on of screen star Clara Bow, the original "It" girl. In addition to playing real-life bedfellow to such notable actors as Bela Lugosi and Gary Cooper, she was also reported to have indulged in sexual scrimmages with the entire University of Southern California football team. Her adventures may have inspired at least one fledgling actor—the team at the time included tackle Marion Morrison, later known as John Wayne. USC coach Howard Jones, a stodgy teetotaler, put an end to this off-the-field scoring by declaring Bow off-limits. The Trojans may have suffered because of his strictness: they enjoyed few winning seasons for years to come.

In the late 1930s, a reform-minded organization called CIVIC began investigating the shady dealings of Mayor Frank Shaw and the corrupt Los Angeles vice squad. With the firm backing of the *Los Angeles Times*, Shaw was able to hold his own, and the city's pimps, whores, bootleggers, gamblers and hucksters continued to operate without such nuisances as municipal law enforcement. Then a CIVIC investigator, Harry Raymond, got in his car on the morning of January 14, 1938, on his way to give damaging testimony against the mayor. The car exploded when he turned the key, but miraculously, despite massive shrapnel wounds, he survived. The bomb was traced to LAPD Lt. Earl Kynette, a notorious figure whose methods of persuasion were known to veer toward the thuggish. The scandal brought down the administration. This mini-Watergate earned L.A. the dubious distinction of being the only major American city to ever recall its mayor.

In February 1949, Robert Mitchum, wholesome star of the American screen, was arrested during a party at the Laurel Canyon home of actress Lila Leeds. The charge was—gasp—"conspiracy to possess marijuana." His trial buzzed with speculations about Mitchum being framed, since (among other things) before his arrest, for some inexplicable reason, his house was being bugged. Unlike previous celebrity victims of drug scandals, Mitchum came out of his two-month prison sentence with his career intact, though the city fathers did feel it behooved them to cancel Mitchum's speech in celebration of National Youth Week.

WINNERS & LOSERS

The disillusionment of Hollywood's countless young aspirants was embodied in the person of Lillian Millicent (Peg) Entwhistle. Entwhistle is best known not for her acting talents, which were fairly accomplished, but as "the woman who jumped off the Hollywood sign." Actually, at the time, the sign read, HOLLYWOODLAND. Entwhistle plummeted to her sad death from the 50-foot-high H, although many versions had her leaping from the final D; this legend was preferred because the D was the thirteenth letter in the sign, and Entwhistle's first, and last, screen performance was in a movie called *13 Women*, thus giving the story a satisfying superstitious confluence. Also incorrect is the widespread notion that her death leap precipitated a fad among suicides who took to jumping off the sign in droves. No one else has ever been known to repeat poor Peg's final performance.

By all accounts, Eben Ahbez was a strange man. He eschewed such amenities as shoes, shaves and haircuts and wandered the streets of Hollywood preaching Oriental philosophy. In 1947 he confronted Nat King Cole's manager, Mort Ruby, and shoved a dirty sheet of paper into his hand, imploring Ruby to show the song it held to Cole. Amazingly, the song did find its way to Cole, and from Cole, to Irving Berlin. Berlin was sufficiently impressed with the tune to want to buy it—the only problem was, nobody knew how to find Ahbez. As legend has it, Ahbez was finally located sleeping under the Hollywood sign. The song, "Nature Boy," recorded by Nat King Cole, sold more than one million copies.

"Marie Prevost did not look her best / The day the cops burst into her loneliness." So sang new-wave pop star Nick Lowe, who put to music the oft-told tale of one of Hollywood's ugliest suicides. Prevost, a silent-screen star, was one of the many human casualties to fill the morgues and sanitariums when talking pictures came along, destroying many careers. In 1937, driven to despondency, Prevost holed herself up in her Hollywood apartment with her pet dachshund and literally drank herself to death at the age of 38. She remained in her apartment for many days, and when she was finally discovered, her body was . . . well, as Lowe sang, "Even the dog, he's a-gotta eat."

MURDER MOST FOUL & SUSPICIOUS SUICIDES

Few homicide investigations so captured the public's imagination as the one that followed the grisly murder of Elizabeth Short, better known as the Black Dahlia. So called because of her habit of always wearing black, Short, like many other lost, star-struck women in Tinseltown, hopped from casting couch to casting couch in search of fame. Fame, unfortunately, finally found her when her mutilated body was discovered dumped in an open field. The massive manhunt yielded plenty of dirt on the tawdry goings-on on the Dream Machine's fringes, but little in the way of actual clues. Thousands of loonies descended on the police with bizarre confessions. The case, which was never solved, spawned a TV movie, a novel and miles of thrilling copy for a public looking for some exciting reading in those dull days following the hubbub of World War II. Short apparently is not resting in peace—her ghost is said to be seen scurrying around her old Hollywood apartment.

Another unsolved mystery with a subsequent haunting is that of the so-called suicide of actor George Reeves, star of the old *Superman* TV series. Reeves was found dead in his Benedict Canyon bedroom after a bullet fired at his head failed to ricochet off harmlessly, as they always did on TV. The gun was found next to him, and his death was ruled a suicide, though many people close to Reeves didn't buy it. His mother dedicated her life, unsuccessfully, to proving he was murdered. The case remains a mystery; numerous ghost sightings and séances at the house have failed to shed any light on the subject.

In 1935 actress Thelma Todd was found dead in the garage above the building that housed her restaurant and her apartment. Her body was bruised and bloodied, slumped behind the wheel of her Packard. It looked like murder, but the coroner said accidental death by carbon-monoxide asphyxiation. Tongues began wagging—too many suspicious circumstances. Words like "scandal" and "cover-up" were bandied about. Todd's ex-husband had known mob connections. Rumors began circulating that the mob wanted to use the Pacific Coast Highway restaurant that she owned as a high-class gambling den, which could be patronized by Todd's high-rolling friends. As the story goes, Todd was not one to be pushed around, and she refused the offer and was summarily rubbed out. Her property was more fortunate: the building that was once Thelma Todd's Roadside Rest still stands, about a half mile north of Sunset on PCH.

COMEDIES OF ERROR

A bbot Kinney had a dream. Already a successful developer at the turn of the century, he decided to create a Venice of America. Not just the physical Venice, with the canals and such, but a cultural duplicate as well. Symphonies and classic dramas would, Kinney believed, make his city one of rare refinement. Unfortunately, it didn't work out that way. Concessions to public tastes required Kinney to make Venice into something closer to Coney Island, complete with kiddie rides and carny shows. Drainage problems caused the canals to turn into swamps, prompting the city of Los Angeles, which by then had incorporated Venice, to fill in most of them. Kinney's idyllic community fell into decline and today, despite awe-inspiring real estate prices, is still home to an unparalleled collection of loonies (not to mention a considerable homeless population). There are, however, some remaining signs of Kinney's dream: what's left of the canals and a lingering artistic sensibility in many of its residents and businesses.

During a longshoremen's strike in San Pedro in 1915, social critic Upton Sinclair addressed the strikers on private property that they had secured permission to use. He began reading to them from the U.S. Constitution. Finding this scene inexplicably offensive, the police arrested him on the spot. Another speaker who read from the Declaration of Independence, and one who commented favorably on the agreeability of California's climate, also suffered the same fate.

In the early 1900s William Mulholland rose to the level of chief engineer of the city water department without ever having stepped inside a university. He is most famous for tapping water from the Owens Valley and carrying it, via a huge aqueduct, hundreds of miles to parched Los Angeles. In 1924, heady with that success, Mulholland decided to build a dam in the Santa Clara River valley north of Los Angeles. Although geologists and engineers who had actually endured the tedium of formal education thought the plan unsafe, Mulholland would not be deterred. The St. Francis Dam was completed in 1927, and it immediately began to develop leaks. Brushing public concerns aside, Mulholland examined the dam on March 12, 1928, and declared it to be completely safe. That very evening, the St. Francis Dam burst with a mighty roar, obliterating three towns—and Mulholland's career.

An old Hollywood story that's been told as often as its veracity has been disputed concerns the fate of actor John Barrymore's body after it was left at the mortuary. The cast of characters changes with each telling. So does the mortuary, for that matter. But the general thrust is this: as a joke, director Raoul Walsh, and/or some accomplices, bribed or cajoled the undertakers to let them borrow Barrymore's body for a few hours. The corpse was then driven up to the Hollywood Hills and deposited in an armchair in Errol Flynn's mansion. Upon returning home, Flynn found himself eye to eye with what he thought to be the late John Barrymore, now apparently making himself at home chez Flynn. The macho, swashbuckling Flynn promptly screamed, ran out of the house and hid behind an oleander bush until the offending body could be, ahem, spirited away.

BASICS

GETTING AROUND

AIRPORT

Though the expansion of Los Angeles International Airport (LAX) has lessened traffic and made the airport considerably more serviceable, it can still get chaotic and crowded at peak travel times. Most travelers have friends or family pick them up from (and take them to) LAX, which can often lead to great frustration when the parking lots are full and the ramps are backed up. It's sometimes wise to consider using the airport shuttle services, which are generally convenient and efficient. Among the biggest shuttle services are: Airport Flyer Express (Los Angeles, 216-1006, Orange County, 714-533-7500, Ventura County, 805-582-0144); Super Shuttle Ground Transportation (338-1111, 714-973-1100); and Prime Time Shuttle (558-1606, San Fernando Valley, 818-901-9901, Ventura County, 805-522-9500). The services are competitively priced: a one-way trip to LAX from most L.A. hotels will cost between $10 and $18 for the first passenger, and between $6 and $10 for each additional passenger in the same party. It's advisable (and sometimes required) to book your shuttle reservation at least one day in advance. If you're planning to rent a car at the airport, note that most rental companies have shuttle services; limousine chauffeurs will, naturally, pick you up at the arrival gate. You'll find cabs (both licensed and "gypsy") waiting outside the terminals, but be warned that if you're going all the way across town, a cab will cost almost as much as a limo!

BUSES

Despite the efforts of the RTD (Rapid Transit District), traveling Los Angeles by bus can be extremely unpleasant and time-consuming and should be avoided whenever possible. There are a few express lines that are reasonably fast, but for the most part, RTD buses are slow and don't seem to follow any sort of time schedule. Ground has been broken for Metrorail, the city's fledgling subway system, but it won't be in use for at least several years.

CARS

Don't think you can survive Los Angeles without access to a car; you can't. The distances here are unlike those in any other city—it seems that every destination is at least a twenty-minute drive away. If you don't have the use of a car or limo, there are dozens of rental agencies throughout the city that are well stocked with high-mileage, low-power American and Japanese compacts and sedans. The biggest companies, with branches everywhere, are Hertz (800-654-3131) and Avis (800-331-1212). For more unusual rentals, try Rent-a-Wreck in West L.A. (classic American cars from the '50s, '60s and '70s, including convertibles, at very low prices; 478-0676, 818-762-3628); Luxury Line (the city's leading renter of such class cars as Ferraris and Rollses; 659-5555) and Budget Rent-a-Car in Beverly Hills (a good stock of Mercedeses and every sort of luxury car; 274-9173). And before you drive your rental *anywhere*, get the indispensable Thomas Brothers map book for Los Angeles and Orange counties. It's available at most bookstores, and it will become your bible for finding your way in the city.

TAXIS

Cabs aren't a very viable means of transportation in L.A., unless you're keeping to one specific area. Since the distances are so vast, cabbing it can become prohibitively expensive; you'll generally come out ahead renting a car. But sometimes a cab is your best alternative, and we can recommend several of the more established companies: Yellow Cab (384-1995), Checker Cab (481-1234), L.A. Taxi (627-7000), United Independent Taxi (653-5050) and Celebrity Red Top Cab (278-2500, 818-988-8515). Unless you're at a hotel, airport or train station, you'll have to callde; the cabs are radio-dispatched, and the wait is usually no more than fifteen minutes.

AT YOUR SERVICE

FOREIGN EXCHANGE

Los Angeles is home to a few more foreign-exchange brokerages each year, but there are still relatively few in the city. Outside of LAX, your best bets for exchanging money on the weekends, when the banks are closed, are the Beverly Hills branch of Deak International, 452 N. Bedford Drive (274-9176; open Saturday 10 a.m. to 4 p.m.), one of Deak's two other branches (Glendale Galleria, 818-242-6883, Sherman Oaks Galleria, 818-907-0160; both open Saturday 10 a.m. to 6 p.m.) or Associated Fine Exchange (AFEX, 433 N. Beverly Drive, Beverly Hills, 274-7610; open Saturday 10 a.m. to 4 p.m.). Bank of America also operates exchange counters at two of its branches (1101 Westwood Boulevard, West L.A., 209-3912, and 525 S. Flower Street, downtown, 228-4622; both open Saturday 9 a.m. to 1 p.m.). The L.A. Currency Exchange (646-9346) has six airport counters that are open until 11 p.m. nightly. Many of the more established banks have exchange windows, but you're limited by bankers' hours, and the rates may not be as good.

LATE NIGHT

BABYSITTER

Baby Sitters Guild
6362 Hollywood Blvd., Hollywood
469-8246
Mature, bonded, reliable sitters are on call 24 hours a day.

BOOKS & NEWSSTANDS

Circus of Books
8230 Santa Monica Blvd., W. Hollywood
656-6533
4001 W. Sunset Blvd., Hollywood
666-1304
L.A.'s only around-the-clock general-interest bookstore. At the time of this writing, the Santa Monica Boulevard store is fighting a battle with local residents to remain open 24 hours. But win or lose, it will doubtless continue to stay open until at least 2 a.m. or so.

Robertson Magazine & Bookstore
1414 S. Robertson Blvd., W.L.A.
858-1804
Come here for art, science-fiction, music and entertainment magazines as well as international magazines and newspapers. Open 24 hours.

Sherman Oaks Newsstand
14500 Ventura Blvd., Sherman Oaks
(818) 995-0632
This good, well-rounded newsstand stocks sports and racing magazines, a large selection of maps and international magazines and newspapers. Open 24 hours.

Victory Boulevard Newsstand
14501 Victory Blvd., Van Nuys
(818) 782-2446
Financial, horse-racing, photography, car and sports magazines are a strong suit. Open 24 hours.

World Book and News
1652 N. Cahuenga Blvd., Hollywood
465-4352
Notable for film and specialty magazines and a wide selection of domestic and foreign periodicals and newspapers, World Book and News has an excellent selection of publications. Open 24 hours.

CAR REPAIR

A-1 Automotive
4430 Santa Monica Blvd., Hollywood
661-5352
These mechanics are on duty 24 hours.

DENTIST

Los Angeles Dental Society
481-2133
Call for a referral to a late-night dentist.

LIMOUSINE

White Tie Limousine Service
553-6060
If you have a pressing need for a Rolls-Royce Phantom Classic at 4 a.m., White Tie

will supply one for $75 per hour. There's a two- or three-hour minimum for most limousines (five-hour minimum for a Rolls).

LOCKSMITHS

Vans Locksmith
463-1982

A large firm with radio-dispatched service. Hours are 8 a.m. to midnight.

Wilshire Lock and Key
389-8433

This locksmith is well established, reliable and on call 24 hours a day.

PHARMACY

Horton & Converse Pharmacy
6625 Van Nuys Blvd., Van Nuys
(818) 782-6251

Pharmacists are on duty 24 hours a day. Another store (11600 Wilshire Boulevard, West L.A., 478-0801) fills prescriptions until 2 a.m.

PLUMBER

Residential Services
277-0770

Licensed, insured and very skilled plumbers are on call 24 hours a day.

POST OFFICE

Van Nuys Main Post Office
15701 Sherman Way, Van Nuys
(818) 908-6701

You can send Express Mail packages from the "Firms" window throughout the night.

Worldway Postal Center
5800 W. Century Blvd., Inglewood
337-8845

This post office near LAX is open until midnight, but you can send Express Mail 24 hours a day.

RESTAURANTS

L.A. is not a late-night town, and the 24-hour culinary pickings are slim. You'll find few gourmet meals at 4 a.m. in this town—but here are a few suggestions for decent all-hours eating.

Canter's
419 N. Fairfax Blvd., Wilshire District
651-2030

Classic, if rather mediocre, Jewish deli food in a quintessential brightly lit, garish deli/coffee-shop setting.

Edie's Diner
4211 Admirality Way, Marina del Rey
823-5339

Another rider on the '50s-diner bandwagon, with average food. Open 24 hours on Friday and Saturday and until 2 a.m. weekdays.

Gorky's Russian Brewery & Café
536 E. 8th St., Downtown
627-4060
1716 N. Cahuenga, Hollywood
463-4060

A hip cafeteria with heavy, hearty, Russian-inspired food, low prices and an eccentric crowd, especially late at night. Open 24 hours.

Jerry's Famous Deli
12655 Ventura Blvd., Studio City
(818) 980-4245

Popular Valley nightspot that serves good New York–style deli fare.

The Original Pantry
877 S. Figueroa St., Downtown
972-9279

The Pantry has been serving continuously for more than 50 years, and very little has changed in all that time. Plain, hearty, all-American meals (roast beef, steak) are served at very low prices. Always open and always crowded. No liquor.

Pacific Dining Car
1310 W. 6th St., Downtown
483-6000

The most attractive, most comfortable and most expensive 24-hour restaurant in town. It has its good dishes and its not-so-good ones; best bets are the delicious (but pricey) steaks and the hearty breakfasts.

Larry Parker's Beverly Hills Diner
206 S. Beverly Dr., Beverly Hills
274-5655

Aside from being open 24 hours, the distinctive feature of this plant-filled diner is the fact that there are telephones in every booth, presumably for those who can't tear themselves away from their work even at 3 a.m. There are always people snacking on hamburgers, omelets and Mexican dishes in the middle of the night here. A comfortable place with mediocre food.

Ships
10705 Washington Blvd., Culver City
839-2347
1016 S. La Cienega Blvd., Wilshire District
652-0401

At these traditional family-style coffee shops you can make your own toast at the table.

Tommy's
2575 Beverly Blvd., Downtown
389-9060

For those with sturdy constitutions, Tommy's serves its famous chiliburgers 24 hours a day. The neighborhood is questionable, but there are guards in the parking lots.. This is one L.A. landmark that's always jumping no matter what the hour..

Zucky's
431 Wilshire Blvd., Santa Monica
393-0551

This popular westside deli's main virtue is that it is always open. You won't exactly be eating four-star cuisine, but you can order everything from omelets to cheesecake 24 hours a day—the perfect place to satisfy your 2 a.m. craving for cheese blintzes after a night of dancing.

TELEPHONE NUMBERS

Amtrak, 624-0171

Beach Information, 305-9545

Burbank Airport, (818) 840-8847

Directory Assistance, 411

Emergency: Fire/Police/Paramedic, 911

Fire Department, 384-3131

Highway Conditions, 626-7231

Library Information, 612-3200

Los Angeles International Airport (LAX), 646-5252

Los Angeles Times, 237-5000

Police Department, 625-3311

Time, 853-1212

Travelers Aid Society of Los Angeles, 625-2501

Visitors Bureau, Los Angeles, 624-7300; Beverly Hills, 271-8126

Weather Conditions, 554-1212

GOINGS-ON

No matter what time of year, there's always some sort of event going on in Southern California—from a date festival to a Shakespeare festival to a surfing contest. We've put together a calendar of the more prominent and/or interesting events (dates are provided when possible).

JANUARY

Rose Parade (Jan. 1), Pasadena, (818) 449-7673 or (818) 449-4100. Renowned parade of floats decorated entirely with flower petals.

Rose Bowl Football Championship (Jan. 1), Rose Bowl, Pasadena, (818) 449-7673. The classic college football showdown.

Chinese New Year (late Jan.-early Feb.), Chinatown, 617-0396.

Whale-watching peak season, Cabrillo Beach Marine Museum, 548-7562; Dana Wharf, (714) 496-5794; and Redondo Beach, 372-3566.

Bob Hope Chrysler Classic, various courses, Palm Springs, (619) 346-8184. Men's golf tournament.

L.A. City Tennis Tournament, Griffith Recreation Center, (818) 246-5614.

"Oshogatsu" Japanese New Year celebration, Little Tokyo, 628-2725.

Pacific Serenades Concert, Biltmore Hotel, (818) 767-2434. Chamber music by the L.A. Philharmonic, the Long Beach Symphony and the L.A. Chamber Orchestra.

FEBRUARY

Black History Month Exhibit, Watts Towers Arts Center, 569-8181. Art exhibition featuring the life and philosophies of Dr. Martin Luther King, Jr.

L.A. Open Golf Tournament, Pacific Palisades, 482-1311.

Laguna Beach Winter Festival (mid-Feb.), Laguna Beach, (714) 494-1018. Art show and arts festival.

National Date Festival, Indio, (619) 347-0676. Festival celebrating Indio's prized fruit. Don't forget to drink plenty of ultra-caloric date shakes.

Pismo Beach Clam Festival, (805) 773-4382. Jazz festival, parade, fair and clams galore: fried clams, clam chowder, raw clams and so on.

MARCH

Environmental Education Fair, L.A. Arboretum, (818) 446-8251. Nature games, exhibits and tours for children and adults.

St. Patrick's Day Parade, Downtown, 413-1273.

Newsweek Champions Cup, Hyatt Grand Champions Resort, Indian Wells, (619) 341-1000, ext. 7002. Men's tennis tournament.

Swallows return to Capistrano (March 19), Mission San Juan Capistrano, (714) 493-1111. These days there may be more tourists than swallows, but the birds are still returning, year in and year out.

Wildflower Walks, Lancaster, (805) 948-4518. Spectacular desert flowers in bloom.

Long Beach Grand Prix, Shoreline Dr., Long Beach, 436-7727. High-energy automobile race through the streets of Long Beach.

Camellia Show, Descanso Gardens, (818) 790-5571. Over 100,000 camellia plants in full bloom.

Kite festivals: Venice (822-2561) and Redondo Beach (437-2552). Bring a picnic and a colorful kite.

APRIL

Academy Awards (early April), Music Center, 278-8990.

American Film Institute Los Angeles International Film Festival, 856-7707. Unusual, eccentric and sometimes excellent films from every corner of the globe.

Blessing of the Animals (weekend before Easter), Olvera St., Downtown, 625-0605. Traditional Mexican parade and celebration.

Easter Sunrise Services, Hollywood Bowl, 850-2000; Forest Lawn, (818) 241-4151; and atop the Palm Springs Aerial Tramway, (619) 325-1391.

Renaissance Pleasure Faire (April-May), San Bernardino, 395-0063. Huge, popular festival with music, theater, food, crafts and costumes of Elizabethan times.

Nabisco–Dinah Shore Invitational Golf Tournament, Rancho Mirage, near Palm Springs, (619) 324-4546.

Cherry Blossom Festival, Little Tokyo, 680-8861. Crafts, food and music to celebrate the arrival of spring.

Los Angeles Dodgers baseball season begins, Dodger Stadium, 224-1500.

MAY

Bullfight season opens, Tijuana.

Affaire in the Gardens—Fine Arts and Crafts Show, Beverly Hills, 550-4628. Artists from around the country display their work.

L.A./California Science Fair, Museum of Science and Industry, 744-7400. Lots of gee-whiz gadgets, gizmos and experiments.

Cinco de Mayo (May 5), Olvera St. and many other L.A. locations, 680-2525. Parades and celebrations honoring Mexico's defeat of the French.

UCLA Mardi Gras, Spaulding Field, UCLA, 825-8001. An ever-popular collegiate carnival and festival.

JUNE

Grand Irish Faire and Music Festival, L.A. Equestrian Center, 202-8846. A cheerful celebration of Irish music, dancing, food, crafts and culture.

Playboy Jazz Festival, Hollywood Bowl, 450-9040. One of the best.

Hollywood Bowl outdoor-concert season begins, 850-2000. Reserve seats for an enchanting musical night under the stars.

Shakespeare Festival (runs all summer), Old Globe Theatre, Balboa Park, San Diego, (619) 239-2255. Many of these productions have been quite admirable.

Ojai Festival, Ojai, (805) 646-2094. Excellent festival featuring innovative modern classical music.

JULY

Fireworks (July 4), throughout the city.

Laguna Beach Arts Festival/Pageant of the Masters (runs several weeks), Laguna Canyon Rd., Laguna, (714) 494-1018. Art show and popular pageant featuring live "reproductions" of great paintings.

Sawdust Festival, Laguna Canyon Rd., Laguna, (714) 494-3030. Crafts show across the street from the arts festival.

Ringling Brothers and Barnum & Bailey Circus, Great Western Forum, Inglewood, 673-1300. The granddaddy of circuses.

Grand Prix Bicycle Race, Manhattan Beach, 545-5313.

Volvo Tennis Los Angeles, L.A. Tennis Center, UCLA, 208-3838. Men's tennis tournament.

AUGUST

Fiesta Days, Santa Barbara, (805) 965-3021. Music, food and crafts of Santa Barbara's early Spanish days.

Nisei Week, Little Tokyo, 620-8861. Celebration of Japanese culture.

Yiddish Culture Festival, Plummer Park, 938-7339. Festival honoring Jewish and Yiddish history and culture.

International Surf Championship and Festival, South Bay beaches, 772-1886.

Old Miners' Days, Big Bear Lake, (714) 866-4601. Local merchants sponsor events celebrating Big Bear's history.

Saint Anthony's Celebration, Pismo Beach, (805) 773-4382. Portuguese seafaring festival and parade.

Virginia Slims Women's Championship Tennis, Manhattan Beach, 546-5656.

SEPTEMBER

Danish Days, Solvang, (805) 688-3317. Danish-heritage town east of Santa Barbara celebrates its roots.

Hollywood Bowl season ends, 850-2000. Gala fireworks finale.

Day in the Park—Belizean Independence Day, Rancho Cienega Park, 732-9742. Celebration with reggae music and Belizean dancing, foods and crafts.

Korean Festival, Koreatown, 730-1495. L.A.'s fast-growing Korean community honors its heritage.

Long Beach Blues Festival, Cal State Long Beach, 985-5566. Top blues artists from across the country perform in a casual festival-style setting.

L.A. County Fair, County Fairgrounds, Pomona, (714) 623-3111. A giant, old-fashioned county fair where farmers show off prize livestock, women compete in pie-baking contests, and kids eat cotton candy.

Los Angeles's birthday, 680-2525. Various civic celebrations.

OCTOBER

Art Expo, L.A. Convention Center, 741-1151. Exhibition of works from artists around the country.

Los Angeles Garden Show, L.A. Arboretum, (818) 446-8251.

NEC World Cycling Invitational, L.A. Velodrome, 649-2466. International competition of top cyclists.

Festival of Masks, Hancock County Park, 315-9444. Exotic folk-art masks from around the work are displayed.

Old Home Town Fair, Manhattan Beach, 545-5313. Beachy small-town festival.

Sea Fest and Sandcastle Building Contest, Corona del Mar, (714) 644-8211.

L.A. Philharmonic opens season at the Music Center, 972-7211.

Los Angeles Lakers basketball season begins, Great Western Forum, Inglewood, 673-1300. The great Chick Hearn loosens up his vocal cords for another season of play-by-play.

NOVEMBER

Dia de los Muertos (Nov. 1), Olvera St., Downtown, 628-7833. Colorful Day of the Dead parades and festival.

Santa Claus Ln. Parade (first Sun. after Thanksgiving), along Hollywood Boulevard, Hollywood, 469-8311. The one and only.

Doo-Dah Parade (after Thanksgiving), Pasadena, (818) 796-2591. Wacky free-for-all parade that spoofs famous parades.

Death Valley Days, Furnace Creek and Stovepipe Wells, Death Valley, (619) 852-4524. This dramatic desert is at its most beautiful during this festival.

Beverly Hills Holiday Pageant, (800) 345-2210. Features youth choir, Santa and local celebrities.

DECEMBER

American Indian Festival, Natural History Museum, 744-3488. Cultural celebration with arts and activities.

Winter Wildland, L.A. Zoo, Griffith Park, 666-4090. The zoo is decorated for Christmas and offers special activities for children.

Corona del Mar Christmas Walk, 644-8211. Merchant open house and street festival along Pacific Coast Highway.

Christmas water parades, in Los Angeles Harbor, 519-3400; Naples Canal in Long Beach, 590-8427; and Marina del Rey, 821-7614. Light-draped and decorated boats of every size and type parade through local waterways.

Las Posadas (nightly from Dec. 16-Dec. 24), Olvera St., Downtown, 628-7833. Traditional Mexican candlelight Christmas march.

L.A. County Holiday Music Program (Dec. 24), Dorothy Chandler Pavilion, Music Center, 972-7211. Free concert of Christmas carols and holiday classics.

Sing-along performance of Handel's *Messiah,* Dorothy Chandler Pavilion, Music Center, 972-7211.

MAPS

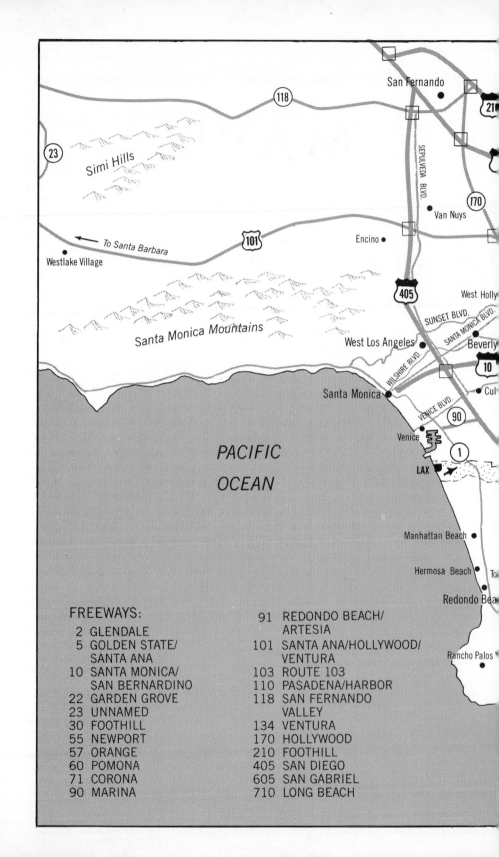

San Fernando

118

23

Simi Hills

SEPULVEDA BLVD.

170

Van Nuys

← To Santa Barbara

101

Encino

Westlake Village

405

West Holly

SUNSET BLVD.

SANTA MONICA BLVD.

Santa Monica Mountains

West Los Angeles

Beverly

WILSHIRE BLVD.

10

Santa Monica

Cul

VENICE BLVD.

90

Venice

PACIFIC

OCEAN

1

LAX

Manhattan Beach

Hermosa Beach

To

Redondo Bea

Rancho Palos

FREEWAYS:

2	GLENDALE	91	REDONDO BEACH/ ARTESIA
5	GOLDEN STATE/ SANTA ANA	101	SANTA ANA/HOLLYWOOD/ VENTURA
10	SANTA MONICA/ SAN BERNARDINO	103	ROUTE 103
22	GARDEN GROVE	110	PASADENA/HARBOR
23	UNNAMED	118	SAN FERNANDO VALLEY
30	FOOTHILL	134	VENTURA
55	NEWPORT	170	HOLLYWOOD
57	ORANGE	210	FOOTHILL
60	POMONA	405	SAN DIEGO
71	CORONA	605	SAN GABRIEL
90	MARINA	710	LONG BEACH

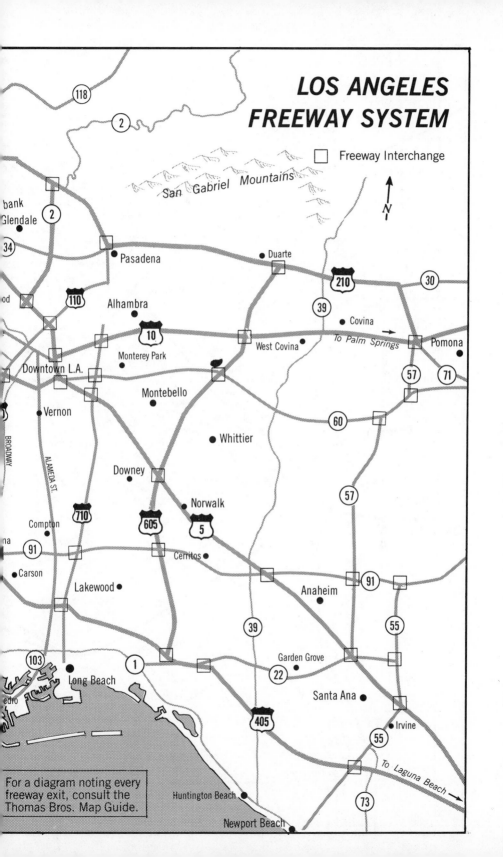

LOS ANGELES FREEWAY SYSTEM

☐ Freeway Interchange

N↑

San Gabriel Mountains

118

2

bank
Glendale   2
34

od
110

Pasadena

Alhambra

10

Monterey Park

Downtown L.A.

Vernon

BROADWAY

ALAMEDA ST.

Downey

710

Compton

91

Carson

Lakewood

103

Long Beach

edro

Duarte

210

30

39

Covina

West Covina

To Palm Springs   Pomona

57   71

Montebello

60

Whittier

57

Norwalk

605   5

Cerritos

Anaheim

91

55

39

Garden Grove

22

Santa Ana

1

Garden Grove

405

Irvine

55

To Laguna Beach

For a diagram noting every
freeway exit, consult the
Thomas Bros. Map Guide.

Huntington Beach

73

Newport Beach

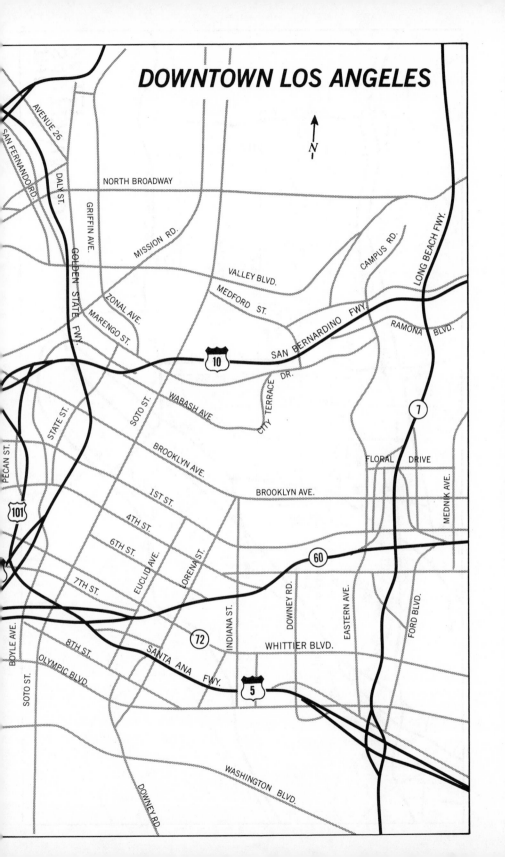

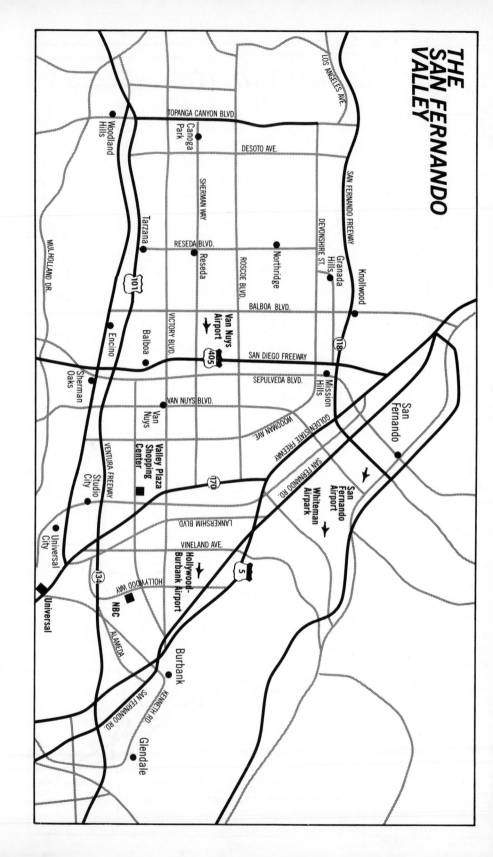

THE
SAN FERNANDO
VALLEY

LOS ANGELES AVE.

TOPANGA CANYON BLVD.

Woodland
Hills

Canoga
Park

DESOTO AVE.

SAN FERNANDO FREEWAY

SHERMAN WAY

DEVONSHIRE ST.

Knollwood

Tarzana

RESEDA BLVD.

Reseda

ROSCOE BLVD.

Northridge

Granada
Hills

MULHOLLAND DR.

BALBOA BLVD.

Van Nuys
Airport

118

Encino

Balboa

VICTORY BLVD.

405

SAN DIEGO FREEWAY

SEPULVEDA BLVD.

Mission
Hills

San
Fernando

Sherman
Oaks

VAN NUYS BLVD.

Van
Nuys

WOODMAN AVE.

GOLDEN STATE FREEWAY

SAN FERNANDO RD.

San
Fernando
Airport

Whiteman
Airpark

Studio
City

VENTURA FREEWAY

Valley Plaza
Shopping
Center

170

LANKERSHIM BLVD.

Universal
City

VINELAND AVE.

Hollywood-
Burbank Airport

5

134

HOLLYWOOD WAY

NBC

Universal

ALAMEDA

SAN FERNANDO RD.

Burbank

KENNETH RD.

Glendale

INDEX

O

N

MORE GAULT MILLAU "BEST" GUIDES

Now the guidebook series known throughout Europe for its wit and savvy reveals the best of major U.S., European and Asian destinations. Gault Millau books include full details on the best of everything that makes these places special: the restaurants, diversions, nightlife, hotels, shops, arts. The guides also offer practical information on getting around and enjoying each area. Perfect for visitors and residents alike.

Please send me the books checked below:

☐ The Best of Chicago $15.95
☐ The Best of London $16.95
☐ The Best of Los Angeles $16.95
☐ The Best of New England $15.95
☐ The Best of New York $16.95
☐ The Best of Paris $16.95
☐ The Best of San Francisco $16.95
☐ The Best of Washington, D.C. $16.95
☐ The Best of France $16.95
☐ The Best of Italy $16.95
☐ The Best of Hong Kong $16.95

PRENTICE HALL TRADE DIVISION
Order Department—Travel Books
200 Old Tappan Road
Old Tappan, NJ 07675

In the U.S., include $2 (UPS shipping charge) for the first book, and $1 for each additional book. Outside the U.S., $3 and $1 respectively.

Enclosed is my check or money order made out to Prentice Hall Trade Division, for $ _____

NAME_____

ADDRESS_____

CITY _____STATE _____

ZIP_____COUNTRY _____

QUESTIONNAIRE

The Gault Millau series of guidebooks reflects your demand for insightful, incisive reporting on the best (and worst) the world's most exciting destinations have to offer. To help us make our books evern better, please take a moment to fill out this anonymous (if you wish) questionnaire. return it to:

Gault Millau Inc.
P.O. Box 361144
Los Angeles, CA 90036

1. How did you hear about the Gault Millau guides: bookstore, newspaper, magazine, radio, friends or other ? (please specify) _____

_____

2. What cities (and/or countries) are you most interested in seeing covered in a Gault Millau guide? Please list in order of preference:_____

_____

_____

3. Do you refer to the Gault Millau guides only on your travels, or do you use the Gault Millau guide for your own city, too?

☐ Travels   ☐ Own city   ☐ Both

4. What are the three features you like most about Gault Millau guides?

1._____

2._____

3._____

5. What are the features, if any, you dislike about the Gault Millau guides?

_____

_____

_____

6. Please list any features you would like to see added to the Gault Millau guides.

_____

_____

_____

Please turn over →

7. Do you use any other travel guides in addition to Gault Millau? If so, please list below:
1. _____
2. _____

8. If you use another guidebook series, please list the features you enjoy most or find most useful about it:_____
_____
_____

9. How many trips do you take per year?
Business trips: Domestic _____ International _____
Pleasure trips: Domestic _____ International _____

10. Please check the category that reflects your annual household income:
☐ $20,000-$39,000   ☐ $80,000-99,000
☐ $40,000-$59,000   ☐ $100,000-$120,000
☐ $60,000-$79,000   ☐ Other (please specify)_____
_____

11. We thank you for your interest in the Gault Millau guides, and we welcome your remarks and recommendations about restaurants, hotels, nightlife, shops and services around the world.
If you have any comments on the Gault Millau guides in general, please list them in the space below.

NOTES

NOTES

NOTES